FreeBSD®

Brian Tiemann
Michael C. Urban

SAMS

Unleashed

FreeBSD® Unleashed

Copyright © 2002 by Sams Publishing

International Standard Book Number: 0-672-32206-4

Library of Congress Catalog Card Number: 2001089508

Printed in the United States of America

First Printing: August 2001

04   03   02   4   3

Trademarks

All terms mentioned in this book that are known to be trademarks or service marks have been appropriately capitalized. Sams Publishing cannot attest to the accuracy of this information. Use of a term in this book should not be regarded as affecting the validity of any trademark or service mark.

Warning and Disclaimer

ASSOCIATE PUBLISHER
Jeff Koch

ACQUISITIONS EDITOR
Katie Purdum

DEVELOPMENT EDITOR
Mark Cierzniak

MANAGING EDITOR
Matt Purcell

PROJECT EDITOR
Andy Beaster

COPY EDITOR
Nancy Sixsmith

INDEXER
Becky Hornyak

PROOFREADERS
Bob LaRoche
Plan-It Publishing

TECHNICAL EDITOR
Tim Hicks

TEAM COORDINATOR
Chris Feather

MEDIA DEVELOPER
Dan Scherf

INTERIOR DESIGNER
Gary Adair

COVER DESIGNER
Aren Howell

PAGE LAYOUT
Mark Walchle

Contents at a Glance

Contents

About the Authors

Michael Urban is a biology student at the University of Minnesota. He has been working with various forms of Unix-like operating systems for several years including FreeBSD, Linux, and Solaris. Michael has worked as a technical analyst, and is now a systems administrator and webmaster for the Lion Research Center. He also does software development for them, including the development of Web-enabled database applications. When he is not studying for exams, or writing new Perl or Java code, he can usually be found immersed in research material on African lions.

Brian Tiemann has been a constant user of FreeBSD since his student days at Caltech, where he used it to build a movie fan Web site that has continued to grow and sustain more and more load until the present day. Born in Ukiah, California, Brian has remained in the state all his life; he currently lives in San Jose and works in the networking appliance field. Aside from FreeBSD, his other interests include Macintoshes, motorcycles, and animation.

About the Tech Editor

Tim Hicks is a Sr. Unix Engineer for HomeSide Lending, Inc. He is an HP Certified IT Professional in HP-UX Systems Administration and has been working extensively with HP-UX 10.10 – 11.00 as well as some work with Solaris 8 and AIX 4.1 for five years. He has in-depth knowledge and experience with Highly Available Clusters using HP's MC/ServiceGuard and HP-UX 11.00 with Sybase and Oracle. Mr. Hicks graduated from Florida State University with a B.S. in Finance and a B.S. in Management Information Systems in 94 and 96 respectively.

Dedication

To my parents, Chris and Bonnie, and my sister Beth. And to the Serengeti lions. I hope my work helps contribute to the difference that the Lion Research Center is making for them.

-Michael C. Urban

I dedicate this book to my parents, Keith and Ann, and to my brother, Mike. And to Douglas Adams, wherever in the Galaxy you are.

-Brian Tiemann

Acknowledgments

A project of this magnitude would not have been possible without the efforts of a lot of people. We would like to thank the staff at Sams Publishing who worked with us on this book, including Kathryn Purdum, Mark Cierzniak, Andrew Beaster, Nancy Sixsmith, and Dan Scherf. Also, we would like to thank Tim Hicks for doing the technical editing on this book. In addition, we would like to thank the rest of the staff who worked on this book, and also for putting up with our frequent changes as we wrote for FreeBSD 5.0, which was a moving target that was still in development at the time.

Of course, without the efforts of the FreeBSD developers, this book would not exist. So, we would also like to thank Jordan Hubbard and the rest of the FreeBSD core team for their efforts. Also, the volunteer FreeBSD developers all over the world who donate their personal free time to make FreeBSD an operating system that is better than similar commercial operating systems that cost hundreds or even thousands of dollars.

In addition, Michael would like to thank Dr. Craig Packer and Peyton West of the Lion Research Center (located at the University of Minnesota) for providing some of the photographs used in this book. Please give the Lion Research Center's Web site a visit at www.lionresearch.org. I would also like to thank my co-author, Brian Tiemann, for allowing me to use his Web server to test my latest programming creations and toys.

Brian would like to thank Paul Summers for his untiring efforts doing all the hard and expensive site-admin work while I philosophize and hack and rant from afar; Lance, Kris, Chris, Brian D., David, Drew, Zjonni, Gerrit, Marcus, Matt, and the rest of my friends who have helped me solidify my opinions and passions about operating systems and software; Adam, Ian, Jarrod, and Sean for inspiration; and Cirque du Soleil and Brak for the music to write by. Finally, I thank all the members of the TLK-L and lionking.org for supporting me so steadfastly all these years and making me feel as if I know what I'm talking about. Maybe a copy of this book will find its way into the γδβ-library, as would be appropriate.

Tell Us What You Think!

As the reader of this book, *you* are our most important critic and commentator. We value your opinion and want to know what we're doing right, what we could do better, what areas you'd like to see us publish in, and any other words of wisdom you're willing to pass our way.

As an Associate Publisher for Sams, I welcome your comments. You can fax, e-mail, or write me directly to let me know what you did or didn't like about this book—as well as what we can do to make our books stronger.

Please note that I cannot help you with technical problems related to the topic of this book, and that due to the high volume of mail I receive, I might not be able to reply to every message.

When you write, please be sure to include this book's title and author as well as your name and phone or fax number. I will carefully review your comments and share them with the author and editors who worked on the book.

Fax: 317-581-4770

E-mail: feedback@samspublishing.com

Mail: Jeff Koch, Associate Publisher
              Sams Publishing
              201 West 103rd Street
              Indianapolis, IN 46290 USA

Introduction

Twenty years ago, when the first personal computers were being sold, could anyone have accurately predicted what they would be used for at the turn of the century? Could anyone have guessed that Microsoft would become as omnipresent a force in the computer industry as IBM was at that time? Was there any indication to predict the rise of open-source software and its contention against Microsoft for market share? Could anyone have imagined that in 2001, IBM would be funding Linux development, seemingly facing off against Microsoft itself?

Even today, it's not necessarily any easier to tell what the picture is like, thanks to the fast pace of technology development. Determining which products and which companies are the ones that will be with us for another 20 years, and which ones are doomed to failure is a fruitless pursuit, made even more difficult by the inherent limitations on the accuracy of any kind of survey mechanism to find out what's actually being used on the Internet. Even so, it's clear from recent general trends that Internet server roles are being filled decreasingly often by commercial UNIX operating systems, increasingly often by versions of Microsoft Windows, and even more increasingly often by open-source UNIX systems or workalikes. Chief among these in the industry news headlines is Linux in its myriad forms. Linux, developed as a grass-roots effort with more and more corporate backing in recent years, has achieved legitimacy through its market success and reputation for reliability and performance, and even through Microsoft's recent attempts to denounce it as a great enemy to the concept of intellectual property. Whether you love it or hate it, open-source software like Linux is here to stay.

However, a frequently overlooked fact is that Linux is not UNIX; it's properly called "UNIX-like," in that it performs the same functions as most commercially sold UNIX variants do, but was developed entirely by its user community. The guiding principles of the project are embodied in the GPL, the GNU General Public License, which states in part that any code developed under it must be made freely available. This extends to commercial software development bodies who must re-release as freely available source any software that they develop from earlier materials.

If there is any single strong point of contention between the supporters of open-source and those of commercial software, it is this seemingly innocent license. The problem is that many companies are unwilling to abide by its terms because to them, giving away the source code that they develop is tantamount to publishing trade secrets as soon as they're conceived. GPL-based software embodies an ideal: the notion of software written by the people, for the people, owned by nobody, and leveraged by nobody. It is the absolute antithesis of commercial, closed-source software that is sold in compiled, executable form from only one supplier. Linux adheres to that ideal in a number of important ways, but the unattractiveness of the spirit of the GPL to businesses that otherwise would have bought into it has slowed down its progress.

Enter FreeBSD, another freely available UNIX-based operating system that has been around for as long as GNU/Linux has, and whose roots go back even further.

FreeBSD is open-source with a twist. It is not based on software developed under the GPL, but instead favors the BSD open-source license that allows code originally developed at the University of California at Berkeley (and later commercially) to be used in current software development, whether the results are published in source form or not. This is part of the reason why Apple (and earlier, NeXT) chose the freely available BSD (Berkeley Software Design) operating system core to form the NeXTSTEP platform that became Mac OS X, and why Microsoft appears to favor FreeBSD over Linux in maneuvers such as its recent announcement of plans to port the C# programming environment to FreeBSD. The BSD license is friendlier to commercial software developers than the GPL is. It strikes a balance that encourages grass-roots contributions from users, but does not place undue restrictions on companies with the resources to develop BSD-licensed software into truly great products.

Naturally, one might assume that Linux and FreeBSD are rivals. In part, or at least in some people's estimation, they are. The percentage of open-source operating systems currently in use that are not Linux is dominated by FreeBSD, but that "domination" currently corresponds only to about 15% of a segment of the market that is by no means the only major one. Even if FreeBSD has a number of high-profile reference installations to help it wave its flag—such as Yahoo!, The Apache Project, and Walnut Creek CD-ROM—these installations don't exist in such numbers as to give FreeBSD the high profile that Linux enjoys, for better or for worse.

Perhaps one of the biggest differences between FreeBSD and Linux is that of advocacy. FreeBSD has very little of it by comparison. The voices that aggressively promote Linux do not have comparable analogs in the FreeBSD world. In a way, this makes sense; Linux is a more "extreme" example of the open-source ideal, and FreeBSD is a moderate compromise between open-source enthusiasm and corporate stodginess. The vibrancy of Linux contributes to its higher visibility, but also means it's a more chaotic platform and community. FreeBSD attempts to be more attractive to traditionalists, and so it's not as flashy, but it's in many ways more sturdy and predictable—it's a true UNIX, with original commercial UNIX code that has the same stability as traditional "big-iron" UNIX variants. It's hard to say whether Linux or FreeBSD is more "cutting-edge" or has the more modern features, but in many ways FreeBSD trails Linux as a "showcase" platform for the newest Windows-challenging features that attempt to bring open-source to the desktop. That's really not where FreeBSD is targeted.

If you're reading this book, it might well be because you're a Linux user who wants to try a less-volatile platform for what has to be a reliable corporate network server; it might be because you're a commercial UNIX user who wants to build a familiar-to-use but inexpensive server or workstation; or it might be because you're a Windows administrator who wants an alternative to the completely closed and welded-shut status quo of Microsoft's server offerings. In all these capacities, FreeBSD is an excellent choice.

I had my first exposure to FreeBSD in 1997, with release version 2.2.2. What attracted me was the fact that even at this early point in its development, Yahoo! had given it the nod as the platform of choice rather than Linux, and Hotmail (before it was taken over by Microsoft) used it side-by-side with Solaris machines to handle its already extraordinary load of "Web-mail" users. (Microsoft in 2000 finally was able to migrate most of Hotmail onto Windows 2000, but FreeBSD is known still to be in wide use there for many major functions.) I considered these to be strong testimonials, and the convenient floppy-based "net install" feature sealed the deal.

Since that time, FreeBSD has undergone a massive evolution. The layout of the system has become more and more organized; the security model has been tightened and enhanced over and over; the revolutionary "ports collection" has been successful enough that it has been ported to NetBSD, OpenBSD, and Mac OS X; and a Linux binary compatibility module allows software that is commercially developed for Linux, such as RealPlayer and StarOffice, to run on FreeBSD. Centralized configuration files and a tightly controlled filesystem structure lend to the platform's predictability and easy administration, perhaps more so than any other widely used UNIX. Although FreeBSD doesn't enjoy the notoriety of Linux or suffer from the backlash against that notoriety, it does provide nearly all the meaningful benefits one can have by running Linux, and many that are uniquely its own.

When it comes to open-source operating systems, Linux has the spotlight, and probably will continue to have it for the foreseeable future. However, FreeBSD continues to gain in popularity, simply by being there as a sane alternative for companies that want out of the Microsoft hegemony, but are put off by the politics or distribution-proliferation of Linux. Other BSD-licensed operating systems keep a firm grasp on their respective corners of the market: OpenBSD is focused on being the most secure OS available, and NetBSD has bragging rights for being able to run on a vast number of different hardware platforms, from Intel's x86 architecture to the Motorola PowerPC to the Sega Dreamcast. FreeBSD's appeal is more general; it excels in the role that's so important in this age where anybody with a few hundred dollars can launch a Web site or a home network to write software, run a small business, or simply share thoughts with the world: the role of a full-featured Internet server or workstation. It does so without excessive specialization and without being so politically charged as to alienate all-important corporate finance managers. It holds to a course that runs squarely between the extremes, and in the coming years it's likely to gain in popularity and reputation as more and more users discover what it can do for them.

Twenty, or ten, or even five years ago, the current state of the computer industry could hardly have been accurately predicted. We can't hope to imagine what the next decade or two will bring, but if FreeBSD's thus-far successful history is any indication, it will be with us as long as the open-source movement is relevant. Someday, the compromise between open-source and commercial assurance that FreeBSD represents might well be the only kind of platform that anyone can imagine.

Conventions Used in This Book

Features in this book include the following:

> **Note**
>
> Notes give you comments and asides about the topic at hand, as well as full explanations of certain topics.

> **Tip**
>
> Tips provide great shortcuts and hints on how to program more effectively in FreeBSD.

> **Caution**
>
> Cautions warn you against making your life miserable and help you avoid pitfalls in programming.

In addition, you'll find the following typographic conventions throughout this book:

- Commands, variables, directories, and files appear in a monospaced font.
- Commands and such that you type appear in **boldface type**.
- Placeholders in syntax descriptions appear in *monospaced italic* type. This indicates that you should replace the placeholder with the actual filename, parameter, or other element that it represents.

What's on the CD-ROMs

CD 1 includes the FreeBSD operating system, version 5.0-RELEASE.

CD 2 includes the following:

- **mkpasswd.pl**—A Perl script to help in migrating a Linux user database to FreeBSD format (see Chapter 20, "FreeBSD Survival Guide")

- **simpledemo.pl**—A simple Perl program that demonstrates basic programming techniques (see Chapter 21, "Introduction to Perl Programming")

- **sendcomments.cgi**—A sample CGI Perl program that demonstrates a common use of server-side programming (see Chapter 26, "Configuring a Web Server")

- **portsentry.sh**—A shell script that aids in the automatic startup of the PortSentry program, and an example for other such programs (see Chapter 29, "Network Security")

- **StarOffice 5.2**—Sun's Office Suite for Linux, which runs great on FreeBSD and includes word processing, spreadsheet, presentation, drawing programs, and more.

Introduction to FreeBSD

PART

I

IN THIS PART

What Is FreeBSD?

CHAPTER 1

In a nutshell, FreeBSD is similar to a UNIX operating system. It runs on Intel x86 and Alpha architectures, although there are some efforts underway to create Sparc and PowerPC ports. Volunteers from all over the world develop FreeBSD, and the source code for the system is available free of charge to anyone who wants it.

Why Use FreeBSD?

There are probably as many reasons to use FreeBSD as there are the number of people who use it. Perhaps the most obvious reason is that FreeBSD is free, and there are no expensive licensing fees. You can install a single copy of FreeBSD on as many computers as you want without paying a dime. There are also no "per-connection" or "per-user" fees for FreeBSD on a server, as there are for some commercial network operating systems. But just because FreeBSD is free does not mean it is of low quality. Here are some other very convincing reasons to look into using FreeBSD:

- **It is extremely stable** In Netcraft's (www.netcraft.com) "longest uptime" survey as of March 14, 2001, no fewer than 47 of the top 50 sites in the "sites with the longest uptime" survey are running FreeBSD. The #1 Web server in the list runs FreeBSD, and it has been running for an amazing 1,133 days since its last reboot!

- **It's trusted by some of the largest companies and busiest sites in the world** Some of the companies and sites running FreeBSD include Sony; Yahoo!; The Apache Project; and freesoftware.com, the busiest FTP site in the world.

- **It's open source** The entire source tree for the operating system is available to you. You can change it, perform security audits on it, or do whatever else you like.

- **There are thousands of free software packages available** Take advantage of the thousands of free software packages available for UNIX that do everything, including the following: playing chess, simulating the division of cells and bacteria growth, word processing, image editing, and Web serving on the most popular Web server software in the world.

What Can You Do with FreeBSD?

Because FreeBSD comes with compilers for multiple programming languages, what you can do with FreeBSD is really limited only by your imagination and the technical limits of your hardware. Various organizations are using FreeBSD for everything from low-end file sharing on an old 486, to creating high-end special effects and computer-generated animation rendering for motion pictures on multi-processor FreeBSD systems linked together in powerful clusters.

> **Note**
>
> The special effects for the Warner Brother's motion picture "The Matrix" were rendered on a cluster of FreeBSD systems.

The following lists some of the more common uses for FreeBSD that don't require any programming skill or custom software:

- **Economical file and print sharing**   Create an economical file- and print-sharing solution. The freely available Samba software (covered in Chapter 32, "File and Print Sharing with Microsoft Windows") allows file and print sharing with Microsoft Windows-based computers. Using Samba, FreeBSD can even serve as a primary domain controller (PDC) for a Windows network.

- **Web serving**   As mentioned previously, FreeBSD powers some of the busiest Web sites in the world. Even if you aren't setting up a Web site for the Internet, FreeBSD can make a great intranet server for your business.

- **Email services**   Set up an email server for your company with FreeBSD. Even an old 486 will perform quite well in this role.

- **Routing, DNS services, and Internet sharing**   Once again, you can turn even a low-end 486 into a very serviceable router, DNS server, or a gateway for sharing a single Internet connection with multiple computers.

- **Economical database solutions**   Using FreeBSD and one of the several freely available SQL databases for it, you can create a database solution for free that could easily cost tens of thousands of dollars to implement with commercial software. If the freely available databases don't have enough horsepower for your needs, you can run Oracle on FreeBSD.

- **Economical custom solutions**   FreeBSD has a very liberal license agreement that allows you to use its code in other applications free of royalties. This makes it a perfect solution if you are an embedded systems designer. There are many other applications in which you might want to use BSD code as well. Apple's OS X uses a lot of BSD code, for example.

FreeBSD: It's Not Just for Servers Anymore

"Well, that's all well and good," you might be saying. "But I don't need any of that stuff. I'm not setting up a server or anything."

Well, don't put this book back on the shelf quite yet. There are plenty of workstation uses for FreeBSD that you might also be interested in. For example:

- **Web site development and testing**   The days of Web pages that display static HTML content are history. These days, Web pages use server-side technologies such as CGI, embedded scripting, and database backends to display content that is dynamic and interactive. This means that testing your Web site by loading the pages into your browser from your hard drive are also history. To design a Web site of any complexity these days, you need to have a Web server available for development and testing. Even if you will not be running a Web server for public use, you can still use Apache, PHP, and one of the free SQL databases on a FreeBSD workstation to allow you to do all the Web site development and testing offline without uploading any pages to your hosting service for testing. This can save you a lot of time and money.

- **Offline database development**   This kind of ties in with the first point, but FreeBSD can allow you to develop and test a database for your Web site entirely offline. When you finish, simply upload the database to your hosting service (assuming that your hosting service supports the database you use for development).

- **Software development or learning programming**   If you ever wanted to learn a programming language, you might be happy to know that using FreeBSD doesn't require you to spend hundreds of dollars on compilers and debuggers. All the software you need to learn programming and write powerful applications is already there, waiting for you to learn how to use it.

- **Learning about OS design and/or UNIX**   If you are a computer science student and need to learn the ins and outs of operating system design, having access to all the source code for a real UNIX operating system can be a great help. Suppose that you need to learn UNIX for your job or for a course you are taking in college. FreeBSD can help you learn at home on your own time, instead of having to spend all your time in the UNIX terminal lab.

- **Inexpensive workstation**   With all the free software available, FreeBSD can make a very powerful and inexpensive workstation for just about anything you might want to do. Some of the free applications available for FreeBSD include email programs, Web browsers, word processors, spreadsheets, databases, CAD programs, and image editors. And yes, there is a Winamp clone for FreeBSD and your mp3 collection.

Chances are, you found something in the previous list that whets your appetite to learn more about FreeBSD, and maybe even try it out. The next section gives you some history of FreeBSD and UNIX in general, and also explains some of the excellent design philosophies behind UNIX that have kept it a driving force in computers today; more then 30 years after it was written.

A Brief History of FreeBSD and UNIX

The original UNIX operating system was developed at AT&T Bell Laboratories. Two men named Ken Thompson and Dennis Ritchie were the main driving forces behind UNIX.

The origins of UNIX can probably be traced to the spring of 1969. It was an offshoot of a largely unsuccessful effort by a conglomeration of companies to develop a time-sharing operating system. This operating system was called MULTICS. Although it was developed, it was never very successful.

UNIX was originally written in assembly language for the DEC PDP-7, and was then ported to the DEC PDP-11. Then, an entirely new language called "C" was written for the purpose of rewriting the UNIX operating system. The UNIX operating system was then rewritten in C. The C programming language and UNIX are two of the most important developments in the history of the computer. The C programming language was the first portable language that allowed applications written in C to be ported to other types of computer platforms relatively easily. Because UNIX was written in C, it was also portable and could be made to run on other types of computer platforms relatively easily. This is one of the many points that made UNIX so popular.

BSD Is Born

Because AT&T Bell Laboratories was not really in the business of selling computer operating systems, it licensed the UNIX operating system and its source code to various academic institutions relatively cheaply. One of the institutions that did a lot of early work on UNIX was the Computer Systems Research Group (CSRG) at the University of California at Berkeley. The CSRG at Berkeley made some very important contributions to UNIX, including the development of the UNIX File System (UFS) and adding TCP/IP networking to UNIX. Eventually, the CSRG made so many changes to UNIX that it released its own version, known as the Berkeley Software Distribution. Contrary to popular belief, CSRG did not do the first port of UNIX to the DEC VAX. The first VAX port was done at AT&T Bell Laboratories. But the port that Bell Labs had done did not support the VAX's virtual memory system. So, CSRG ported BSD to the VAX and added support for the VAX's virtual memory system.

BSD on Intel x86 Platforms

CSRG made much of the BSD source code available to the public for free, and a man named Bill Jolitz ported BSD to the Intel x86 platform in 1991. The port was called

386/BSD. In addition, a commercial spin-off company of CSRG named Berkeley Software Distribution, Incorporated, sold a commercial version of BSD for the x86 platform that included source code.

FreeBSD Is Born

In 1993, it became apparent that because of full-time jobs and such, Bill Jolitz was no longer going to enhance 386/BSD. Two different groups decided that the project was worth doing though, and so two spin-off projects were formed. The first was NetBSD, which seemed to focus on universal availability. If it's a platform, chances are there is a version of NetBSD that runs on it. The second was FreeBSD, which focused on making the system easier to use for non-technical users, and also focused primarily on Intel x86 hardware (although, as mentioned previously, FreeBSD is now available for Alpha as well). Today, FreeBSD is the most popular of the BSD-based, UNIX-like operating systems.

There are several more interesting events in the history of FreeBSD and UNIX, such as the lawsuits over the Net/2 Tape, and more on the development of UNIX. If you are interested in learning more about the history of FreeBSD and UNIX, I recommend the following links:

- `http://www.bell-labs.com/history/unix/`   Contains a detailed history of the development of UNIX at Bell Labs, including some rare photographs.
- `http://daemonz.org/bugs/history.ehtml`   Contains a detailed history of the Berkeley Software Distribution.
- `http://www.freebsd.org/handbook/history.html`   Contains more history of FreeBSD in particular.

The Design Philosophy of UNIX

Several things have kept UNIX going strong even after 30 years. One of these is its portability, as mentioned previously. In my opinion, however, the most important thing that has kept UNIX on the cutting edge, when most other software that old is considered obsolete, is its design philosophy about how an operating system should work.

Many people tend to think of UNIX as an extremely complicated, complex, and confusing operating system. But in my opinion, UNIX is the ultimate example of the KISS (Keep It Simple, Stupid) design in an operating system. One of the amazing things about UNIX is that it is both KISS and extremely powerful at the same time. Here is how the designers of UNIX did it.

The UNIX design philosophy is made up of a lot of small programs that do relatively simple tasks, and do them well. But the designers of UNIX had a brilliant idea—that these programs should be able to be combined together by the user to do things that a single program could not do by itself.

> **Note**
>
> This combination concept is known as *piping*. Doug McIlory of Bell Labs is cred-ited with coming up with the idea. Thompson implemented it in UNIX. (We cover pipes in detail when we learn about working with the shell in Chapter 8, "Working with the Shell.")

Here is an example of the way pipes work. Suppose that you have a plain-text file that serves as a simple address book. It uses one line per person and contains names, addresses, phone numbers, email addresses, and so on. Fields in this file are separated by a tilde (~). A few sample lines from the file might look like these:

```
Doe, John~505 Some Street~Anytowm~NY~55555~505-555-1212~jdoe@email.com
Doe, Jane~121 Any Street~Sometown~NY~12121~121-555-1212~jadoe@isp.com
Bar, Foo~501 Some Street~Anytown~NY 55555~505-123-4567~foobar@email.com
```

This file could contain 50 names or 500 names—it really doesn't matter. In this case, however, you want to get a list of all the people that live in Anytown, just their names and phone numbers, the list sorted alphabetically, and to create a hard copy of the list.

There is no single command that will do everything you want, but you can combine sev-eral commands together in a pipe to do what you want. Here is one of several ways that this task could be accomplished:

```
awk 'BEGIN {FS="~"} $3 == "Anytown" {print "%s\t%s\n",$1,$6}'
➥address.txt | sort | lp
```

In simple terms, the code sets the field separator to the tilde; selects lines where the third field (the field that contains the city name) is equal to Anytown; and then prints the first and sixth fields (the name and phone number) of these lines, separated by tabs (\t), with a new line at the end of each line (\n). The file it gets the information from is address.txt. The output is then piped to the sort command, which sorts it in alphabetical order. It is then piped to the lp command, which will print it on the default printer. Here is what the output looks like using our simple three-record data file:

```
Bar, Foo     505-123-4567
Doe, John    505-555-1212
```

Although this command string may seem somewhat arcane right now, it is really quite amazing. Basically, what you did is create a simple database that can search by any field and present output in any form you want, all with only a single line of code.

Just so you can see how powerful this single line of code can be, here is a second example that modifies the previous example slightly to print a simple mailing list:

```
awk 'BEGIN {FS="~"} $3 == "Anytown" {printf "%s\n%s\n$s, $s
$s\n\n",$1,$2,$3,$4,$5}' address.txt | lp
```

The output of the previous code is as follows:

```
Doe, John
505 Some Street
Anytown, NY 55555

Bar, Foo
501 Some Street
Anytown, NY 55555
```

For those who are willing to learn, UNIX is about as close to an infinitely customizable and flexible operating system as you can get. There is immense power locked up inside UNIX (and thus FreeBSD) that can be unleashed and used to do things you probably didn't even know your computer could do without buying expensive software. This book will teach you how to unleash that power (hence the name of the book).

It is this design philosophy that has kept UNIX from becoming obsolete and falling by the wayside, as so many other programs have done.

FreeBSD Compared to Other Operating Systems

Here, we will compare the Windows 2000 and Linux operating systems to FreeBSD.

Windows 2000

Microsoft has done a good job of listening to what its customers want in an operating system. Windows 2000 doesn't allow you to "get under the hood" much. It is designed to work reasonably well for a wide variety of tasks without the user having to learn about the internals of the system. It does this at the expense of some performance and efficiency. Windows 2000 has relatively steep hardware requirements, but many users are willing to accept this in exchange for ease of use. In addition, because of the graphical design of Windows 2000, "power users" can easily hit limits. There is only so much that can be done from a graphical user interface. The following lists some of the important differences between FreeBSD and Windows 2000:

- **The kernel cannot be customized**   The kernel is the core of the operating system; it controls virtually every other aspect of how the system works. FreeBSD allows you to build a new kernel for the operating system that is customized for your specific system. This can increase performance and reduce memory usage. Windows 2000 does not allow you to rebuild the kernel. This is one of the areas where Windows 2000 sacrifices some efficiency and performance for ease of use.

- **Windows 2000 uses a GUI (graphical user interface) for almost all tasks. FreeBSD relies much more on the command line**   The GUI in Windows 2000 is laid out so that things are easy to find, and tasks are easy to perform. For example, setting up a network in Windows 2000 is done from a network control panel, and there are "wizards" that walk you through the process. FreeBSD, on the other hand, uses text-based configuration files for network configuration. Setting up the network involves editing one or more configuration files by hand.

- **The GUI in Windows 2000 is always running; the GUI in FreeBSD is optional**   Although a GUI can make a workstation easier to use, it is wasteful overhead on a backroom server in which no one ever sees the screen, anyway. FreeBSD gives you the option of turning off the GUI or not using it at all.

- **Because everything in FreeBSD can be done from the command line, it is very easy to administer remotely**   In FreeBSD, all system administration tasks can be done from the command line. This makes remote administration easy. It can be done from any terminal—even a terminal that cannot display graphics. It can also be done from any type of system that is capable of running a terminal emulator. FreeBSD can be administered from another UNIX-like system, a Windows system, a Macintosh, and so on. Windows 2000, on the other hand, requires the GUI to do many tasks. Although remote administration is possible on Windows 2000, special software is required to do it. Also, most of this software is available only for Windows. Because of this, most remote administration tasks for Windows can be done only from another Windows system.

- **By nature, a GUI has limits that are not present in a command-line interface**   Only so many features can be crammed into a GUI. Sooner or later, a "power-user" will want to do something that the operating system designers didn't think about. For example, the simple address book database demonstrated in the previous section could not be done with the software that is included with Windows. A similar system would require third-party software in Windows. The mailing list example could not be done with the software included with Windows, either. Although third-party GUI software is available for simple tasks like this, after you get familiar with the command line, you will actually find that you can type the command line much faster than you can go through the menus in a GUI-based system.

Linux

Unless you have been living in a cave for the last few years, you have at least heard of Linux, even if you don't know what it is. Linux is a clone of UNIX that has become rather popular in recent years. Like FreeBSD, it is open source and developed by volunteers. Unlike FreeBSD, there is no single controlling authority for Linux, and there are well over 30 different distributions of Linux.

There are more similarities than differences between FreeBSD and Linux. Both are excellent operating systems, and both can serve the needs of most users quite well. Although there is more software available for Linux than for FreeBSD, FreeBSD can run almost all Linux software that is available, so this is not really an issue. When running Linux software under FreeBSD, performance is not really an issue, either, because FreeBSD actually runs some Linux software faster than Linux itself does.

Here are some of the most important differences between FreeBSD and Linux:

- **There is only one distribution of FreeBSD, whereas there are more than 30 distributions of Linux**   FreeBSD will work the same way on all systems in which it is installed. This is not true with Linux. Each Linux distribution has a slightly different way of doing things. For example, Slackware Linux uses BSD-type run control scripts. Debian Linux uses Sys V run control scripts. And Redhat Linux uses Sys V run control scripts, but stores them in a different location than standard Sys V UNIX does. This can be confusing for users who move from one distribution of Linux to another, because things may not work the same way in the other distribution.

- **FreeBSD is a complete operating system maintained by a core team; Linux is a kernel maintained by Linus Torvalds**   Linux is not a complete operating system. It is a kernel. As mentioned in the section on Windows, the kernel is the core of the operating system. It controls virtually all aspects of the operating system. The various companies that sell Linux distributions take the Linux kernel and package it with a bunch of other programs designed to work with Linux. Because each company has its own idea about what should be included in a distribution, you may find that a program you had available on one Linux system does not exist on another Linux system (although you could download and install it). This fact can also cause dependency problems when upgrading Linux. For example, you may upgrade your Linux kernel, only to find out that you need to upgrade several other packages as well. Because FreeBSD is a complete operating system,

upgrades are generally easier to do because any dependencies are upgraded at the same time.

- **Anyone can contribute code to Linux; contributions to FreeBSD must be reviewed and accepted by the core team**   Although anyone can contribute to the FreeBSD project, it is much more of a coordinated effort than Linux is. Contributions to the FreeBSD source code need to be approved by the core team before they will be merged into FreeBSD. This is good for most users because you can be sure that the code has been checked for problems by people who know what they are doing. It also helps to ensure that the code will not cause problems with other code that already exists. (This is sometimes a common problem with Linux, which is why many Linux distributions seem to come with at least some part "broken" out of the box. Because there is only one FreeBSD base of FreeBSD code (commonly known as a "source tree"), this is far less of a problem with FreeBSD).

These are some of the most important differences between Linux and FreeBSD. Because FreeBSD has a single source tree that is controlled by a core team, it tends to be more stable than Linux, and therefore is often more suitable for a production environment. The main drawback to this is that new features are not always implemented as quickly in FreeBSD as in Linux. There is a trade-off here. Do you want stability for a production environment? Or, do you want the latest gizmos and gadgets to play with at the expense of performance and stability?

FreeBSD Mascot

A quick word on the FreeBSD mascot is probably in order here because it is often a source of confusion for new users. Sometimes, people even get offended at the FreeBSD mascot. Well, the FreeBSD mascot is not a reference to a satanic cult or anything like that. It is a joking reference to background processes in UNIX systems that handle various tasks. These background processes are called "daemons," which is pronounced "demons". Daemons are actually wonderfully helpful things. If you've ever sent an email or visited a Web page, you have used the services of a daemon without even knowing it. Windows 2000 also has daemons. They just aren't called that. Microsoft calls them "services" instead.

So, what about the pitchfork? That is a reference to an important system call known as "fork." You will learn more about forking later in the book, but for now, simply know that a *fork* causes a program to make a copy of itself in memory and then run that copy. Once again, if you have ever visited a Web page, you have used the services of the fork system without even knowing it. Without fork, the Web server could only handle one visitor at a time. And you can imagine how much fun that would be. You would get a lot of errors about the site being too busy.

Installing FreeBSD

CHAPTER 2

IN THIS CHAPTER

Before you can use FreeBSD, you need to install it on to your system's hard disk. This is a relatively painless process and you shouldn't have any problems if you follow the directions in this chapter carefully. Depending on how fast your system and your CD-ROM drive run, the installation process will take anywhere from about 20 minutes to an hour or more. Most of this time is spent copying files, so you will not always have to sit in front of your computer.

I strongly suggest that you read this entire chapter before beginning the install. Mistakes in the install can result in losing some or possibly even all of the existing data on your hard disk. Poor planning can also result in an install that has to be redone because the decisions you made don't work for the environment in which you will use FreeBSD. Read this whole chapter (and also Chapter 3, "Advanced Installation Issues," if necessary) before beginning the install. This will ensure that you make the best decisions possible during the installation because you will know what to expect.

> **Caution**
>
> Make sure to pick a time to do the installation when you will not be distracted. You will be performing actions during the installation that are potentially hazardous to existing data on your system if you make mistakes.

> **Tip**
>
> Now is a good time to look over the hardware compatibility list in Appendix B, "Hardware Compatibility Lists," to make sure that your hardware is supported. There is no sense in continuing the install if you find out that a key piece of hardware in your system is not supported by FreeBSD.

Checking Your Hardware

Before you begin the installation, you should have some information about your hardware available. Here is a list of the information that you should have:

- Type of video card and amount of video RAM installed.
- The manual for your monitor: You need to know the horizontal and vertical refresh rates for setting up X-Windows.
- If you have a modem, the com port and IRQ it is using.

- The type of mouse you have (serial, PS/2, or bus) and what port it uses.
- If you have a network card, the address and IRQ it uses.
- If you are connected to a network, the network information such as your hostname, IP address, DNS server, gateway, and such. If you are unsure, obtain these values from your network administrator.

If you don't have this information available and you currently have Microsoft Windows installed on your system, you can often get it from the Device Manager in the Windows Control Panel. See your Microsoft Windows documentation or Windows Help for information on how to do this.

Creating Boot Disks

The FreeBSD CD-ROM included with this book is bootable. If you plan to install on a system that supports booting from the CD-ROM drive, you can probably skip this section. If your CD-ROM does not support booting, or if you plan to install from some method other than from the CD-ROM (such as installing over a network), read on.

If you will install over a network, or if your system doesn't support booting from a CD, you need to create two boot disks.

The boot floppies are located in the `floppies` directory on the CD-ROM. If you can't use the CD at all (presumably because you don't have a CD-ROM drive), you can also download the boot floppies from the FreeBSD FTP server at `ftp.freebsd.org`. They are located in `/pub/FreeBSD/releases/5.0-RELEASE/floppies`—assuming that 5.0 is the RELEASE version of FreeBSD. If it isn't, replace 5.0 with whatever the current RELEASE version is. The two files you need to download are `kern.flp` and `mfsroot.flp`. If you create the floppies on a DOS or Windows system, you also need the `fdimage.exe` program located in the `/pub/FreeBSD/tools` directory on the ftp server.

> **Tip**
>
> For better response time, and also to cut down on the traffic load on the main FTP server, you might want to try one of the mirrors. In many of the mirrors, `ftp` is simply followed by a number (for example `ftp1.freebsd.org` or `ftp2.freebsd.org`). Using a mirror can speed up the transfer.

Next, you need two blank 1.44MB formatted floppies.

Note

The boot floppy files cannot simply be copied to a floppy disk. They have to be written to floppies using one of the procedures described as follows.

Tip

Use brand-new floppies to create the boot disks. The boot disks write raw data to the floppies with no regard for the format of the floppy. There can't be even one bad sector on the floppy because bad sectors on the floppy can make tracking down installation problems difficult. Save yourself the headaches and just use brand-new floppies.

The next several sections show you how to create the boot floppies in various environments.

Creating the Boot Floppies from a DOS or Windows System

Before creating the boot floppies from a Windows system, you should boot into plain DOS mode. Trying to create the boot floppies from a DOS window while Windows is running could cause problems. If you can't access your CD-ROM drive from DOS mode, copy the following files off the CD-ROM to some temporary place on your hard disk before creating the boot floppies:

- `D:\TOOLS\FDIMAGE.EXE`
- `D:\FLOPPIES\BOOT.FLP`
- `D:\FLOPPIES\MFSROOT.FLP`

Assume that drive letter D is your CD-ROM drive. If it isn't, replace D with whatever drive letter is assigned to your CD-ROM drive.

After you reboot your system into DOS mode, this is how to create the boot floppies.

Using Your CD-ROM Drive

Insert the included CD-ROM into your CD-ROM drive, and put the first blank floppy disk into your floppy drive. Then, type the following commands from the DOS prompt. Once again, if your CD-ROM is not drive D, replace D with whatever drive letter is assigned to your CD-ROM drive.

```
C:\> cd d:\tools
D:\TOOLS> fdimage \floppies\boot.flp a:
```

When the program has finished running, remove the first floppy from the drive and insert the second one. Then, type the following at the DOS prompt:

```
D:\TOOLS> fdimage \floppies\mfsroot.flp a:
```

The a: is the drive letter of your 3½-inch, 1.44MB floppy drive. Unless you have a system that can boot from the B drive (most can't), your A drive will have to be a 3½-inch, 1.44MB floppy drive.

Can't Access the CD-ROM Drive or Downloading from the FreeBSD FTP Server

Change to whatever directory you copied fdimage.exe, boot.flp, and mfsroot.flp to. Type the following commands at the DOS prompt, replacing the directory temp with whatever directory you copied the files to:

```
C:\> cd temp
C:\TEMP> fdimage boot.flp a:
```

When the program finishes running, remove the first floppy from the drive, and insert the second one. Then, type the following at the DOS prompt:

```
C:\TEMP> fdimage mfsroot.flp a:
```

Creating the Boot Floppies from Another FreeBSD or UNIX System

If you are creating the floppies from another FreeBSD or UNIX system, you do not need the fdimage.exe program. (You still need the boot.flp and the mfsroot.flp programs, though.)

Use the UNIX dd utility to write the files to the floppies. On a FreeBSD system, it looks like this:

```
dd if=boot.flp of=/dev/rfd0
```

When the copy finishes, remove the first floppy from the drive, and insert the second one. Once again, use dd to create the second floppy. On a FreeBSD system, it would look something like this:

```
dd if=mfsroot.flp of=/dev/rfd0
```

Note that for the previous commands to work, you must have write access to the raw floppy device. Also, on other versions of UNIX, the device name may be different. See the documentation for your version of UNIX to find out the name of the floppy device.

Now that you have created the installation disks, you are ready to begin the installation.

Booting in to the Install Program

> **Caution**
>
> If you are installing on a system that already has Windows or some other operating system on it, and you don't want to lose that operating system and all the data that is installed on it, stop here and read Chapter 3. It is VERY IMPORTANT that you read this first. Failure to follow the instructions in that chapter could result in the loss of all data on your hard disk!

The next few sections assume that you either plan to wipe out everything currently on your hard disk to install FreeBSD, that you are installing on a new disk, or that you have already followed the instructions in Chapter 3 to create space for FreeBSD on a system that already has another operating system installed on it. The next few sections also assume that you are installing from the included CD. If this is not the case, stop here and read the relevant sections in Chapter 3 on NFS installs, FTP installs, or floppy installs. After you do that, come back and continue with the instructions given here.

When you are ready to begin the installation, insert the included CD into your CD-ROM drive. If you need to boot from floppy disks, also insert the floppy disk that you installed boot.flp onto into your A drive. Reboot your system. If necessary, enter your BIOS setup program, and enable booting from the CD-ROM drive. Some BIOSs also have a security feature that prevents booting from the floppy drive. If you have to boot from the floppy drive, you might need to check for this option and set it to allow booting from the A drive. See your system documentation for the way to configure the BIOS settings to control boot devices.

As the system boots, you should see some messages on your screen. You should also see a "twirling baton." As long as the baton keeps twirling, the system is doing something. If the baton stops twirling for a long period of time, it probably means that your system is

hanging. If that happens, refer to Appendix C, "Troubleshooting Installation and Boot Problems." The system will load a few things and then you should see a message like this:

```
FreeBSD/i386 bootstrap loader, Revision 0.8
   (jkh@bento.freebsd.org, Mon Nov 20 11:41:23 GMT 2000)
   |
   Hit [Enter] to boot immediately, or any other key for command prompt.
   Booting [kernel] in 9 seconds... _
```

Go ahead and press Enter to continue. At some point during this process, you will also be asked to remove the boot floppy and insert the mfsroot floppy. When you are asked, simply do what it says and then press Enter.

When the kernel finishes loading, you are put into the UserConfig program, which looks like this:

```
                  Kernel Configuration Menu

Skip kernel configuration and continue with installation.

     Start kernel configuration in full screen Visual mode.
     Start kernel configuration in CLI mode.

Here you have the chance to go into kernel configuration mode, making
any changes which may be necessary to properly adjust the kernel to
match your hardware configuration.

If you are installing FreeBSD for the first time, select Visual Mode
(press Down-Arrow then ENTER).

If you need to do more specialized kernel configuration and are an
experienced FreeBSD user, select CLI mode.

If you are certain that you do not need to configure your kernel then
simply press ENTER or Q now.
```

Most users can probably get away with selecting Skip kernel configuration and then continue with the installation. I suggest you try this option first. If you have problems during the installation, or if the hardware probe hangs, see Appendix C for information on how to use the UserConfig program to resolve hardware conflicts.

After you leave the UserConfig program, the kernel will finish booting. A flurry of messages will go past your screen as the kernel detects and initializes the hardware in your system. If your system hangs at any point during this period, see Appendix C for help on troubleshooting installation problems.

Introduction to the FreeBSD Sysinstall Program

After the kernel has finished booting (and assuming you didn't run into any problems), you will be placed into the FreeBSD Sysinstall program. The first screen you see looks like Figure 2.1.

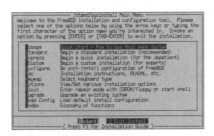

Navigating the Sysinstall Program

You can't use the mouse in Sysinstall, but it is still easy to navigate. Table 2.1 lists the navigation keys you can use in Sysinstall.

TABLE 2.1   Navigation Keys

Navigation Key	Command
Up arrow	Moves up to the previous option in the menu.
Down arrow	Moves down to the next option in the menu.
Left/right arrow	Toggle between the choices on the bottom of the menu. For example, on the main menu the left and right arrow keys toggle between Select and Exit Install.
Spacebar	In menus in which multiple options can be selected, the spacebar toggles the current highlighted option on and off.
Tab key	Has the same effect as the left and right arrows in menus. Tab between fields in screens in which you need to fill in blanks.

In addition, you can also select most options by selecting their highlighted letter—usually the first letter in the option name.

If you want to read more about using Sysinstall, you can press Enter on the highlighted option Usage, but because it will all be explained here, I suggest you arrow down to the second option to begin a standard install.

After you select the Standard option, you will be given a message informing you that you need to set up a DOS-style (fdisk) partitioning scheme for your hard disk. After you read this message, simply press Enter to continue.

Creating Partitions and Assigning Mount Points

After you press Enter on the informational message telling you about creating a DOS-style (fdisk) partitioning scheme, one of two things will happen:

- If you have only one hard disk in your system, you will be placed directly into the FreeBSD partition editor. In this case, you can skip the next section, "Selecting Hard Disks," and continue with "Partitioning the Disk(s)."

- If you have more than one hard disk in your system, you will be given a menu to select which hard disk or disks on which you want to install FreeBSD. If this is the case, read the next section, "Selecting Hard Disks."

Selecting Hard Disks

If you have multiple hard disks in your system, you will see a menu that looks similar to Figure 2.2.

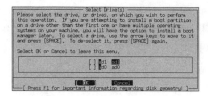

Your menu might not look the same. Table 2.2 lists some of the values you might see in
the menu and what they mean.

TABLE 2.2   Menu Values

Menu	Value
ad0	The first physical ATA hard disk on the system. This is the master drive on the primary IDE controller. If you have DOS or Windows installed on your system, they will be located on this drive.
da0	Similar to ad0, except that it indicates a SCSI disk instead of an ATA disk. Once again, this would be the first SCSI disk in your system. If you have only SCSI drives on your system and you have DOS or Windows installed, they will be located on this drive.
ad1	The second ATA disk on the system. Depending on how your system is set up, this can be either a slave disk on the primary controller or a primary disk on the secondary controller.
da1	The second SCSI disk on the system.

You might also have an ad2 and ad3 in your list, or a da2 or da3, and so on. Just remember that the number is the number of the drive in your system, and that FreeBSD starts numbering the drives at zero instead of one.

Use the spacebar to select which disk or disks you want to use for FreeBSD. You can select more than one disk for the FreeBSD installation. This is fairly common, and the end result is transparent for everyday operation. In other words, even if FreeBSD is installed across multiple disks, it appears to the end user that everything is on a single disk. You will see in the next section, "Partitioning the Disk(s)," why it might be advantageous to install on multiple disks.

When you select a disk from this menu, it puts you into the FreeBSD partition editor, where you will edit the partition table for that disk. After you finish editing the partition table for that disk and leave the partition editor, you are placed back at this menu. You can then select another disk to edit, or press Enter to leave this menu and continue with the installation. After you finish editing disks, you are placed into the FreeBSD disk label editor (more on that after the next section, which explains the partition editor).

Caution

If you will install FreeBSD on a second hard disk, you have another operating system on the first hard disk, and you don't plan to make any changes to the first hard disk, you need to install a boot manager so that you can choose which operating system you want to boot at system startup. FreeBSD will give you the option of installing the boot manager later in the process. However, the boot manager *must* be installed on the first disk in your system. In order for this to happen, you *must* select the first drive in this menu. If you do not want to make any changes to the first disk, simply select it in the menu and then exit the Partition Editor menu without making any changes to the disk. You can then select a different disk in the menu and partition it for use with FreeBSD. This allows FreeBSD to install the boot manager on the first disk. If you do not do this, the boot manager will not be installed on the first disk, and you will not be able to boot FreeBSD after the installation is finished.

2

INSTALLING
FREEBSD

Partitioning the Disk(s)

Here is what the partition editor looks like:

```
Disk name:     ad0                              FDISK Partition Editor
DISK Geometry:  4336 cyls/146 heads/63 sectors = 39882528 sectors (19473MB)

Offset     Size(ST)        End    Name PType      Desc Subtype    Flags

       0   39882528   39882527   ad0s1      3   freebsd     165   C




The following commands are supported (in upper or lower case):

A = Use Entire Disk    G = set Drive Geometry    C = Create Slice
D = Delete Slice       Z = Toggle Size Units     S = Set Bootable
T = Change Type        U = Undo All Changes      Q = Finish


Use F1 or ? to get more help, arrow keys to select.
```

In this case, the first line tells us that we are working on the disk ad0, which—as mentioned previously—is the first ATA disk in the system. The second line gives us information about the geometry of this disk. (See Chapter 19, "Understanding Hard Disks and Filesystems," if you need help with this. It's not important to understand it unless FreeBSD is having trouble detecting your disk's geometry.) The next several lines give us information about each currently defined partition on the system. If this is a new disk, or if you deleted all of the partitions on it before installing FreeBSD, there will be only one partition with the description "unused" that takes up the entire disk. Table 2.3 explains what each column of information means.

> **Note**
>
> If you are unfamiliar with the terms used in the next section (such as *sectors*), please see Chapter 19, which gives an introduction to hard disks and the terminology related to them.

TABLE 2.3 Partition Table Information

Column	Information
Offset	The starting sector of the partition.
Size (ST)	The size of the partition in sectors.
End	The last sector in the partition.
Name	The FreeBSD assigned device name of this partition (if known).
Ptype	A number representing the partition type.
Descr	Type of partition.
Subtype	More information about partition type.
Flags	The following symbols can appear in this column:
	=: The slice is properly aligned.
	>: This slice extends past the 1024th cylinder on the hard disk. This becomes an issue later on when you create the disk labels as boot partitions that extend past the 1024th cylinder can cause problems on some systems (a BIOS limitation, not a limitation of FreeBSD).
	R: This slice contains the root filesystem, which is the top-level filesystem on the FreeBSD system.
	B: This slice uses BAD144 bad-spot handling.
	C: This slice is a FreeBSD partition.
	A: This slice is the active partition. (The slice is the bootable slice.)

Tip

Press z to toggle the display units between sectors, kilobytes, and megabytes.

To assign all available space on this hard disk to FreeBSD, simply select A for "Use Entire Disk". This will create a FreeBSD partition that takes up the entire disk.

Caution

In previous versions of FreeBSD, there was an option called "Dangerously dedicated". This could be used to get around geometry detection problems on older systems. These days, FreeBSD rarely has problems detecting the proper

> geometry, and the "dangerously dedicated" option has been deprecated. It is still available by pressing F, but it is intentionally undocumented and its use is not recommended.

After you select Enter, you should see a line that shows a single partition of subtype 165 with the description freebsd and C in the Flags column. Press Q to exit the partition editor.

> **Caution**
>
> This operation deletes everything currently on this disk. If you have anything you want to keep, make sure you do a backup first. If you don't want to delete everything on this disk, see Chapter 3 first.

> **Note**
>
> Unlike Linux, you do not create multiple partitions on a single disk for FreeBSD, even if you will probably be creating more than one partition on the disk to hold your FreeBSD filesystems. You use the Disk Label Editor to create the separate areas for your different filesystems.

If you have only a single hard disk in your system, you will receive a message that tells you to create BSD partitions inside the fdisk partition(s) just created. Go ahead and press Enter to go to the Disk Label Editor. If you have multiple disks, you go back to the disk selection menu.

If you want to spread your FreeBSD installation out across more than one disk (either because you don't have enough space on one disk for a complete install or for performance reasons), select any other disks you want to use for FreeBSD, repeating the previous steps under "Partitioning the Disks." When you have partitioned all the disks that you want to use for FreeBSD, make sure that OK is highlighted, and press the Enter key. You then receive the message about creating BSD partitions inside the fdisk partition(s) just created. Press Enter again, and you go to the Disk Label Editor.

The Disk Label Editor

The Disk Label Editor is where you will actually create the filesystems that will hold the FreeBSD installation. When you first enter it, it will look like this:

```
                    FreeBSD Disklabel Editor

Disk: ad1       Partition name: ad1s1   Free: 30033360 blocks (14664MB)
Disk: ad0       Partition name: ad0s1   Free: 39882528 blocks (19473MB)


Part      Mount             Size Newfs   Part      Mount             Size Newfs
----      -----             ---- -----   ----      -----             ---- -----
```

```
The following commands are valid here (upper or lower case):
C = Create        D = Delete    M = Mount pt.
N = Newfs Opts    Q = Finish    S = Toggle SoftUpdates
T = Toggle Newfs  U = Undo      A = Auto Defaults

Use F1 or ? to get more help, arrow keys to select.
```

Notice that there are two disks listed at the top of the menu in the example. Your system may have only one disk listed, or it may have more than two disks listed. It depends on how many disks you selected to use with FreeBSD.

There is an option A (for Auto Defaults). If you are setting up a workstation and you have only one disk to use for FreeBSD, you might be able to get away with this as a quick-and-dirty way to set up the filesystems. If you use more than one disk, you need to manually set up the partitions. Also, if you are setting up a server, you need to manually set up the partitions because the Auto Defaults option doesn't allocate nearly enough space for the /var filesystem. In addition, it puts the /tmp filesystem in the root partition (the meaning of /var and /tmp will be explained later in the chapter). This is unsafe in my opinion, so I recommend that you take the time to set up your partitions manually.

At a bare minimum, you need to create two partitions: a root filesystem and a swap partition. You might be tempted to do this because it ensures that you won't end up in a situation in which you run out of space on a partition where you need it and have 150 zillion gigabytes of free space on a different partition that you can't use for what you need. In fact, there is at least one well-known Linux distribution that encourages putting everything in the root filesystem. This is a dangerous way to live, for the following two reasons.

First of all, FreeBSD and all other versions of UNIX are powerful multitasking operating systems. They are almost always doing something—especially on a busy server. These systems usually have several files open at the same time, and they often write to the disk. If the system crashes, if there is a power failure, or if the janitor runs the vacuum cleaner over the server's power cord while a write is in progress, the filesystem can be damaged. Depending on what was being written when the crash occurred, the damage can be severe enough to destroy the filesystem. Filesystem damage is far less likely to occur if the filesystem is not being written to when the crash or power failure occurs.

This is why it is a good idea to use multiple filesystems. It not only helps to restrict damage to one area instead of the entire system, it also helps protect the all-important root filesystem. In a properly laid-out filesystem, the root partition is almost never written to.

The second reason that having everything in one partition is dangerous is that it opens a server to various DoS (Denial of Service) attacks. Whether these attacks are intentional or not, they can occur. For example, on a system in which user disk quotas are not enforced, a user could either intentionally or accidentally (through the misuse of the command that copies files) create a file that fills up the entire partition where the home directory is located. If all the filesystems are located on that same partition, this would do far more than prevent users from saving files in the home directory. Other fallout from this event could include denial of mail service because there is no room in the mail spool directory, denial of print service because there is no room to queue print jobs, and the Web server could stop serving because it can't write its log file. Syslogd (the program that logs system messages) will be unable to record important messages, which could allow crackers to enter your system undetected. Any programs that need to write temp files will fail because there is no room left in the tmp filesystem. Although running out of space on all filesystems is somewhat unpredictable, running out of space is not a good situation.

Hopefully, by now I have convinced you that despite the convenience of having everything in one partition, the risks simply aren't worth it. Now that we agree on that, let's go ahead and look at creating the partitions.

Creating the Partitions and Disk Labels

I recommend a minimum of four partitions: one for the root filesystem (/), one for the swap space, one for the user filesystem (/usr), and one for the var (/var) filesystem. Some people recommend placing the /var filesystem in the same partition as /usr because it is difficult to judge how much space to give /var. I don't like to do this, however, because this subjects your system to various possible denial of service attacks again—especially if users' home directories are also located in the same partition as the /usr filesystem.

> **Note**
>
> FreeBSD has the capability to use more memory than is actually installed in the system. This is called *virtual memory*. To use virtual memory, FreeBSD moves memory pages that are not currently in use out to the disk. This way it can make room in memory for memory pages that are currently needed. When the memory page that was moved out to disk is needed again, FreeBSD moves it back into the memory, and if necessary, something else in memory is moved out to the disk to make room. These operations are known as *swapping*, and the area of the disk that the swapped out memory pages are stored on is called the *swap partition*.

To help you better decide what filesystems you want to put on each partition, Table 2.4 describes some of the directories in FreeBSD and what they are used for. Note that this is not a complete list; it has only the directories for which you might want to have separate partitions. For a complete list of all directories and their purposes, please see Chapter 9, "The FreeBSD Filesystem."

TABLE 2.4 FreeBSD Directories and Their Purposes

Directory	Purpose
/	This is the root filesystem. It is the directory under which all other filesystems will appear (even if they may be located on different partitions, different disks, or even different computers on different continents.) It is also the directory where the kernel is located on versions of FreeBSD prior to 5.0. The root filesystem needs to have a partition. 100MB should be enough for this partition. If you are really tight on space, you could probably get away with cutting it down to 75MB, but I wouldn't go any lower than that.
/boot	On versions of FreeBSD prior to 5.0, this directory contains the FreeBSD boot loader configuration files and some other files necessary for the system startup. Beginning with FreeBSD 5.0, the kernel and various other files needed to start the system are also located in this directory. You can now have a root partition that extends past the 1,024th cylinder by putting boot on its own partition. (Note that /boot would have to be contained completely in the first 1,024 cylinders).
/usr	The /usr filesystem contains most of the utilities and programs that will be accessed by normal users. /usr should definitely have its own partition.

TABLE 2.4 continued

Directory	Purpose
/usr/local	This is where third-party software that is not part of the operating system is installed (Web servers and database programs). Some people like to put /usr/local on its own partition separate from the /usr partition. Personally, I don't recommend this for normal operations. The only time I would recommend this is if you have multiple disks and need to split /usr for space reasons.
/var	This is where the system stores files that will have a variable size. I like to put /var on its own partition. Some of the things stored in /var include incoming mail, system logs, Web server logs, and jobs queued for the printer. The size you need to make /var depends on whether you will be running a print server, mail server, or Web server. Note that on a busy Web server, log files can easily grow to more than 100 megabytes in only a couple of days. If you are going to be running a busy Web server, either give /var a lot of space or make sure you rotate your logs often. If you expect to receive a lot of mail, you will also want to make /var quite large.
/tmp	This is where programs and users can write temporary files. This directory is usually cleaned out at each reboot. Properly behaved programs that need to write very large temp files should not use this directory; they should use /usr/tmp or /var/tmp instead. You can either give /tmp its own partition or link it to a place in /usr. Also, note that if a particular operation requires more temp space than is available, you can temporarily change the location where temp files are written for that one operation.
/home	This is where users' home directories are located. It is often located under the /usr partition. If you aregoing to have a lot of users, and you expect them to have a lot of files, you might want to put /home on its own partition, or possibly even give /home an entire disk.

Optimizing Performance

If you have more than one hard disk on your system, you can optimize the performance of your system by carefully dividing up disk-intensive tasks between multiple hard disks.

For example, if you run a Usenet news server (rather disk-intensive) and a Web server (also quite disk-intensive), you should put the news directory and the directory where the Web server keeps its pages on separate disks.

The Root Partition

If you aren't using a /boot partition, the first partition on your drive should be the root partition (/). To create the root partition, use the up or down arrow key to highlight the disk at the top of the Disk Label Editor that you want to put the root partition on. Then, press C for Create Partition.

You then see a dialog box that asks you for the size of the partition (see Figure 2.3).

FIGURE 2.3

Setting the size of the partition.

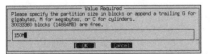

As mentioned previously, 100MB should be sufficient for the root partition. If you are not pressed for space, this is the size I recommend. As the dialog box says, you can specify a size in megabytes by adding an "M" to the end of the number. So, assuming that you want to make your root partition 100MB in size, enter 100M at the prompt and then press Enter. You are then asked to choose a partition type for this partition. Because this will hold the root filesystem, select the FS   A filesystem option, and press Enter. You are then asked to specify a mount point for this partition. The *mount point* is the directory under which the filesystem will be available. Because this is the root filesystem, enter / in this box, and press Enter.

Your screen should now look similar to this:

```
                    FreeBSD Disklabel Editor

Disk: ad1      Partition name: ad1s1    Free: 30033360 blocks (14664MB)
Disk: ad0      Partition name: ad0s1    Free: 39882528 blocks (19473MB)

Part        Mount          Size Newfs  Part      Mount          Size Newfs
----        -----          ---- -----  ----      -----          ---- -----
ad0s1a      /              100MB UFS Y
```

```
The following commands are valid here (upper or lower case):
C = Create        D = Delete    M = Mount pt.
N = Newfs Opts    Q = Finish    S = Toggle SoftUpdates
T = Toggle Newfs  U = Undo      A = Auto Defaults

Use F1 or ? to get more help, arrow keys to select.
```

This code shows that we now have a filesystem at `ad1s1a` (the device name and slice entry that FreeBSD uses to refer to this filesystem), it is mounted on `/`, the size is 100 megabytes, and it is of type UFS (the standard filesystem for FreeBSD). Next, we deal with the swap partition.

The Swap Partition

FreeBSD is a virtual memory operating system: It can use more memory than it has available in physical RAM. It does this by swapping memory pages of programs that are not currently being used out to the hard disk. When those pages are needed again, FreeBSD swaps them back into memory from the hard disk, and if necessary, swaps something else out to the hard disk to make room for the pages it is bringing in. Of course, accessing something from the hard disk is many times slower than accessing something from RAM, so swap space is no alternative for having enough RAM in a system. But still, swap space is very useful and is often used, especially on busy servers that have many processes running at the same time.

The proper (or improper) placement of your swap partition can have a significant impact on the performance of your system. So here are some guidelines for choosing where to put your swap partition.

- Put the swap partition as close to the beginning of the disk as possible. Lower-numbered cylinders on the disk can be accessed slightly faster than higher-numbered cylinders.

- If you have multiple drives in your system, as a general rule, you should put the swap partition on the fastest drive in your system.

- If the fastest drive on your system is also the most heavily accessed by users, Web servers, mail transfer agents, and so on, you will probably want to violate the previous point and put the swap partition on the least-accessed drive in your system. Not only does this allow more time for the drive to access the swap space instead of accessing other things, but it also increases the chances that the hard disk heads will already be positioned within the swap partition when swapping is needed. Little things like the time it takes the hard disk heads to cross the disk to where the swap partition is located really can make a difference during high loads and heavy swapping.

So, how much space should you give your swap partition? Long ago, when RAM was an expensive commodity and most users made do with 4MB to 16MB of RAM, the rule of thumb was to have 2.5 times as much swap space as you had RAM. But today, RAM is cheap and affordable. A high-end workstation with 512MB of RAM and servers with 1GB or more of RAM are not uncommon these days. Today, the average user can afford to have more RAM than they actually need. So with that in mind, if your workstation has 512MB of RAM, it probably doesn't make much sense to create a 1.2GB swap partition. More than likely, this would just be a huge waste of disk space because a workstation with 512MB of RAM would rarely need to swap at all, much less need anything close to 1.2GB of swap space.

256MB of swap space is a nice number to use if you have 256MB of RAM or less, and you aren't really pressed for disk space. If at all possible, you should try to have at least as much swap space as you have RAM. If you plan to do development or track the FreeBSD CURRENT branch, this is practically a necessity. Here is why.

Occasionally, something funky that the operating system's kernel doesn't know how to handle can happen. When an event occurs that the kernel doesn't know how to handle, it gives up, "panics" (you get a message that says "Kernel panic"), and then reboots the system. However, if the kernel is configured to do so, it attempts to dump the contents of RAM into the swap partition when it panics before it reboots. The contents of RAM when the panic occurred are essential to programmers for debugging what is causing the panics. So, what happens if there is more information in RAM than can fit in the swap space? One of two things can happen:

- The kernel will refuse to dump the RAM contents. This is the most likely scenario. In this case, no debugging information will be available to attempt to diagnose what caused (or is causing, if it is happening on a regular basis) the panic.

- If the panic was caused by some state of confusion in the kernel over something regarding the filesystems, it's conceivable that the kernel could dump the RAM contents to the swap partition and keep right on going when it hits the end boundary of the swap partition. The result would likely be irreparable damage to whatever filesystem came after the swap partition on the disk.

Kernel panics don't happen often in FreeBSD, but when they do happen, it's nice to be able to use the RAM dump feature so that you or someone else can examine the contents of RAM when the panic occurred and attempt to figure out what is causing the panic. So, try to make your swap partition at least as big as the amount of RAM you have in your system.

> **Note**
>
> UNIX kernel panics are similar to the infamous BSOD (Blue Screen Of Death) errors in Windows NT/2000. But if you are used to working with Windows NT/2000, you can breathe a sigh of relief. You won't be seeing nearly as many kernel panics with FreeBSD as you see blue screens in Windows NT/2000. This author has only had one kernel panic on his FreeBSD workstation in nearly seven years of working with FreeBSD.

After you decide on a size for your swap partition, create it just like you created the root partition, except this time select Swap when prompted for the filesystem type. The swap partition does not get a directory mount point, so you will not be asked the question about where you want to mount the partition when you are creating a swap partition.

Creating the Rest of the Partitions

After you create the root (and possibly boot) partition and the swap partition, create the rest of the partitions as filesystems, give them the size you decided on earlier, and set the mount points to the proper directories when asked (for example /usr, /var). Don't forget to include the leading slash.

If you have more than one hard disk in your system, and you need to switch between them, use the up and down arrow keys to move the highlighted line over the disk at the top of the screen that you want to create the partition on.

Here is an example of what a final result might look like:

```
                      FreeBSD Disklabel Editor

Disk: ad0       Partition name: ad0s1   Free: 0 blocks (0MB)
Disk: ad1       Partition name: ad1s1   Free: 0 blocks (0MB)

Part        Mount          Size Newfs   Part      Mount          Size Newfs
----        -----          ---- -----   ----      -----          ---- -----
ad0s1a      /             100MB UFS Y
ad0s1b      swap          256MB SWAP
ad0s1e      /var          200MB UFS Y
ad0s1f      /tmp          100MB UFS Y
ad0s1g      /usr        18817MB UFS Y
ad1s1e      /home       14664MB UFS Y




The following commands are valid here (upper or lower case):
C = Create         D = Delete    M = Mount pt.
N = Newfs Opts     Q = Finish    S = Toggle SoftUpdates
T = Toggle Newfs   U = Undo      A = Auto Defaults

Use F1 or ? to get more help, arrow keys to select.
```

In this example, there are two hard disks in this system, and the /home directory is on a partition in the second hard disk that takes up the entire second disk.

> **Note**
>
> When creating a partition, if you get an error message at the bottom of your screen that says You can only do this in a master partition (see top of screen), it means that you have to highlight one of the filesystem partitions. Use the up arrow until the highlight is on the main disk at the top of the screen that you want to create the partition in, and try again to create the partition.

Notes on SoftUpdates

Starting with FreeBSD 5.0, you have the option of enabling SoftUpdates on the filesystem directly from the Disk Label Editor. SoftUpdates are covered more in Chapter 9, but for now simply know that they can greatly increase the performance of most filesystems.

So, you probably want to enable these. To enable SoftUpdates on a filesystem, move the highlight over the filesystem you want, and press S to toggle SoftUpdates on or off. A filesystem that has SoftUpdates enabled will have a +S following the filesystem type (for example, UFS+S).

After you finish creating partitions, press Q to leave the partition editor. Once again, do not use the W option because this is intended for making changes to existing filesystems, not installing new ones. The next screen will ask you what you want to install.

Selecting a Canned Distribution Set

Figure 2.4 shows the Choose Distributions menu.

FIGURE 2.4

Selecting the distribution.

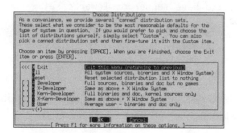

If you have the space, I suggest that you select the All option. If you are running a server, and you are sure you will not need the X-Windows system, you can select the Developer option instead. If you select an option that doesn't include the source code, you cannot build a new kernel or upgrade the system through cvsup (unless you download all the sources while doing the cvsup, which negates the space-saving of not installing the sources here). If you select an option that only installs the kernel sources but not the rest of the sources, you will be able to build a new kernel, but you still can't upgrade the system with cvsup. I don't recommend the custom option for inexperienced users because this will give you the ability to select each and every package that gets installed. If you are a new user, you probably won't know what most of these packages are for. Therefore, I suggest you stick to one of the canned distributions—preferably, the All distribution.

> **Note**
>
> cvsup is a system that allows automatic updating of the FreeBSD operating system by connecting to servers and automatically determining what has changed since the last time you ran cvsup. Any changes are automatically downloaded from the server and applied to the FreeBSD source code. This is much faster than having to download the entire source tree because with cvsup, only things that have changed need to be downloaded. cvsup is covered in detail in Chapter 18, "Keeping Up to Date with FreeBSD."

To select a distribution, highlight the one you want, and press the spacebar. If you selected the All distribution, you will then be asked whether you want to install the FreeBSD ports collection or not. You really should install it if you can afford the space because it provides an easy way to download and install additional software for your FreeBSD system that handles most of the dirty work for you. Installing additional software is a breeze if you have the ports collection installed. Use the Tab key to select the option you want and then press Enter.

Next, you return to the Choose Distributions menu. Don't worry if it looks like nothing is selected here. If you selected the All option previously, it is still selected. Arrow up to the Exit option, and press Enter.

Choose the Installation Media

The next screen asks you to choose the installation media (see Figure 2.5).

FIGURE 2.5

Choosing the installation media.

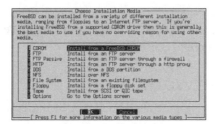

This chapter assumes that you are installing from the CD included with this book (or from an official CD set). If this is not the case and you need to do a network, tape, or floppy install; or you are installing from an existing filesystem; please see the relevant sections of Chapter 3 before continuing.

Assuming that you plan to install from CD, make sure that the CDROM option is highlighted and press Enter.

The system will then print a warning message:

```
                     User Confirmation Requested

 Last Chance! Are you SURE you want to continue the installation?

 If you're running this on a disk with data you wish to save then WE
 STRONGLY ENCOURAGE YOU TO MAKE PROPER BACKUPS before proceeding!

We can take no responsibility for lost disk contents!
```

> **Caution**
>
> Up to this point, no changes have actually been made to your hard disk. This is your last chance to back out of the installation. After you select Yes here, the partitions you created will be formatted and the installation will begin. Any existing data on the partitions you selected to use WILL BE LOST!

Assuming that you are happy with the installation choices that you made, select Yes here. The system then prints a message telling you it is Starting an emergency holographic shell on vty4 and then proceed to format the partitions. After partition formatting is done, Sysinstall will begin copying files to your hard disk(s).

Post-Installation

When the file-copying process is completed, you will see a screen that congratulates you for making it to this point and informs you that Sysinstall will now move on to the final configuration questions. Select Ok here to continue.

Configuring the Network

Next, you are asked if you want to configure any Ethernet or SLIP/PPP network devices. If you have the values from your system administrator, you can go ahead and set these up now. If you don't have the values available, or if this is a new network you are setting up and you are unfamiliar with networking, you can always re-enter this utility later after you have read the chapters on networking.

> **Caution**
>
> If you are on a network and you do not configure the network device(s) now, be aware that when the system reboots, you cannot access the network until you configure the network devices to work with your network. With that said, if you don't have a network or you don't know what values should go in the fields for the network configuration, go ahead and skip this section and come back to it later after you have read the networking chapters.

If you don't want to configure any network devices now, simply select No to this question, and move on to the next section of this chapter. If you do want to configure network devices at this time, select Yes, and you see a screen such as that shown in Figure 2.6.

FIGURE 2.6

Selecting the network interface to configure.

Select the network device you wish to configure from the list, and press Enter. Note that depending on the make and model of your Ethernet adapter, it may have various names. It will usually have the number zero, though, if it is the first Ethernet adapter in the system.

After you select the network device that you want to configure, you are asked if you want to try the IPv6 configuration of the interface. Unless you are sure that your network has an IPv6 server on it that is set up to send you configuration information, you should select No here.

The next question asks you the same thing about the DHCP configuration of the interface. If your network has a DHCP server on it, FreeBSD will attempt to contact that server and obtain its network information from it. If your network does not have a DHCP server, you should select No here.

The next screen allows you to enter the information about your network. This will be covered in much more detail in Chapters 22, "Introduction to Networking," and 23, "Configuring Basic Networking Services," but here are a few guidelines to get you started.

Figure 2.7 shows what the network configuration screen looks like.

FIGURE 2.7

Configuring the network interface.

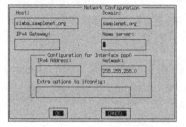

Table 2.5 lists what the fields are for.

TABLE 2.5 Network Configuration Fields

Field	Description
General Network Options for This System	
Host	The hostname and domain name of your system go here (in this example, `simba.samplenet.org`).
Domain	The domain name that your system is located in (in this example, `samplenet.org`).
IPv4 Gateway	If your system will use another host to access non-local network resources (the Internet), put the address of that host here. If this system has direct Internet access, this field should be left blank.
Name server	The IP address of your DNS server, which is the server that resolves network names into IP addresses.
Network Options Specific to This Network Interface	
IPv4 Address	The IP address of this system.
Netmask	The netmask value for the network that this interface accesses.
Extra Options to `ifconfig`	Any extra options you need to pass the network configuration should go here.

If you are unclear about any of the previous concepts, you should read Chapters 22 and 23 before configuring the network.

> **Caution**
>
> If your system is connected to a network, simply inserting random numbers in the IP address field or a random hostname in the host field is a sure way to get on the bad side of the network administrators as well as other network users. If you select an IP address that conflicts with an existing system on the network, bad things will happen, including possible denial of service to an important network resource if your IP address conflicts with that of a major server. So, if you aren't sure what numbers or names should go here, ask someone who will know. Never ever simply fill in random numbers or names if your system is on a network.

Use the Tab or Enter key to move between fields. When you are done, select OK to leave the configuration screen.

Depending on the type of network interface you set up, you may now be asked if you wish to bring the interface up right now. Select no here, since we are almost done with the install and will be rebooting the system soon anyway.

Sysinstall will then ask you a series of questions about the network:

- **Will this machine be a leaf node (for example, will it not forward packets between interfaces)?**

  Unless this machine will be a gateway that other systems on the network will use to get to the Internet, or a router that will handle network traffic intended for other systems, you should select Yes here.

- **Do you want to grant only normal users FTP access to this host (for example, no anonymous FTP connections)?**

  I suggest that you select Yes here unless you have already read the chapters on networking. You can always configure anonymous FTP access later on.

- **Do you want to configure this machine as an NFS server?**

  The NFS server allows you to share directories on your hard disk so that users on other systems can mount them and read and/or write files to them. Once again, unless you have read Chapter 31, "The Network Filesystem (NFS)," I suggest you select No for now, even if you know that you will need this service. NFS can be a security problem if not set up properly. After you read Chapter 31, you can come back and set this up.

- **Do you want to configure this machine as an NFS client?**

  If you need to mount filesystems on your drive that are located on other systems, you need to set up the NFS client. Once again, see Chapter 31 for more information on configuring NFS.

- **Do you want to select a default security profile for this host (select No for medium security)?**

  Unless high security is absolutely critical in your environment, I suggest you select No here. Later, you can customize the security settings by editing the system configuration files. These settings are very easy to change in the system configuration files.

After you select No for this option, you see another message that tells you about the services that will be enabled in this profile. The "high" security profile will disable services such as X, so you can't even start the X-Server on your local machine. So, I suggest using the default medium security profile for now unless you will run the server in an environment in which security is critical. After you read this message, press Enter to continue.

Customizing the Console

Next, you have the opportunity to customize the FreeBSD console settings. You can use these settings to customize the behavior of your keyboard, to choose which font will be used on the screen display, and to select which screensaver should be used. If you select Yes to the question asking you whether you want to customize your console setting, you see a menu that looks like Figure 2.8.

FIGURE 2.8

Customizing the console settings.

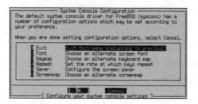

Most of the options here are self-explanatory. Simply select any options you need to onfigure and then follow the onscreen instructions.

Setting the Time Zone

Next, Sysinstall asks you whether you want to set the system's time zone. Select Yes here. Your system's clock is probably not set to UTC (known also as Coordinated Universal Time, Greenwich Mean Time, and Zulu Time). So, unless you are sure your clock is set to UTC, select No here. The next menu asks you to select your region, your country, and other information about where you are located. After you provide Sysinstall with all the information it needs about your time zone, it shows you an abbreviation and asks Does the abbreviation *xxx* look reasonable?, where *xxx* is your time zone. If it looks correct, select Yes. If it doesn't, select No; you can do it again.

Linux Compatibility

The next question is Would you like to enable Linux binary compatibility?

If you answer Yes here, Sysinstall will install a "mini-Linux filesystem" in your /usr partition that will include the Linux share libraries and other necessary programs for Linux to run on FreeBSD. Unless you are sure that you will not run any Linux programs, I suggest you select Yes. This can be a very useful option. In fact, I wrote much of the manuscript for this book on StarOffice for Linux that ran on my FreeBSD workstation.

> **Note**
>
> Your first thought might be that you wouldn't want to do this because if you worked with emulators under other operating systems, you know how slow they can be. With FreeBSD, this is not the case, however. Linux support in FreeBSD is not done through an emulator, but rather is implemented at a kernel level. FreeBSD's Linux support is so good that it runs most Linux applications as fast as native Linux. In fact, FreeBSD will even run some Linux applications faster than Linux itself runs them!

Configuring the Mouse

FreeBSD comes with a console mouse daemon that allows you to cut and paste text from the console using the mouse. The next question asks you if you have a non-USB mouse attached to your system. If you do, select Yes, and you will see the mouse configuration menu (as shown in Figure 2.9).

2

INSTALLING
FreeBSD

> **Caution**
>
> At the time of this writing, the console mouse daemon seems to cause problems with Xfree86 4.0 (the version of X-Windows that is included with FreeBSD 5.0). If you plan to use X-Windows as the graphical user interface for FreeBSD most of the time, you should probably select "Disable the mouse daemon" from this menu. You do not need to use the console mouse daemon to cut and paste from X-Windows terminal prompts (similar to DOS windows in Microsoft Windows). So, if you will be using X-Windows most of the time, you will not need the mouse daemon. If you do select "Disable the mouse daemon," you can skip this section and continue with the section "Configuring the X-Server."

FIGURE 2.9

Configuring the mouse.

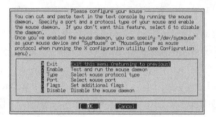

Use the menu options to select the type of mouse you have and the port it is connected to. Read the instructions at the top of each menu to help you determine which protocol and port to select.

X-Windows makes use of all three buttons on a standard mouse. If you have a mouse with only two buttons on it, you need to emulate a three-button mouse by telling the mouse driver to interpret the clicking of both buttons at the same time as the third button. You can do this by selecting the Flags option on the menu and typing -3 in the dialog box that pops up. Some other useful options you might want to put in here are -r high to make the pointer move faster if it moves too slowly, or -r low if the pointer moves too fast and you want to slow it down.

After you finish configuring the mouse settings, select the option Enable to test and run the mouse daemon. If the mouse is set up correctly, you should now be able to move the mouse pointer around on the screen. When you are done testing the mouse, select Yes (note that the mouse still doesn't work in the menu—you still need to use the arrows and the Tab key) if the mouse worked, or choose No if it didn't.

You are then returned to the mouse configuration menu. Assuming that the mouse worked, select the Exit option.

Configuring the X-Server

> **Note**
>
> This section applies only to FreeBSD 4.4 running XFree86 3.3.6. If you are running FreeBSD 5.0, you will be using XFree86 4.x. In this case, please follow the configuration instructions in chapter 34, "Advanced X-Windows Configuration" for XFree86 4.x.

Assuming that you installed the X-Windows system, you will now be asked if you want to configure the X-Server. Select Yes at this option, and you will be given a menu that looks like figure 2.10

FIGURE 2.10

Selecting the X-Server configuration method.

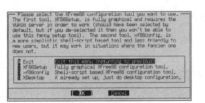

If you have never set up X-Windows before, you should definitely select XF86Setup option to configure the server as it is much easier then using the shell script based xf86config tool.

Press [Enter] at the message about "You have configured and are now running the mouse daemon". Also press [Enter] at the message about switching to graphics mode.

At this point, your screen may go blank for a little bit, and then display a checkered background with an "X" in the middle. Sooner or later, you should see a screen like Figure 2.11. This can take some time, so be patient.

> **Note**
>
> Avoid moving the mouse until you have completed the mouse setup portion of XF86Setup. Moving the mouse before it is set up could cause XF86Setup to fail to properly detect it later when you do set it up.

FIGURE 2.11

*The XF86Setup
Main Menu.*

The first thing you will want to configure here is your mouse so that you can use it for the rest of the setup. Since the mouse configuration will be the option currently selected by default, simply press [Enter] to start the mouse configuration.

Configuring the Mouse

You should have a help screen that looks like figure 2.12 in front of you.

FIGURE 2.12

*The Mouse
Configuration
Help Screen*

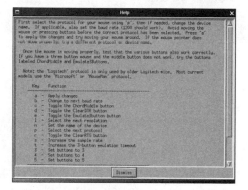

When you are finished reading the help screen, simply press [Enter] to get rid of it. You should then be left with a screen like figure 2.13.

Use the Tab key to move between options. You will notice that as you press the Tab key, a black border will move between the various buttons available to select.

Because we configured the mouse daemon for cutting and pasting text from the console, we want to use it as our X-Windows mouse as well. First, use the Tab key Sysmouse is selected under the "Select the mouse protocol" menu. When it is, press [Enter] to select it. The button will change color and have a "pressed" look to it.

FIGURE 2.13

*The Mouse
Configuration
Screen*

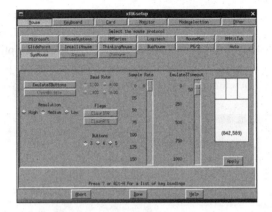

Now use the Tab key to move into the "Mouse device box". From here, you can use the up and down arrows to move through the different mouse devices available. Select the /dev/sysmouse option and press [Enter]. The box should not reflect the choice you made.

Now Tab until the "Apply" button is selected under the drawing of the mouse. Press [Enter] on the button, and in a second or two, your mouse should become active. See if you can move the mouse around and also test the buttons to make sure they work properly. If you have problems getting the mouse to be detected, please see Appendix C.

If you have a two button mouse and you need to emulate three buttons by pressing both buttons at the same time, also select the Emulate3Buttons button. You can then use Emulate3TimeOut to control how long the X server waits before activating a left click or right click, to see if you intend to press both buttons to emulate the third button.

Many of the other options here such as "Resolution" have no affect because you are using the FreeBSD mouse daemon.

Assuming your mouse is now working, you can use the mouse for the rest of the XF86Setup process.

Configuring your Keyboard

Click on the "Keyboard" button in the menu across the top of the screen. Here you can select the model and type of keyboard you have (figure 2.14).

The default selection will be "Generic 101-key PC". These days however, most people have a 104 key keyboard (sometimes known as a "Windows Enhanced" keyboard because of the additional Windows keys). There are programs and utilities for X-Windows that can make use of these additional keys and reprogram them to do something useful in X-Windows. So if you have a 104 key keyboard with the extra Windows keys, select the "Generic 104-key PC" option in model. If you happen to have a Microsoft Natural keyboard, or one of the various other keyboard listed, select those options instead. The "Generic 101-key PC" or "Generic 104-key PC" options should work for most keyboards though. If are outside of the United States, or just happen to have a non-US keyboard, you can also select various other keyboard layouts here.

FIGURE 2.14

Configuring the Keyboard.

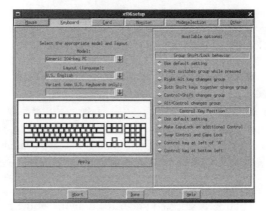

On the right side of this screen, you can remap some keys to do other things than what they would normally do. I don't recommend this unless you are familiar with a different keyboard layout than the PC keyboard has (for example, some UNIX keyboards place the CTRL key where Caps Lock key is on a PC keyboard. If you are an Emacs guru in UNIX you might want to remap the Caps Lock to the CTRL key since the CTRL key is used so often in Emacs).

Configuring the Video Card

Next click on the "Card" button at the top of the screen. This brings up the video card menu where you tell XF86Setup what type of video card you have (figure 2.15).

FIGURE 2.15

Configuring the Video Card.

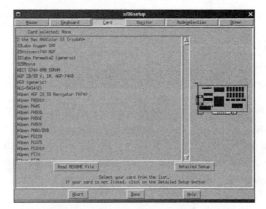

The list of video cards here is quite extensive, and chances are quite good that you will find your card in this list. Scroll through the list and look for your video card. When you find it, click on it so that it is selected.

If you can't find your video card in this list, all might not be lost. If you can manage to come up with various technical details about your video card including the Chipset it uses, the RamDac, and the ClockChip, you might be able to configure your card manually by using the "Detailed Setup" option. A discussion of the Detailed Setup option is beyond the scope of this chapter. If you need it, please see chapter 34 on Advanced X-Windows Configuration.

Once you have selected your video card, click on the "Monitor" button to select your monitor type and set the refresh rates on it.

Configuring Monitor Settings

Caution

STOP: This is about the only place in the installation where it's possible that a mistake could actually cause physical damage to your hardware. Although most monitors have built in protection circuits these days, and will shut themselves down if you try to drive them with a refresh rate higher than they support, some monitors will try to display the screen at the given refresh rate, even if the monitor's hardware is not capable of handling it. The result could destroy your monitor. If you really do a number on it, you might even get smoke coming out of the top. So make sure that you do not select refresh rates higher than your monitor can support! There is also the slight possibility of pushing your video card past its limits and destroying it.

Now that you have read the above warning, you are ready to configure your monitor settings. After you have clicked on the "Monitor" button, you will have a screen that looks like figure 2.16.

Enter the horizontal and vertical refresh rates for your monitor in the respective boxes. You should be able to get this information from your monitor's manual. If you have a multi-frequency monitor (and almost all monitors are multi-frequency these days), you can specify the frequency range with a dash.

If you don't know what the frequency range that your monitor supports is, you can select one of the generic monitor types from the list that closely matches your monitor type.

If you want, or need a detailed discussion of how monitors work, see chapter 34 on "Advanced X-Windows Configuration".

2

INSTALLING
FreeBSD

FIGURE 2.16

Configuring the Monitor Refresh Rates.

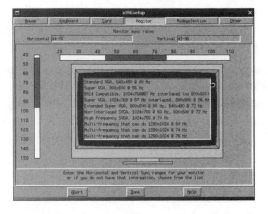

Selecting the Video Mode

Click on the Modeselection button to switch to the menu where you can select your video mode (figure 2.17). Note that your screen may look slightly different as resolutions not supported by your hardware will not be displayed.

FIGURE 2.17

The Video Mode Selection Menu

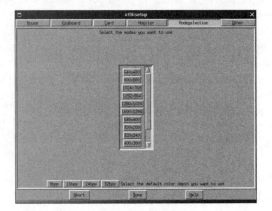

X-Windows works best with a resolution of at least 1024x768. If you have a 17 inch monitor, this will be fine. If you have a 15 inch monitor, it might be tolerable. If not, you may want to go down to 800x600 on a 15 inch monitor. It is difficult to use 14 inch monitors with X-Windows, but if you must, then you will not want to go higher than 800x600 resolution, and you might even want to stick to 640x480. If you have a 19 or 21 inch monitor, you may want to go higher then 1024x768. Note that you can select multiple resolutions. Toggle a resolution on or off by clicking on it. If you select multiple resolutions, you will be able to change the resolution of your screen from within X-Windows (assuming your video card supports this).

On the bottom of the screen, you need to choose your color depth. This is the number of colors that can X-Windows can produce:

- 8 bit color is the least desirable as it only allows 256 colors. In addition, since it uses a system wide palette to store color information, those 256 colors have to be shared by everything that is currently displayed on the screen. This can make for some very grainy looking colors sometimes, especially if you are displaying photographs on your screen, or using photographs or other high color images as background images for your desktop.

- 16 bit color can display over 64,000 different colors. Unlike 8 bit color, 16 bit color doesn't use a palette. This means that applications and displays on the screen aren't all limited to sharing the same palette of colors.

- 24 bit color can display 16.7 million colors This is more then the human eye is capable of distinguishing.

- 32 bit color can still only display 16.7 million colors, but it uses four bits per pixel instead of 3 bits per pixel like 24 bit color does.

Testing the X-Server

When you are finished configuring the resolution and color depth, click the "done" button at the bottom of the screen (I don't suggest you make any changes in the "Other" section at this point). Click Ok on the message that appears about starting the X server with the configuration you have selected.

You will then get a message about "Attempting to start the X server". Once again, your screen will go dark for a little bit. It shouldn't take long though before the checkered background appears again with the "X" in it.

Caution

If your screen comes back up and looks all garbled and strange looking and/or if you hear a high pitched whine coming from your monitor, IMMEDIATELY turn off your monitor or press the keys [CTRL][ALT][BACKSPACE] at the same time to kill the X server. Both of these signs are indications that you have overdriven the refresh rate of your monitor, and your monitor's flyback transformer is getting ready to fry.

If your monitor stays dark, or appears to go into a power saving mode or turn itself off (the power light starts blinking or changes color or something), it probably indicates that you selected a refresh rate higher than your monitor can handle and it has turned itself

2

INSTALLING
FreeBSD

off to prevent damage. Press the [CTRL][ALT][BACKSPACE] keys at the same time to kill the X server and try again.

> **Note**
>
> If you press [CTRL][ALT][BACKSPACE] and you end up with a checkered screen with a very large X in the middle and you never get a menu back, you will need to press [CTRL][ALT][BACKSPACE] again to exit XF96Setup. After this, you will have to restart the configuration, beginning with the mouse.

In a few moments, you should get a box with "Congratulations. You've got a running X server!"

If the image on your screen is off center or is the wrong size, you can use xvidtune here to adjust it as suggested. You can also use the controls on your monitor to adjust the image.

Using xvidtune

If you decide to use xvidtune, you will first get a ominous warning on your screen about improper use of the program causing damage to your monitor and/or video card. Once you have clicked OK here, you will have a screen like figure 2.18.

FIGURE 2.18

The xvidtune screen.

Here is what the various buttons in xvidtune do:

TABLE 2.6   xvidtunde controls

Button	Action
Left, Right, Up, and Down	Move the display image in the respective direction on the screen.
Wider, Narrower. Shorter, Taller	Adjust the size of the display image respectively.
Quit	Quit xvidtune.

TABLE 2.6 continued

Button	Action
Apply	Apply the changes to the current video mode.
Auto	This button acts as a toggle. When active, it causes the changes made to the image to be applied immiediately rather than wating for you to press the Apply button. Allows you to see the effects of your changes in real time.
Test	Test the display with the new changes you made. The original display will be restored after a few seconds. Has no real effect if Auto is also active.
Restore	Restore the settings to their original values.
Fetch	Fetches the current settings from the X server. This will also cause Restore to now revert to the settings that were active when Fetch was selected.
Show	Shows the current modeline from the XF86Config file on the standard out (more on that in Chapter 34 on "Advanced X-Windows Configuration").
Next, Prev	Switches to the next or previous video mode respectively (if you have defined multiple resolutions).

Once of the important things to watch here is the horizontal and vertical sync rates shown on the right lower half of the screen. As you make changes in xvidtune, make sure that these values don't go out of range of what you know your monitor can support.

> **Caution**
>
> Do not click Apply or Test when the horizontal sync or vertical sync values are outside of what you know your hardware can support. Although you may simply get an error meesage saying that the configuration is not supported by your hardware, if xvidtune does try to apply the settings, it could cause permanent damage to your monitor and/or video card.

Once you have finished making changes here, click Apply to apply the final changes, and then Quit to leave xvidtune.

Saving the Configuration and Quiting XF86Setup

After you have left xvidtune (or if you elect not to use xvidtune), Click on the "Save configuraiton and Exit" option. Answer yes to the question about whether you want to create an 'X' link to the server.

Selecting the Default Desktop

Note that now you are back to familiar text based Sysinstall program. The mouse can no longer be used. Go back to the arrow keys, tab keys, space bar, and Enter keys.

In the next screen, you can select which desktop you want to use as your default FreeBSD desktop in X-Windows. Unlike Microsoft Windows, FreeBSD allows you a wide choice of desktops with different features, looks, etc. There are far more desktops available then are in this list and they are very easy to change.

If you are an old Linux guru or something, and you already know which desktop you would like to use, select whatever you want here. If you have never worked with X-Windows before, I suggest you select the Gnome + Sawfish option here as this desktop is easy for new users to work with and it is the one I will be using in the next few chapters. If you later decide you don't like the desktop, you can always change is to a different one.

Once you have made your selection here, the packages for your chosen desktop will be loaded onto your system.

Note

In FreeBSD 5.0, one of the options available in this menu is xf86cfg. This is a graphical interface to help you configure the X-Server. However, at the time of this writing, the xf86cfg tool does not work properly and may leave you with a blank screen. Therefore, this section does not cover it. Instead, go to Chapter 34, "Advanced X-Windows Configuration," and read the section "Configuring X-Windows with the xf86config Script." After you have finished xf86config, return to this chapter and continue with the next section.

Caution

If you decide to try using xf86cfg anyway, you should be aware that improper refresh rate settings can cause damage to your monitor. So, make sure you do not use monitor settings that your monitor is not capable of supporting. This is discussed in more detail in Chapter 34.

Installing Additional Software Packages

Answer Yes to the question about whether you want to browse the FreeBSD package collection. Here, you can install some additional software that will be useful in the next couple of chapters. Feel free to browse through the collection as long as you want only to see what is available. For now, however, I don't recommend that you install a ton of software at this point because it is very easy to add more later. There are a few packages that I recommend you install for use in the next few chapters, however.

If you are asked where you want to install the packages from in the Choosing Installation Media menu, select CDROM, assuming that you are installing FreeBSD from the included CD.

Figure 2.19 shows the main menu for the package installation system.

FIGURE 2.19

Installing additional packages.

To navigate through the package installation system, use the arrow keys to move between packages and categories, the spacebar to select or unselect a package, and the Enter key to get back to the main selection menu (in which you can select the category you want to browse). Packages that are already installed will have an X next to them. Unselecting these packages causes them to be uninstalled. Packages that have a D by them are dependencies, meaning that that package is required by some other package that is currently installed. At the bottom of the screen is a short description of the currently highlighted package.

The following sections describe the categories I suggest you browse and the packages I suggest you install for now.

Note

By the time this book goes to press, some of the version numbers on the software listed as follows may have changed. In this case, select the option that appears closest to what I list here. For example, I list Bash-2.04. If your menu has Bash-2.07 instead, select it.

Shells

- **Bash-2.04**—This is a very powerful and easy-to-use shell for the FreeBSD command-line interface. Linux users will be familiar with this shell because it is the default shell on almost all Linux distributions.

UNIX gurus can also install any other shell in this list that they want to be available to work with.

Gnome

If you followed my advice earlier and installed `Gnome + Sawfish` as the default desktop environment, you may want to install several packages from this category to make Gnome use more productive (and more fun). You should not go overboard on installing software because it is very easy to add this software later. But there are a few packages that you will want to install for what we will do in the next couple of chapters:

> **Note**
>
> Some of these packages may already be selected because you selected Gnome as your default desktop. If this is the case, leave those packages alone, and just select the ones that do not already have an X or a D next to them.

- **`eog-0.5_1`**—The Eye of Gnome Image Viewer. Handles most popular image formats.
- **`gaddr-1.1.4`**—A simple address book for Gnome.
- **`gedit-0.9.3`**—A graphical text editor for Gnome. Somewhat like Notepad in Windows, but with more features.
- **`glunarclock-0.11`**—An applet that can display a picture of the moon in its current phase on the Gnome panel. Useful for keeping track of the next time you will turn into a werewolf.
- **`gno3dtet-1.6.0`**—A classic time-waster. This is a 3D version of Tetris for Gnome.
- **`gnomeapplets-1.2.4`**—A set of panel applets for Gnome.
- **`gnomefind-1.0`**—Similar to "Find" in Windows, this utility helps you find file locations that you can't remember.
- **`gnomegames-1.2.0`**—A package that contains multiple time-wasters.

- **gnomemc-4.5.51**—Gnome Midnight Commander. A Windows Explorer-like file manager for Gnome, required if you want to be able to have icons on the Gnome desktop.

- **gnomemedia-1.2.0**—Multimedia applications for Gnome (a CD player and such).

- **gpaint-0.1.1**—Similar to the Paint program in Windows.

After you finish selecting packages, make sure that you are at the main package installation menu (as was shown in Figure 2.19), use the Tab key to highlight Install at the bottom of the screen, and press Enter. Sysinstall proceeds to install the packages you selected, along with any dependencies.

Adding a User

When the package installation is complete, you are asked whether you want to add any user accounts to the system. Select Yes to create a normal user account for yourself. It is dangerous to use the root account for normal operations because root has no restrictions and can damage or destroy important system files if you make a mistake. Using your normal user account for most operations prevents you from making mistakes like this.

On the screen that looks like Figure 2.20, select User to add a new user to the system.

FIGURE 2.20

Adding users and groups to the system.

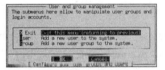

You are then taken to a form you need to fill out to add the new user (see Figure 2.21).

FIGURE 2.21

The Add a new user form.

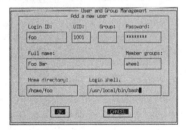

Not all of the fields on this form have to be filled in, and actually you should leave some of them blank so the system can make a default choice for you. Use the Tab key to move between the various fields. The following sections describe what each field means.

Login ID:

The name you use to identify yourself to the system when you sign in. It should not be more than eight characters long. Common conventions are to use initials, nicknames, or combinations of initials and first or last name. For example, I might use mikeu, murban, or mcu as my login name. Each user on the system must have a unique login name. Names are case-sensitive and, by convention, use all lowercase letters.

UID:

A numeric ID that the system uses to keep track of users. You should leave this field alone and let the system pick the number for you.

Group:

The primary group that you will be a member of. Once again, leave this field alone and let the system pick for you.

Password:

The password you use to log in. Passwords are case-sensitive. Here are some guidelines for choosing good passwords that crackers (commonly known as "hackers," but "hackers" is not the correct term for these people who illegally break into computer systems) can't figure out.

- Use at least eight characters. Short passwords are easier for programs designed to try random combinations of letters and numbers to crack.
- Use a combination of uppercase and lowercase letters, numbers, and at least one special character such as $ or !.
- Don't use words found in a dictionary. Password-cracking programs exist that go through the dictionary trying various words until they hit one that works.
- Don't use things that other people know about you, or can easily find out about you. In other words, the name of your child, your cat, the city you were born in, etc., do not make good passwords.

At the same time, it's good to pick something that you will remember easily. Some techniques for doing this include combining parts of various words together (remembering, of course, to include both uppercase and lowercase letters, and stick a few numbers and at least one special character in it somewhere). You can also use "keyboard substitution," what I call a technique where you pick a word that means something to you (but that others will not know) and then substitute the character to the upper-left, upper-right, lower-left, or lower-right as the actual character in the password.

After you decide on a password, enter it carefully as you will not be asked to verify it. (The password will show up on the screen as asterisks, *.) If you mistype it, you will not be able to log in (if you accidentally do mistype it, you can read how to fix it in Appendix C).

After you decide on your password, do not write it down anywhere. Do not write it on the bottom of your desk. Do not write it down in your appointment book. Do not have it tattooed on your arm. And whatever you do, do not write it on a Post-It Note and stick it on your monitor. (I know that seems like stating the obvious, but you would be surprised how many users do just that.) Also, do not tell your password to anybody. Do not tell it to your coworkers, your spouse, or your children.

Full name:

You can either put your name in here or leave it blank. Note that some programs, such as the UNIX mail program, will use this field to determine what to put in the From: field of e-mail that you send. So, it is probably a good idea to put your name in here.

Member groups:

I suggest you type wheel in this box. This will make you a member of the group "wheel" which will allow you to assume the identity of the root user (superuser or system administrator) without having to log out and log back in as a different user (you still need to supply the root password to do this).

Home directory:

The place where your home directory will be located on the hard disk. You should leave this field alone and let the system choose for you.

Login shell:

The default command-line shell you will be placed in after you log in. Assuming that you installed the Bash shell, as suggested earlier, I suggest you type /usr/local/bin/bash in this field (including the slashes). If you later decide that you do not like the Bash shell, it is easy to change your default shell to a different one.

After you finish entering the information, tab over to the OK button and press Enter. The user account will be created for you, and you will be returned to the menu shown in Figure 2.20. Select the Exit option.

Setting the Root Password

Press Enter at the message about setting the system manager's password. You are then given a prompt at the bottom of the screen that asks you to enter a root password. It looks like this:

```
Changing local password for root.
New password :
```

All the guidelines I gave you about choosing and protecting your normal user password are doubly important here. Anyone who knows your root password (or can find it out) can access anything on your entire system, as well as do anything to your entire system. They will have access to read confidential information, e-mail it to other places, destroy data on your system, change data on your system, and do whatever other evil things they decide to do. After you decide on a root password, enter it at the prompt. Notice that it will not show up onscreen as you type it. This prevents someone from looking over your shoulder and getting your password. After you enter the password, press Enter. You will be asked to verify it. Type it again, and press Enter. Assuming that you typed it the same way both times, the installation will ask you if you want to visit the general configuration menu for a chance to set any last options. Select No here, and you are returned to the main menu.

Exiting the Install and Rebooting the System

At the main menu, tab over to Exit Install, and press Enter. The system asks you to confirm that you wish to exit, and asks you to remove any CDs or floppies from the drives on your system. After you remove the CD and/or floppy from the drive(s), select Yes, and the system will reboot.

> **Note**
>
> You may find that you press the Eject button on your CD-ROM, and nothing happens. Don't worry. FreeBSD didn't break your CD-ROM drive; it just locked it to ensure that you couldn't accidentally eject the CD in the middle of the install or something. If you can't open your CD-ROM, select Yes anyway, and wait until just after your system has started to reboot (when it is counting the memory and such). Then, press the eject button on your CD-ROM. It should now open and you should be able to remove the FreeBSD CD.

> **Tip**
>
> When the system reboots, you might want to go into your BIOS setup utility right away and configure the system so that it will not try to boot from the CD anymore. Some systems can hang for a long time while trying to boot from the CD if there is no bootable CD in the drive (or no CD at all). Although most systems will eventually give up and boot from the hard disk, it can sometimes take as long as a minute or more before the system decides it can't boot from the CD and goes to the hard disk instead. Disable CD booting in the BIOS to avoid this problem. (See your hardware documentation for information on how to configure your system BIOS settings.)

Booting FreeBSD for the First Time

When your system restarts, one of two things should happen: You should either get a boot menu asking you which operating system you want to boot; or, if FreeBSD is the only operating system on the drive, the system should begin to boot straight into FreeBSD. If this is not the case, and your system either hangs or boots right into some other operating system without giving you the option of starting FreeBSD, see Appendix C.

Assuming that the restart is successful, you should get a flurry of messages going past your screen as the kernel finds and initializes your system hardware. Kernel messages are in a bright white color. After the kernel is finished, it will pass control to a program called init, which starts up various other processes and programs in the system. These messages have a light gray color. There will be a short pause the first time the system boots as it generates RSA and DSA encryption keys for your system (which are used for secure communication across networks or the internet). Eventually, after init is finished, you should be left with the following:

```
FreeBSD/i386 (simba.samplenet.org) (ttyv0)
```

```
login:
```

Your display, of course, will have the name of your host and network instead of (simba.samplenet.org). If you didn't set up the network, it will have the system default hostname, which will probably be Amnesiac.

Log in using the name root, and after pressing Enter, enter the password you gave to root (once again, the password will not display on the screen).

Assuming that you type the username and password correctly, you will see a welcome message that tells you a little bit about FreeBSD and where you can get help (as well as how you can change this message or get rid of it), and then left with a shell prompt. It will look something like this:

```
Copyright  1980, 1983, 1986, 1988, 1990, 1991, 1993, 1994
        The Regents of the University of California.  All rights reserved.

FreeBSD 4.4 RELEASE (GENERIC) #0: Mon Mar 26 00:47:09 CST 2001

#
```

The # is the command prompt. And it means the shell is waiting for you to give it something to do.

Shutting Down FreeBSD

FreeBSD (like other versions of UNIX) is a multitasking and multiuser operating system. It is constantly doing something, and usually has many files open at the same time. Because of this, you cannot simply turn off the power when you want to shut down a FreeBSD system. First, you have to tell FreeBSD to shut itself down so that it can terminate programs it is running and save any files it has open in an orderly fashion. The proper way to do it right now is with the following command:

```
shutdown -h now
```

This tells FreeBSD to perform a system shutdown, to halt after the shutdown is complete (as opposed to reboot or going into single user mode), and that we want the shutdown to happen now instead of five minutes from now, for example. (Usually, you put a delay here so that users will get a warning of the coming shutdown and have time to save whatever files they are working on.)

Type `shutdown -h now` at the prompt, and press Enter.

You see a few messages on your screen, including `Broadcast message from root` and various status messages from some processes as they shut down.

Look for the following message:

```
System halted
Please press any key to reboot
```

Then, and only then, is it safe to turn off your computer.

Caution

Never shut down a FreeBSD system, or any other UNIX system, by simply turning off the power. Doing so can cause serious damage to the filesystems. You should always issue a proper shutdown first.

Advanced Installation Issues

CHAPTER 3

This chapter serves mostly as a supplement to Chapter 2, "Installing FreeBSD." If you wish to install FreeBSD on a system that already has another operating system on it, you will want to read this chapter before doing the installation. After you have completed the preinstallation tasks necessary for your situation, you should return to Chapter 2 and proceed with the normal installation.

Most often, you will install FreeBSD on a workstation that is already running Windows. This chapter shows how the two can operate side-by-side. We will also look briefly at installing on a system that is running Linux.

In addition, we will briefly cover NFS and FTP network installs.

Backing Up Existing Filesystems

Before you go any further, back up any existing filesystems that you want to maintain. Although the next section will show you how to nondestructively create space for FreeBSD, mistakes can still happen, and programs can cause errors. It is best to have a backup of anything you want to keep.

> **Caution**
>
> If you are not taking regular backups of your system, it is a good idea to get into the habit of doing so anyway. Hard disks are mechanical devices. They can and do fail sometimes. When they do, you will want a backup to restore your data from.

Media that can be used for backup purposes include recordable CDs, Zip or Jaz disks, tape drives, or—if the amount of data you need to save is small—floppy disks. Backing up the operating system and installed programs, such as word processing programs, are not necessary because they can be easily reinstalled. The primary things to worry about are your files containing data that cannot be easily replaced.

If you do not have an actual backup program, you can use an archiving program such as WinZip to help you compress data for backup and also to place that data onto disks.

The exact procedures for doing the backup are beyond the scope of this book. Please see the documentation for the program you plan to use for doing the backup for information on how to complete the backup.

Once you have backed up any existing files that you wish to keep, you will need to free up some space on your hard disk for installing FreeBSD. There are several ways that this can be done:

- Simply delete the partitions and start over. This will cause you to lose all the existing data on your system, and you will have to reinstall everything that is currently on your system once you have re-created the partitions.

- Use a commercial partitioning program such as Partition Magic. If you have Partition Magic, by all means use it. A discussion of how to use this commercial program is beyond the scope of this book. Please see Partition Magic's documentation for instructions.

- Use the FIPS utility. This freely available program allows you to split an existing partition to create free space. FIPS is included on the CD with this book, and it is the method that will be discussed here.

Nondestructive Hard Disk Partitioning with FIPS

FIPS is a program designed to run under DOS or Windows in DOS mode. It will split an existing DOS partition into two partitions at the point you specify. You can then use the new partition it creates as the space for FreeBSD. Note that FIPS works only with DOS-style partitions (FAT16 or FAT32). FIPS will not work with Windows NT/2000 NTFS partitions, nor will it work with Linux EXT2FS partitions. If you happen to be running OS/2, FIPS will not work with HPFS partitions, either.

FIPS has a couple of limitations that you need to be aware of:

- It cannot split an extended DOS partition—only a primary one. If you are like most people running Windows 95 OSR2 or Windows 98, this will not be a problem since you likely have one primary partition that takes up the entire disk.

- You cannot currently have more than three partitions on your disk. FIPS creates a new primary partition with the free space it is assigned. Since you can only have four partition entries on a disk, you will need to have no more than three existing already.

If neither of the previous issues applies to you, and assuming you have made a backup, you are ready to begin the partitioning process.

Run Scandisk and Defragmenter

Before you use FIPS, you should run DOS or Windows Scandisk to fix any problems on the disk. After Scandisk has finished running, you will need to run the disk defragmenter.

FIPS needs contiguous free space at the end of the drive in order to split the partition. It cannot split before the last sector on the disk that contains data. Running the disk defragmenter moves all the data to the beginning of the disk without leaving holes in the middle.

Depending on the speed of your computer, the size of your hard disk, how fast the disk is, and how badly fragmented it is, the defragmentation process could take anywhere from a few minutes to several hours.

Obtaining FIPS and Creating a Boot Disk

Once the defragmentation process is finished, you are ready to start FIPS. FIPS is located on the included CD in the TOOLS directory with the name FIPS.EXE. You will also want the files named RESTORRB.EXE and ERRORS.TXT. You can also download FIPS from the FreeBSD ftp server at ftp.freebsd.org or one of its mirror sites in the directory /pub/FreeBSD/tools/fips.exe. Also, you will want the files restorrb.exe and errors.txt from the same directory.

You should create a bootable floppy, and copy the three files mentioned previously to it. In DOS or Windows, you can create a bootable floppy from a DOS prompt with the command format a: /s, assuming that you have a blank floppy in drive a. Following is a sample procedure to create the boot disk:

```
C:\> format a: /s
Insert new diskette in drive A:
and press ENTER when ready...

Checking existing disk format.
Verifying 1.44M
Format complete.
System transferred

Volume label (11 characters, ENTER for none)?

    1,457,664 bytes total disk space
      388,608 bytes used by system
    1,069,056 bytes available on disk

        512 bytes in each allocation unit.
        2,088 allocation units available on disk.
```

```
Volume Serial Number is is 031B-0831

Format another (Y/N)?n

C:\>d:
D:\>cd tools
D:\TOOLS>copy fips.exe a:\
    1 file(s) copied
d:\TOOLS>copy restorerb.exe a:\
    1 file(s) copied
D:\TOOLS>copy errors.txt a:\
    1 file(S) copied
D:\TOOLS>
```

Once you have done this, reboot your system from the floppy you just created. After the system has finished booting, type `fips` at the DOS prompt to start the FIPS program.

Working with FIPS

When FIPS first starts, it will give you a warning about not using it in a multitasking environment, among other things. Once you have read all the information, press any key to continue. If you have more than one hard disk in your system, FIPS will ask you which one you want to work on. Select the disk you want. FIPS will then show you the partition table of your disk. It will look something like the following:

```
    |        |   Start           |      |     End           | Start  |Number of|
Part.|bootable|Head Cyl. Sector|System|Head Cyl. Sector| Sector |Sectors  |  MB
-----+--------+-----------------+------+----------------+--------+---------+----
1    |   yes  |  1   0      1| |  06h|  12  983      32|     32| 409312| 199
2    |   no   |  0   0      0|    00h|   0    0       0|      0|      0|   0
3    |   no   |  0   0      0|    00h|   0    0       0|      0|      0|   0
4    |   no   |  0   0      0|    00h|   0    0       0|      0|      0|   0

Checking root sector ... OK

Press any Key
```

If you have more than one partition on your disk, FIPS will ask you which one you want to split. Select the partition you would like to split. If you only have one partition on your disk, you will simply be asked to `Press any Key`, as in the preceding example. After you have pressed a key to continue, FIPS will read the boot sector and present some more information on the disk:

```
Bytes per sector: 512
Sectors per cluster: 8
Reserved sectors: 1
Number of FATs: 2
```

```
Number of rootdirectory entries: 512
Number of sectors (short): 0
Media descriptor byte: f8h
Sectors per FAT: 200
Sectors per track: 32
Drive heads: 13
Hidden sectors: 32
Number of sectors (long): 409312
Physical drive number: 80h
Signature: 29h
```

When FIPS has finished presenting information, you will be asked to choose the starting cylinder for the new partition. The size of the new partition and the size of the old partition are presented. Use the left and right arrow keys to decrease and increase the number that the new partition will start on. In addition, you can use the up and down arrow keys to increase and decrease the size of the new partition in increments of 10 cylinders. When you have finished, press Enter to continue.

Tip

Write down the starting cylinder information for the new partition that you create. This will help you verify later on during the FreeBSD install that you have selected the correct partition to install FreeBSD on.

Once you have pressed Enter, FIPS will show you what the new partition table will look like. You will then be given the option to re-edit the partition table, or continue. If you select Continue, FIPS will ask you one last time if you are sure you want to write the changes to the partition table. Selecting y will cause FIPS to write the changes and then exit. At this point, you need to reboot your system.

If FIPS exited with any errors see the "Troubleshooting FIPS Problem" section at the end of this chapter.

Caution

It is very important that you do NOT write anything to the hard disk until after you have rebooted. Doing so could corrupt the disk since DOS will not be aware that the partition table has changed until the system has been rebooted.

Once you have rebooted, you should run FIPS again with the -t option. This will check to make sure that the partition was split correctly. If errors are reported, restore the previous partition table by running RESTORRB.EXE and then reboot again.

Caution

Once you have made ANY changes to the filesystems on the disk, you will no longer be able to use RESTORRB.EXE to restore the old partition table. Therefore, it is very important that you run fips with the -t option after you reboot before you do anything else.

If fips -t doesn't report any errors, remove the floppy from the drive, and reboot. When Windows or DOS has finished restarting you should run Scandisk on the partition you split to check for any errors.

Potential Problems with and Limitations of Dual Boot Systems

It is possible to have a dual boot system in which you can have two (or even more) operating systems on the hard disk, and you can select which one you want at each system boot. There are some potential problems that you need to be aware of when doing this, though.

The first one is that all of the information necessary to boot FreeBSD must be located within the first 1024 cylinders of the hard disk. This means that either the root partition must be completely located within the first 1024 cylinders, or you can use a separate boot partition that is completely located in the first 1024 cylinders. If you choose this option, the root partition does not have to be completely located in the first 1024 cylinders. Note that "completely located" means that the partition has to both start and end below the 1024th cylinder. Simply starting below the 1024th cylinder is not good enough.

If you need more space for Windows or DOS than is available below 1024 cylinders, you will need to split the Windows or DOS partition into two partitions, giving you a C drive and a D drive in Windows or DOS. In between these C and D drives, you will need to put a small partition for FreeBSD to boot from. This partition will be used as /boot later on during the install. 30 megabytes should be more than enough for this partition.

The second thing to be aware of if you will be reinstalling everything is that you should install DOS or Windows before you install FreeBSD. DOS and Windows assume that they are the only operating system on the hard drive, and will overwrite the master boot record without asking. If you install FreeBSD first, installing DOS or Windows later will clobber FreeBSD's boot manager, and you will no longer be able to boot into FreeBSD. This problem is easily fixed, but save yourself the headaches, and just install DOS or Windows first.

Dual Booting with DOS, Windows 95, Windows 98, or Windows ME

FreeBSD comes with a boot manager that will allow you to dual boot with various operating systems. If you already have DOS, Windows 95, Windows 98, or Windows ME installed, it is easy to set up the boot manager. You will be given the option to install it during the FreeBSD installation. DOS, Windows 95, Windows 98, or Windows ME will automatically be added to the boot menu.

Dual Booting with Linux

If you wish to dual boot with Linux and load Linux from the FreeBSD boot manager, install LILO at the beginning of your Linux boot partition rather than in the MBR. See the LILO documentation for instructions on how to do this. After you have done this, you will be able to boot Linux from the FreeBSD boot manager. If you wish to boot FreeBSD from LILO, please see the section later in this chapter titled "Booting FreeBSD from LILO," later in this chapter.

The FreeBSD Boot Manager

The FreeBSD boot manager can be installed during the installation to allow you to boot multiple operating systems. After the install, the boot manager can be configured with the boot0cfg program.

boot0cfg is command-line driven. Fortunately, you probably do not need to be concerned with most of the options. There are a couple of options that you might be interested in, though.

boot0cfg -B will install the boot manager onto the hard disk's MBR. This is one way to restore the boot manager if Windows should wipe it out. Of course, you would have to boot from a FreeBSD boot disk to use this if the boot manager had been wiped out. In addition, if you wish to make changes to the boot manager configuration, you will need to reinstall it using this command, followed by the changes you wish to make. The following list (see Table 3.1) of options is supported for making changes to the boot manager configuration:

TABLE 3.1   Boot Manager Configuration Options

Option	Description
-v	boot0cfg will be more verbose about what it is doing.
-b *image*	Where *image* is the name of the boot image to use. The default is /boot/boot0.
-d *drive*	Where *drive* is the drive number used by the PC's BIOS for referencing the disk. Usually this is 0x80 for the first drive, 0x81 for the second, and so on.
-f *file*	Where *file* is the name of a file that the original MBR should be backed up to in case there are problems. If the file already exists, it will be truncated.

The -o option is also supported and it contains a comma-separated list of options. Here are some of the options:

TABLE 3.2   Boot Manager Configuration Options

Option	Description
packet	If the PC's BIOS supports it, this will tell boot0cfg to use int 0x13 extensions instead of CHS for disk IO. This will get around the 1024 cylinder boot limit described previously. However, if the PC's BIOS does not support this option, it may cause the system to hang on the next reboot.
noupdate	By default, the boot manager can write to the MBR and update it (to set the active flag, etc). This can cause problems if you have hardware antivirus support enabled that prevents writing to the MBR and such. The noupdate option will prevent the boot manager from attempting to write to the MBR.

boot0cfg also supports the -s *n* option, where *n* is a number from 1 to 5 that specifies the *default slice* (commonly referred to as *partitions* in MS-DOS/Windows) to boot if no selection is made. The -t *n* option is also supported, where *n* is a number representing the number of "ticks" to wait before booting the default operating system. There are approximately 18.2 ticks in a second.

Booting FreeBSD from LILO

If you are running Linux and want to boot FreeBSD from Linux's LILO, it is fairly easy to do.

In Linux, edit the file `/etc/lilo.conf`, and add the following lines:

```
other=/dev/hda2
    table=/dev/hda
    label=FreeBSD
```

You will need to change the other line to reflect whatever device Linux recognizes your FreeBSD drive as.

After you have changed the configuration file, you will need to reinstall LILO by typing **lilo** as the root user.

Alternate Installation Methods

If you can't, or (for whatever reason) don't want to install FreeBSD from the CD included with this book, there are several other options available. These include network installs with FTP or NFS.

Installing FreeBSD over FTP

FTP stands for *File Transfer Protocol*. It is one of the earliest methods of transferring files over the Internet from one system to another. FTP is still widely used.

If you wish, you can install FreeBSD directly from an FTP server. If you want to do this, however, it is recommended that you have a full-time, fast Internet connection available. Doing an FTP install over a modem will take a very long time.

The first thing you need to determine if you want to do an FTP install is whether you can log in to the FTP server using the username anonymous. This is a common way of logging into public FTP servers. If you will be installing FreeBSD from the FreeBSD sites or one of the official mirrors, you can log in as anonymous. In this case, you can skip the next section. If however, you will be installing from an FTP server that does not allow anonymous logins (such as an internal FTP server on a LAN), you will need to follow the procedures in the next section to configure the username first.

Configuring the Username

From the sysinstall main menu (see Figure 3.1), arrow down to Options and press Enter. This will bring you to the screen shown in Figure 3.2.

FIGURE 3.1

The FreeBSD sysinstall *main menu.*

FIGURE 3.2

The Options menu, in which you can set the FTP login name.

In this screen, arrow down to the option that says FTP Username and press the spacebar. A dialog box will ask you to enter the username. Enter the name you need to use to log in to the FTP server and press Enter. You will then be asked to supply a password. Enter the password you need to use and press Enter again.

After you have finished, press Q to quit, and you will be returned to the Main sysinstall menu.

Selecting an FTP Install

After you have set the FTP username and password (if necessary), follow the instructions in Chapter 2 until you get to the screen where you are asked to Choose Installation Media. From this screen, select FTP or FTP Passive if the server you intend to install from is behind a firewall. (Ask your system administrator if you are not sure). You will then be asked to select a distribution site (see Figure 3.3).

FIGURE 3.3

Selecting the FTP server to install FreeBSD from.

If you are installing from one of the FreeBSD mirror sites, you can select the site from the list. Otherwise, select URL to specify an FTP server manually. In the dialog box that comes up (see Figure 3.4), you will be asked to specify the name of the FTP server, as well as the path to where the FreeBSD installation files are located. Figure 3.4 shows a sample for an ftp site with a hostname of `lion` located on the network `samplenet.org`, with the FreeBSD files located in the `/FreeBSD` directory.

FIGURE 3.4

Configuring the FTP server to install from.

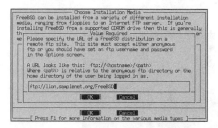

Once you have configured the FTP server you wish to install from, you will need to configure the network (see Figure 3.5).

FIGURE 3.5

Configuring the network.

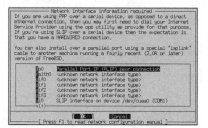

Follow the procedure in Chapter 2 under the "Configuring the Network" heading for instructions on how to do this.

Once you have finished configuring the network, the installation continues as in Chapter 2. When files have finished copying, you can go ahead with the "Post Installation" section of Chapter 2. Because you have already configured the network to do the installation, you can skip the network configuration portion.

Note that this chapter has covered only how to install FreeBSD from an FTP server. If you want to set up an "Installation server" that can be used by clients to install FreeBSD, see Chapter 27, "Configuring an FTP Server." Once you have an FTP server set up and the FreeBSD installation files available on it, you can have other systems install from it using the procedures in this chapter.

Doing an NFS Install

NFS stands for *Network File System*. It is a way for filesystems located on a server to be accessed by the local system. FreeBSD can be installed over NFS, assuming that there is an NFS server on your network that has the installation files available.

If your NFS server will work only on a secure port (or if you have a slow Ethernet adapter, follow the procedure in the following section. Otherwise, you can skip the next section.

Configuring `sysinstall` for a Secure Port or Slow Connection

At the `sysinstall` Main Menu (shown previously in Figure 3.1), select Options and press Enter. This will bring up the screen shown previously in Figure 3.2. The first option is NFS Secure. If your NFS server only works on a secure port (ask your system administrator) press the spacebar to toggle this to Yes. The second option (NFS Slow) should be toggled to Yes if you have a slow Ethernet card. Once you have made these changes, press Q to return to the `sysinstall` Main Menu.

Installation then continues, as discussed in Chapter 2, up to the point where you are asked to Choose Installation Media.

Selecting an NFS Install

At the Choose Installation Media screen, select NFS. You will then be asked to enter the name of the NFS server followed by the path where the FreeBSD installation files are located. In the example in Figure 3.6, the server is lion and the installation directory is install/FreeBSD.

FIGURE 3.6

Configuring an NFS server for installation.

Once you have entered this information, you will need to configure the network (shown previously in Figure 3.5). Follow the procedure shown in Chapter 2 under the "Configuring the Network" heading for instructions on how to do this.

Once you have finished configuring the network, the installation continues as discussed in Chapter 2. When files have finished copying, you can go ahead with the "Post Installation" section of Chapter 2. Because you have already configured the network to do the installation, you can skip the network configuration portion.

Note that this chapter has covered only how to install FreeBSD from an NFS server. If you want to set up an Installation server that can be used by clients to install FreeBSD over NFS, see Chapter 31, "The Network Filesystem (NFS)." Once you have an NFS server set up and the FreeBSD installation files available on it, you can have other systems install from it using the procedures discussed in this chapter.

Using FreeBSD

PART II

IN THIS PART

Your First Session with FreeBSD

CHAPTER 4

Unlike Windows, when you first start up FreeBSD, you are given a text mode command prompt. Also, unlike some versions of Windows, FreeBSD requires you to log in to the system before you can use it. This chapter will show you how to log in to FreeBSD and how to start the X-Windows system. It will also help you become acquainted with the Gnome Desktop Environment.

FreeBSD Startup Process

When you first start FreeBSD, it prints a flurry of messages on your screen from the kernel and also from the various processes that are starting up. We won't go into detail about what all of these messages mean right now, but the following sections give a quick rundown of the FreeBSD startup procedure.

The BIOS

Note

The following sections apply only to FreeBSD running on x86 (Intel) hardware. Although the startup process on Alpha systems is similar, some of the details are slightly different.

BIOS, which stands for *Basic Input/Output Services*, is a small piece of software that is on a ROM or EPROM chip on your computer's system board. Among other things, it is the job of the BIOS to test hardware when the computer is first turned on, and to find and load the first part of the operating system off of the hard drive.

The POST

The first thing your computer does when you turn it on is run the *POST*, which stands for *Power On Self Test*. During this phase, your computer's BIOS basically checks out all its hardware and makes sure that everything is working. RAM is counted, and PnP (Plug and Play) devices are probed to see what resources they can use.

The Bootstrap

After the POST is complete, the BIOS searches for a device on your system that it can boot from. The devices that are searched and the order they are searched in depend on the configuration you have set up in your BIOS setup program. The normal device to boot from is the first hard disk in the system, but other possible devices include the floppy drive, the CD-ROM drive, and even the network card for systems that have no hard disk and support loading the operating system over the network from a server. The system normally boots from the first bootable device it finds. After a bootable device is found (in this case, we assume that it is the hard disk), the BIOS begins the *bootstrap* procedure. The bootstrap is a multistage process, starting with *boot0*.

boot0

After the BIOS finds a bootable hard disk, it reads whatever is in sector 0 of the hard disk. Sector 0 is also known as the *Master Boot Record*, or *MBR*. The program located in the MBR can be only 512 bytes long. Therefore, it is a very simple program that knows just enough about the disk to be able to present a menu of the slices that can be booted from. Here is an example of a screen that might be produced by boot0:

```
F1 DOS
F2 FreeBSD
F3 Drive 1

Default: F2
```

Here, you can use the function keys to select which slice you want to boot—and, therefore, which operating system you want to boot. After you make a selection, boot0 finds and loads whatever is in the *boot sector* of the slice you selected. If FreeBSD is the only operating system on your hard disk, you will not see this menu, and the boot sector will be loaded immediately. This begins the next stage of the bootstrap known as *boot1*

boot1

boot1 is located on the first sector of the slice that is being booted. Like boot0, it can only be 512 bytes in size and therefore is very simple. It knows just enough to be able to find and load *boot2*.

boot2

boot2 knows enough to be able to load actual files off of the hard disk. Normally, boot2 loads a program called *loader*, although boot2 is capable of loading the kernel directly. The loader program is the next stage of the bootstrap.

boot3

The loader program is normally stored in /boot/loader. It is the program that allows you to control various options of the FreeBSD startup process, including which kernel should be booted, and so on. We will cover working with the loader in detail in Chapter 11, "System Configuration and Startup Scripts." For now, simply be aware that ultimately, the loader finds and loads the kernel and passes control to it. After the kernel is booted, the bootstrap is complete.

The Kernel

The standard kernel is normally located in /boot/kernel, and is started by the loader. As mentioned before, the kernel is the core of the operating system. It controls all access to hardware resources from both programs and users.

The white messages that you see onscreen when FreeBSD starts are messages from the kernel as it finds and initializes your hardware. Most of these messages will go by too fast for you to read, but after you log into the system, you can use the command dmesg | more to view them one screen at a time, and use the spacebar to advance to the next screen. Some example messages from the kernel on the system are shown as follows. This example does not show all the messages, but it gives you an idea of the kind of messages you will see and what they mean. Your messages will probably be different, depending on the type of hardware in your system.

```
Copyright  1992-2001 The FreeBSD Project.
Copyright  1979, 1980, 1983, 1986, 1988, 1989, 1991, 1992, 1993, 1994
        The Regents of the University of California. All rights reserved.
FreeBSD 5.0-CURRENT #0: Sun Apr 8 15:17:26 CDT 2001
    root@simba.samplenet.org:/usr/obj/usr/src/sys/SIMBA
```

The first three lines don't really need any explanation. They are simply copyright information.

Line 4 gives the operating system and the version of the kernel (the kernel version number will increase by one each time you rebuild the kernel). It also tells the date and time that the kernel was built.

The first part of Line 5 gives the username and local e-mail address of the person who built the kernel. In this case, the root user built the kernel, and it was built on the same system that I am currently writing this on. The second part of Line 5 tells where the directory is that this kernel was built in. (For you C-programming gurus, this is where you will find some of the C source files, the header files, and the object files that this kernel was built from; as well as the Makefile for the kernel.)

```
CPU: AMD-K6(tm) 3D+ Processor (400.91-MHz 586-class CPU)
  Origin = "AuthenticAMD"  Id = 0x591  Stepping = 1
  Features=0x8021bf<FPU,VME,DE,PSE,TSC,MSR,MCE,CX8,PGE,MMX>
  AMD Features=0x80000800<SYSCALL,3DNow!>
```

Here, the kernel has detected the CPU type, and it is simply printing out some information about it and the features it supports.

```
psm0: <PS/2 Mouse> irq 12 on atkbdc0
psm0: model Generic PS/2 mouse, device ID 0
fdc0: <NEC 72065B or clone> at port 0x3f0-0x3f5,0x3f7 irq 6 drq 2 on isa0
fdc0: FIFO enabled, 8 bytes threshold
fd0: <1440-KB 3.5" drive> on fdc0 drive 0
```

The kernel found the mouse, and also detected that it is a PS/2 type mouse. In addition, the mouse is device `psm0`.

The kernel also found the floppy controller and the floppy drive. `fdc0` is the device name of the floppy controller, and `fd0` is the device name of the floppy drive itself. (The `fd0` is analogous to `A:` in Windows/DOS. It is the device name you use when you want to access this device.)

```
sbc0: <Creative SB AWE64> at port 0x220-0x22f,0x330-0x331,0x388-0x38b irq 5 drq
1,5 on isa0
pcm1: <SB16 DSP 4.16> on sbc0
```

The kernel found the SoundBlaster AWE 64 sound card and gives information about the resources it is using. Note that in this case, `sbc0` is actually the name for a group of devices related to the sound card. The sound card uses several devices, depending on what features you want to access—including `dsp`, which is where output such as wav and mp3 files go; and `mixer`, which controls the levels of various audio devices.

```
unknown: <PNP0303> can't assign resources
unknown: <PNP0f13> can't assign resources
unknown: <PNP0501> can't assign resources
unknown: <PNP0700> can't assign resources
unknown: <PNP0401> can't assign resources
unknown: <PNP0501> can't assign resources
```

You may see some of these on your startup message. This means that the kernel has found some Plug and Play devices in the system, but it doesn't know anything about them, and can't assign resources for them. These messages are harmless. If you don't like seeing these messages, as the FreeBSD FAQ says "The FreeBSD project will happily accept driver contributions via send-pr." (This is for you C gurus who are good at writing device drivers).

```
ad0: 19473MB <Maxtor 92049U6> [39566/16/63] at ata0-master UDMA33
ad1: 14664MB <IBM-DJNA-351520> [29795/16/63] at ata0-slave UDMA33
```

The kernel found the hard drives, and gives various information about the device name of the drive, size of the drive, manufacturer and model of the drive, geometry, and what controller the drive is located on. It also tells what access mode the drive is using. In this case, both of my drives are using Ultra DMA 33 (this will be covered in more detail in Chapter 19, "Understanding Hard Disks and Filesystems").

```
Mounting root from ufs:/dev/ad0s1a
```

Here, the kernel mounted the root filesystem. After the root filesystem is mounted, the kernel passes control to a process called *init*. Messages in light grey are triggered by things happening during the init stage. This is how you can differentiate kernel messages from non-kernel messages. Kernel messages are in white; non-kernel messages are in light grey.

init

When a FreeBSD system is properly shut down, it runs a program called sync on each disk to ensure that all data is written out, dismounts the filesystems, and then sets the *clean* flag on the filesystems. This is similar to the process that Windows goes through when it shuts down. If a FreeBSD system is not properly shut down, the clean flag will not be set.

Filesystem Consistency Check

One of the first things that init does is check whether or not the clean flag is set. If it is, init mounts the filesystem for use. If it isn't, init first runs the fsck program on the filesystem to make sure it isn't damaged and to repair any damage it finds that it knows how to repair. fsck is similar to the Scandisk program in Windows, and this process is similar to the Your system was not properly shut down procedure you see on a Windows reboot if you didn't properly shut it down first. If fsck encounters an error it cannot fix at this point, it drops the system into single user mode so the system administrator (which is probably you, if you are reading this book) can make the necessary repairs manually.

Assuming that the clean flag was set, or that fsck was able to repair the damage if it was not set, init then proceeds to mount each filesystem listed in the /etc/fstab file that has the mount at boot flag set. (This file will be covered in detail in Chapter 9.)

Tip

If you need to, you can also run fsck manually. More information on fsck and its various options can be found in Chapter 9.

System Configuration Scripts

After the filesystems are mounted, init reads the system configuration scripts (known as *run control scripts*, or *rc scripts*) located in /etc and /etc/defaults. In addition, init checks the /usr/local/etc/rc.d directory for any additional scripts it should run at boot (these might be scripts to start Web servers, database servers, or any other program you want to run automatically at startup). If you are familiar with Windows and/or DOS, this part of the boot process is similar to config.sys, autoexec.bat, system.ini, and the parts of the Windows Registry that control Windows startup options.

Note

For the sake of completeness, it should be mentioned that init also checks for and reads a file called /etc/rc.local, which can be used to start programs such as Web servers. However, this file is deprecated and may not be supported in future versions of FreeBSD. Therefore, it is recommended that you put your startup scripts in the /usr/local/etc/rc.d directory instead of in the /etc/rc.local file.

BSD versus Sys V Run Control

If you come from a Sys V UNIX background, you may be a little bit confused after that last section. So, here is a clarification. In BSD init, the concept of run levels doesn't really exist. You pretty much have single user mode and a multi-user mode with network support. There is no multiuser mode without network support, as there is in Sys V run levels. There is no inittab file in BSD, as there is in Sys V. Also, startup options are mostly controlled by a single file called rc.conf. There are not separate files to start most services with links in different run-level directories, as there is in Sys V. (This will all become clear in Chapter 11.)

getty and Login

After reading the run control scripts, init starts a program on the console (and several virtual terminals). This program is normally the getty program, but it doesn't have to be. Another common program used in place of getty is *xdm*, which starts a graphical login session for the X-Windows system immediately after system boot (similar to an NT login session). The program that is started is defined in the file /etc/ttys. For the purposes of this discussion, we will assume that it is the getty program.

The `getty` program initializes the terminal (or console), and controls various security options and terminal-type options. Once again, these options and their values are defined in `/etc/ttys`. The `getty` program then starts the login program to validate your login name and password.

Logging In to FreeBSD

After all the startup processes are complete, you see a screen that looks something like this:

```
FreeBSD/i386 (amnesiac) (ttyp0)

login:
```

Assuming that you didn't configure any network information during the installation, the default host name for your system is `amnesiac`. We'll show you how to change it later in this chapter.

Enter the login name of the normal user (not the root user) that you created for yourself during the installation. Press [Enter] and then enter the password you gave yourself when prompted. Note that the password will not be displayed onscreen. Actually, nothing will be displayed onscreen. Don't worry, though. Your password is being read.

After you enter the password, the login program checks the password database for a match. If it finds one, you see get a screen that looks something like this:

```
Last login: Tue Apr 10 15:19:17 on ttyp0
Copyright  1980, 1983, 1986, 1988, 1990, 1991, 1993, 1994
        The Regents of the University of California.  All rights reserved.

FreeBSD 5.0-RELEASE (GENERIC) #0: Sun Apr  8 15:17:26 CDT 2001

bash$
```

Because this is probably the first time you log in with your normal user account, you probably won't see the first line about `Last login`. In the future when you log in, however, this line will be present.

> **Caution**
>
> It's a good idea to pay attention to the `Last login` information. If, for example, FreeBSD says your last login was on Sat., Sept 15, 14:05:29; and you were out of town on vacation that day, and you know you did not log in to the system on that day, someone else logged into your account. If something like this ever

happens, change your password IMMEDIATELY (use the `passwd` command and follow the instructions it gives), and also notify your system administrator of the security breach (assuming that you are not the system administrator).

The rest of the information here is copyright information, and information about the kernel and when the kernel was built. The final line is the shell prompt. It means that FreeBSD is waiting for you to give it something to do.

Caution

Notice the difference between the command prompt you get this time and the command prompt you got last time—when you logged in as the root user. The root user's login prompt is the pound sign (#). A normal user's login prompt will usually be either $ for Bourne-style shells, or % or > for C-style shells. Either way, the type of prompt you have serves as a constant reminder when you are logged in as root, and as a warning to be extra careful when issuing potentially dangerous commands.

If you mistype either the login name or password, FreeBSD will respond with the following:

```
Login incorrect
login:
```

If this happens, simply try again, starting with your login name.

Tip

If you mistype your login name or password three times in a row, it may appear that the system has hung because it looks as if nothing is happening. Don't worry. The system hasn't hung. This delay is a security feature that helps reduce the effectiveness of password-cracking programs that simply try random words as passwords to break into an account. The delay may get progressively longer on each mistype after three. Wait several seconds, though, and the login prompt will reappear.

Starting the X-Windows System

Assuming that you configured X-Windows during the installation, you should now be able to type `startx` at the command line to start the X-Windows system.

Introduction to the Gnome Desktop Environment

If you selected Gnome as the default desktop environment during the installation, and if you also installed the packages suggested in Chapter 2, "Installing FreeBSD," you should get a screen that will look similar to Figure 4.1.

FIGURE 4.1

The Gnome desktop environment.

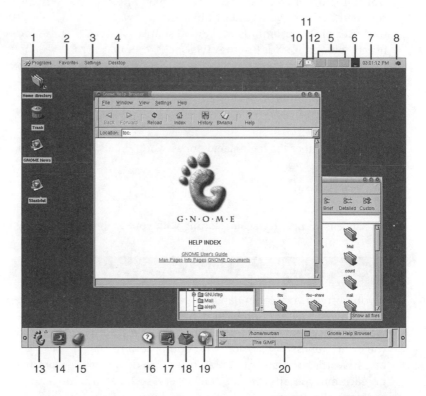

If you worked with Windows or Macintosh in the past, you will probably quickly notice some similarities between the desktops. But you will also notice quite a few differences. Here is a list of what each of the numbered items in Figure 4.1 does:

1. Where you can start programs that have been added to the Gnome menu. Similar to Start - Programs in Windows.

2. You can create a list of favorites of just about anything here: Web site URLs, FTP site addresses, programs, and so on.

3. Allows you to access the various Gnome configuration tools.

4. Arranges icons on the desktop, or logs out of the desktop.

5. Allows you to switch between four different virtual desktops. The downward-pointing arrow on the left gives you a window list.

6. A 3D rotating envelope appears here when you have new e-mail. Right-click here to configure this e-mail notification tool. (It can check either a local mail spool directory or a remote POP3 or IMAP server.)

7. You can right-click on the clock to change the format in which it displays. If you installed Gnome-PIM, you can also access appointment calendars from the right-click menu of the clock.

8. Clicking here brings up a shortcut to various Gnome Web pages (such as the news site, FAQ, and so on).

9. Brings up the window menu.

10. Iconifies the window.

11. Maximizes or restores the window.

12. Closes the window.

13. The Gnome footprint is the equivalent of the Start button in Windows.

14. Logs out of Gnome.

15. Locks the system if xscreensaver has been installed

16. Accesses the Gnome help system.

17. Starts a Gnome terminal session (accesses the command prompt in a window).

18. Starts the Gnome configuration tool.

19. Starts a Web browser. By default, it tries to start Netscape, but you can change it to start a different browser.

20. The task list (like the taskbar in Windows).

Gnome is extremely customizable, and it is possible to modify the desktop so it looks nothing like what you see here. You will see how to customize Gnome in Chapter 6, "Customizing the Gnome Desktop Environment." So, before you decide you hate Gnome, have a look at Chapter 6 to see how you can change just about every aspect of Gnome. If you still hate Gnome, I will also show you some alternative window managers in Chapter 34 under the section, "Changing the Window Manager."

Also note that most items in Gnome have ToolTips turned on by default. If you aren't sure what an item does, move the mouse over it, and leave it there for a moment. A short description of the item and its purpose will pop up (try this on the title bar of one of the windows that is open).

Stopping the X-Windows System

The next chapter will provide a detailed discussion on how to work with Gnome. For now, we'll show you how to log out of X-Windows.

There are three ways to shut down Gnome and get back to the command prompt:

- Click on the monitor icon with the moon in it that is on the Gnome Panel at the bottom of your screen.
- Click on Desktop on the menu at the top of your screen and then select Log Out.
- Click on the footprint icon on the Gnome Panel, and select Log Out.

Whichever method you use, you will get a dialog box asking you if you really want to log out. There will also be a check box in this dialog box called Save current setup. Selecting this check box will cause Gnome to remember the panel applets you had running, any file manager windows you had open, and any Gnome terminal windows you had open. The next time you access Gnome, it will have this same setup, and continue to have this same setup until the next time you check this box.

After you have told Gnome that you really do want to log out, you should be back at your command prompt. You may see a bunch of odd messages on your screen above the command prompt. Don't worry about them; they are messages generated by the X server and also by Gnome while X-Windows is running.

Logging Out of FreeBSD

When you are done using FreeBSD (or you are going to lunch or something), you should log out of the system if you are in an area in which others have access to your computer or terminal. This prevents other users from being able to access your account. To log out of FreeBSD, simply type exit at the command prompt. This should return you to the login prompt, as you saw when FreeBSD first finished booting.

> **Tip**
>
> If you were working on something that you do not want others to be able to see if they happen to walk past your screen, you can clear the screen before logging out by typing clear at a command prompt. After that, log out of the system as described earlier.

Shutting Down the FreeBSD System

As mentioned in Chapter 2, it is very important that you always shut down a FreeBSD (or any other UNIX) system properly before turning off the power. Failure to do so can result in serious damage to the filesystem.

Using the `shutdown` Command

The normal way to shut down the system is with the `shutdown` command. You saw one way to do it in Chapter 2. Before we actually shut down the system now, however, I am going to show you several other options for this command.

The basic syntax of the `shutdown` command is as follows:

```
shutdown [action] [when] [broadcast message]
```

In other words, the first option tells `shutdown` what to do, the second option tells `shutdown` when to do it, and the third option tells `shutdown` the message it should send to all logged-in users. Table 4.1 lists the options that can be used for *action* in `shutdown`, and what they do:

TABLE 4.1　Shutdown Options

Action	*Result*
nothing	Kick everybody off the system, and bring the system down to single user mode with no network support.
-h	Halt the system.
-p	Halt the system and turn off the power (if the system supports automatic power-off and the kernel is configured to support power management).
-r	Reboot the system.
-k	Kick everybody off the system, and disable any further logins (except from the root user). Leaves the system in multiuser mode and connected to the network, though.
-o	Shut down without sending a signal to `init`. This is not usually a good idea because it prevents program-specific shutdown scripts from running.
-n	If the -o option has also been specified, this prevents the file system cache from being flushed before the shutdown. This is probably never a good idea because it can cause data loss.

4

YOUR FIRST
SESSION WITH
FREEBSD

The "when" part of shutdown can be specified in several ways. As we saw in Chapter 2, the keyword now tells shutdown to perform the action now. It also recognizes the format *+n* where *n* is the number of minutes shutdown should wait before performing the action (this gives users time to save their files and close their programs). The format yymmhhmm is also supported to specify an exact time the action should be performed. Here, *yy* is the year, *mm* is the month, *hh* is the hour (in a 24-hour format), and *mm* is the minute. If the year and month parts are eliminated, shutdown will assume that the shutdown should happen today. If you specify a time that has already past, shutdown will complain.

The "broadcast message" part of shutdown is a message that will be broadcast at regular intervals to all logged-in users. These messages start coming 10 hours before the impending shutdown and get more frequent as the shutdown time gets closer.

Don't enter this command because you don't want to wait 10 minutes for the system to shut down, but I am going to walk through a typical shutdown process; in this case, using a 10-minute delay.

```
# shutdown -h +10 Hard disk needs to be replaced
```

This starts the shutdown command and runs it in the background. The system will halt in 10 minutes. In addition, the following broadcast message is displayed on all users' terminals:

```
*** System shutdown message from root@simba.samplenet.org ***
System going down in 10 minutes

Hard disk needs to be replaced
```

Five minutes before the impending shutdown, a file called /var/run/nologin will be created. This file disables any further logins, and displays its contents when someone attempts to log in. The shutdown command places the time of the shutdown and the broadcast message in this file. For example, in this case, anyone who attempts to log in will see:

```
NO LOGINS: System going down at 17:57

Hard disk needs to be replaced.
```

When the countdown clock runs out, the following actions are performed:

- A TERM signal is sent to init, which ceases creating any new processes.
- init reads the file /etc/rc.shutdown, and runs any program-specific shutdown scripts it contains.

- All processes are sent a TERM signal and given time to terminate themselves gracefully.
- Any processes that did not respond to the TERM signal in a reasonable amount of time are sent a KILL signal, which cannot be ignored, and will force the process to terminate ungracefully.
- Cache data is written out to the filesystems with the sync command, the filesystems are dismounted, and the clean flag is set.
- The kernel is halted.

In addition, shutdown writes an entry in the system log noting the time of the shutdown and who performed the shutdown.

Note that you need to be the root user to shut down the system—either by logging in directly as root or by using the su command to become root.

To shut down your system now, type su and press [Enter]. Then, enter the root password when prompted. If you receive a message complaining that you are not in the proper group to su to root, log out and then log back in as root. Then (assuming there are no other users logged into the system), issue the following command:

```
shutdown -h now
```

As mentioned in Chapter 2, on a multiuser system, you would not normally do this. Instead, you would give users some warning about the impending shutdown.

After the shutdown has completed, you will see the following message:

```
System halted
Please press any key to reboot
```

Then, and only then, is it safe to turn off your system.

Notes on halt and reboot

Two other commands—halt and reboot—can be used to halt and reboot the system, respectively. However, I do not recommend that you get in the habit of using either one. Neither of these commands runs the rc.shutdown script, which can cause some programs to terminate improperly. Also, neither of these programs allows you to specify a delay, and neither of these programs gives users any warning about the impending shutdown. Therefore, you should always use the shutdown command to halt the system.

Note

If you have used DOS and/or Windows, you might be in the habit of using the Ctrl+Alt+Delete combination to reboot a system. By default, FreeBSD will trap the signal sent by this combination, and do the equivalent of running the reboot command. This can be a problem when normal users have access to the server's keyboard because it allows them to reboot the system without being root. In Chapter 11, you will see how to configure FreeBSD to trap the Ctrl+Alt+Delete sequence to prevent it from rebooting the system.

Working with the Gnome Desktop Environment

CHAPTER 5

The last chapter gave you a brief introduction to the Gnome desktop environment. This chapter will discuss in detail how to work with Gnome.

If you are coming from a Microsoft Windows or Apple Macintosh environment, some background information on window managers is called for. If you feel you are sufficiently familiar with how X-Windows works, feel free to skip the next session. If you are familiar with X-Windows, but are unclear about the differences between a window manager and a desktop environment, you should probably read the next section.

Window Managers

The window manager runs on top of the X-Server. It is what controls how the graphical environment looks and behaves. Figure 5.1 shows what a default X-session would look like.

FIGURE 5.1

A very bland and rather useless X session.

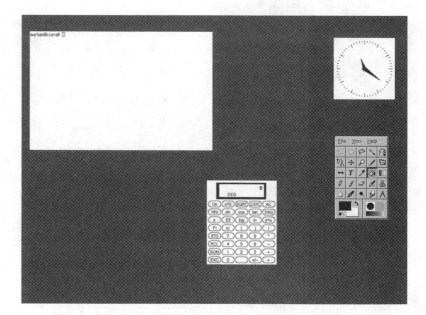

In Figure 5.1, there are several applications running in the X-Windows session: an xterm, a clock, a calculator, and the GIMP image-processing program that I used to take this screen shot. There are no title bars on the windows and the windows have no borders. The windows are not resizable or movable. Nor can they be minimized or maximized. Obviously, this makes for a pretty useless graphical user interface. This is where the window manager comes in.

The X-Server provides the "framework" for a graphical environment; the window manager controls how that graphical environment looks and works. There are dozens of different window managers available for X-Windows, so it is almost infinitely customizable. If you don't like the way X-Windows looks or feels, you can either customize your existing window manager or switch to a completely different window manager.

Figure 5.2 shows the same session that is shown Figure 5.1, but this time it is running under the Sawfish window manager.

FIGURE 5.2

This X session is now running under the Sawfish window manager.

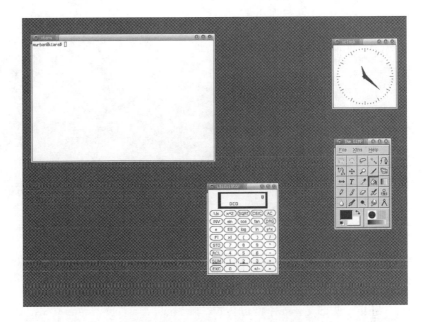

Now, things are beginning to look a little user-friendly—we actually have a title bar with a menu button; and minimize, maximize, and close buttons. Now, we actually have borders on the windows, and the windows can be moved and resized. But we can go further than this and really make this thing user-friendly, which is where the concept of the *desktop environment* comes in (specifically in this case, the Gnome desktop environment).

The Gnome Desktop Environment

Figure 5.3 shows the same X session again. This time, however, it is running under the Gnome desktop environment, and it is quite user-friendly. We have a panel across the top

and bottom that allows us to easily access features, a taskbar that lists running applications, and we also have the ability to place icons on the desktop (the icons are mostly
hidden in this figure).

FIGURE 5.3

*The same X ses-
sion, this time
running under
Gnome.*

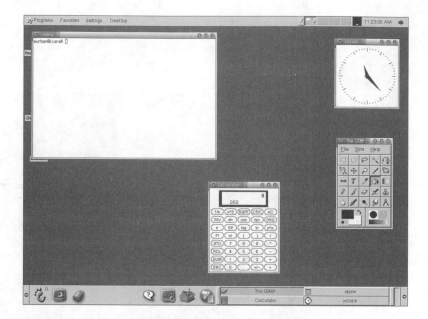

Notice that the window borders and controls look the same because Gnome does not
have its own window manager. Instead, it uses the services of a Gnome-aware window
manager to manage the windows. A Gnome-aware window manager recognizes when it
is running under Gnome, and modifies its behavior accordingly to work better with
Gnome. In this case, Gnome is using Sawfish to manage Windows. Sawfish is pretty
much the window manager of choice for Gnome these days. Besides Sawfish, there are
other Gnome-aware window managers to choose from, such as IceWM and
Enlightenment. You will see how to change the window manager in Chapter 6,
"Customizing the Gnome Desktop Environment."

The distinction between a window manager and a desktop environment is somewhat
blurred these days. Basically, the differences are usually in the number of features.
Window managers often have the capability to manage windows, present menus of
applications, and so on. Desktop environments, on the other hand, usually add features
such as panels, drag-and-drop capabilities, and often a suite of integrated "mini-
applications".

There are several different desktop environments available for X-Windows. The two most popular of these for open source UNIX systems (such as FreeBSD and Linux) are Gnome and KDE. Gnome is likely to become the de facto standard UNIX desktop environment because Sun Microsystems, Hewlett Packard, and IBM have all put their support behind Gnome and have committed to using Gnome as the default desktop in future versions of their UNIX operating systems. Therefore, we will concentrate on Gnome. However, if you would like to try KDE, it is included on the CD and will be covered briefly in Chapter 7, "Working with Applications."

Navigating the Desktop

If you used Windows or Macintosh before, it probably won't take you too long to become comfortable with the Gnome desktop. Figure 5.4 shows the Gnome desktop environment, after you close the Help and File Manager windows, which open by default the first time you run Gnome.

FIGURE 5.4

The default Gnome desktop environment.

You may need to rearrange the icons on the desktop slightly if the top panel is covering some of then. Move an icon, just as you do in Windows, by holding down the left mouse button and dragging it. Gnome remembers where you left the icons the next time it starts, so you won't have to do this each time.

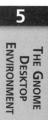

5

THE GNOME
DESKTOP
ENVIRONMENT

Most of the mouse-driven behavior of the desktop is similar to the behavior in Windows. Double-clicking an icon on the desktop opens it; holding down the left mouse button allows you to drag an item or select multiple items if you click on a blank spot on the desktop. In addition, you can drag items into other items, such as dragging an item to the trash. Clicking the right mouse button over the desktop or over an item brings up a menu of options similar to the menu you see after a right mouse-click in Windows.

The main difference between Microsoft Windows and X-Windows is that X-Windows also makes good use of the middle mouse button. Clicking this button activates an "all-purpose" menu. From here, you can launch programs, change to a different window, change to a different virtual workspace, customize the appearance of the window manager, and get help on various topics. Remember that if you don't have a middle mouse button, you should be able to emulate it by pressing the left and right buttons at the same time (assuming that you configured that option during setup).

> **Tip**
>
> If you don't have any icons on your desktop, and right-clicking on the desktop seems to have no effect, it probably means that you didn't install gnomemc during the installation. To install it now, see the section titled "Installing Packages" in Chapter 15, "Installing Additional Software."

> **Tip**
>
> The function of the middle and right mouse buttons may change if you decide to use a window manager other than Sawfish with Gnome. The previous section assumes that you are using Sawfish, which is the de facto standard window manager for Gnome these days.

The Gnome Panel

Gnome allows you to create as many panels as you want, and allows you to customize virtually every aspect of the panel—such as in what direction it is oriented, where it appears on the screen, and what is on the panel. By default, the FreeBSD install of Gnome creates two panels—one on top of the screen and one on the bottom of the screen. Chapter 4, "Your First Session with FreeBSD," covered what each of the default panel icons does.

Clicking on the Gnome footprint brings up a menu similar to the Start menu in Windows. That little upward-pointing arrow on the right side of the Gnome footprint indicates that clicking this item brings up a submenu. Notice the dashed line at the top of the menu. Clicking on it detaches the menu and allows you to place it anywhere you want onscreen, just like any other window. Note that this creates a copy of the menu rather then moving it off the panel. In other words, when you detach a menu from the panel, you can still access the menu from the panel as well as from the window created when you detach the menu (see Figure 5.5).

FIGURE 5.5
Detached menu panels in Gnome.

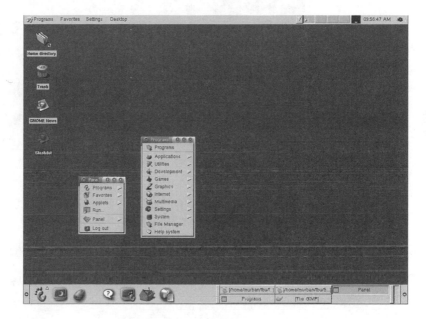

Many Gnome applications also allow you to detach their menus as well. For example, the GIMP image-processing program has detachable menus such as these.

Note also that right-clicking on an empty spot in the panel brings up the same menu that clicking on the Gnome footprint brings up.

The Taskbar

The Gnome taskbar simply gives you a list of tasks that are currently active on the desktop. A shaded icon in a taskbar item indicates that the item is minimized. Clicking on a task bar entry will bring it to the foreground, just like in Windows. Right-clicking on a taskbar entry will bring up a submenu like that shown in Figure 5.6.

5

THE GNOME DESKTOP ENVIRONMENT

FIGURE 5.6

The taskbar submenu.

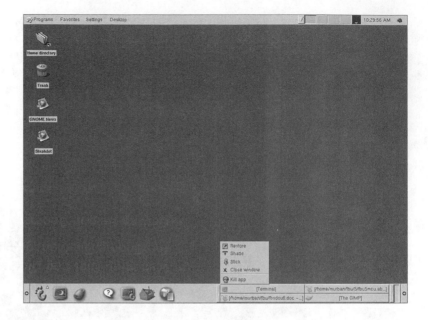

Here is a list of the options on the submenu and what they mean:

- **Iconify/Restore**—This is a toggle that either iconifies (minimizes) the corresponding window, or raises (restores) it.

- **Shade/Unshade**—"Rolls" the window up so only the tile bar is visible. Unrolls it if it is already rolled up.

- **Stick/Unstick**—A "sticky" window is one that shows up on all virtual desktops. "Sticky" windows are covered in more detail later in this chapter.

- **Close window**—Closes a window and terminates the program it is running in a normal fashion.

- **Kill app**—Also terminates a windowed application, but with SIGKILL. SIGKILL cannot be ignored, and cannot be trapped by the application. This forces a program to terminate ungracefully. You should generally use this option only if a program is hung and is not responding.

The other icons on the Gnome panel generally start applications. Notice that they do not have the upward-pointing arrow next to them. If you are unsure what an icon does, you can move the mouse over the icon and leave it still for a moment. This causes a small "tool tip" to pop up, giving you a short description of what the item does.

In the next chapter, I will show you how to customize the Gnome panel to your liking.

Working with Windows

For the most part, working with Windows in Gnome is very similar to working with Windows in Microsoft Windows or Macintosh. There are a few things worth noting however, particularly on the window pull-down menu.

You will notice that there are quite a few more options on the pull-down menu in Gnome than in the pull-down menu in Microsoft Windows. Here are some of the more important ones and what they do:

- **Delete**—Terminates the application in the window normally.

- **Destroy**—Terminates the application with a SIGKILL, forcing the application to terminate ungracefully. This signal cannot be trapped or ignored.

- **Toggle**—Contains a submenu of operations that will be discussed in detail later in this chapter.

- **Maximize/Minimize**—Performs basically the same function as the equivalent options in Windows.

- **In Group**—This option is discussed in detail later in the chapter.

- **Send window to**—Allows you to move or copy windows to different virtual workspaces. This option is discussed in detail in the section on virtual workspaces later in this chapter.

- **Depth**—Allows you to place a window in the foreground, move it to the background, and so on.

- **Frame type**—Allows you to control various aspects of the window frame, such as whether the title bar or frame borders should be present.

- **Frame style**—Allows you to change the complete appearance of the window, such as the appearance of the title bar and the title bar buttons. Note this may also change the behavior of the controls.

- **History**—Clicking one of the Remember options causes the desktop to remember that aspect of the window. The next time you open this program, the window will appear in the same position, with the same dimensions, or with the same attributes as when you clicked on this option. Clicking Forget saved state causes the desktop to forget that it ever stored any information about the state of the window.

Although the capability to display things in windows is a great addition to facilitate the multitasking capabilities in FreeBSD, you can fit only so many windows onscreen. Sometimes, you might want to have more windows open and available than will fit on a single screen. This is where virtual workspaces come in.

Virtual Workspaces

Like the name implies, *virtual workspaces* allow you to have more than one desktop on a single physical monitor. You can switch between the different workspaces using the Desk Guide on the right side of the panel at the top of your screen, or by middle-clicking on the desktop, selecting Workspaces, and then selecting the workspace that you want from the pop-up list. The different workspaces can have different windows open and have different arrangements of the windows.

Sticky Windows

If you want a certain window to be available from all of the virtual workspaces, you can set the sticky property on the window. There are two ways to set the sticky bit:

- Right-click on the windows entry in the taskbar and then click on Stick.
- Click on the window menu at the top left of the title bar, select Toggle, and then select Stick.

To "unstick" the window, simply repeat the same procedure.

If you want to move a window from one virtual workspace to another, there are two ways to do it.

- Set the sticky property on the window, switch to the virtual desktop where you want the window to be, and then unset the sticky property.
- Click the window menu on the top left of the title bar, select Sent window to, and then select Previous workspace or Next workspace to move the window to the respective location.

Adding and Removing Virtual Workspaces

By default, FreeBSD gives you four virtual workspaces, but it is easy to add or remove workspaces.

There are two ways to create a new virtual workspace:

- While you are on the last virtual workspace in the list (the last one on the right), middle-click on the desktop, click Workspaces, and then click Insert workspace. A new blank workspace is created, and you are placed in the new workspace.
- While on the first or last workspace, middle-click on the desktop, click on Move workspace left or Move workspace right, respectively. A new workspace is created and the contents of the current workspace are moved to the new workspace.

To destroy a workspace, make sure that you are on the workspace that you want to destroy, middle-click on the desktop, click on `Workspaces`, and then click on `Merge with next` or `Merge with previous`. The current desktop will be destroyed, and its contents will be merged with the next or previous desktop respectively.

The Window Menu Toggle Option

Clicking on the window menu in the upper left-hand corner of the title bar brings up a pop-up menu. One of the options in the menu is `Toggle`. The following lists the options the `Toggle` menu contains, and what they do.

- **Sticky**—This option was already covered in the previous sections. It allows you to set a window so that it is visible from all virtual workspaces.

- **Minimize**—This option minimizes the window to the task manager on the Gnome panel.

- **Shaded**—When set, this option rolls the window up so that only the title bar is visible. When unset, it rolls the window back down to its normal size.

- **Ignored**—Selecting this option causes the window manager to completely ignore this window as if it does not exist. This means it will not show up in the window list, it will not be resizable or movable, and it will have no title bar or borders.

- **Focusable**—When selected, the window can be given focus (made active). When the option is unselected, the window can be brought to the foreground so it is visible, but it can't be made active (you can't do anything with whatever is running in the window).

- **Cyclable**—If selected, the window will be included when cycling through the windows. If unselected, it will not be included.

- **In window list**—If selected, this window shows up by middle-clicking on the desktop and selecting `Windows`. When unselected, it does not show up in the window list.

- **In GNOME task list**—Toggles whether or not the window will show up in the Gnome taskbar on the bottom panel in the screen.

The Window Menu In Group Option

You can use this option to place windows into groups. These groups show up as submenus in the window list when you middle-click on the desktop. For example, if you are working on a project and have multiple files open for the same project, you can group them all under one submenu in the window list.

Send Window To

This option was covered in a previous section. It allows you to move a window to a different virtual workspace.

Depth

This option allows you to move windows to the foreground and background. Unlike Microsoft Windows, windows in Gnome that are not in the foreground can still have focus and be active. In the next chapter, you will see some of the various configuration options for this and learn why this can be useful.

Frame Type

This option allows you to control various things about the appearance of the window frame around the window. You can turn off borders, title bars, and so on.

Frame Style

Here, you can change the style of the frame. There are several different styles available that change the appearance and also sometimes the behavior of the controls. Figure 5.7 shows an example of two of the different frame types available.

FIGURE 5.7
Two different frame styles in Gnome.

History

This option was already covered in a previous section. It causes the window manager to remember various aspects of this window so that the next time you open it, it appears in the same size, position, and so on, as it was when you selected these options.

Exploring the Gnome and X-Windows Applets

If you installed the recommended packages in Chapter 2, "Installing FreeBSD," you have access to several Gnome and X-Windows applets. These applets are similar to the applets in Microsoft Windows or Macintosh. The applets (and other programs in Gnome) can be accessed in one of three ways:

- Click the Gnome footprint, and select Programs.
- Click the Programs entry in the top panel.
- Middle-click on the desktop, and select Programs from the pop-up menu.

> **Note**
>
> Some of the X-Windows applets may not yet be available in the Gnome menus. If this is the case, you can access them by clicking on the Gnome footprint, selecting Run, entering the name of the program listed in the following sections in the dialog box, and then clicking the Run button. In the next chapter, you will see how to add applications to the Gnome menus.

We do not cover all the applets here, but we will cover some of the ones that you are likely to find the most useful. Regular applications will be covered in detail in Chapter 7.

gedit

Knowing how to work with a text editor is important to becoming proficient with any UNIX system. Although eventually you should learn one of the shell editors (for those times when you can't start X-Windows), until you are comfortable with the shell, you might prefer working in the graphical environment that gedit gives you.

Like Windows Notepad, gedit is not a full-featured word processor. It is designed to handle plain-text files; it cannot do all the fancy formatting that a full-featured word processor can do. However, gedit does have many more features than Windows Notepad.

Figure 5.8 shows the main editing window of gedit.

I'm going to assume that you are familiar with an editor such as Notepad, so here I will explain only some of the more interesting and less-common features of gedit that are not found in Notepad.

FIGURE 5.8

The gedit text editor. Notice the menu at the top, which is similar to the menu in Windows.

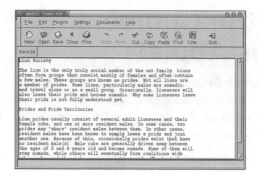

gedit is capable of editing multiple files at the same time. The current file can be selected by clicking on one of the tabs at the top of the editing window. Open files in gedit just as you do in Notepad by selecting File, Open.

gedit can do some interesting things from the Plugins menu. If you select Browse from the menu, you can load text mode Web pages into the editor. Although you will not be able to see the images or anything, this can be quite useful if you need to cut and paste text from a Web document or something into your text file.

Also available from the Plugins menu is the ability to load two documents, compare them, and generate a third document automatically that contains the differences between the two documents.

You can also email documents directly from the editor by using the Email option in the Plugins menu.

The Shell Output option in the Plugins menu allows you to run a command-line program and have the output of that program automatically inserted in the file you are working on wherever the cursor is currently located (see Figure 5.9). For example, click on Plugins and then Shell Output. Now, type ls in the Enter Shell Command dialog box (ls is the shell command to list the contents of the current directory). After you click on Ok, the contents of the current directory will be placed into your text file at the cursor position. Notice that there is also a Directory dialog box, in which you can change the directory that the command you issue works on. You can use the Shell Command option with any shell command that will display output to STDOUT (normally the screen).

gedit is also quite customizable using the Preferences dialog box under Settings.

FIGURE **5.9**

*The Shell
Command dialog
box. Here, you
can type a shell
command that will
automatically
paste its output
into the text editor.*

Eye of Gnome

Eye of Gnome is a quick-and-dirty image-viewing program for Gnome. Note that this
is not an image-manipulation program. It is only a viewer. Its usage is mostly self-
explanatory. (GIMP, which is an image-manipulation program, is covered in Chapter 7.)

CD Player

The Gnome CD Player has support for the CDDB system (the ability to automatically
download CD information such as artist, title, and track name from the Internet).

You may need to do some configuration before the Gnome CD player will work. This
usually involves setting a link to the symbolic device /dev/cdrom from the actual device
name of the CD-ROM drive. If the player complains that it can't find your CD-ROM
drive when you start it, you need to set this link. (Please see the links section under
"Basic File Manipulation" in Chapter 9, "The FreeBSD Filesystem," to see how to set
links. Remember: Everything in UNIX is a file. You work with devices just as you work
with any other file.)

After you have the device link properly set, you should be able to access the CD player.
If you have an Internet connection, the player probably automatically retrieves the CD
information from an Internet CDDB database in a few seconds. (See Chapter 24,
"Connecting to the Internet with PPP," for information on how to configure a dial-up
Internet connection.)

You can control the CDDB options, as well as several other options by clicking on the
middle button in the last row of the CD Player controls. Figure 5.10 shows the Gnome
CD Player in action.

5

THE GNOME
DESKTOP
ENVIRONMENT

*The Gnome CD
Player. Holding
the left mouse but-
ton down on the
left and right
arrows will cause
the CD to search
the current track
rather than skip to
the next one.*

Gnome Terminal

The Gnome Terminal is like the MS-DOS box in Windows. It allows you to access the UNIX command line from within X-Windows. You can start the Gnome Terminal by clicking on the icon on the bottom panel that has the screen with a footprint over it. Click on Settings to customize various aspects of the Gnome Terminal, such as the fonts and colors it uses.

xcalc

The equivalent of the Windows calculator, this is a scientific calculator for X-Windows. To access it, enter xcalc in the Run dialog box, as previously discussed in the note under "Exploring Gnome and X-Windows Applets."

xmag

This option allows you to magnify any portion of the desktop or window. You can change the magnification factor by starting xmag with the mag option. For example, xmag -mag 2 causes xmag to magnify the selected area by two.

When xmag is started, the mouse pointer changes to a pointed bracket pointing at the top left. It represents the upper-left corner of the area that will be magnified. Move to the area you want to magnify, hold down the middle mouse button, and drag until you select all the area you want to magnify. When you release the mouse button, a magnified view of the selection will open in a window.

xman

xman allows you to browse the FreeBSD manual pages from a user-friendly graphical interface. It opens a small window with a few buttons in it. Select the Manual Page button to browse the manual pages. More information on manual pages, such as what is contained in the various sections, can be found in Chapter 8, "Working with the Shell."

xclock

Displays an analog clock in a window on your desktop. This can be useful if you switch to a different window manager that does not have a built-in clock.

xfontsel

Allows you to preview the various fonts that are installed. It also gives you the *X Logical Font Description*, which is the full name for the font. This can be useful for some applications (such as designing custom themes for certain window managers). Figure 5.11 shows the xfontsel tool.

FIGURE 5.11

The xfontsel tool.

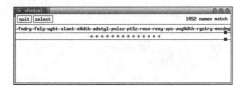

xfontsel works on the process of elimination. When you select an option from any one of the categories across the top, it will narrow down the font list in the other categories to only those fonts that match. To see all the options in a particular category, select the asterisk at the top of the list.

Managing Files and Directories with the Gnome File Manager

To access the Gnome File Manager, double-click on the Home directory icon on the desktop. The file manager looks like Figure 5.12.

FIGURE 5.12

The Gnome File Manager.

If you are used to the Windows Explorer File Manager, you will probably become comfortable with the Gnome File Manager fairly quickly. It looks and behaves very much like Windows Explorer.

Dragging the object with the left mouse button moves the object to whatever location you drag it to. Dragging with the middle mouse button opens a submenu similar to the submenu in Windows that allows you to select what you want to do with the object (move, copy, or create a link).

Clicking the right mouse button over an object brings up a submenu of options.

> **Caution**
>
> Note the important difference between the Move to trash and Delete options on this submenu. Move to trash moves the object to the trash can, from which it can be recovered, just as you do in Windows, by dragging the object out of the trash. Delete permanently deletes an object and does not put it in the trash. After you delete an object, it is gone for good and cannot be recovered.

You can also drag objects out of the File Manager and onto the desktop if you want to create links (shortcuts) to various items on your desktop and such.

Clicking the Home icon in the File Manager will immediately take you to your home directory (which is your personal space on the FreeBSD system). The Icons, Brief, Detailed, and Custom options will give you different views of the files in the File Manager.

Don't worry if you don't fully understand the information provided by the Gnome File Manager yet. It will become more clear in Chapter 9.

Getting Help in Gnome

To access the Gnome Help System, click on the question mark icon in the bottom panel. This will open up the Gnome Help system (see Figure 5.13).

The Gnome Help system is a hypertext-based system that works just like Web pages on the World Wide Web, so it shouldn't take you long to become comfortable with the system.

FIGURE **5.13**

The Gnome Help system.

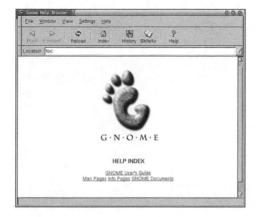

The system is divided into four sections:

- **Gnome user's guide**—The user's guide for Gnome.

- **Man pages**—The FreeBSD manual pages. These can also be accessed from the command line using the man command and from the xman command, as discussed in a previous section of this chapter.

- **Info pages**—The GNU info pages. Many GNU programs come with an info page, which is similar to a man page, but is usually much more detailed and often more tutorial rather than reference in nature. Many of the utilities that are part of the FreeBSD system are GNU utilities, and thus include an info page. Many programs such as grep (to search for patterns in text files) include both a man page and an info page.

- **Gnome documents**—The various documents on Gnome that are installed on the system, but are not part of the Gnome user manual. These often include documentation for third-party Gnome software that is not installed by default in Gnome. You will find documentation for the various Gnome applets and such here.

You can add a bookmark to a particular section in Help that you access a lot by clicking File and then Add Bookmark. You can then of course, click the Bookmark icon in the Help system to access your list of bookmarks. There is also a History icon that allows you to jump to any page you have already looked at (see Figure 5.14).

Finally, you can click the Index icon at any time to take you back to the Gnome Help index page.

FIGURE **5.14**

The Gnome Help history.

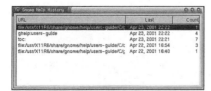

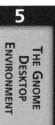

5

THE GNOME
DESKTOP
ENVIRONMENT

Customizing the Gnome Desktop Environment

CHAPTER 6

As mentioned in previous chapters, the FreeBSD X-Windows system allows you to customize it in a number of different ways, including tinkering with the Gnome Desktop Environment. However, for those of you not satisfied with Gnome, there is a section at the end of this chapter that discusses alternative window managers.

Adding New Icons to the Desktop

There are several ways to add new icons to the desktop. As discussed in Chapter 5, "Working with the Gnome Desktop Environment," you can simply drag items from the Gnome File Manager and onto the desktop. Dragging with the left mouse button will move the item from its current location to the desktop. Dragging with the middle mouse button will give you a menu of options, asking you what action you wish to perform. You can use the "Link" option to create a symlink, which is virtually identical to a shortcut icon in Windows. Figure 6.1 shows an example of a symlink. The arrow in the lower-right corner indicates that the item is a symlink.

FIGURE 6.1

A symlink in Gnome. The arrow on the lower-right corner of the icon indicates that this is a link.

As in Windows, if you delete the file that the symlink points to, the link becomes an orphan (see Figure 6.2), and will no longer work. Unless you have manually changed a link's icon to something other than the default, its icon will automatically change to look like that in Figure 6.2 when and if the link becomes an orphan.

FIGURE 6.2

An orphaned symlink whose file has been removed.

Other than dragging programs to the desktop in order to create shortcuts, you can also create new items on the desktop by right-clicking anywhere on the desktop and then selecting "New" from the pop-up menu. This will bring up several options. Here is what each one does:

Customizing the Gnome Desktop Environment

CHAPTER 6

127

6

CUSTOMIZING THE
GNOME DESKTOP
ENVIRONMENT

TABLE 6.2 Options for Adding New Items to the Desktop

Option	Description
Terminal	This opens a new command line window on the desktop.
Directory	Creates a new directory (often called a folder in GUI environments) on the desktop.
URL link	Creates a shortcut to a Web site on the desktop. By default, the Web site will open in Netscape when the icon is double-clicked.
Launcher	Creates a new shortcut for a program on the desktop. This is the option whose dialog box may not be immediately clear, so it will be explained in the next section.

Adding a Program Launcher to the Desktop

A *program launcher* is simply an icon shortcut on the desktop to start a program or application. There are two ways to add one. The first is using the Gnome File Manager and navigating to the directory where the program is located. Then, you can use the middle mouse button to drag the program's icon in the File Manager out to the desktop and then click "Link".

The second way is by right-clicking on a blank spot in the desktop, selecting "New", and then clicking "Launcher". This method gives you more control over setting up the properties of the launcher than the previous method. It is also sometimes quicker because of the way the FreeBSD directory structure is set up. With the first method, you have to know where the program file is located. With the second method, you usually don't. All you have to know is the name of the executable program file. FreeBSD installs almost all executable files in directories that will be in your search path. Because of this, you can simply type the name of the file without having to worry about where it is actually located in the filesystem. Figure 6.3 shows the new launcher dialog box.

FIGURE 6.3

Configuring a new launcher for the desktop.

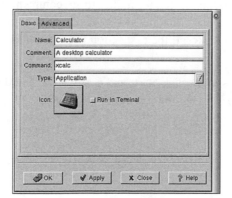

For example, assume that we want to create a shortcut on the desktop to the xcalc calculator program. Here is a walk-through of the procedure we would use, along with a description of each option.

1. **Name**—This is the name that will appear under the icon on the desktop. This is only for human reference, and it does not have to correspond to the actual name of the program at all. You could enter "Jim" here, and FreeBSD wouldn't care. But it is best of course, to use descriptive names. So you might enter "Calculator" instead.

2. **Comment**—A brief description of what the icon does. In this case, you don't really have to put anything here because it is obvious by the name what the icon does. But you could enter `"A desktop calculator for X"`, or another comment here. Once again, this is only for the benefit of the users.

3. **Command**—The actual command used to launch the program. As mentioned previously, you only need to know the name of the command—not the directory path where it is located. In this case, the name of the calculator executable is `"xcalc"`, so that is what we will enter in this box.

4. **Type**—Clicking the downward-pointing arrow on the right brings up a pull-down menu. Here, you select `"Application"`; this launcher is intended to launch an application.

5. **Run in Terminal**—If checked, Gnome will start the application in a command prompt window. You would use this for text-based applications. Because xcalc is not a text-based application, you leave this box unchecked.

   You will probably want to click the raised button that says `"No Icon"`; too, so you can choose an appropriate icon for the application. By default, Gnome looks for icons in /usr/X11R6/share/gnome/pixmaps. But you can use the "Browse" button to look in other places for icons.

6. **Advanced Tab**—The "Advanced" tab at the top of the dialog box contains options you will probably rarely use, including the ability to set comments for different languages, and the ability to have Gnome attempt another action before the primary action that the icon invokes. If the first action fails, the main action of the icon will not be carried out.

Once you have completed this, simply click `"Ok"`, and a new icon should appear on your desktop. Double-clicking this new icon should start the calculator.

Customizing the Gnome Panel

Most of the Gnome panel customization options can be accessed by right-clicking a blank spot on the panel, selecting "Panel", choosing "Properties", and then selecting one of the various options from the submenus under Properties. You can also select "Global Preferences" from the Panel menu to change global preferences affecting the Gnome Panel. This will open the panel section of the Gnome Control Center. The Gnome Control Center is covered in detail later on in this chapter.

> **Note**
>
> Make sure that you are clicking on a blank spot on the panel itself to bring up the panel submenu. Some spots appear to be blank spots in the panel, but are actually blank spots in some applet running on the panel. For example, clicking a blank spot in the taskbar (delimited by the two vertical dimpled bars) will not bring up the correct menu.

Working with Panel Icons

There are three different kinds of icons you may see on the Gnome panel. The first one is a launcher, as was just discussed. The second is an integrated Gnome application, such as the footprint icon, which launches the Start menu. The third is a running Gnome applet (more on this later). The different types of icons will have different submenus when you right click them. Right click any icon on the panel to bring up a menu of actions that can be performed on the icon. To move an icon for example, right-click it and then select "Move". You can now move the icon to a different location on the panel. To drop the icon when you have moved it to where you want it, click the left mouse button.

If you want to change the behavior of a panel launcher, you can right-click it and then select "Properties". For example, if you want to change the Web browser launcher so that it launches a Web browser other than Netscape, you can right-click it and then click "Properties". You see a dialog box like that shown in Figure 6.4.

Customizing the "Start" Menu

The Gnome footprint icon is similar to the Start menu in Windows. Some applications (particularly those that were designed for Gnome) will automatically appear in the panel when the application is installed. However, many applications that are not specifically designed for Gnome will have to be added manually if you want to access them from the menu.

FIGURE 6.4

The Properties dialog box for the Web browser panel launcher.

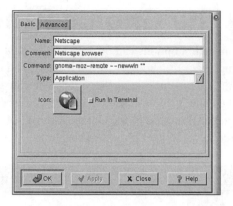

To add, remove, or customize items in the menu, right-click the Gnome footprint icon and then click "Edit Menus". The Gnome menu editor looks like Figure 6.5.

FIGURE 6.5

The Gnome menu editor. Here, you can customize the programs that will be available from the Gnome footprint.

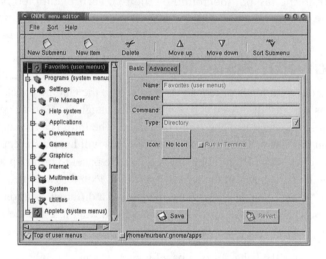

Notice that the right half of the menu editor looks virtually identical to the dialog box in Figure 6.3 and Figure 6.4 that you used to create an application launcher on the desktop. The operation of the right half of the menu editor is virtually identical as well. The left part presents a tree view of the menu. A plus sign (+) on the left side of an item indicates that the item is a submenu and has objects underneath it. (They can be more submenus or application launchers. Submenus can be nested many layers deep.) Clicking the plus sign will expand the tree to show the items underneath the current item. The plus sign will then change to a minus sign (-). Clicking the minus sign will collapse the view.

> **Note**
>
> As a normal user, you will only be able to add, change, or delete items that are located in the "Favorites (User Menus)" section of the menu. Only the root or superuser can change any of the other menu items because they are system-wide menus that affect all users that use the system.

Clicking on either "New Submenu" or "New Item" will insert the respective item just before the item that is currently highlighted. You can then edit the item using the right side of the menu editor, just as you did when you added the xcalc application launcher to the desktop. Note that no changes will take effect until you have clicked the "Save" button.

Clicking on any item within a submenu and then selecting "Sort Submenu" will sort all items under that submenu into alphabetical order in the list. Selecting "Sort" from the menu bar and then choosing "Sort Submenu Recursive" will sort the current submenu as well as all submenus below the current one.

Working with Panel Applets

Panel applets are small applications that run directly on the Gnome panel. Panel applets available for Gnome do anything from monitoring battery status on a laptop, to checking email, to presenting useless quotes when clicked on (see the "Wanda the Gnome Fish" applet). An example of four panel applets that are running by default are the taskbar, the clock, the pager (which allows you to switch to different virtual workspaces) and the mail checker. All of these applets can be removed, moved to different locations on the panel, or even moved to a different panel.

The various panel applets have different submenus, depending on what they do; as a general rule, however, you can right-click any running applet to get its submenu of options.

To remove an applet from the panel, right-click it and then click "Remove from Panel". In some cases, you will have to right-click the edge of the applet to have this option because right-clicking on the main part of the applet presents the applet's submenu instead. An example is the taskbar. If you click one of the items in the taskbar itself, you will get a menu of actions that can be performed on that taskbar entry. Click the dimpled vertical bar on the left of the taskbar to get the menu in which you can control the applet itself (such as moving or removing it).

To add an applet to the panel, right-click a blank spot on the panel, select "Applets", select one of the submenu categories of applets, and then click the applet you want to add.

Most applets can be customized by right-clicking on the applet itself or on its border (as in the case with the taskbar) and then selecting "Properties". This allows you to control how the taskbar displays items, the frequency with which the mail checker checks mail, what mailboxes it should check, and so on; and in what time format the clock displays the time.

Adding Launchers and Drawers to the Panel

An application launcher is used to launch an application from the Gnome Panel. A drawer is used to contain a pop-up menu that contains applications or can even contain more drawers.

To add an application launcher to the panel, right-click a spot on the panel that is not occupied by an applet (it's okay if there is already a launcher there), select "Panel", choose "Add to Panel", and then select "Launcher". You will see a dialog box like that shown in Figure 6.6.

FIGURE 6.6

Adding an application launcher to the panel. Once again, this dialog box looks similar to the dialog box that we used to add a launcher to the desktop.

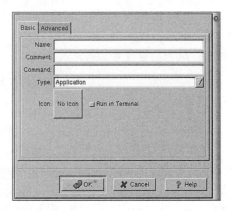

If, for example, you want to add a launcher for the calculator to the panel, you could do the following:

1. Enter a name for the application in the first field; in this case, enter "Calculator".

2. If you enter a comment in the comment box, it will be used as the ToolTip that pops up when the mouse is left over the icon for a moment. You could enter "A desktop calculator" here.

3. Leave the "Type" field set to "Application".

4. Click the raised icon box that says "No Icon" to select an appropriate icon for the application.

Once again, you can probably leave the advanced tab alone. After you have clicked "Ok", the new launcher will appear on the panel.

A *drawer* is basically an icon on the panel that holds another panel. Clicking on the drawer will open the panel that it holds. To add a drawer to the panel, simply click a spot on the panel that is not occupied by an applet, select "Panel", choose "Add to panel", and then select "Drawer". A new drawer will be added to the panel. Clicking on the drawer will expand the panel that is in the drawer, or collapse it if it is already expanded. Once you add a drawer to the panel, you can expand it and then modify the panel inside of it, just as you can modify any other panel. Figure 6.7 shows an expanded drawer with several application launchers added to it.

FIGURE 6.7

An expanded drawer with several application launchers in it, including the calculator.

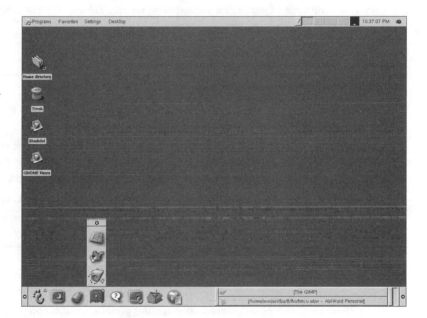

You can, of course, modify the properties of the drawer itself (such as the icon it uses) by right-clicking on it and selecting "Properties".

Adding and Removing Panels

To delete an existing panel from the desktop, simply right-click it, select "Panel", and then click "Remove this panel". You will receive a warning about losing the panel and all its applet settings. If you remove a panel that currently has applets running on it, you may receive warnings that say "The applet appears to have died unexpectedly" (see Figure 6.8), and asking you if you want to reload the applet. If you click "Reload", the applet will be reloaded on a different panel. If you click "Cancel", the applet will not be reloaded.

FIGURE 6.8

The "Applet has died unexpectedly" dialog box.

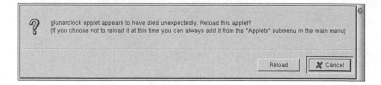

To add a panel, right-click an existing panel, select "Panel", choose "Create panel", and then click the type of panel that you want to create. Table 6.1 shows the different types of panels.

TABLE 6.1   Different Panel Types in Gnome

Panel Type	Description
Edge panel	A panel that extends from oneedge of the desktop to the other.
Aligned panel	A panel that expands and contracts dynamically to the size required to hold all the information in it. An aligned panel can be aligned to the left edge, center, or right edge of the top or bottom of the screen; and the top edge, center, or bottom edge of the left or right of the screen.
Sliding panel	A sliding panel will resize itself to the largest icon it contains.
Floating panel	A floating panel can be placed anywhere on the desktop rather than just on one of the sides.

After you have added a new panel, you can change its properties—such as its location on the screen and its alignment—by right-clicking on the panel, selecting "Panel", and then choosing "Properties". If you want to change the panel's location onscreen or its orientation (horizontal over vertical), select the "All properties" option. The available settings under "All properties" will change, depending on what type of panel you are working with (edge, aligned, sliding, or floating). Figure 6.9 shows a sample "All properties" dialog box.

FIGURE 6.9

The "All proper-ties" dialog box for an edge panel in Gnome.

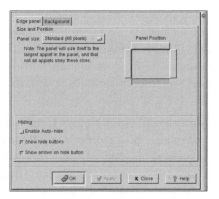

Customizing the Gnome File Manager

The Gnome File Manager, which was covered in Chapter 5, "Working with the Gnome Desktop Environment," is similar to Windows Explorer.

To customize the Gnome File Manager, click "Settings" on the menu bar and then choose "Preferences" (see Figure 6.10).

FIGURE 6.10

Customizing the Gnome File Manager.

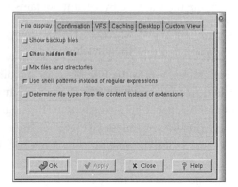

The File Display Tab

The first tab, labeled "File display", controls how files are displayed, and also a little about how file searches are done. Here is what each option does:

- **Show backup files**—Backup files generally end with a tilde (~). By default, the Gnome File Manager does not show these files. Checking this box will cause it to show them.

- **Show hidden files**—Hidden files are also known as *"dot files"* because they begin with a period. Files that begin with a period do not normally show up in the directory listing. Checking this box will cause these files to show up in the listing. Normally, you will probably want to leave this option unchecked because dot files tend to clutter up the listing, and you rarely want to work with the dot files anyway.

- **Mix files and directories**—Normally, all directories are listed first in alphabetical order and then all files are listed in alphabetical order after all the directories. If you would rather just sort by alphabetical order, you can uncheck this box. Directories and files will then be mixed together, and sorting will only be done based on alphabetical order.

- **Use shell patterns instead of regular expressions**—This controls how pattern matching is done when using the File Manager's `"find"` utility to search for a file. Unless you understand regular expressions, you should not change this setting from the default. Regular expressions are covered in Chapter 8 in the section "Searching for Text with grep"

- **Determine file types from file content instead of extensions**—This is another option you should probably leave alone unless you are sure you know what you are doing. By default, the File Manager determines the file type in a Microsoft fashion by using the extension on the file. Changing this option will cause the File Manager to attempt to determine the file type by what it contains rather than based on the extension.

The options under the "Confirmation" tab are self-explanatory.

The VFS tab contains options that configure how the File Manager handles virtual file systems. For our purposes now, a virtual file system is any file system that is not an actual FreeBSD file system. The options here apply mostly to FTP (file transfer protocol) servers. The Gnome File Manager can allow seamless FTP access, from which you can manipulate files on an FTP server just as if they were on your own disk. This means you can drag and drop files to the FTP server, just as you can from locations on your hard disk. Listed as follows are options under the VFS tab:

- **VFS timeout**—The number of seconds of inactivity before the connection to the FTP server times out and closes itself.

- **Anonymous FTP password**—Most anonymous FTP services expect you to log in with your email address as the password, so this is what you should probably put in this box.

- **Always use FTP proxy**—If you are behind a proxy server and cannot directly connect to an FTP server, you will need this option checked.

The "Caching" Tab

The settings you have configured under this tab can increase (or decrease if set incorrectly) the performance of the File Manager. Here is what the various options are for:

- **Fast directory reload**—If this option is enabled, the File Manager will cache directory contents (store them in RAM) so that when you go back to the directory again, it does not have to reread the contents from the hard disk. Note that this may sometimes cause new files in the directory not to show up until you click the "Rescan" button.

- **Compute totals before copying files**—You should probably not change this option. By default, it is enabled. The File Manager will compute the total number of files you have selected for copying, so it can give you a status report while the copying is actually being done. Disabling this option may speed up performance slightly, but the benefit will likely be negligible.

- **FTP directory cache timeout**—The File Manager caches the contents of FTP directories, so it does not have to rescan the directory each time you go back to it. This controls the number of seconds that the cache information is good for. Once again, if the directory contents are being cached, new files will not show up until the "Rescan" button is clicked. You should probably leave this value alone, though, unless you have a fast connection to the FTP server. Not caching the directory contents can greatly decrease performance.

- **Allow customization of icons in icon view**—This allows you to customize the appearance of the icons that show up when the File Manager is in icon view. The Gnome documentation says that turning this option on may result in a slower system. That is an understatement. When you turn this option on, the time it takes to display the contents of a directory increases greatly. You probably want to leave this option disabled.

The Desktop Tab

This section allows you to customize various aspects about the way the icons on the desktop behave.

- **Automatic icon placement**—If enabled, icons will be automatically aligned against the left edge of the desktop. You will not be able to move icons to different locations and drop them there (you will still be able to drag items to the trash and such, though).

- **Snap icons to grid**—When enabled, icons are automatically aligned to an invisible grid on the desktop. So, when you drop an icon, it will automatically be aligned in the nearest invisible grid square. This can be useful to help you align icons in neat columns or rows on the desktop.

- **Use shaped icons**—When this option is enabled, icons on the desktop will have a transparent background. If disabled, they will have an ugly square opaque background around them. You probably want to leave these options alone, unless you are having strange video-related problems.

- **Use shaped text**—Like the `"Use shaped icons"` option, except that this one affects the text under the icons. Enabling this option can make the text under the icons difficult or impossible to read, especially if you are using vivid wallpaper as a desktop background. Disabling the option will cause the text to be written on an opaque box and thus solve the problem with it being hard to read on wallpaper backgrounds.

The Custom View Tab

Here, you can customize what information is included in the custom view mode of the File Manager. To select the custom view, click the `"Custom"` button in the File Manager.

Working with the Gnome Control Center

The Gnome Control Center is the equivalent of the Windows Control Panel. From here, you can control almost every aspect of Gnome's behavior. To access the Gnome Control Center, click the toolbox icon on the lower panel. Figure 6.11 shows the Gnome Control Center.

FIGURE 6.11

The Gnome Control Center.

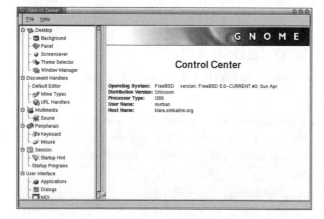

Like the File Manager, it uses a tree view on the left side, with the various options grouped under the relevant heading. Click any option in the left side of the Control Center to activate it in the right side.

We will cover some of the ones you will most likely use in this section.

Changing the Background

By now, you might be sick of looking at the bluish-green background on the desktop. This is where you can change it. Click "Background" to bring up the background options (see Figure 6.12).

FIGURE 6.12

Configuring the desktop background.

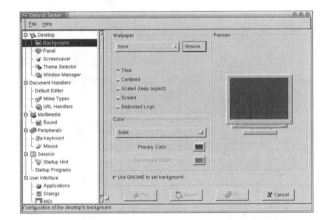

As you can see, you can set an image to use as the background wallpaper for the desktop. Gnome supports most common image formats for background wallpaper, including BMP, JPEG, GIF, PNG, and XPM.

The options for the way the image should be displayed are self-explanatory.

If you do not want to use an image as the background, you can set a solid color or a color gradient. When you select a color gradient, you can set the gradient to either horizontal or vertical; you then select the two colors that should be used in the gradient.

Panel

Here, you can control various aspects of the panel, such as whether the icons should have textured tiles around them or not.

The "Menu" tab allows you to control various aspects of the Gnome "footprint" menu (see Figure 6.13).

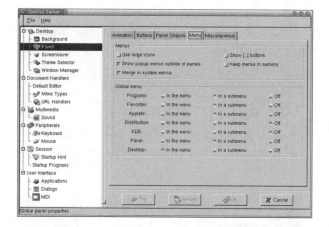

The section labeled `"Global menu"` controls whether items appear in the menu at all, and, if so, how they appear. For example, Selecting `"In the menu"` for programs will cause the items in the program menu to show up in the main menu (see Figure 6.14).

FIGURE **6.14**

*Programs listed in
the main menu
with the "In the
menu" option
checked.*

Selecting `"In a submenu"` will cause a "Programs" submenu to show up in the main menu, under which will be the items in programs (see Figure 6.15).

FIGURE **6.15**

*Programs listed as
a submenu with
the "In a sub-
menu" option
checked.*

Customizing the Gnome Desktop Environment

CHAPTER 6

141

6

CUSTOMIZING THE
GNOME DESKTOP
ENVIRONMENT

Finally, selecting "Off" will cause programs not to be in the menu at all (see Figure 6.16).

FIGURE 6.16

Programs do not show up in the menu at all with the "Off" option checked.

Theme Selector

Here, you can change the desktop theme that Gnome uses. Thousands of different themes and instructions for installing them can be found at gtk.themes.org.

Window Manager

As mentioned previously, Gnome does not have a built-in window manager. Instead, it uses the services of a Gnome-aware window manager. The default Gnome window manager is Sawfish, which is what we have been working with up to this point. But if you don't like Sawfish, you can tell Gnome to use a different window manager here. Note that if you change the window manager, some of the various controls and menus that were discussed in the previous chapter may change as well.

Figure 6.17 shows the control panel for changing the Window manager, and Figure 6.18 shows Gnome running with the IceWM Window Manager. Note the differences in the window appearance.

FIGURE 6.17

Changing the window manager from the Control Center.

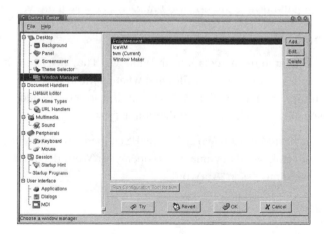

Figure 6.18

Gnome running with the IceWM window manager.

For best results, it is recommended that you use a Gnome-aware window manager with Gnome. Although other window managers will work, Gnome will usually behave rather strangely while running under them. As of this writing (and this is not likely to change soon), the three most Gnome-compliant window managers available are Sawfish, IceWM, and Enlightenment.

Document Handlers

The options here control the way various documents should be handled. These options relate to how the File Manager handles various different file types. We will look at each of these options in detail.

Default Editor

This is the default editor that the Gnome File Manager should use when opening text files for editing. If you are a new user to FreeBSD, you might want to change this to "gEdit" from the pull-down menu because Emacs is not very intuitive for new users.

Mime Types

Mime types are similar to file associations in Windows. They determine how the Gnome File Manager handles various types of files and what application it should use to open those files when they are double-clicked. Now, you'll learn how to add a mime type and also how to associate an application with that mime type.

Although you can't get Microsoft Word for FreeBSD, there are different word processors available that can handle word documents. To open your Word documents you can use the open source word processor "AbiWord".

> **Tip**
>
> Abiword is available in the FreeBSD ports collection under the "editors" directory. See Chapter 15, "Installing Additional Software," for more information.

When you click a Word document, a dialog box will ask what application you want to use to open it with (see Figure 6.19).

FIGURE 6.19

The "Select application" dialog box.

Obviously, this gets a little old after a few times of doing it. So, you will want to set a mime type so the Gnome File Manager will automatically recognize this type of document as a word document, and choose the appropriate application to open it (in this case, AbiWord).

Looking through our the list of mime types in the Control Center (see Figure 6.20), you see that Gnome currently knows nothing about Microsoft Word documents (there is no Word mime type to be found in the list).

Looking at the list of mime types, you can see that there are certain conventions that are followed. Application-specific files usually start with the word `"application"`, followed by a slash and then some type of identifier that represents the type of document. For example, pdf (Adobe Portable Document Format) documents are of type "application/pdf". Documents that consist of plain text generally start with `"text"`, followed by a slash, and then something about the type of document. For example, a Web page document is type "text/html". A plain-text file is type "text/plain".

FIGURE **6.20**

The mime types list in the Control Center.

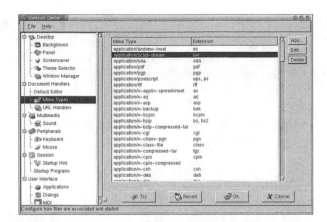

Note

Mime stands for *multipurpose Internet mail extensions*. As the name suggests, mime was originally developed to allow files rather than just text to be transferred through email. The concept was later extended to the World Wide Web. When you visit a Web page, for example, the Web server sends a header that tells your browser what type of document it is going to send. This header is invisible to you, and you will not see it even if you look at the source code for the page. The information in this header is a mime type, and your browser uses the mime type in the header to determine how to handle the document it is about to receive (display it in a browser window, open an external application to handle it, or download it to disk). Different file types have different standard mime type names to go with them that browsers and email clients know about.

If you want to learn the details of mime types, the standard is defined in the IRFC (request for comment) 2045 and 2046.

Although Gnome doesn't really care what you call the mime type, it is a good idea to follow these conventions, including the use of common mime type names. There are several places on the Internet that list the common mime types. One site is http://www.isi.edu/in-notes/iana/assignments/media-types/media-types.

Looking through the list in this Web site, you can determine that the mime type for Microsoft Word documents is "application/msword". Use this term to call the mime type that you create.

To create the mime type, click "Add", and a dialog box like that shown in Figure 6.21 appears.

FIGURE 6.21

Adding a mime type for Microsoft Word documents (fields already filled in).

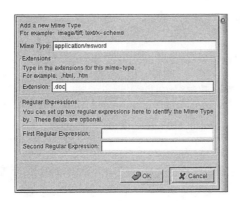

You enter `"application/msword"` in the "Mime type" field. Because Microsoft Word documents have a .doc extension, you enter doc in the "Extensions" field.

The "Regular Expression" fields should be left blank in this case. If they are set, the File Manager will look at the document itself and try to find these regular expressions in the document to identify the mime type.

After you have entered the information, click `"Ok"`, and the new mime type appears in the list. Now, you want to edit the mime type to associate an application with. So, click the new mime type and then click `"Edit"`. Figure 6.22 shows the Edit dialog box.

FIGURE 6.22

Editing the new Word mime type.

In the "Open", "View", and "Edit" fields, we enter `"abiword %f"`. The %f tells the File Manager to supply the name of the file as an argument to the program. You will probably also want to change the icon to something more easily distinguished as a Word document, so click the raised square that contains the icon and then you can select a new one from the list.

> **Note**
>
> An *argument* is an option passed to the program to tell it what data it should work on. For example, in this case, the %f contains the name of the file that was selected in the File Manager. This is supplied as an argument to abiwor so that abiword is invoked using the command `"abiword filename"` and will open `"filename"` for editing.

> **Note**
>
> There are more icons available than you see listed. Click the `"Browse"` button to change the directory in which the icons should be looked for.

After you have selected an icon, click `"Ok"` and then click `"Ok"` again in the Control Center window to save the changes. Now, you can open the File Manager, find a Word document, double-click it, and abiword will be opened and display the document rather than us having to select which application we want to use each time.

Customizing Sawfish Window Manager Options

Most aspects of the window manager behavior cannot be controlled from the Gnome Control Center. Instead, you have to use the Sawfish Configurator to change these. To start the Sawfish Configurator, middle-click a blank area on the desktop, select `"Customize"`, and then select `"All Features"` (see Figure 6.23).

To make the desktop environment easier to work with, make the following changes.

Choose `"Focus"` and check `"Focus windows when they are first displayed"`. This will cause new windows to automatically be made active when they open. Make sure that `"Dialog windows inherit the focus from their parents"` is checked. `"Raise windows when they are first focused"` should also be checked, and `"Delay in milliseconds until focused windows are raised"` should be set to `"0"`.

Other than that, you can look through the other settings in this Configurator, and decide to change them or not. For example, the `"Appearance"` option allows you to change the appearance of the window frames (and might also change their operation). When you are finished making changes, click `"Ok"` to exit the Sawfish Configurator.

FIGURE 6.23
*The Sawfish
Configurator.*

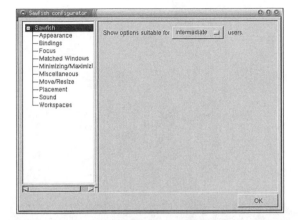

Caution

When making changes to these settings, you should be aware that they may change the default behavior and appearance of the environment. For example, changing the window frame could change the behavior of the window control buttons.

Working with Applications

CHAPTER

7

A computer that can't do any work is not very useful, and neither is an operating system that doesn't have any applications. FreeBSD has thousands of applications available, ranging from scientific applications that do biological modeling, to office packages, to games. All of the applications covered in this chapter are available for free.

In addition to the thousands of applications that are available natively, FreeBSD can also run most Linux applications. This gives you a very wide variety of applications to choose from for virtually any purpose.

Of course, this chapter cannot even begin to cover all the applications available for FreeBSD, but it does give a good sampling of some of the more popular ones in various areas.

Note

This chapter covers applications for workstation use. It does not cover server applications such as Web servers, ftp servers, and e-mail servers. If you are look-ing for information on setting up services such as these, you should read the appropriate chapters in Part IV of the book, "FreeBSD Networking," which cover the services you are interested in configuring.

Tip

Although this chapter will tell you where to obtain the applications it covers, it will not explain the procedure for *installing* the software. If you are unsure about how to install software on FreeBSD, please see Chapter 15, "Installing Additional Software," for information on this topic.

Working with Text

One of the most common applications that almost everyone needs is a basic text editor.

Unlike a word processor, a text editor simply works on plain-text files. It does not have the ability to store font changes, margins, or any other such information in the document. Here are some common uses of a text editor:

- **Editing system configuration files:** FreeBSD, like most other versions of UNIX, relies heavily on text-based configuration files to control system behavior. To edit these files, you will need a text editor that can write a plain-text file. Using a word processor on these configuration files would ruin them because the operating system would not understand the strange formatting that the word processor saves with the document. This will have unpredictable results, which could even render the system unbootable. (The system configuration files and how to configure them will be covered in Chapter 11, "System Configuration and Startup Scripts.")

- **Creating or modifying programming source code:** You will use a text editor to write the code that tells the computer what you want it to do. Although in many languages, this code will be converted to machine language by a program called a compiler, your original instructions are still written in plain-text. These instructions are called *source code*. Chapter 13, "Shell Programming," and Chapter 21, "Introduction to Perl Programming," introduce two popular programming languages in FreeBSD in which you would use a text editor to write the code.

- **Creating or modifying Web pages:** Web pages are written in HTML, which stands for *hypertext markup language*. Although there are many GUI-based, WYSIWYG (what you see is what you get) programs available for designing Web pages, the end result is still a plain-text file with formatting control tags that the Web browser understands. Many people still choose to write Web pages by hand in a plain-text editor because it gives them total control over all of the features of HTML. In addition, you would use a text editor to write PHP code, JavaScript, and other such extended features of Web design that allow you to give your pages interactive content.

- **Sophisticated typesetting:** There are some very sophisticated typesetting languages available for FreeBSD. Like HTML, typesetting languages generally use plain-text files with special formatting tags in them to control the layout and appearance of text. Although the word processor has largely replaced these languages (the word processor is easier to work with, and shows you what the output will actually look like), there are still situations in which you might want to use a typesetting language. TeX, and its extended macro package LayTeX, might interest you if you are a scientist or engineer because of their extremely sophisticated mathematical equation-formatting capabilities.

We will start by looking at a couple of the GUI-based editors available for the X-Windows system because they will be more familiar to you if you have a Windows or Macintosh background. After that, we will look at some of the text-based editors available for FreeBSD.

gedit

`gedit` is pretty much the standard text editor for the Gnome Desktop Environment. It is similar to Windows Notepad in that its controls behave much the same way. However, it

has many more features than Windows Notepad. gedit is available in the packages
included on the CD and also in the ports tree under the editors directory. Figure 7.1
shows what gedit looks like.

FIGURE 7.1

The gedit *text
editor. You can
switch between
open documents
by clicking on the
tabs across the
top.*

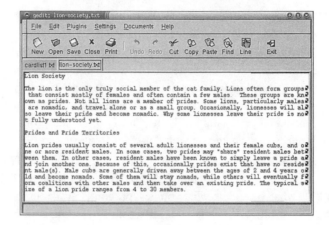

If you've worked with any text editor in Windows before, the first two menu options will
look familiar to you. As you would expect, the File option allows you to save, print, and
open files. The Edit option allows you to do search and replace functions, and so on.
Some of the other options may be less familiar because they allow you to access some of
the advanced features of gedit.

Plug-ins

gedit can use plug-ins to extend its functionality. Plug-ins are external programs that
interface with gedit.

To select a plug-in, simply click Plug-ins on the menu bar and then select the plug-in that
you want from the list. There are five plug-ins installed by default. Here is what they do.

Browse

If you have the Lynx Web browser installed, this plug-in will allow you to load the text
from Web pages directly into the editor. The text from the Web page can then be saved as
a text file, edited, and so on. Note that only the text portions of the page will be loaded
and that you will not be able to follow any links. Figure 7.2 shows the dialog box asking
you to enter the Web page address you wish to load.

FIGURE 7.2

Viewing a Web page in gedit. The change button allows you to specify a different location for where Lynx is located.

Tip

As mentioned previously, the Lynx Web browser needs to be installed for this feature to work. Lynx is available in the packages included on the CD and also in the ports tree under the directory www.

Diff

This plug-in compares two existing documents and then creates a third document that contains the differences between the two documents. Figure 7.3 shows the `diff` dialog box.

FIGURE 7.3

Comparing two documents in gedit.

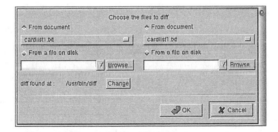

The plug-in can compare both documents that are loaded in the editor currently, as well as documents that are stored in a file on disk by selecting the appropriate check boxes.

An example of how you might use this is if you write a document, send it to someone else, and then that person makes some changes and sends it back to you. Rather than go through the whole document and look for the changes, you can use this plug-in to automatically compare the original document with the changed one and show you the changes that were made. Suppose you have two files that look like the following:

File 1:

```
Line 1
Line 2
Line 3
Line 4
Line 5
Line 6
Line 7
Line 8
Line 9
Line 10
```

File 2:

```
Line 1
Line 2
Line 3
Line four
Line 5
Line 6
Line 7
Line eight
Line nine
Line ten
Line 11
```

To compare these two documents, select Plugins and then Diff. In the dialog box (refer
to Figure 7.3), either select the From document checkbox, and then select the name of
the two documents from the pull-down lists, or select the From a file on disk checkbox
and then either enter the name of the file in the box below or click the Browse button and
browse to the file. Note that the output the plug-in will produce is based on what would
have to be done to the first document (the one on the left) to make it the same as the second document (the one on the right). Don't worry if that statement seems really confusing right now; it will make sense after the output is displayed.

Here is the output of the diff plug-in when run on the two samples shown previously.
Note that the line numbers are just for reference purposes and do not appear in the actual
output:

```
1.   --- /tmp/gedit-991687757-2758-1    Mon Jun  4 15:49:17 2001
2.   +++ /tmp/gedit-991687757-2758-2    Mon Jun  4 15:49:17 2001
3.   @@ -1,10 +1,11 @@
4.    Line 1
5.    Line 2
6.    Line 3
7.   -Line 4
8.   +Line four
9.    Line 5
```

```
10.  Line 6
11.  Line 7
12. -Line 8
13. -Line 9
14. -Line 10
15. +Line eight
16. +Line nine
17. +Line ten
+Line 11
```

Lines 1 and 2 show the names of the two files that are being compared and the date and times that the files were created. In this case, they are temporary files because they were compared from the document windows instead of being files on the disk.

Lines 4, 5, and 6 are common between both documents, so they are displayed as is.

Line 7 exists only in the first document, and therefore it has a minus sign in front of it. This indicates that you would have to remove this line from the first document to make it the same as the second document.

Line 8 exists only in the second document, and therefore it has a plus sign in front of it. This indicates that you would have to add this line to the first document to make it the same as the second document.

Lines 9, 10, and 11 are common between both documents, so they are shown as is.

Lines 12, 13, and 14 exist only in the first document, and again, the minus sign indicates that they need to be removed to make the first document the same as the second document.

Lines 15, 16, 17, and 18 exist only in the second document, and once again, the plus sign indicates that they would need to be added to the first document to make it the same as the second document.

Notice that the output from the plug-in created a new tab in gedit. In effect, the output is a new document. It can be saved and modified just like any other document.

E-mail

The E-mail plug-in simply allows you to e-mail the current document to the specified recipient. Figure 7.4 shows the dialog box for e-mailing the document.

FIGURE 7.4
E-mailing the current document. The From, To, and Subject headers work exactly as expected.

Caution

In order for the e-mail function to work, you must have Sendmail or some other mail transfer agent installed, running, and configured to work with your mail setup. Information on how to configure Sendmail can be found in Chapter 25, "Configuring E-mail Services."

Shell Output

The shell output plug-in lets you run a shell command and automatically have the output pasted into the current document at the position of the cursor. Figure 7.5 shows the dialog box of the shell output plug-in.

FIGURE 7.5
The Shell Output dialog box. The Directory box is where you enter the directory you want the shell command to operate on.

For example, to insert a long listing of the contents of the root directory into the document at the current location of the cursor, you could enter / in the Directory box, and enter `ls -l` in the Enter shell command box. This would run the `ls` command with the `-l` option and print the output in the currently active document wherever the cursor currently located.

Insert Time

This plug-in simply inserts the current date and time into the document at the cursor position. Here is an example of how the date and time is formatted:

```
Mon Jun  4 17:26:11 CDT 2001
```

Preferences

You can change several settings of gedit to suit your work style. The Preferences dialog box is found under the Settings menu option. Figure 7.6 shows the first screen of the Preferences dialog box.

FIGURE 7.6

The Preferences dialog box for gedit*. The tabs across the top allow you to select different categories of preferences to customize.*

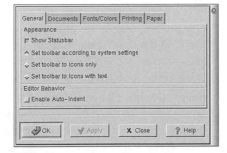

7

WORKING WITH
APPLICATIONS

ee

ee (Easy Editor) is installed by default along with FreeBSD. It is a basic text editor that is designed to be easier to work with than some of the other traditional UNIX text editors.

ee can be invoked either by simply typing ee at the command line or by typing ee followed by the name of a file you wish to edit. Figure 7.7 shows a sample ee session with a blank document.

FIGURE 7.7

A sample ee *session. The top part of the screen shows the key combinations used to access various features.*

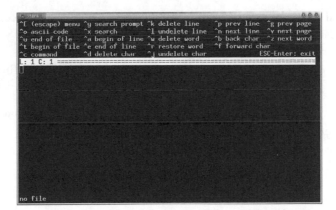

The carat (^) in the options menu means the Ctrl key. Most of the options in the menu are self-explanatory, but there are a few that deserve greater discussion. Table 7.1 shows these options and their meanings.

TABLE 7.1   Ctrl Key Options in ee

Key Combination	Action
Ctrl+o	Brings up a prompt where you can enter an ASCII value. Useful for inserting special characters that do not exist on the keyboard and require their ASCII values to be entered directly.
Ctrl+c	Changes the top menu and also brings up a prompt at the bottom of the screen where you can type one of the commands listed at the top. Simply press Enter to leave the prompt without entering a command.
Ctrl+y	Brings up a search prompt. Here, you can type an expression to search for in the file. When you press Enter, the first occurrence of the expression after the current location of the cursor will be found.
Ctrl+x	Repeats the previous search done with Ctrl+y, causing ee to find the next occurrence of the expression.
Ctrl+g and Ctrl+v	As the menu says, these will move forward and backward one page at a time. You can also use the Page Up and Page Down keys on your keyboard to accomplish the same thing. Ctrl+G and Ctrl+V exist in case you are on a terminal that does not have Page Up/Page Down keys.

Setup and Configuration of ee

If a file called .init.ee exists in your home directory, ee will read the configuration options in this file each time it starts. You can create this file by hand or you can press Esc in ee to bring up the menu (see Figure 7.8); then press e for settings, or use the down arrow to highlight the settings option in the menu and then press Enter (see Figure 7.9).

In Figure 7.9, you can either press the letter corresponding to the option to toggle the option on or off, or you can use the arrow keys to highlight the desired option and then press Enter to toggle the option on or off.

FIGURE 7.8
The menu in ee.

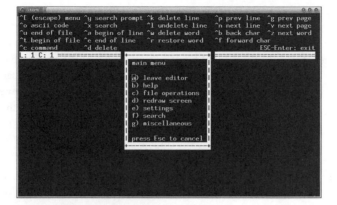

FIGURE 7.9
Setup options for
ee.

Table 7.2 shows the various setup options and what they do.

TABLE 7.2   ee Setup Options

Option	*Description*
Tabs to spaces	Off by default. This converts hard tabs into the equivalent number of spaces. It is useful for some programming languages, where whitespace is important (for example, Python and FORTRAN).
Case-sensitive search	Off by default. This controls whether searches are case-sensitive.
Margins observed	Off by default. When it is on, ee wraps at the right margin and starts a new line automatically. When it is off, wrapping does not occur unless a new line is inserted manually.

TABLE 7.2 continued

Option	Description
Auto paragraph format	Off by default. When it is on, ee tries to reformat the paragraph automatically when text is being inserted into the middle, similarly to the way a word processor behaves. When it is off, no reformatting is attempted. Note that turning this option on automatically turns the margins observed option on as well. Turning off the margins observed option automatically turns this option off, too.
Eightbit characters	On by default. When it is on, 8-bit extended ASCII characters are displayed. When it is off, those characters are not displayed.
Info window	On by default. When it is on, the top part of the screen shows the menu/help window. When it is off, this is not displayed. You should probably leave this on until you are familiar with the various key commands.
Emacs key bindings	On by default. When it is on, the Ctrl key sequences behave similarly to Ctrl key sequences in the Emacs editor. Even if you do not know what this is, you probably shouldn't change this option. If you do, some of the key bindings will change and will no longer work the way they are described here.
Right margin	The column at which the right margin is set. By default, it is set for the width of a standard 80-column terminal display.
16 bit characters	This controls how 16-bit characters are handled (whether they are handled as two 8-bit characters or one 16-bit character). You shouldn't have to worry about this option unless you are using a Chinese character set or something similar.

The final option in the menu, Save editor configuration, writes the configuration information to the file `.init.ee`. If that file already exists, it will be overwritten.

When you choose to save the configuration information, you will be asked if you want to write the configuration file to the current directory or to your home directory. If you write it to your home directory, the configuration will be the default configuration for all files you create and open in ee. If you write it to the current directory, the settings will override the default settings from the configuration file in the home directory any time ee is started from this directory.

The `vi` Editor

`vi` was one of the first editors developed for UNIX-like operating systems. To this day, it is still one of the most powerful editors available, and it comes standard on virtually every UNIX-like operating system. It has also been ported to several non-UNIX systems, including Microsoft Windows and OS/2. Unfortunately, vi also has a reputation among newbies for being notoriously arcane and difficult to learn. This is because there are no menus, for example. Everything must be done by keystrokes and combinations of special key presses that take some time to learn.

So why learn vi? There are two primary reasons, really. The first is that you can be virtually assured that vi will be available on any UNIX-like system you might ever have to work on. Because of this, vi is a very nice thing to know if you may have to work on other UNIX-like systems because it might be the only editor you will have available.

The second reason for learning vi is that once you have learned its various keystrokes and commands, it is a very powerful editor. If you are a touch typist, it is also an extremely fast way to work because you do not have to remove your hands from the home keys to access most vi commands.

To start vi, you can either type `vi` to start it with an empty file, or `vi` followed by a name to load the file with that name into the editor for editing. If the filename you specify doesn't already exist, vi will assume that this is a new file. Figure 7.10 shows a vi session with a new file ready for editing.

FIGURE 7.10

The vi editor, editing a new file. The status line at the bottom of the screen gives information about the file being edited.

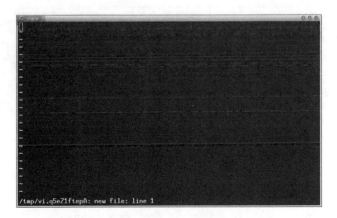

Looks rather plain and boring, doesn't it? One of the first things you may notice if you start trying to type text is that vi does nothing except beep at you and not insert any of the text you are typing. You may also hit certain keys and see strange-looking messages on the status line at the bottom of the screen. This is because vi has different modes of operation.

When vi first starts, it is in command mode. In command mode, key presses are interpreted as commands to the editor rather than as text to be inserted into the document. To switch into the mode in which you can enter text into the document, you must press the a, i, or o key.

The a key stands for *append*. In this mode, the text you type will be inserted after whatever character the cursor is currently on.

The i key stands for *insert*. In this mode, the text you type will be inserted before whatever character the cursor is currently on.

Finally, the o key stands for *open*. This will cause a new line to be inserted after the line the cursor is currently on. Then, the cursor will move to the new line, and vi will enter insert mode, allowing you to enter text on the new line.

There are also some other commands to enter text entry mode that are less used, but still available. They are O, which adds a blank line above the current line; and A, which begins inserting text at the end of the current line.

If you wish to get back into command mode after entering text entry mode, press the Escape key. By default, vi will beep when entering command mode.

> **Tip**
>
> Remember that if you are trying to enter text and vi simply keeps beeping at you or doing other strange things, you are probably in command mode. Press a, i, or o to enter text mode. Also, if you are ever unsure what mode you are in, simply pressing Escape will put you in command mode (if you are already in command mode, it will have no effect). You can then press a, i, or o to enter text entry mode.

Moving Around in vi

In text entry mode, you can usually use the arrow keys and the Page Up/Page Down keys to move around. However, these may not always work while on a terminal. Also, some terminals don't even have arrow keys or Page Up/Page Down keys. In this case, there are other keys that can be used in command mode to move around in a document. There are also several command mode keys that can be used to move in ways that cannot be done with the arrow keys and the Page Up/Page Down keys.

To use the movement keys, press Escape to get into command mode. You can then use the h, j, k, and l keys on the keyboard to move the cursor left, down, up, and right, respectively. The following four tips may help you remember which key moves the cursor in which direction.

- The l key is the furthest to the right, and it moves the cursor right.
- The j key looks somewhat like a downward-pointing arrow. It moves the cursor down.
- The h key is the furthest to the left, and it moves the cursor left.
- The remaining key, k, moves the cursor up.

There are several other movement keys available in command mode. Table 7.3 shows the various keys and their functions.

TABLE 7.3   The Movement Keys Available from vi's Command Mode

Key	Action
h	Moves the cursor left one character.
j	Moves the cursor down one character.
k	Moves the cursor up one character.
l	Moves the cursor right one character.
w	Moves the cursor forward one word.
b	Moves the cursor back one word.
e	Moves the cursor to end of the next word.
0	Moves to the beginning of the line.
$	Moves to the end of the line.
)	Moves to the beginning of the next sentence.
(	Moves to the beginning of the previous sentence.
}	Moves to the beginning of the next paragraph.
{	Moves to the beginning of the previous paragraph.
G	Moves to the bottom of the current document.
^	Moves to the first character in the line that is not a space.
H	Moves the cursor to the first line on the screen.
L	Moves the cursor to the last line on the screen.

Note that each of the commands in the table (with the exception of G) uses the unit of one by default. j moves the cursor down one line, k moves it up one line, w moves one word to the right, and so on. You can modify the default behavior by typing a number before the command. For example, the following line causes the cursor to move down five lines instead of one line:

5j

The following line causes the cursor to move to the 75th line in the current file that is being edited:

75G

The following line causes the cursor to move to the line that is five lines up from the bottom of the screen:

5L

This syntax works for all of the commands in Table 7.3, except for the ^ command that moves to the first non-space character in the document.

> **Tip**
>
> If you enter a number followed by one of the previous commands, and vi seems to do nothing except beep, it probably means you entered a number out of range. For example, if you enter 560G to move to line 560, and the document has only 557 lines, vi will simply beep at you—indicating that the number you entered is out of range. Unfortunately, no error message will be printed telling you what is wrong.

Other Movement Keys

In addition to the cursor movement keys described previously, there are also some key combinations that are related to scrolling the screen (Table 7.4 lists them).

TABLE 7.4 Scrolling in vi

Key Combination	Action
z then Enter	Moves the line the cursor is on to the top of the screen.
z then -	Moves the line the cursor is on to the bottom of the screen.
z then .	Moves the line the cursor is on to the center of the screen.
Ctrl+u	Scrolls up one-half screen.
Ctrl+d	Scrolls down one-half screen.

TABLE 7.4 continued

Key Combination	Action
Ctrl+f	Scrolls forward one full screen.
Ctrl+b	Scrolls backward one full screen.
Ctrl+e	Scrolls down one line.
Ctrl+y	Scrolls up one line.

Text-Editing Commands

The Backspace and Delete keys will not do what you expect in vi. Instead, you will have to use various keystrokes from vi's command mode in order to delete text, and so on. Table 7.5 lists the various text-editing commands available in vi.

TABLE 7.5 Commands for Text Editing in vi

Key	Action
D	Deletes the text from the cursor position to the end of the line.
dd	Deletes the entire current line.
*n*dd	Where *n* is the number of lines you wish to delete. For example, 5dd will delete the current line, as well as the next four lines.
rc	Where *c* is a character. This will replace the character under the cursor with the character that follows r.
R	The text typed after R will overwrite the current text, starting at the cursor position until Escape is pressed to get back into command mode.
S	Deletes the current line and begins inserting text in the now blank line.
x	Deletes the character under the cursor, and moves the character to the right over to close the gap.
X	Deletes the character before the cursor, and moves the character to the character under the cursor over to close the gap.
~	Change the case of the letter under the cursor.
J	Joins the current line with the previous line, and removes the resulting blank line.

7

**WORKING WITH
APPLICATIONS**

File Operations and Exiting vi

These operations are related to loading and saving files in vi. Table 7.6 shows the various commands available for these actions.

TABLE 7.6   File Operations in vi

Key	*Action*
ZZ	Saves changes to the current file and then exits.
:wq	Saves changes to the current files and then exits (the same as ZZ).
:w	Saves changes to the current file.
:w!	Saves changes to the current file, overwriting a file of the same name if it already exists.
:q	Quits vi. If there are unsaved changes, vi complains and does not quit.
:q!	Quits vi even if there are unsaved changes. All unsaved changes will be lost.
:e *filename*	Loads the specified file into vi for editing. If the specified file does not exist, a new file will be created.
:e!	Loses all changes, and reloads the saved file from the disk.

Caution

Note that the ! option on the end of several of the commands in Table 7.6 forces the action to take place. You will not be prompted before the action is taken if you have unsaved changes in your document. For example, :q! will exit vi immediately without asking first if you want to save any changes. Use the ! option with care.

Searching and Replacing Text in vi

There are several commands for doing a search-and-replace in vi. Table 7.7 lists the available commands and their actions.

TABLE 7.7   Search and Replace Commands in vi

Key(s)	Action
/pattern	Where *pattern* is what to search for. vi searches forward in the file for the first occurrence of the specified pattern.
/	Repeats the last search, finding the next occurrence of the pattern in the file.
?pattern	Where *pattern* is what to search for. vi searches backward in the file for the first occurrence of the specified pattern.
?	Repeats the last search, finding the previous occurrence of the pattern in the file.
%	Moves to the matching parenthesis or brace for the one that the cursor is currently on. It is useful for programmers.
:s/pattern1/pattern2	Replaces each occurrence of *pattern1* with *pattern2* on the current line.
:%s/pattern1/pattern2	Replaces every occurrence of *pattern1* with *pattern2* in the entire file.

There are a few other search-and-replace functions that are not used as often, and will not be covered here. The previous operations are the ones that you will probably use most often.

Copying, Cutting and Pasting Text in vi

To copy text to a buffer in vi, use the y command. y is short for "yank," and it basically yanks text into the buffer. Table 7.8 shows the various ways the yank command can be used.

TABLE 7.8   Yank Commands in vi

Command	Action
yw	Yanks the word that the cursor is currently on into the buffer.
y$	Yanks from the current cursor position up to the end of the current line into the buffer.
yy	Yanks the entire current line into the buffer.
nyy	Where *n* is the number of lines you wish to yank into the buffer. For example, 5yy yanks the current line, as well as the next four lines into the buffer.

Once you have yanked text into the buffer, you can paste it into any location in the document by moving to the correct location in the document and then using p or P to "put" the text. p places the text into the document after the cursor; P places the text into the document before the cursor. After you have put the text, it continues to remain in the buffer. You can use p or P again to copy the text to another location in the document.

If you want to cut instead of copy, use one of the deletion commands. For example, 5dd will cut the current line as well as the next four lines. They can than be pasted into the document in another location by using p or P.

> **Caution**
>
> vi stores only the last text that was yanked or deleted. In other words, if you use dd to delete a line of text, and you later use yy to copy a line of text, the text from the dd operation will be replaced with the text from the yy operation. This means the text from the dd operation will no longer be available, nor will you be able to undo the delete.

vi has many more powerful features that cannot be covered here due to lack of space. Once you get to know vi, it is a very powerful editor and also a very fast way to work. If you would like to learn more about vi, there are a few books available on the subject including *Learning the vi Editor* and *vi Editor Pocket Reference*, both available from O'Reilly.

Graphics and Images

There are several graphics programs and image-editing programs available for FreeBSD such as the Gimp for image editing and Xfig for drawing figures and illustrations. All the programs below are available for free in the FreeBSD ports collection.

The GIMP

The GIMP stands for The GNU Image Manipulation Program. It is a freely available and open-source image-editing program maintained by the GNU project. It has many advanced features such as the layers and filters. If you have worked with a program such as Adobe Photoshop before, most of GIMP's features will be familiar to you. Getting used to the layout of GIMP however, may take some time.

GIMP recognizes most image formats, including BMP, GIF, JPEG, PNG, PCX, and TIFF. GIMP can also read PostScript files.

GIMP is available in the FreeBSD ports collection under the `graphics` directory. Once you have installed GIMP, you can simply type **gimp** from a terminal in X-Windows, or use the Run dialog box and type **gimp** in it. See Chapter 5, "Working with the Gnome Desktop Environment," for more information on how to start applications from within X-Windows. For information on how to add GIMP to the Gnome menu or create a desktop icon for GIMP, see Chapter 6, "Customizing the Gnome Desktop Environment."

Figure 7.11 shows the main control panel for GIMP.

FIGURE 7.11

The main control panel for GIMP. This is where you can select the various tools available in GIMP as well as Load and Save files.

The File option from the menu bar is usually your starting point for GIMP. Here, you can open an existing file, create a new file, or acquire an image—either from a screen shot (this will be explained in a later section) or from a supported scanner, if installed.

Opening an Existing File

Figure 7.12 shows the File, Open dialog box in GIMP.

FIGURE 7.12

Opening a file in GIMP. Notice that there is a primitive file manager built in to it.

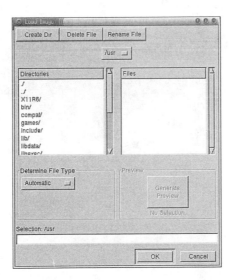

The pull-down menu in the middle of the top part of the box will list the directory tree from the current directory up to the root directory. This can be a quick way to jump to a directory that is several layers above the current directory.

You can select directories from the left half of the screen; then select the file you want to work on from the right half of the screen. If you double-click the file, it will be opened immediately. Otherwise, you can click it once and then click the OK button to open the file.

The Determine file type pull-down menu will default to Automatic. Normally, you will not have to change this unless GIMP cannot properly detect the type of file you are trying to open, for whatever reason.

Finally, you can click the Generate Preview button to generate a thumbnail-sized image of the file that is currently highlighted.

Tip

If you have already generated a preview of an image, that preview will be saved, so the preview will automatically show up the next time you click the image. If you make changes to the file, those changes will not be reflected in the preview unless you click the preview image to refresh it with the newly saved file with the changes.

Figure 7.13 shows an image loaded into GIMP.

FIGURE 7.13

The image window in GIMP. Note that the GIMP control panel is still available.

Tip

If you load an image into GIMP and can't see the control panel any more, it has probably just been covered up with the image window.

Creating a New Image in GIMP

To create a new image in GIMP, select File, New. This will bring up a dialog box like that shown in Figure 7.14.

FIGURE 7.14

The New Image dialog box in GIMP. Here, you can control various properties of the image—such as size and background color.

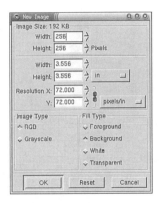

You can set the new size of the image by either specifying the height and width in pixels at the top of the dialog box, or by specifying it in some other unit of measurement, such as inches. The pull-down box allows you to select different units to specify the size in.

You can also specify the resolution of the image. The higher the resolution, the greater the quality of the image will be. But it will also increase the file size. The "chain link" icon next to the resolution means that changing either the X or Y resolution will cause the other resolution to change accordingly. If you wish to set each resolution manually, you can do so by clicking the chain link icon. When you have, the chain will change and appear broken. Click it again to restore the link.

The image type can be set to either RGB or Grayscale initially. RGB, which stands for "Red Green Blue," indicates the color of the three electron guns in your computer's monitor. All the colors can be made up by combining different combinations and intensities of red, green, and blue.

Finally, you can set the fill type to either the foreground color, the background color, white, or transparent.

The current foreground and background colors are shown in the lower-left corner of the GIMP control panel (refer to Figure 7.14).

Clicking either the foreground or the background color will allow you to change the respective color. Figure 7.15 shows the dialog box for changing the color.

FIGURE 7.15

Changing the color in GIMP. The tabs on the top allow you to select different methods of setting the color. The default method (GIMP) is shown in this figure.

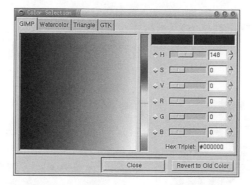

If you happen to know either the hexadecimal value of the color you want, or the RGB or HSV numbers, you can enter the values manually by clicking in the appropriate boxes and then typing the number for the color. Most commonly, you would probably know the hexadecimal value for the color (for example, you are trying to match a Web page background color or something).

If you do not know the value of the color you want, select the approximate color from the vertical color bar by clicking the mouse in an area of the bar. Then, you can drag the mouse in the large square to control the color. Note the right half of the screen at the top. The color box on the left will change in real time as you drag to reflect the current color. The color in the right color box is the old color. If you click the Revert to Old Color button, this is the color that it will go back to. You can then use the vertical slider bar again to fine-tune things. Keep switching back and forth between the vertical slider and the large square until you have the color you want.

Notice that the color value numbers update to reflect the current color. If you are creating an image that will be used on a Web site, you can write down the hex triplet value. You can then use this as the background color in your Web page to prevent the image border from showing up. This is handy for image formats such as JPEG and PNG, in which transparencies are not supported.

Using the tabs at the top of the Color Selection dialog box, you can select other ways to set the color. Figure 7.16 shows the Watercolor tab.

FIGURE 7.16

Setting the color with the Watercolor tab. This allows you to mix the colors in the large square.

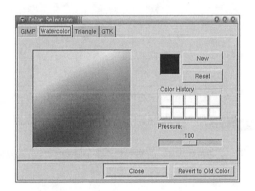

Clicking on any area of the large square will cause that color to be added to the small box on the right. Clicking again on the same spot will increase the amount of that color. You can control how much the amount is increased on each click by dragging the Pressure slider control. The Color History box will store the last several colors you created. Each time you press New, a new color will be stored. When all the boxes have been filled up, GIMP will start over at the beginning.

The Triangle tab presents a color triangle. You can drag the outside circle around the color ring on the outside, and the inside circles around in the triangle (see Figure 7.17).

FIGURE 7.17

The color triangle. The triangle will rotate as you drag the outer circle around the color ring.

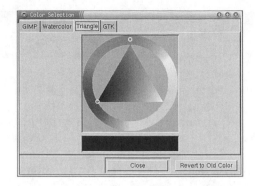

Finally, there is the GTK tab. This allows you to select colors in a way similar to the GIMP tab, except that moving the circle changes the color in the vertical slider bar. Once you have selected the approximate color from the circle, you can drag the bar in the vertical slider up and down in order to change the intensity of the selected color. Figure 7.18 shows the GTK tab of the color selector.

FIGURE 7.18

The GTK tab of the color selector.

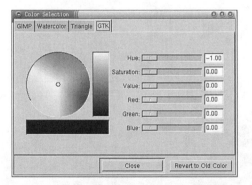

Tip

With any of the color selectors, you can drag the color from the current color box into an image window to flood the selected area with that color. To drag the color, simply hold down the left mouse button over the color box and then drag the color into the area you wish to flood in the image window.

Capturing a Screen Shot in GIMP

You can also obtain an image in GIMP by capturing a screen shot. To do this, click File in the control center's menu bar, and then click Acquire. In the submenu under Acquire, click Screen Shot. This will bring up a dialog box like the one in Figure 7.19.

FIGURE 7.19

*The Screen Shot
capture dialog box
in GIMP.*

The first option is to capture just a single window. If the With Decorations dialog box is also checked, the window frame will be included in the screen shot. If it is not checked, only the window will be included in the screen shot. If you wish to capture just a single window, you can ignore the After Seconds Delay option at the bottom of the dialog box. Click Ok, and your mouse pointer will change to a crosshair. Now, simply move the pointer over the window you wish to capture, and press the left mouse button. GIMP will beep twice, and a new image window will open with the captured screen. You can then edit the image, or simply save it to a file in any one of the formats that GIMP supports.

If you wish to capture the entire screen instead of just one window, check the Whole Screen option. You can then set a delay in seconds. After you press OK, GIMP will wait the specified number of seconds before doing the screen capture. This will give you time to minimize the GIMP windows and perform any other operations you need to do before the screen is captured. After the allotted time has passed, GIMP will beep twice, and the screen shot will appear in a new window. You can then edit the image, or save it to a file in any of the formats that GIMP supports.

Editing Images

Once you have an image window open in GIMP, the majority of editing controls are accessed from the GIMP control center window or by right-clicking the image. Let's start by looking at the commands available by right-clicking on the image. Figure 7.20 shows the pop-up menu that is given by right-clicking on the image.

We aren't going to cover all of the options available, but we will cover some of the more common ones.

Tip

If you make a change that you do not like, or if you make a mistake while making changes, you can undo the change by right-clicking somewhere on the image, clicking Edit, and clicking Undo. GIMP supports multiple undo levels, so you can repeat the action to undo multiple changes.

FIGURE 7.20

The image-editing menu in GIMP. This menu is obtained by clicking the right mouse button anywhere on a loaded image.

Changing the Image Mode

The image mode stores what color mode the image uses. There are three possibilities: RGB (16.7 million colors), Grayscale, and Indexed (uses a palette that contains a maximum of 256 colors). This menu can be accessed by right-clicking on the image editing window, selecting Image and then selecting Mode.

Clicking on RGB or Grayscale will cause the mode of the image to be converted immediately. A color image that is changed to grayscale will have the color removed from the editing window and be changed into shades of gray. Changing an image to indexed mode requires a few more steps. Selecting Index will cause a dialog box like the one shown in Figure 7.21 to be displayed.

FIGURE 7.21

Converting an image to indexed mode in GIMP.

The Generate Optimal Palette option will create an optimal palette for this image using the exact number of colors specified in the # of Colors box. The Use Custom Palette option will allow you to select a predefined palette or create a new palette. One of the useful options here is the Web palette. This uses a palette that will work with a Web browser running on a display that is set to 256 colors. The final option is a 1-bit palette. This will use only black-and-white pixels.

The dither options are beyond the scope of this book. If you are a graphics designer, you will probably know what they mean already. If you are not, you may want to simply play with the different options to determine which one looks best for the image you are working on.

Brightness, Color Balance, and so on

Brightness, contrast, color balance, color curves, and so on, can be controlled by right-clicking on the image, clicking Image, and then clicking Colors. Note that to control most of these properties, the image must be either an RGB image or a grayscale image. If it is indexed, most of the options will be grayed-out and unavailable. If you want to change the properties of an indexed image, you will need to convert it to RGB or grayscale first. After you have made the desired changes, you can then convert it back to indexed format.

Filters

There are many filters available in GIMP that can be accessed by right-clicking on the image and then selecting Filters. For most of these filters to work, the image must be in RGB format. Filters usually cannot be applied to indexed images. If you want to apply a filter to an indexed image, you will need to convert it to RGB first. After you have applied the desired filter, you can then convert it back to indexed format.

Script-Fu

The options under Script-Fu can produce some interesting effects, such as making images look like old photographs, adding simulated coffee stains, making an image look like it is embroidered on cloth, and so on. They usually perform several operations on the image, including applying several filters. To access the Script-Fu options, right-click somewhere on the image and then select Script-Fu.

> **Caution**
>
> If you are unsure of what the effects of applying one of the Script-Fu options might be, and you have made other changes to the image already, you should save it first before using Script-Fu. Script-Fu may run multiple filters on your image when doing its changes. The result might be that Script-Fu makes so many changes that you will not be able to back out all of the changes using the undo feature. Some of the Script-Fu options will make the changes and present the image in a new window, leaving the original image as is. But not all of them will.

Making Changes to Images

The various tools to make changes to images are available from the GIMP control center (see Figure 7.22).

FIGURE 7.22
The GIMP tools.

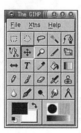

Table 7.9 shows each of the buttons available and what its function is. Note that double-clicking on the tool icons brings up a dialog box of configuration options for that tool.

TABLE 7.9   The various image tools available in GIMP.

Icon	Function
	Rectangular selection tool. Hold down the left mouse button and drag to select rectangular areas in the image.

TABLE 7.9 continued

Icon	*Function*
	Circular selection tool. Hold down the left mouse button and drag to select circular areas in the image.
	Freehand selection tool. Hold down the left mouse button and move the mouse to select areas of the image freehand.
	Magic wand tool. Clicking the left mouse button causes this tool to select areas of similar color adjacent to the spot that was clicked. Double-clicking the tool brings up a dialog box where you can control the sensitivity.
	Bezier curve tool. This tool allows you select areas by using a bezier curve.
	Intelligent scissors. This tool allows you to select shapes from the image.
	Move tool. This tool allows you to move layers as well as sections of the image that are currently selected by using one of the other selection tools.
	Zoom tool. This tool zooms in when the left mouse button is clicked on the image, centering the part of the image where the pointer is when the left button is clicked. Holding down the Ctrl key while pressing the left mouse button causes it to zoom out.
	Cropping and resizing tool.
	Rotation and perspective tool. Clicking this tool and then clicking on the imageplaces a grid over the image and brings up a dialog box. You can then drag the grid to rotate the image. Clicking Rotate causes the changes to take effect.
	Flip tool. When the image or selection is clicked on, this tool flips it, basically providing a mirror image.
	Text tool. This tool brings up a dialog box where you can add text to an image. You can control font sizes, types, and so on, from the dialog box.
	Color picker. Selecting this tool and then clicking anywhere on the imagecauses the foreground color to be set to that color. It also brings up a dialog box that tells you the RGB values and the hex number of the color.

TABLE 7.9   continued

Icon	Function
	Flood tool. Clicking on an area of the image causes that area to be flooded by either the foreground color, the background color, or a pattern, depending on the configuration of the flood tool (which you can change by double-clicking it).
	Gradient fill tool. This is similar to the flood tool, except that it fills with a gradient instead. The gradient by default is the foreground to background color, but you can change this by double-clicking on the tool.
	Pencil. Draws in sharp strokes when the left mouse button is held down. You can change the opacity of the tool by double-clicking it.
	Paint brush. Similar to the pencil, except that it draws in fuzzy strokes. You can change the opacity of the tool by double-clicking it.
	Eraser tool. This tool erases areas of the image and replaces those areas with the background color. You can change the opacity of the eraser by double-clicking it.
	Airbrush tool. Paints with variable pressure. The longer the airbrush is left in an area, the more dense the color becomes.
	Clone brush/pattern brush. In clone mode, hold down the Ctrl key and click the left mouse button on an area of the image. Then move to another area and hold down the left mouse button while painting. This clones the area that was clicked on while holding Ctrl. To change to pattern mode, double-click the tool to bring up its dialog box.
	Blur/sharpen tool. Dragging this tool over various areas of the image either blurs or sharpens that area, depending on the tool's settings. Double-click it to change the settings.
	Ink tool. Draws in a style that emulates a fountain pen.
	Burn tool. Dragging this tool over an area of the image gives it a burned look.
	Smudge tool. Dragging this tool over an area of the image gives it a smudged look.
	Measuring tool. This tool measures distances and angles in an image.

Brush Selection

Figure 7.23 shows the Brush selection tool circled on the GIMP control center.

FIGURE 7.23

The Brush selection tool in GIMP. Depending on the currently active brush, yours may look different from what is shown here.

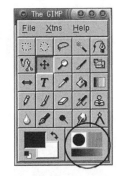

Double-clicking the Brush selection tool will bring up a dialog box that allows you to select which brush you want to use (see Figure 7.24).

You can also create new brushes by clicking the New button. You can also edit or delete existing brushes that you have already created. (You cannot edit or delete brushes that come standard with GIMP. Those options are grayed out.)

Patterns and Gradients

Next to the Brush selection tool shown in Figure 7.23 is the Pattern selection tool, and underneath it is the Gradient selection tool. Use these in the same way you use the Brush selection tool to select patterns and gradients. The patterns and gradients can be used by various tools such as the Clone brush and the Flood tool, depending on how they are configured.

Saving Files in GIMP

To save a file in GIMP, right-click on the image window that contains the image you want to save. Select File, Save to save the file under the same name and format, or select File, Save As to save the file under a different name and/or format (see Figure 7.25).

To select the file format, you can either have GIMP determine it automatically from the extension you provide in the "Selection" box, or you can select the file type from the pull-down menu. Note that depending on the mode that the image is in (RGB, grayscale, or indexed) some of the file formats will be grayed out and unavailable. An RGB image for example, cannot be saved as a GIF. An indexed image cannot be saved as a JPEG.

FIGURE 7.24

The Brush selection dialog box.

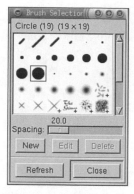

FIGURE 7.25

The Save as dialog box in GIMP.

Different file formats will have different options, and some may have no options at all. For example, the GIF file format has the option of making the file interlaced so it appears to gradually fade in when being loaded over a Web browser, and also of having a transparent background. The JPEG option allows you to control the compression level and thus reduce or increase the file size. Note that JPEG uses lossy compression, meaning that it throws out some information about the file to compress it. Too much compression can result in files that have low quality. Not enough compression will result in huge files. Try to find a happy medium between image quality and compression level.

> **Caution**
>
> Saving files in formats other than native GIMP format will cause layer information to be lost. Because of this, if your image uses layers, you may want to keep a copy of the image around in GIMP format in case you ever need to make changes to the layers. When you save the file in a format that can be used on the Web for example, all the layers in your image will be merged into one layer. This means you will no longer be able to work on individual layers in the image.

The GIF Image Format

The GIF image format is a popular image format that is used on the Internet. However, future versions of GIMP may not support the GIF format. This is due to a patent issue with Unisys, which holds a patent on the LZW compression used to make GIF images. Basically, Unisys now wants to charge royalties to anyone who uses the GIF image format in their software. Because of this sudden move on the part of Unisys, many software programs that used to support GIF with no problem decided to simply drop support for the format rather than pay Unisys' newly requested royalties. All is not lost, however. A group of people got together shortly after Unisys announced its decision to charge royalties and began working on a new royalty-free image standard for the Internet. The result is PNG, which stands for *Portable Network Graphics*. In general, PNG is superior to GIF, and most browsers support it these days. Microsoft and Netscape have both thrown their support behind PNG.

The only current drawback to PNG is that most browsers do not support PNG transparency. This is not usually a problem, however, because unless you are using a tiled background on your Web page, you can get around this by simply making the background color of the image the same color as the background color of your page.

If you absolutely need transparency, you will need to use GIF. But if you do not need this, it is recommended that you use PNG instead. PNG is superior to GIF in most ways, and is rapidly becoming the standard of choice for Internet graphics. At the same time, GIF is rapidly falling out of favor due to Unisys' decision to start charging royalties on GIF use (something they had not done for years).

Note that you should continue to use JPEG images on the Web for photographs. PNG should generally be used for logos and line art.

This section has only scratched the surface of all the features that are available in GIMP. To cover all that can be done with GIMP would require an entire book. If you are interested in using the advanced features of GIMP, there are several books available on this powerful image software, including *Teach Yourself GIMP in 24 Hours,* from Sams Publishing.

GQview

GQview is an image-viewing program designed for Gnome. It is available in the FreeBSD ports collection under the graphics directory, and it supports most popular file formats. Figure 7.26 shows GQview with an image loaded.

FIGURE 7.26

GQview with an image loaded on the right side of the window. The images and directories can be selected on the left side.

Two of the nicest features of GQview are its slideshow mode and its ability to display images in full-screen mode. You can create slides using GIMP or some other image-editing program, and you can use GQview in full-screen mode to display your slides. Combined with a projector or large monitor, this allows GQview to be used as a primitive form of presentation program. And if all you need to do is a simple presentation of a few slides or something, GQview will be a lot easier to learn than PowerPoint, or some other full-featured presentation program.

To use GQview in this fashion, simply save each slide in your presentation into a special directory created for that presentation. Be sure to use names that will make the slides show up in the right order. Names such as slide-01.jpg, slide-02.jpg, and so on, will do the trick. Note that if you have more than nine slides, it is important to use the leading 0 for slides numbered less than 10. Otherwise, slide-10.jpg will show up before slide-2.jpg because of the order in which files are stored.

> **Caution**
>
> If you are using GQview to design a simple presentation, make sure that you design your image files that will be the slides for the proper size. Basically, the size of the images should be the same size that your monitor or projector will be running at. Although GQView can resize the images on-the-fly to fit the screen, the results will be less than optimal, and images will appear grainy and distorted if they were much larger or much smaller than the screen. So, try to design your images for the proper resolution when you design your presentation.

Once you have all your images saved in the correct directory, start up GQView (by typing gqview at an X terminal window or by adding an icon to your desktop or menu). Then, select the correct directory from the left side of the GQview window. Note that unlike many other applications, you need only to click the directory once for it to become the current one. Once you are in the current directory, press v to switch to full-screen mode. Pressing the left mouse button will advance to the next slide. Pressing the middle mouse button will back up to the previous slide. Pressing the right mouse button will bring up a menu of options.

To get out of full-screen mode, you can either press v again, press the Escape key, or right-click somewhere onscreen and then select Exit full screen from the menu.

If you want to have the slides advance automatically without having to press the mouse button, right-click onscreen and then click Start slideshow. You can control how long each slide displays before moving to the next one by clicking Edit and then Options in GQView's menu bar. This will bring up the GQView configuration dialog box (see Figure 7.27). The General tab contains the options for configuring the slideshow properties.

Note that you will need to be in normal mode (not in full-screen mode) to access the menu bar and get to the configuration dialog box.

You can stop or pause the running slide show by right-clicking onscreen (or on the image if not in full-screen mode) and selecting the appropriate option from the menu.

FIGURE 7.27

The GQview configuration dialog box. For the slide show, you can control how many seconds each slide will display before moving to the next one.

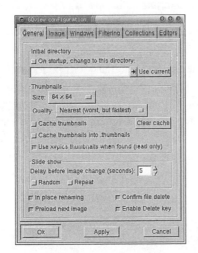

StarOffice Office Suite

StarOffice is a full-featured office suite available from Sun Microsystems. It can be purchased on CD-ROM for a very modest cost or downloaded free. StarOffice has features similar to Microsoft Office, Lotus SmartSuite, and so on. StarOffice includes a word processor, spreadsheet, presentation program, drawing program, e-mail client, HTML editor, and PIM. There is also a database available. StarOffice can be installed from the FreeBSD ports collection under the editors directory.

> **Caution**
>
> If you plan to download StarOffice from the Internet rather than purchase it on CD, be aware that it is about a 95MB download. If you have a modem connection to the Internet, the download can take eight hours or more. Make sure you do the download sometime when you will not need to use your Internet connection for some time. Of course, if you don't have a dedicated phone line for the Internet, you will also want to make sure you do the download when you do not need your phone and are not expecting any calls for awhile.

Follow the instructions included in the FreeBSD port for installing StarOffice. Once you have completed the setup procedure and answered the various questions about your name, and such, you will be able to run StarOffice in one of two ways:

- If you did a network installation, by typing **soffice** at an X terminal window or Run dialog box.

- If you did a local installation, the StarOffice binary will be located in a directory called office52 in your home directory. You can start it by typing office52/ soffice at an X terminal window if you are in your home directory. You might want to add this directory to your path (see Chapter 12, "Customizing the Shell," for information on how to add directories to your path). Once you have added the directory to your path, you can start it simply by typing **soffice** at an X terminal prompt or a Run dialog box. Of course, you can also add a desktop shortcut or create a menu entry.

> **Tip**
>
> StarOffice is cross-platform that is also available for Microsoft Windows, Solaris x86, and Solaris Sparc. If you want to standardize your office package on all your systems, you might also want to look into the Microsoft Windows version

for your Windows-based systems. Virtually all the information on StarOffice given in this section applies to the Windows version as well. The only real difference is that some of the file locations (such as where the templates are found) will vary. To obtain StarOffice for Microsoft Windows or other platforms, visit www.sun.com/products/staroffice/get.html. Here, you will find information on how to download StarOffice or order CDs from Sun. The Deluxe package comes with printed manuals, and so on, and retails for $39.95, which is a real bargain considering that comparable products generally top $300 and $400. You can also order just the CDs without the manual. You can also find StarOffice at most large retail software stores.

Working with documents in StarOffice is much the same as working with documents in any other office package, so this section will not cover issues such as how to set margins, control fonts, and so on. Instead, it will introduce some of the other features of StarOffice that do not have to do directly with document editing.

The StarOffice Desktop

Figure 7.28 shows the StarOffice desktop.

FIGURE 7.28

The StarOffice desktop. The icons allow you to create various new types of documents. The start button and taskbar at the bottom of the screen behave just like their Microsoft Windows counterparts.

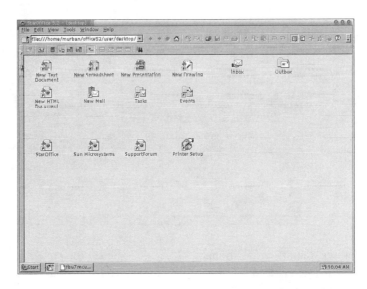

Opening a New Document

There are several different ways to create a new document in StarOffice:

- Double-click one of the new document icons on the desktop. For example, to open a blank word processor document, simply double-click the New Text Document icon.
- Click File on the menu bar, click New, and select one of the available document types.
- Click File on the menu bar, click New, and then click From template to create a document from a template. This process will be covered more in the next section.

Document Templates

Clicking File on the menu bar, clicking New, and then clicking From template will allow you to create a new document from a template. There are several predefined templates available, or you can create your own. You can also import most word templates and use them, although any VBScript macros included in the template will not transfer. Importing Word templates is shown in the next tip box.

Figure 7.29 shows the Template dialog box.

FIGURE 7.29

Creating a new document from a template. Clicking the Preview check box will cause a preview of what the template looks like to be displayed in the box below it.

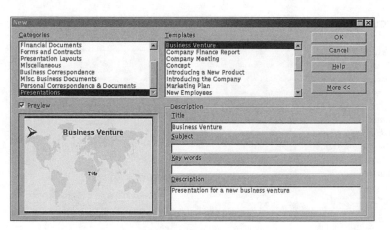

As you can see, templates are arranged by category. Select the proper category from the window on the left and then select the type of document you would like to create from the window on the right.

Creating New Templates

If you would like to create a new template, you can do so simply by creating a new document; adding the features you want; selecting File, Save As; and then selecting one of the available template formats under File type. The available formats will vary, depending on what type of document you are working on (a word processor or spreadsheet, for example). In the word processor, for example, the correct document type is StarWriter 5.0 Template.

Templates should be saved in the `office52/share/template/english` directory, assuming that your templates are in English. Under this directory, there are several subdirectories for different types of templates related to different things. Here is the default subdirectory listing:

```
educate        internal       officorr       presnt
finance        layout         offimisc       sfx.tlx
forms          misc           personal       wizard
```

If you can't find a suitable directory/category to place your new template under, you can create new directories in here to store them in. The directory name you create will show up in the Categories window of the Template dialog box.

> **Tip**
>
> To a limited extent, you can import and use Microsoft Word and Excel templates into StarOffice. To do so, simply load the template as a normal document (by selecting File, Open from the menu bar); then select File, Save as. In the File type pull-down menu, select the appropriate StarOffice template type. Make sure you save the template in the correct directory (`office52/share/templates/english` if this is an English template). Also remember to choose a subdirectory under `english`.

StarOffice Integrated Web Browser

> **Tip**
>
> Before you can use the StarOffice integrated Web browser, you of course have to have an Internet connection configured and working properly. If you need help doing this, see the relevant chapters in Part IV, "FreeBSD Networking." Chapter 23, "Configuring Basic Networking Services," should help you if you are on a LAN. Chapter 24, "Connecting to the Internet with PPP," should help you if you are using a dial-up connection.

StarOffice has an integrated Web browser that works well for displaying most Web pages. To access the Web browser, simply select File, Open; in the filename dialog box, simply type the URL of the Web site you wish to open. For example, typing www.sam-spublishing.com will open a new window that will load the Web site for Sams Publishing. This new window will also appear on the StarOffice taskbar. Figure 7.30 shows an example of the StarOffice Web browser.

Notice that the taskbar at the bottom of the screen now lists both this document, and the Sams Publishing Web Site. You can switch back and forth simply by clicking on the relevant taskbar entries.

Because of the integrated nature of StarOffice, Web sites can also be opened in the same window that you are working on a word processing document in, for example. StarOffice will attempt to detect Web site addresses that are embedded in documents you are working on or reading. These addresses will be underlined and printed in a different color. Just as in a Web browser, clicking them with the left mouse button will cause them to open. If you have any unsaved changes in the document you are currently working on, you will be prompted to save them before the Web page opens. Once you have done so, the Web page will load inside of the current window. You can then switch back and forth between the Web page and the word processor document using the back and forward arrows on the StarOffice icon bar. This is just like using the back and forward buttons on a Web browser. The only difference is that StarOffice extends the concept to include all types of documents.

FIGURE 7.30

The Sams Publishing Web site loaded into the StarOffice Web browser. Note that each time you open a new Web page with File, Open, it will be opened in a new window.

Customizing the StarOffice Integrated Web Browser

You can customize various aspects of the StarOffice Web browser by clicking Tools, Options from the menu bar. This will bring up a configuration dialog box like the one shown in Figure 7.31.

FIGURE 7.31

The Options dialog box in StarOffice. Clicking the plus sign (+) next to Browser will expand it to show the various Web browser options that are configurable.

Among the configurable options are the size of the cache, the way cookies are handled, and so on.

If you wish to have URLs in documents open in a browser other than StarOffice, you can select Use external browser (see Figure 7.32).

FIGURE 7.32

The External Browser configuration dialog box. Check the Use external browser box and then type the name of the browser you would like to use in the box next to it.

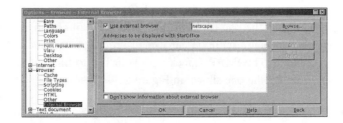

If you wish, you can provide a list of Web sites that will open in the StarOffice browser instead of the external browser. The reverse is also true. If you have the Use external browser check box off, you can provide a list of Web sites that will open in an external browser. This is handy if you want to use the internal browser for most sites, but you visit a few sites that do not display correctly in StarOffice's internal browser.

StarOffice E-mail

StarOffice also has an integrated e-mail program that can handle your e-mail needs. This can be handy if you do a lot of work in StarOffice because the e-mail program integrates quite nicely with the other StarOffice applications.

However, the StarOffice e-mail program requires some configuration before it can be used.

The first thing you will need to do if you want to allow StarOffice to handle your e-mail is make sure that your e-mail address is specified in your user profile. To check this, click Tools, Options in the menu bar. In the dialog box that pops up, click the plus (+) next to General, if it is not already expanded, and then click User Data (see Figure 7.33).

FIGURE 7.33

The User Data for StarOffice. Make sure that your e-mail address is listed in the box in the lower-right corner.

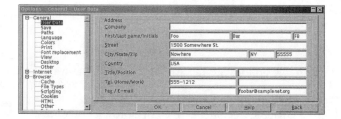

Once you have made sure that your e-mail address is correctly configured, you will need to create a new e-mail account for receiving mail. To do this, right-click somewhere on the StarOffice Desktop. In the pop-up menu, select the type of e-mail account that you would like to create. If you are setting up an e-mail account with your ISP, this is probably POP3, but it could also be IMAP. Check with your ISP to find out for sure. This will bring up a dialog box like the one shown in Figure 7.34.

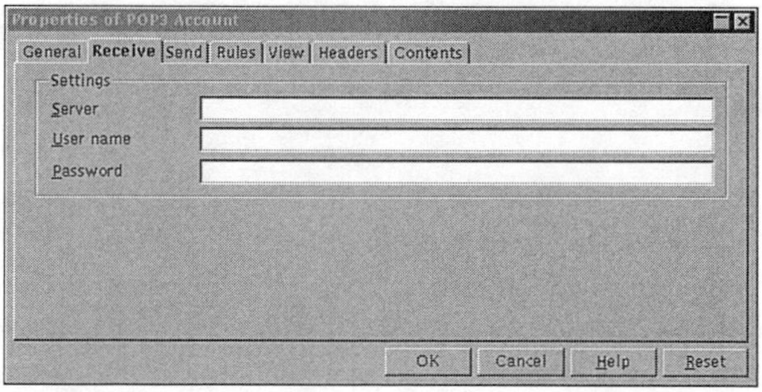

FIGURE 7.34

Configuring a new POP3 e-mail account in StarOffice.

Enter the address of the mail server that you get mail from, as well as the user name and password required to access the server. You can then click the General tab, and enter a name for this account in the first box that has the envelope with the hand underneath it on the left. The name you enter here is what will show up on the StarOffice desktop with the icon for the new account that will be created. If you have a full-time Internet connection, you might also want to click the Contents tab, in which you can configure the e-mail program to automatically check for new e-mail at regular intervals (see Figure 7.35).

To configure the e-mail program to automatically check e-mail at certain times, check the Include in update function check box and then set the plus every entry to the number of minutes between checks.

You will probably also want to check the Remove messages from server and Save document contents locally options. Otherwise, your e-mail will stay on the server and will be unavailable when you are not connected to the Internet.

FIGURE 7.35

The Contents tab in the POP3 configuration dialog box.

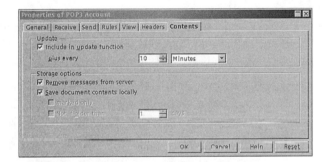

Once you have finished configuring the incoming mail account here, click Ok. You will then be given information, informing you that an outbox is required to send messages, and asking you if you want to create one. Select Yes here to create the outbox. You will then be given a dialog box like the one shown in Figure 7.36.

FIGURE 7.36

Configuring the outbox for sending e-mail from StarOffice.

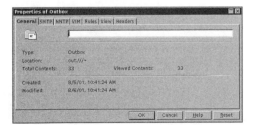

In the first box with the folder by it, type a name that you would like to call this outbox. This is the name that will show up underneath the icon that is created on the desktop for this outbox. You can call it anything you want. If you will have only one outgoing e-mail account, something as simple as Outbox will work fine.

After you have entered a name for the outbox, click the SMTP tab. In the Server box, enter the address of your outgoing mail server (check with your ISP if you are unsure). Also, verify that the information in Sender is correct. You do not need to put anything in the Reply to box, unless you want people to send replies to your e-mail to a different address than what is listed in Sender.

Once you have entered these settings, you can click Ok, and both the inbox and the outbox will be created.

You can change the settings for the inbox and outbox at any time by right-clicking the respective icon and then clicking Properties.

Receiving New Mail

When you have new e-mail, the globe icon next to the clock on the StarOffice taskbar will blink. In addition, you can double-click the icon at any time to force StarOffice to check for new mail immediately rather than waiting until the next scheduled update.

When you have new e-mail, double-click the new icon that was created on the desktop for the inbox. This will bring up the e-mail window (see Figure 7.37).

FIGURE 7.37

The StarOffice inbox, where incoming mail is stored.

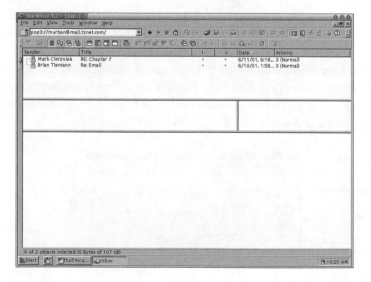

The various icons on the bar at the top of the window can delete messages, reply to messages, or send new messages. Move the mouse pointer over each item, and leave it for a moment to get a pop-up message about what each item does.

Sending Mail

There are several ways to start a new mail message:

- Click File, New, Mail from the File menu of any StarOffice application.
- Right-click on the StarOffice desktop; in the pop-up menu, click New, Documents, Mail.
- Click the New Mail icon from within the inbox or outbox (see Figure 7.38).

FIGURE 7.38

The New Mail screen in StarOffice's inbox and outbox.

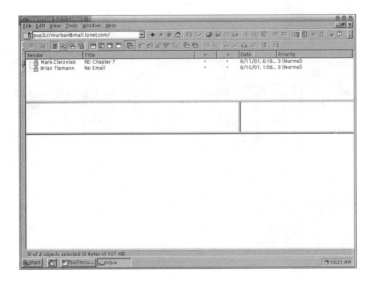

This will bring up a blank message window like the one shown in Figure 7.39.

When you have finished entering the message, press the Send Message icon (see Figure 7.40) to send the message.

Sometimes, you might not want StarOffice to attempt to deliver the message immediately. For example, you may be on a laptop and not have access to the Internet right now. For this reason, StarOffice provides both an online and offline mode.

7

WORKING WITH
APPLICATIONS

FIGURE 7.39
Creating a new mail message in StarOffice.

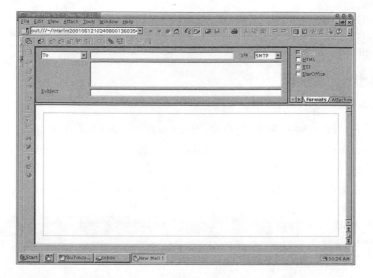

FIGURE 7.40
The Send Message screen.

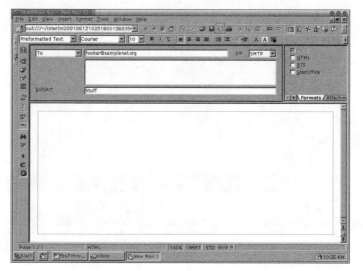

Online vs. Offline Modes in StarOffice

Figure 7.41 shows the online/offline mode toggle icon in the StarOffice icon bar.

While in online mode, e-mail messages will be sent immediately as soon as the "Send Message" icon is clicked. In offline mode, they will be held and StarOffice will not attempt to send the messages. Later, when the network connection is available, you can click the icon again to switch StarOffice into online mode. Any pending e-mail messages will be delivered immediately as soon as StarOffice is placed in online mode.

FIGURE 7.41

Click this icon to toggle between online and offline mode in StarOffice. When the icon appears pressed, it is in online mode. When it does not appear pressed, it is in offline mode.

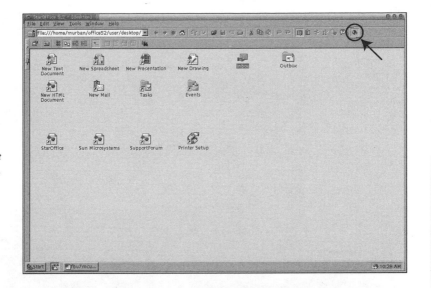

Tip

You can also instantly send any document you are working on by clicking "File", then "Send", and the "Document as E-mail". You will then be given a dialog box asking how you want to send the document. Usually, you will select "Save and attach". This will open a new e-mail message that already has the current document attached to it.

The StarOffice Explorer

The StarOffice Explorer allows you quick access to your documents, the gallery of samples, the StarOffice recycle bin, etc. The explorer can be in one of three modes: Visible, hidden, or turned off. Whether the explorer is on or off is controlled by the icon shown in Figure 7.42.

When the Explorer is turned on, it can either be visible, or hidden. Figures 7.43 and 7.44 show the Explorer in visible and hidden mode, respectively.

Clicking the arrow shown in Figure 7.44 will cause the Explorer to "slide out" from the left edge of the screen, covering part of the existing screen. Clicking the pin will cause the Explorer to "slide out" from the left edge of the screen and the existing window to be resized so that the Explorer does not cover part of it.

FIGURE 7.42

This icon toggles the StarOffice Explorer on and off. When it is on, the icon will appear pressed. When it is off, it will not.

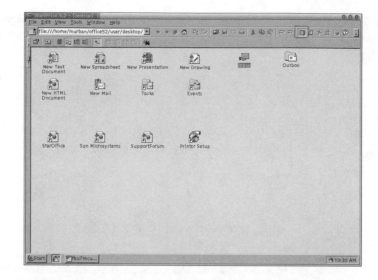

FIGURE 7.43

The StarOffice Explorer. Clicking the arrow button on the right edge will hide the Explorer.

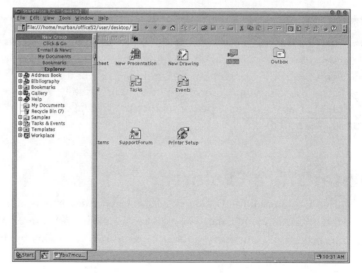

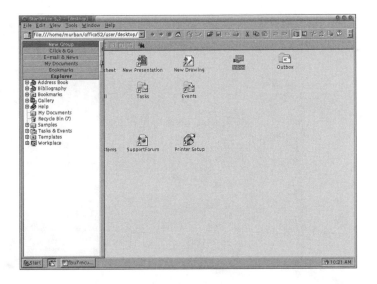

FIGURE 7.44

The StarOffice Explorer in hidden mode. The circled arrow and pin buttons can be usd to make the Explorer visible.

Note in particular, the Recycle Bin. The number in parentheses after it tells you how many items are currently in it. Any items deleted from within StarOffice including files, e-mail messages, etc., are placed in the Recycle Bin. Double-clicking on the Recycle Bin will open it in the main window so you can view its contents. You can then delete items permanently either individually by right-clicking on the item and then clicking "Delete", or you can empty the entire bin by right-clicking somewhere on a blank space in the Recycle Bin window and clicking "Empty Recycle Bin". Whichever method you choose, you will be asked to confirm that you really want to delete the file(s) or empty the Recycle Bin. Once you have deleted files out of the Recycle Bin or Emptied the Recycle Bin, the files are gone forever and cannot be recovered.

Other items of interest in the Explorer include the "My Documents" button. This will show you a list of all the documents that are stored in StarOffice's "My Documents" directory.

Help in StarOffice

There are two primary ways to get help in StarOffice. The first is the Help Agent. It provides context-sensitive help on whatever you are currently doing. To enable the Help Agent, click the icon in the StarOffice icon bar shown in Figure 7.45.

FIGURE 7.45

This icon toggles the Help Agent on and off.

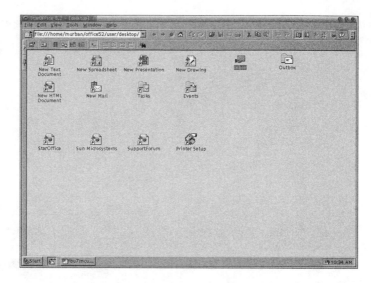

The Help Agent is shown in Figure 7.46

FIGURE 7.46

The StarOffice Help Agent. It is dynamically updated to show context-sensitive help on what you are currently doing.

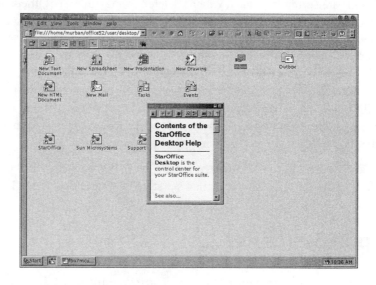

The second way to obtain help in StarOffice is from the "Help" entry in the menu bar. This is also somewhat context sensitive as you will be automatically placed in the help section for whatever StarOffice program you are currently working in. Figure 7.47 shows the main help screen.

FIGURE 7.47

The main help screen in StarOffice. It is hypertext-based and the links can be clicked on to view more information on the listed topics, similar to navigating a Web page.

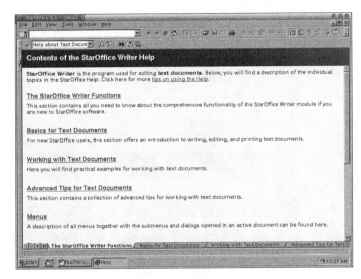

The tabs at the bottom of the help screen allow you to quickly jump between various topics. The pull-down menu at the upper left also allows you to select various topics. You can search the help index by clicking on the binoculars icon in the icon bar.

One of the really nice features of StarOffice help that is lacking in most other help systems is that it allows you to write your own comments and notes directly into the help file. Click the icon in Figure 7.48 to bring up a dialog box where you can write a comment. The dialog box looks like Figure 7.49. Type a comment in the box and then click OK to write it to the help file. You can also click Insert to copy whatever is currently on the clipboard into the help file.

After you type a comment and click OK, the title on this help section has a little page icon in front of it. Figure 7.50 shows an example. Notice the little page icon in front of the Contents of the StarOffice Writer Help title. Compare this figure to Figure 7.47.

FIGURE **7.48**

*This icon allows
you to write a
comment to the
StarOffice help
file.*

FIGURE 7.48

*This icon allows
you to write a
comment to the
StarOffice help
file.*

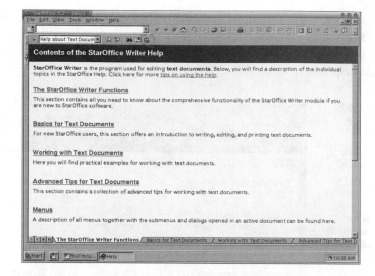

FIGURE 7.49

*The Write
Comment dialog
box.*

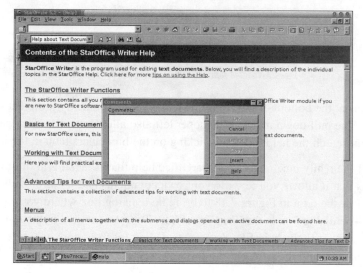

FIGURE 7.50

A help section that has a user comment attached to it.

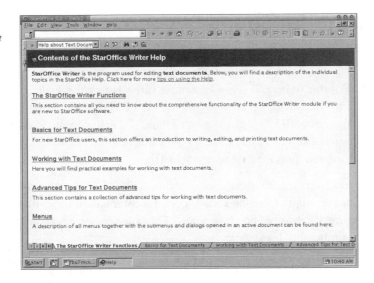

To access the user comment, you can click the page icon in front of the title. This will bring up the same dialog box that was shown in Figure 7.49. You can then view the comment, make changes to it, or delete it.

This section has only touched on the features available in StarOffice. Covering everything in StarOffice would require a book in itself, and indeed there are several books on StarOffice. For a complete tutorial on using StarOffice, check out *Teach Yourself StarOffice 5 for Linux in 24 Hours* from Sams Publishing. Even though the title contains the word "Linux" everything in this book will also apply to running StarOffice under FreeBSD.

For a complete reference guide to StarOffice, check out *Special Edition Using StarOffice* from Que. This mammoth book weighs in at over 1,500 pages and contains virtually everything you could ever want to know about StarOffice.

Multimedia

The multimedia support in FreeBSD has gone from virtually nonexistent to quite good in a rather short period of time. If you have any one of the common sound cards, chances are good that FreeBSD supports it natively. Even if FreeBSD does not have native support for your sound card, all is not lost. There is a good chance that the commercial sound drivers from a company called 4Front Technologies will support your sound card. If you would like to look into the commercial drivers, the Web site for 4Front's sound drivers is located at www.opensound.com. There are free trial versions available, so you can try the drivers before purchasing them.

Checking for Sound Support

Before you can use any of the multimedia applications presented in this section, you will need to make sure that you have sound support available in FreeBSD.

At the time of this writing, it is not known for sure whether the sound driver will be included in the default kernel or not. To see if the PCM driver is loaded, examine your kernel configuration file for the line `device pcm`. If this line exists, sound support is compiled into the kernel. If you have not built a custom kernel, the kernel configuration file will be located in `/sys/i386/conf/GENERIC`.

Once you have verified that the kernel contains the PCM driver, type `dmesg | more` to check the `dmesg` output from the kernel. Look for information indicating that your sound card was correctly detected on system boot. For example, the `dmesg` output on my system contains the following lines:

```
sbc0: <Creative SB AWE64> at port 0x220-0x22f,0x330-0x331,0x388-0x38b irq 5 drq
1,5 on isa0
pcm1: <SB16 DSP 4.16> on sbc0
```

This output shows that FreeBSD detected a SoundBlaster AWE 64, as well as giving the addresses it is on.

If FreeBSD doesn't seem to find your sound card, you might want to try to get sound working using the 4Front sound drivers. Once again, they can be obtained at `www.opensound.com`.

Note that if you decide to try using the 4Front drivers, you will probably need to remove or comment out the `device pcm` line from your kernel configuration file and then rebuild the kernel. Otherwise, you may have problems with the kernel sound driver and the 4Front driver conflicting.

For complete instructions on kernel configuration and kernel building, see Chapter 17, "Kernel Configuration."

Creating Device Nodes

In FreeBSD 4.4, you will need to create the device nodes for the sound devices. To do this, simply type the following command in the `/dev` directory as the root user:

```
./MAKEDEV snd0
```

This command will create the various devices needed to support sound.

FreeBSD 5.0 uses the DEVFS file system which dynamically builds the device nodes at each system boot. Because of this, you do not need to create device nodes using `MAKEDEV` in FreeBSD 5.0.

The Mixer

Once the device links have been created, you should be able to access the FreeBSD mixer from the command line. From a shell prompt or X terminal window, type the command `mixer`, and press Enter. Your system will output something similar to the following:

```
Mixer vol      is currently set to   75:75
Mixer bass     is currently set to   50:50
Mixer treble   is currently set to   50:50
Mixer synth    is currently set to   75:75
Mixer pcm      is currently set to   75:75
Mixer speaker  is currently set to   75:75
Mixer line     is currently set to   75:75
Mixer mic      is currently set to    0:0
Mixer cd       is currently set to   75:75
Mixer igain    is currently set to    0:0
Mixer ogain    is currently set to   50:50
```

This shows what levels (in percentage values ranging from 0 to 100) each audio device in the system is set to. As you would expect, the number on the left of the colon indicates the level for the left audio channel, and the number on the right of the colon indicates the level for the right audio channel.

Most of the items in the list are self-explanatory, but a few of them deserve some more attention:

- **Mixer vol**—This is the master volume for all of the audio devices.
- **Mixer pcm**—This is the device through which most audio is played. This will control the volume of .wav files, MP3s, Real Audio files, and so on.
- **Mixer synth**—This controls the volume of the synthesizer. This generally affects MIDI files.
- **Mixer cd**—This controls the volume of audio CDs.
- **Mixer line**—This controls the volume of a device connected to the line in the jack on a sound card.
- **Mixer igain**—This controls the input gain level.
- **Mixer ogain**—This controls the output gain level.

To make changes to any one of the levels, you can type `mixer`, followed by the name of the device and the desired level. For example, the following will set the `cd` volume to 90% on both the left and right channels:

```
mixer cd 90
```

If you want to set the left and right channels to different values, you need to include both values, separated by a colon. For example, the following will set the cd volume to 100% for the left channel, and 80% for the right channel:

```
mixer cd 100:80
```

At system boot, most of the mixer values will default to 75%. If you wish to have different default values at system boot, there are two ways to accomplish this.

The first way is by creating a startup file in /usr/local/etc/rc.d. In the file, simply include a list of the desired mixer commands. You can name the file anything you want. For example, you might call the file mixerset. Here is an example of what the file might contain:

```
mixer vol 80:80
mixer cd 90:90
mixer pcm 50:50
```

As root, create this file in the directory /usr/local/etc/rc.d, and save it as mixerset, for example. Next, make the file executable by issuing the following command:

```
chmod u+x mixerset
```

The commands inside this file will now be run at each system boot and cause the mixer to be set to the desired values.

Tip

If the previous steps are unclear to you, see Chapter 8, "Working with the Shell" and Chapter 11 for more information on these topics.

The second way you can change the default mixer values is by adding commands to your login profile to change the desired values. If you are using a Bourne-compatible shell, the file you will want to add these commands to is .profile. If you are using a C type shell, the file you will want to add these commands to is .login. Both of these files are located in your home directory. If this is unclear to you, please see Chapter 12 for further details.

Basically, what you will want to do is open either .profile or .login in your favorite text editor, and add the mixer commands that you want to set. For example, you might want to add the following lines to the file:

```
mixer vol 80:80
mixer cd 50:50
mixer pcm 90:90
```

Unlike the changes made to the startup file, these do not need to be made as root, and they also will not take effect at system boot. They will take effect as soon as you log in to the system. The benefit of this method is that if more than one person uses this system, each person can create his own customized set of mixer settings to suit his listening preferences. Each time that user logs in to the system, his custom mixer settings will be applied.

MP3 with XMMS

Now that you have the audio device configured properly, you will probably want to play something with it. Yes, your MP3 collection will work with FreeBSD. XMMS is a Winamp clone for FreeBSD and other UNIX-like systems. It is available in the FreeBSD ports collection under the `audio` directory.

Once you have XMMS installed, you can start it with the command `xmms`. Like the other programs in this chapter, the command to start XMMS can be issued from either an X terminal or the Run dialog box, or you can create menu entries or desktop shortcuts for the program.

Figure 7.51 shows XMMS with the mixer and playlist windows also open.

FIGURE 7.51

The XMMS MP3 player. Windows users who have used Winamp will be quite comfortable with XMMS because its controls are virtually identical.

Yes, it even supports Winamp skins. And you don't even have to unzip them first. Simply place your zipped Winamp skins in the directory `.xmms/Skins` located in your home directory. Click the icon at the very upper-left corner of XMMS; then select Options, Skin Browser from the pull-down menu. This will bring up a dialog box in which you can select the desired skin.

> **Tip**
>
> In order for you to be able to use zipped skins, you will have to have the unzip program installed. It can be installed from the FreeBSD ports collection, and is located in the `archivers` directory.

In addition to Winamp skins, there is also a large number of XMMS skins available at www.xmms.org/skins.html. Like the Winamp skins, they can simply be copied into the .xmms/Skins directory and do not need to be unzipped first.

XMMS skins are normally distributed as gzipped tar files with a .tar.gz extension. This is a popular archive format for UNIX-like systems that is similar to zip files.

XMMS also supports various visualization and audio effect plug-ins. Many of these are available as FreeBSD ports in the audio directory.

MP3 with mpg123

If you aren't running X-Windows, but still want to be able to play your MP3 files, there are several command-line MP3 players available. One of the best and most popular is a program called mpg123. It is available in the FreeBSD ports collection under the audio directory.

In its most basic form, mpg123 is started by typing mpg123 *filename,* where *filename* is the name of the MP3 file that you wish to play. It supports wild cards (see Chapter 8). For example, mpg123 *.mp3 will play every file in the current directory that ends in .mp3. You can also supply a list of files on the command line that you want mpg123 to play. The -z option will cause the files to play in random order. You can also use the -@ option followed by the name of a text file. mpg123 will then treat the contents of the text file as a list of MP3 files to play. The text file should contain the list of MP3s, one on each line.

mpg123 has many more options. For a complete list of all the features, type man mpg123 to read the manual page for the program.

X-Based Mixers

If you are not keen on the idea of controlling the mixer from the command line, as described previously in this chapter, there are several X-Windows-based interfaces to the mixer available. This section covers xmixer, which is available in the FreeBSD ports collection under the audio directory.

xmixer can be started using one of two commands. The command used changes the appearance of the mixer. The first way to invoke xmixer is simply by typing xmixer at an X terminal or Run dialog box, or by creating a desktop shortcut or menu entry for it. xmixer uses the Athena toolkit (a programmer's toolkit for designing graphical interfaces). Figure 7.52 shows what xmixer looks like.

FIGURE 7.52

xmixer when invoked using the xmixer *command. This version uses the Athena toolkit (a programmer's toolkit for creating graphical user interfaces).*

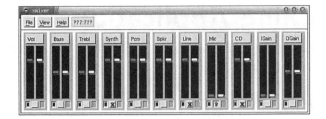

The sliders in the mixer can be moved up and down by holding the left mouse button down. At the bottom of each slider are three buttons. The one on the left locks the sliders so that the left and right levels are changed at the same time and kept synchronized. Clicking this button will cause the black box inside of it to disappear, and now the left and right levels can be adjusted individually.

The right button controls whether the device is on or off. When it is green, the device is on. When it is red, its level is set to zero, thus cutting it out of the mix.

The middle button turns recording on and off for input devices such as the microphone and the line in. It is disabled on devices that are output only.

The second way xmixer can be invoked is with the command 1. This invokes the GTK version of the program. It is exactly the same as xmixer. The only difference is that the use of the GTK toolkit instead of the Athena toolkit gives it a different appearance. Figure 7.53 shows xgmixer.

FIGURE 7.53

xmixer when invoked with xgmixer. The functionality is exactly the same. The appearance is different because this version uses the GTK toolkit instead of the Athena toolkit.

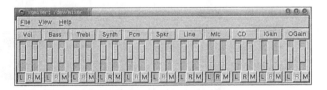

There are several other audio applications available for FreeBSD including various CD players, more MP3 players, the Real Audio player, and tools for ripping CD audio tracks to MP3. Browse through the audio category in the FreeBSD ports tree to see what is available.

Networking Applications

There are many networking applications available for FreeBSD. This section will concentrate on Web browsers, e-mail, FTP, and so on.

Configuring Netscape

The Netscape Communicator Web browser is available for FreeBSD. The latest version that is available for FreeBSD is 4.76. If you want to run Netscape 6, you will need to run the Linux version of Netscape in FreeBSD. In addition, you will also need to run the Linux version if you want to use most plug-ins such as Flash and Shockwave. These plug-ins are available only for Linux versions of Netscape. Running the Linux version of Netscape in FreeBSD allows you to use these plug-ins.

All the Netscape browsers, including the Linux versions, are available as ports in the www directory. This allows you to install and run the Linux versions just like they were normal FreeBSD applications.

Once Netscape has been installed, you can start it with the command `netscape` for Netscape 4.76, or with the command `netscape6` for Netscape 6. This section will cover Netscape 4.76, but Netscape 6 is similar.

Most users have probably used Netscape before, and the configuration in FreeBSD is the same as the configuration in Windows. To change Netscape options, click Edit in the menu bar and then click Preferences. This brings up a configuration dialog box like the one in Figure 7.54.

FIGURE 7.54

The configuration dialog box for Netscape. It is similar to configuring Netscape in Windows.

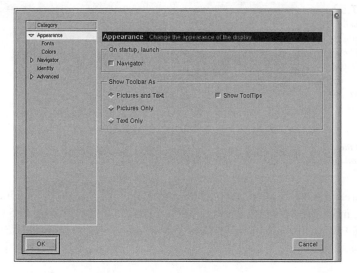

To configure the various Netscape settings, click the plus sign (+) by the desired category of options to expand it. Then, click the item you wish to configure to bring up its configuration dialog box in the right side of the window.

Lynx Web Browser

Lynx is a Web browser that runs in text mode and has no graphical capabilities. Although it can still be used, it is getting more and more difficult to navigate the Web with Lynx because it does not support images, frames, or Java. Because many sites are using images as links and not making use of ALT tags, this can cause navigational problems in Lynx that are difficult or impossible to get around. Figure 7.55 shows Lynx with the FreeBSD Web site loaded into it.

FIGURE 7.55
The FreeBSD Web site in Lynx.

Lynx can still work on quite a few sites, although navigation is not always easy. Use the arrow keys to move between links in the browser window. The spacebar will advance to the next page. Type **G** to change to a different Web site. You will be asked to enter a URL after typing **G**. **Q** quits Lynx after asking you if you are sure you want to quit.

For more information on Lynx, including customization options, see the Lynx man page by typing `man lynx`.

FTP

FTP stands for *File Transfer Protocol*. It is a method of transferring files between systems. Although it is not commonly used directly anymore (often, files are downloaded from FTP by clicking Web site links), it is still handy to know if you need to move files to another server.

To start an FTP session, type `ftp` followed by the name of the server you wish to connect to at the shell prompt or X terminal. For example, to connect to the FreeBSD FTP server, you would type the following:

```
ftp ftp.freebsd.org
```

Once you have done this, and assuming the connection is successful, you will eventually see something like the following:

```
Connected to ftp.beastie.tdk.net.
220 ftp.beastie.tdk.net FTP server (Version DG-4.1.73 983302105) ready.
Name (ftp.freebsd.org:murban):
```

At the Name prompt, you need to enter your login name for the FTP server. If your login name is the same as your login name on the system you are currently on, you can simply press Enter without entering a name here, and your local login name will be used.

If you do not have a login name for the system, you can log in to public FTP servers with the name anonymous. For example, this is how you would log in to the FreeBSD FTP server. Once you have entered anonymous as the username and pressed Enter, the remote host will respond with something like the following:

```
331 Guest login ok, send your e-mail address as password.
Password:
```

Simply do what it says, and enter your e-mail address as your password. Note that the password will not echo to your screen.

After you have logged in, you may get a welcome message, and finally something that looks similar to the following:

```
Remote system type is UNIX.
Using binary mode to transfer files.
ftp>
```

At the prompt, you can use many of the same shell commands that you use at your local shell to navigate through the FTP server. See Chapter 8 for details on how to work with shell commands. Table 7.10 provides a list of some of the most commonly used commands in an FTP session.

TABLE 7.10 Commonly Used FTP commands.

Command	Action
ls	Lists the directory contents of the remote host.
cd	Changes the directory on the remote host.
pwd	Displays the current directory you are in on the remote host.

TABLE 7.10   continued

Command	Action
lcd	Changes the directory on the local host.
binary	Transfers files in binary mode (this mode should be used for anything other than plain-text).
ascii	Transfers files in ASCII mode (this mode should be used ONLY for plain-text. Note that plain-text can also be transferred in binary mode, in most cases, with no problems).
put *filename*	Copies *filename* to the remote host. *filename* is assumed to be in the current directory unless a path is specified. If no destination file is specified, the file will be placed in the current directory in the remote host and have the same name as the local file. (This command works only if you have permission to write to the directory on the remote machine.)
mput *file1 file2*	Copies multiple files in a list to the remote host. The files will be placed in the current directory on the remote host. (This command works only if you have permission to write to the directory on the remote machine.)
get *filename*	Copies a file from the remote host to the local system. If no path is specified, the file is assumed to be located on the current directory on the remote host. If no destination file is specified, the file will be copied to the local system using the same filename.
mget *file1 file2*	Gets multiple files in a list from the remote host. The files will be placed in the current directory on the local system.
mkdir *dirname*	Creates a directory called *dirname* on the remote machine (assuming you have permission to do so).
rmdir *dirname* or rm *dirname*	Removes the directory called *dirname* on the remote machine (assuming you have permission to do so).
del *filename*	Deletes the file *filename* from the remote machine (assuming you have permission to do so).
bye or quit	Closes the connection with the remote host and quits the FTP program, returning you to the shell prompt.

7

WORKING WITH
APPLICATIONS

You can also type `help` at the `ftp>` prompt to get a list of available commands. Type `help` followed by one of the commands in the list to get a short description of what that command does. For example:

```
ftp> help
Commands may be abbreviated.  Commands are:

!               disconnect      mdelete         preserve        runique
$               edit            mdir            progress        send
account         exit            mget            prompt          sendport
append          form            mkdir           proxy           site
ascii           ftp             mls             put             size
bell            get             mode            pwd             status
binary          gate            modtime         quit            struct
bye             glob            more            quote           sunique
case            hash            mput            recv            system
cd              help            msend           reget           tenex
cdup            idle            newer           rename          trace
chmod           image           nlist           reset           type
close           lcd             nmap            restart         umask
cr              less            ntrans          restrict        user
debug           lpwd            open            rhelp           verbose
delete          ls              page            rmdir           ?
dir             macdef          passive         rstatus
ftp> help mdir
mdir            list contents of multiple remote directories
ftp>
```

For more information on using FTP, read the manual page for ftp by typing `man ftp` at the shell prompt. You might also want to read the sections in Chapter 8 on file-manipulation commands because the commands used in FTP are similar.

The following shows what a sample FTP session might look like:

```
bsh$ ftp ftp.freebsd.org
Connected to ftp.beastie.tdk.net.
220 ftp.beastie.tdk.net FTP server (Version DG-4.1.73 983302105) ready.
Name (ftp.freebsd.org:murban): anonymous
331 Guest login ok, send your e-mail address as password.
Password:
230 Guest login ok, access restrictions apply.
Remote system type is UNIX.
Using binary mode to transfer files.
ftp> ls
ftp> ls
227 Entering Passive Mode (62,243,72,50,88,26)
150 Opening ASCII mode data connection for 'file list'.
total 2
dr-xr-xr-x  2 root   wheel   512 May 15 18:30 etc
drwxr-xr-x  3 root   wheel   512 May 13 15:26 pub
```

```
226 Transfer complete.
ftp> cd pub/FreeBSD/tools
ftp> get gunzip.exe
local: gunzip.exe remote: gunzip.exe
227 Entering Passive Mode (62,243,72,50,89,241)
150 Opening BINARY mode data connection for 'gunzip.exe' (37178 bytes).
100% |**************************************************| 37178        00:00 ETA
226 Transfer complete.
37178 bytes received in 9.55 seconds (3.80 KB/s)
ftp> bye
221 Goodbye!
bash$
```

If you would rather work with a graphical FTP client in X-Windows, there are several graphical FTP client ports available in the `ftp` directory.

E-mail Applications

E-mail was one of the first applications of the Internet, and it is still the most popular use of the Internet. There is no shortage of e-mail clients available for FreeBSD. There are clients available for text mode shell use, and also graphical clients available for X-Windows. This section will look at some of the more popular e-mail clients available for both the shell and for X-Windows.

> ### Tip
>
> In addition to having an Internet connection configured and working properly, you will also need to have a mail transfer agent such as Sendmail configured and working properly before you can use some of these e-mail clients. In addition, if you need to retrieve your mail from a POP3 or IMAP server at your ISP, you will also need to have Fetchmail configured and working properly. Not all of the clients listed here will require this because some can transfer mail on their own. It is better to use the mail transfer agent / `Fetchmail` setup, though. This allows much greater flexibility in dealing with e-mail because it uses FreeBSD's native mail-handling system. This will allow the shell to notify you when you have new e-mail, as well as allow mail-checking utilities for X-Windows such as `xbiff` to notify you of new mail. These features will not work if you use the mail clients built in mail handing functions. See Chapter 25 for details on how to set up and configure FreeBSD to send and receive e-mail.

Balsa

Balsa is a graphical mail client for Gnome. It is available in the FreeBSD ports collection under the `mail` directory.

Once Balsa has been installed, it can be invoked with the command `balsa`. The first time you run it, it will ask you some questions in order to set it up correctly for receiving and sending mail.

The first dialog box (see Figure 7.56) will ask you for information such as your name, e-mail address, the SMTP server (that handles outgoing mail), and where you want to store your messages.

FIGURE 7.56

This dialog box helps you configure Balsa to work with your e-mail setup. You will be asked these questions only the first time you run the program.

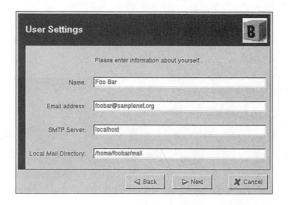

Most of the options except for the third one are self-explanatory. The third option can be left set at the default `localhost` if you are have Sendmail or some other mail transfer agent configured to handle your outgoing mail. If you do not have Sendmail or another MTA configured to do this, change this box to reflect the outgoing mail server at your ISP. Contact your ISP if you are not sure what the address of the outgoing mail server is.

The local mail directory option is the directory within your home directory that incoming, outgoing, and sent mail messages will be stored in. Unless you have a specific reason for changing this, simply accept the default that Balsa suggests.

After you have configured these two options, click Next to move onto the next configuration screen (Figure 7.57).

Once you have clicked Next on the second configuration screen, you will be given a message informing you that you have successfully set up Balsa. After clicking Finish on this screen, you will be taken to the main Balsa screen, as shown in Figure 7.58.

FIGURE 7.57

The files where various messages are stored. You should probably just accept the defaults here.

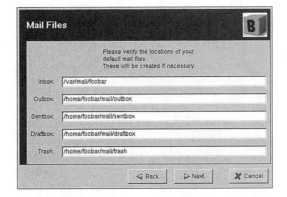

FIGURE 7.58

The main Balsa screen. Microsoft Outlook Express users will find the layout fairly familiar, and shouldn't have much trouble adjusting to Balsa.

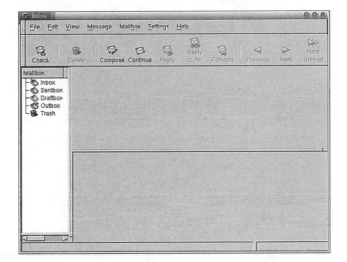

Although Balsa is now set up to send messages, it cannot yet receive messages. To set up an incoming mail account in Balsa, click the Settings item in the menu bar and then click Preferences. This will bring up the dialog box shown in Figure 7.59.

To add an incoming mail account, click the Mail Servers tab to bring up the dialog box shown in Figure 7.60.

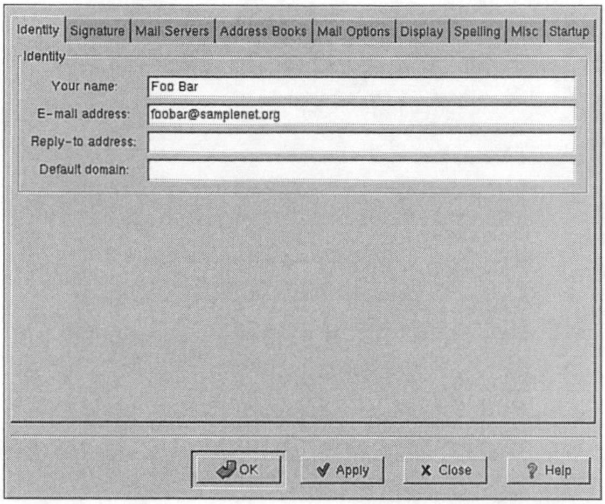

FIGURE **7.59**

The configuration dialog box for Balsa. Here you can control all aspects of Balsa's behavior including mail servers and address books.

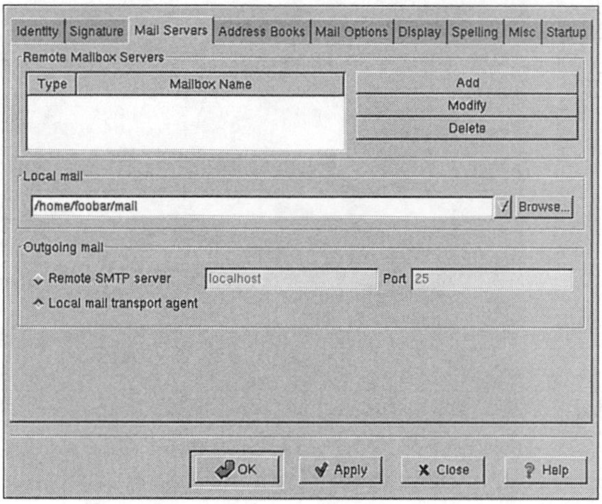

FIGURE **7.60**

Configuring the mail servers in Balsa. Note that you can also make changes to the outgoing mail server from this dialog box.

To add a new mail server, click the Add button to bring up the dialog box shown in Figure 7.61.

After entering a name for the mailbox, set the server to the name of your ISP's POP3 mail server. The port should be left at the default value of 110 unless your ISP has specifically told you that the mail server is on a different port. The Username and Password options are self-explanatory.

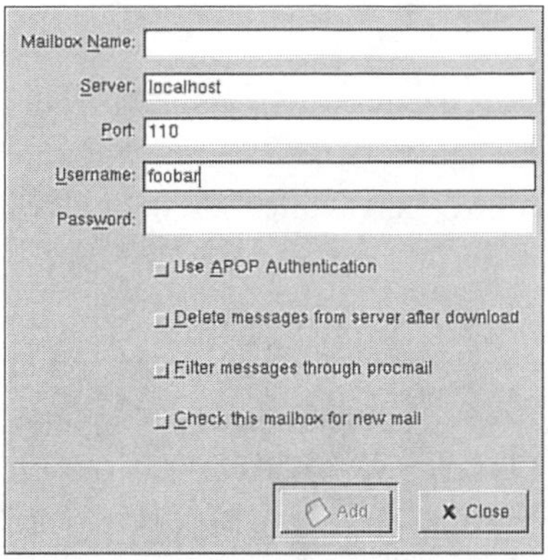

FIGURE 7.61

Adding a new incoming mail server in Balsa. The Mailbox Name can be anything that you want.

The check boxes below the server information have the following effects:

- **Use APOP Authentication**—This will attempt to log in to the mail server securely (assuming that the remote server supports it). This prevents your password from being sniffed out as it is sent over the network.

- **Delete messages from server after download**—This will remove the messages from the server after they are downloaded. If the option is not checked, messages will remain on the server. You will probably want to check this option.

- **Filter messages through procmail**—procmail is a separate program that is available in the FreeBSD ports collection under the `mail` directory. The program allows you to create rules that filter incoming mail to various different folders or directories. A discussion of writing procmail rules and configuring procmail is beyond the scope of this book, but resources that contain instructions on writing procmail rules can be found at `www.procmail.org`.

- **Check this mailbox for new mail**—When checked, this mailbox will be automatically checked for new mail at intervals specified (more on that later in this section). If unchecked, this mailbox will not be checked automatically, and will be checked only when it is manually selected.

You can set Balsa to automatically check for new mail at specified intervals under the Mail Options tab.

Once you have finished making configuration changes to Balsa, click the OK button to make the changes take effect.

This should get you up and running with a basic Balsa configuration. See the Balsa Web site at `www.balsa.net` for more information on using and configuring Balsa.

7

WORKING WITH APPLICATIONS

Pine

Pine is a text-based e-mail client that was designed with the non-technical user in mind. It is menu-driven, and is designed to be intuitive and easy to use for the average computer user. Pine is available in the FreeBSD ports collection under the mail directory. Figure 7.62 shows the main menu of Pine.

FIGURE 7.62

The main menu of Pine. It is menu-driven, and can be navigated with the arrow keys or by pressing the letter in front of the menu entry.

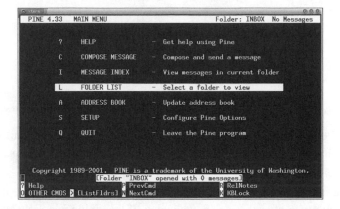

Pine is very popular with end users because of its ease of use. Since it is text-based, it also allows e-mail to be checked remotely over a dumb terminal.

Unfortunately, Pine has a reputation of being poorly programmed and having a lot of security problems. Although all of the known problems have currently been fixed, many security experts believe that there are many more security holes in Pine that have not yet been discovered. Some even place the likely number of undiscovered holes in the thousands. You will also be warned of these potential security issues with Pine when you install the port.

If you do decide to make Pine available to your users, you should make sure that your users are aware of the potential security hazards involved in using Pine.

If security is a high-level concern on your system (for example, if you have confidential data on the system that these users have access to), it is probably best to forbid the use of Pine altogether (in other words, don't install Pine, or uninstall it if it is already installed). Your users may have fits, but in some situations, security may be more important than user convenience. There are other mail programs available that your users can use (one popular alternative, Mutt, is discussed in the next section). Although they may not be as easy to use as Pine, they are generally much more secure.

> **Caution**
>
> Although it is generally a bad idea to open any e-mail while logged in as root, it is even more so with Pine. This is because of the nature of some of the potential holes in Pine that might allow someone to execute arbitrary code on your system as the user running Pine simply by sending a bad e-mail header. It is a much better idea to forward root's mail to a normal user account and then read the e-mail using that account instead. Instructions on e-mail forwarding can be found in Chapter 25.

Mutt

Mutt is another text-based e-mail client for FreeBSD and other UNIX-like operating systems. It is available in the FreeBSD ports collection under the `mail` directory. Figure 7.63 shows the main screen of Mutt.

FIGURE 7.63

The main screen in Mutt. Although it does not have the simple menu-driven interface of Pine, Mutt is much more secure than Pine and is also more configurable.

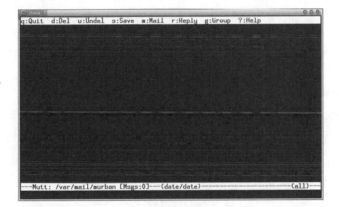

Mutt has its name because it is known as "the mongrel of mail clients." This is because it is a relatively new mail client that attempts to combine the best features of Elm (a very old e-mail client that is not widely used anymore) and Pine (which was designed to be much easier to use than Elm). Mutt has many users that would agree that the client successfully fulfills these goals.

Mutt is a very complex program with a rich set of features. Its use and configuration is beyond the scope of this book. The Mutt Web site located at www.mutt.org has very good online documentation and reference manuals that explain the use and configuration of this powerful program.

uuencode and uudecode

A brief word on uuencode and uudecode is in order here. uuencode is basically a method of sending binary files as plain-text so that they can be sent through e-mail. Often, the e-mail client will handle encoding and decoding of the attachments automatically. However, this is not always the case. Sometimes, you may receive an e-mail that has an attachment and the attachment may appear as several hundred lines of what appears to be garbage text. It will look something like the following:

```
begin 644 gunzip.exe
M35HZ`4D```"""`.I6___/6H`````.``,,4(```""`$0:.3'_\8X&W"<H_S9(`/M8
M`'_X!H&`#'E'"'X"X9"'#'!"^+[F@(8^F%O_$'$`!!4!`!!'`U%"'>0X!`??=
M#}B;_\7X4A3H07?2`0%%???.[($7&H``L,&.#'_`(`&!'*!!+"`#B&
M0<F<+[F<H(@'##'{$[[#?}@B`@_[;'7(I`,Q([>@{!`_"`]H}'&\$$#IH}(K#.]
M$>G}UQ'#F#^]@^}+'\0}_O}C_#k~I&<1}!D$_I/~Z,<'0#{,~_}X=~XN.'C0
M^!~}#".{X$E}U"E=6Q"{Z$!~`'10'?C48(k~l.~'-^P;{FE(#QP4&",,&WB"C/B&)
```

These are what the first several lines of a uuencoded file may look like. The `begin` line contains the name of the file that this file will be saved to when uudecoded.

To decode the file, save the attachment (and/or e-mail message that contains the garbage text) to a file in the directory where you want to decode it. For example, suppose you save the file as `program.txt`. You can now use the following command to decode the file:

```
uudecode program.txt
```

This will decode the file and write the contents to whatever filename is given in the encoding. In the previous example, this would write an output file called `gunzip.exe`.

If you need to encode a file, you can do so with a command like the following. Assume that the file you want to encode is called `gunzip.exe`.

```
uuencode gunzip.exe gunzip.exe > gunzip.txt
```

The three arguments in the previous command are the name of the file you want to encode (in this case `gunzip.exe`); the name of the output file that should be produced when the file is decoded (usually this will be the same as the input file, as in this example); and then we redirect the output to a file called `gunzip.txt`, which will contain the encoded file. If we do not do this, the output will be sent to the screen instead. This allows the output to be piped directly into a mail program or something if you wish to send the encoded file to someone.

See Chapter 8 for more information on input/output redirection and pipes.

Working with the Shell

Up to this point, we have worked mostly with the graphical user interface (GUI) in X-Windows and Gnome. Although this is the easiest way to work with an operating system, the real power of FreeBSD can be unleashed only if you learn how to work with the shell. The design philosophy behind the UNIX command line and UNIX shells is one of the things that has kept UNIX as one of the most powerful operating systems available for more than 30 years after it was originally written. This chapter introduces several shells available for FreeBSD, gives a feature comparison of the various shells, and then shows how to work with the shell.

Introducing the Shell

The UNIX shell is the command-line interface between the user and the operating system kernel. If you have worked with MS-DOS, you can think of the DOS prompt as being the same thing. In a looser sense, you could also think of the Windows or Macintosh desktop as being a shell. The shell acts like a translator—translating human language into machine language that the kernel can understand. The shell also translates machine language from the kernel into language that humans can understand. Figure 8.1 shows the relationship between the system hardware, the kernel, and the shell.

FIGURE 8.1
Relationship between hardware, kernel, and shell.

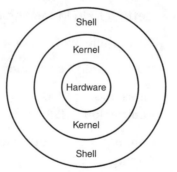

We will cover the role of the kernel in detail in Chapter 17, "Kernel Configuration." For now, simply be aware that the *kernel* is a special piece of software that controls and regulates all the interactions of other software (and the actions of users) with the computer's hardware. Normally, you do not need to concern yourself with the kernel because it is transparent to the user, does its job in the background, and is "out of sight, out of mind."

Types of Shells Available

There are a lot of different shells available for FreeBSD, ranging from bare-bones to loaded with features. We aren't going to talk about all of the shells here, but we will look at some of the more popular ones. Let's begin with the earliest shell that is still in common use: the Bourne shell, commonly known as sh.

The Bourne Shell (sh)

The original Bourne shell was developed at Bell Labs by Steven Bourne for the AT&T UNIX operating system. FreeBSD, like many other versions of UNIX, has replaced the Bourne shell with the POSIX shell, which is basically an enhanced version of the Bourne shell that supports things such as command-line editing, command history, and aliases— all things that the original Bourne shell did not support. We will discuss command-line editing and command history later in this chapter.

The C Shell (csh)

The C shell is the traditional BSD shell. The researchers at Berkeley saw all of the limitations that the original Bourne shell had, so they created their own shell for the BSD operating system. The C shell is so named because it has a syntax that looks a lot like the C programming language. The C shell has many enhancements over the Bourne shell for interactive use, such as job control and command history. It also has a logout configuration file, which is something that most Bourne shells don't. The C shell also supports a configuration file that gets read every time a new sub-shell that is not a login shell is started (the original Bourne shell does not support this).

The C shell is the reverse of the Bourne shell in that it is great for interactive use, but absolutely terrible for shell programming. There are programmers who insist upon writing shell programs in the C shell, but because of its more cryptic and demanding syntax it can be an exercise in frustration and futility.

Although, as I said, the C shell is great for interactive use and has been a very popular interactive shell, it is somewhat dated these days and there are better choices available for an interactive shell.

> **Note**
>
> Modern versions of FreeBSD have replaced the original C shell with the tcsh shell. More on that later in this section.

The Korn Shell (ksh or pdksh)

This is my personal favorite shell. Not to be outdone by Berkeley, AT&T released the Korn shell in 1986. This shell was written by David Korn, and was AT&T's answer to the C shell. The Korn shell is backward-compatible with the Bourne shell. Like the C shell, it supports job control, command history, command aliases, and a configuration file for sub-shells. The Korn shell goes even further though, by supporting vi and Emacs style history editing (the capability to recall a previous command and edit it before running it again). It also includes a number of very useful enhancements for shell programmers, such as extensibility with new commands and syntax compatibility with many other shells and command interpreters. The Korn shell has been very popular, and is included with most commercial versions of UNIX these days.

There is a public domain version of the Korn shell available: pdksh. This is the version you can get for FreeBSD by installing it from the ports collection, as we will see in Chapter 15, "Installing Additional Software."

Users who are familiar with vi and Emacs will like the Korn shell, but users new to UNIX will probably prefer the bash shell (discussed next) because vi and Emacs editing commands are not exactly intuitive (although once you get used to them, they are great productivity enhancers).

The Bourne Again Shell (bash)

The Bourne Again Shell is a Bourne-compatible shell developed by the Free Software Foundation (FSF). There is a version included on the CD-ROM with this book. The bash shell is the default shell on virtually all Linux distributions. It is similar to the Korn shell, but adds even more features, including built-in help, intuitive command-line editing and history editing that uses the arrow keys, extremely powerful history functions, and more environment variables than you can shake a stick at.

The only real problem with bash is that it is not standard software on most commercial UNIX versions. Because of this, shell programs written in bash are not very portable across different versions of UNIX.

The Tcsh Shell (tcsh)

The tcsh shell is an enhanced version of the C shell. (What does the "t" stand for? It refers to TENEX, an operating system for the DEC PDP-10, whose command-line behavior tcsh originally was intended to mimic.) It adds many new features to the C shell, including filename completion and command-line editing with intuitive editing controls like in bash (it uses the arrow keys). tcsh also has some nice features that even bash doesn't support, including the capability to watch your back for you by recognizing potentially dangerous commands and then asking if you are sure you want to continue (for example, "Are you sure you want to delete ALL files?").

tcsh is a great shell for interactive use. In many ways, it is even better then bash. Unfortunately, it is still plagued by many of the problems of the C shell when it comes to shell programming. Although some of the problems have been fixed, you should still write your shell programs for a Bourne style shell and avoid C shell programming like the plague.

Which Shell to Choose?

So, which shell should you choose? For most of this chapter, it doesn't really matter. Most of the standard FreeBSD commands work the same way under all shells. It is only when you want to start doing advanced tasks such as changing shell variables, setting aliases, and shell programming that the differences between the shells become really apparent.

If you don't plan to do any shell programming, pick Korn, bash, or tcsh as your shell. If you are interested in learning shell programming, pick Korn or bash because you won't have to unlearn anything when you start programming. Also, if you pick Korn or bash, everything you learn will be applicable to shell programming.

Changing Your Shell

For most of this chapter, we will use the bash shell because it is the easiest shell for new users to work with. To see what shell you are currently running, type the following command, where foo is your logon name and # is the command prompt:

```
$ grep foo /etc/passwd
```

Don't worry if you don't know what this command line means. You will understand it and far more before you are done with this chapter. The command returns a line that looks something like the following:

```
foo:*:1001:1001::Foo Bar:/home/foo:/usr/local/bin/ksh
```

The line on your screen will probably be different from this one. For now, all you need to worry about is the last field (the one that says /usr/local/bin/ksh in the example). This is your default shell—in this case, the Korn shell. Your shell will probably have one of the following values:

- /bin/sh: The POSIX Bourne shell.
- /bin/csh: The C shell, which is now actually a link to the tcsh shell. So, if your shell is /bin/csh, you are actually running the tcsh shell.
- /bin/tcsh: The tcsh shell.

- /usr/local/bin/ksh: The Korn shell.
- /usr/local/bin/bash: The bash shell.

If you are not already running the bash shell, simply type bash at the command prompt to change to the bash shell. In Chapter 12, "Customizing the Shell," you will see how to permanently change your shell.

> **Caution**
>
> Unlike DOS, Windows, or VMS, UNIX and FreeBSD are case-sensitive. The names *Grep*, *grep*, and *greP* are completely unrelated to each other as far as FreeBSD is concerned. This is a common source of errors for newcomers. If you are getting No such file or directory errors when you type commands in this chapter, make sure that you are using the correct case.

Getting Help in the Shell

This chapter can't even begin to cover all the commands that are available from the shell; nor can it even cover all of the options that are available for the commands that it does cover. But FreeBSD includes an extensive set of online manuals that document each command and its various options. To access the manual page for a command, type man commandname. For example, to read the manual page for the man command itself, type man man.

You can use the spacebar, the arrow keys, and the Page Up/Page Down keys to review the contents of the manual page.

Searching for Manual Pages

Sometimes, you might know what you want to do, but you are not sure of the name of the command to do it. In this case, you can use the -k option to the man command. Sometimes, you have to be fairly creative about what you search for in order for man -k to return the results you want. For example, suppose that you want to find out about commands that can search text files for certain words or phrases, and show each place in the text file where that word or phrase occurs. First, you might try the man -k search command, as shown in Listing 8.1.

LISTING 8.1   Using man -k

```
$ man -k search
apropos(1), whatis(1) - search the whatis database
```

LISTING 8.1   continued

```
bios(9), bios_sigsearch(9), bios32_SDlookup(9), bios32(9) - Interact
with PC BIO
S
bsearch(3)                - binary search of a sorted table
devclass_find(9)          - search for a devclass
device_find_child(9)      - search for a child of a device
lkbib(1)                  - search bibliographic databases
lookbib(1)                - search bibliographic databases
lsearch(3), lfind(3)      - linear searching routines
manpath(1)                - determine user's search path for man pages
res_query(3), res_search(3), res_mkquery(3), res_send(3), res_init(3),
dn_comp(3
), dn_expand(3) - resolver routines
tsearch(3), tfind(3), tdelete(3), twalk(3) - manipulate binary search
trees
Search::Dict(3), look(3) - search for key in dictionary file
bash$
```

Not exactly what you had in mind. The results seem to be geared toward search routines for programmers using C. For the next attempt, try searching for the keyword "pattern" (as shown in Listing 8.2)because you'll want a command to find patterns in text files.

LISTING 8.2   Another Attempt with man -k

```
$ man -k pattern
gawk(1) - pattern scanning and processing language
glob(3), globfree(3)      - generate pathnames matching a pattern
grep(1), egrep(1), fgrep(1), zgrep(1)   print lines matching a pattern
lptest(1)                 - generate lineprinter ripple pattern
menu pattern(3)           - get and set a menu's pattern buffer
bash$
```

Now *that* looks more useful—especially the grep series of commands. These seem to be tools for searching for patterns within files, as we hoped. You could now type man grep to read the man page for grep, and you would find that indeed this command does what you need.

Command Summaries

At other times, you might know the name of a command, but are not sure what it does (if you are poking around in /usr/bin or /usr/games, for example). You can use the -f option to man to get a short, one-line description of a command. For example, suppose that you find the command pom in the /usr/games directory, and you want to know what it does:

```
$ man -f pom
pom(6) - display the phase of the moon
bash$
```

The (6) at the end of the command name is the section of the manual that the command comes from.

Manual Sections

The online manuals are divided into nine sections, as shown in Table 8.1.

TABLE 8.1 Manual Sections

Section	Description
1: User Commands	Information on user commands such as ls, rm, cp, and grep. This is the section you will probably use most often while working with and learning FreeBSD.
2: System Calls	Contains information on various APIs for FreeBSD. This section is primarily of interest to C programmers.
3: Subroutines	Also known as library functions. This section contains information on library functions. Once again, mostly of interest only to C programmers.
4: Devices	More stuff for C programmers. Contains information on interfacing with device drivers in FreeBSD.
5: File Formats	Contains information on the formats of various system configuration files, such as the crontab files for scheduling of regular jobs and the rc files that control system startup.
6: Games	The most important section of the manual. This section contains instructions for playing the various games and other amusements that come with FreeBSD.
7: Miscellaneous	If it doesn't fit anywhere else, it will be found here.
8: System Administration	Contains information on commands related to system administration, such as fsck for checking filesystems.
9: Kernel Interfaces	More information for programmers. This section contains information on interfacing with the kernel in C.

Some commands have more then one entry. For example, the crontab entry has an entry in section 1 for the crontab command, and also an entry in section 5 for the format of the crontab file. By default, you will get the first entry that man comes to, which, in the case of crontab, means that you will get the entry for section 1. If you want to see the entry for section 5, use man 5 crontab. If you want to specify only certain sections of the manuals when doing a search, use the -S option with a colon-separated list of section numbers.

Basic Shell File Manipulation

If you've worked with MS-DOS before, most of this chapter will come fairly easily to you. If you haven't worked with MS-DOS before, then some background information is necessary.

How FreeBSD Stores Files

Like most other modern operating systems, FreeBSD stores files in a hierarchal tree structure. You can think of the FreeBSD filesystem as a system of filing cabinets as in an office. You can think of the hard disk as a group of filing cabinets. FreeBSD is organized into multiple directories. You can think of these directories as individual filing cabinets within the group of cabinets. Directories can contain files and also other directories. These directories and files are analogous to the folders and papers in a filing cabinet. Windows and Macintosh systems both use this same type of filing system. The only real difference is that in Windows and Macintosh, you see a graphical representation of folders and files from a graphical file manager. From the FreeBSD command line, you are seeing a textual representation, as we will see shortly.

In Windows or DOS, you are usually placed at the top directory when you log in. This is not true with FreeBSD. When you log in to FreeBSD, you are placed in your home directory, which is located a few levels down from the top directory. We will look in detail at directory structures in Chapter 9, "The FreeBSD Filesystem." For now, we are only concerned about your home directory.

There's No Place Like Home

Each user on a UNIX system (with certain exceptions) has his own home directory. Your home directory is like your own private "virtual hard disk." Here, you can create and delete files, copy files, move files, and create and remove directories. Your home directory is your personal space on the FreeBSD system. Being able to manage the files and directories in your home directory is an important skill. The next few sections will take a look at the various commands available to manage your files and directories.

Listing Directory Contents

Use the ls command to list the contents of the directory you are in. By itself, with no options, the ls command produces output similar to the following:

```
$ ls
Mail      letter-to-boss    program       proposal-draft
fbu       mail              program.c
```

By itself, this output is not very useful because it tells us nothing about the contents of the files, or even whether they are files or directories. `ls` supports several options to modify its default behavior. One of the most useful is the `-F` option, which provides you with more information on the type of each file in the list. For example:

```
$ ls -F
Mail/     letter-to-boss    program*      proposal-draft
fbu@      mail/             program.c
```

Now we know a little bit more about the entries in the list. Here is what each symbol following the various files means:

- `/`: The item is a subdirectory of the current directory.
- `*`: The item is an executable binary file or script.
- `@`: The item is a link to another location on the hard disk. These are analogous to shortcuts in Windows or to aliases in Mac OS.

Notice the executable file "`program`" here. Unlike Windows, FreeBSD does not require a file to have a `.com`, `.exe`, or `.bat` extension to denote it as being executable. Whether a file is executable or not is a "permissions" bit that is stored in the files i-node entry. You will almost never see an executable FreeBSD file with an `.exe` or `.com` extension.

There are more symbols that are not in this list. Type `man ls`, and look at the `-F` option for a complete list.

Modern versions of the `ls` command also support the `-G` option, which tells `ls` to use different colors to denote different types of files. Not all terminals can display colors, though, and as a general rule, an xterm cannot display colors unless it is configured as a color xterm.

By default, `ls` does not display hidden files, also known as *dot files*, because they begin with a period. To display hidden files, use `ls` with the `-a` option:

```
$ ls -a
.                .forward       .mailrc          ..profile      Mail
..               .hushlogin     .mysql_history   .project       fbu
.addressbook     .login         .rhosts          .login.conf    mail
.muttrc          .sh-history    .cshrc           .mail_aliases
```

Most of these hidden files are configuration files that store various things, such as profile information on how you want your shell set up, your address book for the mail program, and a list of the commands you have typed for the history functions of the shell. The two main benefits of having these files hidden and begin with a period are that they don't clutter up the directory during normal operation because they are not shown, and also that it makes it more difficult to accidentally delete important configuration files because "dot files" are not matched by shell wildcard operators when used by themselves.

If you want more detail about the files and directories (see Listing 8.3) in the list, use the -l option:

LISTING 8.3 Sample Output of ls -l

```
$ ls -l
total 3
drwx------ 2 murban murban    512 Feb 15 16:04 Mail
lrwxr-xr-x 1 murban murban     15 Mar 20 06:55 fbu ->
/home/murban/documents/books/fbu
-rw-r--r-- 1 murban murban    782 Mar 15 09:21 letter-to-boss
drwx------ 2 murban murban    512 Mar 24 15:12 mail
-rwx------ 1 murban murban  15221 Feb 21 18:11 program
-rw-r--r-- 1 murban murban   1571 Feb 21 17:51 program.c
-rw-r--r-- 1 murban murban   2521 Feb 25 18:51 proposal-draft
```

Each entry has seven different fields of information. From left to right they are:

- **Permissions and other file attributes.** The first field in the ls -l list tells you the permissions and attributes of the file. This field will be covered in detail in Chapter 10, "Users, Groups, and Permissions." For now, simply be aware that the information in this field tells you who has read, write, and execute permissions on each file or directory.

- **Number of links.** This field contains the number of links that exist to that file. All regular files will contain at least one which is to itself, and all directories will contain at least two links—one to itself and one to its parent.

- **User name of the file's owner.** This field and the next are covered in detail in Chapter 10. For now, just be aware that they tell you who the owner of the file is and what group the file belongs to.

- **Group name that the file belongs to.** See the previous field.

- **Size of the file.** This is the size of the file in bytes.

- **Date and time of last modification of the file.** This is the time the file was last modified.

- **Name of the file.** This is the name of the file. Files that look like the following are links:

```
fbu -> /home/murban/documents/books/fbu
```

8

WORKING WITH
THE SHELL

In this case, the entry `fbu` is actually a link to `/home/murban/documents/books/fbu`. I can use this link any time I want to reference the directory rather than having to type the entire pathname of the directory.

Moving Around the Filesystem

The `cd` command is used to change from one directory to another in the filesystem. You can give it directory names in several forms, as shown in Table 8.2.

TABLE 8.2   Usage of the `cd` Command

Command	Result
`cd`	Instantly takes you to your home directory from anywhere else.
`cd /`	Directories that begin with a / are known as "absolute paths". They always start at the root directory of the system (which is the very top directory). A / by itself takes you to the root directory.
`cd /usr/local/bin`	Takes you to the directory "bin", located under the directory "local", which is located under the directory "usr", which is located under the root (top) directory.
`cd bin`	Takes you to the "bin" directory (if there is one) located directly under whatever directory you currently happen to be in. If there is no such directory, `cd` returns an error. Directory or filenames that do not begin with a / are relative to the current directory you are in.
`cd ../`	The special "`../`" notation means the parent directory of the directory you are currently in. This takes you to the directory one level above where you are right now. The trailing slash is not required.
`cd ../bin`	Takes you to the directory "bin", if one is located in the parent directory of the directory you are currently in.
`cd ../../bin`	Takes you to the directory "bin", located two levels above the directory you are currently in.

Lost in the Filesystem?

Sometimes, it's easy to forget where you are in the filesystem hierarchy. The `pwd` command prints the current directory that you are in on your screen. Use it whenever you need to refresh your memory about where you are. (Yes, you can set your shell prompt to show you where you are. We'll show you how in Chapter 12.)

Copying Files and Directories

Use the `cp` command to copy files from one place to another. It takes as its arguments a list of files to copy, followed by where to copy the files. If you specify more then one file to copy or use a wildcard, the destination to copy to must be a directory. A few examples are shown in Table 8.3.

TABLE 8.3 Usage of the `cp` Command

Command	Result
`cp file1 file2`	Copy an existing file called `file1` to a new file called `file2`.
`cp file1/archive`	Copy `file1` to the directory "archive", which is a subdirectory of the root directory.
`cp file1 mystuff/newfile`	Copy `file1` to the directory `mystuff` in the current directory. If "newfile" is a subdirectory, `file1` will be copied to the subdirectory "newfile" under "mystuff". If "newfile" is not a subdirectory, `file1` will be copied to the subdirectory "mystuff" and given the name "newfile".
`cp file1 file 2 /archive`	Copy `file1` and `file2` to the directory "archive", located under the root directory.

> **Caution**
>
> By default, the `cp` command simply overwrites the contents of an existing file if you accidentally copy a file to a filename that already exists. For example, `cp file1 file2` overwrites `file2` with the contents of `file1` if `file2` already exists. You can use the `-i` (for "interactive") option with `cp` to cause it to ask you before overwriting any existing files.

If you want to recursively copy a directory and everything under it, including subdirectories to another location, use the `-R` option to `cp`. For example:

```
$ cp -R dir1 /dir2
```

This copies everything under `dir1` to a new directory called `dir2`. If `dir2` already exists, a new directory will be created under `dir2` called `dir1`, and the contents will be placed there. If `dir1` already exists in `dir2`, the contents of `dir1` in the current directory will be added to the `dir1` directory under the `dir2` directory. Any files in the directory that have the same name will be overwritten by the copy, so be careful when using the `-R` option (or combine it with the `-i` option so it will warn you before overwriting anything).

8

WORKING WITH
THE SHELL

> **Caution**
>
> Be careful that you do not do something like this when using `cp -R`:
>
> ```
> $ cp -R /* /old
> ```
>
> This command recursively copies everything in the root directory to a subdirectory called `old`, which is also in the root directory. Of course, this also means that the contents of `old` are copied into a subdirectory in `old` called "old". The result is a loop that will copy the contents of `old` indefinitely. On a fast hard disk, this can quickly fill up the entire disk.

Moving and Renaming Files and Directories

The `mv` command can be used to move or rename files and directories. Some examples are shown in Table 8.4.

TABLE 8.4 Usage of the `mv` Command

Command	Result
`mv file1 file2`	Renames `file1` to `file2`.
`mv /dir1 /dir2`	Renames `dir1` to `dir2`. Generates an error message if `dir2` already exists and is not empty.
`mv file1 /dir2`	Moves `file1` to `dir2` located under the root directory.
`mv file1 /dir2/file2`	If `file2` is a directory, `file1` is moved into the directory `/dir2/file2`. If `file2` does not exist, `file1` is moved into `dir2` and renamed to `file2`.

Deleting Files and Directories

To delete files, use the `rm` command. With no options, `rm` deletes the list of files it is given on its command line. It does not delete directories. If you want to delete a directory and everything under that directory, use the `-R` option with `rm`. Table 8.5 shows some examples of using the `rm` command.

TABLE 8.5 Usage of the `rm` Command

Command	Result
`rm file1`	Deletes `file1`.
`rm file1 file2`	Deletes `file1` and `file2`.
`rm -R dir1`	Deletes directory `dir1` and everything under it.

Table 8.6 shows a list of some (but not all) of the other options that are supported by the rm command:

TABLE 8.6   Options for Use with the rm Command

Option	Result
-f	Causes rm to force the deletion without asking questions, even if the file is marked read-only. Use with care.
-i	Prompts before deleting each file. Useful when using rm with wildcards (more on that later) or with the -R option.
-P	Overwrites files three times with patterns of bytes before deleting. Useful for deleting sensitive files because it reduces the chance that they can be recovered with the option.
-W	Attempts to undelete a file that was previously deleted with the rm command.

Removing Directories

Use the rmdir command to remove directories. rmdir will only remove a directory if it is empty. Used with the -p option, it will remove a directory and its subdirectories, provided that the subdirectories are also empty. If you need to remove directories that have files in them, use the rm -R command instead.

The touch Command

The touch command serves two primary purposes: It can be used to create an empty file, and it can be used to modify the last access or last modification time of an existing file. Its basic format is:

- touch filename where *filename* is the name of the file that you wish to create or modify.

- touch supports a few options that control how the last accessed or last modified times are set. See the man page for touch for full details.

Creating Links

As mentioned briefly, you can create links that point to other places in the filesystem. This is useful to avoid having to type long pathnames or having to navigate through many sublevels of folders from the GUI. You can think of links as being similar to shortcuts in Windows. There are a few important differences, though, which we will look at in the following sections. There are two kinds of links: hard links and soft links. Let's look at hard links first.

Hard Links

A *hard link* is a directory entry that points to the same i-node (physical location on the hard disk) as another file. There is actually only one file. There are just two or more directory entries that point to the same physical data on the hard disk.

By default, the `ln` command creates hard links. For example:

```
$ ln /home/foo/documents/books/fbsd/file1.txt ./file.txt
```

This creates an entry in the current directory called `file1.txt` that points to the same location on the hard disk as `/home/foo/documents/books/fbsd/file1.txt` does. I can now access the same file by using either directory entry (presumably I would create a link like this so I only have to type `vi file1.txt` after I log in to edit this file rather than `vi documents/books/fbsd/file1.txt`). If I now do an `ls -l` on this link, it will look something like the following:

```
-rw------- 2 foo bar 26896 Mar 25 19:18 file.txt
```

It looks like any other plain old file, right? That's because it *is* a plain old normal file, for all practical purposes. The only visual cue we have that this is a link is seeing that number 2 after the permissions. This indicates that there are two directory entries pointing to this i-node (physical location) on the hard disk. Any changes I make to this file or its directory entry will affect the other directory entries that point to this same location. For example, if I change the permissions on this entry, the original directory entry in `/home/foo/documents/books/fbsd/file1.txt` will reflect the changes as well. The modification time here reflects the same modification time as the original directory entry. The size also reflects the size of the original directory entry.

If I delete the original directory entry in `/home/foo/documents/books/fbsd/file1.txt`, the directory entry will be removed, and the link count will be decremented by one to show the change. However, the file still exists because there is another link pointing to that same location on the hard disk (the link we created). The file will not actually be deleted until all of its hard links have been removed, and the link count is decremented to zero.

Hard links have two important limitations:

- They cannot be used to link directories.
- They cannot cross filesystem boundaries.

If you need to link a directory or cross a filesystem boundary, you will have to use a soft link.

Soft Links

Soft links (also called *symbolic links* or *symlinks*) are virtually identical to shortcuts in Windows. Unlike hard links, a soft link is a separate file that has its own i-node on the hard disk. The soft link is simply a file that contains a pointer to another file. Use the `-s` option with `ln` to create a soft link. For example:

```
$ ln -s /home/foo/documents/books/fbsd/file1.txt file.txt
```

If you do an `ls -l` on this file, it will look something like this:

```
lrwxr-xr-x 1 foo bar 31 Mar 25 19:56 file.txt ->
➥/home/foo/documents/books/fbsd/file1.txt
```

Notice the differences between this version and the hard link:

- The permissions do not indicate the permissions of the actual file. Also, you cannot change the attributes of a soft link (permissions, owner, or group). You must do this from the actual file.

- The link count is only one instead of two. This is because the soft link is an actual file that points to the other file. It is not simply a directory entry that points to a location on the hard disk (as the hard link is).

- The file size is lying to us. The size listed here is the size of the file containing the link—not the size of the actual file it points to.

- The file modification time is lying to us. It tells us the time that the link was last modified, but it tells us nothing about the time that the actual file the link points to was last modified.

- The filename tells us the name of the file that this file points to after the `->`.

Also, unlike the hard link, if you delete the original file that this link points to, the file's data blocks are removed and the link becomes an orphan that no longer works. However, if you delete the link with `rm` the original file remains untouched.

> **Tip**
>
> If you are trying to access a file, and you keep getting "No such file or directory" errors, and yet when you do an "ls", the file is clearly there, you are probably trying to use a soft link that has become an orphan, meaning that its target (or parent) no longer exists. Use the `-l` option to `ls`, and see if the file is a soft link. If it is, check to see whether the file it points to actually exists or not. Note that either deleting or simply moving a file can cause its soft links to become orphans.

As a general rule of thumb, use hard links if you are pointing to a file located on the same filesystem as the one you are currently on. Hard links have the advantages of providing you with information about the actual file and of not becoming orphans if the original file is deleted or moved. However, if you need to link a directory or link to a file that is located on a different filesystem, you must use soft links.

> **Note**
>
> Hard links also have one other advantage over soft links: They don't take up an i-node. This may not seem like a huge issue, but there is a fixed number of i-nodes available on the hard disk. It is possible to run out of i-nodes if you have a lot of very small files on the disk, even if you have a lot of space left on the hard disk. When you run out of i-nodes, no more files can be created until you have deleted some files and thus freed up some i-nodes.

Universal Options

Most (but not all) of the commands mentioned in this section support the options shown in Table 8.7.

TABLE 8.7   Universal Options for Most Shell Commands

Option	*Result*
-i	Run in interactive mode,prompting before taking action on each file if that action would cause damage to an existing file.
-v	Be verbose about what the command is doing. In other words, print messages on the screen for each operation as the command performs it.
-f	Force the action without asking, even if the file permissions prohibit the action (for example, delete a file without asking if the file is set read-only, assuming that you have write privileges in the directory where the file is located).

> **Caution**
>
> As you may have noticed, most UNIX commands that deal with file and directory manipulation will pretty much do whatever you tell them to do without asking any questions, even if the action you tell it to do will destroy existing

files. UNIX doesn't hold your hand, like Windows or DOS does. UNIX assumes that you know what you are doing when you tell it to do something. Because of this, if you aren't completely sure of what you are doing (you aren't sure if there might be existing files of the same name in a directory you are copying another directory to, for example), it is often a good idea to use the -i option with many of these commands. This way, you will be prompted before the command does anything that will damage existing files.

Meta-Characters and Wildcard Operators

All the previous commands also support meta-characters and wildcards. These allow you to match one or more unknown characters.

Caution

DOS users: Before you get any ideas of skipping this section because you think you know all about wildcards, just remember that UNIX and FreeBSD wildcards DO NOT behave like DOS wildcards. Part of this is because the period is just another character in a filename as far as UNIX is concerned. UNIX gives no special treatment to the period, like DOS does. This means that although del * would do virtually nothing in DOS, it will delete every file in the current directory in UNIX! Be careful with UNIX wildcards, especially if you are used to wildcards in DOS.

There are three primary wildcard operators that you will use in FreeBSD, shown in Table 8.8.

TABLE 8.8   Wildcard Operators

Operator	Meaning
?	Match any single unknown character. For example, file?.txt will match the files file1.txt, file2.txt, and fileA.txt. It will not match file10.txt or fileAB.txt.
*	Match any number of unknown characters. For example, f* will match the files "f", foo, file, file1.txt, file2.txt, fileA.txt, file10.txt, and fileAB.txt.
[]	Matches a range of characters (explained as follows because it requires more explanation than can fit well in this table).

8

WORKING WITH
THE SHELL

Matching Ranges of Characters

You can match ranges of characters by enclosing them in brackets. For example, file[1-3] will match file1, file2, and file3, but not file4. This also works with characters. Also, file[a-c] will match filea, fileb, and filec.

Tip

When dealing with ranges of characters, it is important to remember that the matching is based on the ASCII number value of the character. For example, file[A-b] will match fileA and fileb; but it will also match fileB, fileC, fileD, fileE, and so on—all the way up to fileZ. This is because uppercase letters come before lowercase letters in the ASCII chart. So, any time you specify an uppercase letter as the starting point for the match and a lowercase letter as the ending point, all the uppercase letters between the one you specify and "Z" will also be matched.

You can also match one of several characters simply by including them in a list. For example file[1234]* will match any file beginning with file1, file2, file3, or file4, no matter what follows it. Notice that I combined two wildcard operators. That is perfectly legal.

Finally, you can use the logical NOT operator with wildcards. For example, file[!1234]* will match all files that do NOT begin with file1, file2, file3, or file4.

Caution

Be extremely careful when using wildcards with commands such as rm because it is easy to make disastrous mistakes. For example, suppose that you accidentally type rm note * when you meant to type rm note*. The shell interprets the space as an argument separator. So, a typo as simple as putting a space between the note and the asterisk changes this command from "Remove all files beginning with note" to "Remove the file note and then remove ALL other files in the directory"! So, double- and triple-check your typing when using wildcards with commands such as rm. Better yet, use the -i option.

Notes on Filenames

Although UNIX will technically let you get away with using just about any character in a filename (although some can't simply be typed—they have to be entered explicitly), to save yourself from migraines, you should use only letters, digits, periods, -, and _ (underscore) characters in filenames. You should not begin a filename with a dash because UNIX interprets the dash as a special character that means an option is to follow. This makes it hard to do things with the files. It is all right to include spaces in files, but you will need to quote the filenames if you are going to do that to tell the shell to interpret the string as one argument, not two separate files. A common practice, and the one I recommend, is to use underscores in filenames instead of spaces. This makes them easy to read and also eliminates the need to quote filenames.

Avoid using filenames with special characters.

Dealing with Funky Filenames

Sooner or later, you will probably somehow end up with a file that has a funky name. For example, here is a directory listing that contains several files with funky names:

```
*               File\1.txt      file4.txt      file6.txt
File 1          file"3".txt     file5.txt
```

These filenames are for demonstration purposes only. Don't create filenames like this in practice.

The first one is the file `*`. How can you remove this file? When you are new to UNIX, your first reaction might be simply to type `rm *` and that would remove a file named "*", right? Well, it will remove this file, but the shell interprets the asterisk as a wildcard character. Because of this, it would remove this file and also every other file in the directory! This is obviously not what you want to happen.

The shell provides an "escape" character for cases such as this one. The escape character is the backslash (\). It tells the shell that it should interpret the next character as a normal character instead of giving it special treatment. So, in this case, the command `rm -i \*` would remove the offending file while leaving the other characters untouched.

The second one is the file named `File\1.txt`. In this case, the filename itself contains the escape character. Typing `rm File\1.txt` will result in `File1.txt: No such file or directory`. The solution here is to simply escape the escape character itself like this: `rm -i File\\1.txt`.

Then, we come to `File 1`. The shell interprets spaces as argument separators, so `rm File 1` will not remove this file. Instead, it would attempt to remove two files: one named `File` and the other named `1`. In order to get the shell to interpret the string as a single argument, you need to quote it. `rm -i "File 1"` will do the trick here.

So what about `file"3".txt`? Once again, if you simply try `rm file"3".txt`, you will see `file3.txt: No such file or directory`. This is because the shell interprets the `"` as a special character. Once again, you need to escape it with the backslash. The command `rm file\"3\".txt` will do the trick.

> **Tip**
>
> Notice that I used the `-i` option to `rm` in all the previous examples. This is a good habit to get into when trying to remove files with funky names. This way, you can be sure that the command you are issuing will actually have the effect you intend it to have, and it won't delete some files you don't want to delete.

Where Did I Put That File Again?

It happens to all of us. Once in awhile, we create files or save files and then we simply can't remember where we put them. For situations such as this, FreeBSD provides the `find` command, which has a somewhat nonstandard syntax. Here is an example of how to use it:

```
$ find . -name "lostfile*"
```

This command will find all files that begin with the name `lostfile` that are in the current directory or any directory under the current directory. Note that a search done from the root directory will check every subdirectory on the entire system—even subdirectories located on other disks or across NFS mounts. This can take quite some time on large disks. There are various options to control how far into the directory hierarchy `find` will go, and whether or not it will traverse filesystems or only look on the current filesystem. You can also use `find` to search for files based on criteria other than their names, such as their owner, group, and size. See the `man find` page for full details on this command.

There is another command, called `locate`, that does not actually search for the file, but rather instead searches a database list of files on the system. Because of the database feature, `locate` is many times faster than `find`. The drawback is that there could be files on the system that the `locate` database doesn't know about and won't find. Depending on the system, the `locate` database is usually updated once a day or sometimes once a week (you can control how often it is updated). See the `locate` man page for more details.

That about covers the majority of the things you need to know to manipulate files from the command line. There are options to these commands that were not covered here, but the most important ones that you are likely to use on a regular basis have been discussed. For more information on each of these commands and their options, see the man pages for the commands.

Text-Related Commands

One of the original design goals of UNIX at AT&T was for processing of text data. UNIX and FreeBSD include a large number of commands for processing text data from the command line. I'm not going to try to cover every single command available, but I am going to cover the most useful ones.

Counting Lines, Words, and Characters

Use the wc command to count the number of lines, words, and characters in a text file. With no options, it will give all three. For example, the following tells me that there are 1160 lines, 7823 words, and 51584 characters currently in the text file that contains this chapter of the book:

```
$ wc fbu8mcu
    1160    7823    51584 fbu8mcu.html
```

wc supports the -1 option to only display number of lines, the -w option to only display words, and the -c option to only display characters. These options can be combined to control what information wc displays.

Viewing Text Files...More or Less...

Once two separate commands, the more command is now actually a hard link to the less command. Despite its name, the less command actually is more powerful than the more command.

You can use the less (or more) command to display text files on your screen, one screen at a time. In addition, you can search the file you are currently viewing for text, and scroll back and forth through the file by any number of lines you specify.

Table 8.9 shows some examples of commands that can be used in less.

TABLE 8.9 Commands Allowed Within the less Program

Command	Usage
/pattern	Replace pattern with the pattern you want to search for, and less will find the specified pattern in the file.
SPACE or f	Scroll forward one screen. If you type a number before pressing SPACE, then less will scroll forward that number of lines.
b	Scroll back one screen. If you type a number before pressing b, less will scroll back that number of lines.

8

WORKING WITH
THE SHELL

TABLE 8.9   Continued

Command	Usage
Up and down arrows	Move up or down one line at a time in the file.
$ g	Replace # with a number and then type g. less will move to that exact line in the file.
$ %	Replace # with a number between 0 and 100. less will move that percentage location in the file.

These are probably the most common options you will use with less. There are many more options available, however. The man page for less is nearly 2,000 lines long. See this page for more information on the other options and commands that less offers.

Searching for Patterns

You can use the grep series of commands to search for patterns in text files. There are three different grep commands available. There is plain old grep, which simply searches for patterns; there is egrep, which can search for extended regular expressions; and there is fgrep, which searches for fixed strings. Some earlier UNIX manual pages also referred to fgrep as "fast grep" because it was supposed to be faster than regular grep. In reality though, fgrep is almost always slower than regular grep. Most man pages these days no longer refer to fgrep as "fast grep".

Suppose that you want to search the file textfile for the pattern cat. In its simplest form, grep looks like this:

```
$ grep cat textfile
```

This command will search through every line of the file textfile and print each line where the pattern cat is matched. Note that the command matches a pattern and not a word. This means that in addition to "cat", the words catnip, catbird, catfish, and concatenate would also be matched because they all contain the string cat. If you only want to match the actual word cat, enclose the string in quotes and include spaces on each side like this:

```
$ grep " cat " textfile
```

Some common options to grep include -i to do a case-insensitive search, -c to suppress the display of matching lines and print the number of times the match occurred instead, -n to display the line number of the line in front of each line where a match occurs, and -v to reverse the operation and print only lines that do not match the specified pattern.

The extended regular expression matching of egrep is beyond the scope of this chapter, but extended regular expressions will be covered in detail in Chapter 13, "Shell Programming."

Sorting Text in a File

Sometimes, you might want to sort the text in a file into a certain order. For example, you might want to do an alphabetical sort, or a numerical sort. You can use the sort command for this.

By default, sort sorts based on the ASCII value, and does not ignore leading whitespace. Some of the common options are shown in Table 8.10.

TABLE 8.10 Options for Use with the sort Command

Option	Result
-d	Sort using "telephone book" sorting. This ignores anything other than letters, digits, and blanks when sorting.
-b	Ignore leading whitespace in lines when sorting.
-f	Fold lowercase letters into uppercase letters when sorting. Has the effect of creating a case-insensitive sort.
-n	Sort according to numeric value of a field.
-t	Change the field separator that sort uses to indicate the end of a field and the beginning of the next field. By default, sort uses whitespace to separate fields.
-u	If there are identical lines in the input to be sorted, display only one of the lines in the sorted output.
-r	Reverse the output of the sort.
-o	Send the results to an output file instead of to the screen. The name of the desired file should be supplied after the -o. This option has the same basic effect as redirecting the output to a file (more on input/output redirection later in this chapter).

If given more than one file on its command line, sort will concatenate the two files. If you use the -m option when supplying multiple files, sort will work faster. However, for the -m option to work properly, each input file should already be individually sorted.

8

WORKING WITH
THE SHELL

Replacing Strings with tr

You can use the tr command to search a text file for each occurrence of a certain string and replace it with a new string. The basic form of the command is as follows:

```
$ tr 'a-z' 'A-Z'
```

This command would replace all lowercase letters with uppercase letters. By default, tr gets its input from standard input (which is normally the keyboard), and sends its output to standard output (which is normally the screen). This is not very useful in most cases, so normally tr is used with input and output redirection. You will learn more about input and output redirection later, but here is the basic form of tr that will make it receive input from a file, and also direct output to a file:

```
$ tr 'a-z' 'A-Z' < file1 > file2
```

This command will read file1, replace all lowercase letters in the file with capital letters, and store the new file in file2.

You can also use the -d option with tr. In this case, tr will simply go through the file and delete each occurrence of a specified character. For example, the following will delete each occurrence of either uppercase A or uppercase B from file1 and store the results in file2:

```
$ tr -d 'AB' < file1 > file2
```

Showing Only Certain Parts of Lines in Text Files

Sometimes, you might be interested in only a certain part of a line in a file. You can use the cut command to cut only certain fields or parts thereof from a file for display. For example, suppose that you have a text file named phone.txt that contains the following simple address book:

```
Doe, John~105 Some Street~Anytown~NY~55555~123-555-1212
Doe, Jane~105 Some Street~Anytown~NY~55555~123-555-1212
James, Joe~251 Any Street~Sometown~CA~51111~321-555-1212
```

If you only want to see five characters of each line, you can use cut -c1-5 phone.txt:

```
Doe,
Doe,
James
```

A more useful application of cut is to cut only certain fields. By default, cut expects fields to be separated with tab characters. However, you can change the field separator to any character you want.

```
$ cut -f1 phone.txt
```

In this case, our address book text file doesn't use tab characters as field separators. So we can specify which character we want to use with the -d option.

```
$ cut -f1 -d'~' phone.txt
Doe, John
Doe, Jane
James, Joe
```

Here, we have told cut to display only the first field, and also told it that fields are delimited by tildes (~). Since the first tilde comes after the name, this will list only the name of the person and leave out the rest of the information.

Similarly, you can get a listing of all the users on your system by using cut on the /etc/passwd file:

```
$ cut -f1 -d':' /etc/passwd
frank
bob
alice
joe
simba
lee
```

Formatting Text with fmt

The fmt command formats text into nice 65-character lines (by default). This is most useful for preparing a text file to be sent through email, but it can be used for other simple formatting tasks as well. For example:

```
Until he extends his circle of compassion to include all living things, man
➥will not himself find peace.
-- Dr. Albert Schweitzer
```

The first line contains 105 characters, which is too long to display on one line of a character-based display (and even some graphical displays if the resolution is low). The result is that either the mail reading program will break the line in an odd place (such as in the middle of a word), or the text will go off the right end of the screen, forcing the reader to scroll right to read the rest of it. (If you've ever gotten one of those email messages that looks like it is just one long line, the mail program is not breaking lines when mail is written.)

```
$ fmt quote.txt
```

```
Until he extends his circle of compassion to include all living
things, man will not himself find peace.
-- Dr. Albert Schweitzer
```

This output could then either be redirected to a mail program or to a file that could then be mailed.

Here is an example that makes it easier to see the results of the `fmt` command:

```
Until he extends
his
circle of
compassion to
include all living
things
man
will not himself
find peace

-- Albert Schweitzer
```

It will look like this after being run through `fmt`:

```
Until he extends his circle of compassion to include all living
things man will not himself find peace

-- Dr. Albert Schweitzer
```

This section presented some of the most useful commands for working with text. By combining these various commands, you can do some rather sophisticated things such as analyzing Web server logs for trends and other such tasks. Of course, these commands have their limits. When you run into them, you might want to look into `sed` and `awk` for text processing. `sed` and `awk` are beyond the scope of this chapter, but you should be aware that they exist on your FreeBSD system, and can be used to handle some very sophisticated text processing tasks.

So, how can you combine the commands we used to do more useful things? That is where pipes and input/output redirection come in to play.

Pipes and Input/Output Redirection

One of the things that makes UNIX so powerful is the fact that output from one command can be used as the input to another command, and output can be redirected to other places. For example `ls`, which would normally display the directory list to the screen, can easily have that output redirected to a file like this:

```
$ ls > filelist.txt
```

This will create a text file called `filelist.txt` that contains the directory list of the current directory. This is known as *output redirection*.

If the directory list is too long to fit on the screen, I can pipe its output to the more pro-gram like this:

```
$ ls | more
```

You may recall that the more command displays text sent into it one screen at a time. This will prevent the directory list from scrolling off the screen before you get a chance to read it.

What if I want to mail the Albert Schweitzer quote to someone? Rather than type the quote into an email message, send the file that contained the quote as the input to the mail command. There are actually two ways you can do this, and both have the same effect. First, you can use the cat command, which would normally print the file to the screen, and pipe the output to the mail program like this:

```
$ cat quote.txt | mail useraddress
```

The following command uses input redirection to accomplish the same thing:

```
$ mail useraddress < quote,txt
```

In this case, you have told the mail command that instead of getting the message to send from the keyboard, it should get it from the file quote.txt. Although both of these com-mands accomplish the same thing, the second one would be more efficient because it doesn't have to call the cat program. Instead, it lets the shell handle redirection.

You can do both input and output redirection in the same command. For example, the tr command we used previously tells tr to get its input from file1, and send its output to file2:

```
$ tr 'a-z' 'A-Z' < file1 > file2
```

(If you ever get confused about whether to use < or >, remember that the arrow points in the direction that the data is going.)

You can combine multiple pipes into a single command:

```
$ cut -f1 -d' ' access.log | sort | uniq -c | more
```

This is a quick-and-dirty way of extracting useful information from an NCSA-compliant Web server log file. Specifically, this information would extract field 1, which contains the network address of each hit, pipe it to sort, and then pipe the sorted output to uniq -c. This counts the number of occurrences of identical lines and then displays each unique line, preceded by the number of times that line was repeated and then pipes the output to more, so you can read it without it scrolling off the screen. Specifically, this command would tell me how many hits each network address generated on my Web server.

8

WORKING WITH
THE SHELL

You can also combine pipes and input/output redirection:

```
$ cut -f1 -d' ' /var/log/httpd-access.log | sort | uniq -c > hits.txt
```

This is the same as the first command, except that it records the information in a file instead of displaying it on the screen.

A creative use of pipes and input/output redirection is where the power of FreeBSD is really unleashed.

Command Completion and History Editing

Now that we have seen some of the basic commands available at the command line, let's examine a few of the advanced features of the more modern shells.

If you're not sure whether bash (or any program) is installed on the system, you can easily figure it out by taking advantage of the built-in command-completion features of tcsh and other feature-rich shells. Type enough of the command name for it to be unique—the first two or three letters, just to see how it works—and then press Tab. If you've entered enough of the program name for it to be uniquely determinable, the rest of the command will complete itself.

If you haven't specified enough of the program name for the shell to figure out what you want, you will get a "bell" signal (which will beep at you or give you another kind of alert, depending on your terminal program). You can then get a listing of all possible completions to the command, either by pressing Tab again (in bash) or with Ctrl+D (in tcsh). Note that Ctrl+D is also the keystroke for deleting the character to the right of the cursor, and also (if entered on a blank line) for logging out of a tcsh session—so be careful!

```
$ bas[Tab]
basename  bash      bashbug
```

Tab-completion also works on filenames:

```
$ ls show[Tab]
showchars.cgi*     showfavepics.cgi* showprofile.cgi*  showuploads.cgi*
showcomments.cgi* showpopular.cgi*  showrequests.cgi*
```

History editing is also a fundamental feature of the advanced shells. As you enter commands, each one is held in a buffer for the duration of your current login session, up to a limit set in your shell configuration file (100 by default in `tcsh`). You can scroll up and down through the commands you've entered with the up and down arrow keys; then, either press Enter to re-execute whatever command you've selected, or edit it with the other arrow keys to correct mistakes or alter the desired result.

Each command is also entered into a history file in your home directory: `.history` for `tcsh` and `.bash_history` for `bash`. This allows your command history to span even beyond your current login session, back into previous ones; however, although the history file is readable only by its owner, any user might still consider it a security risk. After all, who wants to have a file sitting around with a record of all the commands he's entered? If that's the case, the history file can safely be deleted without any detrimental effects other than commands from previous login sessions not being available in scrollback. A user can delete his history file by entering `rm ~/.history` or `rm ~/.bash_history`, depending on the shell.

8

WORKING WITH
THE SHELL

Administering FreeBSD

PART
III

CHAPTER 9

The FreeBSD Filesystem

To understand how FreeBSD operates, it is essential to have a clear idea of how the system manages files, and the critical differences between FreeBSD's method and the way other operating systems do it.

FreeBSD uses *FFS*, the BSD Fast File System. It is a common misconception that modern BSD UNIXs use *UFS* (*Universal* or *UNIX File System*, depending on who you ask). It is a common source of confusion because many of the tools we'll be discussing in this chapter (such as mount) refer to UFS as the default filesystem type. This isn't the case. FFS is colloquially called UFS by many, and you can do the same as long as you remember that the "true" UFS was used only in very early BSD-style UNIXs, and is no longer what you're dealing with in FreeBSD.

FFS is the typical filesystem type used in FreeBSD, OpenBSD, NetBSD, and others—including Mac OS X (whose foundation, called Darwin, is based on FreeBSD and the core BSD). Linux uses Ext2FS most commonly, Windows NT uses NTFS, and Windows 95/98/Me use VFAT; this information will be useful to know later in this chapter when we discuss mounting filesystems from other operating systems.

> **Note**
>
> A fuller reference and discussion of the filesystem types used in the computing world can be found at `http://www.penguin.cz/~mhi/fs/`.

The FreeBSD Directory Structure

If you have used any UNIX or UNIX-like operating system, FreeBSD's directory structure will undoubtedly look familiar (see Figure 9.1).

However, there are some key differences between the FreeBSD filesystem and the one used by Linux, and between those from Solaris and other UNIXs. For users coming from a Windows or Macintosh background, the directory structure can be extremely cryptic. As with much in the UNIX realm, the original reasons for such things as the quirky traditional naming scheme are lost in the mists of time, but we can try to shed a little light on it—or at least to become familiar enough with its quirks that we can be comfortable using the system (see Table 9.1).

If you issue an ls / command, you will see the top-level view of the FreeBSD filesystem, including the following items, as well as probably a few more. Directories are indicated with a following slash (/), symbolic links with an @ sign, and executables with an asterisk (*).

FIGURE 9.1

The FreeBSD filesystem, showing part of the hierarchical structure beginning at "/", or the root directory.

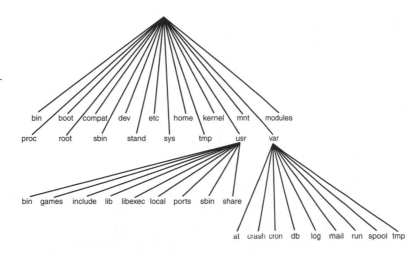

TABLE 9.1 Key Elements of the FreeBSD Filesystem

Directory	Purpose
bin/	Statically linked binaries are contained here. These can be used even when you're doing an emergency boot and don't have access to any dynamically linked programs or any filesystems other than /.
boot/	This directory contains configuration files and executables that are used during boot. In addition, in FreeBSD 5.0, this directory also contains the kernel. The kernel manages all devices and handles networking, along with a host of other tasks. See chapter 17, "Kernel Configuration", for more information.
compat@	This is a symlink to directory structures, which provides compatibility with other operating systems, such as Linux.
dev/	A special directory. Files in here are mostly devices, which are special file types that give programs an interface into any devices that the kernel supports.
etc/	Long ago, this was merely a directory for random files that didn't fit elsewhere. It is now where most system-wide configuration files go, including your user (password) databases and startup scripts.
home@	Possibly a plain directory; possibly a symbolic link to /usr/home, depending on your installation. All regular users' home directories are contained here.
mnt/	An empty directory, provided for your convenience as a mount point if you need to mount another disk.

TABLE 9.1 continued

Directory	Purpose
modules/	Loadable kernel modules are here.
proc/	The procfs, or process filesystem. This is an interface to the process table. Used for convenience by some programs, but not essential to the operation of the system (it can safely be unmounted).
root/	The root user's home directory. It's not in /home for security reasons, and so it will be available during an emergency boot.
sbin/	System binaries that are statically linked. These programs differ from the ones in /bin in that they generally alter the system's behavior, whereas the /bin programs are simply user tools.
stand/	Contains a set of hard-linked programs that provide a "mini-FreeBSD" environment during system installation and emergencies when running in standalone mode. The only program you will likely be interested in is sysinstall, which was covered in Chapter 2, "Installing FreeBSD."
sys@	A link to the kernel sources if you installed them.
tmp/	Temporary files. Any user can write files into this directory.
usr/	The gateway to the rest of the system—dynamically linked programs, user files, and programs you installed yourself. In upcoming chapters, we will spend most of our time here.
var/	Variable files. These include runtime files used by programs, log files, spool directories, and other items that change with the normal operation of the system.

These files and directories make up the core of a FreeBSD system. However, there are some important features to point out regarding the differences between the FreeBSD directory structure and that of similar operating systems, such as Linux.

FreeBSD's structure is tightly controlled, and the clearest rule is that "Anything installed by the administrator goes into /usr/local". Although other systems might allow user-installed programs the freedom to install files wherever they want, FreeBSD maintains strict structural guidelines in its ported programs and packages (see Chapter 15, "Installing Additional Software"). Although a program might, by default, put its libraries in /var/lib and its configuration files into /etc, FreeBSD patches (modifies) the installation scripts so that the files would go into /usr/local/lib and /usr/local/etc, respectively. In fact, all configuration files for any software you might install will go into /usr/local/etc; and if the program installs a startup script to be launched on boot, the script is placed in /usr/local/etc/rc.d. Anything in that directory is run at boot time, after the scripts in the analogous /etc/rc.d (the base system's startup scripts) are run.

The advantage of a structure this carefully controlled is that a FreeBSD system is relatively easy to maintain, and especially easy to re-create on a new machine (if you're upgrading to new hardware, for instance). You could theoretically copy the entire /usr/local directory tree from one machine to another, and everything would work as on the previous machine. However, this is a risky proposition, and there will undoubtedly be unforeseen snags. Still, this is an ideal toward which FreeBSD strives.

An obvious disadvantage, though, is that if you're used to Linux or Solaris, and trying to port a program from there to FreeBSD, it may cause you some pain in fixing the expected paths. For instance, if you have programs written in Python on Linux, in which the Python interpreter is installed as /usr/bin/python, the programs will not run on FreeBSD because Python is not part of the base installation and is therefore installed as /usr/local/bin/python. This can be easily fixed for one or two files, but migrating an installation with hundreds of such programs can quickly become painful. In the interest of cross-platform compatibility, it may turn out to be simplest to violate FreeBSD's structural guidelines by making a symbolic link /usr/bin/python to point to /usr/local/bin/python.

A still more detailed description of FreeBSD's filesystem layout can be found by entering man hier.

Monitoring Filesystem Usage

One concept with UNIX-style operating systems that is quite foreign to Windows users is the idea of mount points. In Windows/DOS, each disk in your system is assigned a drive letter (such as C:), and each drive has its own independent filesystem. For example, a machine with two hard drives and a CD-ROM drive has C:, D:, and E: drives that the user can switch between. In UNIX, the concept is a bit different. There is only one system-wide directory structure, and all disks in the system are mounted at different points in the structure. An appropriate analogy would be that a Windows system resembles a vineyard, with a row of similar trees or vines; whereas a UNIX system is more like a single large tree with smaller trees grafted onto it at the trunk and on branches, all forming a single hierarchical structure (see Figure 4.2).

The advantage of this type of structure is that it's really easy to add more disk space to your system; to increase the pool of storage available to some part of the hierarchy, just mount a new disk or partition there (as we will demonstrate later in this chapter). However, a corresponding disadvantage is that it's much harder in a filesystem like this to move the entire contents of a disk wholesale to another disk. In Windows or Mac OS, you can move your entire system to a new larger disk with a simple drag-and-drop operation because each disk is a separate filesystem. This task is a more cumbersome one in FreeBSD. The hierarchical structure is better suited to a server machine with a long

9

lifetime on the same hardware than to a desktop computer where the data often outlive the hardware.

FIGURE 9.2

Diagrams of the FreeBSD (UNIX) and Windows filesystem structures, using the "tree" analogy.

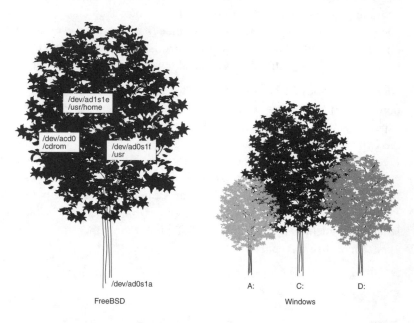

/dev/ad1s1e
/usr/home

/dev/acd0
/cdrom

/dev/ad0s1f
/usr

/dev/ad0s1a

FreeBSD

A: C: D:

Windows

df (Disk Free) command

The df command (which stands for "disk free," historically) is the most direct way of finding out the status of your system's disk usage; a df reading is part of every daily status check (more on this in Chapter 14, "Performance Monitoring, Process Control, and Job Automation"), and it nicely encapsulates all the relevant information about your different filesystems and their respective device names.

Enter the command df. You will get output similar to this:

```
Filesystem  1K-blocks     Used    Avail Capacity  Mounted on
/dev/ad0s1a     49583    28427    17190     62%    /
/dev/ad0s1f   4254901  1959405  1955104     50%    /usr
/dev/ad0s1e     19815    12058     6172     66%    /var
procfs              4        4        0    100%    /proc
```

Each disk slice or partition is regarded as a "filesystem", and can be mounted at any point in the directory structure. The previous output shows that this system has three slices on its main IDE disk (/dev/ad0), and that they are mounted at /, /usr, and /var. This is the default setup for a FreeBSD installation. Note that the / file system has only about 50MB allocated to it, and /var only has about 20MB; all the rest of the disk is allocated to /usr. This means that the system defaults expect very little to ever be placed into the directories other than /usr or /var, and still less to go into /var.

> **Caution**
>
> Allocating a small /var slice can be dangerous because log files traditionally go into /var/log; many administrators choose to move /var to /usr/var and create a /var symlink to point to it because log files can grow to be extremely large. We will discuss the pros and cons of different styles of partitioning in Chapter 19, "Understanding Hard Disks and Filesystems."

du (Disk Usage) command

Aside from the df command, you also need to have a more specific method for monitoring disk usage, especially if you're running a network server and you have a lot of users, any of whom might suddenly dump gigabytes of data into their home directories. For this, the tool of choice is du ("disk usage").

```
# du -d 1 /home/
22572     /home/bob
9         /home/fred
31        /home/alice
1520      /home/tom
66211     /home/pat
```

The du command will tell you the size, recursively, of every directory below the one you're currently in (or the one you specify on the command line). You can specify the -d switch along with a number, which will tell du to recurse only down to that depth (a necessity unless you want to be flooded with output). You can also use the -s option, which forces "summary" mode—you only get a single line of output, listing the aggregate size of everything in the directory you specified. More options to du, including controls for the way it handles symbolic links, can be found in man du.

All this, of course, places the burden of watching the filesystems on you, the administrator. Wouldn't it be great if we could rely on the system to keep tabs on these things for us? Fortunately, we can—with quotas. Quotas will be discussed at the end of the chapter, but there are a few important topics to cover first.

Mounting and Unmounting FreeBSD Filesystems

Now, we will see how the versatility of UNIX-style filesystems can really shine. Let's say that your system outgrows its single disk (/dev/ad0), and you install another disk as the primary slave so that it appears as /dev/ad1. (A SCSI disk would be available as

/dev/da0, and so on.) After you partition and label the disk (a procedure that is described in detail in Chapter 19), you will have one or more new filesystems you can add to your system's directory structure at any point, like grafting a new branch onto the side of a tree.

mount Command

Suppose, for instance, that you have a system in which you have been adding new users left and right, and they keep uploading large files into their home directories; you notice (through the use of df and du) that the /usr partition is almost full, almost entirely because of /usr/home. What you want to do is add another pool of storage space, and dedicate it to your users and their home directories.

You bought a new 50GB disk, and you divided it into three partitions within the single FreeBSD slice—they are available as /dev/ad1s1e (100MB), /dev/ad1s1f (8GB), and /dev/ad1s1g (40GB). You made the third partition the largest because it's the one you want to make into the new home for your users; the other two partitions are chunks of space you want to add to other parts of the system. But for now, all you're interested in doing is turning /home into a new 40GB partition for nothing except users' home directories.

Right now, /home is most likely a symbolic link to /usr/home, so you will first want to use rm /home to get rid of the symlink. (The actual /usr/home directory that the symlink points to is not touched by this.) If /home in your system is not a symlink, but instead a plain directory, do something like mv /home /home.old to rename it for this process.

Now, create a mount point for the new filesystem. Mount points (or nodes) must be plain directories; they don't need to be empty, but after a device is mounted on a non-empty directory, whatever was originally located in that directory will no longer be accessible. (To have them simultaneously accessible, union filesystems are needed, but this feature is not fully supported as of this writing.) So, to create the new mount point, issue mkdir /home.

We're now ready to mount the new filesystem. For standard FreeBSD filesystems, this is done with the mount command. Our 40GB partition is labeled as /dev/ad1s1g, so give the following command:

```
# mount /dev/ad1s1g /home
```

If the command executes without any errors, you should be able to use the new file system immediately. Check df to see if it worked:

```
Filesystem  1K-blocks    Used    Avail Capacity  Mounted on
/dev/ad0s1a    49583    28427    17190    62%     /
```

```
/dev/ad0s1g   39245453   3362491   32119340    12%   /home
/dev/ad0s1f    4254901    892410    3140012    22%   /usr
/dev/ad0s1e      19815     12058       6172    66%   /var
procfs               4         4          0   100%   /proc
```

Looks like it's ready to go! You can now move the files from /usr/home (or /home.old, depending) into the new /home filesystem, and your users will be free to upload to their hearts' content.

It isn't always this easy, however. Mounting filesystems is one of the areas of system administration that have the most potential pitfalls for the unwary. You may get an error message about "Incorrect super block", for instance, or the even less informative "Invalid argument". These messages usually stem from improperly specifying the name of the device on the mount command line; the naming conventions used by the FreeBSD labeling conventions can lead to serious confusion. A filesystem might be labeled as /dev/ad1s1e, /dev/acd0, or /dev/ad3s1, depending on whether it is being addressed in "slice mode" or "dedicated mode"; and certain device names with suffixes can be interchangeable with shorter names. This will all be discussed thoroughly in Chapter 19.

mount has a -f option, which will force a mount operation. However, if a filesystem won't mount, it's usually for a good reason, and it's a much better idea to find the cause for any error and fix it, rather than use the -f option. Some of these reasons might include an unformatted disk, a filesystem of an unrecognized type, or a "dirty" filesystem that was not shut down properly, and might have some inconsistencies that must be repaired using fsck (as we will see later in this chapter) before the filesystem can be mounted.

One other useful argument to note is the options field, in which you can specify any of a large list of code words (flags), separated by commas. Most useful are the ones specifying whether the filesystem is read-only or read/write; it is read/write by default, but you can use the -r or rdonly options to make it read-only. See man mount for a full list of mount options.

The umount Command

There will also come the time when you have to unmount a filesystem; the command for this is umount (rather than "unmount"). To unmount the /home filesystem, issue the following command:

```
# umount /home
```

You can also use umount /dev/ad1s1g to accomplish the same result, or even umount -a to unmount everything except for the root filesystem.

Unmounting filesystems is a much simpler procedure than mounting them, with only one major complicating factor: For a filesystem to be unmounted, it cannot be in use. This means that to unmount filesystems such as /usr and /var, you will probably have to be in single-user mode. For the /home partition in the example in the previous section, any connected users will likely be in their home directories, so they will have to be kicked off the system before /home can be unmounted. This is what leads to the most common surprise most users find when first experimenting with mount and umount: *You can't be inside a filesystem you're trying to unmount!* If you are, you'll get a "Device busy" error message. To be safe, be in the habit of entering cd / before you attempt to umount anything.

Like mount, umount has a -f option to force an unmount. But again, it's best to avoid using it unless absolutely necessary; filesystem operations have the potential to destabilize the system if done in a messy manner.

Mounting and Unmounting Filesystems from Other Operating Systems

This is all well and good for standard FreeBSD filesystems. But what if you need to mount a disk from a Linux box, or from a Windows 98 or NT machine? You can do that. FreeBSD supports the following filesystems in the GENERIC (default) kernel (see Table 9.2).

TABLE 9.2   Filesystems Supported in the GENERIC Kernel

Filesystem	Name
FFS	Berkeley Fast Filesystem
MFS	Memory Filesystem
NFS	Network Filesystem
MSDOSFS	MS-DOS Filesystem
CD9660	ISO 9660 (CD-ROM) Filesystem
PROCFS	Process Filesystem

There is also support for the following other filesystems, but they need to be compiled into a custom kernel in order to work (see Chapter 17).

TABLE 9.3   Additional Available Filesystems

Filesystem	Name
FDESC	File Descriptor Filesystem
KERNFS	Kernel Filesystem
NTFS	NT Filesystem
NULLFS	NULL Filesystem
NWFS	NetWare Filesystem
PORTAL	Portal Filesystem
UMAPFS	UID map Filesystem
UNION	Union Filesystem
CODA	CODA Filesystem
EXT2FS	Ext2 Filesystem (Linux)

Some of these latter filesystems are more stable than others; as we saw earlier, union filesystems are available as an option, but are only partially in a working state (and can damage your system), so it is not recommended that you use it unless absolutely necessary. Ext2FS and NTFS support are also given caveats about their completeness and stability. Filesystems that are not built into the GENERIC kernel, in general, are not included for a reason.

The ideal circumstance for a filesystem type that isn't part of the existing kernel is that it will be available as a kernel module in /modules; if it is, as many of the previous filesystems are, it will be automatically loaded when you try to mount the filesystem. At the time of this writing, these available modules include CODA, PORTAL, NWFS, NULL, NTFS, UNION, and some others that are already compiled into the GENERIC kernel and are provided in /modules for compatibility.

If you're mounting a filesystem that is supported in the default kernel (MSDOSFS, for example), or if you decide to accept the risks and plunge ahead with mounting a filesystem that isn't initially built in, you'll find that FreeBSD does provide some handy tools for doing the actual mounting. You'll find the following tools in /sbin:

```
mount_cd9660*      mount_mfs*        mount_portal*
mount_devfs*       mount_msdos*      mount_procfs*
mount_ext2fs*      mount_nfs*        mount_std*
mount_fdesc*       mount_ntfs*       mount_umap*
mount_kernfs*      mount_null*       mount_union*
mount_linprocfs*   mount_nwfs*
```

Each of these variations on mount corresponds to one of the supported filesystems, and operates in the same way as mount; the idea is that these mount_* tools serve as an extension to the -t option to mount. The -t option recognizes only a couple of internal filesystem types; if you give it an unrecognized argument, it will execute the corresponding tool from the previous list. For example, if you say mount -t nfs /mnt, it will actually execute mount_nfs /mnt. Knowing this, it is often easier simply to run the latter tool directly.

> **Note**
>
> A further note on stability and completeness issues with the not-fully-supported filesystem types: Read the man mount_* pages. Each one will give a good account of what is deficient in that filesystem's support; man mount_ntfs discusses the lack of full write capabilities and support for compressed files, and man mount_union warns about the feature's limited functionality and potential to damage data. Be informed!

Mounting a Windows/MS-DOS Filesystem

Let's first look at mounting a Windows 98 disk, which will be MSDOSFS for FreeBSD's purposes. The command we will be using is mount_msdos. This command can take some special options, which we do not need to cover fully here; examples are -W and -L, which control the locale-based character mapping for the long filenames associated with FAT32/VFAT filesystems. We can content ourselves for this example with the default settings, which assume ISO 8859-1 encoding and that you will read and write to the filesystem as root.

```
# mount_msdos /dev/ad1s1 /mnt
```

Bear in mind that for reasons that will be discussed in Chapter 19, what DOS and Linux systems call "partitions" are called "slices" in FreeBSD, to avoid confusing them with traditional BSD "partitions" (which are subdivisions of slices). So, because our Windows 98 filesystem on /dev/ad1s1 is effectively using a "slice" rather than a "partition", we can address it simply by its slice number rather than specifying additional suffixes, as described earlier in the section about mounting standard FreeBSD filesystems (where we used /dev/ad1s1g).

If you're using an extended DOS partition, you may get an "Invalid argument" error. If this happens, note that extended DOS partitions are numbered beginning with 5, so your device name will be /dev/ad1s5.

You can perform additional tricks when mounting MS-DOS filesystems, such as mounting it as a non-root UID/GID, mounting it with a permissions mask for controlling users' access to the filesystem's contents, listing it with long versus short filenames, and so forth. Refer to man mount_msdos for full documentation on these options.

Tip

A Windows floppy disk contains filenames that can be in the standard MS-DOS "8.3" short format or in the Windows 95/98 long format, which is derived from metadata in the filesystem. If you mount a Windows floppy disk using mount_msdos, FreeBSD attempts to find any of these long filenames on the disk. If it finds any, it uses that format to list and interact with the files. However, if it finds none of these long filenames, but it does find short ones, it will use the short format. To force mount_msdos to use the long format, use the -l option; the -s option forces the use of the short format.

Mounting a Linux Filesystem

Most Linux systems use Ext2FS. Because Ext2FS is not built in to the GENERIC kernel, this task involves an extra step. (Ext2FS support will eventually be available in a loadable kernel module, but not as of the time of this writing.) Chapter 17 discusses the steps involved in compiling and installing a custom kernel; the line you want to add is the following:

```
options    EXT2FS
```

After your system is up and running with the new kernel, you can use the following command:

```
# mount_ext2fs /dev/ad1s1 /mnt
```

Other than the kernel support, mount_ext2fs behaves almost identically to standard mount, so the surprises should be minimal.

Using fdisk to Gather Partition Information

You can determine what filesystem you're working with by using the fdisk command:

```
# fdisk /dev/ad1
******* Working on device /dev/ad1 *******
parameters extracted from in-core disklabel are:
cylinders=1247 heads=255 sectors/track=63 (16065 blks/cyl)
```

```
Figures below won't work with BIOS for partitions not in cyl 1
parameters to be used for BIOS calculations are:
cylinders=1247 heads=255 sectors/track=63 (16065 blks/cyl)

Media sector size is 512
Warning: BIOS sector numbering starts with sector 1
Information from DOS bootblock is:
The data for partition 1 is:
sysid 131,(Linux filesystem)
    start 63, size 2104452 (1027 Meg), flag 0
        beg: cyl 0/ sector 1/ head 1;
        end: cyl 130/ sector 63/ head 254
The data for partition 2 is:
sysid 130,(Linux swap or Solaris x86)
    start 2104515, size 787185 (384 Meg), flag 0
        beg: cyl 131/ sector 1/ head 0;
        end: cyl 179/ sector 63/ head 254
The data for partition 3 is:
sysid 131,(Linux filesystem)
    start 2891700, size 17141355 (8369 Meg), flag 0
        beg: cyl 180/ sector 1/ head 0;
        end: cyl 1023/ sector 63/ head 254
The data for partition 4 is:
<UNUSED>
```

For each partition (or slice, as FreeBSD has it), there's a "sysid" number. 131 is an Ext2FS Linux filesystem, 165 is FreeBSD—and everything else `fdisk` recognizes can be found in `/usr/src/sbin/i386/fdisk/fdisk.c`.

Mounting and Unmounting CD-ROM and Floppy-Based Filesystems

Now that you've had some experience mounting different foreign filesystems, it should be a snap moving on to CD-ROMs and floppy drives. CD-ROMs will usually be mounted as CD9660, but floppies will generally either be FFS (the FreeBSD standard) or MS-DOS.

Mounting CDs and Floppies

For CD-ROMs, the main trick is to determine the device name. IDE drives will be of the form `/dev/acd0c`, SCSI drives will be of the form `/dev/cd0c`, and miscellaneous types of non-standard drives have other prefixes. As for the suffix, use "c" to indicate that you are addressing the entire disk in "dedicated" mode.

Tip

See `http://www.FreeBSD.org/handbook/disks-naming.html` for the current reference to disk names.

```
# mount_cd9660 /dev/acd0c /cdrom
```

Mounting a floppy disk is also fairly straightforward. The device name you will want to use is /dev/fd0; the kernel contains a confusing entry for fdc0, which refers to the actual ISA floppy disk controller device; but fd0 and fd1 are the device names for the drives that hang off the controller.

```
# mount /dev/fd0 /floppy
# mount_msdos /dev/fd0 /floppy
```

Be careful: Floppy disks can be write-protected and CD-ROMs are physically read-only, but FreeBSD does not check at mount time whether they are writable or not! If you mount a write-protected floppy without specifying the -r or rdonly options, you will get I/O errors whenever anything tries to write to the disk—and what happens as a result can vary with the stability of whatever program is doing the writing. Anything from a simple console error message to a complete hang of the system can happen. So, if you must mount a write-protected floppy or CD-ROM from the command line, make sure to specify the -r or rdonly option to prevent programs from *trying* to write to it!

Unmounting CDs and Floppies

The other tricky thing about CD-ROMs and floppies is that because they are removable devices, there exists the potential to remove the disk while the system still thinks it is mounted. Windows (for comparison's sake) dynamically mounts and refreshes the devices whenever they are accessed for reading or writing, and Mac OS keeps track of such things by having disk mounting and physical insertion/ejection controlled entirely by software, and therefore interdependent. FreeBSD (and other x86 UNIXs) do not have the latter luxury or the former sophistication, so you must shoulder the burden of making sure that the system's impression of its mounted disks is an accurate one.

Most CD-ROM drives will lock when the operating system has the disk mounted because they have soft eject mechanisms; it will not respond when you press the eject button until you have unmounted the device. Floppies, however, can be ejected on a whim, and even CD-ROMs can be ejected through determination and the use of a paper clip. If a mounted device is ejected without being properly unmounted, and some program tries to read from or write to the device, the same kind of system destabilization can occur as described previously.

The bottom line is this: Always remember to umount /cdrom or umount /floppy before ejecting the disk. Your system will thank you.

Other Removable Media

The field of removable media is becoming more complex every day, with USB and FireWire-based external media and rewritable CD and DVD drives coming into the market at an ever-increasing pace. Zip drives and their relatives have been around for some time; FreeBSD supports parallel-port Zip drives as the vp0 device and USB Zip drives as the umass devices. But these are due soon to be joined by dozens of new devices, each with its complications regarding writability, removability, and mountability. However, we have now laid the groundwork for them by gaining an understanding of how to deal with CD-ROMs and floppies—their ancestors.

Understanding the `/etc/fstab` File

You may be asking whether there is a shortcut to all this mounting—a way to program recipes for all the mountable devices on a system, since chances are that all the flexibility offered by the mount tools becomes less useful over the lifetime of a system. After you figure out the commands needed to mount your second IDE hard drive, your NFS volume from across the network, your MS-DOS floppy, and your SCSI CD-ROM, do you really have to remember those commands every time you want to mount them? No, there is indeed a better way. That way is the /etc/fstab file.

Take a look at the file now, using cat /etc/fstab:

```
# Device           Mountpoint      FStype   Options      Dump      Pass#
/dev/ad0s1b        none            swap     sw           0         0
/dev/ad0s1a        /               ufs      rw           1         1
/dev/ad0s1g        /home           ufs      rw           2         2
/dev/ad0s1f        /var            ufs      rw           2         2
/dev/ad0s1e        /usr            ufs      rw           2         2
/dev/acd0c         /cdrom          cd9660   ro,noauto    0         0
/dev/fd0           /floppy         msdos    rw,noauto    0         0
proc               /proc           procfs   rw           0         0
```

This file tells the system everything it needs to know about a given mount point: what device attaches to it, what filesystem type to expect, the mount options, and in what order it should perform filesystem checks when the system is booted. The `fstab` file is closely interrelated with the `mount` command; used in conjunction, the two tools can make filesystem management a relative breeze.

The main function of the `fstab` file is to give the system a profile of mounted devices that can all be activated at once at boot time. With all your mount points specified here, you can issue the command `mount -a` to mount them all. This is what happens during boot, when the system goes through its filesystem checks; the system runs `fsck -p` (to "preen" the filesystems, making sure they are all marked "clean"—more on this later in this chapter). It then runs `mount -a -t nonfs` to mount all but the NFS filesystems listed in `/etc/fstab`.

Beyond this function, though, is an even more convenient effect of this setup. After a mount point is specified in `/etc/fstab`, you no longer need to remember the `mount` command necessary to bring it online; now, the only thing you have to know is the name of the mount point:

```
# mount /home
```

This reads in all the necessary information from the `fstab` file. It knows that the device you want is `/dev/ad0s1g`, that it's a UFS (well, FFS) filesystem, and that you want it mounted read/write. Similarly, to mount a floppy disk, all you need to enter now is the following:

```
# mount /floppy
```

Now, it's starting to look almost user-friendly!

The `noauto` option on the `/cdrom` and `/floppy` entries tells `mount` that these filesystems should not be mounted at boot time. As with NFS resources, there is no guarantee that a CD-ROM or floppy disk will be available when the system boots, so the `noauto` option prevents `mount` from spending pointless time trying to mount a disk that isn't there. It doesn't prevent you from easily mounting it later, however; the previous command is all you need.

You can specify any of the `mount` options in the fourth column of the `fstab` file that are applicable to the filesystem in question. For instance, anything listed in `man mount` can be used, as well as anything in the filesystem's `man mount_*` page if it's a non-standard filesystem type.

The rightmost column in /etc/fstab, the "Pass#" field, is a flag for fsck (a tool we will examine in a moment); numbers above zero indicate the order in which the filesystems should be checked. The root filesystem has a pass number of 1, meaning that it is checked first; mounts with a pass number of 2 are checked next, in as parallel a manner as the hardware permits. A pass number of zero means that the filesystem should not be checked; this is what you want for CD-ROMs, floppies, swap partitions, and other resources that either can't become corrupted or that don't matter if they do become corrupted.

To the left of the pass number is the dump level number. This is for the benefit of the dump command, which is a venerable UNIX backup utility that operates based on levels. The dump level number tells dump at what level to trigger a backup for that filesystem when it is run. For example, filesystems with a dump level number of 1 are backed up only when the dump level is 1 or lower (a dump level of zero means "full backup of all filesystems"). Note that specifying zero in /etc/fstab omits that filesystem from ever being dumped.

A fuller discussion of backup and restoration procedures can be found in Chapter 20, "FreeBSD Survival Guide," in which dump will be covered in more detail, along with other backup/mirroring methods such as CVSup.

Checking and Repairing Filesystems with fsck

The fsck program, which stands for File System Consistency checK, is the equivalent of Microsoft ScanDisk and other disk utilities, at least as far as its role in the boot process and its interactive nature go. Its purpose is primarily to run at boot time just before mounting the filesystems out of /etc/fstab, and to make sure that all the filesystems are "clean" and eligible for mounting. This is the "preen" mode that is called with the -p option. But it also exists to repair any inconsistencies that it finds and to clean filesystems that have not been marked "clean" by a proper shutdown method.

The most likely place you'll encounter fsck is at boot time, no matter what role it's going to play in your life. In the happiest circumstances, it runs invisibly just after all the devices have been identified, and all you see are a few lines like this:

```
/dev/ad0s1e:
103469 files, 858450 used, 9066025 free
(25777 frags, 1130031 blocks, 0.3% fragmentation)
```

> **Note**
>
> Don't worry about the "fragmentation" figure that fsck prints out. It looks pretty dire, but be aware that even fragmentation of 2–3% (which is the highest you'll likely see) is miniscule compared to the kind of fragmentation that occurs under traditional desktop operating systems. It is not unusual to see a DOS/VFAT disk with 50% or more fragmentation; that is why defragmenting utilities sell so well in the desktop market. UNIX filesystems, however, are designed with mechanisms to keep related sectors together on the fly, so fragmentation is kept to a vanishingly small level. You won't ever need to defragment a UNIX hard drive. See "Blocks, Files, and Inodes," later in this chapter, for a closer look at the mechanics of data storage and fragmentation.

Where you may run into more trouble is if the system has not been shut down cleanly—if power has failed, or if someone has hit the power switch without running shutdown first. UNIX filesystems keep track of their structural information by writing that *metadata* to the disk in a synchronous manner, which may take multiple write cycles. If the system goes down while it's in the middle of the write sequence, the metadata becomes corrupted, and the filesystem cannot be used until it is made consistent again. This is what fsck is for.

If a filesystem is brought up in this "unclean" state, fsck drops into its investigative mode. It then walks through the filesystem block by block, examining the metadata and making sure it is consistent. This can take a very long time, depending on the size of the filesystem and the speed of the disk. When it finds an inconsistency that it cannot repair automatically while guaranteeing data integrity (see man fsck for details on these), fsck prompts you about whether you want to fix it. In most cases, you do. However, if you are being prompted, it's most likely that the inconsistency is so severe that you will have lost some data—usually the file or files that were being written at the time of the crash, which tends to mean that data loss is fairly small.

After fsck finishes running, you may be dropped to a # prompt; type boot to continue booting or reboot to go through the entire boot process again. This might be a good idea, just to make sure it will come up cleanly without intervention—you don't want to lock the server in a cabinet and drive away, only to have it not come up the next time it crashes.

9

THE FREEBSD FILESYSTEM

Boot time is not the only place for fsck, though. It can also be run from the command line at any time on mounted filesystems, although it's a bad idea to do so when the system is fully up and running! It's important that the filesystem in question not be changing while you're trying to give it a consistency check. If you have to run fsck on one of your system's main devices, a useful precaution to take is to drop to single-user mode:

```
# shutdown +5
```

This will close down multiuser mode in five minutes from when you issue the command. Naturally, everything from this point on has to be done at the physical console. You can't remotely administer the system in single-user mode!

With the system in this quiescent state, you can now fsck to your heart's content. This may be necessary if during runtime you find a message in your dmesg output (part of the daily monitoring scripts that get sent to root) that says it found a bad inode or file descriptor, and you want to go directly to the root of the problem without rebooting. After you run fsck on one or all of your devices (use syntax such as fsck -p /dev/ad1s1g), you can then simply exit from the single-user shell (type exit) to bring up the rest of the multiuser system.

One case where it is safe to use fsck while still in multiuser mode is if you're trying to mount a second disk with a non-critical or new filesystem that you're trying to add. The fsck that runs at boot time will only check the filesystems that are listed in /etc/fstab; rather than adding the new device to the fstab file and rebooting, you can simply try to mount the device; if it fails, telling you that you need to run fsck, do so with the syntax shown previously. Then try mounting the disk again. This can be done safely in multiuser mode, since nobody will be writing to a device that hasn't been mounted!

Journaling Filesystems and Soft Updates

Many different solutions to the synchronous-write issue have been developed. You will hear about journaling (or logging) filesystems, which keep a log of all metadata writes before they are executed; this dramatically speeds up fsck, since it no longer needs to comb the entire filesystem[md]it knows where the inconsistencies are and how to fix them.

FreeBSD does not include support for journaling filesystems; what it does have, though, is Soft Updates. While journaling filesystems work by maintaining a log file of write actions, Soft Updates (which is built into the GENERIC, or default, kernel as of FreeBSD 5.0) is a potentially superior technique which uses pre-calculated, ordered writes to eliminate the need for an external log while still protecting the integrity of the metadata, providing filesystem consistency as good as or better than journaling offers. It has performance advantages over journaling as well; a filesystem can be brought up immediately at boot time, and the consistency checking is done afterwards through the use of automated snapshots in a background task.

In FreeBSD 5.0, a daemon called `diskcheckd` supports Soft Updates. Enabled by default, `diskcheckd` runs in the background and performs periodic filesystem integrity scans, dramatically reducing the reliance on `fsck` at boot time and the risks associated with abrupt shutdowns. The configuration file is `/etc/diskcheckd.conf`; see `man diskcheckd` for instructions and examples for using this file. Any errors that `diskcheckd` finds are logged through the `syslogd` service, described in Chapter 11 ("System Configuration and Startup Scripts"). While `diskcheckd` is running, you can use `ps` to view its progress:

```
# ps -ax | grep diskcheckd
  251 ??  Ss    0:00.28 diskcheckd: ad0 13.26% (diskcheckd)
```

> **Note**
>
> FreeBSD's `fsck` is pretty similar in functionality to `fsck` on similar operating systems; however, it does lack one or two nice interface features, such as the progress bar on the Linux `fsck`. Be assured, though, that the core features behave almost exactly the same way.

You will find more information on Soft Updates and comparisons between it and journaling filesystems at `http://www.mckusick.com/softdep/` and `http://www.ece.cmu.edu/~ganger/papers/CSE-TR-254-95/`.

Using `fsck` to Recover a Damaged Super Block

Chances are, you'll never have to use this technique, but according to Murphy's Law, the best way to ensure that a precaution will be unnecessary is to take that precaution.

A common kind of filesystem corruption is a damaged super block. This is when the system, for whatever reasons, cannot read the block that contains the critical data for the device's filesystem, which is known as the *super block*, and located on sectors 16 through 31 at the beginning of the device. It's such an indispensable part of a filesystem that FreeBSD keeps an alternate super block at the beginning of every cylinder group, so that if your main super block becomes corrupted, there are dozens of backups throughout the device that you can use. The first alternate is always at block 32, and the rest are at regular intervals throughout the disk—but are much less easily predictable.

Let's say you try to mount a filesystem that you know is otherwise valid—for example, a removable hard disk that worked the last time you had it in the machine. Upon issuing the mount command, you get an error of "/dev/ad1s1h on /mnt: Incorrect super block". As dire as the situation sounds, this is easily dealt with using fsck.

```
#  fsck /dev/ad1s1h
** /dev/ad1s1h
BAD SUPER BLOCK: MAGIC NUMBER WRONG
LOOK FOR ALTERNATE SUPERBLOCKS? [yn] y
USING ALTERNATE SUPERBLOCK AT 32
** Last Mounted on /home2
** Phase 1 - Check Blocks and Sizes
** Phase 2 - Check Pathnames
** Phase 3 - Check Connectivity
** Phase 4 - Check Reference Counts
** Phase 5 - Check Cyl groups
148 files, 15660 used, 7038840 free (208 frags, 879829 blocks, 0.0%
fragmentation)
UPDATE STANDARD SUPERBLOCK? [yn] y
***** FILE SYSTEM WAS MODIFIED *****
```

FreeBSD makes it easy: Other platforms make you use command-line options to specify where the alternate super block is that we want to use, and the one at 32 is really the only one that you know for sure is there. Using fsck in this manner, the first available alternate super block is copied over the primary one, and you should be able to mount the filesystem cleanly.

Note

You can determine where all the super blocks on the device are, if you're really interested, by using the newfs utility, with the -N parameter (which prints out the filesystem's stats without actually making any changes to the disk):

```
# newfs -N /dev/ad1s1h
Warning: 2672 sector(s) in last cylinder unallocated
/dev/ad1s1h: 14558608 sectors in 3555 cylinders of 1 tracks, 4096 sectors
 7108.7MB in 223 cyl groups (16 c/g, 32.00MB/g, 7936 i/g)
super-block backups (for fsck -b #) at:
 32, 65568, 131104, 196640, 262176, 327712, 393248, 458784, 524320, 589856,
 655392, 720928, 786464, 852000, 917536, 983072, 1048608, 1114144, 1179680,
 1245216, 1310752, 1376288, 1441824, 1507360, 1572896, 1638432, 1703968,
 1769504, 1835040, 1900576, 1966112, 2031648, 2097184, 2162720, 2228256,
 2293792, 2359328, 2424864, 2490400, 2555936, 2621472, 2687008, 2752544,
 2818080, 2883616, 2949152, 3014688, 3080224, 3145760, 3211296, 3276832,
 3342368, 3407904, 3473440, 3538976, 3604512, 3670048, 3735584, 3801120,
 3866656, 3932192, 3997728, 4063264, 4128800, 4194336, 4259872, 4325408,
 4390944, 4456480, 4522016, 4587552, 4653088, 4718624, 4784160, 4849696,
```

```
4915232,  4980768,  5046304,  5111840,  5177376,  5242912,  5308448,  5373984,
5439520,  5505056,  5570592,  5636128,  5701664,  5767200,  5832736,  5898272,
5963808,  6029344,  6094880,  6160416,  6225952,  6291488,  6357024,  6422560,
6488096,  6553632,  6619168,  6684704,  6750240,  6815776,  6881312,  6946848,
7012384,  7077920,  7143456,  7208992,  7274528,  7340064,  7405600,  7471136,
7536672,  7602208,  7667744,  7733280,  7798816,  7864352,  7929888,  7995424,
8060960,  8126496,  8192032,  8257568,  8323104,  8388640,  8454176,  8519712,
8585248,  8650784,  8716320,  8781856,  8847392,  8912928,  8978464,  9044000,
9109536,  9175072,  9240608,  9306144,  9371680,  9437216,  9502752,  9568288,
9633824,  9699360,  9764896,  9830432,  9895968,  9961504,  10027040, 10092576,
10158112, 10223648, 10289184, 10354720, 10420256, 10485792, 10551328,
10616864, 10682400, 10747936, 10813472, 10879008, 10944544, 11010080,
11075616, 11141152, 11206688, 11272224, 11337760, 11403296, 11468832,
11534368, 11599904, 11665440, 11730976, 11796512, 11862048, 11927584,
11993120, 12058656, 12124192, 12189728, 12255264, 12320800, 12386336,
12451872, 12517408, 12582944, 12648480, 12714016, 12779552, 12845088,
12910624, 12976160, 13041696, 13107232, 13172768, 13238304, 13303840,
13369376, 13434912, 13500448, 13565984, 13631520, 13697056, 13762592,
13828128, 13893664, 13959200, 14024736, 14090272, 14155808, 14221344,
14286880, 14352416, 14417952, 14483488, 14549024
```

As you can see, there are plenty of available backups, but all except for the one at 32 are at odd locations. `fsck` does all the dirty work for us. However, it does let you specify a certain super block if you don't want to let it pick one automatically: `fsck -b 2490400 /dev/ad1s1h` is the command to use the super block at sector 2490400.

Setting and Enforcing User Filesystem Quotas

Remember those users from earlier in the chapter, who wouldn't stop uploading files and forced you to buy a new disk to accommodate them? Well, suppose you decided that you didn't want any single user to be able to use more than 20MB unless they got special permission from you. This can be done with quotas.

Quotas are not built in to the GENERIC kernel. To enable them, you have to add the following line to your kernel configuration:

```
options     QUOTA
```

See Chapter 17 for information on building a custom kernel. Then there are a couple of switches in `/etc/rc.conf`, which enables support for quotas when the system is brought up; you'll want to add these lines:

```
enable_quotas="YES"
```

```
check_quotas="NO"
```

The first line turns on quota support globally; the second line tells the system to skip a long, time-consuming consistency check (quotacheck -a) at boot time, which ensures that the quota database is properly synchronized. If you want to enable this check, change the second line to have a "YES" (or remove the line altogether—"YES" is the default).

The last step is to turn quotas on (or off) per filesystem. This is done in /etc/fstab by adding the userquota and/or groupquota option to the fourth field in each filesystem on which you want to enforce quotas. For example:

```
/dev/ad0s1g      /home    ufs    rw,userquota,groupquota    2    2
/dev/ad0s1f      /var     ufs    rw,userquota               2    2
/dev/ad0s1e      /usr     ufs    rw,gropquota               2    2
```

Reboot after all these things are done. Now that you're armed for battle, you're ready to start assigning quotas to users. You can do this either user-by-user (hardly practical on a high-load server), or on a range of UIDs (by setting one user's quota and then using it as a prototype to apply the same settings to a range of UIDs). To set the quota for that first user, you'll need to use the built in edquota utility, which lets you edit the attributes as a text file (much like chfn, which we will discuss in the next chapter). The text editor that edquota uses is whatever is specified in your EDITOR environment variable—vi in the default installation, but you may choose to change it to something more user-friendly, such as pico or ee by using a command such as setenv EDITOR pico.

```
# edquota -u bob
Quotas for user test:
/usr: blocks in use: 65, limits (soft = 50, hard = 75)
      inodes in use: 7, limits (soft = 50, hard = 60)
/var: blocks in use: 0, limits (soft = 50, hard = 75)
      inodes in use: 0, limits (soft = 50, hard = 60)
```

After this user's quota has been set up, you can then clone the settings throughout your system as follows:

```
# edquota -p bob 1001-9999
```

This will apply the same quota settings to the entire range of UIDs specified, even those that haven't been created yet!

Note the difference between blocks and inodes. Both limits will be enforced. *Blocks* refer to total space used (in 1K units), and *inodes* can be understood to mean "files".

Blocks, Files, and Inodes

The different ways of looking at data on a disk can get fairly confusing, but the details are important for understanding how to read the output of tools such as df and fsck. Let's take a closer look at how storage is divided up and used.

The default size for a data block is 8192 bytes. This is the unit of data storage. The data block is divided into eight fragments of 1024 bytes each. A file that does not take up an entire data block is stored in fragments and shares that block with other files. This is actually what fsck is counting when it reports fragmentation.

However, if a file that is currently sharing a data block with another file grows to the point where it will no longer fit in the current data block, FreeBSD moves the entire file to a different data block, rather then simply fragmenting the file into an adjacent block (as Windows does). This ensures that for files smaller than 8192 bytes, all the fragments for a single file are always stored in one data block; it also ensures that a file of any size is stored across as few different blocks as possible. You will never have a file that has fragments in more then one data block. This, of course, improves access time, and it prevents fragmentation from getting to the dizzy levels seen in consumer-grade operating systems.

A file is really just a way of looking at an *inode*, which is the fundamental grouping of related data that we think of as a file. This model is necessary for a true multiuser operating system to be able to share files efficiently. Here is all the information that is contained in an inode:

- Type of file and the access modes
- UID and GID of the owner
- Size of the file
- Time the file was last accessed and modified, and the inode changed
- Number of data blocks used by or allocated to the file
- Direct and indirect pointers to these data blocks

FreeBSD accesses data blocks with pointers located in the inodes. There are 12 direct pointers, which can access one block each. This allows direct access to a file up to 96 kilobytes. In addition, there are three levels of indirect pointers: single, double, and triple. The *single* indirect pointer refers to a filesystem block that contains pointers to data blocks. The filesystem block contains 2,048 additional addresses of 8K data blocks, allowing access to a file up to 16 megabytes in size. The *double* indirect pointer refers to a filesystem block containing 2,048 addresses that each point to a filesystem block containing a single indirect pointer, and each one of those 2,048 single indirect pointers refers to a filesystem block containing 2,048 addresses of 8K data blocks. This allows access to a file up to 32 gigabytes in size. Finally, the *triple* indirect pointer contains 2,048 addresses that each point to a filesystem block containing a double indirect pointer. Each of these double indirect pointers contains 2,048 addresses that each point to a single indirect pointer. And each of these single indirect pointers contains 2,048 addresses that point to a filesystem block that contains addresses for 2,048 8K data blocks, thus allowing the triple indirect pointer to access a file that is 70 terabytes in size! UFS limits the maximum file size to one terabyte, though, so don't get too excited.

A word about hard and soft limits—and the grace period—are in order here.

- A *hard limit* is strictly enforced. If a user's disk usage reaches the hard limit, the system will not permit any more space to be allocated to that user.

- A *soft limit* does not prevent the user from creating more files or using more space; instead, it triggers a timer for the *grace period*, which is seven days by default (but can be changed using edquota -t). After this grace period expires, the soft limit is enforced the same way as a hard limit. This allows users to use more than their allocated space (up to the hard limit) for brief periods. If the user's disk usage drops below the soft limit, the grace period is reset.

Once you have set these limits, you can view them as follows:

```
# quota bob
Disk quotas for user bob (uid 1015):
Filesystem  blocks   quota   limit   grace   files   quota   limit   grace
/home        1812    20000   40000           37      0       0
```

The quota command shows the quota information for the user specified as the final argument, or for the current user if that argument is omitted. If the user is over either of the limits, an asterisk (*) will appear after the number of blocks or files that is over the limit, and the "grace" column will report the amount of time left before the soft limit is enforced:

```
# quota bob
Disk quotas for user bob (uid 1015):
Filesystem  blocks   quota   limit   grace   files   quota   limit   grace
/home       28121*   20000   40000   6days   189     0       0
```

> **Note**
>
> To make sure that quotas are running properly, use the `mount` command with no arguments. The following is output from `mount` on a system in which the `/home` partition is using quotas:
>
> ```
> /dev/ad0s1a on / (ufs, local)
> /dev/ad0s1f on /home (ufs, local, with quotas)
> /dev/ad0s1e on /usr (ufs, local)
> procfs on /proc (procfs, local)
> ```
>
> If you don't see the `with quotas` flag, the filesystem did not get properly mounted with quotas. Check your `/etc/fstab`, `/etc/rc.conf`, and kernel configuration, and try rebooting if all look correct.

Quotas can be turned off easily enough, in one of three ways: globally, by setting `enable_quotas="NO"` in `/etc/rc.conf`; per filesystem, in `/etc/fstab`; or per user, by using `edquota` and setting the hard and soft limits to zero. Then, use `edquota -p` to propagate these settings throughout a range of UIDs, if you wish.

Filesystem management isn't an easy task, but once you have a few of these concepts that we've discussed at your disposal, the versatility of UNIX filesystems becomes readily apparent. Multiuser operating systems such as FreeBSD bring up all kinds of issues that don't exist on desktop systems, such as handling multiple filesystem types, monitoring usage, and enforcing quotas; but these features are what separates UNIX from its less-capable contemporaries. We will be continuing this discussion into the area of formatting and labeling new disks in Chapter 19, "Understanding Hard Disks and Filesystems."

9

THE FREEBSD FILESYSTEM

Users, Groups, and Permissions

In this chapter we will cover users and file permissions—concepts that form the central pillars of a UNIX system. Administering a system that is designed for multiuser operation imposes many more restrictions for a person who is accustomed to working from a single-user desktop background, but these restrictions serve to prevent much of the uncontrollable complexity that occurs when every operation on a machine is done effectively by the "super-user" (as is the case in Windows and other such systems).

Traditional desktop operating systems, such as Windows 95/98/Me and classic Mac OS, give the impression of being multiuser operating systems; however, strictly speaking, they are not. What they have are simply profiles, or ways of presenting data according to each user's preferences. Any action the user wants to take on the local machine—whether reading files, installing programs, or shutting down the computer—is permitted because there is only one "user" with absolute control over the machine. Access to network resources is done on a "guest user" basis, without the user or the machine participating in any true authentication with a domain or its equivalent.

Windows NT and 2000, however, have each taken successive steps toward becoming true multiuser operating systems like FreeBSD. Each user in the system has a separate account and a set of permissions that control access to files, printers, and other resources. Both systems have a concept of a "root" user, or "administrator," who has absolute power over the local machine. Both systems have groups and different layers of accessibility; in fact, Windows NT/2000 permissions have such complexity—inheritance upward, inheritance downward, domain users versus local users, and up to three accounts with administrative power—that even the most veteran user can get swamped. But there is one crucial element of multiuser functionality that is native to UNIX-like operating systems and foreign to desktop-bred ones: remote accessibility.

Most NT machine usage takes place at the console, sitting in front of the actual computer. To do otherwise requires specialized "terminal server" software. In fact, an NT user cannot directly execute any processes on the server. Access to an application on the server has to be done through that application's client software, and the server application has to be running already. Windows 2000 includes "terminal server" software, which enables users to execute GUI applications on the server side, which brings it a step closer to UNIX-style accessibility.

FreeBSD and similar operating systems thrive on remote accessibility. In fact, almost nothing on a UNIX system takes place at the physical console, but rather through terminal connections (such as Telnet or SSH), which provide a user with a command-line interface over the network. The upshot of this is that your FreeBSD machine will likely be accessed wholly from other locations and by many different users at once. Therefore, user and group permissions will play a much more important part in your life as an administrator than they would on an NT system, in which the administrator can always predict which applications will be running.

Introduction to Users and Groups

The users and permissions model that FreeBSD (and most UNIXes) use is a fairly simple and single-layer one. There are only two types of users: regular users, and the "super-user," or "root." Regular users are subject to user permissions that restrict what they can do; only the super-user is free of these restrictions. Other permissions models (such as that of Windows NT/2000) involve more complex layering, which is intended to facilitate certain system functions such as authentication services and system-level processes. The simpler mode that we will deal with means that we'll have to do a few more gymnastics when it comes to tasks such as setting up a Web server with proper permissions (covered in Chapter 26, "Configuring a Web Server"). However, the alternative—a more complex permissions system—more than likely means a less secure system, since there's so much more that can go wrong.

Everybody on a FreeBSD machine has limited permissions and a place to dwell, a home directory. To gain elevated status, you need to promote yourself to super-user status using the su command. This prompts you for the root password, which is the "key to the kingdom" and the most important piece of information you'll have to remember in maintaining your system. After you gain root access, you have as much freedom to create—or destroy—anything on the computer as you would on a single-user Windows machine. Any time you are logged in as root, you should cultivate a heightened sense of security consciousness, a wariness that someone malicious could be eavesdropping to get the kind of access that you have. The root password should never be transmitted over the network in cleartext (see Chapter 29, "Network Security," for details on network security), and it should be changed every few months as a rule. You cannot be too careful with this vital piece of information.

In order to execute the su command, you need to be a member of an elite group called "wheel." Although it is true that FreeBSD has only two types of users (as described previously), regular users and the super-user, this "wheel" group effectively creates a special class of regular users: those who are allowed to *become* root (using su). This is how you can delegate administrative responsibility to others that you trust.

> **Note**
>
> FreeBSD differs slightly from most distributions of Linux and many other UNIX-based operating systems in that it does not allow you to connect directly to the system (via Telnet or SSH) as root. This is a security measure. To gain root access, you must connect as a regular user—specifically, a user that is a member of the "wheel" group—and use the su command to promote yourself to super-user status. This means that for someone unauthorized to gain root access to your system, the root password alone will do him no good; he also has to gain access to a user's password in the "wheel" group. A determined hacker will find ways to do this, but the added step is a significant deterrent.
>
> If you really, *really* must turn off this feature, you can do so by editing the file /etc/ttys and adding the keyword secure in the field to the right of network in the first few entries in the "Pseudo terminals" section:
>
> ```
> ttyp0   none                    network     secure
> ttyp1   none                    network     secure
> ttyp2   none                    network     secure
> ```
>
> This is, however, considered an extremely risky maneuver, and not one that you should use if you can possibly stand simply logging in as yourself and using su.

Another kind of distinction among regular users is between actual login users (people who connect to the system) and automated users (such as bin, operator, daemon, nobody, and others). These user accounts exist in order to "own" certain system processes. It is important to realize that processes, just like files, are all owned by some user—and those processes are bound by that user's permissions when interacting with files and other processes.

Users never really access their files directly; everything a user does to his or her files by giving commands is effectively done by executing processes, running with the user's assigned permissions, which then operate on files and other processes, as illustrated in Figure 10.1. The processes owned by user1 can only operate on the files and processes owned by user1; permission would be denied if any of those processes tried to change any of user2's files or processes in any way. In the simplest setup, each user can change only those files and processes that he or she owns.

Imagine what would happen if user1 were the super-user. Then, that user's processes would have absolute power over any other user's files and processes. If one of user1's processes was, for instance, a program that would read a configuration file and then modify items on the system specified in that file, imagine what would happen if an unauthorized user managed to modify the configuration file. Your system would be vulnerable to complete annihilation. This is why most system processes, except those that are absolutely trusted, run under the ownership of one of these automated pseudo-users, instead of running as root.

FIGURE 10.1

A user executes processes, which then operate on files and other processes.

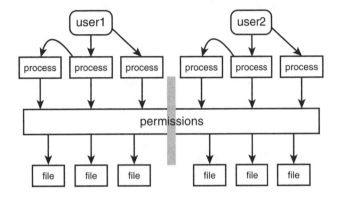

Why Use Groups?

Every user belongs to some primary group, generally a group of one, which has the same name as the user. This can be changed as you see fit; for instance, you may decide to have all users belong to the "users" group as their primary group. However, having a different group for every user gives you more flexibility, as we will see a little later—and it is also a more secure model. There is also more information on unique "personal" groups in man adduser.

Any user can also belong to any other groups in the system, such as other users' "personal" groups, the "wheel" group, or any other groups that you create (by adding them to the /etc/group file, as we will see later). However, the super-user is the only one who can control who belongs to what groups.

We have seen the purpose of the "wheel" group: to indicate a special clique of users who have the privileges to su to root. There are other applications for groups that are geared toward granting special privileges to certain users. In the most general case, a group exists to give one user the same permissions on a set of files or processes as another user—for example, to enable different engineers working on a software project to modify the source code files in a single central location, as illustrated in Figure 10.2. It wouldn't be very desirable if the two users had to share an account or tell each other their passwords; groups enable the two users to "own" the same group of files, and to both have the same permissions to operate on them.

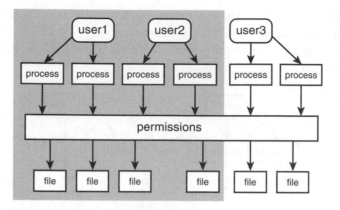

FIGURE 10.2

Two users in a group working on the same set of files, which are still protected from other users.

File Ownership

This brings us to our file ownership model. All UNIXes have the same kind of ownership structure: Every file and directory is owned by both a *user* and a *group*. However, as you will see in a moment, this does not necessarily mean that either the user or the members of the group have any particular permissions to access the file or directory.

Let's take a look at the permissions and ownership details of a set of files (see Listing 10.1). Use the -l option to ls to give a detailed listing, and the -a option to show all files, including "hidden" ones (whose names begin with a dot):

LISTING 10.1 Set of Files Showing Ownership and Permissions

```
# ls -la /home/frank
total 3126
drwxr-xr-x   3 frank     users      512 May 12  2000 .
drwxr-xr-x  52 root      users     9216 Mar  7 13:37 ..
-rw-r--r--   1 bob       users   291090 Jan 23  2000 1.bmp
-rw-rw-r--   1 bob       bob       2703 Dec 22  1998 contents.html
-rw-r--r--   1 frank     users     3657 Jan  9 14:11 file.txt
-rw-r--r--   1 bob       users    92195 Sep 11 21:31 1.uu
drwxr-xr-x   2 root      users      512 Jan  2 14:19 files
drwxr-xr-x  12 root      wheel     1024 Feb 18  1999 more-files
```

Pretty cryptic, isn't it? Not really. In this chapter, you will learn how to decode those "drwxr-x" strings, which define the *mode* of a file.

There are three modes of owner permissions on a file (or directory): *user*, *group*, and *others*. There are also three modes of access: *read*, *write*, and *execute*. These six pieces of information, referred to as *bits*, define the permissions on a file. For instance, a file's permissions configuration might tell us that the user who owns it can read and write to the file, but members of the group who owns it can only read from it, and anybody else in the system can also only read from it. (This is the default file mode.) Similarly, it can tell us that anybody—user, group, or others—can read or execute the file (running it as a program), but that only the user and group who own it can write to it. Literally any combination is possible; we will look in more detail at the permission modes and how to set them a little later in this chapter.

For now, it is necessary to realize that a user can only read his or her own files if those files have their permissions set so that the user can read them. Similarly, the necessary permissions must be in place if members of the owner group are to read the files. Most of the time, this is the case; it is important to recognize, though, that ownership and permissions are not inextricably tied together.

Note

The one exception—the one thing that really ties ownership and permissions together—is that a user can delete a file owned by another user, *if that file is in a directory owned by the first user*. The rm (remove) command will prompt for whether the user wants to override the file's ownership and permissions, and proceed. Other than this, though, there is nothing inherent in the permissions of a file that gives its owner special power over it.

```
# ls -l tempfile
-rw-r--r--  1 root   users  0 Aug  7 21:44 tempfile
# rm tempfile
override rw-r--r--  root/users for tempfile? y
```

Using chown to Change File Ownership

As the super-user, you have the ability to change which users own any files on the system. This is one of those things that only the super-user can do; regular users cannot "give" their files to another user or "take" them from another user. (If they could, it would sort of defeat the purpose of users and file ownership!)

The command to change ownership is chown (for "change owner"):

```
# chown bob file.txt
```

This will change the *user* owner—not the group owner—of the file file.txt to the user "bob". The file used to be owned by "frank", but now "bob" can read and write to the file while "frank" can no longer write to it.

You can also use `chown` on a directory:

```
# chown bob /home/frank
```

This command, when used on a directory, operates on the "." entry in the listing we saw earlier in Listing 10.1. This entry is a pointer that refers to the current directory, while the ".." entry refers to the parent directory. (This behavior is the same as in MS-DOS.) Looking back at the permissions on the `/home/frank` directory, we see that it was writable only by its user owner; therefore, "bob" is now the only one who can create or delete files in the directory, even if he owns the files he wants to delete. He can, however, modify any file that he owns in any directory. This interrelation between ownership and permissions will be made clearer in Table 10.1 after we have covered file permissions more thoroughly.

> **Tip**
>
> There's a useful option to `chown` that you as an administrator will need to know: `-R`. This makes `chown` act recursively, meaning that if you run it against a directory, the function will operate on the current directory, all files within the directory, and all files in all subdirectories below it. You'll need to use this if you have to re-create an account, for example, and need to transfer ownership of all the user's files:
>
> ```
> # chown -R bob /home/frank
> ```

Using `chgrp` to Change File Group Ownership

Now that you know how to use `chown`, it's a simple matter to extend this to the use of `chgrp`, a very similar command. Its purpose is to change the group owner rather than the user owner of a file or directory, and it works exactly the same way:

```
# chgrp users contents.html
```

After issuing this command, the permissions for `contents.html` will look like this:

```
-rw-rw-r--  1 bob      users   2703 Dec 22  1998 contents.html
```

Because both the user and group owners have write permissions, you've just created a situation in which any member of the "users" group can write to the file just as "bob" can.

FreeBSD by default creates a new group for every user, so there will be a "bob" group as well as a "bob" user, and "bob" belongs to it as his primary group. All the user's files will by default be created with the user and group owners set to "bob". Now, if another user (for instance, "frank") belongs to the "bob" group, he can write to those files, and we now have a file-sharing mechanism in which both "bob" and "frank" have the same access over the files.

chgrp is really just another way of executing chown; if you prefer, you can use the following syntax:

```
# chown bob.users contents.html
```

This changes the ownership on contents.html to the "bob" user and the "users" group. And the following will change the group owner only:

```
# chown .users contents.html
```

Both chown and chgrp support the -R option, described previously, in the same way.

File and Directory Permissions

Refer to the files in Listing 10.1. It's now time to examine the permissions strings on these files and directories more carefully. The first thing we should notice is that on directories, the first bit in the string is a d. This is simply a flag, and doesn't really indicate permissions that can be controlled; it is, however, a useful means of distinguishing between files and directories.

The rest of the bits in the string are fairly straightforward: three groups of three, showing respectively the read, write, and execute permissions for the user owner, the group owner, and others. For instance, contents.html is readable and writable by both the user and group owners, and only readable by anyone else.

Note that a directory must have the "execute" bit set in order for its contents to be viewable; for directories, the x bit is construed as "search" rather than "execute".

The Relationship Between File and Directory Permissions

Table 10.1 shows the relationship between a user, a group to which the user belongs, and the permissions that the directory offers to the user and group depending on its mode.

TABLE 10.1   Capabilities Granted by Various Types of File Permissions

	Directory Writable by User	*Directory Writable by Group*	*Directory Writable by Other*
create file	yes	yes	no
delete file owned/writable by user	yes	yes	no
delete file owned/writable by group	yes	yes	no
delete file owned/writable by other	yes	yes	no
rename file owned/writable by user	yes	yes	no
rename file owned/writable by group	yes	yes	no
rename file owned/writable by other	yes	yes	no
modify file owned/writable by user	yes	yes	yes
modify file owned/writable by group	yes	yes	yes
modify file owned/writable by other	no	no	no

Any time you try to delete (rm) a file for which you do not have write permissions, you will see the following prompt:

```
# rm file.txt
override rw-r--r--  bob/users for 1.uu? y
```

Note that you still might not have permissions to delete the file! The override prompt appears any time you try to delete a file that isn't yours, regardless of whether you'll be successful if you say "y". You can suppress the override prompt with rm -f.

A file that can be deleted can be renamed because you use the mv (move) command to rename a file in FreeBSD—and mv operates by copying the file and then deleting it. A file that can be read can be copied.

Beyond the standard permissions that apply to the user, group, and others, there are a few additional file modes with special meanings. We will discuss these next as we cover the mechanisms for changing file permissions.

Using chmod to Change File and Directory Permissions

Now that we know how to read permissions on a file or directory, it's time to learn how to set them. The command for this is chmod, for "change mode." A file's permissions set is often referred to as its *mode*.

The chmod command can operate in two ways, depending on your preference: numerically or symbolically.

Changing Modes Numerically

The most direct way to change permissions is by setting a three-digit, octal (base 8) number that uniquely specifies the permissions for each type of ownership. Each digit refers to a certain ownership mode, controlling the permissions that correspond to the user, group, and others, respectively. (There is a fourth digit as well, which we will cover shortly.) A mode digit is constructed by adding together the numbers corresponding to the permission bits you want to grant. The available bits are shown in Table 10.2.

TABLE 10.2   Permissions Mode Bits and Their Meanings

Bit	Meaning
0	no permissions
1	execute (or, for directories, search)
2	write
4	read

Thus, you can make a mode of "read and write" with a 6, a mode of "read and execute" with a 5, or a mode of "read, write, and execute" with a 7.

Combine these digits into a three-digit number, and you've got a numeric way of specifying the standard permissions for a file. Table 10.3 shows a few examples.

TABLE 10.3   Some Complete Numeric Permissions Modes

Mode	Meaning
755	read/write/execute by user, read/execute by group and others
644	read/write by user, read-only by group and others
600	read/write by user, no access for group and others

You can then apply the permissions to a file or directory like so:

```
# chmod 755 testscript.sh
```

But that's only three of the four digits mentioned earlier. The fourth controls some "extra" features that address certain specific behaviors of files and directories under special circumstances. We will now look at the bits that make up this fourth digit and what they do.

- 0—normal permissions.

- 1—The sticky bit. This can only be set (with any effect) on directories; within a directory with this bit set, a user can only delete or rename files if he owns them *and* if he has write permissions on the directory. Does not apply to executable files.

- 2—Set group ID, or "setgid". If this bit is set on an executable file, it will be executed with the effective group permissions of the file's group owner, rather than that of the user executing it.

- 4—Set user ID, or "setuid". If this bit is set on an executable file, it will be executed with the effective user permissions of the file's user owner, rather than that of the user executing it. This fourth digit is the highest-value digit (in other words, the leftmost one), so in the earlier example where we showed what permissions of 755 mean, we could have used the equivalent value 0755. We use the same method to construct the value for that digit as we do for the other digits, so the value 3755 would create a directory with the sticky bit and the setgid bit set, in addition to regular 755 permissions.

Changing Modes Symbolically

As clever as the octal numeric system is, it's often helpful to have a method for setting modes that's easier to remember. Fortunately, we have a symbolic method for doing just that.

Instead of giving chmod a number, we will give it between one and three flags in a single string. This string can be formatted in a large number of ways, but we can briefly cover the most common usages here.

> **Note**
>
> See man chmod for complete coverage of the flexible syntax of chmod and its symbolic modes.

Table 10.4 shows some examples of symbolic modes. Each is made up of a string of characters. The first character specifies the ownership mode(s), the second character is the modification you're making (+,-,=), and the third is the permission bit(s).

TABLE 10.4 Symbolic Permissions Modes

Mode String	Meaning
go+w	add "write" permissions to the group owner and others
+x	add "execute" permissions for everyone

TABLE 10.4   continued

Mode String	Meaning
o-r	remove "read" permissions for others
ugo=rw	set "read" and "write" permissions for everyone
a=rw	same as ugo=rw
+t	add the "sticky bit"
+s	add both the setuid and setgid bits

```
# chmod g+w file.txt
```

This symbolic method lends itself more readily to memory than the numeric method, and it will probably be a much easier way for you to do most of your typical chmod operations.

> **Tip**
>
> The -R option works on chmod too, the same as with chown and chgrp.

Access Control Lists (ACLs)

> **Note**
>
> The following sections on Access Control Lists (ACLs) applies only to FreeBSD 5.0. FreeBSD 4.x does not support ACLs).

Access Control Lists (ACLs) are a new addition to FreeBSD 5.0 that give you tighter control over who can and cannot access files and directories. Instead of just allowing or denying access based on owner, group, and everyone else, you can now grant access to individual users and individual groups. You can also set a maximum permission mask for the users and groups that are granted access through the ACL that will override the actual permissions given by the ACL.

For ACL to work, UFS extensions must be compiled into the kernel. The next section explains the options that must be added.

10

USERS, GROUPS, AND PERMISSIONS

Configuring the Kernel to Support ACL

At the time of this writing, it is not known for sure whether UFS Extensions will be enabled in the default kernel for the release version of 5.0. If they are, you do not need to rebuild the kernel. If they are not, you will need to add the UFS extension options to the kernel configuration file and then rebuild the kernel.

To see whether your kernel has UFS extensions enabled or not, look for the following lines in your kernel configuration file. Unless you have already built a custom kernel, your kernel configuration file will be `/usr/src/sys/i386/conf/GENERIC` on an Intel x86-based system, and `/usr/src/sys/alpha/conf/GENERIC` on an Alpha-based system. The following lines should be present in order for ACL to work:

```
options     UFS_EXTATTR
options     UFS_EXTTR_AUTOSTART
options     UFS_ACL
```

If these options are already present in your kernel configuration file, you don't need to do anything. If they are not present, you will need to add the options and then build a new kernel. See Chapter 17, "Kernel Configuration," for full details on how to configure, build, and install a new kernel.

After you have installed the new kernel and rebooted, you will need to configure the filesystems that you want to use ACL with.

Configuring Filesystems to Use ACL

The `extattrctl` command is used to control the extended attributes on filesystems. You will need to use it on each filesystem that you want to use ACL with. For example, to enable ACL on the filesystem mounted as `/usr`, the following procedures will work:

First, as the root user, create the directories `/usr/.attribute` and `/usr/.attribute/system`:

```
mkdir /usr/.attribute /usr/.attribute/system
```

Next, change to the newly created `/usr/.attribute/system` directory (`cd /usr/.attribute/system`). Then, run the `extattrctl` command to initialize the ACL attributes on the filesystem:

```
extattrctl initattr -p /usr 388 posix1e.acl_access
```

On large filesystems, this command can take several minutes to complete, so be patient as the command generates the backing files needed to support ACL.

When the first command has finished executing, you will need to run the `extattrctl` command one more time with a different filename as the argument:

```
extattrctl initattr -p /usr 388 posix1e.acl_default
```

Once again, on a large filesystem, this command can take several minutes to complete. So be patient.

> **Caution**
>
> The files created by the previous two commands can be extremely large, possibly taking up several gigabytes of disk space on large filesystems. Make sure you have plenty of free disk space before running the commands.

Once you have run the preceding commands, you will need to reboot the system or remount the filesystems in question for the changes to take effect. After you have done so, the ACLs for the filesystem will be enabled.

Getting Information About Current ACL Settings

Use the `getfacl` command to obtain information about existing ACL settings on files or directories. For example, on a newly created file named `acltest.txt` with no ACL set and with default 644 permissions, issuing `getfacl acltest.txt` will return the following:

```
#file:acltest.txt
#owner:0
#group:0
user::rw-
group::r--
other::---
```

The first line simply shows the name of the file. The next two lines show the UID and GID of the owner and group the file belongs to (in this case, the file is owned by root). And the final three lines show the current file permissions on the file. Notice that `other` does not have any permissions on this file.

Setting the Maximum Permissions Mask

The *maximum permissions mask* controls the maximum permissions that will be given to any user or group added to the ACL list. Note that the mask applies only to users and groups that are given access to the file or directory with an ACL entry. It does not affect the permissions that the owner has. It also does not affect the permissions that the default group has, nor does it affect the permissions of the rest of the world. For anyone not listed in an ACL entry, the standard file access permissions apply.

The `setfacl` command is used to add, modify, or delete entries from the ACL list. The syntax is

```
setfacl action permissions filename
```

where `action` is the action that should be performed (adding an entry, modifying an entry, deleting an entry, and so on); `permissions` are the ACL permissions that should be set; and `filename` is, of course, the name of the file or directory that the ACL should be applied to. The following example adds an ACL maximum permissions mask of read to the file `acltest.txt`:

```
setfacl -m m::r acltest.txt
getfacl acltest.txt
#file:acltest.txt
#owner:0
#group:0
user::rw-
group::r--
mask::r--
other::---
```

In the `setfacl` command, the `-m` option means that we want to add or modify the ACL entry. The `m::` specifies that we want to set a mask, and the `r` simply means "read". If we wanted to also set the mask to allow write permissions, we would have used `m::rw`. The last entry is of course, the name of the file we want this operation to be performed on.

After we have set the mask, `getfacl` shows us the same information it showed us the first time, but this time it shows that there is a mask set.

Adding a User or Group to the ACL

To add a user or group to the ACL, we will once again use the `setfacl` command. For example, to give the user `foobar` read access to this file, the following command can be used:

```
setfacl -m u:foobar:r acltest.txt
getfacl acltest.txt
#file:acltest.txt
#owner:0
#group:0
user::rw-
user:foobar:r--
group::r--
mask::r--
other::---
```

As you can see, an entry has been added to the ACL list for the user `foobar`. This user will now have read access to the file, even though the standard file permissions would not normally give it to him.

So, what happens if we try to give the user write permissions as well as read permissions? The following command would give `foobar` both read and write permissions on the file:

```
setfacl -m u:foobar:rw acltest.txt
#file:acltest.txt
#owner:0
#group:0
user::rw-
user:foobar:rw-
group::r--
mask::rw-
other::---
```

The `getfacl` output shows that `foobar` was indeed given write permissions to the file. Notice also that the mask has been updated automatically to give a maximum permission of read and write. If this behavior is undesirable (in other words, you do not want the mask to be updated), use the `-n` option when setting the ACL. For example, the following command will set an ACL that gives the user `foobar` read and write access to the file, but will not update the mask, even if the current mask does not allow write access:

```
setfacl -n -m u:foobar:rw acltest.txt
```

> **Tip**
>
> The order of the options is important. The `-n` option must come before the action option (in this case, `-m`). If you reverse the order of the two options, you will get an error that says `setfacl: acl_from_text() failed: Invalid argument`.

> **Caution**
>
> Remember that if you set a new ACL without using the `-n` option, the maximum permissions mask will automatically be updated to allow them. For example, if the mask is currently set to allow maximum permissions of read only, and you add an ACL for a user that allows read and write, the mask will automatically be updated to allow both read and write privileges. Always remember to use the `-n` option if you do not want this to happen.

> **Tip**
>
> When the `-n` option is not used and the mask is automatically updated, as you have seen, it will increase the permissions if a new ACL is added that has greater permissions than the mask currently allows. The mask will also automatically be lowered to the maximum permissions needed to support all the entries in the ACL. For example, if you delete an ACL entry that allows read and write access to a certain user, and after you delete this entry there are no other entries left that require write access, write access will automatically be removed from the mask. Just like the automatic raising of the mask, the automatic lowering of the mask can also be prevented with the `-n` option.

After giving `foobar` read and write access to the file, our ACL should now look like this:

```
#file:acltest.txt
#owner:0
#group:0
user::rw-
user:foobar:rw-
group::r--
mask::rw-
other::---
```

If we want to change our mask back so that it allows maximum ACL permissions of read only, we use the following command:

```
setfacl -m m::r acltest.txt
```

If we then run the `getfacl` command again, we get the following output:

```
#file:acltest.txt
#owner:0
#group:0
user::rw-
user:foobar:rw-          # effective: r--
group::r--
mask::r--
other::---
```

Notice that the user `foobar` still has read and write permissions listed. However, because of the mask, `foobar`'s effective permissions are read-only.

You can also add several ACLs with a single command line by separating them with commas. For example:

```
setfacl -n -m u:foobar:rw,u:guest:r,g:visitors:r acltest.txt
```

This command will give read and write access to the user `foobar`, read access to the user `guest`, and read access to the group `visitors`. In addition, the use of the `-n` option prevents the mask from being updated, even if the current mask doesn't allow some of the permissions we assign in this statement.

Denying Access with ACL

Just as an ACL can be used to allow users or groups that otherwise would not have access to that file or directory to access a file or directory, it can also be used to deny access to users or groups who otherwise would have access to it. For example, the following command will create an ACL entry for the user `foobar` that contains no permissions:

```
setfacl -m u:foobar: acltest.txt
```

In this case, the user `foobar` will be denied all access to the file `acltest.txt`, even if `foobar` is a member of the group that owns the file and that group has access to the file. The ACL will overrule the standard file permissions and deny the user access, even if the standard file permissions would allow the user access.

Deleting an ACL Entry

Use the `-x` option with `setfacl` to delete an ACL entry. For example, the following command will remove the entire entry for the user `foobar`:

```
setfacl -x u:foobar: acltest.txt
```

Removing All ACL Entries

Use the `-b` option to remove all of the ACL entries. For example:

```
setfacl -b acltest.txt
```

For more information on the capabilities of ACL, including the capability to set default ACLs for directories, please see the `man` pages for `getfacl` and `setfacl`.

Adding and Removing Users

Now that we covered permissions and ownership, we need to turn our attention to expanding the system's user base to include more users and groups.

Use the `adduser` script to add users to the system. This program differs somewhat in workflow from the `adduser` or `useradd` scripts you might be used to using on a Linux system, but what it accomplishes is the same. You must be root in order to run `adduser`.

The first time you run adduser, the script sets up a configuration file with a set of defaults; the next time you run it, you can use the -s ("silent") option to use these defaults and it will only ask you for the basic details on each user. Listing 10.2 shows a sample initial run of the script:

LISTING 10.2   A Sample adduser Session

```
Use option ``-silent'' if you don't want to see all warnings and questions.

Check /etc/shells
Check /etc/master.passwd
Check /etc/group
Enter your default shell: csh date ksh no sh tcsh [ksh]:
Your default shell is: ksh -> /usr/local/bin/ksh
Enter your default HOME partition: [/home]:
Copy dotfiles from: /usr/share/skel no [/usr/share/skel]:
Send message from file: /etc/adduser.message no
[/etc/adduser.message]:
Use password-based authentication (y/n) [y]: y
Enable account password at creation (y/n) [y]: y
Use an empty password (y/n) [n]: n

Ok, let's go.
Don't worry about mistakes. I will give you the chance later to correct any
➥input.
Enter username [a-z0-9_-]: joe
Enter full name []: Joe User
Enter shell csh date ksh no sh tcsh [ksh]:
Enter home directory (full path) [/home/joe]:
Uid [1005]:
Enter login class: default []:
Login group joe [joe]:
Login group is ``joe''. Invite joe into other groups: guest no
[no]:
Use password-based authentication (y/n) [y]: y
Use an empty password (y/n) [n]: n
Enter password []:
Enter password again []:
Enable account password at creation (y/n) [y]: y

Name:     joe
Password: ****
Fullname: Joe User
Uid:      1005
Gid:      1005 (joe)
Class:
Groups:   joe
HOME:     /home/joe
Shell:    /usr/local/bin/ksh
OK? (y/n) [y]:
```

LISTING 10.2   continued

```
Added user ``joe''
Send message to ``joe'' and: no root second_mail_address [no]:

Joe User,

your account ``joe'' was created.
Have fun!

See also chpass(1), finger(1), passwd(1)

Add anything to default message (y/n) [n]:
Send message (y/n) [y]: n
Copy files from /usr/share/skel to /home/joe
Add another user? (y/n) [y]: n
Goodbye!
```

Hitting Enter after every prompt accepts the default value, which is shown in brackets. Many of the prompts give you a space-separated list of choices, such as the prompt for the shell; when these choices include no, that option can be used to disable or decline whatever that prompt is offering. For instance, entering no for the shell will create the user without a valid shell, meaning that the user cannot log in to the system.

> **Tip**
>
> As of FreeBSD 4.0 and later, the "csh" built in to the base system is actually tcsh, an extended version of csh (the C shell). You can still specify tcsh as a shell, but it's the same thing as csh.

If you like, you can put a file at /etc/adduser.message, which will be e-mailed to the new user at the new local account. The user will be able to read it the first time he or she logs in to the system and runs a mail program (more on reading mail can be found in Chapter 25, "Configuring E-mail Services"). To make it easier, if you have elected to send the adduser.message file, the script will prompt you for a second address to send it to (for instance, an address that the person is already using), so you can be sure the user receives it.

The "dotfiles" that the script mentions are the semi-hidden shell configuration files (they are only visible if you use the -a option on ls):

.cshrc	.login_conf	.mailrc	.rhosts
.login	.mail_aliases	.profile	.shrc

These files will be explained in more detail in Chapter 12, "Customizing the Shell."

Each user and group has a numeric equivalent to its name, the user ID and group ID (or UID and GID), respectively. This ID is actually what is listed in the ownership information of a file or directory, and what is used to control processes. If you remove a user from the system, that user's files become owned by the UID number that the user left behind.

Removing a user is a fairly simple matter. The command here is `rmuser`, which takes the username as an argument (`adduser` does not), as shown in Listing 10.3.

LISTING 10.3   A Sample `rmuser` Session

```
# rmuser joe
Matching password entry:

joe:IRBpIrE/nkDQo:1008:1008::0:0:Joe user:/home/joe:/bin/csh

Is this the entry you wish to remove? y
Remove user's home directory (/home/joe)? y
```

LISTING 10.3   continued

```
Updating password file, updating databases, done.
Updating group file: (removing group joe -- personal group is empty) done.
Removing user's home directory (/home/joe): done.
Removing files belonging to joe from /tmp: done.
Removing files belonging to joe from /var/tmp: done.
Removing files belonging to joe from /var/tmp/vi.recover: done.
```

That line about the "matching password entry" describes the database in which all the user information is kept, which brings us to our next topic.

The `/etc/passwd` and `/etc/master.passwd` Files

All UNIX-flavored operating systems have an `/etc/passwd` file, but its specific role differs from platform to platform. For some systems, it is the sole repository of user information (including passwords). In these cases, adding a user requires you only to add a line to it using a text editor (`vi`, `pico`, `ee`, `emacs`, and so on). More modern operating systems, though, use a "shadow passwords" structure—a way of storing the encrypted password strings not in `/etc/passwd`, but in a different file that is readable only by root. This file's name varies, depending on the platform. On some, it's `/etc/shadow`; on some, it's `/etc/security/master.passwd`; and on FreeBSD, it's `/etc/master.passwd`.

Both of these `passwd` files are simple text databases, containing a line for each user with fields delimited with colons (`:`). The files contain the username, the user ID, the group ID of the primary group, the home directory, the login shell, and the full name (which also has embedded comma-delimited fields such as "Office Location", "Office Phone", and "Home Phone").

The permissions on /etc/passwd are 0644, and /etc/master.passwd is 0600. This security scheme means that any user can access the information in /etc/passwd; but root is the only one who can see into /etc/master.passwd, which differs from /etc/passwd only in that it contains the users' encrypted passwords in the second field. Passwords are encrypted in FreeBSD using a hash scheme based on the MD5 algorithm.

```
/etc/passwd:
joe:*:1008:1008:Joe User:/home/joe:/bin/csh
```

```
/etc/master.passwd:
joe:$1$32iknJXS$TnJUUj9LzYGwWRZonOu/I0:1008:1008:Joe User:/home/joe:/bin/csh
```

These two files aren't the only ones that store user information, though. Flat text databases are fine for a fairly small number of users, but as the user base grows, the need for a faster, hash-table-based lookup database becomes more and more obvious. On a system with 25,000 users in a linear text database, it can take a significant amount of time to look up a user's information—while the user is waiting to log in!

So, in FreeBSD, we also have /etc/pwd.db and /etc/spwd.db. These files are hash tables in db format, corresponding to the "insecure" /etc/passwd and the "secure" /etc/master.passwd, respectively; they also have the same permissions as their corresponding cleartext files. They provide a fast lookup mechanism for large user databases, and they're generated by the pwd_mkdb program automatically every time you alter a user's information with the chfn, passwd, or adduser/rmuser commands.

Speaking of which, the chfn command (or "change full name") is the tool you will use to change a user's information. Like the edquota command that we examined in the last chapter, chfn operates by invoking the editor specified in your EDITOR environment variable (vi, by default). You can then modify any of the text fields; and upon saving and exiting, the /etc/master.passwd file is rewritten, and pwd_mkdb -p is automatically run to rebuild the other three files.

It is important to understand that /etc/master.passwd is truly the "master" user database file; if you want to rebuild a user list or port one from another FreeBSD machine, you can simply place the new master.passwd file into /etc (or anywhere within the / partition) and then give the following command:

```
# pwd_mkdb -p /etc/master.passwd.new
```

This example assumes that your new master.passwd file is in /etc as master.passwd.new. The /etc/master.passwd file will be replaced with your new file; and /etc/pwd.db, /etc/spwd.db, and /etc/passwd will be rebuilt. The -p option tells pwd_mkdb to generate a new /etc/passwd file; if omitted, /etc/passwd will be left unchanged. You will probably want to use -p at all times to keep the two files synchronized.

10

USERS, GROUPS, AND PERMISSIONS

> **Note**
>
> In FreeBSD, the /etc/passwd file itself is never consulted; it only really exists for compatibility with third-party applications. Most modern utilities look up user information from /etc/pwd.db.

The /etc/group File

Groups are handled in much the same way as users—with a text database in /etc—but because groups do not normally have passwords, there is no need for special security on the /etc/group file (the group equivalent of /etc/passwd), other than having it writable only by root.

Following is a sample line from /etc/group. Note that there are only four fields: the group name, a "dummy" field (in which passwords would go if they existed), the group ID, and then a comma-separated list of the users in the group.

```
wheel:*:10:root,bob,frank
```

There is no hash database for /etc/group because generally the information in it is referenced much less frequently than the /etc/passwd information; also, there are usually far fewer groups than users on a system. FreeBSD's "unique groups" policy, however, makes that latter point a moot one. Future development may eventually produce a hash file for groups.

Managing Groups

Without passwords, user access, or a hash file to worry about, adding a group to the system is extremely easy by comparison to adding a user. You can simply open the /etc/group file in any text editor and create a new line in the format listed earlier. Make sure to give the new group a group ID that has not yet been used.

New groups are added automatically by the adduser script when it creates unique per-user groups; the group IDs typically match the corresponding user IDs, but that is not a requirement. You will most likely only be interested in adding systemwide groups—for example, for tasks such as running a Web server or a database backend. These groups generally ought to have group IDs in the range between 100 and 1000. The numbers above 1000 are usually used for unique per-user groups, to match the corresponding user IDs. The numbers under 100 tend to be populated by system groups that are part of the core operating system.

To add a user to a group, type the user's name into the fourth field. If there are already usernames in the fourth field, separate them with commas, as shown previously. You can remove a user just as easily—by erasing the name.

CHAPTER 11

System Configuration and Startup Scripts

IN THIS CHAPTER

FreeBSD's startup process, like that of most UNIX-like operating systems, provides you with a lot of information before it gives you a command prompt. This startup can be more complex than operating systems such as Windows or Mac OS. However, as long as you run the right system on the correct hardware, a full startup (including the launch of all its services, or "daemons") can be just as quick as that of a desktop OS.

Because every UNIX-like operating system does things a bit differently, FreeBSD's startup process may be unfamiliar, even if you're a veteran with Linux. For example, you won't have the handy fsck progress meter or the neatly formatted check box columns of some distributions of Linux, and the boot manager operates quite differently from LILO (the Linux boot loader). Neither does FreeBSD have the large variety of runlevels that Linux or Solaris have. Because FreeBSD's model is simpler and more direct, it can be easier to understand and deal with, but it also has pitfalls and complexities that other platforms lack.

With a little exploration, though, we'll soon have the process fully analyzed and under control.

Understanding the FreeBSD Startup Process

FreeBSD's bootstrapping (startup) process is a multistage one, with each stage typically having a very limited function and scope, and executing one crucial step before passing off control to the next stage. We will now go over these stages in detail. Chances are that you won't ever need to know the details of what happens when the system is starting up, but knowing them can't hurt!

When you first power on the machine, the first thing it does is run the hardware checks and probing that are specified by the BIOS and the CMOS configuration. The hardware check and probe runs the memory check and the IDE or SCSI exploration that you see before the screen is cleared for the first time. This step is not OS-specific; it happens the same way, no matter what you have installed on the machine. After it prints the table showing the hardware data it has collected, the BIOS reads the Master Boot Record (MBR) of the primary disk for the first preliminary *boot block*. It is the job of this and the next two boot blocks to find and run the loader, which configures and loads the kernel. Each of the boot blocks is sequentially a little more complex than the last; the first two are limited to 512 bytes in size (by the size of the MBR and the size of the boot sector of a slice), so they are both very simple. We will now look at each of the boot blocks in turn to see what their functions are.

- **Boot block 0 (boot0)**. This preliminary boot block is what sits in the MBR, like LILO, and lists the available slices (the F-key commands that follow) from which you can choose what you want to boot.

```
F1 FreeBSD
F2 Linux
F3 ??

Default: F1
```

You can press the appropriate F-key to select the slice you want, or else just wait for several seconds—it will choose the default selection and continue.

- **Boot block 1 (boot1)**. This a very simple program that runs from the boot sector of the slice you selected in boot0, and its job is to use a stripped-down version of disklabel (what divides a slice up into BSD-style partitions, which we will cover thoroughly in Chapter 19, "Understanding Hard Disks and Filesystems") to find and run boot2 in the appropriate partition. There is no user-interface portion to boot1.

- **Boot block 2 (boot2)**. Finally, we reach a boot block that has enough elbow room to have the necessary complexity to read files on the bootable filesystem. In earlier versions of FreeBSD, this boot block used to provide a prompt so you could tell it where to load the kernel from, if not from the default location in the bootable slice. Now it automatically runs a program called loader, which gives you this interface and a lot more.

- **loader**. You can find this program in the /boot directory. It reads the /boot/defaults/loader.conf and /boot/loader.conf configuration files, and loads the kernel and modules specified there. (The /boot/loader.conf file contains the overrides to /boot/defaults/loader.conf, in a similar fashion to the way /etc/rc.conf works, which we will cover later in this chapter.)

The loader counts down 10 seconds while it waits for a key press from you; if it doesn't get one, it boots the kernel in its default state. However, if you press Enter, it will put you into its command prompt interface, in which you can control precisely your kernel boot procedure. You can boot in single-user mode (boot -s), boot an old kernel (boot kernel.old), boot from CD-ROM (boot -C), load and unload kernel modules one by one, view the contents of files (more), or perform a number of other tasks (see man boot for details). This should all be unnecessary most of the time. Usually, you will boot in the default configuration. Let's say, though, that you want to load a certain kernel module (/modules/portal.ko) at boot time, rather than waiting until the system has completely booted. You also want to view the currently loaded kernel modules. This is done at the ok prompt, as follows:

```
ok load portal.ko
/modules/portal.ko text=0x1d18 data=0x1f4+0x4 syms=[0x4+0x8d0+0x4+0x6bf]
ok lsmod
 0x100000: kernel (elf kernel, 0x355be4)
 0x455be4: /boot/kernel.conf (userconfig script, 0x4c)
 0x456000: portal.ko (elf module, 0x3eb0)
```

Pressing ? at the ok prompt gives you a list of available commands. The two we just saw are load, which loads modules into the kernel, and lsmod, which lists currently loaded modules. This can be very useful during troubleshooting or if you use kernel modules that must be loaded in a specific order. For further details on the options available at the loader command line, consult man loader.

This concludes the boot block phase of the bootstrapping process. We're now well on the way to bringing the system all the way up. The final phase of the boot process is where the complete FreeBSD system starts to come into play; where the kernel loads itself into memory, probes its available devices, and runs the "resource configuration" scripts that construct a working environment and start up the various system services.

- **kernel**. After loader transfers control, the kernel begins to probe all the devices it can find, and the results of each probe are echoed to the screen. This is the time where you will see many boot messages. These messages are logged into the dmesg files, which you can read with the dmesg command if you need to see what the kernel had to say about a certain device.

Tip

dmesg is a fairly rudimentary tool, listing the contents of the system message buffer that have accumulated since the system last booted. Simply enter dmesg to view the list of messages, or enter dmesg | less to view the output in an interactive pager for easier access.

- **init**. After the kernel loads, it passes control to the init process, the final stage in the startup procedure. This is signaled by the "Automatic reboot in progress" message, which involves init running the Resource Configuration script (/etc/rc). This script first checks all the filesystem devices in /etc/fstab for consistency, as we discussed in Chapter 9, "The FreeBSD Filesystem."

  If fsck finds no problems that it cannot correct on its own, it will mount all the filesystems (using mount -a -t nonfs) and continue running the rest of the startup processes. If fsck finds an unresolvable problem with the disks, it will exit to single-user mode for you to run fsck manually and repair the damage. Exit the single-user shell to continue rebooting into multiuser mode.

Finally, if all goes according to plan, you get a login prompt. This whole process usually takes no more than a minute.

Securing the Boot Process

Of concern to the security-conscious administrator is the fact that by default, if you choose to boot into single-user mode (`boot -s` at the `loader` prompt), you are not prompted for a password—the system comes up automatically with full root access. If you're sharing the machine with anyone else—so that they can sit down in front of the machine and physically reboot it if they want to—this constitutes a grave and gaping security hole.

Fortunately, it's easy to plug this hole. In `/etc/ttys`, which contains terminal settings for the various access methods (the console, virtual terminals, serial terminals, and network [pseudo] terminals), you can change the setting on the `console` line from `secure` to `insecure`:

```
console none                              unknown off insecure
```

This tells the system to treat the console as an insecure access point, and to present a challenge (login prompt) to anyone who tries to boot into single-user mode.

Note

The `console` terminal method is only used in single-user mode; when booting fully multiuser, multiple virtual terminals are available at the physical terminal (switch between them with Alt+F1, Alt+F2, and so on). These terminals always present a login prompt. The `secure` and `insecure` settings in this case control whether you can log in as root, or whether it requires that you log in as a regular user and then su to gain root access.

A second security hole to plug, which is a very good idea if others have access to the physical terminal (even if you've secured the single-user console), is the fact that Ctrl+Alt+Delete causes the system to reboot, whether or not you're logged in as root—or logged in at all. The three-finger-salute works even at the login prompt. This is appropriate behavior in some situations (a rack-mounted server in a trusted machine room, for example), but not in others. To disable it, you'll need to add an option to your kernel configuration and rebuild the kernel:

```
options         SC_DISABLE_REBOOT
```

For a detailed discussion of kernel options and configuring your kernel, see Chapter 17, "Kernel Configuration."

What Can Slow Down the Boot Process?

Your system might take longer than this. However, because of the scripted, serial nature of the boot process, it's fairly simple to see where it's hanging. Two common culprits are sendmail and httpd (Apache); in both cases, the typical reason for their slowness is a network connectivity problem or misconfiguration.

Both Sendmail and Apache have to figure out your machine's hostname; to do this, they need to do a reverse lookup against the DNS (domain name server) configured in /etc/resolv.conf. (TCP/IP setup will be covered thoroughly in Chapter 23, "Configuring Basic Networking Services.") This lookup will have to time-out for every configured name server before it fails and allows the startup process to proceed. Network timeouts are often fairly long, which is why networking is the most common cause of boot hangups. One solution to this problem is to make sure that the name server listed first in /etc/resolv.conf is reachable from your FreeBSD machine; this ensures that Sendmail and Apache will be able to determine the machine's hostname and start up without delay. If this is not possible, list 127.0.0.1 (localhost) as the first name server and disable the rest.

Incidentally, this is why init uses mount -a -t nonfs when doing its initial "preen" to see if it can safely go into multiuser mode. NFS has an astonishingly long timeout period, and a process waiting for that timeout to occur can be almost impossible to kill. The mount command, which we saw in Chapter 9 avoids mounting NFS resources until later in resource configuration, so that it can come up properly in multiuser mode without user intervention. However, init does mount all filesystems later in /etc/rc, including NFS ones. Any NFS resources that you configured for automatic mounting in /etc/fstab (for example, without the noauto option) have the potential to freeze the system for a long time when the /etc/rc script reaches that point. Don't auto-mount NFS resources at boot unless you're sure you'll always be able to reach them!

Resource Configuration Scripts

Anything in /etc that has a filename beginning with rc is a resource configuration script, a program that starts up parts of FreeBSD according to the system's configuration. Some are called recursively from other programs, some do nothing in the out-of-the-box configuration, and some will probably never even be run. However, there is only one rc file in /etc that you should ever edit to change system startup behavior, and that is

/etc/rc.conf. All the resource configuration scripts that FreeBSD uses are described in Table 11.2.

TABLE 11.1   Resource Configuration Scripts

Script Name	Description
/etc/rc	The main resource config script.
/etc/rc.diskless1	init reads these scripts if you're doing a diskless boot via BOOTP.
/etc/rc.diskless2 /etc/defaults/rc.conf	init reads in this file early to fill in its laundry list of tasks to do.
/etc/rc.conf	This is the file you edit to override defaults set in /etc/defaults/rc.conf. *This should be the ONLY resource config file in /etc that you edit!*
/etc/rc.sysctl	Sets runtime kernel variables. Does nothing by default.
/etc/rc.serial	Sets up terminals and other serial devices.
/etc/rc.pccard	Runs the PC-card daemon for laptops.
/etc/rc.network	Sets up TCP/IP networking.
/etc/rc.network6	Same as rc.network, except for IPv6 services.
/etc/rc.atm	Called from rc.network; sets up ATM devices for WAN machines.
/etc/rc.firewall	Called from rc.network; configures an ipfw firewall.
/etc/rc.firewall6	Called from ro.network0; configures an ip6fw firewall.
/etc/rc.i386	Architecture-specific startups for the x86 platform, such as console options and APM.
/etc/rc.shutdown	Executed by init when it is shut down (using shutdown).
/etc/rc.suspend	Scripts used for the APM power management daemon.
/etc/rc.devfs	Configures the device filesystem.
/etc/rc.local	Obsolete method of adding your own startup script extensions. Use the rc.d method (following) instead!
/usr/local/etc/rc.d/ /usr/local/X11R6/etc/rc.d/	Directory trees containing any new startup scripts you add (or are installed automatically by programs).

Of the files listed previously, the only ones that concern us are /etc/defaults/rc.conf, /etc/rc.conf, and the local rc.d directory trees. Everything else should be left untouched so that future installations of FreeBSD can upgrade the files while preserving your customizations.

The `/etc/defaults/rc.conf` File

Take a look through the `/etc/rc` script. You'll see that it's completely automated; it works by checking whether certain variables are defined that control system configuration or whether certain files exist; if so, it executes a predefined, abstracted launch loop, which takes its parameters from those variables and files. Nothing in `/etc/rc` itself should be edited. In other systems, the system startup process is altered and extended by making changes to the resource configuration scripts themselves; in FreeBSD, though, the model is to automate and abstract as much as possible of the process and centralize the control files that specify the parameters.

In earlier versions of FreeBSD, there was only `/etc/rc.conf`; it contained all the variables that `/etc/rc` and related scripts would need in their default states, and any modifications to the system would be made to that file. This quickly became unmanageable as the list of variables grew and the role of the file expanded. An administrator upgrading the system would painstakingly have to merge the old `rc.conf` with the new. This was hardly an improvement over just editing `/etc/rc` in the first place.

So, the solution was to create an `/etc/defaults` directory, and put a copy of `rc.conf`, with all the defaults filled in, into this directory. Now, `/etc/rc.conf` still exists, but it can be empty and the system will still boot. Its purpose is to fill in overrides for the defaults in `/etc/defaults/rc.conf`; typical overrides are for the networking configuration (IP address, hostname, gateway address, and so on) and for running daemons like `sendmail` and `sshd`.

Let's look at a typical block in `/etc/defaults/rc.conf`, shown in Listing 11.1.

LISTING 11.1   Excerpt from `/etc/defaults/rc.conf`

```
# named. It may be possible to run named in a sandbox, man security for
# details.
#
named_enable="NO"              # Run named, the DNS server (or NO).
named_program="named"          # path to named, if you want a different one.
named_flags=""                 # Flags for named
#named_flags="-u bind -g bind" # Flags for named
```

Now, you can find what `/etc/rc` will do by default. In this case, we see that the default behavior is to not run `named` at all.

Typically, variables in `/etc/defaults/rc.conf` are grouped into these blocks, with similar prefixes keeping them related, and with a single `"YES"`/`"NO"` variable serving as a "master switch" at the top. If the variable is set to `"NO"`, generally none of the rest of the variables will matter; if it is set to "YES", they will all apply unless commented out (as with the second named_flags line in the previous example, which we can see is provided as an example in case we wanted to create a bind user and group for named to run as).

The /etc/rc.conf File

Let's say we do want to run named. In the simplest case, all we would have to do is edit /etc/rc.conf (the overrides file) and add the following line anywhere in the file:

```
named_enable="YES"
```

The rest of the named_* variables in /etc/defaults/rc.conf do not need to be copied into the overrides file; remember, every variable in the defaults file is loaded into memory by init, and they only matter if the "master switch" for that block has been turned to "YES". If it has, the variables will be used in the execution loop in /etc/rc to launch whatever process is controlled by the block we're working on (in this case, named).

You can use these other variables for fine-tuning, though, and override them just as easily. Let's say that your name server program was a customized version called mynamed. Let's also say that you created a bind user and group, intending that the name server should run as this user and group so it won't be susceptible to as many security hacks. Well, to handle that, all you need to do (assuming that mynamed has the same behavior and command-line options as named) is add these two lines to /etc/rc.conf:

```
named_program="mynamed"
named_flags="-u bind -g bind"
```

Just for curiosity's sake, let's see what init is doing with these variables:

```
# grep "named_enable" /etc/rc*
/etc/rc.network:        oaoc ${named_enable} in
```

Okay, so it's launched from /etc/rc.network. Looking in that file, we find this loop:

```
network_pass2() {
        echo -n 'Doing additional network setup:'
        case ${named_enable} in
        [Yy][Ee][Ss])
                echo -n ' named';        ${named_program:-named} ${named_flags}
                ;;
        esac
```

Here, we can see all the named_* variables from both rc.conf files being invoked; now, when you boot the system and see "named" appear in the console messages after "Doing additional network setup:", you know that it's applying your overrides over the defaults and running the name server automatically.

> **Note**
>
> See Chapter 13, "Shell Programming," for a tutorial on shell scripting, which will help in reading the resource configuration scripts.

The most typical variables that appear in /etc/rc.conf are the TCP/IP configuration parameters because they will naturally be different for every system; FreeBSD can't very well specify them in the defaults, after all. Listing 11.2 shows a typical /etc/rc.conf just after a new FreeBSD installation:

LISTING 11.2   A Newly Installed /etc/rc.conf

```
# This file now contains just the overrides from /etc/defaults/rc.conf
# please make all changes to this file.

# Enable network daemons for user convenience.
# -- sysinstall generated deltas -- #
kern_securelevel="1"
kern_securelevel_enable="YES"
linux_enable="YES"
sendmail_enable="YES"
sshd_enable="YES"
portmap_enable="NO"
nfs_server_enable-"NO"
inetd_enable="NO"
network_interfaces="fxp0 lo0"
ifconfig_fxp0="inet 10.6.7.101   netmask 255.0.0.0"
defaultrouter="10.6.1.1"
hostname="freebsd1.testnetwork.com"
usbd_enable="YES"
```

Some of these variables are in fact redundant with the defaults file; still, it can be useful to also have them in the overrides file because many of these features (such as the NFS server) now have a one-touch toggle control, as it were.

Many programs, when you install them, will have to install a way for themselves to start up at boot time; /etc/rc.conf is not, however, the place for them. That file is supposed to be touched only by you, the administrator, and by the sysinstall program when it makes changes to the core system. For user-installed programs (ports and packages), and for any scripts that /etc/rc and friends do not know about, there is another structure in place for their startup scripts and configuration files: the /usr/local/etc hierarchy.

The `/usr/local/etc` and `/usr/local/X11R6/etc` Directories

Remember in Chapter 9 where we noted that "anything installed by the administrator goes into `/usr/local`?" This is as true of startup scripts as it is of programs and shared libraries. The `/usr/local/etc` directory is the "local" equivalent of `/etc`, and into it go all the configuration files that are installed by programs that you choose to install, rather than the ones that are controlled by the FreeBSD base system distribution.

> **Note**
>
> It's important to note that the difference between the `/etc` files and the `/usr/local/etc` files is *not* that the former are non-editable and the latter are; just as most of the files in `/etc` should not be tampered with, many of the ones in `/usr/local/etc` also contain no user-serviceable parts, or are designed not to need any modification by you in order to function (although the directory also contains customizable configuration files for installed programs). The distinction is that `/etc` controls the base system—for example, only those programs that are always part of a FreeBSD installation. The ones in `/usr/local/etc` are instead the analogous files that control programs that you install after the fact, from the ports collection or from packages (which we will cover in Chapter 15, "Installing Additional Software"). `/usr/local/etc` also doubles as the location for any startup scripts that you yourself write.

The main local configuration directory `/usr/local/etc` contains configuration files that the administrator will edit to tune their respective programs' behavior; we will see specifically how they work in Chapter 15 when we look at ports and packages. However, what we are interested in right now is the `rc.d` subdirectory (which stands for "Resource Configuration for Daemons").

`init` turns its attention to `/usr/local/etc/rc.d` after it has run through all the other `/etc/rc.*` scripts. Any executable file within the directory that ends in `.sh` will be executed in lexicographical order. Examples of files that will be installed in here include `apache.sh`, `mysql-server.sh`, and `samba.sh`. These scripts are custom-built as part of the ports or packages, and each one is tuned to take a `start` or `stop` argument; when `init` runs each script, it uses the `start` argument. Note that you can just as easily run these scripts yourself during runtime—for instance, to start a newly installed service without rebooting:

```
# /usr/local/etc/rc.d/apache.sh start
```

Some ports or packages will install with a secondary suffix of `.sample` (for example, `samba.sh.sample`). This is because the program that it's part of has to be properly configured before it can run successfully. Apache, for instance, will run immediately after installation without any further modification to its `config` files (though you will no doubt be modifying them anyway!), so it installs an `apache.sh` file, which could run the program cleanly if you rebooted it right then. But Samba must be tuned first to run on your machine; if you ran the script right after installing it, it would fail to start the daemon. You need to rename the script to remove the `.sample` extension before it will be run on startup by `init`.

The `/usr/local/X11R6/etc` directory is analogous to `/usr/local/etc`, except it is specifically tasked to X11-based programs: GNOME panels, graphical tools, games, window managers, and so on. This directory also has an `rc.d` subdirectory, and scripts in it are executed immediately after the ones in `/usr/local/etc/rc.d`. The local startup-script directories are configurable. Override this `rc.conf` line to add more directories if you need to:

```
local_startup="/usr/local/etc/rc.d /usr/X11R6/etc/rc.d" # startup script dirs.
```

Creating Scripts to Run Programs on System Boot

It is perhaps a bit idealistic to imagine that you will never need to have the system perform any startup tasks that are not tied to any of the carefully crafted ports/packages or the core system. You may want to run a custom daemon that you wrote yourself, for example, or clear out a common file-sharing directory every time the system boots. To do this, you can write your own shell script and put it into `/usr/local/etc/rc.d`.

Recall that `init` expects every script in the `rc.d` directory to be able to handle the `start` argument, and that its name has to end in `.sh` in order to be run automatically. The following is an example script from the `man rc` page:

```sh
#!/bin/sh -
#
#     initialization/shutdown script for foobar package

case "$1" in
start)
        /usr/local/sbin/foo -d && echo -n ' foo'
        ;;
*)
        echo "unknown option: $1 - should be 'start'" >&2
        ;;
esac
```

You might call this file `foo.sh`. Make sure it is set executable (`chmod +x foo.sh`)!

Technically, the program doesn't actually have to be a shell script; you can write it in perl if you want, or even C or anything else that will run, as long as it has a `.sh` extension. This is fairly bad form, though. You shouldn't have to try to fool the system! For more on shell scripting, consult Chapter 13.

The `inetd` Daemon and the `inetd.conf` Configuration File

Although there are a fair number of daemons in the base system that have `.conf` files in the `/etc` directory, the most important (and sensitive) one you will have to deal with is `inetd`, the "super-server." We will take a brief look at `inetd` here, and discuss how to configure it.

The job of `inetd` is to listen for connections on a specified set of network ports and fire off the appropriate server process when a request comes in. For instance, `inetd` is in charge of telnet connections; if your system allows telnet, you can open a connection to it and receive a login prompt without any `telnetd` process running on the server beforehand. Every time the system receives a connection request on Port 23, it creates a new `telnetd` process to handle the connection. Executable programs that run out of `inetd` (and other similar daemons) are in `/usr/libexec`. These programs are not generally part of your command path and are not supposed to be run from the command line; instead, they are spawned from within another process and passed certain resources (such as environment variables and network connections).

> **Note**
>
> The use of `inetd` eliminates the need for a "master" `telnetd` process running as root, which is a situation that could be particularly dangerous if a security vulnerability were to be uncovered in `telnetd`. Many daemons (among them `sshd`, `httpd` (Apache), and `sendmail`) do run in this "standalone" mode rather than being called out of `inetd`. The master process (running as root) listens for the new connections and spawns new processes, owned by an unprivileged user, to handle each transaction. This allows for greater flexibility and speed in the program, at the expense of a centralized security risk. `inetd` also runs as root, so it is just as dangerous if it is compromised. The more daemons that run as root, the more possibilities there are for security holes to be found.

Examining the /etc/inetd.conf file shows us that nearly all entries in it are disabled in the out-of-the-box configuration. The only ones that are enabled are listed in Table 11.2.

TABLE 11.2 System Services Controlled by inetd that Are Enabled by Default

Service	Description	Port(s)/Resources Used
ftp	File Transfer Protocol	Port 21/TCP
telnet	Remote terminal	Port 23/TCP
comsat	"biff" server (notifies users of incoming mail)	Port 512/UDP
ntalk	command-line chat server	Port 518/TCP,UDP
ftp (IPv6)	File Transfer Protocol	IPv6
telnet (IPv6)	Remote terminal	IPv6

Other services that you'll probably want to enable are as follows in Table 11.3.

TABLE 11.3 Other Useful inetd Services

Service	Description	Port(s)/Resources Used
pop3	Post Office Protocol	Port 110/TCP
imap4	Interim Mail Access Protocol (server-side mail)	Port 143/TCP
smtp	Qmail (alternative to Sendmail SMTP server)	Port 25/TCP
netbios-ssn		
netbios-ns	Samba file sharing with Windows	Port 139/TCP
		Port 137/TCP
finger	Lookup user information	Port 79/TCP

To enable any one of these services, simply remove the comment (#) from the beginning of the line and then restart the inetd server, as follows:

```
# ps -waux | grep inetd
root    110  0.0  0.6  1032  752  ??  Ss   11:57PM   0:00.01 inetd
# kill -HUP 110
```

Tip

If you have selected to run the system at security level 1 or higher (an install-time option—level 1 is the "Medium" security level mentioned in the installer),

> `inetd` will not be running. This is indicative of the risky nature of many of the
> services that run out of `inetd`. If you are running at this security level and want
> to run `inetd`, you can run it by entering `inetd -wW`. To enable it permanently,
> remove or toggle this line in `/etc/rc.conf`:
>
> `inetd_enable="NO"`

`inetd` is one of the areas of FreeBSD without a lot of automation built in or safety nets
to prevent bad configurations. If you must enable services in `/etc/inetd.conf`, be aware
that you're venturing into a nonstandard type of setup, and you should know what you're
getting into. For instance, the `cvs` services come with a dire warning about a security
hole that can be opened up with a misconfigured parameter. The Samba services (`net-
bios-ssn` and `netbios-ns`) expect to find the `smbd` and `nmbd` binaries in
`/usr/local/sbin`, but they won't be there unless you installed Samba from the ports or
packages. (Running Samba from `inetd` instead of standalone is a nonstandard, alternative configuration.)

Similarly, other services (such as `pop3`) try to run services installed into
`/usr/local/libexec`. But remember, this directory is inside `/usr/local`, meaning that
unless you explicitly installed a program there, it won't be there. Installing the `popper`
port/package will put the necessary binary into that directory, so you can enable the service in `inetd`. However, if you choose instead to install the `qpopper` port/package
(another POP3 server), the binary will be `qpopper` instead of `popper`, and you'll have to
modify the line accordingly:

```
pop3    stream  tcp     nowait  root    /usr/local/libexec/qpopper       qpopper
```

Numerous other pitfalls await the unwary. Be sure not to modify the `inetd` services any
more extensively than you really have to. The `man inetd` page provides a more extensive
discussion of the syntax and technique of handling `inetd`.

The System Logger (`syslogd`) and the `syslog.conf` File

System messages are logged to files in `/var/log`. The mechanism that does this is called
`syslogd`, the system logger daemon. Its behaviors are set in `/etc/syslog.conf`, which
defines various different log files for different services. Each service or "facility" that it
knows about (which can be any of `auth`, `authpriv`, `console`, `cron`, `daemon`, `ftp`, `kern`,
`lpr`, `mail`, `mark`, `news`, `ntp`, `security`, `syslog`, `user`, `uucp` and `local0` through `local7`)

has a number of different "severity" levels for which you can control logging. These levels include `emerg`, `alert`, `crit`, `err`, `warning`, `notice`, `info` and `debug`, listed in decreasing order of severity.

Each daemon or service that you run in FreeBSD can log through the pre-defined facilities of `syslogd`; for instance, Sendmail and other mail programs can use the system's `syslog()` routines to send out messages at various levels of severity, using the `mail` facility; the messages would be handled by `syslogd` as defined in `syslog.conf`.

By default, `syslog.conf` defines several logging rules as follows:

```
*.err;kern.debug;auth.notice;mail.crit          /dev/console
*.notice;kern.debug;lpr.info;mail.crit;news.err /var/log/messages
security.*                                       /var/log/security
mail.info                                        /var/log/maillog
lpr.info                                         /var/log/lpd-errs
cron.*                                           /var/log/cron
*.err                                            root
*.notice;news.err                                root
*.alert                                          root
*.emerg                                          *
```

We can interpret this to mean that all `err` messages from any service, `debug` messages from the kernel, authorization `notice` messages, and `crit` messages from mail programs will be printed out to the system console, and you will see them if you have a monitor hooked up to your FreeBSD machine. Similarly, all security-related messages go into the `/var/log/security` file, and all messages from mail programs at the `info` level go into `/var/log/maillog`. Almost everything else goes into `/var/log/messages`, the general system log file. (If you're used to Linux, this file is equivalent to what is usually called `syslog`.)

Certain types of messages are not merely written to log files, but are sent to a variety of other types of handling mechanisms. In the default `syslog.conf`, messages from any service at the `err`, `notice`, or `alert` level are printed to any terminal where root is logged in, and `emerg` messages are printed to the all users at all terminals. Table 11.4 shows the possible actions for `syslogd` messages and the syntax for each.

TABLE 11.4   Syntaxes for `syslogd` actions

Syntax	*Action Taken*
`/path/to/file`	Messages are written to the specified file.
`@some.hostname.com`	Messages are forwarded to the `syslogd` at `some.hostname.com` using the `syslog` network service.

TABLE 11.4 Continued

Syntax	Action Taken
user1	Messages are printed to any terminal where user1 is logged in.
root,user1,user2	All specified users receive messages on all their terminals.
*	Messages are written to all logged-in users.
| "mail root"	Messages are mailed to root.

Further details on how to configure syslogd can be found in the man syslogd and man syslog.conf pages.

> **Note**
>
> Each log file in /var/log is rolled-over according to a different set of rules. For instance, the /var/log/maillog file is archived and restarted every day by the periodic program. Other log files, such as /var/log/cron and /var/log/messages, are refreshed through other means (often internally by the programs that write to them). Archived log files are generally compressed with gzip. To search through old log files, use gzcat in conjunction with the conventional grep:
>
> ```
> # gzcat /var/log/messages.2.gz | grep "rejected"
> ```

Notes on the /etc/rc.local File

A resource configuration script mentioned earlier in this chapter received almost no mention, except that it was obsolete: /etc/rc.local. This file will be familiar to administrators who used earlier versions of FreeBSD or certain distributions of Linux. Its purpose is much the same as the /usr/local/etc/rc.d directories—to provide you with a mechanism to extend the system's startup behavior.

The rc.d method described earlier is the preferred method of accomplishing this. It is more structured: It keeps each startup task in its own script with a common interface—corraled into /usr/local and out of /etc. However, if you must use it, /etc/rc.local still works, although it doesn't exist in the default installation. You can create the file (with the proper interpreter line modeled after the other rc.* files) and put any set of shell commands into it, and it will be executed just before the rc.d scripts.

Support for `rc.local` is for backward-compatibility only, and it may eventually be removed from FreeBSD. To make sure that your system supports it, check `/etc/rc` for mention of the `rc.local` file, as shown in Listing 11.3.

Listing 11.3   Excerpt from `/etc/rc` Showing Support for `/etc/rc.local`

```
# grep -A 5 rc.local /etc/rc
# Do traditional (but rather obsolete) rc.local file if it exists. If you
# use this file and want to make it programmatic, source /etc/defaults/rc.conf
# in /etc/rc.local and add your custom variables to /etc/rc.conf, as
# shown below. Please do not put local extensions into /etc/rc itself.
# Use /etc/rc.local
#
# ---- rc.local ----
#       if [ -r /etc/defaults/rc.conf ]; then
#             . /etc/defaults/rc.conf
#             source_rc_confs
#       elif [ -r /etc/rc.conf ]; then
#             . /etc/rc.conf
--
# ---- rc.local ----
#
if [ -r /etc/rc.local ]; then
        echo -n 'starting local daemons:'
        sh /etc/rc.local
        echo '.'
fi

# For each valid dir in $local_startup, search for init scripts matching *.sh
#
```

The loop that runs `sh /etc/rc.local` is what you're looking for. if it's there and not commented out, you can use `rc.local`. It is still a much better idea, however, to use the `rc.d` script method.

CHAPTER 12

Customizing the Shell

Whether you choose to operate your FreeBSD system through the X-Windows GUI or not, the facts of life are that you're going to have to deal with a shell, particularly as an administrator. A shell gives you all the flexibility you need to accomplish even the most complex tasks, but meanwhile dictates a user experience that's arcane at best. In this chapter, we'll make ourselves at home in the shell, comfortable enough to use it as a programming environment and "captain's chair" as well as a user interface.

What Is a Shell?

We've already talked about the basics of the shell and what you can do with it back in Chapter 8, "Working with the Shell." That chapter introduced the shell as a command-line interface, and discussed the various shells you can use in FreeBSD and what kinds of commands are available in the shell for controlling the system. Now, though, we'll be looking at the shell itself in more detail as it applies to the multitudes of users you might be supporting on your system, and how to customize it to your taste.

We already know that a shell (in brief) is a command-line interface in which you can enter the typed commands that make the UNIX computing experience so markedly different from a fully GUI-based one such as Windows or Mac OS. It's similar in function to the COMMAND.COM command interpreter in MS-DOS and its descendants in Windows, but vastly more complex and useful, since it plays a much more important role than in a GUI-based operating system.

However—why is it called a "shell?" Well, it has to do with the terminology used in UNIX architecture to describe the various levels of system operation that separate the innermost, most automated functions from the outermost, user-triggered functions. On the inside is the *kernel*, which we have mentioned in earlier chapters and will cover thoroughly in Chapter 17, "Kernel Configuration." On the outside is the user. How does the user interact with the kernel and its surrounding support programs? Through the shell, naturally. This relationship is illustrated in Figure 12.1.

The job of the shell is to give the user a safe, structured way to access the kernel. As a command interpreter, the shell takes your commands and translates them into processes that access files and devices through the kernel. It prevents you from executing unsafe code that could crash the kernel, and it eases your ability to find and execute the programs that run the system.

In a more practical sense, the shell is simply a program—a forking-capable utility that is executed by the system whenever you log in, presents you with a command prompt, interprets your commands, and terminates when you log out. In fact, these are the only things a shell really needs to be or do; any program can act as a shell, which is a fact that can be used with great creativity, as we will see.

FIGURE 12.1

The kernel surrounded by the shell.

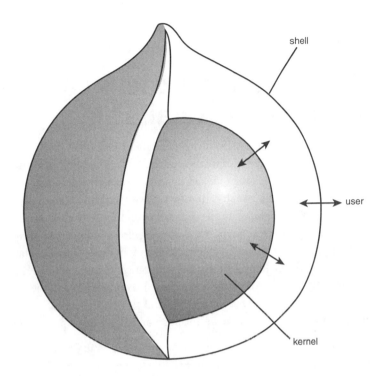

shell

user

kernel

You will also probably encounter the term "shell" used in a number of slightly different contexts. For instance, any program running on top of another and providing an interface to it is a type of shell; Windows 95 is technically a shell, albeit a better-disguised one than its predecessors (Windows 3.1, DESQview, and the short-lived MS-DOS Shell). Many programs will offer you the option to "shell out" to DOS or the command-line interface; this is common in older programs that predate multitasking operating systems or terminal-based programs in which you're likely to have only one window open to the system. In their case, "shelling out" means executing a shell program (such as the DOS or UNIX command line) from within the program you're in, suspending the program while you perform operations "above" it.

In Chapter 8, we looked at the various choices of programs for FreeBSD that are specifically designed to be shells, in the sense that they are command interpreters capable of running scripts in specialized shell scripting languages. Some of these programs are sh, csh, bash, ksh, and tcsh; these shells differ subtly in their behavior and in the programming languages they support. Chapter 13, "Shell Programming," will cover scripting in the Bourne shell (sh) environment, the most popular by far. However, for now we will turn our attention to a somewhat more pedestrian and everyday topic: configuring your chosen shell to fit your taste and needs.

Before we can do this, we must look at how to add shells to FreeBSD that are not included with the base system, and how to change from one shell to another.

Adding Shells to the System and Making Them Available

Most users will probably be satisfied with the default FreeBSD shell, /bin/tcsh (the same as /bin/csh). It provides command-line editing, tab-completion, history, and the rest of the advanced shell features lacked by the more rudimentary shells. However, the fact that FreeBSD defaults to tcsh rather than bash (which is commonly used in Linux) reflects the subtle philosophical differences between the BSD tradition and the System V structure (which accounts for much of the architecture of Linux), an argument as old as UNIX itself. These philosophical differences used to mean a lot more than they do today. Commercial flavors of UNIX generally fall into one camp or the other, and haven't changed materially in years; between Linux and FreeBSD, though, the more significant philosophical difference is between the GNU and BSD license structures. That's where we see the roots of Linux's preference for bash and FreeBSD's preference for tcsh.

Because bash is a GNU-oriented program, and because Linux tends to prefer software developed under the GNU Public License (GPL), bash is the default Linux shell. The feature sets of bash and tcsh are quite similar, but these features are accessed in different ways, and the configuration process and runtime behavior of the two shells differ subtly. Readers who are used to Linux may want to install bash in order to remain in a familiar environment. Or, you might come from a system in which your shell was ksh or zsh. This is no problem; we'll now look at how to go about installing these shells and using them seamlessly.

The remainder of this chapter will examine both tcsh and bash in each section, showing the differences in configuration and usage for each one. For additional shells, you're on your own—you'll need to install the shells and read their man pages for details.

Installing Shells from the Ports or Packages

The preferred way to install software on FreeBSD is through the ports or packages, which is described in detail in Chapter 15, "Installing Additional Software." You can get instructions in that chapter on how to use the ports collection and the packages for all your software management needs. For now, we'll cover the most basic commands and procedures for installing new shells.

Installing from Packages

The simplest way to install a new shell is through `sysinstall` and its interface to the package manager. Run `/stand/sysinstall`; select "`Configure`" and then choose "`Packages`". Select your installation media—CDROM if you have the FreeBSD installation CD handy, or FTP otherwise.

After you've received the package list, go into the "shells" subsection, and scroll through the list of available shells. Press the spacebar to place an "X" on each shell you want to install. Press Enter once you're done selecting shells to install, and you'll be returned to the main package selection screen. Use the right-arrow key to select "`Install`".

The software will now download automatically and install itself. Once it's done, exit out of `sysinstall` by returning to the "`Exit`" option at the top of the Configuration menu, then "`Exit Install`" from the bottom of the screen. The shell (or shells) you've selected are now installed. You can verify this installation by looking in `/usr/local/bin`, and by reading the `man` page for the shell you've installed, for example `man bash`.

Installing from the Ports

An alternate way to install software, also described in Chapter 15, is the ports collection. This is a rigorously structured way to compile and install the software on your own machine while guaranteeing that the installed files will be put in the proper locations (for instance, inside `/usr/local`, according to the FreeBSD hierarchy rules). If installed, the ports collection is in `/usr/ports`, and contains the same hierarchical structure found in the packages as browsed through `sysinstall`.

Go into /usr/ports/shells and look around. This is a fairly small section of the ports collection; most of the other categories have lots more available programs for you to install.

44bsd-csh/	es/	osh/	rc/	vshnu/
Makefile	esh/	pash/	ruby-shell/	wapsh/
README.html	flash/	pdksh/	sash/	zsh/
bash1/	ksh93/	perlsh/	scsh/	zsh-devel/
bash2/	mudsh/	pkg/	tcsh/	

All you have to do is go into the directory, and type `make`; the system will retrieve the distribution file, unpack it, patch it, configure it, and compile it. Then, type `make install` to install the package, and type `make clean` to delete all the temporary files created during the build process:

```
# cd /usr/ports/shells/bash2
# make
  ...
# make install
  ...
# make clean
  ...
```

Once this process is complete, the new shell will be installed and available for use.

> **Note**
>
> You may need to type `rehash` (if you're using `tcsh`) to force the shell program to reread your shell configuration files and the available programs in your path after installing any new programs; otherwise, you won't be able to access those programs unless you log out and then back in.

The `/etc/shells` File

A very important system file that you'll need to know about when working with shells is `/etc/shells`. This is simply a list of the installed shells on the system, listed with their full paths. Following is an example of an `/etc/shells` on a working system with three extra shells installed:

```
# cat /etc/shells
# $FreeBSD: src/etc/shells,v 1.3 1999/08/27 23:23:45 peter Exp $
#
# List of acceptable shells for chpass(1).
# Ftpd will not allow users to connect who are not using
# one of these shells.

/bin/sh
/bin/csh
/bin/tcsh
/usr/local/bin/bash
/usr/local/bin/zsh
/usr/local/bin/ksh
```

The purpose of `/etc/shells` is to specify the shell programs that you, the administrator, consider "valid". This allows you to ensure that a user cannot change his default shell to a program that isn't designed to be used as one. Especially problematic are setuid programs, or programs that run with the effective UID of the user that owns them (as we saw in Chapter 10, "Users, Groups, and Permissions"). If a `setuid` program is owned by root, it can execute any action with root's privileges; it's clearly not desirable for a user to be able to attain these privileges simply by logging in. The `chsh` program (which we will discuss shortly) will not allow a regular user to change his default shell to any program that you have not listed in /etc/shells.

A user's shell is specified in the /etc/master.passwd user database, in the tenth field of each user's record (or the seventh field in /etc/passwd), as we saw in Chapter 8:

```
/etc/master.passwd:
foo:*:$1$LXZkCuzD$7Oa8LyRgbjYOb.XrXiBad.:1001:1001::999066364:0:Foo
Bar:/home/foo:/usr/local/bin/ksh
/etc/passwd:
foo:*:1001:1001::Foo Bar:/home/foo:/usr/local/bin/ksh
```

If that field's value (/usr/local/bin/ksh in this example) is set to a shell that appears in /etc/shells, the user will be allowed to log in using services such as FTP. If not, access will be denied. Also, /etc/shells is used to generate the list of available shells that you can assign a user during the adduser process, which we covered in Chapter 10.

An entry is added automatically to /etc/shells each time you install a shell through the ports or packages, as described earlier. Note that although only the administrator (root) can change a user's shell to a program not listed in /etc/shells, a user can log in as a shell user whether or not the assigned shell appears in /etc/shells. The shells database also controls access to the system via FTP; a common trap is for an administrator to install a shell without using the ports or packages (thus not adding an entry to /etc/shells), and then to switch another user to that new shell (because the administrator is allowed to do so). The regular user can telnet or ssh to the machine without any trouble—but as soon as he tries to FTP to it, he will be inexplicably denied access. The solution to this is simply to make sure that his shell is listed in /etc/shells Always use the ports or packages to install shells properly.

Using Alternate Shells

Any user can change his or her assigned shell at any time. The reasons for doing this are myriad: Someone might be accustomed to Linux and bash, as described earlier, or he might have a highly customized shell environment from another system that is only in a certain shell's configuration format (as we will discuss shortly). Regardless of the reason, changing a user's shell is pretty easy.

Changing Your Shell While Logged In

The simplest way to use an alternate shell is simply to run it. If your default shell is tcsh, and you want to use bash (assuming that bash is available on the system), just type bash to open a new bash environment within your tcsh session.

```
# bash
bash-2.04#
```

Now, when you log out, you'll have to do it twice: once to exit the `bash` process, and again to exit the original `tcsh` process. When your login shell program exits, you are disconnected from the system.

Changing Your Default Shell

Running a shell, other than your default one, every time you log in can get tedious; while you can do it automatically by adding the command for the second shell into your `.login` file (an initialization script which runs when the shell is started, as we will discuss shortly), this still means you're running a shell within a shell, which isn't very efficient. Fortunately, any user can change his shell to any program listed in `/etc/shells`. The `chsh` (change shell) program is used for this task. This program differs in its behavior from platform to platform; on some, such as Linux, `chsh` is a command-line, interactive tool that prompts for new values one by one. In FreeBSD, however, `chsh` is really the same program as `chpass`, `chfn`, and other user-management tools: They're all hard links to each other. They all have the same function.

The behavior of `chsh` (and its identical siblings) is to open your user information in a text editor and allow you to change the values in any of the available fields. The editor used by default is `vi`, although this can be overridden by setting the `EDITOR` environment variable to the name of a different program, such as `ee` or `pico`. (We will talk about environment variables in just a moment.)

To change your own shell, simply enter `chsh`. If you're root, you can modify another user's shell by supplying that user's login as the argument.

```
# chsh frank
#Changing user database information for frank.
Shell: /bin/tcsh
Full Name: Frank Allen
Office Location:
Office Phone:
Home Phone:
Other information:
~
~
```

Using `vi` is no easy feat for a beginner; there are whole books just on its usage, utilitarian though the program's design is. For now, let's concentrate on the necessary commands you'll need for changing the user's shell. Part of what makes `vi` so challenging is that its internal commands are so arcane and must be entered so exactly that it's easy to get to a point at which crucial data has been accidentally deleted or mangled, and can't be retrieved. If you make a mistake, enter a colon (`:`) followed by `q!`, then press Enter; this will force an exit without saving changes.

```
~
~
:q!
```

Let's say we want to change frank's shell permanently from `/bin/tcsh` to `/usr/local/bin/bash`. Once in the `vi` screen, obtained by typing `chsh frank`, use the arrow keys to move to the beginning of the word `tcsh`, immediately after the second slash (`/`). Press `c` (for "change") and then `w` (for "word"). A `$` sign will appear at the end of the word you're changing:

```
Shell: /bin/tcs$
```

Type `bash` in place of the word `tcsh` and then press Escape to exit change-word mode. Now the shell is `/bin/bash`. The next step is to place the cursor on top of the first slash, just before `bin`, and press `i` (for "insert") to get a usable cursor. Enter `/usr/local` and then press Escape. The shell string should now be `/usr/local/bin/bash`.

Now, enter a colon (`:`) to go into the in-program command line and then follow it with `w` (for "write"); press Enter to save the file. Finally, enter `:q`, and press Enter to quit.

The file you've now written is actually a temporary file in `/etc`. If your changes are valid, they will be read from that file and automatically rebuilt into `/etc/master.passwd` and `/etc/passwd`. From now on, every time the user in question logs in to the system, it will be under `/usr/local/bin/bash` rather than `/bin/tcsh`.

If the changes you've made are not valid (for example, if the shell you specified is not listed in `/etc/shells`), you are given the choice to re-edit the user profile or to cancel the operation.

Non-Shell Programs as Shells

It's possible to set a user's shell to a program that isn't specifically designed to be a shell; there are programs (such as `/sbin/nologin`) that do nothing but print out a text banner and exit. There are also some programs tailored to command-line interaction with services other than the UNIX filesystem (such as TinyFugue) that a user might prefer. You can set a nonexistent program as a user's shell to prevent the user from logging in at all. You can even set a user's shell to `/usr/bin/mail` (the shell-based mail reader) if you want, although this will mean that the user can't do much but read mail. On the other hand, this might be the server policy you decide to set.

The `chsh` program will warn you if you specify a shell that doesn't exist, but it will still dutifully write it into the user database. There's nothing wrong with having a user's shell

set to a nonexistent program; it simply means that the user won't be able to log in.
Remember, the way a login shell works is that if the program can be successfully executed and attached to a pty (pseudo-terminal), the login will be successful and will not
end until the shell program terminates and releases the pty. If the shell program can't be
executed, nothing will bind to the pty, and the user won't get a command line—just an
error, which (depending on the terminal program) might take the shape of a password-
authentication error, a protocol failure error, or (in command-line `telnet`) an explicit
failure to execute the shell program after displaying the various login banners:

```
FreeBSD/i386 (stripes.somewhere.com) (ttyp2)

login: frank
Password:
Last login: Sat May  5 18:35:52 from w044.z064002043.
Copyright (c) 1980, 1983, 1986, 1988, 1990, 1991, 1993, 1994
        The Regents of the University of California.  All rights reserved.

FreeBSD 4.3-RELEASE (STRIPES) #0: Wed Jan 31 18:45:43 PST 2001
--------------------------------------------------------------------
Welcome to the system! Today's news: nothing.

You have mail.
login: /usr/local/bin/foosh: No such file or directory
Connection closed by foreign host.
```

You can leverage this behavior of displaying the general login banners before executing a
user's shell. For instance, if you have a troublesome user or group of users who have vio-
lated system policy in some way (such as by hacking), you can prevent them from logging in by setting their shells to a nonexistent program and giving an explanation of a
system-wide policy enforcement change in `/etc/motd` (a regular text file that is displayed as a banner to every user immediately after their password is accepted). Edit
`/etc/motd` in your favorite text editor to reflect anything you want all your users, including ones without valid shells, to read upon login.

Even more usefully (and correctly), you can set the user's shell to a program that isn't
really a shell, but merely a program that prints out informative text. `/sbin/nologin` is a
built-in example of this that you can set as a user's shell to disable his login. It's nothing
more than a shell script that prints out a single line of text and then exits. This line of
text is short and sweet:

```
You have mail.
This account is currently not available.
Connection to stripes.somewhere.com closed.
```

Notice that `/sbin/nologin` executed, attached to the pty, exited properly, and released
the pty. The fact that it never presented any kind of interactive command line doesn't

make it any less valid as a shell; this method of disabling an account works for any terminal program, whether using `telnet` or `ssh`, and it involves no errors or warnings. It's very elegant and extensible. You can, in fact, assign any program as the shell, whether interactive or not. You can make your shell `/bin/ls` or `/usr/bin/finger`, if you like. More usefully, you can create your own script or program to execute when a certain user logs in. This is a way for you to set up interesting services on your system, such as a customized "library" system in which guests can log in and interact with a menu, execute a certain limited set of commands, or simply get a screenfull of information. The possibilities are endless!

> **Caution**
>
> A word of warning is in order. If you write a login handler for this kind of purpose in C or another such language in which you have to allocate your own buffer space, beware of potential buffer overflows! These are the most common types of security holes found in network services; if an attacker is able to find and exploit a buffer overflow in a program you devise yourself, and there is any way for the program to run executable code as root (for example, if it's a `setuid` program owned by root), your system belongs to that attacker. Be very careful in this area!

Shell Initialization Files

It's now time to discuss how to customize your shell to do what you want. You can create aliases to simplify common commands, you can automatically execute certain programs every time you log in, you can set various environment variables to your taste, and much more. These tasks are handled in the shell initialization and configuration files, which exist both at the global and per-user levels.

Since `tcsh` and `bash` have completely different sets of configuration files, we will cover them both sequentially. FreeBSD includes system-wide and default per-user config files for both shells, so that you can switch from `tcsh` to `bash` on a system-wide basis if you really want to. This almost certainly won't be necessary.

> **Note**
>
> When a new user is created, default shell config files are copied from `/usr/share/skel` (the dot prefix on each of the files is dropped) into the new user's home directory. If you like, you can copy these default files into

/usr/local/share/skel, modify them to your taste, and then alter the
/etc/adduser.conf file to copy its default "dotfiles" from this new location.
This is the way you can make a global, pre-emptive change to all users' default
shell configurations before they're even created.

tcsh/csh Files: .cshrc, .login, and .logout

The first file that tcsh looks at when it is executed is the system-wide config file,
/etc/csh.cshrc, followed immediately by /etc/csh.login. Note that in FreeBSD, both
these files exist, but their only contents are commented out (see Listing 12.1).

LISTING 12.1   The global /etc/csh.cshrc and /etc/csh.login files

```
# cat /etc/csh.cshrc
# $FreeBSD: src/etc/csh.cshrc,v 1.3 1999/08/27 23:23:40 peter Exp $
#
# System-wide .cshrc file for csh(1).

# cat /etc/csh.login
# $FreeBSD: src/etc/csh.login,v 1.19.2.1 2000/07/31 20:13:26 rwatson Exp $
#
# System-wide .login file for csh(1).
# Uncomment this to give you the default 4.2 behavior, where disk
# information is shown in K-Blocks
# setenv BLOCKSIZE      K
#
# For the setting of languages and character sets please see
# login.conf(5) and in particular the charset and lang options.
# For full locales list check /usr/share/locale/*
#
# Read system messages
# msgs -f
# Allow terminal messages
# mesg y
```

This listing shows that these config files don't really do anything, but they could if you
so chose. Any change you make in either of these files, for example to enable mesg (terminal messages) globally, is applied globally and only overridden if set differently by the
per-user config files, which are analogous to the system-wide ones and read immediately
afterwards from the user's home directory: .cshrc, followed by .login.

The default .cshrc file, which comes from /usr/share/skel/dot.cshrc, does a number
of generally useful things to set up the shell environment. It creates several aliases to
shorten commands:

```
alias h        history 25
alias j        jobs -l
alias la       ls -a
alias lf       ls -FA
alias ll       ls -lA
```

It sets the search path for programs:

```
set path = (/sbin /bin /usr/sbin /usr/bin /usr/games /usr/local/sbin
➡/usr/local/bin /usr/X11R6/bin $HOME/bin)
```

It sets various environment variables, which control the behavior of many different shell tasks:

```
setenv  EDITOR  vi
setenv  PAGER   more
setenv  BLOCKSIZE     K
```

And a few other things are set as well. You can look at the .cshrc file in your own home directory to see them all.

The .login file, which is read next, is where the user can place any programs he wants to run every time he logs in. For example, the fortune program is provided in the default .login (from /usr/share/skel/dot.login), and encapsulated in an existence-test conditional, but it's commented out:

```
# Uncomment to display a random cookie each login:
# [ -x /usr/games/fortune ] && /usr/games/fortune -s
```

You (or the user) can also specify certain things to happen whenever the user logs out; for instance, you might write a script to clean out any temporary files owned by that user in /tmp; you could put a call to this script into /etc/csh.logout, which in its default state has no material contents:

```
# cat /etc/csh.logout
# $FreeBSD: src/etc/csh.logout,v 1.3 1999/08/27 23:23:41 peter Exp $
#
# System-wide .logout file for csh(1).
```

The logout process will also read a .logout file in the user's home directory if it exists, but there is no such per-user file installed by default.

> **Note**
>
> These files are the ones run by tcsh when it is executed as a login shell. There are various other circumstances under which it can be run; for instance, as a non-login shell (for example, a shell executed in order to run a shell script, invoked from the interpreter line of the script). In this case, the .login and .logout files (and their system-wide equivalents) are ignored.

12

CUSTOMIZING THE SHELL

bash Files: `.profile`, `.shrc`, and `.bash_logout`

If you've chosen to use bash rather than tcsh, it will operate in much the same way: first, reading the system-wide config and initialization files and then proceeding to the per-user ones. First comes /etc/profile, which (like /etc/csh.cshrc) is materially blank, but contains a few examples for options you might decide to enable (as shown in Listing 12.2).

LISTING 12.2   The Global /etc/profile File

```
# cat /etc/profile
# $FreeBSD: src/etc/profile,v 1.12.2.1 2000/07/31 20:13:26 rwatson Exp $
#
# System-wide .profile file for sh(1).
#
# Uncomment this to give you the default 4.2 behavior, where disk
# information is shown in K-Blocks
# BLOCKSIZE=K; export BLOCKSIZE
#
# For the setting of languages and character sets please see
# login.conf(5) and in particular the charset and lang options.
# For full locales list check /usr/share/locale/*
# You should also read the setlocale(3) man page for information
# on how to achieve more precise control of locale settings.
#
# Read system messages
# msgs -f
# Allow terminal messages
# mesg y
```

Notice that /etc/profile combines the functionality of both /etc/csh.cshrc and /etc/csh.login. It's the only bash-related global file in the system; there is no system-wide logout script for bash.

The next step for bash is the user's .profile file, which primarily sets various environment variables (including the PATH), and exports them in the Bourne shell style:

```
# remove /usr/games and /usr/X11R6/bin if you want
PATH=/sbin:/bin:/usr/sbin:/usr/bin:/usr/games:/usr/local/bin:/usr/X11R6/bin:$HOM
E/bin; export PATH

BLOCKSIZE=K;     export BLOCKSIZE
EDITOR=vi;       export EDITOR
PAGER=more;      export PAGER

# set ENV to a file invoked each time sh is started for interactive use.
ENV=$HOME/.shrc; export ENV
```

This last line sets the ENV variable to the .shrc file, also in the user's home directory, which is then read in sequence with .profile. Its purpose is to define the various aliases that tcsh sets in .cshrc, as well as a few other optional things, such as customizing the prompt, which are commented out by default:

```
# some useful aliases
alias h='fc -l'
alias j=jobs
alias m=$PAGER
alias ll='ls -laFo'
alias l='ls -l'
alias g='egrep -i'

# # set prompt: ``username@hostname$ ''
# PS1="`whoami`@`hostname | sed 's/\..*//'`"
# case `id -u` in
#       0) PS1="${PS1}# ";;
#       *) PS1="${PS1}$ ";;
# esac
```

As with .logout for tcsh, bash will read and execute a .bash_logout file if it's present; there isn't one installed by default, though.

> **Note**
>
> These are the files sourced by bash if it's executed as a login shell. If it's a non-login shell, though, the file it reads is .bashrc rather than .profile. This file doesn't normally exist in FreeBSD.

Customizing Your Shell Environment

We've seen a few examples already, in both tcsh and bash style, of how to customize how your shell works—the default settings in the shell config files. These can serve as perfectly valid examples of how to extend your shell's functionality. There are a few extra things you can do, though, and some options that aren't clearly demonstrated in the default files. We'll look at how to accomplish this in tcsh and in bash. In most cases, these are built-in shell commands that can be issued either from the command line directly or from within any of the shell configuration files.

> **Note**
>
> Full details on a large number of available built-in commands—some of which appear in csh/tcsh, some of which appear in sh/bash, and some of which appear in both—can be found in man builtin.

Customizing tcsh

The most common shell customization is an alias. This sets a substitution of the first word of a command for whatever you choose to replace it with. Aliases can greatly simplify your work, especially if there are certain complex commands that you find yourself using on a regular basis. The simplest alias is of the type seen in .cshrc:

```
alias ll     ls -lA
```

This, as you would expect, replaces a command such as ll /usr/local with ls -lA /usr/local. But what if you want to do argument substitution as well—reformatting the command's parameters according to what you enter each time? That can be done with the extremely versatile and equally convoluted command-line parsing syntax of tcsh. The man tcsh page will explain this in full detail, but for our purposes, we can note that the first argument to a command in an alias assignment can be referred to as \!^ (or \!:1), and further arguments can be indicated as \!:2, \!:3, and so on. So, you can do something like the following:

```
alias lookup    grep \!^ /etc/passwd
```

This would allow you to enter commands such as lookup frank to extract a user's information. The unalias command allows you to remove an alias:

```
unalias lookup
```

You can customize your prompt's appearance. This is done by setting the prompt shell variable: You can embed the output of any command by enclosing it in backticks, much as is done in Perl scripts. You can also echo the "command number" variable, which specifies an event in the editable history, with the ! character. The following example is a fairly complex one that incorporates all these tricks, plus the use of sed (a "stream editor" text processor which operates non-interactively on text fed to it at any time) to shorten the output of hostname to its first element:

```
# set prompt="{`whoami`@`hostname | sed 's/\..*//'`:!} "
{root@www:23}
```

Another use of the prompt shell variable is to reflect the directory you're currently in, which can be echoed using the pwd ("present working directory") command:

```
# set prompt="{`pwd`:!} "
{/root:24}
```

Setting the command path in `tcsh` also involves setting a shell variable (we will cover shell variables and environment variables in a moment). You can't add elements to the parenthesized array "on-the-fly"; you have to add the new path element to the string and reissue the entire `set` command, which is why the path is best set from within one of the config scripts rather than from the command line. The syntax is to specify a list of pathnames in parentheses, separated by spaces:

```
set path = (/sbin /usr/sbin /bin /usr/bin /usr/local/bin /usr/contrib/bin
/usr/X11R6/bin /usr/local/sbin /usr/games . /usr/local/mystuff)
```

Another useful built-in tool is `stty`. This allows you to redefine various character mappings, which you might find very useful in cases where your terminal program sends unexpected characters to your programs—most commonly seen in confusion between "delete" and "backspace" characters, or in line-delimiter characters. The first step is to see what's currently set:

```
# stty -a
speed 38400 baud; 60 rows; 80 columns;
lflags: icanon isig iexten echo echoe -echok echoke -echonl echoctl
        -echoprt -altwerase -noflsh -tostop -flusho pendin -nokerninfo
        -extproc
iflags: -istrip icrnl -inlcr -igncr ixon -ixoff ixany imaxbel -ignbrk
        brkint -inpck -ignpar -parmrk
oflags: opost onlcr -oxtabs
cflags: cread cs8 -parenb -parodd hupcl -clocal -cstopb -crtscts -dsrflow
        -dtrflow -mdmbuf
cchars: discard = ^O; dsusp = ^Y; eof = ^D; eol = <undef>;
        eol2 = <undef>; erase = ^?; intr = ^C; kill = ^U; lnext = ^V;
        min = 1; quit = ^\; reprint = ^R; start = ^Q; status = ^T;
        stop = ^S; susp = ^Z; time = 0; werase = ^W;
```

Now, if you want to set your "erase" character to `^H`, specify it in just that two-character form:

```
# stty erase ^H
```

You can turn on "watch" mode, telling you who's logged in on the system and who has the various ptys, with the following sequence:

```
set watch=(1 any any)
set who="%n has %a %l from %M."
```

One thing about `tcsh` that you'll likely want to disable is the `autologout` shell variable, which is set by default to 60 minutes, and can quickly become annoying if you ever leave

12

a terminal idle for more than an hour—it closes your connection. You can disable this easily enough with a single config file line:

```
unset autologout;
```

Finally, if you set any of these built-in customization variables by editing the configuration scripts, you don't have to log out and back in to incorporate them; you can force a reread of all the config scripts with the `rehash` built-in command.

Customizing bash

Aliases in `bash` work slightly differently from those in `tcsh`. The alias and substitution text are separated by an = sign rather than a space or tab; also, there is no mechanism for doing argument substitution as there is in `tcsh`, so the `lookup` alias we created for `tcsh` can't be done in `bash` without more extensive gymnastics.

```
alias ll='ls -laFo'
```

Setting your prompt in `bash` can get interesting. Since `bash` doesn't implement shell variables in the same customized way that `tcsh` does, the best it can really do is to set the "primary" and "secondary" prompts as environment variables (`PS1` and `PS2`), from which the shell reads the strings it displays to you. To get the "email address" prompt we saw earlier in `tcsh`, we'd use the following, noting the backslash behind the `!` character (which doesn't have the same special meaning as it does in `tcsh`):

```
# PS1="{`whoami`@`hostname | sed 's/\..*//'`:\!} "
{root@www:17}
```

Similarly, to get a prompt that reflects the present working directory, use the following:

```
# PS1="{`pwd`\:!} "
{/root:18}
```

Setting the command path in `bash` involves setting the `PATH` environment variable. In this context, it's a colon-separated string of pathnames, together with an `export` statement to publish the variable into the environment.

```
PATH=/sbin:/bin:/usr/sbin:/usr/bin:/usr/games:/usr/local/bin:/usr/X11R6/bin:
➥$HOME/bin; export PATH
```

The need to export your variables is something we'll talk about in the next section.

Shell and Environment Variables

One of the biggest differences between `tcsh` and `bash` is how they respectively handle variables. There are two kinds of variables to work with, as we'll see in greater detail in Chapter 13. Let's take a look at how the variable types differ and where they're used.

Environment Variables

No matter which shell you're using, you always have environment variables. These kinds of variables contain values that travel with you throughout your login session, as well as being propagated to any program spawned from within that session. Environment variables dictate the behavior of certain programs that you run. For instance, the chfn program will launch the text editor specified in the EDITOR environment variable, and the TERM variable tells the shell how to format text to display properly on your screen. The BLOCKSIZE variable controls what the output numbers in such commands as du and df signify: kilobytes, half-kilobytes, or whatever the value of the variable is. A program doesn't have to be a login shell to have access to environment variables—every program has access to the same set of variables as the program that spawned it.

Whichever shell you're using, you can view all your environment variables using the printenv command, as shown in Listing 12.3.

LISTING 12.3   Sample Output of the printenv Command

```
# printenv
PATH=/sbin:/usr/sbin:/bin:/usr/bin:/usr/local/bin:/usr/contrib/bin:/usr/X11R6/
bin:.
MAIL=/var/mail/frank
BLOCKSIZE=1k
FTP_PASSIVE_MODE=YES
USER=frank
LOGNAME=frank
HOME=/home/frank
SHELL=/bin/tcsh
SSH_CLIENT=192.168.173.230 50095 22
SSH_TTY=/dev/ttyp0
TERM=vt100
HOSTTYPE=FreeBSD
VENDOR=intel
OSTYPE=FreeBSD
MACHTYPE=i386
SHLVL=1
PWD=/home/frank
GROUP=users
HOST=stripes.somewhere.com
REMOTEHOST=192.168.173.230
PATHSET=true
EDITOR=vi
VISUAL=pico
```

To set an environment variable from within the shell, you would use one of two syntaxes, depending on the shell you're using. To set a variable called COLOR to gold in tcsh, enter the following:

```
# setenv COLOR gold
```

In bash, you have to first set the variable in the local session context and then export it to the shell's environment:

```
# COLOR=gold
# export COLOR
```

Note that an environment variable must have a value; it can't simply exist in the environment with a null or undefined value.

Shell Variables

There's another separate set of variables available to your login session. These *shell variables* apply only to the current login session and have no bearing on any other processes; they're comprehensible only to the shell process itself. In programming terms, shell variables exist in the "local" context, whereas environment variables exist in the "global" context and can be inherited by other programs.

Shell variables in tcsh *must* be lowercase, and shell variables in bash *must* be uppercase. They can be viewed using the set command. Setting a shell variable in tcsh is also done, not surprisingly, with set. It's possible to set a shell variable in tcsh without assigning a value to it:

```
# set history 100
# set noclobber
```

In bash, simply set the variable without exporting it:

```
# VISUAL=pico
```

You can also remove a variable with unset:

```
# unset autologout
```

Shell and environment variables, and the way their inheritance properties interact and apply to shell scripting techniques, will be described more fully in Chapter 13.

13

Shell
Programming

IN THIS CHAPTER

In Chapter 8, "Working with the Shell," you saw how to work with the shell interactively at the command line. What you may not have known is that there is a powerful programming language built into the shell. You can use shell programming to do everything from automating a repetitive list of commands, to writing sophisticated interactive programs that process text data, to storing and retrieving information in simple databases.

Due to the modular design of the FreeBSD operating system, you can call any FreeBSD command from within a shell program. And if you can't find a FreeBSD command to do what you want, you can string commands together in "pipelines" to create new commands. *Pipelines* take the output from one command and use it as the input for another command. They will be explained in detail later in this chapter. FreeBSD has hundreds of these modular commands that each serve a small but highly specialized purpose. There are commands for searching text file; combining text from two files into a single file; formatting text in columns; cutting only certain fields from text files; counting the number of characters, words, and lines in a file; performing math operations; doing file backups; compressing and uncompressing files; and much more. If you can't find a command or pipeline that does what you want, chances are you can find a free program available on the Internet that you can use in your shell program.

Shell programming is sometimes shunned in favor of Perl or other languages, and thought of as simply a "glorified DOS batch programming language," but this simply is not true. In its simplest form, shell programming is like DOS batch programming in that it can be used to execute a list of commands stored in a file that you could also execute from the command line. But if you take the time to learn how to understand the shell, how it interprets commands, how you can send the output of one command down a pipeline to use as the input for another command, and if you are aware of the hundreds of specialized FreeBSD commands available for performing various tasks, you can write highly sophisticated shell programs.

Here are the top six reasons to learn FreeBSD shell programming:

- It's easy to learn. If you work with the FreeBSD command line on a regular basis, you probably are already familiar with many of the commands you can use in your shell programs.

- For many tasks, you can develop a shell program in 5 or 10 minutes that would take hours or even days to develop in C or some other programming language.

- It can save you hours of tedious work. For example, why go through 100 text files manually to make a single change when you can write a shell program with a "for" loop that will do it automatically?

- It will teach you many new and useful ways to work with FreeBSD. You will discover useful commands you never knew existed, and discover ways to do things you didn't even know could be done. Dare I say, you might even learn to like the

FreeBSD command line, and become excited about the power it gives you. Why spend money to buy a new program to do something when you can string a few FreeBSD commands together in a pipeline that will do the same thing?

- Don't like the way an existing command works? Write a new one in a few minutes with shell programming. One of the things that makes FreeBSD so powerful is the "Do it your own way" philosophy. There are many ways to achieve the same end, and no one way is necessarily the best way.

- It is perhaps the ideal first programming language since it allows you to concentrate on learning programming logic and such while working with commands you may already be familiar with.

So have I whet your appetite? Great! Now let's jump right in and learn how to use this powerful feature of FreeBSD.

> **Note**
>
> The first part of this chapter covers only commands that are available in all Bourne-type shells. The second part covers the enhanced features of the Korn and POSIX shells such as FreeBSD uses. If you need to write shell programs that will be run on other systems, and you cannot say for sure what shells will be available on those other systems, it is best to stick with the commands that are available in all Bourne shells. If you don't, your programs might not work on other systems that have an older Bourne shell.

> **Note**
>
> This chapter does not cover C shell scripting at all. A few notes are in order, however. Although it is possible to write shell scripts using the C shell, this is generally not a good idea because it lacks a lot of very useful shell-scripting features (including functions, and swapping STDOUT and STDERR). C shell scripting can be a real exercise in frustration and futility. Because of this, it is recommended that you always write your scripts using the Bourne shell.

> **Tip**
>
> There is a lot more to learn about shell scripting than we could cover in a single chapter. If you are interested in learning more about shell scripting, refer to *Teach Yourself Shell Programming in 24 Hours*, available from SAMS Publishing, for more information.

13

SHELL PROGRAMMING

A Simple Shell Program

The first rite of passage for any aspiring programmer is to write the "Hello World!" program. So here is one way to write in the Bourne shell programming language:

```
1.  #!/bin/sh
2.
3.  # The legendary Hello World program
4.  # As implemented in the Bourne shell programming language.
5.
6.  echo
7.  echo "Hello World!"
8.  echo
9.  exit 0
```

The line numbers in the previous code are for reference in this text only. When you enter the code, do not include the line numbers.

Enter the previous text in your favorite text editor, and save it as a file. Next, you will need to make the file executable. You can do this with the following command:

```
chmod u+x hello
```

Assuming that you named the file `hello`, this command will give the owner of the file permission to execute it.

Next, execute the file. The following sequence shows the command you type as well as the output of the program:

```
bash$ ./hello

Hello World!

bash$
```

Now let's look at each line in the previous program in detail, and see what each line does.

- **Line 1:** This line contains the magic character sequence #!, which tells FreeBSD that what follows is a script that should be interpreted by the program named after #!. In this case, it tells FreeBSD that it should use the Bourne shell interpreter /bin/sh to interpret what follows. If this were a Perl script, we would use /usr/bin/perl. For a Python script, we would use /usr/local/bin/python, and so on.

- **Lines 2 and 5:** These are simply blank lines. The shell ignores whitespace unless it is quoted (more on that later). It is a good idea to use whitespace to make your program more readable.

- **Lines 3 and 4:** These are comments. Comments in a shell program begin with #
  and extend to the end of the line. They are ignored by the interpreter, and are here
  for the benefit of users who need to revisit a complicated program they wrote six
  months ago and try to figure out what it does again.

- **Line 6:** The echo command takes whatever it receives and echoes it to STDOUT
  (which is normally the screen). This can be redirected, however, so that echo sends
  the output somewhere else, like to a file or something. In this case, echo by itself
  simply prints a blank line on STDOUT.

- **Line 7:** The echo command here prints the string "Hello World!" to STDOUT. The
  quotes tell the interpreter that everything inside the quotes should be interpreted as
  a single argument (the shell should interpret the string as one long unit instead of
  many short units). Without the quotes, the shell will interpret the whitespace as an
  argument separator. In this case, the quotes would not have been strictly necessary.
  But you will see later on in the chapter why quoting is important. It is a good idea
  to get into the habit of quoting strings such as these.

- **Line 8:** The echo command here prints a blank line again.

- **Line 9:** The exit command exits the program and returns an exit status to the
  invoking program. (This is normally the shell, but it could be another program—
  such as another shell program.) An exit status of 0 indicates that the program terminated normally. An exit status of anything other than 0 indicates that an error
  occurred. The exit status can be read by the calling program and used in decision-
  making. The calling program then determines what action it should do next, based
  on the success or failure of the previous program that was run.

In a program this short, setting the exit status would not have been necessary. If the exit
status is not implicitly set, the exit status returned will be the exit status of the last command that was run in the script. It is best to set the exit status, though, since it will
become important as you start to write larger and more complex shell programs. Later in
this chapter, you will see how the exit status of a command can be used in a shell script
to make automatic decisions about the next action that should be performed.

printf

The previous program could also have been written using printf instead of echo. The
printf command performs a similar function, but allows more control over how its output is formatted. The following example shows how the program could be rewritten
using printf instead of echo:

```
1.   #!/bin/sh
2.
```

```
3.  # The legendary Hello World program
4.  # As implemented in the Bourne shell programming language.
5.
6.  printf "\nHello World!\n\n!"
7.  exit 0
```

If this program is run, the output it produces will look exactly the same as the previous program.

If you have ever programmed in C before, the syntax of the printf command will look familiar to you.

The backslash is an escape character that means the character immediately following it has special meaning (or negates the special meaning of the character if the character would have special meaning by itself). In this case, the "n" is a newline character. This is why we could eliminate the two echo commands to insert blank lines when we use printf. Because now we can embed the newlines directly into the string we wish to print. At the end of the string, we used two newline characters because printf does not automatically insert a newline at the end. So, we want two newlines to get a blank line. Following is an example in which printf doesn't automatically insert a blank line at the end:

```
printf "Hello "
printf "World!\n\n"
```

The previous two lines in a shell script would produce the output "Hello World!", even though they are separate statements. This is because printf doesn't automatically insert a blank line at the end of a statement. If we had used echo in the previous two lines instead of printf, "Hello" and "World!" would be on separate lines.

The printf command supports the following formatting characters:

TABLE 13.1 Formatting control characters from printf

Formatting Characters	Description
\a	Ring the terminal's bell. In the old Teletype days, this rang an actual bell on the teletype machine. These days, it usually beeps the computer's speaker.
\b	Print a backspace character.
\f	Print a form-feed character.
\n	Print a newline character.

TABLE 13.1 continued

Formatting Characters	Description
\r	Print a carriage return. The difference between this and the newline character is that the carriage return returns the cursor to the beginning of the line, but does not send to the next line. The result is that the previous output on the line will be overwritten by whatever comes after the \r.
\t	Print a tab character.
\v	Print a vertical tab character.
\´	Print a single-quote character.
\"	Print a double-quote character.
\\	Print a backslash.
\num	Print the ASCII value of the octal 1-,2-, or 3-bit value *num*. You will probably never use this option in a shell program.

Of course, simply being able to echo messages to the screen is not very useful. This is where variables come in.

Variables

In algebra, you learned that you can use letters to stand for unknown quantities in algebraic equations, and that these letters were called *variables*. In programming, the concept is pretty much the same, although variables can hold strings (strings of characters) as well as numbers.

There are two types of variables you will deal with in shell programming: shell variables and environment variables. The primary difference is that environment variables will be available to other scripts or programs that you call from inside your shell program and shell variables will be available only to the script itself.

Variables in shell programming are loosely typed; they do not have to be declared or typeset before they can be used. All variables in shell programming are stored as strings.

Variable Assignment

In its most basic form, a variable can be set in the following manner:

```
myvar=5
```

The value 5 is now stored in the variable `myvar`. To access the information stored in a variable, proceed the variable name with a $. For example `echo ${myvar}` will print 5 to STDOUT, which as you recall, is normally the screen.

> **Note**
>
> Variable assignments are one place where whitespace does matter. The statement "mvar=5" will assign 5 to the variable "myvar". The statement "myvar = 5" will produce an error because the shell will try to interpret "myvar" as a command name to execute rather than as a variable assignment.

The curly braces are optional, but can help to improve code readability since they make variable names easier to spot when quickly scanning code. It's up to you whether you want to use the braces or not.

The value of a variable can also be assigned to another variable. For example:

```
myvarB=$myvar
```

This line assigns whatever is in "myvar" to the variable "myvarB". If "myvarB" already contains something, whatever is there will be overwritten by the new assignment.

In addition, it is also possible to assign the output of a command to a variable or read input from STDIN (which is normally the keyboard) and store it in a variable. We will see how to do this later in the chapter.

Creating an environment variable is pretty much the same as creating a shell variable. The only difference is that it must be exported. This is done with the export statement. For example:

```
MYVAR="5"
export MYVAR
```

will create a shell variable named "MYVAR" and then export it so that it is an environment variable that will be available to other shells started from within this shell.

Variable Names

Variable names are case-sensitive and can contain letters, numbers, and underscores. The variable name cannot begin with a number, though, and it is best to avoid beginning variable names with an underscore. Use descriptive names to make program code easier to read. For example, it is much easier to guess what a variable named "avg_rainfall" probably would contain than to guess what a variable named "xyz123" might contain.

> **Tip**
>
> By convention, local variables use lowercase letters, and environment variables use uppercase letters. However, some people prefer to use a mixture

of lowercase and uppercase letters in local variables to make them stand out from other shell commands, which are almost always in all lowercase.

Interacting with the User

Simply assigning variables inside a script and calling those variables later is not very useful. The shell provides a way for you to get input from STDIN. Normally, this input will be typed in by the user (or received from a file if STDIN has been redirected). The command that can read input from a user is read. Here is a slightly modified version of the "Hello World" program that reads input from STDIN, which is normally the keyboard:

```
1.  #!/bin/sh
2.
3.  # Modified Hello World program that accepts input from keyboard
4.
5.  echo
6.  echo -n "Please enter your name: "
7.  read name
8.  echo
9.  echo "Hello, ${name}!"
10. echo
11. exit 0
```

When run, this program does the following:

```
Please enter your name: Mike
Hello, Mike!
```

There are three new aspects of this program that should be discussed:

- **Line 6:** A new option to the echo command is introduced. The -n option suppresses the newline character that would normally be sent at the end of the echo statement. This causes the cursor to remain on the same line after Please enter your name:.

- **Line 7:** The read command accepts input from STDIN—in this case, the keyboard. The user can enter a string of text here. When Enter is pressed, read takes whatever the user entered and stores it in the variable "name". The read command implies quotes, so therefore the string is stored in the variable exactly as the user enters it with all whitespace preserved.

- **Line 9:** The echo command is used to send the string Hello, followed by the contents of the variable name. Once again, the curly braces are optional.

The read command can take multiple variables as arguments (see Listing 13.1). When it does, whitespace will be used as the delimiter to separate what goes into each variable. Listing 13.1 shows an example.

LISTING 13.1   Using Multiple Variables with read

```
#!/bin/sh

echo
echo -n "Enter three numbers separated by spaces or tabs: "
read var1 var2 var3
echo
echo "The value of var1 is: ${var1}"
echo "The value of var2 is: ${var2}"
echo "The value of var3 is: ${var3}"
echo
exit 0
```

Here is a sample run of the previous program:

```
Enter three numbers separated by spaces or tabs: 557 2024 57240

The value of var1 is: 557
The value of var2 is: 2024
The value of var3 is: 57240
```

It doesn't matter how much whitespace you use in the input from the keyboard. When assigning multiple variables, read interprets any amount of whitespace as argument separators to determine what should go in each variable.

If read gets fewer arguments than there are variables in its list, the remaining variables after the argument list runs out will not be assigned. On the other hand, if read gets more arguments than it has variables, whatever arguments are left over will be assigned to the last variable in the list. For example, here is another run of the program that gives read more than three arguments:

```
Enter three numbers separated by spaces or tabs: 1 2 3 4 5 6 7 8 9 0
The value of var1 is: 1
The value of var2 is: 2
The value of var3 is: 3 4 5 6 7 8 9 0
```

Handling Command-Line Arguments

You can also get information from the user by reading arguments included on the command-line. The shell automatically stores command line arguments in special variables. No programming is required to actually read the arguments. Up to nine arguments can be included on the command line. These arguments are stored in the variables $1–$9.

The FreeBSD POSIX shell also allows additional arguments that be accessed with ${10}, ${11}, and so on. But this should be avoided if these programs will need to run on other systems because the traditional Bourne shell can only handle $1–$9. The variable $0 contains the name of the program itself, the variable $@ contains all the arguments, and the variable $# contains the number of arguments that were passed to the program. For example:

```
#!/bin/sh
echo
echo "The name of the program is: $0"
echo "The total number of arguments received is: $#"
echo "The complete argument string is: #@"
echo "Your first name is: $1"
echo "Your last name is: $2"
echo
exit 0
```

And here is a sample run:

```
bash$ ./yourname Michael Urban

The name of the program is: ./yourname
The total number of arguments received is: 2"
The complete argument string is: Michael Urban"
Your first name is: Michael
Your last name is: Urban

bash$
```

13

SHELL
PROGRAMMING

Note

The POSIX shell that FreeBSD uses also supports the getopts command, which is a more versatile way of handing command-line arguments with a shell program. We will discuss this command when we talk about the advanced features of Korn shell programming. If you are writing Bourne shell programs (that use sh) for other UNIX platforms, however, it is best to avoid the use of getopts because it is not a standard part of the traditional Bourne shell, and may cause the program not to work on some systems.

Command Substitution

Among other things, *command substitution* allows you to run a command and assign the output to a variable. The command to be run should be enclosed in the `. Be careful not to confuse this with the single quote. The ` is a backward quote (usually located with the tilde (~) on the keyboard). For example:

```
TodayDate=`date`
```

will run the `date` command and assign its output to the variable `TodayDate`. You can then access the information in this variable just as you can access the information in any other variable.

Arithmetic in Shell Programs

Although the original Bourne shell has no built-in arithmetic handlers, arithmetic can still be done using command substitution along with the `expr` command. For example:

```
var3=`expr var1 + var2`
```

This adds the values contained in `var1` and `var2` together and then stores the result in `var3`. Note that the arguments and the operator must be separated by whitespace. `expr var1+var2` will not have the intended result.

The `expr` command can do only very simple arithmetic—it can handle only integer arithmetic. Entering floating point numbers will cause an error. In addition, changing the order of operations with parentheses is not supported. Division that does not return an integer value will have the decimal portion dropped. For example, 5 / 2 is 2 as far as `expr` is concerned. If you wish to retrieve the remainder of a division, you can use the modulus operator (%). For example, `expr 5 % 2` will return 1 (5 / 2 = 4 remainder 1).

Characters that have special meaning to the shell must be escaped. For example, `expr 2 * 2` will not work because the shell interprets the * as a wildcard operator. For the operation to work, the multiplication operator (*) must be escaped like this: `expr 2 \* 2`. This protects it from the shell and prevents the shell from giving it special meaning.

`expr` can also evaluate true/false expressions. If the expression is true, `expr` returns a 1. If the expression is false, `expr` returns 0. For example:

```
expr 2 + 2 = 4 + 1
```

This returns 0 (the equation is false).

```
expr 2 + 2 = 3 + 1
```

This returns 1 (the equation is true).

`!=` will reverse the equation. It means "is not equal to." So, for example, the equation `expr 5 != 3` will return 1 (true).

`expr` can of course, also evaluate less than/greater than expressions. Once again, because the < and > characters have special meaning to the shell, they must be escaped when used with `expr` to protect them from the shell. It is a true/false evaluation just like the equal to operator. If the expression is true, expr returns 1. If the expression is false, expr returns 0. For example, expr 5 \> 4 returns 1 (the expression is true). In addition, greater than or equal to (\>=) and less than or equal to (\<=) evaluations are also supported.

expr is not limited to comparing numbers. It can also compare strings. For example, expr "The quick brown fox jumped over the lazy dog" = "The quick brown fox jumped over the lazy dg" will evaluate to 0 (the expression is false unless the strings are exactly equal).

Although expr is great for simple shell scripting, as mentioned previously, its capabilities are rather limited. If you need to do floating point math, complex expressions that change the order of operations, and so on, you can use a command called bc. bc is a programming language in itself for working with math. It is possible to embed expressions into your shell program and feed them to bc. The program in Listing 13.2 uses bc to compute both the circumference and the area of a circle.

LISTING 13.2   Using bc to Compute the Circumference and Area of a Circle

```
1.  #!/bin/sh
2.
3.  # The Following program computes both the circumference and the area
4.  # of a circle.
5.
6.  pi="3.14159265"          # Assign the value of pi to a variable.
7.
8.  # Tell the user what the program does and ask them for the radius of
9.  # the circle.
10.
11. echo
12. echo "This program computes both the circumference and the area of"
13. echo "a circle."
14. echo
15. echo -n "Please enter the radius of the circle: "
16. read radius
17.
18. # Now we will use bc to compute the answers and store them in variables.
19.
20. circumference=`echo "$radius*$pi" | bc -l`
21. area=`echo "$radius^2*$pi" | bc -l`
22.
23. # Last, we display the answers to the user and exit.
24.
25. printf "\n\nThe circumference is:\t$circumference\n"
26. printf "The area is:\t\t$area\n\n"
27. exit 0
```

13

SHELL PROGRAMMING

Most of the concepts used in this program have already been explained, so rather than go through the program line by line, I am only going to cover the concepts that are new and/or important to the operation of the program.

- **Line 6:** This line assigns a reasonably accurate value of pi to a variable called `pi`. I point this out because it shows good programming practice. We could just as easily have typed the number 3.14159265 each time we needed to use pi in the program. But assigning the number to a variable serves two primary purposes. First, it simply makes the program more readable. Second, it makes the program much easier to maintain. If we later decided that we needed more precision for the value of pi, we would only have to change one number where we assign the value to the variable `pi`. If we had used the actual number each time in the program when we needed it, we would have to find and change each occurrence of pi when we decided we need more precision.

- **Line 16:** As shown earlier, the `read` command gathers data from STDIN. In this case, we gather the value typed by the user and store it in the variable `radius`.

- **Line 20:** Line 20 uses command substitution and a pipe to compute the circumference of the circle and store the value in the variable circumference. Since `bc` does not accept expressions directly on the command line, we need to use the `echo` command to echo the expression we want computed and then pipe the output of `echo` to `bc`.

- **Line 21:** This line is similar to line 20. The caret (^) in the expression is the `bc` exponent operator. In this case, it raises the value stored in `$radius` by the power of 2 (you may recall from geometry that the area of a circle is obtained by squaring the radius and then multiplying by pi). We do not need to use parentheses to change the order of operation because, as you may recall from algebra, exponents have higher precedence than multiplication. Therefore, we can be assured that the exponent will be evaluated before the multiplication is done.

- **Lines 25 and 26:** These lines display the results to the user. I used `printf` here because it gives me a nicer layout than `echo`. The use of the hardware tabs with the \t causes the numbers to line up in a nice column.

This is only a very simple use of `bc`. `bc` is quite powerful and can do much more than what I have shown you here. As I said before, `bc` is a programming language itself. See the man page for `bc` if you are interested in learning more about its capabilities, both inside shell scripts and in standalone programs.

Loops

Sometimes you might want an operation to repeat until a certain condition becomes true (or until a certain condition is no longer true). This is where looping statements come into play. The Bourne shell supports three different looping constructs for these situations. These are the *while* loop, the *until* loop, and the *for* loop. We will look at each one separately.

The while Loop

The while loop repeats the statements inside the loop as long as the condition that is being tested is true. Depending on your point of view, it could also be said that the while loop repeats the statements inside the loop until the condition that is being tested becomes false. If the condition is already false the first time it is evaluated, the loop will never be executed. For example, the following program uses a while loop to count to 20 and display the numbers on the screen.

```
1.  #!/bin/sh
2.  # Count from 1 to 20
3.  i=1
4.  while [ $i -le 20 ]
5.  do
6.        echo $i
7.        i=`expr $i + 1`
8.  done
9.exit 0
```

This program introduces a few new concepts:

- **Line 3:** This line simply assigns the variable i the initial value of 1. i is a variable that is universally understood to be a loop control counter, so this is one case where you can get away with not using a descriptive variable name.

- **Line 4:** The while command contains the condition to test enclosed in brackets. The bracket is actually a shorthand notation for a command called test. You will use this command a lot in shell scripting.

Unfortunately, the test command uses a somewhat strange syntax. -le in this example means "is less than or equal to". So this means the loop will repeat as long as the variable "i" is less than or equal to 20. For mathematical evaluations, Table 13.2 shows all the operators that this command supports.

TABLE 13.2   Mathematical Operations for the `test` Command

Option	Action
`-eq`	True if operand one is equal to operand two
`-ne`	True if operand one is not equal to operand two
`-gt`	True if operand one is greater than operand two
`-ge`	True if operand one is greater than or equal to operand two
`-lt`	True if operand one is less than operand two
`-le`	True if operand one is less than or equal to operand two

- **Line 5:** The do statement indicates that everything after this should be done for each iteration of the loop. All statements located between the do statement and the done statement are considered part of the loop.

- **Line 6:** Prints the current value of the variable i.

- **Line 7:** Uses command substitution with the expr command to increment the value of i by one and then assign the new value back into i.

- **Line 8:** Indicates the end of the loop. At this point, the program jumps back up to the while statement, and the test condition is evaluated again. If i is still less than or equal to 20, the statements inside the loop are repeated again. If i is greater than 20, the loop exits and control passes to the first statement after the done statement (in this case, line 9, which simply exits the program with a 0, or successful status).

Notice that the statements inside the loop are indented. This makes it easy to pick out the statements that are part of the loop when quickly scanning the program's source code. The shell ignores the indentation, so you could have written this program without using it. I recommend you always indent loops, though, to make them easier to find when quickly scanning program source code.

> **Tip**
>
> The space between the [and the condition to be tested is mandatory. Failing to include it will cause an error. For example [$VarA -gt 5] will work, but [$VarA -gt 5] will cause an error.

The `until` Loop

The until loop is the opposite of the while loop. It performs the operations inside the loop as long as the condition being tested is not true. When the condition being tested becomes true, the loop exits. If the condition is already true the first time it is evaluated, the loop will never be executed.

The while loop and the until loop are very similar. Usually, you can use either one in a program and achieve the same results simply by modifying the condition that is tested for. For example, the counting program that used the while loop can be rewritten to use an until loop by making only two changes in line 4:

```
4.  until [$i -ge 20 ]
```

The program performs the exact same function. The only difference is that now the loop repeats until the value of i is greater than 20, whereas before it repeated while the value of i was less than or equal to 20. The result is exactly the same, however.

Logical AND/OR Statements in while and until Loops

Both the while and the until loop can also work with logical AND/OR statements. A logical AND statement will be carried out if and only if both conditions are true. A logical OR statement will be carried out if either condition is true. The following code sample shows a logical AND statement:

```
#!/bin/sh
# Demonstrate logical AND
VarA=1
VarB=5
while [ $VarA -eq 1 ] && [ $VarB -gt 7 ]
do
        echo "VarA is equal to 1 and VarB is greater than 7"
done
exit 0
```

13

SHELL
PROGRAMMING

In the previous example, the echo statement will not be executed because although $VarA is equal to 1, $VarB is not greater than 7. And since the while loop in this case requires both conditions to be true, the test fails and returns a 0 (false).

The following code sample is identical to the previous one, except we have changed the while test to a logical OR statement. Now, only one of the conditions needs to be true:

```
#!/bin/sh
# Demonstrate logical OR
VarA=1
VarB=5
while [ $VarA -eq 1 ] || [ $VarB -gt 7 ]
do
        echo "VarA is equal to 1 or VarB is greater than 7"
done
exit 0
```

In this case, only one condition needs to be true. And since $VarA will always be equal to 1 in this program, the result will be an infinite loop that prints the echo statement over and over again endlessly. (To break out of this loop, press Ctrl-C on your keyboard.)

The for Loop

The for loop is different from the while or until loops. Instead of evaluating a true/false test condition, the for loop simply performs the statements inside the body of the loop once for each argument it receives in a list. When creating a for loop, you supply it a variable. Each iteration of the for loop changes the value of the variable to the next argument in the list. The for loop continues until the argument list has been exhausted, at which point the loop exists and the first statement after the loop is executed. The following program uses a for loop along with the bc command you learned about earlier to print the square root of all numbers from 10 through 20.

```
1.   #!/bin/sh
2.   # Print square roots of 10 - 20
3.   for num in `jot 10 10 20`
4.   do
5.       square_root=`echo "scale=5; sqrt($num)" | bc -l`
6.       echo $square_root
7.   done
8.   exit 0
```

The output from this program is as follows:

```
3.16227
3.31662
3.46410
3.60555
3.74165
4.00000
4.12310
4.24264
4.35889
4.47213
```

- **Line 3:** Line 3 of the program contains the for loop. It introduces a new command called jot. The jot command can do many useful operations with numbers, including printing a string of numbers and generating random numbers. In this case, we have used jot to print a string of 10 numbers, starting with number 10 and ending at number 20 (10 10 20). The for loop assigns each one of these values to the variable "num" in sequence and then performs the statements in the body of the loop for each value.

- **Line 5:** Line 5 uses the bc command to compute the square root of the value stored in $num. The "scale=5" statement tells bc that the output should be scaled to five significant digits after the decimal point. Notice also the semicolon after the scale statement. Semicolons can be used in place of a new line to separate multiple statements on the same line. The sqrt function of bc takes a number in parentheses, and returns the square root of that number. Since the shell expands the variable to the value it contains, bc actually receives the number contained in the variable rather than the name of the variable itself. Finally, at the end of line 5, the output is piped to the bc command itself. The -1 option tells bc to preload the math function library, which contains the sqrt function.

shift

The shift command is similar to the for loop. Basically, you can use a while loop along with shift to run a loop once for each command-line argument sent to a shell program.

As you recall from the previous discussion, command-line arguments are stored in numbered variables starting at $1 and going to $9. The shift command shifts the variables one position to the left each time it is run. This means that each time shift is encountered, for example, the information currently stored in $1 "falls off" the end, and the information currently stored in $2 is moved to $1. Here is an example:

```
1.  #!/bin/sh
2.  # This program demonstates the use of shift.
3.  while [ $# -ne 0 ]
4.  do
5.      echo "The value of \$1 is now $1."
6.      shift
7.  done
8.  echo
9.  exit 0
```

And a sample run:

```
bash$ ./shift1 a b c d e
The value of $1 is now a.
The value of $1 is now b.
The value of $1 is now c.
The value of $1 is now d.
The value of $1 is now e.

bash$
```

- **Line 3:** This line starts a while loop. You will recall that the magic variable $# contains the number of command-line arguments. This while loop continues as long as the value of $# is not equal to zero. When the value of $# is equal to zero, all the command-line arguments have been used up, and the loop ends.

- **Line 5:** This line prints the current value of $1. Note that to actually print the literal string $1 on the screen, you have to escape the $ with the backslash to prevent the shell from giving the $ a special meaning.

- **Line 6:** When the shift command in line 6 is run, the variables are shifted one position to the left. $1 "falls off" the end, and is no longer available, $2 becomes $1, $3 becomes $2, and so on.

One of the most common applications of shift (and for loops) is in shell programs that accept filenames as command-line arguments and then perform a group of operations on each file specified on the command line.

The true and false Statements

There are two statements available in shell programming called *true* and *false*. The sole purpose of these statements is to return a value of true (0) or false (1), respectively. These statements can be used to create infinite loops. In the next section, you will learn how to break out of an infinite loop. Later on in the chapter, you will see situations where infinite loops can be useful. The following example shows a program that will loop indefinitely.

```
1.  #!/bin/sh
2.  # The following program loops indefinitely.
3.  while true
4.  do
5.      echo "This line will print forever."
6.  done
7.  echo "This line will never print since the program will"
8.  echo "never get past the loop."
9.  exit 0      # The program will never exit cleanly since it will
10.             # never get to this point.
```

Obviously, I cannot show you the output of this program since it would go on forever. Line 3 tests for a true condition. And since the argument it tests (true) will never return a value of false, the loop will repeat indefinitely because the condition will always be true. Lines 7, 8, 9, and 10 will never be executed because the program will never get past the loop. (To end this program, press Ctrl-C on your keyboard.)

Breaking the Loop

Sometimes, you might want to break out of a loop before the condition necessary to exit the loop has occurred. There are two statements that can be used to break a loop. The first is the *break* statement. The second is the *continue* statement.

The break Statement

The break statement will terminate a loop immediately when it is encountered, whether or not the condition required to exit the loop has been met. Listing 13.3 shows a slight modification to the previous endless loop program.

LISTING 13.3   Breaking Out of a Loop

```
1.  #!/bin/sh
2.  # The following program loops indefinitely.
3.  while true
4.  do
5.      echo "This line will print forever... But..."
6.      break
7.  done
8.  echo
9.  echo "The break statement in the loop causes the loop"
10. echo "to terminate immediately and go the first statement"
11. echo "after the loop."
12. exit 0
```

And the output of this program:

```
This line will print forever... But...

The break statement in the loop causes the loop
to terminate immediately and go to the first statement
after the loop.
bash$
```

The continue Statement

The *continue* statement causes the loop to immediately jump back to the top and re-evaluate the test condition. Any remaining statements in the loop are not executed. Listing 13.4 is another example that uses the endless loop program with a slight modification:

LISTING 13.4   Restarting a Loop Before It Has Ended

```
1.  #!/bin/sh
2.  # The following program loops indefinitely.
3.  while true
4.  do
5.      echo "This line will print forever."
6.      continue
7.      echo "But this line will never print even though it is inside"
8.      echo "the loop because the preceding continue statement"
9.      echo "causes the loop to jump back to the top and re-evaluate"
```

13

SHELL
PROGRAMMING

LISTING 13.4   continued

```
10.      echo "the test."
11. done
12. echo "This line will never print since the program will"
13. echo "never get past the loop."
14. exit 0     # The program will never exit cleanly since it will
15.            # never get to this point.
```

This program will indefinitely output "This line will print forever." The rest of the echo statements inside the loop will never be printed because the continue statement before them causes the loop to immediately jump back to the top and re-evaluate the test condition.

Conditional Statements

Conditional statements execute if and only if a certain condition or conditions are true. They generally come in three forms: if statements, case statements, and logical AND/OR statements.

if Statements

if statements test numerical expressions. If the condition is true the statements inside the if block are executed. If the statement is false, one of two things can happen:

- Nothing. The statements inside the if block are not executed, and the program continues as if they were not even there.

- If an else statement is included inside the if block, these statements will be executed if the condition is false. In other words, this can be used to write "Do this if the condition is true, or do this if the condition is false, but do not do both" type of controls in programs.

For example, the following program uses an if statement to test the number of command-line arguments given to the program. If the command-line arguments are 1 or more, the program performs the operations inside the then block. If no command-line arguments were supplied, the program exits without doing anything.

```
1. #!/bin/sh
2. # ifprog: Demonstrate one way to use if statements.
3. if [ $# -ge 1 ]
4. then
5.     echo "You supplied $# command line arguments."
6. fi
7. echo
```

```
8.  echo "Program exiting..."
9.  echo
10. exit 0
```

And here are two sample runs:

Run 1:

```
bash$ ./ifprog file1 file2 file3
You supplied 3 command line arguments.

Program exiting...
bash$
```

Run 2:

```
bash$ ./ifprog

Program exiting...
bash$
```

The `if` statement in line 3 checks to see whether the number of command-line arguments supplied is one or greater (using the magic variable `$#`, which stores the number of command-line arguments). If it is, the statements between `then` and `fi` are executed. ("`fi`" is `if` spelled backward. It marks the end of the if block.) If it isn't, the statements inside the `if` block are skipped and the program jumps to the first statement past `fi`, which in this case simply informs the user that the program is exiting.

We could make this program more user-friendly by including an `else` statement that tells the user how to properly use the program rather than simply having it exit without doing anything as it currently does. Listing 13.5 shows the revised example.

LISTING 13.5   A More Friendly Version of the Previous Program

```
1.  #!/bin/sh
2.  # ifprog: Demonstrate one way to use if statements.
3.  if [ $# -ge 1 ]
4.  then
5.        echo "You supplied $# command line arguments."
6.  else
7.        echo "Usage: $0 file1 file2..."
8         echo
9         exit 1
10. fi
11. echo
12. echo "Program exiting..."
13. echo
14. exit 0
```

Now, if the number of command-line arguments is less than 1, the program will perform the else statements and give the user a usage message (remember that $0 contains the name of the command that was invoked). Notice also line 9, which tells the program to exit immediately and sets the exit status to 1 (which indicates the program terminated with errors). Statements 10–14 will never get executed if the program runs the else statements.

The then part of the if statement is required. The else part is optional. As you have seen, the then part of the if statement performs an action if the expression tested by if evaluates to true. Sometimes, however, you might want to perform an action only if the expression evaluates to false and to do nothing if the expression evaluates to true. You can do this by using a colon as a placeholder. For example:

```
if [ $myvar -gt 5 ]
then
    : # Do nothing and continue after end of if block
else
    # Statements to execute if condition is false go here.
fi
```

elif

Sometimes you might want to test for two or more different conditions and perform a different action, depending on the results. The *elif* statement accomplishes this.

elif is an abbreviation for "else if". When elif statements are used, the program will go through the if statement. If it evaluates to true, its actions will be performed and then program flow will jump to the first statement after the end of the if block (where fi is located). If it evaluates to false, the first elif is checked. If it is true, the statements inside it are executed and flow jumps to the end of the if block. If it is false, the second elif statement is evaluated, and so on. Basically, evaluations are done until the program reaches an expression that evaluates to true. If none of the conditions evaluate to true, either nothing happens, or the statements inside else, if present, are executed. Listing 13.6 uses much of what you have learned up to this point, including if, elif, and else to play a simple number-guessing game.

LISTING 13.6   A Simple Number Guessing Game

```
1.   #!/bin/sh
2.   # Number guessing game
3.   clear
4.   guess_count=1      # Initialize the guess counter to 1
5.   echo
6.   echo "Number guessing game written in bourne shell script."
7.   echo
```

LISTING 13.6   continued

```
8.  echo -n "Enter upper limit for guess: "
9.  read up_limit
10. rnd_number=`jot -r 1 1 $up_limit`   # Get a random number
11. echo
12. echo "I´ve thought of a number between 1 and $up_limit."
13. echo
14. echo -n "Please guess a number between 1 and $up_limit: "
15. read guess
16. # Check the guess against the random number.
17. while true
18. do
19.     if [ $guess -gt $rnd_number ]
20.     then
21.             echo
22.             echo "Your guess was too high. Please try again."
23.             guess_count=`expr $guess_count + 1`
24.             echo -n "Please guess a number between 1 and $up_limit: "
25.             read guess
26.     elif [ $guess -lt $rnd_number ]
27.     then
28.             echo
29.             echo "Your guess was too low. Please try again."
30.             guess_count=`expr $guess_count + 1`
31.             echo -n "Please guess a number between 1 and $up_limit: "
32.             read guess
33.     else
34.             break
35.     fi
36. done
37. # We get to this point when the player guesses the correct number.
38. echo
39. echo "Correct!"
40. echo
41. echo "You guessed the number in $guess_count guesses."
42. echo
43. exit 0
```

And a sample run:

```
Number guessing game written in bourne shell script.

Enter upper limit for guess: 10
I´ve thought of a number between 1 and 10.

Please guess a number between 1 and 10: 5

Your guess was too low. Please try again.
Please guess a number between 1 and 10: 8
```

```
Your guess was too high. Please try again.
Please guess a number between 1 and 10: 7

Correct!

You guessed the number in 3 guesses.
```

Most of the concepts in this program should be familiar to you by now. Line 3 simply clears the screen. Line 4 initializes a variable "guess_count" to store the number of guesses the player has made, and sets the initial value to 1. Lines 23 and 30 increment the value of the variable guess_count by 1 for each incorrect guess made. Line 10 uses command substitution with the jot command to assign a single random number between 1 and whatever the player entered as the upper limit for the guess to the variable rand_number. Line 17 starts an infinite loop. Line 19 checks to see if the number the player entered is greater than the random number that the program picked. If it is, the player is informed of that, the guess_count variable is incremented by 1, and the player is asked to pick another number. After the player has picked another number, it is stored in the variable "guess" and the while loop starts over. If the number the player guessed is not greater than the random number the computer picked, the elif statement is evaluated to check if the number is lower. If it is, the player is informed of this, the guess_count variable is incremented by 1, and the player is asked to try again. After the player has entered a new number the while loop starts over. Finally, if neither condition is true, the else statement is executed (we did not need to perform a test here because if the number is neither higher nor lower, it must be equal). The else statement here simply breaks out of the infinite loop, and program flow passes to the first statement after the done statement. The statements at the end of the program simply tell the user they guessed the correct number and then inform the user how many guesses it took them to get the correct answer by displaying the value of guess_count.

Like loop tests, if tests also support the logical AND (&&) and logical OR (||) tests to perform conditions if and only if both conditions are true, or if one of any number of conditions are true.

case Statements

If you need to test the same variable for multiple conditions, there is a more efficient and cleaner way of doing it than with if statements. The case statement takes a variable as an argument and then uses statement blocks to determine what to do, depending on the value of the variable. Listing 13.7 uses case statements to create a random quote generator.

LISTING 13.7 Using case to Generate Random Quotes

```
1.  #!/bin/sh
2.  # Random quote generator.
3.  quote_num=`jot -r 1 1 5`
4.  case "$quote_num" in
5.      1) echo
6.         echo "\"Until he extends his circle of compassion to include"
7.         echo "all living things, man will not himself find peace.\""
8.         echo" -- Albert Schweitzer"
9.         echo ;;
10.     2) echo
11.        echo "\"With regard to excellence, it is not enough to know, but"
12.        echo "we must try to have and use it.\""
13.        echo "-- Aristotle"
14.        echo ;;
15.     3) echo
16.        echo "\"Imagination is more important than knowledge. Knowledge"
17.        echo "is limited. Imagination encircles the whole world.\""
18.        echo "-- Albert Einstein"
19.        echo ;;
20.     4) echo
21.        echo "\"It is not the strongest of the species that survive, nor"
22.        echo "the most intelligent, but the one most responsive to change.\""
23.        echo "-- Charles Darwin"
24.        echo ;;
25. esac
26. exit 0
```

Once again, we use jot in line 3 to generate a random number between 1 and 4. The case block begins on line 4. The syntax is case *variable* in, where *variable* is the name of the variable that the tests should be performed on. Line 5 begins the first test. Everything to the left of the parenthesis indicates the condition that case tests for. Like the if statement, case stops at the first match it comes to, executes the statements that go with that match, and then jumps down to esac (which is "case" spelled backward). The end of the statements that go along with each condition is marked with a double semicolon. The double semicolon can be on a line by itself, or it can be placed on the same line as the last statement, as is done in the previous example.

The case statement also accepts shell wildcards. For example:

```
case "$myvar" in
    a) #statements to do for a
       ;;
    b) #statements to do for b
       ;;
    *) #statements to do for anything else
       ;;
esac
```

The previous code will check to see if $myvar is equal to a or b, and perform those statements if it is. If it is not, the last test is a wildcard that will match anything. So, if $myvar is not equal to a or b, the last group of statements will be performed.

Other wildcards supported by case include the ?, which works the same way it does in the shell, and the pipe character, which allows case to accept a range of options. Foe example, Y | y) will accept either Y or y as a match for a test. You can also enclose multiple characters in brackets to match a range of characters. For example, [Yy]|[Yy][Ee][Ss]) will accept either "y" or "yes" as a match in any combination of upper- or lowercase letters.

CGI Programming

You've probably seen Web sites that have features such as random quotes that display on the page at each load or a random picture that changes each time the page is reloaded. The program presented previously that used case to display the quotes is one way to do this. This is called a CGI program, and it is a way for the Web server to run external programs and then send the output of those programs over the Internet to a browser. Chapter 26, "Configuring a Web Server," covers more on CGI programming.

Logical AND/OR Conditionals

Logical AND/OR conditionals are basically a short-hand way of doing if statements in some cases. They use the exit status of the first command to determine whether or not to run the second command. For example:

```
tar cvfz backup.tar.gz documents/2000/* && rm -r documents/2000
```

This command basically says, "If the first operation is successful, perform the second operation. If the first operation is not successful, do not perform the second operation." In other words "You have to perform A and B. If A cannot be performed, do not perform B." In this case, it will attempt to archive all the files in the directory documents/2000 into a file called backup.tar.gz. If the archive operation is successful (the tar command exits with 0), the operation after the && will also be performed, which removes the directory documents/2000. If the archive operation is unsuccessful (the tar command exits with some number other than 0), the operation after the && will not be performed (obviously, we do not want to remove the directory if we were unable to successfully archive it).

The || is the OR operator. It basically says, "If you cannot perform A, perform B. But do not perform B if A is successful." Here is an example:

```
tar cvfz backup.tar.gz documents/2000/* || echo "Archive operation failed."
```

In this case, if the archive operation is successful (`tar` exits with 0), the statement after the `||` will not be executed. If however, the archive operation fails (`tar` returns an exit status other than 0), the statement after the `||` will be executed, and an error message will be printed to the screen.

Exit Status

Most programs in FreeBSD return an exit status when they terminate. The exit status is usually 0 if successful, and some number other than 0 if something went wrong. Some programs will return a different exit status, depending on the problem. Often, this information can be found in the program's man page.

The exit status of the last program that ran is stored in the magic variable "$?". Here are a couple of examples:

```
bash$ ls > /dev/null
bash$ echo $?
0
bash$
```

```
bash$ ls -2 /dev/null
ls: illegal option -- 2
usage: ls [-ABCFGHLPRTWabcdfgiklnoqrstu1] [file ...]
bash$ echo $?
1
bash$
```

The first example will set the magic variable $? to 0, as shown (output of the `ls` command was redirected to `/dev/null` for brevity in the example). The second example, however, supplies an illegal option to `ls`. The command fails with an error message, and $? is set to 1.

You can use this exit status to make automatic decisions in your shell programs. The previous logical AND/OR example already introduced this to an extent. It showed how the success or failure of one command can determine whether the next one is executed or not. The logical AND/OR statement used in the previous section could also have been written as an `if` statement like this:

```
if tar cvfz backup.tar.gz documents/2000/*
then
    rm -r documents/2000
else
```

13

```
    echo "Archive operation failed"
fi
```

This example combines the two examples from the previous section. The `if` statement reads the exit status of the `tar` command. If the exit status is 0, the `then` statements are performed, and the directory that was archived is removed. If the exit status is some number other than 0, the `then` statements are not performed, and the `else` statements are performed instead.

Another useful application of this property is with the `test` command. We've already seen how to use the `test` command with mathematical expressions. Another useful application of `test` is to check for the existence of AND/OR properties of a file. For example:

```
if [-f program.conf]
then
    : # do nothing
else
    touch program.conf
done
```

This example checks for the existence of the file "program.conf". If the file exists, a 0 is returned, and the `then` statement is executed. In this case, the `then` statement does nothing. (The colon tells it to do nothing. The rest of the line is a comment). If the file does not exist, a 1 is returned, and the `else` statement is performed, which uses the `touch` command to create the file.

The `test` command can test for more than just the existence of a file. It can also test the attributes and type of file. Table 13.3 is a list of all the options to the `test` command and what they mean.

TABLE 13.3   Testing File Attributes in Shell Programs

Option	Action
-f	The file exists, and is a normal file
-d	The file exists, and is a directory
-s	The file exists, and its size is greater than zero
-c	The file exists, and is a character special file
-b	The file exists, and is a block special file
-r	The file exists, and is readable
-w	The file exists, and is writable
-x	The file exists, and is executable
-d	The file exists, and is a directory

Setting Exit Status

Most of the scripts in this chapter have set the exit status, and by now you have a pretty good idea of what the exit status is used for. You have also seen that the `exit` statement is used to set the exit status. If you do not specifically set the exit status, your program will return the exit status of the last command that ran. When you do set the exit status, whatever you set will be stored in the $? variable just like the exit status of any other program. Also, just like any other program, the exit status of your shell program can be read by other programs to make a decision about what to do next. This can be useful if you are calling a shell program from another shell program, for example.

Also, remember that you are not limited to just 0 and 1 for exit statuses. You can use many more exit statuses. Always use 0 for a successful exit and numbers other than 0 for an error exit. You can use several different exit statuses in the same program to handle different error conditions and then the calling program can act accordingly. Here is a sample of some code that uses multiple exit statuses:

```
if [-r program.conf]
then
    : # do nothing
else
    exit 1
fi
if [touch /tmp/program.lock]
then
    : # do nothing
else
    exit 2
fi
# main program statements here
exit 0
```

The previous sample first checks to see whether it can read the file "program.conf". If it can, the program continues to the next `if` test. If it can't, the program exits immediately with an exit status of 1. If the program was able to read the program.conf file, it will then attempt to create the /tmp/program.lock file. If it can, the program continues. If it can't, the program exits immediately with an exit status of 2. Finally, assuming that both operations succeed, the program will continue with the main part of the program and then exit with a status of 0. This program could be called from another program and then return its exit status to that program. The calling program could then make decisions based on the exit status it received from this program.

13

SHELL PROGRAMMING

Exit Traps

As you know, programs in FreeBSD can be terminated by sending them various kill signals and with various combinations of keyboard commands (Ctrl-C for example). The problem with this is that if, for example, a program creates temp files, and the user interrupts the program with Ctrl-C before it has finished running, the program will not clean up after itself, and will leave its temp files laying around on the disk wasting space. Fortunately, the shell provides a way to trap these types of interrupts. Here is a short sample program that demonstrates the use of trapping interrupts:

```
#!/bin/sh
# Program that demonstrates trapping interrupts
trap `echo "Interrupt received. Quitting." 1>&2' 1 2 3 15
echo -n "Enter a number: "
readln num
exit 0
```

Basically, this program sets a trap for interrupts 1, 2, 3, and 15. The actions performed by the trap are located between the single quotes. If you run this program, and at the prompt that asks you to "Enter a number" you press Ctrl-C, it will send signal 2 (INT) to the program that will set off the trap and cause the message "Interrupt received" to be printed. Then, the program will exit.

We introduced one new aspect of the echo command here. Actually, it is an aspect of shell output redirection. The 1>&2 in the echo statement redirects the output of the echo command to STDERR. This ensures that the output of the command will not accidentally be sent down a pipe to another command or redirected to another location along with the rest of the program's output. It is a good idea any time you create error messages to send the output to STDERR with 1>&2.

Normally, of course, you would use the traps to do things such as clean up temp files and such. If you need to do a lot of things in a trap, it is better to make the trap a function (functions will be covered later in the chapter).

If you want to prevent the user from being able to exit the program with Ctrl-C, you can set a trap and leave the action null. For example:

```
trap `' 2
```

This line causes signal 2 to be completely ignored.

Your program can have more than one trap, and different things can be done, depending on how the program exited. A trap for signal 0 will be set off on all exits, normal or otherwise.

A trap for other signals will be set off only when that signal occurs. Table 13.4 is a list of the most common signals you might want to trap.

TABLE 13.4   Common Interrupt Signals and Their Actions

Interrupt Signal	Action
0	Exit
1	HUP—Session hangup (or disconnect)
2	INT—Interrupt (Ctrl-C)
3	QUIT—Quit (Ctrl-\)
15	TERM—A normal kill command

Note

You can trap signal 15 (the default signal sent by the `kill` command). You can also trap most other signals that can be sent by the `kill` command, however, you cannot trap signal 9 (`SIGKILL`). `SIGKILL` is used as a last resort to terminate a program when all other methods have failed. Therefore, it cannot be trapped and cannot be ignored.

Functions

Functions are basically groups of statements that can be called with a single command. They can almost be thought of as "mini-programs inside programs." Using functions in your shell programs can make your life a lot easier—for two reasons. First of all, if you need to perform the operation in multiple places in your program, you can simply type the name of the function rather than having to retype all the code each time you need to perform the operation. Second, if you later decide you need to make the operation work differently, you only have to change the function rather than go through the code and change it every place it is used. The following shows a simple example of a function that cleans up temp files, and so on, after a shell program exit. It then shows how to call the function:

```
#!/bin/sh
on_exit() {
    rm -rf /tmp/myprogram.*
    mv logfile logfile.old
    mail foo@bar.com < report.txt
}
trap on_exit 0 1 2 3 15
```

The previous sample shows how a function is created. It is given a name, followed by parentheses and a left bracket. Everything between the two brackets is the body of a function. The function can then be called as if it were a program, simply by using its name. As stated previously, functions can almost be thought of as "mini-programs inside programs." Any time you type the name of this function, the statements between its brackets will be performed.

There is one important difference between calling a function and calling another program, though. The function is run in the current shell, whereas a separate program starts in a subshell. This means that a function can modify the variables and environment variables in the program that calls it. But a separate program called from inside a shell program cannot modify any of the variables or environment variables in the calling program.

File Descriptors

File descriptors are numbered IDs that are set up each time the kernel starts a process. These numbers are what the process uses to write output and read input. There are three file descriptors that are opened by default:

F.D. 0   STDIN. This is where standard input comes from. It is normally the keyboard, but it can be redirected to read from a file or some other source.

F.D. 1   STDOUT. This is where standard output goes. It is normally the screen, but as you have seen it can be redirected.

F.D. 2   STDERR. This is where standard error messages go. Once again, it is normally the screen, but it can also be redirected.

File descriptors can be used in shell programs to make your programs both more efficient and easier to write. The "exec" command can be used to open a file descriptor. Here is an example of how file descriptors can make your programs both easier to write and more efficient:

```
#!/bin/sh
# open a file descriptor on F.D. 1 (STDOUT)
exec > testfile.txt
# echo some stuff to STDOUT which will now go to the file testfile.txt
echo "Line 1 of the file"
echo "Line 2 of the file"
echo "Line 3 of the file"
echo "Line 4 of the file"
echo "line 5 of the file"
exit 0
```

The exec statement in line two of the previous code sample causes "testfile.txt" to be opened as STDOUT. As a result, all the echo lines are set to the file "testfile.txt" instead of to the screen, even though the output is not redirected in the echo statements. If you have a lot of things that need to be written to a file, this is more efficient than using shell redirection each time. It is also easier to code since you don't have to redirect the output each time.

This is also very useful when opening a file descriptor for STDIN and using read. Here is a sample:

```
#!/bin/sh
# open a file descriptor on F.D. 0 (STDIN)
exec < testfile.txt
while read string
do
    echo $string
done
exit 0
```

Assuming that you still have the file "testfile.txt" from the previous example, this sample will output:

```
Line 1 of the file
Line 2 of the file
Line 3 of the flie
Line 4 of the file
Line 5 of the file
```

So, what is so great about this? It demonstrates an important concept of using a file descriptor with read. Since the file is not closed between each call to read, read remembers the last line it read, and moves the pointer to the next line in the file. This way, read will read each line of the file in sequence automatically.

Debugging Shell Scripts

If you write shell scripts of any complexity at all, sooner or later bugs are going to creep in. Although there is no full-fledged debugger for the shell, it does provide some primitive debugging capabilities in the form of being able to trace each action that is performed. You turn on the tracing by adding -xv to the end of the #!/bin/sh line in your script, so it looks like this:

```
#!/bin/sh -xv
```

This works best if you pipe the output to more or less, and also if you redirect both STDOUT and STDERR to the same place so that you can see both the output of the script and the errors. Here is a simple example:

```
#!/bin/sh -xv
# Demonstrate the use of tracing in shell script debugging
result=`echo "2 * 12 / (2 + 2)` | bc`
echo $result
exit 0
```

13

SHELL PROGRAMMING

To execute this program so that you will see both STDOUT and STDERR and pipe the output to more, use the following command:

```
./xvtest 2>&1 | more
```

The program will produce the following output:

```
1.  ./xvtest 2>&1 | more
2.  #!/bin/sh -xv
3.  # Demonstrate the use of tracing in shell script debugging
4.  result=`echo "2 * 12 / (2 + 3)" | bc`
5.  + echo 2 * 12 / (2 + 3)
6.  + bc
7.  + result=4
8.  echo $result
9.  + echo 4
10. 4
11. exit 0
12. + exit 0
```

You can now see everything that this program did. The lines with + signs in front of them are results of actions in the program. For example, line 3 in the previous sample assigns the results of a calculation to the variable "result". Lines 4, 5, and 6 show the actions that were taken. Line 4 shows the echo command, line 5 shows the execution of bc, and finally, line 6 shows the variable assignment where 4 is assigned to the variable "result".

This sample also shows how variable expansion works. Notice lines 8, 9, and 10. In line 8, the echo statement is read. In line 9, the variable is expanded so that the echo statement becomes "echo 4". Then, in line 10, the actual output of the echo statement is produced.

Advanced Features of Korn Shell Scripting

The Korn shell contains some advanced features that can make shell programming easier and more powerful. You should think carefully before using these features, however. The reason is that virtually every UNIX system can run a Bourne shell script; some will not be able to run a Korn shell script. If this script will be run only on your local system, this will not be a problem. Also, if you can be sure that this script will be run only on systems that have the Korn shell available, this will also not be a problem. If you are writing a shell script for public consumption, however, or if this script will run on multiple systems within your organization and you cannot be sure which shells will be available on those systems, you are better off sticking to plain old Bourne script.

That being said, this section will cover some of the advanced features of Korn shell scripting.

> **Tip**
>
> Most of the techniques given in this chapter also apply to the POSIX shell that FreeBSD ships with as /bin/sh. However, you definitely should not use these in a /bin/sh script if the script will be run on other systems that do not use a POSIX shell as /bin/sh. Because of the #!/bin/sh at the beginning of the script, the other system will try to run the script anyway. But it will bomb as soon as it hits code that it doesn't understand because it is not part of the Bourne shell syntax.

Obtaining and Installing the Korn Shell

Before you can wrte shell programs for the Korn shell, you need to install a copy of the Korn shell on your system. The Public Domain Korn Shell is available for FreeBSD both on the CD-ROM as a package under shells (which can be installed from sysinstall or from the command line) and also in the ports tree under /usr/ports/shells/pdksh. To tell your program to run with the Korn shell, replace #!/bin/sh at the top of your shell program with #/usr/local/bin/ksh. The Korn shell is completely backward-compatible with Bourne, so any script that was written for a Bourne shell will also run under the Korn shell. The reverse is not true, however. You cannot run a Korn shell script under Bourne.

Now that you have the Korn shell installed, let's look at some of the advanced features that make programming in the Korn shell easier, more powerful, and more efficient.

Built-in Arithmetic

The Korn shell has built-in arithmetic. This means you do not need to call the expr program to do arithmetic in Korn as you do in Bourne. However, like expr, Korn shell arithmetic is limited to operations on integer numbers. Because it is an internal function, however, it can perform these operations much faster than exec.

There are two ways to access the built-in arithmetic functions of the Korn shell. The first is with the `let` statement. For example:

```
let x=7+5
```

This line assigns 12 to the variable `x`.

The other method is by enclosing the expression in double parentheses, for example:

```
if ((x < z))
```

This can be more readable than using `let`. It is also more readable for mathematical comparisons than using the `test` command in Bourne shell syntax since it allows you to use the familiar mathematical notations < and > rather than `-lt` and `-gt`. Also, unlike `"expr"` characters that would have special meaning to the shell do not have to be escaped. In Korn, you can write `((5 * 3))` rather than `expr 5 \* 3`, for example.

Korn shell arithmetic supports the common mathematical operators shown in Table 13.5.

TABLE 13.5   Korn Shell Math Operators

Operator	Description
+	Addition
-	Subtraction
*	Multiplication
/	Division
%	Modulus: Return the remainder of a division.
>	Greater than
<	Less than
>=	Greater than or equal to
<=	Less than or equal to
==	Equal to
!=	Not equal to
&&	True if both expressions are non-zero
||	True if either expression is non-zero
=	Assigns the expression on the right to the expression on the left
+=	Adds the expression on the right to the variable on the left and then stores the result in the variable
-=	Subtracts the expression on the right from the variable on the left and then stores the result in the variable

TABLE 13.5 continued

Operator	Description
*=	Multiplies the expression on the right by the variable on the left and then assigns the result to the variable
/=	Divides the expression on the right by the variable on the left and then assigns the result to the variable
%=	Divides the expression on the right by the variable on the left and then assigns the remainder to the variable

Arrays

The Korn shell also supports arrays. An *array* is a variable that contains multiple elements, each of which contains a separate value. They are useful for grouping related elements together.

You can think of arrays as a box with different compartments in it. Each compartment has a number. You could access the various compartments by giving the name of the box, followed by the compartment number.

Use the set command to load an array. For example, suppose we want to create an array called "temperature" that contains the average temperature for each month of the year for a given area. The following command will do the trick:

```
oot  A temperature 57 52 58 61 63 65 71 70 68 66 64 62
```

This will create an array called "temperature" with 12 elements in it—one for each month of the year. If you are following along at your system, simply enter the previous command from a Korn shell command prompt for now (if you need to start a Korn shell, you can do so by typing ksh at the prompt).

To access the various elements in the array, we use a subscript appended onto the end of the array name. Elements in the array start at 0, and wildcards are accepted. Here are some examples of how this works:

```
ksh$ echo ${temperature[0]}
57
ksh$ echo ${temperature[11]}
62
ksh$ echo ${temperature[*]}
57 52 58 61 63 65 71 70 68 66 64 62
ksh$
```

Arrays can contain up to 512 elements (0–511).

If you wish to change the value of only one element in an array, you can do it by refer-encing the element in a variable assignment. For example:

```
temperature[0]=55
```

There are a couple of points to note here regarding arrays:

- Unlike variables, the brackets are not optional when referencing the array. They are mandatory. echo $temperautre[1] will not have the desired result. It must be written as echo ${temperature[1]}.

- Arrays cannot be exported as environment variables.

So, why not just create a separate variable for each month? Well, we could have done that. But the following program shows an example of how arrays can save a lot of pro-gramming time:

```
1.  #!/usr/local/bin/ksh
2.  # Demonstration of arrays and computing average temperature.
3.  set -A temperature 57 52 58 61 63 65 71 70 68 66 64 62
4.  i=0
5.  printf "\nMonth\t\tTemperature\n\n"
6.  while (( i < 12))
7.  do
8.          (( month = $i + 1 ))
9.          printf "$month\t\t${temperature[$i]}\n"
10          (( total_temp += ${temperature[$i]} ))
11.         (( i += 1 ))
12. done
13. avg_temp=$(( total_temp / 12 ))
14. echo
15. echo  "Average temperature for whole year: $avg_temp"
16. echo
 exit 0
```

And the output of this program:

```
Month           Temperature

1               57
2               52
3               58
4               61
5               63
6               65
7               71
8               70
9               68
10              66
11              64
12              62

Average temperature for whole year: 63
```

This may look scary at first, but really there is not much new here other than the syntax is a little different. There is also some new logic in this program that we haven't used before, but it will make perfect sense once we look at how the program works.

- **Line 1:** Notice the difference here. This shell script starts with `/usr/local/bin/ksh`. If you accidentally put `#!/bin/sh` here instead, the program will not run, and you will get strange errors.

- **Line 3:** Line 3 uses the `set` command to load an array named "temperature" with 12 numbers, each of the numbers being an average temperature for one month.

- **Line 4:** This simply initializes the loop counter to zero.

- **Line 6:** Line 6 starts a loop that will continue as long as `i` is less than 12.

- **Line 8:** This line creates a new variable called month, and sets the value to whatever is in `$i + 1`. This is used in the output of the program to print the number of the current month. Why do we have to add 1 onto `$i`? Because `$i` is currently set to 0, and it is what we will use to get the first element out of the temperature array. Since array elements start with 0, our elements in the temperature array are numbered from 0 to 11. But this is not what we want for our month number display, so we simply add one onto the current value of `$i` for each iteration of the loop.

- **Line 9:** This line prints the current value of month, followed by two tab characters and then a single element from the temperature array. Notice that we use variable substitution here. The value of `$i` is expanded to the number stored in $I, and this is used as the element to retrieve from the array.

- **Line 10:** This line takes whatever value is currently in the variable `$total_temp`; adds the number stored in the array element of temperature represented by `$i` to it; and then stores the new value in `$total_temp`, overwriting the old value. It keeps a running sum of all the temperatures added together that will be used later to compute the average temperature.

- **Line 11:** This adds 1 to the current value of `$i`. So for example, on the second iteration of the loop, `$i` will now be set to 1 instead of 0, and therefore the second element of the array will be printed as well as added to `$total_temp`. This is the last statement in the loop. If `$i` is still less than 12, the loop will repeat.

- **Line 13:** After the loop has completed, the average temperature is computed by taking the sum of all the temperatures stored in `$total_temp` and dividing by 12. The new value is assigned to `avg_temp`.

- **Line 15:** The average temperate for the entire year is printed.

13

SHELL
PROGRAMMING

> **Note**
>
> According to our program, the average temperature for the whole year was 63. This is a good example of how the shell's arithmetic can only handle integers. The actual average temperature for the whole year is 63.083333, but since the shell cannot handle floating point math, it drops the decimal portion and just prints 63. If we needed more precision here we could have used the bc command to do the calculation, as we did in our program that computes the circumference and area of circles with pi.

Do you see how this program saved us some work? Rather than having to go through each month manually, we were able to use a loop that increments a variable and automates the task of getting the value for each month. If we had used separate variables to store the temperatures, this task would have required a good deal more code than we used here.

> **Note**
>
> If you want some good practice, see if you can modify the previous temperature program to use a for loop instead of a while loop. Here is a hint: Remember that the array can accept the asterisk wildcard to show all of the elements in the array.

Command Substitution

The Korn shell also supports a cleaner form of command substitution than the Bourne shell. Rather than putting commands in backquotes, you can use a syntax like the following:

```
today_date=$(date)
```

The old style is also still supported. Which one you use in Korn shell scripts is mostly a matter of personal preference.

Using getopts

getopts is a better way of handling command-line arguments than the simple Bourne style syntax that was used earlier in the chapter. The getopts command allows you to use the standard option syntax of -option that most other FreeBSD commands use. It also allows better handling of arguments to the options.

The general syntax of the `getopts` command looks like this:

```
getopts options variable
```

where *options* are the valid options that can be supplied, and *variable* is the name of the variable that those options should be stored in. If an option letter ends with a colon, it can also take a value. That value will be stored in the special variable $OPTARG. There is another special variable named $OPTIND that stores the value of the current argument being worked on.

The `getopt` command executes once for each option it is supplied with. If used with the `while` loop, the loop will execute once for each command-line argument supplied. The following shows an example of how the `getopt` command syntax works:

```
getopts abc:d: MyVar
```

With this command, the valid options that `getopts` recognizes are a, b, c, and d. In addition, options c and d are followed by a value that will be stored in the variable $OPTARG. The option itself is stored in `MyVar`. For example assuming the program that contains this `getopts` command is named `myprog`, and you invoke it like this:

```
./myprog -a -c foobar
```

the getopts command will be run twice (from a `while` loop, for example). The first time it is run, $MyVar will contain an "a". The second time it is run, $MyVar will contain a "c", and the variable $OPTARG will contain the string `foobar`. Using these variables and the previously mentioned $OPTIND variable, the `getopts` command can be used for decision-making in shell programs using the same procedures used throughout this chapter (loops and conditional statements, for example).

13

SHELL PROGRAMMING

CHAPTER 14

Performance Monitoring, Process Control, and Job Automation

IN THIS CHAPTER

One of the fundamental differences between a desktop operating system such as Windows and a server operating system such as FreeBSD is the process control. FreeBSD lets you control every single process on your system, whether trivial or crucial. Windows, by comparison, gives you control over only certain application processes—and very limited control at that. The only time you ever see the process table in Windows is during an emergency. In FreeBSD, it's an ever-present part of administering the system. For example, in Windows you can press Ctrl+Alt+Delete and get a list of desktop processes, which you can terminate if you choose. That's all you can do—and it's hard to tell what each of the listed processes does or how much of the system's resources it's taking up. But FreeBSD shows you all this information, and gives you the ability to restart processes, alter their priority, give them a number of different types of termination signals, and more—all with complete visibility into which processes might be causing problems. To use a common analogy, desktop operating systems are like cars "with the hood welded shut." FreeBSD lets you pop the hood at any time.

This doesn't mean that FreeBSD is either more arcane or less stable than these GUI-based desktop platforms. The savvy administrator will never end up destabilizing the system through poking at the processes, and neither do you have to comb through an opaque table of numbers just to perform basic system functions. As you will see in this chapter, the process table and the tools that interact with it are instead an embodiment of what makes a UNIX system what it is: a fully accessible machine with all the moving parts exposed, and with all the nuts and bolts showing. This gives you the power to tune everything the system does, no matter how minute. And that's the essence of UNIX.

We will be going through several process-monitoring tools—namely ps, top, and kill. Some are more user-friendly than others, and some are more versatile than others. We will also take a look at the cron program, which is a scheduler for tasks that have to happen periodically—another feature that separates the servers from the desktops.

Performance Monitoring with top

The easiest process-monitoring utility around is top, so named because it was originally designed to list the top-ten processes currently running on the system, in descending order of CPU usage. These days, however, FreeBSD's top, by default, shows you every process currently running, whatever state it's in. On a freshly installed FreeBSD system, this will usually be somewhere around 30 processes.

The benefit that top provides is that it's interactive and real-time. When you run it, it takes over your terminal and udpates itself every second, giving you instantaneous information about the state of the system at that moment. You can also pass it commands, such as the `kill` or `renice` commands (covered later in this chapter), or give it different options for filtering the processes it shows you. This makes it an immensely useful tool for reining in an out-of-control server, fine-tuning the performance of certain tasks, or simply keeping an eye on things as you work in another window.

top Output Explained

Run the `top` program. You'll get output similar to this:

LISTING 14.1   Example Output of top

```
last pid: 30283;  load averages:  0.51,  0.89,  0.87   up 52+15:48:43  11:19:03
126 processes: 1 running, 124 sleeping, 1 zombie
CPU states:  0.7% user,  0.0% nice,  2.8% system,  0.7% interrupt, 95.8% idle
Mem: 142M Active, 35M Inact, 59M Wired, 7496K Cache, 35M Buf, 4256K Free
Swap: 500M Total, 48M Used, 452M Free, 9% Inuse

  PID USERNAME     PRI NICE  SIZE    RES STATE  C   TIME   WCPU    CPU COMMAND
19460 mysql          2    0 25908K 2692K poll   0 112:20  2.20%  2.20% mysqld
30283 bob            2    0  1360K  976K sbwait 1   0:00  6.02%  1.56% qpopper
30282 root          29    0  2076K 1236K CPU1   0   0:00  3.14%  0.93% top
  245 root           2    0   868K  232K select 1 177:39  0.00%  0.00% healthd
18427 root           2    0  7592K 5092K select 0  80:24  0.00%  0.00% named
86694 frank         10    0  1700K   56K nanslp 0  76:46  0.00%  0.00% elm
   86 root           2  -12 1296K  412K select 0   6:28  0.00%  0.00% ntpd
80717 root          10    0  2132K  472K nanslp 0   5:53  0.00%  0.00% telnetd
61945 root           2    0  1868K  360K select 0   3:29  0.00%  0.00% inetd
   80 root           2    0   916K  320K select 0   3:26  0.00%  0.00% syslogd
66061 root           2    0  2100K  504K select 0   3:12  0.00%  0.00% sshd
73772 root           2    0  8956K 2540K select 0   3:12  0.00%  0.00% httpd
40567 www            2    0  9880K 2872K sbwait 1   0:57  0.00%  0.00% httpd
40581 www            2    0 10008K 3796K sbwait 0   0:55  0.00%  0.00% httpd
```

By default, `top` shows us all the system's processes, no matter who owns them; whether they're active, idle, or in "zombie" mode; or how much CPU time they're taking up. The first useful bit of information is in the second line—the number of processes. This will vary from system to system, but chances are that there will be many more processes currently running than will fit on your screen at once. You can press "`i`" to switch `top` into showing you only the processes that are active.

The next things to notice are the "load averages". These are some fairly obtuse metrics that you can use as a yardstick to tell at a glance how busy the system is. The exact derivation of the values is from the number of jobs executed over the last 1, 5, and 15 minutes, respectively; but it's difficult to relate this to real-world applications. Just think of the load average as the "tachometer" of the system, and think "the lower the better".

Load Averages

Eventually, you will get a feel for what constitutes a high load average on your system; typically, loads should not go above 1 on a continuous basis for a server, although a desktop system with lots of graphical tools will bump it up into the 2–3 range. 5 is a high load. Certain daemons stop accepting new requests at a certain load level, for example, 12 for sendmail. If it reaches 20 or 30, chances are that the system is in a feedback-loop situation (which can be thought of as a *race condition*), in which new processes are being created faster than the system can complete them. This only serves to slow it down more and drive the load higher, in what's not-so-affectionately termed a "death spiral".

This is one of those rare times when you might have to reboot a UNIX system because a server under this kind of load can become so tightly wedged that it will never come back—or it will take so long to complete all its processes and return to normal duty that it's faster to reboot. Either way, your remote telnet or ssh session might be unresponsive in this condition, or you might not be running one at the time the "death spiral" occurs (in which case, the system probably won't be able to open a new connection for you to come to the rescue). This is when logging in to the physical console—or even power-cycling the machine as an absolute last resort—might be the only recourse.

The header block also contains more information about the RAM in the system than you probably will ever find useful. You won't find a simple "used/free" graph of all available RAM here; instead, you see the states of all chunks of memory, including swap (virtual memory), in the fourth and fifth lines in Listing 14.1. Don't look at the Free block and assume that it is all the memory available in the system. That block is only the memory that hasn't yet been used at all because the system was last brought online. What you should be looking at is the Active block because that describes memory in use by active processes—programs that are currently running and not idle. The rest of the fields describe other states of use that may or may not be mutually exclusive, so adding up all the fields won't necessarily give you the amount of RAM that you have. It will, in fact, probably add up to more.

The Swap fields are more straightforward. Here, data is paged in and out of the virtual memory space as needed (copied to the disk and out of RAM), and the only fields that top shows us are Used and Free. The numbers here add up predictably. It's probably more useful to look at the Swap fields than at the actual RAM fields to see how well your system is doing; if there's a lot of data in Swap (50% or more Used), it means that data has been paged in fairly recently as a result of your physical RAM being full, and you may want to consider adding more memory. A FreeBSD system will very seldom run completely out of Swap space. If it does, as with most UNIX implementations, the results will usually be benign (you'll see error messages, but the system won't destabilize). The occasional unpredictable behavior or instability will surface, however. You'll want to keep your Swap as little-used as possible—for this reason and also because naturally everything runs faster in RAM than in Swap.

Next, notice that the processes are listed in descending order on the CPU column. This column lists how much of the CPU's cycles are being used currently by each process; don't expect the column to add up to 100 because your CPU will only be lightly used most of the time. Take a look at the headers again; the "CPU states" line tells you how much of the processor is being used in each of the four possible states, and you can relate these values fairly closely to the percentages in the CPU column. The WCPU field is the "weighted CPU" percentage, which we will cover in the next section when we look at the ps command.

The CPU operates in discrete cycles, many millions-per-second (depending on its speed). Each of these cycles is dedicated to some part of some process, and over time a process will have used enough of these cycles to add up to a number measurable in seconds. This is what the TIME column tells you. Don't be fooled by the colon separator into thinking that it's an hours:minutes reading; it's actually the number of CPU seconds that the process used in system states and user states, respectively. It may take minutes or hours for a process to use enough cycles to accumulate a measurable number, so if you see a process that has a large value (such as mysqld in the example output in Listing 14.1), this is usually either because the process has been running for weeks or because it's become a runaway and has been taking up some huge percentage of the CPU during its runtime. In the latter case, you can easily check by looking at the CPU column.

The next parts of top's output that should be clarified are the SIZE and RES columns. SIZE is the entirety of a process' allocated size, including the text, data, and stack components. Because parts of them are shared system-wide, this column is not accurate for seeing how much memory a process is using. Instead, RES is the resident memory value—the column that should add up to the current amount of in-use memory. Both size values are "correct," but use RES for determining the "traditional" amount of memory a process uses, the equivalent to what it would be reported as using in Windows or MacOS.

The rest of the fields in top are less important or are self-explanatory. The C column tells you which CPU a process is using, if there is more than one. The PID is the process ID, a number that is assigned to each process upon execution, and the OWNER is the user that executed the process. STATE tells you which of the possible states a process is in, which

14

PERFORMANCE
MONITORING

isn't very informative unless it's zomb or zombie (which refers to a child process that has terminated, but has not yet fully given up its process table space).

Then, there are the commands you can give top interactively to help you sort through the information. Press i to show only active processes (as mentioned earlier), or press u to be prompted for a username; it will then display only processes owned by that username. (Use + as the username to show them all again.) You can issue a kill command with the k key, which will prompt you for a PID to kill. The t key will toggle whether the top process itself is displayed. These and other options are listed in the man top page.

With this feature set, top serves as a very good all-around summary of what's going on in the system, and allows you to handle the majority of the process management tasks you'll have to do. But it's not a total solution; top doesn't give you detailed information about the processes themselves, and its interactive nature keeps top from being a scriptable tool or something that can be used in conjunction with pipes and other programs. For these functions, we'll use ps.

Process Monitoring with ps

Rather than being an interactive, real-time monitoring program such as top, ps works a lot more like ls (hence the name)—it's an instantaneous listing of all processes at the time you execute it. It provides all information that top does, as well as extra details about many of the values.

By default, if you run ps without any arguments, you will get a listing of only the processes owned by you that are attached to terminals (that is, those that have been run from a login session). There is a large array of command-line options that will give you more wide-reaching results, and each can be found documented in man ps. Specify these options as follows:

```
# ps -waux
```

This combination of options shows the output in wide format (w), which allows the output to wrap to multiple lines and keeps from being cropped to the width of your terminal; it lists usernames along with processes (u); it shows all users' processes, not just your own (a); and it also shows processes, regardless of whether they have an associated terminal (x). In short, this combination of options gives you every process on the system, with as much detail as possible.

You can filter the output in certain ways by using the built-in options. For instance, eliminate the x option to show all processes, whether they're attached to a terminal or not, and drop the a option to show only your processes (or use -U to specify another user—for example, -U frank). Many other options of this type can be found in the man page for ps; beyond the built-in filters, though, you will need to use ps in conjunction with grep (as we saw in Chapter 9, "The FreeBSD Filesystem") to filter based on the process name:

Listing 14.2   Example ps Output, Filtered Through grep

```
# ps -ax | grep httpd
40563  ??  S      0:54.73 /usr/local/sbin/httpd
40564  ??  S      0:55.30 /usr/local/sbin/httpd
40565  ??  S      0:56.03 /usr/local/sbin/httpd
40566  ??  S      1:00.16 /usr/local/sbin/httpd
40567  ??  S      1:05.13 /usr/local/sbin/httpd
```

ps Output Explained

Here is some sample output from ps -waux:

LISTING 14.3   Example Output from ps

```
USER      PID %CPU %MEM   VSZ  RSS  TT  STAT STARTED      TIME COMMAND
root        1  0.0  0.0   528   72  ??  ILs  31Jan01   1:05.94 /sbin/init --
root        2  0.0  0.0     0    0  ??  DL   31Jan01  14:41.63 (pagedaemon)
root        3  0.0  0.0     0    0  ??  DL   31Jan01   2:38.47 (vmdaemon)
root        4  0.0  0.0     0    0  ??  DL   31Jan01   0:33.21 (bufdaemon)
root        5  0.0  0.0     0    0  ??  DL   31Jan01  79:52.61 (syncer)
root       24  0.0  0.0   208    0  ??  TWs  -         0:00.00 adjkorntz  i
root       80  0.0  0.1   916  320  ??  Ss   31Jan01   3:27.80 syslogd -s
```

Processes in the output from ps are sorted by PID rather than any of the reported metrics (unless you used one of the special sorting options described in the man page). You do get most of the same information that top gives you, albeit in a more cryptic format and with a few slight variations.

> **Note**
>
> One exception is that the %CPU column in ps is not the same as the CPU field in top; it's actually equivalent to the WCPU field. This value is a "weighted CPU" percentage that takes into account CPU cycles in which the process was in a "resident" state. Most of the time, this makes no difference, but occasionally it can result in a significantly higher number reported in ps than in top or between the two columns in top. In either case, the %CPU column is calculated as an average over the preceding minute, so the values are approximate at best, and you shouldn't expect them to add up to 100%.

It's generally more useful to use top to gather metrics on your processes; ps is more intended for looking up PIDs of specific processes and seeing the complete command line for each one. It's quicker than top, and scriptable—you can write scripts that extract the PID for a process from the output of ps and send signals to that PID, all through the use of shell commands and pipes. This is particularly helpful when you need to rein in a runaway process, or change the priority on a task—functions that we will now see in detail.

Terminating Misbehaving Processes

Let's say you notice the system running more slowly than you think it should; you su to root, fire up top, and look at the processes. Sure enough, you see something like this:

LISTING 14.4   Output of top Showing a Possible Runaway Process

```
last pid: 67469;  load averages:  8.32,  5.49,  2.47   up 53+01:04:22  20:34:42
90 processes:  1 running, 88 sleeping, 1 zombie
CPU states:  93.2% user,  0.0% nice,  0.2% system,  0.8% interrupt, 5.8% idle
Mem: 153M Active, 23M Inact, 60M Wired, 7252K Cache, 35M Buf, 5112K Free
Swap: 500M Total, 44M Used, 456M Free, 8% Inuse

  PID USERNAME    PRI NICE  SIZE    RES STATE  C   TIME   WCPU    CPU COMMAND
19460 frank         2    0 25908K 2816K poll   0 131:15  0.00% 92.43% testprog
67468 root         28    0  2036K 1024K CPU0   0   0:00  0.43%  0.20% top
  245 root          2    0   868K  232K select 1 178:48  0.00%  0.00% healthd
18427 root          2    0  7592K 5124K select 0  81:01  0.00%  0.00% named
```

Aha! There's your culprit. It seems that frank is running some experimental program that's perhaps not written very well, and it's taking up almost all the CPU's available cycles. Sometimes such a "runaway" process will result from an infinite loop (a piece of code that never reaches a point where it can terminate) or a memory leak (the program keeps trying to grab more memory whether it needs it or not). Chances are that it's not going to exit by itself cleanly; meanwhile, it's becoming more difficult for other processes to execute and terminate. This testprog process has to go.

Press the k key. This brings up the "kill" prompt within top; this is an interface to the kill command, or at least a simplified version of it, and you need to enter the PID of the offending process (19460, in this case). Because you're running with root privileges, the process most likely will immediately terminate, and the system will breathe freely once more. Now, you're safe to track down what happened; you'll probably want to start by sending messages to the user and letting him know what his program did.

There are times when this doesn't work, though, or when you need finer control over what signals you're sending to the processes. The `kill` command within `top` is fine for simple process termination, but it's only a subset of the functionality of the command-line `kill` program.

The `kill` Command

Its name is slightly misleading: `kill` does a lot more than simply terminate processes. Its full charter is to be a signaling mechanism by which processes can give each other commands of a fairly wide variety. Any user can use `kill` against any of his processes, but root is the only user who can `kill` other users' processes.

The simplest usage of `kill` is for its most common purpose: terminating a process:

```
# kill 12553
```

Options to the `kill` Command

This, however, sends only a certain kind of signal to the process: the TERM signal, which is a universal "quit" message that all UNIX programs understand, but isn't guaranteed to work. A number of other signals exist, too; Table 14.1 shows the more important ones.

Table 14.1   Commonly Used Kill Signals

Signal	Symbolic Name and Meaning
1	HUP—hang up, or terminate and restart
2	INT—interrupt
3	QUIT—quit
6	ABRT—abort
9	KILL—non-ignorable kill
14	ALRM—alarm
15	TERM—terminate cleanly

You can use any of these signals by specifying either the signal number or its symbol:

```
# kill -9 12553
# kill -HUP 12553
```

The first command will send a low-level "super-kill" signal that will terminate the process, no matter what; this should be used only if plain `kill` (or `kill -TERM`) doesn't work because it will make the process quit in an unclean fashion, which might leave files open or connections in an orphaned state. The second command will tell the process to shut itself down cleanly and restart itself with the same arguments—rereading any input files and taking on a new PID. This is useful when you've changed something in a program's config file and need to restart the process to incorporate the changes.

All the other signals have meanings, too, but the ones we covered are the only ones you're likely to use in everyday process control. The rest are typically ignored by programs that aren't specifically written to respond to them.

Making Processes "Nice"

We discussed one of the process-management tools that you can use both from the command line and within top, which is the kill command. There was another tool we mentioned, though, which was a way to alter a process' priority; this is the renice command, which alters the priority (or "nice" level) of any currently running process.

The scheduling priority is an integer value between -20 and 20, with -20 being the highest possible priority. Take a look at top; the values in the NICE column are the priorities of each process. Notice that most processes have a priority of zero; this is the default because, in most circumstances, you don't need to specify any particular priority. Still, certain services run at predefined "nice" levels to make sure they will run at a certain time or get out of the way of more important processes.

If you're not root, you can set a process to a lower priority (higher "nice" value), but not to a higher one (lower "nice" value).

From the command line, you can alter a process' priority to 10 using renice:

```
# renice -10 1442
```

> **Note**
>
> The "nice" level is preceded by a dash, which means that positive (lower) priorities are specified as in the previous example, whereas to specify a negative (higher) priority you would have to use the following:
>
> ```
> # renice --10 1442
> ```

Within top, you can type r to get the "renice" prompt; enter a priority level between -20 and 20, followed by the PID of the process you want to change, and you'll see the results in the NICE column. This is an easy, interactive, alternate solution to the "testprog" problem we saw earlier: Rather than killing the runaway process outright, you could simply set its priority to 20, which would theoretically make it back off and allow other processes to run uncontested.

The `nice` command is a way to set the priority level of a process at the time you run it. Precede a command with `nice` and the priority level, like so:

```
# nice 10 ls
```

This starts the `ls` process with a priority level of 10.

Introduction to Job Automation

Now that we've looked at how to manipulate processes directly, we will now examine how processes can be executed automatically, without any intervention on your part. Automating tasks with the scheduler allows FreeBSD to perform daily security audits and system status updates, regularly update its runtime databases, flush log files, and as many other tasks as an administrator can think of. Some operating systems attach schedulers to individual applications (such as the Software Update tool in Mac OS), but the advantage of FreeBSD (and other UNIX-like systems) is that the scheduler is an independent daemon that can run any command-line program or set of programs on any periodic schedule.

The cron Daemon

The scheduler in FreeBSD, as in most UNIX-type systems, is called `cron`. FreeBSD's `cron` program was written by Paul Vixie, and it is the standard version used in most distributions of Linux and other similar systems. Like any standalone daemon, it runs all the time, and looks at its input files (called `crontab` files) each minute to see if they have changed or if they contain a task it needs to execute that minute. The `cron` process itself never needs to be restarted; it will automatically read in any changes when it wakes up every minute.

There is a global `crontab` file (`/etc/crontab`) and a directory (`/var/cron/tabs`), in which individual users can create their own `crontab` files. It can be tempting to add your own scheduled jobs to the `/etc/crontab` file, but, as with `/usr/local/etc/rc.d` versus `/etc/rc.local` (refer to Chapter 11, "System Configuration and Startup Scripts"), you really should leave `/etc/crontab` untouched (so it can be safely overwritten by later upgrades), and create new jobs in root's personal `crontab` file in `/var/cron/tabs`. We will see how to do this in a moment.

Anatomy of a crontab File

Let's take a look inside a user's individual `crontab` file:

```
# DO NOT EDIT THIS FILE - edit the master and reinstall.
# (/tmp/crontab.tqWGz91396 installed on Thu Feb  1 09:29:43 2001)
# (Cron version -- $FreeBSD: src/usr.sbin/cron/crontab/crontab.c,v 1.12.2.1 2000
/11/09 11:05:36 dwmalone Exp $)
0 3 1,15 * * cat ~frank/faq.txt | mail -s "FAQ Auto-Post" mylist@testsystem.com
```

This has one item in it: a task to send a text file into `mail` to be sent out to a mailing list; it will be executed at 03:00 on the first and fifteenth of every month. How is this schedule specified? It's done with the first five fields of the whitespace-separated data line. (The first three lines are auto-generated comments, and are not processed by `cron`.) The fields are shown in order in Table 14.2.

TABLE 14.2   Date and Time Fields in a `crontab` File

Field	Allowed Values
minute	0–59
hour	0–23
day of month	1–31
month	1–12
day of week	0–7

Any field can have multiple numbers separated by commas, or it can be a range (for instance, "1–10"). You can also use an asterisk (*) in a field to specify every occurrence of that interval. The month and weekday (fourth and fifth) fields can also use symbolic names—the three-letter abbreviations for month or weekday names. Names can also be listed as comma-separated strings, though they can't be used in ranges. In the fifth (weekday) field, 0 and 7 are Sunday.

> **Note**
>
> If you want to run a command every *n* minutes, or every *n* hours, you can do that by specifying a "step" value (for example, "*/n*"). In the minute field, */5 would translate to "every fifth minute," or the equivalent of 0,5,10,15,20,25,30,35,40,45,50,55. See man 5 crontab for further details on schedule formatting.

You can also use shorthand strings in place of the first five fields to specify certain often-used schedules, as shown in Table 14.3.

TABLE 14.3 Examples of Symbolic Scheduling Intervals

String	Equivalent
@reboot	Run once, at startup
@yearly	0 0 1 1 *
@annually	Same as @yearly
@monthly	0 0 1 * *
@weekly	0 0 * * 0
@daily	0 0 * * *
@midnight	Same as @daily
@hourly	0 * * * *

After the schedule fields, the formats of the /etc/crontab file and the individual crontab files diverge. The global /etc/crontab file has an extra field before the command field—a who field—that specifies which user should execute and own the process:

```
1      3      *      *      *      root    periodic daily
```

The command field can be as complex as you like; fill it in exactly as you would a command entered at the command line. You can even use a semicolon (;) to separate multiple commands that you want to run sequentially as part of the same automated job. It's important to note that for commands executed from /etc/crontab, cron will not assume the PATH of the user specified in the who field—there's a PATH statement at the top of the file that lists only a few basic system directories. This means you'll want to give the full path to any command you run that isn't in that path, or else cron won't be able to find the programs to run.

If there's any output from any program executed by cron, that output will be gathered into a mail message and sent to the owner of the crontab file (or the owner of the scheduled task for /etc/crontab items).

Creating and Editing crontab Files

It's easy enough for you to edit /etc/crontab as root, and add any schedule items you want. However, because we already said that this should be avoided if at all possible, we need to look at the individual crontab files and how to create them. Because each crontab file will go into a central directory (/var/cron/tabs) and be owned by its

14

PERFORMANCE
MONITORING

creator with permissions `0600`, a security mechanism is in place to allow users to create and edit their own files there without compromising others' files. This mechanism is the `crontab` program:

```
# crontab -e
```

Or, to edit Frank's `crontab` file if you're root:

```
# crontab -e -u frank
```

Much like the `chfn` and `edquota` tools we saw earlier, `crontab` works by invoking the editor specified in the `VISUAL` environment variable (or the `EDITOR` variable, if that one isn't set). The contents of the file (minus the first three comment lines) appear in the editor; after making your changes, save and exit. The temporary file, which resides in `/tmp` while you're making your changes, is copied into `/var/cron/tabs`, and the header lines are added. The `crontab` file will be active the next time `cron` looks at it, at the top of the minute.

Creating Jobs to Run One Time with the at Command

Okay, so `cron` is amazingly useful for regularly scheduled tasks. However, what about a task that you only want to happen once—something you want to postpone until some later time when you won't be around to execute it yourself? You could do this with `cron`, setting up a `crontab` file to have an entry that runs `crontab -u` at the end to delete itself. However, there is a better way: the `at` program.

`at` is actually made up of several commands: `at` (the job creator), `atq` (which displays pending jobs), and `atrm` (which lets you cancel pending jobs listed in `atq`). There is also a `batch` command, which is a version of `at` that will run only if the system load is less than some value (1.5 is the compiled-in default).

When you use `at` to create a job, it reads commands line-by-line in `/bin/sh` script style. These commands can be specified either on the command line (standard input) or with a pre-existing file. Either way, the command you enter is simply `at` followed by a time-formatting string, which can take a number of fairly intuitive forms, as shown in Table 14.4.

TABLE 14.4 Syntax Examples of the at Command

Command String	Meaning
at 10pm	Executes at 10:00pm the current day, or the next day if it's after 10:00pm
at 8:00am May 15	Executes at 8:00am on May 15

Table 14.4 continued

Command String	Meaning
at midnight Jan 1 2000	Executes on the first second of the year 2000
at teatime tomorrow	Executes at 4:00pm the following day

A full discussion of the time-formatting options is available in man at. After you enter this string and press Enter, you will be in standard input mode; enter your commands line-by-line, pressing Enter each time, and when you're done, press Ctrl+D to exit and place the job into the queue. You can alternately specify an input file:

```
# at -f mycommands noon + 5 days
```

This reads a plain text file called "mycommands" that contains your commands, like a batch file, and executes them using /bin/sh at noon five days from the time you enter the command.

You can view existing jobs with the atq command:

```
# atq
Date                    Owner   Queue   Job#
23:00:00 03/28/01       root    c       2
```

This lets you cancel jobs with the atrm command:

```
# atrm 2
```

Note

The way at jobs are executed is with the atrun command, another related tool that runs every five minutes (in the standard FreeBSD installation), and reads all pending jobs for all users, executing all jobs whose execution time has passed. You can modify how frequently atrun runs by changing its entry in /etc/crontab, although this should not be necessary.

14

PERFORMANCE
MONITORING

Controlling Access to the cron and at Commands

Scheduling is so powerful that you as an administrator don't necessarily want your users to be able to have complete access to the cron and at commands. Let's say, for instance, that you have a troublesome user who insists upon running an IRC "eggdrop" bot, and every time you kill the process, it keeps coming back—because the user has set up a crontab file to restart the process if it's not running (checking every hour, for example). The user doesn't respond to email. Your options are either to disable the user's account (a fairly barbaric and messy option) or to restrict the user's access to the cron and at commands. This is done through the deny and allow files for both programs.

Normally, /var/cron/allow and /var/cron/deny don't exist. In this condition, anybody is allowed to create crontab files. If you create /var/cron/allow, the only users (aside from root) who can create crontab files are the ones you listed in it (in a simple text list, one user per line). Alternately, you can put users into /var/cron/deny; this will let everyone create crontab files, except for the ones listed in the file. If both files exist, /var/cron/allow takes precedence.

The /var/at/at.allow and /var/at/at.deny files work the same way, but the filenames are slightly different—take note.

CHAPTER 15

Installing Additional Software

Up until now, we covered topics that are largely applicable to many different types of UNIX systems. Pretty much any system, whether commercial or open source, operates the same way regarding the filesystem structure, process automation, and general administration. But now, we'll get to the good stuff.

What sets FreeBSD apart from its BSD brethren, Linux and commercial UNIX software, more than almost anything else is the model by which the administrator adds new software.

With Solaris, if you want to add a new piece of the software to the system, you have to find a precompiled binary for your particular platform, and install it yourself (usually without the aid of installers that help you put it in the right place), because Solaris typically doesn't come with gcc (the standard GNU C/C++ compiler). Other systems, such as IRIX and HP-UX, do come with gcc—but you still have to find the source code for the program you want to install, run its configuration script, compile it (a step which is often much easier said than done), and install it.

Different flavors of Linux take this a step further with the concept of "packages," essentially all-in-one bundles that contain the proper binary for your system as well as any required libraries, plus the necessary information about where to install everything. The RPM (Red Hat Package Manager) system is a GNU-licensed packager that runs on many systems, including FreeBSD. Its popularity was a large part of what pushed Red Hat to the top of the Linux distributors, edging out the previous favorite, Slackware. RPM allowed administrators to keep tabs on their installed software and upgrade, deinstall, or add new packages with unprecedented ease.

But FreeBSD takes things to yet another level of convenience. It has its own package management system—the pkg_* tools, which we will cover in detail—but it also has a supplementary system called the "ports," which allow you to compile software from its original sources with guaranteed, one-command simplicity. In this chapter, we will look first at FreeBSD's packages, and next at its ports.

Introduction to Packages

Jordan Hubbard, one of the core developers of FreeBSD, is responsible for most of the initial work on the package system. FreeBSD's system has been adopted by NetBSD and other platforms, and refined over the years with the best of the independent development efforts being rolled back into FreeBSD.

By its simplest definition, a package system is a way of bundling up software (including config files, shared libraries, and documentation) and extracting it again onto another machine, in which its configuration will be valid enough that the software can run properly on the new machine. Early package managers were just that. RPM and FreeBSD's packager both have numerous further features: They maintain a database on each machine that shows which software and which version of each package are installed. They can grab a remote file from an FTP site (generally, the primary distribution site). They keep track of dependencies or any additional packages that must be installed for the one you're installing to run. They can do upgrades and deinstalls as well as installations.

The difference between the two packagers is related very closely to the different development philosophies of FreeBSD and Linux. The latter has numerous different distributions, with different versions of glibc (a set of core shared libraries not relevant to FreeBSD), running on many different hardware platforms. RPM must necessarily be quite complex in order to handle all this—and indeed it is. Its command-line interface is fairly arcane, and requires a lot of documentation to be used properly. FreeBSD, however, benefits from a centralized development model and a single supported hardware platform, so the package model can be much simpler, both in architecture and usage.

As we discussed in Chapter 9, "The FreeBSD Filesystem," the /usr/local hierarchy is reserved for items that you install yourself, which refers specifically to software you install from the ports and packages. /usr/local contains the directory structure outlined in Table 15.1.

TABLE 15.1 Directory Structure Within /usr/local

Subdirectory	Purpose
bin	Binaries (compiled programs)
etc	Configuration files
include	C include files, used for building new software
info	Various supporting data for building documentation
lib	Shared libraries
libexec	Supporting binaries used by other programs
man	Manual pages for installed software
sbin	System binaries (programs that alter system behavior)
share	Platform-independent materials (data files, documentation, and so on)
var	Variable files for installed software

In other words, it's the same hierarchy that is found directly within /usr (with the exception that man pages are found at /usr/local/man rather than /usr/local/share/man, as you might expect). FreeBSD's package system keeps anything you install in the

/usr/local tree and out of the /usr tree, maintaining the seamless but strict separation between base and user-installed software.

Shared Libraries and Dependencies

A *shared library* is a centralized file that provides precompiled function calls; using a shared library, a program can access certain functions without having to have those functions built in to itself. This reduces file size and redundancy, and is a technique known as "dynamic linking," as opposed to "static linking" (compiling all necessary functions into every program). Shared libraries exist on nearly all platforms, although they have different names—for instance, Windows calls them DLLs, or Dynamic Link Libraries.

FreeBSD already has a large number of shared libraries installed in the base system—enough to support all the software that's part of the base system, as well as providing hooks for software that you might install later. This doesn't mean, however, that you'll never run across a program that needs a shared library that doesn't exist in the base FreeBSD—indeed, you almost certainly will. In FreeBSD, basic shared libraries are stored in /usr/lib, and any shared libraries that you install go into /usr/local/lib. All programs know automatically to look first in /usr/lib for the shared libraries they need, and they then look in /usr/local/lib (as well as a couple of other places). You can control this search path in /etc/rc.conf, as we saw in Chapter 11, "System Configuration and Startup Scripts."

Every package has a listing of dependencies, which include both shared libraries and executables (programs). If a dependency isn't already installed, the package system will automatically hunt down and install it before proceeding with the installation. If you later remove some program or library (via the package tools) that is a dependency for some other installed package, the tools will tell you about this and refuse to proceed.

Obtaining Information on Installed Packages

The first step of getting to know the packages is to explore the information about the ones we have installed already. Chances are that you have at least some packages installed already, either from earlier in this book or from a custom installation. If not, don't worry—this information will be just as useful to you later.

The tools we will be using are pkg_add, pkg_delete, pkg_info, pkg_update, pkg_version, and pkg_create. Each one does pretty much what you would expect it to (as with the mount_* tools we saw in Chapter 9); one hallmark of FreeBSD's style is to use differently named programs rather than obscure switches and parameters. Each of these tools interacts with a filesystem database at /var/db/pkg, which you can consult by simply using ls if you want a quick glance at your system's package status. This repository has a directory for each installed package, which includes information about the packing list (the manifest of files in the package) and the dependencies. pkg_info uses this database to print out the short descriptions of every package you currently have installed, as we can see in Listing 15.1.

LISTING 15.1 Example Output from pkg_info

```
# pkg_info
ImageMagick-5.2.7_2 An X11 package for display and interactive manipulation of i
analog-4.16         An extremely fast program for analyzing WWW logfiles
apache-1.3.19       The extremely popular Apache http server.  Very fast, very c
arc-5.21e.8         Create & extract files from DOS .ARC files
aub-2.0.5           Assemble usenet binaries
autoconf-2.13       Automatically configure source code on many Un*x platforms
dict-1.4.9          Dictionary Server Protocol (RFC2229) client
elm-2.4ME+68        A once-popular mail user agent, unofficial clone
emacs-19.34b        GNU editing macros
```

You can also get lots of information on any single package with the -v switch. As with RPM, packages in FreeBSD have names with multiple parts separated by dashes— the package name, followed by the version. However, RPM files tend to be geared toward multiple platforms, so the "platform" part of the package name is not used. Instead, a FreeBSD package file takes the form name-version.tgz, or (for example) bzip-0.21.tgz. Packages are generally .tgz files (or "tarballs"), shorthand for .tar.gz (the traditional way of archiving a directory structure under UNIX—first packing it into one file using tar and then compressing it using gzip). To use tools such as pkg_info -v, you need to specify the full package name, including the version, as shown in Listing 15.2.

LISTING 15.2 Verbose Output of pkg_info

```
# pkg_info -v pgp-2.6.3ia
Information for pgp-2.6.3ia:

Comment:
PGP MIT or International version - Public-Key encryption for the masses

Depends on:
Description:
PGP (Pretty Good Privacy) is a public key encryption pack-
age to protect E-mail and data files.  It lets you  commu-
nicate  securely  with  people  you've  never met, with no
secure channels needed for prior exchange of  keys.    It's
well featured and fast, with sophisticated key management,
digital signatures, data compression, and  good  ergonomic
```

LISTING 15.2   continued

```
design.
WWW: http://www.pgpi.org/

Packing list:
        Package name: pgp-2.6.3ia
        CWD to /usr/local
File: man/man1/pgp.1.gz
        Comment: MD5:a0ab17d1fe83aaf159cb80fa1abf5462
File: bin/pgp
        Comment: MD5:625e99562f936a3d9b0ac3c5d5a94ba9
File: lib/pgp/pgp.hlp
        Comment: MD5:d5da3783ea26bc60f4b7584df4227866
File: lib/pgp/pgpdoc1.txt
        Comment: MD5:260ca85cd0263275cb7df6cd276e2b9f
File: lib/pgp/pgpdoc2.txt
        Comment: MD5:e3defe467fbf5c5c4809f8b5c13404a1
File: lib/pgp/language.txt
        Comment: MD5:bcec0f56b207846725fe7e4a612383ef
File: lib/pgp/config.txt
        Comment: MD5:b2518ad2566a9a4bce071936311d3c93
        Deinstall directory remove: lib/pgp
        UNEXEC 'if [ -f %D/info/dir ]; then if sed -e '1,/Menu:/d' %D/info/
➥dir | grep -q '^[*] '; then true; else rm %D/info/dir; fi; fi'
```

This listing tells us everything we need to know about the package, from its long description, to its dependencies, to its packing list (with the MD5 "fingerprint" checksum for each one). Some files have extra information noted, such as "deinstallation scripts," which are tasks the package manager needs to execute if you remove this package. For instance, in this example, the directory lib/pgp within the designated local directory tree (e.g. /usr/local/lib/pgp) would be deleted upon deinstallation. You can deduce from this that this package creates a whole folder for its own shared libraries within /usr/local/lib; it can do that because shared library directories are searched recursively. Similarly, the package manager will run the UNEXEC line as a shell script to remove the /usr/local/info/dir file, subject to some conditionals. As we can see, a well-written and well-behaved package (and just about all packages are well-behaved) will erase cleanly off your system when removed, leaving nary a trace behind.

How do we know that this version is current? This is done easily using the pkg_version tool. It works only if the ports collection has been installed—it should be installed unless you're severely short on disk space. We will cover the ports collection later in this chapter, but all we need to know for understanding pkg_version is that the ports collection (if kept up to date) has a listing of the current version of every package. The pkg_version tool compares the versions of every installed package to the version found in the ports collection, and tells you whether your packages are up to date or not (see Listing 15.3).

LISTING 15.3   Example Output of `pkg_version`

```
# pkg_version -v
ImageMagick-5.2.7_2         <   needs updating (port has 5.2.9_1)
apache-1.3.19               =   up-to-date with port
arc-5.21e.8                 =   up-to-date with index
aub-2.0.5                   =   up-to-date with index
autoconf-2.13               =   up-to-date with index
bash-2.04                   *   multiple versions (index has 1.14.7,2.04)
bnc-2.8.2                   =   up-to-date with index
bulk_mailer-1.12            <   needs updating (index has 1.13)
bzip2-0.9.5d                <   needs updating (index has 1.0.1)
cclient-4.8                 <   needs updating (index has 2000c)
cvsup-16.1                  =   up-to-date with index
demoroniser-1.0             =   up-to-date with index
```

Without the -v option, `pkg_version` wouldn't print the third column; you'd just get the icon in the second column. The version string would also not be appended to the package names in the first column. Either way, this provides you with a quick, at-a-glance method for telling where your maintenance efforts are needed.

Installing Packages

Now, let's go out and find some software to install. The first step is to find out what's available. Just about all software available for Linux is also available for FreeBSD because binary compatibility allows you to do anything up to and including audio/video playback using Linux software.

If you have the ports collection installed, you can see a categorized view of all available software by going to /usr/ports and just looking around at the filesystem. But we'll be covering the ports collection momentarily. In the meantime, there's an even more direct interface: our old friend /stand/sysinstall.

Installing from `sysinstall`

From the main menu of the `sysinstall` program (see Figure 15.1), choose "Configure" and then select "Packages". Choose CDROM as the installation media if you have your FreeBSD install disk handy; if not, and you're on the Net, choose FTP.

15

INSTALLING
ADDITIONAL
SOFTWARE

FIGURE 15.1

The Packages menu in the sysinstall *program.*

After you get the package list from whichever medium you choose, you will be presented with a menu like the one shown in Figure 15.1. Scroll up and down to see the various categories, and press Enter to go into each one.

A Note on Version Branches.

We won't be covering FreeBSD's version branching system until Chapter 18, "Keeping Up to Date with FreeBSD," but before we get there, we should point out at least a few important bits of terminology that are crucial to the proper operation of the packages and ports.

In the "Options" section of the sysinstall program, there is a field to set the release name you'll be working with. Chances are that you will be running a "release" version of FreeBSD (these are the versions that come on CDs). If so, the "Release Name" field will be set correctly for the version you're running. However, if you've upgraded your system to an interim point on either the -STABLE or the -CURRENT branch (which will make sense when you read Chapter 18), this field may be set to a value that won't work when you try to open the Packages menu, namely #.#-STABLE (where the # signs stand for major and minor version numbers). This value is pulled in directly from the output of the uname command, which reports information on the kernel version. The reason this won't work is that the "Release Name" specifies the directory on the FTP server where sysinstall will look for the packages, and the corresponding directory for the packages that match your system's version doesn't necessarily have the same name.

Go to ftp://ftp.FreeBSD.org/pub/FreeBSD/releases/ (and then into your appropriate platform subdirectory) to see the available release directories. If your version is 4.2-STABLE, the release directory you want is 4.x-STABLE. After the next complete version has been released on the branch, the directory will be renamed to 4.2-STABLE. This isn't a foolproof system, and it does take some investigation to make sure it works properly. The FTP site just mentioned is the definitive authority because it's where the packages are that you want to browse. Just copy the directory name from the most recent release within your branch, and you should be all right.

FIGURE 15.2

Browsing a category in the Packages menu.

At the bottom of the screen shown in Figure 15.2, you'll see the one-line "short description" of each package. When you see one you want, press the spacebar to mark it with an "X". Select "Cancel" (press the right arrow) to exit from the category. You can browse through all the available categories this way until you've selected a long list of the packages you want; when you're done, select "Install" from the bottom of the screen to install them all in one fell swoop.

> **Note**
>
> Note that this is the only way to exit from the Package menus. If you don't select any packages for installation, you still need to select "Install" (and accept its dialog about there being nothing to install) in order to exit to the main sysinstall menu.

The program will now go through the list one by one and download each package, unpacking it into /usr/tmp and installing it using the pkg_add program, the command-line element to this phase of the FreeBSD package manager (which you can also use independently of sysinstall, as we will see). If a package has any dependencies, sysinstall will first go out and install them and then return to the packages you selected.

Exit from sysinstall using the "Exit Install" option at the bottom. Your new packages are now installed—that's really all there is to it. Documentation (man pages) is all ready to use, config files are in /usr/local/etc, and the binaries are in /usr/local/bin. Type rehash to refresh the available programs that your current shell knows about (or log out and back in), and you'll be able to use the software.

As we saw in Chapter 11, some programs will need to be configured a bit more before they can be used. Go into /usr/local/etc and check for a config file (usually of the style <program name>.conf, or at least containing the program name). If the file has

.sample at the end, you need to perform some additional configurations and remove the .sample before the program can use it. Open the file with your favorite text editor, and do what needs to be done; it will either be indicated in comments in the file itself, or be available by checking the man page for the program. After you do this, check inside the rc.d subdirectory for similar files, and deal with them in the same way.

> **Tip**
>
> Not all software available for FreeBSD is available as a package. Sometimes it's too new; sometimes it's too rapidly developing; whatever the reason, you won't get the complete list of ported software by reading the package listings. The complete set of software that you can install is found in an up-to-date ports collection, which we will discuss later in this chapter.

Using pkg_add

There are few options to the actual installation process. Because executables and config files and libraries are all kept in a standard centralized location, there's no dialog box that asks where you want to install it, whether you want to do a custom installation of only certain parts, or whether you want any of the other install-time options that you get in the desktop OS world. This is a perfect example, both of the more "closed-box" approach that FreeBSD takes than that of Linux and the centralized distribution model for all the open-source software available for the platform.

However, there are times when you need more control over a package than you can get within sysinstall. Examples include packages that have interactive preinstallation scripts (in which you can set options specific to that package), or if the automated installation in sysinstall fails. For times such as these, the pkg_add tool is what you'll need; it's used in every package installation, whether called directly or run by sysinstall (as we saw earlier).

The pkg_add tool is designed to operate on a .tgz file you already downloaded (from the per-release distribution directory described earlier) or on a remote file specified by its URL. For instance, the following two procedures are roughly equivalent:

```
# fetch ftp://ftp.FreeBSD.org/pub/FreeBSD/releases/i386/4.x-STABLE/packages/
➥www/roxen-1.3.111.tgz
# pkg_add roxen-1.3.111.tgz
```

and

```
# pkg_add ftp://ftp.FreeBSD.org/pub/FreeBSD/releases/i386/4.x-STABLE/packages/
➥www/roxen-1.3.111.tgz
```

Of course, the latter is much more convenient, since not only does it eliminate the separate steps of downloading and installing the package, but it also does all of its work in /usr/tmp (or a similar temp directory) and cleans up after itself when it's done. pkg_add also keeps track of dependencies as if you were using it through sysinstall. If you pkg_add a package that has dependencies, it will automatically download and install the dependencies before proceeding. This ensures that you'll have a fully functional program after it's done working.

> **Tip**
>
> Use pkg_add -nv to do a "dry run" install, showing you the steps that pkg_add would take during the installation, without actually doing anything.

Sometimes, a package installation will finish with a screen that gives you further instructions about how to complete the configuration. This is one benefit of installing packages from the command line rather than through sysinstall. Another is that sysinstall provides no feedback about the file size of any package, so you pretty much have to just let it download with no progress feedback other than data rate. If you used a browser to find the package in its FTP directory, you'll find the package size there and at least know how far you have to go when downloading.

> **Notes on Package Origins**
>
> The directory structure at the FreeBSD FTP site is such that each package is actually a symlink, so the file sizes aren't actually directly available if you reach the files from the preceding URL. A little digging will get you the information, but it may or may not be worth your while.
>
> Note that pkg_add does work on .tgz files grabbed from any location, not just the FreeBSD site. However, beware of files from "suspect" locations; adding packages is an act of trust, allowing whoever wrote the package to specify files to be placed in user-executable locations, possibly overwriting other files. Viruses and "Trojan Horses" are fairly uncommon in the UNIX world, but a conscientious administrator should have those words in mind at all times, and especially when installing packages!
>
> If you stick to sysinstall, or at least to the .tgz files found at the FreeBSD FTP site, you will be assured that all the packages are approved for use, and include an MD5 checksum to verify their authenticity.

15

INSTALLING
ADDITIONAL
SOFTWARE

You can also specify multiple packages, run in verbose mode, or prevent `pkg_add` from running pre-installation or post-installation scripts or even from recording that it's installed the package. These options and more can be found in the `man pkg_add` page.

Removing Packages

There is no front end in `/stand/sysinstall` for removing packages; you really don't need one, since once a package is installed, you have all the tools you need for gathering information about it.

Use `pkg_info` to see which packages you have installed, as we saw earlier. You can also simply look in `/var/db/pkg`; the directory names are the same as the package names. After you have the name of the package you want to delete, simply use `pkg_delete` to remove it:

```
# pkg_delete roxen-1.3.111
```

If the package has any dependencies, `pkg_delete` will detect them and refuse to proceed unless you've run it with the `-f` option to force deinstallation. It will also attempt to run any deinstallation scripts and evaluate any "require" statements; if these fail, `pkg_delete` will also fail (except if running with `-f`). As with `pkg_add`, there are a number of other options you can use, including verbose mode (`-v`) and "dry run" mode (`-n`).

Updating Packages

The `pkg_update` tool allows you to update a package using a newly downloaded `.tgz` of a package you already have installed. It will handle all dependencies and ensure that the new version is installed cleanly. To use it, download the `.tgz` package and then run `pkg_update` on it:

```
# pkg_update newpackage.tgz
```

Introduction to Ports

We've now covered the packages and the tools FreeBSD provides for interacting with them. However, this is where it *really* gets fun. Welcome to the FreeBSD ports.

As convenient as packages are, the traditional "UNIX way" of installing new software has always been to compile it yourself. The administrator finds the distribution site (either HTTP or FTP—or in earlier eras, tools such as `gopher` or `archie`), downloads the source code bundled up in a `.tar.gz` or `.tgz` file, and unpacks it into some temporary directory. He then reads the various README files for special instructions, and usually then runs a `configure` script that examines the system to check for numerous different function calls (because these calls vary from platform to platform within the UNIX world). The next step, finally, is to compile the software by running `make`, an encapsulated compiler-management tool that reads its build targets and necessary steps from a file called `Makefile` within the main source directory. After a (hopefully) clean compile, the administrator must then find the new, freshly baked executable, and manually copy it into the publicly accessible location for binaries (`/usr/local/bin`, for example); or, in the best-case scenario, there will be an "install" target in the `Makefile`, so typing `make install` will result in the proper files being copied into (possibly) the correct locations.

This is (or rather, was) all a very inexact operation. Sometimes it worked, sometimes it didn't, and in the vast majority of cases it worked "sort-of." Maintenance was impossible, performance was unpredictable, and the reputation of UNIX for being arcane and difficult to use only grew stronger.

Enter the FreeBSD ports. Ports are a way for you to compile software directly from the source in a regimented, structured, automated procedure that ensures the safety and integrity of the software you're installing while allowing you to grab the source directly from each program's distribution site. This means you can stay on top of the very latest developments in a piece of software without having to wait for a precompiled binary package that might not run on your system if you've customized it heavily. It also allows thousands of different pieces of software to install all their components into the proper locations in the FreeBSD filesystem without the developers even having to know about it. This is done through a widespread system of port maintainers, who keep track of changes in their assigned ports and maintain scripts that patch a program's build and installation procedures to operate correctly with FreeBSD. A "port," then, is simply these scripts and patches in a bundle, sitting in a particular spot on your FreeBSD machine, with a customized `Makefile` that enables you to install the software simply by typing `make install`. No downloading; no configuring; no tweaking; no copying. All that work has been done for you.

FreeBSD's port system has been so successful that it has been adopted by various other systems, particularly OpenBSD and NetBSD. Its success can be attributed to its capability to keep those UNIX administrators who prefer to compile their own software (either through security awareness or machismo) happy, as well as to provide the simplicity of version tracking and maintenance that the packages can boast. It's truly the best of both worlds.

15

INSTALLING ADDITIONAL SOFTWARE

The FreeBSD Ports Tree

The ports collection lives in /usr/ports. Go into that directory now, and take a look around; what you see should resemble Listing 15.4. You'll notice that every category that you already saw in the sysinstall program is here as a directory. (The list may not be 100% accurate for you because categories are reorganized on a fairly regular basis.)

LISTING 15.4   Directories in /usr/ports

```
# ls -sF /usr/ports/
total 1447
    1 .cvsignore          10 devel/              1 news/
 1296 INDEX                3 distfiles/          1 palm/
   11 LEGAL                4 editors/            3 print/
    4 Makefile             2 emulators/          1 russian/
    1 Mk/                  1 french/             1 science/
    2 README               1 ftp/                4 security/
    4 README.html          6 games/              1 shells/
    1 Templates/           1 german/             3 sysutils/
    1 Tools/               5 graphics/           4 textproc/
    1 archivers/           1 hebrew/             1 ukrainian/
    1 astro/               1 irc/                1 vietnamese/
    4 audio/               9 japanese/           6 www/
    1 benchmarks/          1 java/               3 x11/
    1 biology/             2 korean/             1 x11-clocks/
    1 cad/                 3 lang/               1 x11-fm/
    2 chinese/             4 mail/               1 x11-fonts/
    1 comms/               3 math/               2 x11-servers/
    2 converters/          1 mbone/              3 x11-toolkits/
    2 databases/           4 misc/               2 x11-wm/
    1 deskutils/           7 net/
```

The first few directories (the ones beginning with capital letters, taking advantage of the UNIX convention of alphabetizing capital and lowercase initial letters separately, in accordance with the ASCII character set) are structural elements of the ports system, adjuncts that make the system work. The rest of the directories are categories of ports. Look inside one, and you'll see as many as hundreds of different port directories, such as that in Listing 15.5.

LISTING 15.5   Ports Within a Category (Directory)

```
# ls -sF /usr/ports/audio/
total 230
  1 Maaate/              1 mpg123/
  5 Makefile             1 mpg123.el/
```

LISTING 15.5   continued

11	README.html	1	mpg321/
1	afsp/	1	mpmf20/
1	amp/	1	mq3/
1	ascd/	1	musicbox/
1	aumix/	1	musicbrainz/
1	aureal-kmod/	1	mutemix/
1	autozen/	1	mxv/
1	bladeenc/	1	napster/

Browsing the ports in this way is less than efficient, especially in the larger categories. That's what the README.html file is for. Remember the "short description" that each package had? Well, that description is stored in this file, too, and there's a README.html at both levels of directories, as well as inside (almost) every port directory. You can browse the structure in hypertext using any Web browser on the local machine: Netscape, if you're using the machine as an X-Windows workstation, or lynx if you're logged in remotely (as shown in Figure 15.3).

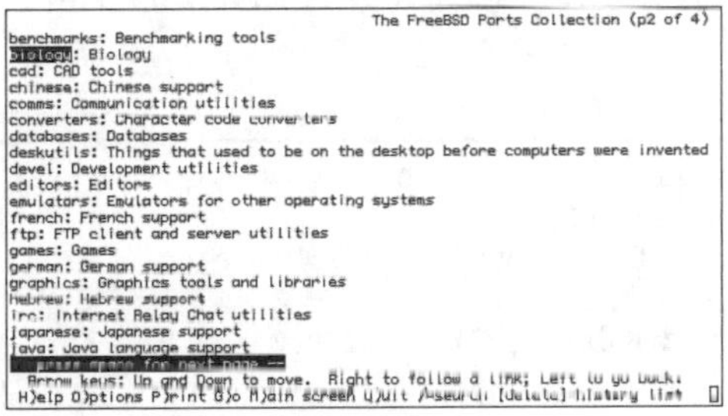

FIGURE 15.3

Browsing a category's README.html *in* lynx.

Anatomy of a FreeBSD Port

Inside each port directory are a few files, totaling no more than a few kilobytes, which completely define all the tweaks and modifications that need to be made to a cleanly downloaded bundle of source code for it to compile and install cleanly on FreeBSD. These files are detailed in Table 15.2.

TABLE 15.2   Files in a port directory

File	*Purpose*
Makefile	Contains certain variables used in the build process, as well as contact information for the maintainer
README.html	Contains the "short description", or comment, for the port in HTML format

15

INSTALLING
ADDITIONAL
SOFTWARE

TABLE 15.2   continued

File	Purpose
distinfo	An MD5 checksum used for verifying the authenticity of the down-loaded tarball
files/ patch-aa patch-ab	Patches that are applied to the source after it's been unpacked
pkg-comment	The "short description" for the port
pkg-descr	The "long description" for the port, which usually includes the URL of the developer's distribution site
pkg-plist	The "packing list," which lists all the files to be installed, as well as keywords telling the port system what to do when the port is dein-stalled (such as removing directories)

The Makefile is the one that has the critical elements for building, configuring, installing, and maintaining a port. Let's take a look at a typical Makefile (Listing 15.6).

LISTING 15.6   A typical port Makefile

```
# New ports collection makefile for:     amp
# Date created:          Jun 23 1997
# Whom:                  Vanilla I. Shu <vanilla@MinJe.com.TW>
#
# $FreeBSD: ports/audio/amp/Makefile,v 1.10 2000/04/08 21:23:11 mharo Exp $
#


PORTNAME=      amp
PORTVERSION=   0.7.6
CATEGORIES=    audio
#MASTER_SITES= ftp://ftp.rasip.fer.hr/pub/mpeg/
# the author's site seems dead.
MASTER_SITES=  ftp://ftp.clara.net/pub/unix/Audio/

MAINTAINER=    vanilla@FreeBSD.org

GNU_CONFIGURE= yes
USE_GMAKE=     yes

MAN1=          amp.1

do-install:
        @ ${INSTALL_PROGRAM} ${WRKSRC}/amp ${PREFIX}/bin
        @ ${INSTALL_MAN} ${WRKSRC}/amp.1 ${PREFIX}/man/man1
.include <bsd.port.mk>
```

The list of variables tells you what you need to know about where the source for the port comes from, what version the Makefile thinks is current, and how to reach the maintainer. The *maintainer* is a volunteer, usually unaffiliated with whoever develops the actual software, whose job is to make sure that the port compiles and installs cleanly, and that the most recent version of the software is reflected in the port.

Most Makefiles contain targets, such as "clean", "install", and "all". The Makefiles in the ports don't have these targets in each one, but what they do have is an included central Makefile (bsd.port.mk, which lives in the /usr/ports/Mk directory along with other included files). This file is what contains the standardized build targets. The individual Makefiles in each port serve as overrides or augmentations (much in the same way as /etc/rc.conf relates to /etc/defaults/rc.conf), setting the necessary variables for the build and defining additional targets that will be used in the automated compile process.

Installing Ports

Let's say that a port catches your eye, and you decide you want to install it. Here's where it gets fun. All you have to do is cd into the port's directory, and type make; this compiles the software. Then, type make install to install it.

It's a simple process on the surface, but there's a lot that goes on under the hood. The make command actually executes a series of sequential make targets (described in Table 15.3), each one of which depends on all the previous targets. You can specify any of these targets directly; this will build all targets up to and including the one you specify.

TABLE 15.3   make Targets in a Port Makefile

Target	Action
fetch	Downloads the source tarball from the master site into /usr/ports/distfiles
checksum	Verifies the authenticity of the tarball using the MD5 checksum
extract	Unpacks the tarball into a work subdirectory
patch	Applies the patches from the files directory to the source
configure	Runs the configure script, which prepares the source for building
build	Compiles the source

So, if you type make extract, it will download the source file, match its MD5 checksum, and unpack it. Although there are other targets, too (listed in

`/usr/ports/Mk/bsd.port.mk`), you won't need to use any of them under most circumstances.

After each step in the process is done (except for `fetch` and `checksum`), a file is created in the `work` subdirectory of the form `.extract_done`. This is how the system keeps track of which steps are completed. To see if the `fetch` step is done, it simply checks for the existence of the file in `/usr/ports/distfiles`. The `extract` step runs the `checksum` step implicitly. After that, the steps are sequential and independent, and check for prerequisite steps by checking for the appropriate `.*_done` files.

If you need to make any changes to the source before compiling, you can `make patch`—bringing the source up to where it's ready to compile—and then make whatever changes you like. Then, complete the process with `make`.

Dependencies are handled automatically by the ports, just as with the packages. Any dependencies are read from the `Makefile` during the `fetch` phase; and downloaded, built, and installed. You will get feedback in the `build` output each time it encounters a dependency, whether that dependency is installed already or not.

After a port is installed, an entry is made in the `/var/db/pkg` database; for all intents and purposes, it is now a package. You can use the `pkg_*` tools on it to gather information and compare its version, just as with packages installed from within `sysinstall`.

Removing Installed Ports

There is a `deinstall` target in the ports (`make deinstall`). This target is used when the installed port version is the same as the one in the `Makefile`—in essence, you're deinstalling exactly the same software package that you installed. If you update your ports so that the version of a package is higher than the installed version, you can't use `make deinstall` to delete it—you have to use `pkg_delete`, the same way as you would a package.

Upgrading a Port

If the version of a port has changed, you can simply `make install` it over the old version. This can be a bad idea, however; most of the installed files will be the same from one version to another, so if you try to `pkg_delete` an older version of the same port or package while a newer one is installed over it, you will end up deleting most of the newer version as well. If you have `pkg_version` output like the following, you're stuck with the earlier versions in your package database, unless you're willing to deinstall all versions of the package and then reinstall the current version:

```
apache-1.3.12          <   needs updating (index has 1.3.19)
apache-1.3.14          <   needs updating (index has 1.3.19)
apache-1.3.17          <   needs updating (port has 1.3.19)
apache-1.3.19          =   up-to-date with port
```

To avoid this situation, always check for a previous version of a port before installing a new one. Use pkg_info, pkg_version, or the /var/db/pkg structure to see what's there already. If there's an earlier version, remove it:

```
# pkg_delete apache-1.3.12
```

You shouldn't have to worry about customized config files for the port. In the apache port, for example, the pkg-plist file contains @unexec commands, which compare the configuration files with the default ones installed by the port, and delete them only if they match. Even so, it's a good idea to back up important config files before removing a package or port.

It's not the end of the world to leave your old versions installed, though. It does provide an audit trail so you can view your system's upgrade history, and it doesn't hurt anything to have the old versions around (except that if a port's files move around, the outdated files on your system will continue to hang around).

Making Sure that Your Ports Tree Is Up to Date

Software changes. There are more than 4,000 ports in the collection, and each one of them is undergoing development (some at much faster rates than others). A fact of system administration is that you can't install or upgrade software fast enough to keep up with the rate of development. The best you can hope to do is keep your ports collection up to date, and use the built-in tools, such as pkg_version, to keep track of what needs to be upgraded.

To keep your ports synchronized, the best tool for the job is CVSup. We will cover CVSup in detail in Chapter 18, "Keeping Up to Date with FreeBSD," but it's a necessary part of working efficiently with ports, so we'll go through how to use it in its simplest form here. There really isn't much to it.

First, install the cvsup-bin package, either by using the package system or by building it from the ports. In fact, it's better to use the package version because CVSup is a tool written in Modula-3, meaning that building it from source involves building several large Modula-3 dependencies. Use the package installation to get past that for now.

Make sure that you're connected to the Internet properly. Now, go into the /usr/ports/net/cvsupit port directory. This is a pseudo-port that doesn't really install anything; instead, it creates a central runtime `config` file for `CVSup` to use. Run `make` and then run `make install`. You will be taken to the `cvsupit` configuration (branch selection) screen (as shown in Figure 15.4).

FIGURE 15.4

The cvsupit *branch selection screen.*

Select the first option—the one called " . " rather than a branch name (this stands for the "HEAD" of the source tree, and is where the current ports are kept on the master server). Accept the defaults for the rest of the screens, and select a `CVSup` server from the list (the higher-numbered servers are usually less busy). When it prompts you, select "No" to elect not to run the `CVSup` update now.

Open the file `/etc/cvsupfile` in your favorite text editor. Comment out the lines beginning with `src-` (tags that specify the operating sources, which we will not be updating now). Do this by placing a hash mark (#) at the beginning of each of these lines.

Now, run the `CVSup` update, as directed by `cvsupit`:

```
# /usr/local/bin/cvsup -g -L 2 /etc/cvsupfile
```

The tool will connect to the selected `CVSup` server and begin synchronizing your ports collection. You will see all changes between your installed version and the current one scroll by. `CVSup` operates by updating only files that have changed, and then by updating only the changed pieces (by using `diff` patches). This allows you to update the entire ports collection while transferring only a minimum of data and using a minimal amount of bandwidth. A `CVSup` update can be done efficiently, even over a very small network link, as we will see when we cover it in more detail in Chapter 18.

After the synchronization is complete, your ports collection will be current and up-to-the-minute. You can now run `pkg_version -v` to see which ports or packages you need to update.

You will probably want to make this synchronization process a part of your system's daily routine, so your ports will never be more than 24 hours out of date. To do this, add the previous `CVSup` command to your daily `periodic` files, as we saw in Chapter 14,

"Performance Monitoring, Process Control, and Job Automation." If it doesn't exist already, create a directory called `periodic` in `/usr/local/etc`, and another directory called `daily` underneath that. Create a file called something like `100.cvsup-ports`, and put these lines into it:

```
#!/bin/sh

/usr/local/bin/cvsup -g -L 2 /etc/cvsupfile
```

Now, every night when the daily `periodic` script is executed, your ports collection will be synchronized. You'll get the output of CVSup mailed to you in your daily system status update.

Notes on Forbidden Ports

Sometimes, a port will be present in the ports collection, but the system will not allow you to build it. This is controlled by a `FORBIDDEN` variable in the `Makefile`. If this variable is present, whatever text string it is set to will be displayed when you try to build the port:

```
# cd /usr/ports/lang/perl5
# make
===>   perl-5.005 is forbidden: perl is in system.
```

There are many reasons why a port might be marked "forbidden". In this example, it's because the program in question has been made a part of the core system, and building it from the ports would be redundant and possibly ruin the system's operation. In other cases, it's because a port might have a recently found security hole that is not yet fixed. In either case, this is a good illustration of the need to keep your ports synchronized to the CVSup server as regularly as possible.

It's seldom a good idea to override a forbidden port, but it's possible to do so by simply removing the `FORBIDDEN` line from the `Makefile`. Some forbidden ports do provide a way to override the block by setting an environment variable, such as in the example of the `security/ssh` port:

```
# cd /usr/ports/security/ssh
# make
===>   ssh-1.2.27_3 is forbidden: OpenSSH is a superior version of SSH which has
been included in the FreeBSD base system since 4.0-RELEASE. This port is now
deprecated and will be removed at some point in the future. To override this
warning set the REALLY_WANT_SSH environment variable and rebuild..
```

As the instructions say, set the indicated environment variable and try again. If you're using `csh` or `tcsh`:

```
# setenv REALLY_WANT_SSH yes
```

Or, if you're using bash:

```
# REALLY_WANT_SSH=yes
```

After setting the variable, run make again, and the port should build cleanly.

Reclaiming Hard Disk Space Used by the Port Building Process

After you're done building and installing a port, the work directory is still sitting there, filled with the unpacked tree of source code and compiled binary objects. This can take up a fair amount of disk space. It's always advisable to clean this directory out after installation—returning the port to its original pristine state—by running one more make command, this time with the clean target:

```
# make clean
```

This deletes the work directory and everything in it. It also cleans out the port directory for each dependency listed. However, it does not remove the tarball files from /usr/ports/distfiles; you'll have to remove these files yourself.

> **Tip**
>
> Unless you really need the disk space, you might want to leave the tarballs intact in the /usr/ports/distfiles directory. You can save a lot of time this way—if you should ever need to rebuild or reinstall a port, the system can use the file it already has, instead of having to download it again.
>
> The beauty of the ports is that if a security hole or critical bug is fixed in a port that you have installed, the ports collection might solve it by placing a patch file in the files directory of the port, not by bumping the revision number of the entire distribution file (and causing you to have to download a new tarball). A simple rebuild allows you to incorporate the new patch into your old sources.

Periodically, you may want to issue a top-level recursive make clean on the entire ports collection. There's a Makefile at both the /usr/ports level and the category level below it, which enables you to do such odd things as building all the ports in a category at once (for example, by running make from inside /usr/ports/www). More usefully, it lets you clean every port at once, in one very long recursive process. Do this simply by going to /usr/ports and entering make clean. You can now go and get a sandwich if you want; like cleaning an oven, this process will be worthwhile, but will probably take forever.

What to Do When a Port Will Not Build

As convenient as the ports collection is, it's not perfect—and with the amount of change that goes on in the tree, especially with so many ports (such as the ones related to GNOME and KDE) interrelated and constantly evolving, chances are that you'll run into some stumbling blocks now and then. The general failure behavior is for the compile process to fail with an "*** Error code 1" or similar message. When this happens, there are a number of things you can try.

First, make sure that you're starting from a clean port. If there is a pre-existing work directory, it's possible that you've mixed new sources with old, resulting in an unbuild-able port. Run a make clean to start over from a clean slate.

If this doesn't work, head to the FreeBSD Web site at http://www.freebsd.org, and go to the "Mailing Lists" link, where you can search the relevant mailing lists. Make sure that you check the "Ports" list as one of the search criteria, and search on the name of your port and some of the relevant text in the last few lines of the compiler output. If there's anything commonly failing that other people have noticed, you'll probably find something useful this way.

Still no luck? There's one more good recourse: the port maintainer. Look in the Makefile for the MAINTAINER variable, which is set to the e-mail address of the maintainer. Send off a politely worded, undemanding e-mail containing the last (relevant) part of the com-piler output, as well as information about your system (the output of uname -a, for instance). The maintainer is usually a very overworked, underappreciated individual, so be sure to express your gratitude for any help!

Upgrade Kits

There may come a time when a port will fail to build, claiming that your system is "too old." It will note that you either need to upgrade your entire system, or to install an "upgrade kit." This latter option is much preferable; despite its name, it doesn't upgrade your system at all, and it's very nonintrusive.

An upgrade kit is a set of updated include files that the ports collection needs in order for its customized build targets to work. Most of these include files are in /usr/ports/Mk, and can therefore be brought up to date with CVSup. However, an unavoidable obstacle is that some required files are not within /usr/ports—they're else-where in the core system, such as /usr/share or /etc. An upgrade kit is a standard FreeBSD package that provides newer versions of these files, enabling you to continue building ports even when your ports tree is much newer than your base system. You can install an upgrade kit using pkg_add, as with any package.

Upgrade kits are distributed from `http://www.freebsd.org/ports`, and there is one available for updating from any supported release version to the current spot in its corresponding `-STABLE` branch. You can install successive upgrade kits if you need to. However, it will eventually become necessary for you to upgrade your entire system, as we will discuss in Chapter 18.

Fresh Ports

The output of the `CVSup` sychronization process is a useful, but hardly ideal way to keep track of which ports have changed. There's a very handy Web site (see Figure 15.5) that should be in the bookmarks or favorites of any FreeBSD administrator: Fresh Ports.

FIGURE 15.5

The Fresh Ports Web site (`www.freshports. org`).

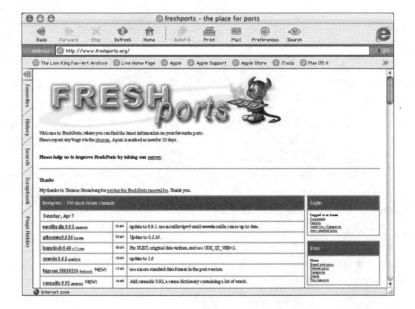

Maintained separately from the FreeBSD project proper, Fresh Ports is a database linked to the main CVS repository for the ports collection. It constantly monitors all checkins, and lists them in reverse chronological order. You can register with the Web site, and set up a watch list for your favorite ports; you'll be e-mailed whenever anything on your watch list changes, and you can view exactly what the changes are to each port, so you can determine whether the change is worth upgrading for. For instance, if a port is bumped up a version or a crucial security fix has been checked in, you may well want to upgrade; but if the only recent change is to fix a typo in an installer error message, don't bother.

Printing

CHAPTER 16

Setting up a printer in FreeBSD is one of the more complex topics you will have to deal with if you administer FreeBSD. Unfortunately, FreeBSD printing is not as simple as installing a driver, selecting the printer from a Control Panel, and then printing. Printing from FreeBSD involves configuring one or more configuration files and possibly installing filters if you need to print anything more advanced than plain text. If you have a printer that is capable of understanding PostScript, it will make your life easier. If your printer cannot understand PostScript, don't worry—you can probably still use it with FreeBSD. It will just require some more configuration because you will have to install an additional software package that allows you to send PostScript data to non-PostScript printers.

> **Note**
>
> GDI printers, sometimes also called "WinPrinters," will not work with FreeBSD. These printers are usually cheaper than non-GDI printers because they move some of the printer control off of the hardware and into a software driver. The disadvantages of these types of printers are that they use more system resources because the computer's CPU has to do much of the processing rather than letting the printer do it, and that they require special drivers that are usually available only for Windows. There is a very long list of operating systems that simply will not work with these types of printers, and FreeBSD is one of them.

The first part of this chapter assumes that you have a printer connected to a parallel port. It is possible to use FreeBSD with printers that connect to the serial port. However, serial printing is very slow, and is obsolete. Only ancient printers use serial printing. In addition, this chapter assumes that you know whether your printer understands PostScript or not. See your printer's documentation to find out.

lpd and the Print Spooler

lpd is the line printer daemon. It is software that runs in the background and waits for print requests. When it receives them, it filters them through any relevant filters, converts the data to a different format if necessary, and sends them to the print queue.

Print Queue

The *print queue* is an area on the hard disk where print data is stored that is waiting to be sent to the printer. Each printer connected to the system has its own separate queue and spool area. The spool area holds the data until it can be sent to the printer. It can hold multiple jobs from the same or different users.

When a user submits a job to be printed, it is put in the queue. The spooler then spools the job to the printer when the printer is available. Jobs can have different priorities that determine what order they will get printed in. The spooler has several advantages over simply printing directly to the printer as DOS used to do:

- It allows the printer to be shared by multiple users because data can be queued up to be printed, and the program that sent the data can then forget about it.

- It allows background printing. Once again, the program that requests a print job can send the job and then forget about it. This means you don't have to wait for the program to finish printing before you can continue working in it. It also means you can shut down the program after the job has been submitted to the queue without losing the print job.

- It allows for some degree of fault tolerance. If the printer has to be reset, you will not lose the jobs that are in the queue and have to resubmit them. After the printer is back online, the remaining jobs in the queue should print normally as if nothing happened.

Generally, the spool directories are located in `/var/spool`. The first printer on the system will normally spool to `/var/spool/lpd` or `/var/spool/output/lpd`. However, this can be changed by editing a configuration file, and we will look at how to do this later on in the chapter.

Kernel, Device, and Communications Mode Configuration

The default kernel has support for the parallel device built into it, so unless you have built a custom kernel and removed support for the parallel port, you shouldn't have any problems. The easiest way to check for parallel support in the kernel is by checking the kernel's `dmesg` output. The command `dmesg | grep lpt0` will check to make sure that the first parallel device (which would be lpt1 in DOS. FreeBSD devices almost always start at 0) is supported in the kernel. If FreeBSD responds with something similar to the following:

```
lpt0: <Printer> on ppbus0
lpt0: Interrupt-driven port
```

Then the printer has support for the parallel port. If FreeBSD responds with nothing, the kernel does not have support for the parallel port. You will need to add the line device lpt to the kernel configuration file, and rebuild the kernel. In addition, the line device ppbus must also exist. See Chapter 17, "Kernel Configuration," for information on how to configure and build the kernel.

Configuring the Parallel Port Mode

You can use the lptcontrol program to configure the mode of the parallel port. Note that you will need to be root to do this, and also that there must be a printer connected to the parallel port for lptcontrol to work.

The syntax of lptcontrol is lptcontrol -x -d /dev/lpt0, where -x is one of the following options depending on the mode you want to set:

TABLE 16.1   lptcontrol Mode Options

Option	Description
-i	Set interrupt-driven mode
-p	Set polled mode
-e	Set extended mode (whatever extended mode the printer supports)
-s	Set standard mode (turn off extended mode)

If your printer and your BIOS support ECP, EPP, or other forms of enhanced communication, you will want to use -e here.

The -d is optional. If you do not specify a device, lptcontrol will use the default device, which is /dev/lpt0.

For example, the following command will set the first parallel port to extended mode:

```
lptcontol -e -d /dev/lpt0
```

If you want these settings to be maintained across reboots, you must add the lptcontrol control command to one of the system startup scripts so that it is run at each system boot. You can add this control command to either /etc/rc.local or create a new file in /usr/local/etc/rc.d that has the command in it. If you create a file in /usr/local/etc/rc.d that has the command in it, you will need to set the permissions on the file so that it is executable. (For example, chmod 655 *filename*)

After you have completed the preceding procedure, you are ready to set up lpd and configure the spooler.

Creating the Spool Directory

The first thing you will need to do is create a spool directory for the printer. Print spool directories are normally located in /var/spool/lpd, although there is nothing that says you can't put them somewhere else.

Decide on a name for the printer you are configuring. You can name the printer just about anything you want. And you can also create aliases to access the printer by other names.

After you have decided on a name for the printer, create a spool directory for it. For example:

```
mkdir /var/spool/lpt/laserjet
```

After this, you will probably want to change the owner of the spool directory and also change the permissions so that users can't snoop around and look at other people's print jobs. All print spool directories should be owned by the user daemon and group daemon; and should have read, write, and execute permissions for the user and group; and no permissions for anyone else. The following commands will correctly set the ownership and permissions on the spool directory:

```
chown daemon.daemon /var/spool/lpd/laserjet
chmod 770 /var/spool/lpd/laserjet
```

After you have set up the spool directory, you will need to set up a text filter for lpd.

Filters

Filters are where most of the actual work is done in printing. When lpd sends data to a filter it sets the filter's STDIN to the file that is to be printed and its STDOUT to the printer device.

Text Filters

As its name implies, the *text filter* is the filter that lpd uses when it receives plain text to print. The text filter can be as simple as a shell script that uses cat to simply pass the raw data to the printer, or as complex as a program that changes the data into a completely different format. An example of a complex filter is one that uses GhostScript, which takes raw PostScript data and changes it into a format that a non-PostScript printer can understand.

A very simple text filter for lpd would look like this:

```
#!/bin/sh
/bin/cat && exit 0
exit 2
```

The generally accepted place to save text filters is in /usr/local/libexec. You may want to call it /usr/local/libexec/if-text, for example. After you have saved it, the file will also need to be made executable so that lpd can run it. The command chmod 555 /usr/local/libexec/if-text will do the trick.

The first line in this filter means that this is a shell program that should be run with /bin/sh (the standard shell).

Tip

If any of this is unclear to you, you might want to refer to Chapter 13, "Shell Programming," before continuing with this chapter. Setting up print filters often involves a significant amount of shell programming.

The second line simply calls the cat program, which by default reads from STDIN and sends to STDOUT. The && means do both of the statements on this line, or do neither one. In other words, if the cat command is successful, the script will exit with status 0, which indicates success. If there is an error, the part of the line after && is not performed, and the third line will be performed instead, which tells the program to exit with a status of 2. (If lpd receives an exit status of 2, it means the filter failed, and lpd will not try to print the file again.)

This simple filter will work fine for printing plain text on most non-PostScript printers. However, PostScript printers cannot handle plain text data. If you have a PostScript printer, you will need a more complex filter that can convert the plain text data into PostScript data.

What Is PostScript?

PostScript is a complex programming language designed to print and format graphics and text. It is device-independent, meaning that any printer that understands PostScript can render a PostScript document with no special drivers. It was invented by Adobe in 1985, and is supported by a wide range or printers today. PostScript became a widely popular language for describing text and images in files because it was so portable and device-independent.

Unfortunately, printers that do not understand PostScript cannot print PostScript documents. (They will print them out as just plain text, which will usually not make any sense.) However, there is a freely available program called GhostScript that translates PostScript into a format that non-PostScript printers can understand. This allows these non-PostScript printers to emulate PostScript with software. GhostScript will be covered later in this chapter.

The first thing you need to do is install a program that can convert plain text to PostScript. The program "a2ps" can be found in the FreeBSD ports tree, and will handle this task for you. (Refer to Chapter 15, "Installing Additional Software," for more information on how to install ports.)

Basically, a filter for a PostScript printer has to be able to test whether it is receiving PostScript data or not. If it is, nothing happens, and the data is passed straight through as it was with the earlier simple text filter. (A PostScript file is a plain text file that simply has complex control codes in it that the PostScript printer can understand.) If it is not receiving PostScript data, the filter must convert the data to PostScript before it sends it to the printer.

All PostScript files begin with the magic character sequence "%!". We can write a shell script that checks to see whether the first line of the file begins with "%!". If it does, we have a PostScript file, and the data can be passed straight through the printer. If it doesn't, we have a plain text file, and the data needs to be passed through a2ps to convert it to PostScript before it is sent to the printer.

The following shell script will do the trick:

LISTING 16.1 Sample Postscript Filter

```
#!/bin/sh
# Simple filter for PostScript printers

read header
ps_test=`expr "$header" : '\(..\)'`
if [ "$header" = "%!" ]
then
        # File is PostScript. Print pass through.
        Echo "$header" && cat && printf "\004" && exit 0
        exit 2
else
        # File is plain text. Convert it first.
        (echo "$header"; cat) | /usr/local/bin/a2ps && printf "\004" && exit 0
        exit 2
fi
```

Save this file somewhere. `/usr/local/libexec/if-ps` might be a good choice. Make the file executable so that `lpd` can run it (`chmod 555 /usr/local/libexec/if-ps` will do the trick).

Basically, this code reads the first line of the input, it is sent by `lpd`, and stores it in the variable `header`. The program then uses the `expr` command to get the first two characters from the file and stores them in the variable `ps_test`. The `if` statement that comes next checks what two characters are stored in `ps_test`. If they are `%!`, this is a PostScript file and the `then` statement is performed, which passes the raw data directly to the printer. It sends the first line; then `cat`s the rest of the input; then sends an escaped `\004` with `printf`; and finally exits with a status of 0. The `&&` connects the different statements and basically says, "Either do all of these commands, or don't do any of them." If for what-ever reason any part of this command line fails, none of it will be performed, and the program will exit with status 2 instead—which tells `lpd` that the data could not be printed, and it should not retry.

If the first two characters are not `%!`, this file is not a PostScript file, and the `else` state-ments are performed instead. The `else` statements on this case first echo the first line of the program; then, `cat` the rest of the input and pipe it to the `/usr/local/bin/a2ps`. The a2ps program does the work of converting the file into PostScript and sending it to the printer.

Finally, when all the data has been sent, an escaped `\004` is sent with `printf`, and the program exits with status 0. Like the `then` statement, if any part fails, the program will exit with status 2 instead.

There are many options to the a2ps program, so if you will be printing plain text files through a PostScript printer on a regular basis, I suggest you read the man page for a2ps. You can then modify the way this script calls a2ps to suit your needs and preference.

Printing PostScript Files on Non-PostScript Printers

If you have a non-PostScript printer, than you have the opposite problem of the preced-ing one. You need to let plain text pass through to the printer, but you need to convert PostScript data to a format that your printer can understand.

If you never plan to print more than plain text, you do not need to worry about this. However, PostScript is the common denominator in UNIX and FreeBSD when it comes to printing anything other than plain text. Virtually all word processing, graphing, draw-ing, and graphics programs can write a PostScript file (or send it directly to the printer). Although some applications (such as StarOffice) may have drivers for your particular printer, most UNIX applications will not. Instead, they will simply output PostScript. Because of this, your printing capabilities will be severely limited if you cannot handle PostScript.

Fortunately, a company called Aladdin makes a freely available program called GhostScript that can simulate a PostScript printer. It takes PostScript input and converts it to a form that your printer can understand.

> **Note**
>
> GhostScript supports a wide variety of printers. A list (which may not be all-inclusive) can be obtained at `http://www.cs.wisc.edu/~ghost/doc/printer.htm`.

GhostScript is available in the FreeBSD ports collection under the "print" category. Refer to Chapter 15 for information on installing ports.

For this to work, we will need a script similar to the one in the previous section. However, the operations will be reversed. In this case, if the script detects that they data being sent is not PostScript data, it will be passed straight through. If it is PostScript, it will be sent through the GhostScript program to convert it to something the non-PostScript printer can understand. A script such as the following, taken from the FreeBSD Handbook will provide PostScript functionality on an HP Deskjet 500 (which is a non-PostScript printer).

LISTING 16.2   Sample GhostScript Filter for an HP DeskJet 500

```
#!/bin/sh
  #
  # ifhp - Print Ghostscript-simulated PostScript on a DeskJet 500
  # Installed in /usr/local/libexec/hpif

  #
  # Treat LF as CR+LF:
  #
  printf "\033&k2G" || exit 2

  #
  # Read first two characters of the file
  #
  read first_line
  first_two_chars=`expr "$first_line" : '\(..\)'`
```

LISTING 16.2   continued

```
if [ "$first_two_chars" = "%!" ]; then
    #
    #  It is PostScript; use Ghostscript to scan-convert and print it.
    #
    #  Note that PostScript files are actually interpreted programs,
    #  and those programs are allowed to write to stdout, which will
    #  mess up the printed output.  So, we redirect stdout to stderr
    #  and then make descriptor 3 go to stdout, and have Ghostscript
    #  write its output there.  Exercise for the clever reader:
    #  capture the stderr output from Ghostscript and mail it back to
    #  the user originating the print job.
    #
    exec 3>&1 1>&2
    /usr/local/bin/gs -dSAFER -dNOPAUSE -q -sDEVICE=djet500 \
        -sOutputFile=/dev/fd/3 - && exit 0

    #
    /usr/local/bin/gs -dSAFER -dNOPAUSE -q -sDEVICE=djet500 -sOutputFile=- -
\
        && exit 0
else
    #
    #  Plain text or HP/PCL, so just print it directly; print a form
    #  at the end to eject the last page.
    #
    echo $first_line && cat && printf "\033&l0H" &&
exit 0
fi

exit 2
```

This script looks complicated at first, but it isn't really that bad. Basically, the script reads the first line of the input, extracts the first two characters, and checks to see whether they are %! or not. If they are, the input is PostScript, and the then statements are executed, which sends the output through GhostScript. If they are not, the file is treated as plain text and is passed straight through.

Note

GhostScript is a very powerful program that has far more options than can be covered here. For more information on GhostScript, see the documentation at http://www.cs.wisc.edu/~ghost/index.html.

lpf print filter

> **Note**
>
> FreeBSD also comes with a program called lpf that can act as a print filter. It has many capabilities including accounting (the capability to track how many pages are printed, by what users, and so on). See the man page for cap for more details on what this program can do.

Conversion Filters

Conversion filters are similar to text filters, except that they are designed to convert file formats into a format that the printer can understand. Conversion filters allow you to print various types of files directly from the command line with lpr and avoid having to load them into a program or convert them by hand before you print them. You specify which filter to use on the command line with an option to lpr (lpr is the command used to print files from the command line. We will cover it in detail later in the chapter). Table 16.2 lists the conversion options that lpr understands:

TABLE 16.2 Conversion Options to lpr

Option	Description
-d	The file is in DVI format (produced by the TeX typesetting system.)
-f	Intended as a filter for printing FORTRAN source files. It is basically obsolete unless you are still writing a lot of FORTRAN code.
-c	The file contains plotting data produced by cifplot. This program is not included with FreeBSD.
-g	The file contains plot data produced by the UNIX plot routines. These routines are included with FreeBSD.
-d	The file contains data from device-independent troff (ditroff). This is not supported by any software included with FreeBSD.
-t	The file contains C/A/T phototypesetter commands for ancient versions of troff. This is probably obsolete for most people.
-v	The file contains a raster image for various image printing devices. Most people will not use this.

By default, none of these filters is installed. Also, the option letter and the filter it calls are not hard-coded into the system. Because of this, if you have no use for a cifplot filter, for example, it is easy to have the -c option call some other filter that you might have use for.

Like text filters, these filters can be shell scripts that call standard UNIX programs or standalone executable programs that may be provided by manufacturers of third-party software.

The following is an example of a very simple conversion filter that converts data in the GNU groff typesetting system (which cannot be understood by the printer) into PostScript (which can be understood by the printer either directly or by sending through GhostScript):

```
#!/bin/sh
exec grops
```

If you read the man page for grops, you will see that it is a program that converts groff to PostScript. In this case, the file will simply be sent through grops before being sent to the printer for printing.

The filter should be saved in the directory /usr/local/libexec. You might decide to call this filter g2ps or something similar because it converts groff to PostScript.

If we assign this to lpr's -t option to this, we can now print a groff source file directly from the command line and have it come out looking correct on the printer. It would be done like this

```
lpe -t myfile
```

where *myfile* is, of course, the name of the groff source file that we want to print.

We will look at how to configure the print system to actually use this filter later in the chapter when we look at setting up the /etc/printcap file (the file that controls how the print system behaves).

Configuring /etc/printcap

The /etc/printcap file is the glue that holds all of what we have covered so far together. It defines the name and aliases of a printer, what filter it uses, the conversion filters it can use, what option should be used to access the filter, where the printer spools to, and more.

There is already an /etc/printcap file on your system, but all of the options are commented out. You will need to uncomment and change options and/or add options.

The format of /etc/printcap is fairly simple. Here is a sample entry:

```
simba|lp|local line printer:\
#       :sh:\
        :lp=/dev/lpt0:sd=/var/spool/lpd/simba:lf=/var/log/lpd-errs:
    :if=/usr/libexec/if-ps:
```

The first line in this entry gives the printer name, followed by any aliases we want to define. In this case, the name of this printer is simba. It also has an alias of lp, which means it will be the default printer. Finally, the last alias is a long description of this printer.

The second line is commented out. If it is uncommented, header pages (cover pages) will be printed that give the name of the user, the name of the file, and so on. This is a good idea if you have a lot of users printing to the same printer—they can easily find which printouts are theirs when they go to pick them up.

The third line gives the information on where the printer is located. :lp stands for "local printer" (as opposed to a remote printer). The printer is located on the first parallel port /dev/lpt0 (which is LPT1 in DOS). :sd is the spool directory that this printer uses, which is /var/spool/lpd/simba (see the section in this chapter on creating and configuring the spool drectory). :lf, which stands for "log file," is where this printer will log errors it encounters.

The fourth line specifies the input filter, or text filter, that should be used with this printer. In this case, we are using the if-ps filter (which is the text-to-PostScript filter that we created earlier).

Installing Conversion Filters

If you want to install any conversion filters, this is also where those are handled. Install them simply by adding the appropriate option (listed next), followed by the name of the filter. The format is the same as the :if line for the input filter.

Table 16.3 is a list of the appropriate options for the various filters:

TABLE 16.3 Filter options for /etc/printcap

Filter	/etc/printcap *option*
DVI	:df
FORTRAN	:rf
cifplot	:cf
plot	:gf

TABLE 16.3   continued

Filter	/etc/printcap *option*
dittroff	:nf
troff	:rf
raster	:if

Remember that these filters are not hard-coded. So, if you have no use for a FORTRAN filter, for example, you can replace it with some other filter.

Here is the line you would add under the :if line to install the groff to PostScript filter that we created earlier:

```
:rf=/usr/local/libexec/g2ps:
```

Note that when you add this line, you will have to make a slight change to the :if line before it and add a backslash at the end. This is because lpd expects the entire line of information to be on one line. The backslash escapes the new line so that multiple lines are treated as a single line when read by the system.

Enabling lpd

After you have configured the /etc/printcap file, you can start lpd. As root, you can simply type lpd from the command line to start it. If you want to have lpd start up automatically each time the system boots, add the following line to /etc/rc,conf:

```
lpd_enable="YES"
```

You should now be able to print from the command line by following the instructions in the next section. If printing doesn't work correctly, see the troubleshooting section at the end of the chapter.

Basic Command Line Printing

The lpr command is used to send a file to the print spooler. In its simplest form, lpr takes the form

```
lpr filename
```

where *filename* is, of course, the name of the file that should be printed. You can specify multiple filenames on the command line to cause multiple files to be printed.

A printer to send the data to can be optionally specified with the -P option. If the -P option is omitted, lpr assumes that the default printer should be used. The default printer is determined by checking the following in the order listed. The first condition that is found to be true will be used as the default printer.

- If the PRINTER environment variable is set, lpr will use the name listed here as the default printer.

- If the LPDEST environment variable is set, lpr will use the name listed here as the default printer.

- The printer name lp is used, which should be an alias to one of the printers in the /etc/printcap file.

- If neither the PRINTER or LPDEST environment variables are set, and there is no printer that has an lp alias in /etc/printcap, the print request will fail.

The lpr command also has several other options. Table 16.4 contains a list of some of the options you are likely to find the most useful:

TABLE 16.4 Options to the lpr Command

Option	Description
-1	Use a filter that will print control codes and suppress page breaks.
-p	Output is formatted with pr. pr formats pages into 66 lines per page with a header at the top containing the date and time the file was created, along with the page number, and five blank lines at the bottom.
-P	Send the job to a printer other than the default one.
-h	Suppress the printing of the "burst" page, also known as the banner or header page. Has no effect if header pages are turned off by default.
-m	Send e-mail to you, notifying you when the print job has completed printing.
-r	Remove the file upon completion of spooling. This option should probably not be used because it will remove the file before it has successfully printed. If it is used with the -s option (described next), it won't remove the file until after it has completed printing.
-s	Use symbolic links. Rather than copying the file to the spool directory, this option will simply create a symbolic link to the spool directory from the exiting file. This allows files too large to fit in the spool area to be printed. If you use this option, be careful that you do not modify or delete the file before it has finished printing.
-#n	Where n is the number of copies of each file that should be printed. (This feature can be disabled.)

Table 16.4 continued

Option	Description
-J *job*	Where *job* is the name of the job that should be printed on the banner page. By default, it will be the name of the first file that is specified.
-T	Title name that pr should use on the header at the top of the page. By default, this will be the filename. This option only applies if the -p option has also been used.
-i *n*	Where *n* represents the number of columns that the printed output will be indented by.
-w *n*	Where *n* represents the page width in columns. Only applies if the -p option has also been used.

Printing from X-Windows

Different X-Windows applications will have different means of printing, but here is a sample from Netscape if you want to print a Web page, for example.

To print a file from Netscape, select File and then choose Print from the menu. The Print dialog box is shown in Figure 16.1

Figure 16.1

The Print dialog box in Netscape. Notice that if you click the File button at the top, the filename will be netscape.ps. *Netscape outputs PostScript data when it prints.*

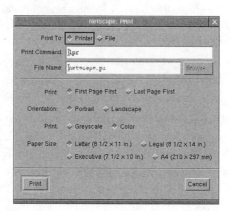

In the Print To: section at the top, you can select whether you want to send the output to a printer or to a file. If Printer is selected, the Print Command: box will be available to type in. Notice that it defaults to lpr, which is the same program you used to print from the command line. If you want, you can supply additional options to lpr here (such as having it e-mail you when it is done, or print more than one copy. See the section on lpr earlier in this chapter for details).

16

Most X-Windows programs can also output to a file. When they do, they will usually create a PostScript file that can then be sent to a PostScript printer directly, or run through GhostScript and sent to a non-PostScript printer.

Also, Netscape sends its output in PostScript, whether it goes to `lpr` or to a file. As mentioned in the configuration section, this is fairly common. Like many other UNIX programs, Netscape has no printer drivers. It simply outputs in PostScript. This demonstrates the need for GhostScript if you are not running a printer that understands GhostScript.

Printing in StarOffice

If you have StarOffice installed, you can configure its printer by double-clicking on the Printer Setup icon on the desktop. You will get a dialog box like that shown in Figure 16.2

FIGURE 16.2

The Printer Configuration dialog box in StarOffice. Notice that StarOffice has printer drivers included (bottom box) for many different printer models.

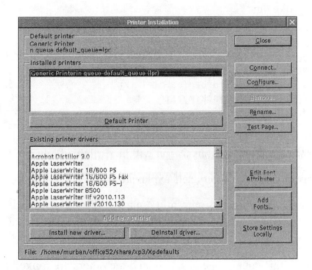

Because StarOffice comes with a large selection of drivers for various printers, it eliminates the need for using GhostScript to translate PostScript. You can simply select your printer model from the list, click Add new printer, and it will be installed as the default printer. You can then use the Configuration button and such to configure the printer.

If you do not install a printer, StarOffice uses the default Generic Printerin queue, which basically sends PostScript output to `lpr`.

Even if you do have GhostScript installed, you will probably want to use one of the native drivers in StarOffice because it may have better support for the various features of your printer that can be accessed directly from StarOffice without having to modify GhostScript filter options.

Checking Status of Print Jobs

The lpq command can be used to check the status of jobs that are waiting in the print queue. If it is called without any arguments, it will report the status of all jobs currently in the queue for the default printer. The default printer is checked in the following order: If the PRINTER environment variable is set, it is considered to be the default printer. If the PRINTER environment variable is not set, the printer that is aliased to lp in /etc/printcap will be used as the default.

lpq can also be called with a job number to show only the status of a particular job or a user name to show only the status of jobs owned by a particular user. The output of lpq will look something like this:

```
bash$ lpq -P simba
simba is ready and printing
Rank    Owner   Job   Files                        Total Size
active  mike    5     /home/murban/sample.txt      2000 bytes
2nd     mike    6     /home/murban/sample1.txt     2500 bytes
3rd     jack    7     /home/jack/myfile.txt        3200 bytes
4th     jack    8     ...                          5500 bytes
```

The -P option tells lpq to report on a printer other than the default—in this case, the printer named simba. All of the options to lpq will be explained later.

The information given by lpq is pretty self-explanatory.

The first line tells what the printer is currently doing. In this case, the printer is ready and printing. If the printer is stalled, out of paper, jammed, and so on, you may see other things listed here instead.

There are four jobs in this queue; one is active, and the others are ranked as to when they will be printed. A few things are worth pointing out though. Column 3, labeled job, is the job ID number assigned to that particular job. If you need to cancel a print job (explained later), you will need this job ID number. Column 4 lists the file or files that are being printed. Notice the fourth job that has just three dots. This means that the pathname of the file was too long to fit in the list, so lpq simply didn't list it.

lpq also has a few other options, shown in Table 16.5.

TABLE 16.5   Options to lpq

Option	Description
-P *name*	Where *name* is the name of a printer. This will cause lpq to show information on a printer other than the default one.
-l	This will cause information about each one of the files in the queue to be displayed, even if the information causes the display to break across a line. (In the previous example, this command would cause the filename to show; it currently shows up as three dots because it is too long to fit.)
-a	Causes lpq to display the status of all local queues for all printers.

Removing Jobs from the Queue

The lprm command can be used to remove print jobs that are currently in the queue and sometimes to remove print jobs that are currently printing. If lprm is run without any command line arguments, it will remove whatever job is currently printing on the default printer if that job belongs to the user that is running lprm. If the currently running job does not belong to the user running lprm, it will have no effect. If the root user runs lprm with no options, it will remove the currently printing job from the default printer, no matter who the job belongs to.

Running lprm with a job number as an argument will remove the job with that ID number from the queue of the default printer, assuming that you own the job and that you are not the root user. Normal users can only remove jobs that belong to them. The root user can remove any job. Here is an example:

```
bash$ lprm 5
dfA001simba.samplenet.org dequeued
cfA001simba.samplenet.org dequeued
bash $
```

The first file that is dequeued in this example is the data file for the job. This is basically a copy of the file in the printer's spool directory. The second file that is dequeued is a control file.

Note that the system may take some time to respond when you run lprm (up to several seconds). It may seem that lprm has hung. Don't worry; it hasn't. Wait a few seconds, and you should get your prompt back.

If you try to delete a job number that does not belong to you, and you are not the root user, lprm will respond with Permission denied.

lprm has several command-line options to modify the default behavior. They are listed in Table 16.6.

TABLE 16.6 Options to lprm

Option	Description
-P *name*	Where *name* is the name of the printer that lprm should remove the job from. If not specified, the default printer specified in the PRINTER environment variable and then the default printer aliased to lp is used.
-	A dash by itself will cause all jobs belonging to you to be removed from the queue. If you are the root user, all jobs in the queue will be removed.
user	Where *user* is the username of someone on the system. This will remove all jobs belonging to that user. This works only for the root user because normal users can only remove jobs belonging to themselves.

Caution

Removing a job that is currently printing will not cause the printer to stop immediately. Depending on the amount of RAM installed in your printer, there could be up to several pages of data already in the printer's buffer. This means that some (or if the document is small enough, almost the entire document) could be printed anyway, even if it has been removed from the queue.

Caution

Print jobs can be removed only from the system they were sent from, even if that printer is available to more than one computer on the network.

Controlling Printers

Printers and their associated queues are controlled with the lpc command. This command is used by the system administrator for printer administration. Some limited functionality is available to normal users, such as displaying the status of queues and restarting the printer daemon if it has died. Among other things, lpc can enable and disable printers, enable and disable printer queues, change the order of jobs in the queue so that files at the bottom of the queue can be printed first, and check the status of queues.

If no command-line arguments are given to lpc, it will start in interactive mode with a prompt. You can also supply command-line arguments when starting lpc. If you do this, lpc will start, run the arguments specified on the command line, and then exit. We will start by looking at the interactive mode of lpc.

lpc in Interactive Mode

If lpc is started with no arguments, it will run in interactive mode. The interactive mode simply gives a prompt like this:

```
lpc>
```

You can type a ? or help, and press Enter to get a list of the available commands. Typing help, followed by the name of one of the commands, will give you a short, one-line description of what the command does.

When you type commands, they can be abbreviated to the shortest form that is not ambiguous. For example, the status command can be abbreviated as stat. It could not be abbreviated as sta, however, because there is also a start command, and lpc would not know which one you wanted.

If you do not provide enough of the command for lpc to know which one you mean, it will respond with ?Ambiguous command, If the command you specify does not exist, it will respond with ?Invalid command.

Queue Status

To check the status of a queue, use the status command, which as mentioned previously, can be abbreviated stat. You also need to specify an argument to the status command. The argument can be either all to display the status of all daemons and queues or the name of a printer to show the status for only that printer. For example:

```
lpc> status lp
lp:
        queuing is enabled
        printing is enabled
        2 entries in spool area
        waiting for lp to become ready (offline?)
lpc>
```

Gives you the status for the system default line printer. In this case, the queue is enabled, printing is enabled, and there are two entries sitting in the queue waiting to be printed;

but nothing is printing because the printer is unavailable, and lpc suggests that it may be offline.

The status command can be run by both normal users and system administrators.

Disabling Printing and Stopping the Daemon

The abort and stop commands can be used by the system administrator to disable printing and also terminate the daemon that handles spooling for that printer. Both commands require an option that can either be all, which will disable printing on all the queues and terminate the daemons; or the name of a printer, which will cause the command to affect only the named printer.

The abort command terminates printing immediately and stops the daemon that handles spooling for that printer. For example:

```
lpc> abort lp
lp:
        printing disabled
        daemon (pid 597) killed
lpc>
```

And here is the output of the status command after the preceding command:

```
lpc> status all
lp:
        queuing is enabled
        printing is disabled
        2 entries in spool area
        printer idle
lpc>
```

There are a few important points to note about this:

- Notice that there are still two entries listed in the spool area. The abort command simply kills the daemon and disables the printer. It does not remove any jobs from the spool area. When the daemon is restarted and the printer is enabled again, the jobs that are in the spool area will print.

- Notice also that queuing is enabled. This means you (and others) can still send jobs to the printer. They will be placed in the queue to wait until the daemon is restarted and the printer is enabled. At that point, any jobs submitted while the printer was disabled will be printed, along with any jobs that were already in the queue.

The stop command works similarly to the abort command except that it will wait until the current job has finished printing before it disables the printer and stops the spool daemon. Like abort, stop does not bring down the queue. The queue will still accept jobs that users submit and hold them for printing whenever the printer becomes available.

Tip

If you will be taking a printer down for an extended period of time (for maintenance, for example), consider aliasing that printer's name and its aliases to another printer in /etc/printcap. If this is the system default printer, make sure that you also alias lp to a different printer. This will redirect any print jobs sent to that printer to a different printer without requiring users to make any changes to their configuration. Preferably, of course, you will want to alias the down printer to a printer that is a similar type and that is located in the building fairly close to where the down printer is located. And you will probably also want to send a system-wide e-mail to the affected users, letting them know where they can pick up their print jobs for the time being until the printer they normally use is available again.

The stop command has a similar effect. It will disable the printer and terminate the spooling daemon after the current job has finished.

Disabling Print Queuing

Neither abort nor stop disables the queue. If you are taking a printer down for maintenance, for example, and you simply issue an abort command to kill the daemon and disable the printer, the queue will still be available. Users will be able to continue to send jobs to this printer as if nothing is wrong, and the queue will happily accept the jobs and store them to print whenever the printer becomes available. Because of this, you will probably want to disable the queue if the printer will be down for an extended period of time. There are two ways that this can be done.

The first is with the disable command. It requires an argument that can either be all to disable all queues on the system or the name of a particular printer to disable the queue for only that printer. For example:

```
lpc> disable lp
lp:
        queuing disabled
lpc> status all
lp:
        queuing is disabled
        printing is enabled
        3 entries in spool area
        waiting for lp to become ready (offline?)
lpc>
```

In this case, the queue is disabled, but printing is still enabled. This means that the printer will continue to print all jobs currently in the queue (if it can), but the queue will not accept any new jobs.

If you try to send a job to a printer with a down queue that is not accepting jobs, you will get an error similar to the following:

```
bash$ lpr myfile.txt
lpr: Printer queue is disabled
bash$
```

The other way that a queue can be disabled is by using the down command. Like the disable command, it requires at least one argument, which can either be all to affect all queues on the system or the name of a printer to affect only one printer.

The down command actually sends a stop command, which disables the printer and the spool daemon after the current job has finished printing and then sends a disable command to bring down the queue. It can also take an optional message as an argument. The message will be written to the status file in the printer's spool directory. This will then be displayed in the output of lpq to let users know why the queue is not accepting their requests. For example:

```
lpc> down lp Printer is down for maintenance.
lp:
        printer and queuing disabled
lpc>
```

If lpq is then run, it will respond with the following:

```
bash$ lpq
Warning: lp is down: Printer is down for maintenance.
Warning: lp queue is turned off
Printer is down for maintenance.
Rank   Owner     Job  Files                          Total Size
bash$
```

To enable a queue that has been disabled, simply type enable followed by all to enable all queues, or type the name of a printer to enable only the queue on that printer. For example:

```
lpc> enable lp
lp:
        queuing enabled
lpc> status lp
lp:
        queuing is enabled
        printing is disabled
```

```
        3 entries in spool area
        Printer is down for maintenance.
lpc>
```

Notice that although this brought the queue back up, it did not re-enable the printer. Currently, the queue will accept jobs, but they will not be printed. If you used the down command to bring down the queue, use the up command to bring it back up. This will re-enable the queue, restart the spooling daemon, and enable the printer. It will not however, clear the status message. To clear the status message, you will need to run the restart command discussed in the next section.

Restarting a Spooling Daemon

If you need to restart a spooling daemon, you can use the restart command. If there is no daemon currently running, this command will start one. If there is currently a daemon running, this command will kill it and restart it (see the following caution, however). This can be used to reset a daemon that seems to have hung or something.

The restart command requires an argument that can be either all to restart all print daemons on the system or the name of a printer to restart only the daemon for that printer. Here is an example:

```
lpc> restart lp
lp:
        daemon (pid 2102) killed
lp:
        daemon started
lpc>
```

Caution

Occasionally, the restart command kills a running daemon, but doesn't restart it again even though it claims it did. Because of this, it is a good idea to check the output of lpq for the printer in question. If lpq says in the status line Warning: no daemon present, it means that lpc stopped the daemon when the restart command was issued, but then failed to restart it again. If this is the case, simply run the restart command again from lpc, and this will take care of the problem.

Cleaning the Queue Directory

The clean command in lpc causes it to clean out the queue directory. Basically, it will remove any control files and so on that cannot be printed because it is not a complete print job. Like most commands in `lpc`, it requires an argument of either `all` or the name of the printer spool directory that you want to clean.

Changing the Priority of Print Jobs

You can use the `topq` command to change the order of print jobs in the queue (that is, move jobs at the bottom or middle of the queue up to the top so they print faster).

Only a system administrator can change the order of the print jobs. The basic syntax of `topq` is `topq *printername jobnum(s)*`, where *printername* is, of course, the name of the printer, and *jobnum(s)* is a list of job numbers that you want to move to the top of the queue. You can specify multiple numbers with the command, and it will print them in the order listed. The first job listed will be moved to the top of the queue, the second will be second in the queue, and so on. For example, suppose the queue looks like this currently:

```
Rank   Owner    Job  Files                      Total Size
1st    murban   8    myfile.txt                 151625 bytes
2nd    murban   9    cardlist.txt               38311 bytes
3rd    murban   10   lions.txt                  1113 bytes
4th    murban   12   schedule.txt               6599 bytes
```

To reverse the order of these jobs in `lpc`, type `topq lp 12 10 9 8`.

```
lpc> topq lp 12 10 9 8
lp:
        moved cfA008simba.samplenet.org
        moved cfA009simba.samplenet.org
        moved cfA010simba.samplenet.org
        moved cfA012simba.samplenet.org
lpc>
```

If we look at the queue again, it now looks like this:

```
Rank   Owner    Job  Files                      Total Size
1st    murban   12   schedule.txt               6599 bytes
2nd    murban   10   lions.txt                  1113 bytes
3rd    murban   9    cardlist.txt               38311 bytes
4th    murban   8    myfile.txt                 151625 bytes
```

`topq` can also take a username instead of a list of jobs. When `topq` is used this way, it will move all the jobs from the named user to the top of the queue.

Note that `topq` does not preempt a job that is currently running. It moves the jobs listed to the top of the queue so that they are next in line, but whatever job was printing before `topq` was used will finish printing before the job moved to the top of the queue starts. If you want the job to print right now, you will have to use `lprm` to remove the job that is currently printing.

Quitting lpc

To quit the lpc program, simply type either quit or exit at the lpc> prompt. This will put you back at the command line.

Using lpc in Non-interactive Mode

lpc can also be run in non-interactive mode. In this case, simply supply the command you want to perform, along with any parameters on the command line.

When lpc is run in non-interactive mode, it expects the first argument to be the command and anything that follows to be arguments to the command. Here is an example:

```
# lpc restart lp
lp:
        daemon (pid 2280) killed
lp:
        daemon started
#
```

All of the same commands that are available in interactive mode are also available in non-interactive mode.

Controlling Who Can Use lpc

Sometimes, you might want to give other people the ability to control printers with lpc, but not give them full root privileges on the system. The operator group allows you to do this.

Basically, any user who is a member of the group operator can make full use of lpc without having full root access to the system. This will allow that user to change the priority of print jobs, start and stop print daemons, and bring queues up and down.

Refer to Chapter 10, "Users, Groups, and Permissions" for more information on groups and how to add users to a group.

Basic Network Printing

Basic network printing is similar to local printing. To set up a network printer in /etc/printcap, use a line like the following:

```
simba|lp|local line printer:\
        :lp=::rm=nova:rp=simba:sd=/var/spool/lpd/simba:lf=/var/log/lpd-errs:
```

This entry will connect to a remote printer named simba on the host named nova. Note that the local name (on line 1) does not have to be the same as the remote name of the printer. You can call the local name whatever you want. What printer the job is actually sent to is controlled by the rp entry in line 2. The local spool directory will hold the file only until the remote spool directory has room. Then, the file will be moved into the remote host's spool directory.

Notice that we did not have to specify an input filter here. That is because all the filtering will be handled by the remote host.

The printer on the remote host should be configured using the instructions provided earlier in the chapter for configuring a printer.

Troubleshooting

There are several things that can go wrong when using printers. Here is a short list of some of the most common problems you might run into and some solutions for them.

Printer Does Not Receive Data; Jobs are Sitting in Queue

Check lpq and make sure that the spooling daemon is running. If it says Warning: no daemon present, you will need to use lpc to restart the spooling daemon. Also check lpc, and make sure that the printer is not disabled.

Data Light on Printer Flashes, but Printer Will Not Print

This is often a symptom of sending non-PostScript data to a PostScript printer. Check your filter and make sure that it is filtering text correctly and converting it to PostScript.

Printing an Image File in GIMP or a Web Page Results in Hundreds of Pages of Garbage Being Printed

This can often be a symptom of feeding PostScript data to a printer that doesn't understand PostScript. The non-PostScript printer will try to print this file as plain text. Check out the GhostScript program, and see the section in this chapter on "Printing PostScript Files on Non-PostScript Printers."

The Printer Is Slow

Try setting the printer to polled mode (assuming this printer is on the parallel port). Use the following command:

```
lptcontrol -p
```

Remember that you will need to add this to a startup file if you want to take effect at each system boot. See the section at the beginning of the chapter on lptcontrol.

Printed Output "Stair Steps"

The symptoms of the stair step problem look something like this:

```
Line one of the file.
                Line two of the file.
                                Line three of the file.
                                                Line four of the file.
```

This pattern will continue until the text runs off the end of the page. This is a fairly common problem caused by differences in the way UNIX and DOS/Windows interpret the line feed (LF) character. When DOS/Windows advances to a new line, it sends both a carriage return and a line feed. UNIX, on the other hand, sends only a line feed character, and expects a carriage return to be implied. If your printer is expecting DOS-style carriage return and line feed combinations, but is only receiving a line feed, it will advance the paper, but never return the print head to the beginning of the line. There are a few ways you might be able to solve this problem.

The first is to look for an option in your printer's configuration that changes the way it interprets a line feed character. See your printer documentation to see whether there is a way you can do this.

The second way is to create a filter that converts the LF to a combination of CR and LF.

If your printer understands HP-PCL language, the following filter is recommended by the *FreeBSD Handbook* for performing this task:

```
#!/bin/sh
#
# hpif - Simple text input filter for lpd for HP-PCL based printers
# Installed in /usr/local/libexec/hpif
#
# Simply copies stdin to stdout.  Ignores all filter arguments.
# Tells printer to treat LF as CR+LF.  Ejects the page when done.

printf "\033&k2G" && cat && printf "\033&l0H" && exit 0
exit 2
```

See the section on text filters earlier in this chapter for more information on how to install a text filter.

If your printer does not understand HP-PCL, you might be able to use the `tr` command to convert the LF into a CR LF. A filter such as the following may do the trick:

```
#!/bin/sh
# Filter that fixes the stair stepping effect on non PCL printers.
/bin/cat | tr '\13' '\13\10' && exit 0
exit 2
```

Once again, see the section on text filters earlier in this chapter for more information on how to install a text filter.

All the Text Prints On One Line, Creating a Mess and Writing Over the Top of the Existing Text

This is basically the opposite of the stair-stepping problem. This problem is rare, but it does happen occasionally. Basically, the LF is being interpreted as a CR by the printer. The print head is getting returned to the beginning of the line, but the paper is not being advanced.

To fix this problem, you will need to make changes to your printer's configuration settings so that it interprets CR and LF properly. See your printer's documentation for details on how to do this.

If you find that you cannot change the hardware settings of your printer to fix this problem, the same filter used earlier to fix the stair-stepping problem might fix this problem.

CHAPTER 17

Kernel Configuration

This chapter covers a topic that's likely to be one of the most intimidating to a newcomer to UNIX: how to configure and rebuild your kernel. This is a task that simply does not happen in the desktop PC world. However, it's a necessary part of life when dealing with an open-source system under constant development, in a world in which new devices constantly demand more functionality from a kernel. Unfortunately, it's not an easy matter to do.

Configuring the kernel is at the heart of customizing FreeBSD and other operating systems like it. A well-tuned kernel will serve 100% of the demands that a system and its users place on it while eliminating all the unnecessary baggage that an unoptimized kernel might have, making it operate significantly faster. This chapter intends to provide enough insight into the kernel-configuration process to eliminate the mystery and enable this kind of customizability.

The Role of the Kernel

The kernel is the master executable of the system. It's the first thing that is executed from the boot blocks when you power on the system, and it constantly runs throughout the machine's uptime. Its job is to oversee all the processes running on the system, handle TCP/IP and other networking duties, manage access to all the devices on the system, and control memory usage—to name just a few of its tasks.

Every operating system has a kernel—from MS-DOS, to Windows, to the highest-end mainframe. Some systems take greater pains to hide it from the user than others do: In Windows, it's an executable in `C:\WINDOWS\SYSTEM`; in classic Mac OS, it's hidden from the filesystem entirely. In many UNIX systems, its traditional place is in the root directory at the top of the filesystem. FreeBSD puts it in `/boot`. With each of these operating systems, a default (or "generic") kernel is part of every released version of the system, and every time a new version comes out, its changes are mostly additions to accommodate drivers for new devices that it supports. The kernel is responsible for knowing about every kind of device that can be connected to the system. This is why when you install drivers for a new and previously unsupported device in Windows, you generally have to reboot—it's because your kernel has been modified. The system has to be restarted in order to use the new kernel unless it is able to load the new device as a kernel extension or module.

FreeBSD uses a *microkernel* architecture, which means that the kernel is fairly small and modular. Windows NT and Mach (the kernel upon which Mac OS X is built) are other examples of microkernels, in which new devices are more frequently added through kernel modules—which can be loaded and unloaded during runtime—than by recompiling the kernel. Linux and Windows 95/98 are instead *monolithic* kernels, in which the kernel's code is more optimized for performance and to minimize context switching, an architecture that makes for kernel code that's cleaner and easier for developers to maintain, but more frequently requires the administrator to recompile the kernel every time support for a new device is added.

This isn't a terribly clear delineation—Linux operates fairly heavily on kernel modules today, and FreeBSD's kernel does have to be recompiled for a number of different reasons. The difference between a microkernel and monolithic kernel architecture is largely a philosophical one, and has to do with a good deal more than simply device support; the biggest fundamental difference is that a microkernel has a mechanism for passing certain non-core system calls to a user-level processing level, or "ring," instead of handling them all internally, and stripping down the core of the kernel to only the bare essentials, only what absolutely requires the highest level of supervisor-mode execution status. The purpose of this is to increase runtime robustness and make the kernel processes more understandable and manageable, as well as providing for easier support for modularity when it comes to devices.

Although this is all well and good, unfortunately a kernel in which every possible kind of device and option is modular and loadable during runtime is as theoretical as perpetual motion. Chances are that as you gain experience with FreeBSD, you will come to a point where you can't avoid recompiling your kernel, and it's at that time that you'll undergo the rite of passage that initiates you into the circle of kernel hackers.

Why Configure a Custom Kernel?

FreeBSD comes with a GENERIC kernel installed by default. This kernel is tuned to support as wide a user base as possible, so that FreeBSD will work "out-of-the-box" on as many different machines as there are users in the world. Given the nature of x86-based hardware, this means there must be a truly astounding number of drivers built in. An operating system built for a tightly controlled set of hardware (such as SGI's IRIX or Apple's Mac OS X) can afford to get away with much less of this generic support, but FreeBSD is stuck with it. The GENERIC kernel also has various options for memory allocation and optimization set to low-common-denominator levels, and other optional elements are left out in order to keep the kernel as streamlined as possible under the circumstances. These are all aspects of the kernel that can almost certainly be configured more efficiently for your particular system.

The kernel probes at boot time for every single kind of device that it knows about. This is where you see that scrolling screen full of white text while the system is coming up;

the kernel is looking for dozens of different kinds of devices that are enabled in the GENERIC kernel. Although it doesn't hurt anything for the kernel not to find most of them, it does take time to do each probe, and you can speed up boot time significantly by removing the unnecessary devices from the kernel. This also helps reduce the size (and therefore the memory footprint) of the kernel. Modern systems with hundreds of megabytes of RAM don't need to worry about this, but it's a worthy consideration on a machine that barely meets FreeBSD's minimum requirements.

> **Note**
>
> Even with the GENERIC kernel, it's possible to suppress probing for every device under the sun. That's what the boot configurator (covered in Appendix C, "Troubleshooting Installation Problems") does: It allows you to explicitly remove support for various devices that it can tell will cause IRQ or memory address conflicts (or that you know you don't have). This process does not actually change the kernel or its compiled-in elements at all, but it does prevent it from wasting time looking for nonexistent devices when it's booting.

As you add devices to your system, such as USB peripherals, sound cards, SCSI controllers, or numerous other possible additions, you won't be able to use many of them unless you add support for them in the kernel. The same is true of new filesystem types (such as EXT2FS, as we saw in Chapter 9, "The FreeBSD Filesystem"). Many devices and filesystems are available today as kernel modules, but the majority still have to be compiled into the kernel, and so you have little choice but to rebuild it. However, this gives you the chance to tweak other things in the system (such as the number of memory buffers, custom memory management features, or the kernel's name), so you can probably enhance your system's performance fairly significantly with one rebuild.

SMP (Symmetric Multi-Processing) support is not present in the GENERIC kernel either, by the way. If you have a system with more than one CPU, you'll need to build a custom kernel in order to take advantage of all of them.

Using `dmesg` to Get Information About the Kernel Startup

If you will be stripping the unnecessary devices out of your kernel, it is imperative that you find out what devices you do have, so you don't end up accidentally removing support for your existing hardware. As mentioned earlier, the kernel probes for all its known devices at boot time, and it prints out the status of each probe, telling you which devices you must keep in the new kernel. This information isn't just printed out to the screen at boot time; it's also echoed into an internal runtime message buffer for reference at any time. The tool to use for recalling this information is dmesg.

The output of dmesg can be very long, so you'll probably want to pipe it through less, as shown in Listing 17.1.

LISTING 17.1   dmesg Output Piped through less for Readability

```
# dmesg | less
Copyright (c) 1992-2001 The FreeBSD Project.
Copyright (c) 1979, 1980, 1983, 1986, 1988, 1989, 1991, 1992, 1993, 1994
        The Regents of the University of California. All rights reserved.
FreeBSD 4.2-STABLE #1: Sun Mar  4 14:05:42 PST 2001
    btman@stripes.arclight.net:/usr/obj/usr/src/sys/STRIPES
Timecounter "i8254"  frequency 1193182 Hz
CPU: Pentium III/Pentium III Xeon/Celeron (598.06-MHz 686-class CPU)
  Origin = "GenuineIntel"  Id = 0x683  Stepping = 3
  Features=0x383f9ff<FPU,VME,DE,PSE,TSC,MSR,PAE,MCE,CX8,SEP,MTRR,PGE,MCA,CMOV,
➥PAT,PSE36,MMX,FXSR,SSE>
real memory  = 132907008 (129792K bytes)
config> di sn0
config> di lnc0
config> di ie0
config> di fe0
config> di ed0
config> di cs0
config> di bt0
config> di aic0
config> di aha0
config> di adv0
config> q
avail memory = 125018112 (122088K bytes)
Preloaded elf kernel "kernel" at 0xc044a000.
Preloaded userconfig_script "/boot/kernel.conf" at 0xc044a09c.
Pentium Pro MTRR support enabled
md0: Malloc disk
npx0: <math processor> on motherboard
npx0: INT 16 interface
pcib0: <Host to PCI bridge> on motherboard
pci0: <PCI bus> on pcib0
pci0: <Intel model 1132 VGA-compatible display device> at 2.0 irq 11
pcib1: <PCI to PCI bridge (vendor=8086 device=244e)> at device 30.0 on pci0
pci1: <PCI bus> on pcib1
fxp0: <Intel PLC 10/100 Ethernet> port 0xde80-0xdebf mem 0xff8fe000-0xff8fefff
➥irq 11 at device 8.0 on pci1
fxp0: Ethernet address 00:d0:b7:c7:74:f1
fxp1: <Intel Pro 10/100B/100+ Ethernet> port 0xdf00-0xdf3f mem 0xff700000-0xff7f
ffff,0xff8ff000-0xff8fffff irq 11 at device 9.0 on pci1
```

LISTING 17.1   continued

```
fxp1: Ethernet address 00:d0:b7:bd:5d:13
isab0: <PCI to ISA bridge (vendor=8086 device=2440)> at device 31.0 on pci0
isa0: <ISA bus> on isab0
atapci0: <Intel ICH2 ATA100 controller> port 0xffa0-0xffaf at device 31.1
➥on pci0
ata0: at 0x1f0 irq 14 on atapci0
ata1: at 0x170 irq 15 on atapci0
```

The output continues throughout all device checks, filesystem validations, and daemon startup blocks; and then continues into runtime errors generated since you booted by various devices. You can ignore everything after you begin seeing date stamps and regular error messages. What we're interested in is the boot messages, such as the ones in the block shown previously.

The first part of the boot messages, after the copyright and CPU information lines, is the kernel configuration that you have set in the boot configurator; each line beginning with `config>` is a command you issued in visual config mode, most likely (as with the `di` lines) to delete unwanted devices from the probe process. These devices won't appear later in the `dmesg` output. If you haven't removed these devices in the configurator, it will probe for them.

Anywhere in the output that you see a "not found" message, it's a driver that you can delete from the kernel. Keep the `dmesg` window open while you configure your kernel, and don't delete anything that the system reports as found.

The Kernel Configuration Files

At the time of this writing, FreeBSD doesn't have a visual kernel configuration utility such as Red Hat Linux's `linuxconf` or the `make config` dialog-driven process in other Linux distributions. FreeBSD's kernel is configured using text files, a method that may seem quite arcane, but which does provide some flexibility that the visual methods don't allow.

A visual configuration tool provides interactive feedback, allowing you to enable and disable devices and options on a one-by-one basis. What it doesn't do, though, is allow you to maintain multiple configurations side-by-side, comparing them using tools such as `diff` and `grep`, and using the base-level GENERIC configuration, previous known valid configurations, and the reference NOTES file as guidelines. It also allows you to see all your device options at a glance. An interactive visual tool can become needlessly complex and convoluted, and in asking you to decide individually whether to include every different option, it actually can detract from useful feedback. Unless you can remember the importance and consequences of every different option, it's hard to keep track of which options you should be selecting. With the FreeBSD method, you can tune your config file until you're happy with it—incorporating changes since a previous version or even copying a "standard" configuration from another FreeBSD system—and then build the kernel from it.

Assuming that you installed the FreeBSD sources on your system, go into the `/sys/i386/conf` directory, the location for the kernel config files. You'll see the GENERIC file, among other items.

> **Note**
>
> If you're running on Alpha hardware instead of x86, use `alpha` in the previous pathname instead of `i386`. A number of other details in this chapter will be slightly different as well, but the process remains the same.

The GENERIC Configuration File

Open up the GENERIC file in your favorite text editor. Scroll through the various options, but don't actually make any changes just yet (you don't want to alter the GENERIC file itself). You'll see that there's a lot of redundancy built in, in order to remain compatible with all kinds of machines. This is the block of "required" lines:

```
machine         i386
cpu             I386_CPU
cpu             I486_CPU
cpu             I586_CPU
cpu             I686_CPU
ident           GENERIC
maxusers        32
```

Below this block are the "optional" lines: items that are part of the GENERIC kernel by default, but don't have to be present in order for the kernel to be valid (it just wouldn't be a very useful kernel without them). These include the block of useful kernel options shown in Listing 17.2.

LISTING 17.2 Built In GENERIC Kernel Options

```
options         MATH_EMULATE        #Support for x87 emulation
options         INET                #InterNETworking
options         INET6               #IPv6 communications protocols
options         FFS                 #Berkeley Fast Filesystem
```

Listing 17.2   continued

```
options          SOFTUPDATES          #Enable FFS soft updates support
options          MFS                  #Memory Filesystem
options          MD_ROOT              #MD is a potential root device
options          NFS                  #Network Filesystem
options          NFS_ROOT             #NFS usable as root device, NFS required
options          MSDOSFS              #MSDOS Filesystem
options          CD9660               #ISO 9660 Filesystem
options          DEVFS                #Device Filesystem
options          PROCFS               #Process filesystem
options          COMPAT_43            #Compatible with BSD 4.3 [KEEP THIS!]
options          SCSI_DELAY=15000     #Delay (in ms) before probing SCSI
options          UCONSOLE             #Allow users to grab the console
options          USERCONFIG           #boot -c editor
options          VISUAL_USERCONFIG    #visual boot -c editor
options          KTRACE               #ktrace(1) support
options          SYSVSHM              #SYSV-style shared memory
options          SYSVMSG              #SYSV-style message queues
options          SYSVSEM              #SYSV-style semaphores
options          P1003_1B             #Posix P1003_1B real-time extensions
options          _KPOSIX_PRIORITY_SCHEDULING
options          KBD_INSTALL_CDEV     # install a CDEV entry in /dev
```

The remainder of the file is taken up with device lines. These lines specify all the devices that the GENERIC kernel has built in, and there are a lot of them. These are mostly what you will want to strip out of your custom kernel in order to optimize it. The following is an example block of device lines, of which there are several in the file, as shown in Listing 17.3.

Listing 17.3   Some of the Device Drivers Built In to the GENERIC Kernel

```
# PCI Ethernet NICs that use the common MII bus controller code.
# NOTE: Be sure to keep the 'device miibus' line in order to use these NICs!
device           miibus          # MII bus support
device           dc              # DEC/Intel 21143 and various workalikes
device           fxp             # Intel EtherExpress PRO/100B (82557, 82558)
device           pcn             # AMD Am79C79x PCI 10/100 NICs
device           rl              # RealTek 8129/8139
device           sf              # Adaptec AIC-6915 (''Starfire'')
device           sis             # Silicon Integrated Systems SiS 900/SiS 7016
device           ste             # Sundance ST201 (D-Link DFE-550TX)
device           tl              # Texas Instruments ThunderLAN
device           tx              # SMC EtherPower II (83c170 ''EPIC'')
device           vr              # VIA Rhine, Rhine II
device           wb              # Winbond W89C840F
device           xl              # 3Com 3c90x (''Boomerang'', ''Cyclone'')
```

Device Hints

Note

The following section on device hints applies only to FreeBSD 5.0. FreeBSD 4.*x* does not use device hints.

FreeBSD operates using *device hints*, which are a way of abstracting the attributes of various devices so the system can find them without needing the attributes to be compiled statically into the kernel. These attributes used to be defined like this, in the kernel config file itself:

```
device          ata0    at isa? port IO_WD1 irq 14
device          ata1    at isa? port IO_WD2 irq 15
```

Now, however, the kernel configuration file only needs to have this line:

```
device          ata
```

This is because the `ata` device has its attributes in the `/boot/device.hints` file, which is consulted by the kernel at boot time. Here are the relevant lines for this example:

```
hint.ata.0.at="isa"
hint.ata.0.port="0x1F0"
hint.ata.0.irq="14"
hint.ata.1.at="isa"
hint.ata.1.port="0x170"
hint.ata.1.irq="15"
```

With these attributes kept in a central location, the kernel knows on what bus, memory address, and IRQ (interrupt request) to find the `ata` device; and you can change these attributes without having to recompile the kernel. If you prefer, though, you can still compile the attributes statically into the kernel by enabling this line:

```
#To statically compile in device wiring instead of /boot/device.hints
#hints          "GENERIC.hints"         #Default places to look for devices.
```

The `LINT` File

Fortunately , we're not alone when it comes to identifying each of these ugly looking options and devices, or knowing which other ones are available. There is a file called `LINT`, also in `/sys/i386/conf` that describes all possible options and devices available in the current system. It's another file that you don't want to modify. Just open it in a text editor and look through its contents.

Everything in GENERIC has an entry in LINT as well. Nothing is commented out of it except for actual comments. You can theoretically copy any configuration line into your custom config file and run with it. This will generally be necessary only if you add some particularly unusual device or kernel option, but LINT is the first thing you should consult in that event.

One of the long running ideals (or myths) about FreeBSD is the capability to build a kernel based on the LINT file, incorporating every possible supported option and driver. This is almost certainly not possible because many of the kernel options are mutually exclusive or unstable.

Note that in FreeBSD 5.0, the LINT file does not exist, and instead you will find a file called NOTES in the same directory. The NOTES file is similar to the LINT file except that it contains comments and device hints. If you wish, you can use the NOTES file to build a LINT file by running `make lint` from within the directory. This creates a config file that you can theoretically use to build a really huge, all-encompassing kernel that probably won't have a change of booting or even compiling.

Creating a Custom Kernel Configuration File

Here's where we actually begin the process of creating a new kernel. You won't actually want to modify the GENERIC file itself; it gets updated with the system sources every time you synchronize or upgrade. So, to make sure that your changes don't get overwritten, make a copy of it to use as your custom kernel config. The name for the copy should be a single word in all caps, according to tradition. Our example custom kernel will be called CUSTOM:

```
# cp GENERIC CUSTOM
```

You can now modify the CUSTOM file all you like. The first thing you should do is go through it, and change every mention of GENERIC to CUSTOM (or whatever name you choose). You also should remove redundant entries for cpu, and possibly modify the value of maxusers. The following is a block from a customized kernel config on a Pentium II-class machine operating as a high-profile server:

```
machine       i386
cpu           I686_CPU
ident         CUSTOM
maxusers      64
```

Note

Don't be fooled by the `maxusers` setting: It doesn't actually limit the number of current logins the system will support. (That limit is controlled by the `device pty <num>` line.) What `maxusers` does is much more subtle: A number of internal table sizes are derived from it, such as the maximum number of processes allowed (16 times the `maxusers` setting, plus 20) and several others. It should be set approximately to what you expect the average number of users to be, but don't set it lower than 4—you'll run out of processes quicker than you expect.

You can now start customizing the options and devices. Refer to `NOTES` to keep yourself informed about what you're modifying, and keep your other window with the `dmesg` output open. Don't delete anything from the config file that `dmesg` says the kernel found! It's in fact a good idea not to actually delete any lines; just comment them out by putting a hash mark (#) at the front of the line.

If you have any doubt about whether or not to disable a line that's in `GENERIC`, don't disable it. `GENERIC` definitely contains a lot of items that aren't needed on every system, but it's better to err on the side of caution when it comes to kernels, especially if you're making these changes on a production server.

Compiling and Installing the Custom Kernel

After your config file is ready to go, building the kernel is a fairly simple process. In theory, it's at most three commands:

```
# cd /usr/src
# make buildkernel KERNCONF=CUSTOM
# make installkernel KERNCONF=CUSTOM
```

The `KERNCONF` argument specifies the kernel config file to use; if you omit it, the `GENERIC` config file will be assumed. The first step parses the config file, sets up the build directory, builds the dependencies, and then builds the kernel itself. The second line installs it into `/boot`, moving the current kernel to `/boot/kernel.old`. You must then `reboot` to use the new kernel.

If you're really sure of yourself, you can combine both the `make` lines into a single one:

```
# make kernel KERNCONF=CUSTOM
```

> **Note**
>
> The kernel has the schg (system-immutable) flag set on it, meaning that even root can't delete or overwrite it without removing that flag. The make installkernel target attempts to remove that flag before installing the new kernel. However, if you're running with a securelevel of 1 or higher (a system-wide security setting that you select during installation or in /etc/rc.conf; see man securelevel for details), it won't be able to remove the flag. You'll have to reboot into single-user mode (dropping to single-user via shutdown won't work) in order to complete the kernel installation.

Adding Device Nodes to the /dev Directory (if Necessary)

> **Note**
>
> If you are using FreeBSD 5.0, this section does not apply. FreeBSD 5.0 uses the DEVFS filesystem interface to the system's devices and builds the /dev virtual filesystem dynamically at boot time.

Many devices will be missing an entry in /dev when you add them to the kernel configuration; devices in /dev include only those devices that have either been part of the base system or added afterward explicitly. You have to create device nodes for new devices that you add to the kernel—they're not generated automatically.

Fortunately, this is done fairly simply. All you have to do, after you reboot with the new kernel, is go into the /dev directory, and run the MAKEDEV shell script:

```
# ./MAKEDEV
```

All devices supported by the running kernel will be created as device nodes or "special files" in /dev, and you now have a target you can use with your command-line tools to interact with each new device. A more efficient, direct solution is to make the device node only for the new device(s) you've installed (for instance, if you've enabled the snd0 sound driver). Enable it by running the MAKEDEV command on it alone:

```
# ./MAKEDEV snd0
```

Recovering if Something Goes Wrong

Compiler errors are not uncommon. If you're running the same source tree that you've had since you installed the system, an error in the compile process (where the compiler fails to complete, usually citing "`*** Error code 1`") is probably the result of some unstable kernel option or device that you've enabled. See if you can determine which one it is by inferring from the last few lines of the compiler output. If it's not obvious, you can find some guidance by visiting the FreeBSD Web site (`http://www.freebsd.org`) and searching the mailing list archives on some of the unique words in whatever compiler errors were generated.

If you've updated your sources since installing your system (a process described in the next chapter, "Keeping Up-to-Date with FreeBSD"), it's quite likely (especially if you're tracking -CURRENT or -STABLE) that the code is in an unstable state, and whatever errors you've encountered will probably be corrected within a few days. You should be subscribed to the `freebsd-current` or `freebsd-stable` mailing lists if you're such a cutting edge FreeBSD user (again, see the FreeBSD Web site for details on subscribing), and you can get help there.

However, there is always the chance that your kernel will build cleanly, install cleanly, reboot cleanly, and then explode without warning when it tries to boot. It might fail to mount its filesystems, it might freeze up with a kernel trap error, or it might behave according to a number of other failure modes. If this happens, don't panic—even if your kernel might be doing just that—there's an easy way to get out of this predicament.

Reboot the machine. Press the appropriate F-key to get past the bootloader, but when you're offered the `loader` prompt (when it counts down from 10 seconds, giving you the option to press any key but Enter for the prompt), take it. Enter `boot /boot/kernel.old` at the prompt, and it will use your previous working kernel.

Keep in mind that if you next try to rebuild the kernel and install it, your `/boot/kernel.old` will get overwritten by the previous kernel that you built and was broken. To avoid this, copy your `kernel.old` to some filename that won't get overwritten by any automated process (for instance, `/boot/kernel.frank`). You can use this kernel to boot from the `loader` prompt next time if it happens again.

Another possible problem is that your system might boot properly and completely come up, but system utilities such as `ps`, `top`, and `w` no longer work. If this happens, it's most likely because you're building your kernel from a newer source tree than your system is built from, and the libkvm library has become outdated by your newer kernel. To get around this, you can rebuild your libkvm library. A still better solution, though, is to always build your kernel from the same sources that your full system is built from, and only build a kernel on updated sources if you're doing a complete make world, as described in the next chapter.

CHAPTER 18

Keeping Up to Date with FreeBSD

Every operating system has to have a way of keeping up with the times. Security patches, bug fixes, and support for new technologies have to get into people's installed systems without forcing them to wait for new full releases, which can take anything from six months to three years in the operating system world. In a world that operates on "Internet time," in which you could find your system compromised by a hacker hours after a security breach is made public, an up-to-the-minute operating system is a must.

No operating system maker completely neglects this need. Microsoft provides large periodic "service pack" upgrades to users of Windows NT/2000, and security patches are made available for individual applications on consumer Windows operating systems and Macintoshes in a matter of days after the need is discovered. Similar patch mechanisms are in place for Linux. FreeBSD can be kept up to date through these methods, but because it's a system largely founded on its users' access to the source code, even more so than its open-source cousins, it has some even better methods for keeping your system buttoned up against even the most current conditions.

Major versions of FreeBSD (4.0, 5.0) appear every one to two years, and interim releases (3.4, 4.1.1) generally appear every three to six months. But no matter how frequently a patch release becomes available, it's too infrequent to address the pressing day-to-day needs of a security-conscious administrator. In this chapter, we will be covering the more real-time methods that FreeBSD provides (for example, CVSup and `make world`).

Tracking the FreeBSD Sources

The easiest and most common upgrade path is simply to wait for each new official release. This involves little more than obtaining the CD or disk image file and then installing the new version of the operating system from it by using the same methods covered in Chapter 2, "Installing FreeBSD," or described at the FreeBSD Web site. But this is hardly a real-time solution to the upgrade procedure. To really keep up with the times, you have to track the sources.

The source tree for FreeBSD is kept in a central CVS repository, mirrored across a number of redundant servers, and maintained by a fairly small core of contributors and committers. Rather than Linux's model—in which the sources for the kernel are available but each individual distribution has its own set of executables and libraries, its own filesystem structure, and its own policies for how the source for those resources should be made available—FreeBSD is structured so that the entire system is available in source form at all times for anybody to use. Whether a person intends to modify and develop the sources and check them back in to the main tree, or intends only to maintain a server with a current source distribution, the mechanism used for handling its structure and revisions is CVS, putting developers and administrators on the same level of accessibility to the code.

The STABLE and CURRENT Source Branches Explained

Between complete releases, the FreeBSD code is in a state of constant flux. Bugs are being fixed, utilities are being patched and extended, features are being added, and the structure of the system is being reorganized. There are also multiple different branches of the code tree that are being maintained in parallel. Generally, there is active development on two different branches at once, with only sporadic maintenance work on earlier branches. Think of the code repository as a tree, growing upward with a central trunk that sprouts new branches at the top every so often. The topmost branch is called CURRENT, and the next highest is STABLE.

FIGURE **18.1**

The FreeBSD code branches, showing the relationship of the CURRENT and STABLE branches.

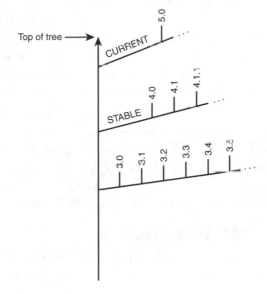

Each time a new version (3.x, 4.x, 5.x, and so on) is initiated, it branches off from the main development codebase, or the "trunk" of the tree. This is a fairly common development model: It allows developers to freeze a certain feature set and allow it to mature without adding more instability to it—new features are added in blocks, with each new feature set or restructuring being introduced with each new branch.

The thing to remember here is that CURRENT is not the branch you want for a production server! CURRENT refers to the very most cutting-edge branch of the code—the one where brand-new features are being tested, and consequently where the most instability in the entire code tree will be found. CURRENT is intended only for developers and people who absolutely, without any possibility of alternative, must have the new features that are introduced in it, without waiting for it to be declared STABLE.

At some point during development on a CURRENT branch—usually after the first release, for example 5.0-RELEASE—it is deemed STABLE, and the CURRENT and STABLE designations each move up one branch on the tree. CURRENT becomes the tag for the newly created topmost branch, and the STABLE designation means that it—the former CURRENT branch—is now recommended for use on production servers. New releases are announced on both branches every few months until the feature set in CURRENT has matured and the STABLE branch no longer meets the needs of the community. The tree then branches again, starting the cycle over.

Selecting Your Upgrade Target

Upgrading your system can be done at any time, no matter how far along the development in the tree is. You have two choices for how to go about it: You can select any release in which the code is frozen and kept in a static repository; or, you can simply synchronize your source using CVSup (in much the same way as we discussed synchronizing your ports in Chapter 15, "Installing Additional Software"), and build a new system any time you want to.

The rest of the chapter will discuss how to synchronize your source to one of these targets, and build a new system. The only difference between the two following methods, in practice, is the target tag you use in your CVSup configuration. All tags begin with RELENG, a prefix that stands for RELease ENGineer. It signifies that a branch has been officially initiated by the release engineer on the core FreeBSD team.

Upgrading to a Release Version

The release version tags each have three digits, separated by underscores rather than periods, and have a suffix of RELEASE. Table 18.1 shows how release tags map to version numbers.

TABLE 18.1   Mappings Between Release Tags and Version Numbers

Release Tag	Version Number
RELENG_5_0_0_RELEASE	FreeBSD 5.0
RELENG_4_2_0_RELEASE	FreeBSD 4.2
RELENG_4_1_1_RELEASE	FreeBSD 4.1.1
RELENG_3_5_0_RELEASE	FreeBSD 3.5

Upgrading to an Interim Build

To specify a branch that's in development, leave off the RELEASE suffix and the third digit (which signifies the patch release number). You probably won't need the second digit, since recent releases of FreeBSD have tended more to treating the second digit as the patch release number, moving toward a two-digit numbering system, as shown in Table 18.2.

> **Tip**
>
> Note that Table 18.2 is current as of summer 2001. Due to the dynamic nature of development branches, this information will become obsolete with time. Refer to http://www.freebsd.org/handbook/cvsup.html for a definitive and current table of the appropriate branch tags.

TABLE 18.2 Branch Tags and Version Designations for Interim Versions

Branch Tag	Version Designation
RELENG_5	FreeBSD 5-CURRENT
RELENG_4_3	FreeBSD 4.3-STABLE
RELENG_4	FreeBSD 4-STABLE (No longer maintained)

What Is make world?

Rebuilding your entire system is certainly a more low-level, less "prepackaged" way of upgrading than simply dropping in a CD, but it's in accordance with the FreeBSD way of doing things: a sensibility that building your binaries from pure source is the only way to ensure that your system will truly be compatible with your hardware and your setup. It does involve a lot of steps and a fair amount of risk. However, the regimented structure of FreeBSD helps to mitigate the risk and allows us to enjoy the advantages that this method provides us.

The process of rebuilding the system is known as make world. It provides safeguards that would not normally be available if you were to install precompiled binaries from a CD— for example, if there's anything broken in the source code, it will fail during the compile process, rather than waiting until it's installed on your system before revealing itself to be unusable. The clearest philosophical difference, though, is that it blurs the line between release software and interim builds. A *release* is just a snapshot of the source where it appeared particularly stable, and the process of synchronizing to that snapshot is functionally the same as synchronizing to any other point in the branch—a developer-friendly approach. It encourages administrators to keep their code trees in sync, which is where the real advantage comes in: The most recent security patches and bug fixes are always at your fingertips. All you typically have to do to update an individual part of your system is to go to that part of the source, build it, and install it. You're instantly up to date. We will discuss updating individual components through this method when we discuss network security in Chapter 29; for right now, we will concentrate on rebuilding the entire system—the entire world—on a periodic basis.

Making the world consists of four main steps: building and installing the world (or everything in the core system aside from the kernel) and then building and installing the kernel. Before you do any of these things, though, there are naturally some preparations and precautions that must be addressed.

Things to Consider Before Making the World

The risks of building your system from scratch are not insignificant. On a high-profile production server, you may deem them too great for making the world to be a viable upgrade method. It's a simple matter to wait for each full release on CD, and you may prefer to go that route instead. Let's look at the risks involved, though, so the decision not to build a system from interim sources can be an informed one.

First of all, and most obviously, a make world will involve at least one reboot. If you're concerned about your uptime, or if your system absolutely must be online at all times (as with a high-profile network server), you would probably be best served by upgrading to each successive RELEASE version and applying the necessary patches in between releases.

It's also not a guaranteed process. The FreeBSD Group makes no claims that a make world will not completely destroy your system (though the same is true for any upgrade path, really). The real issue is that frequently rebuilding the operating system gives it that many more chances to blow up. It's absolutely the best way to keep on top of all the latest bug fixes, but it's also an excellent way to find yourself running a system with untested new features or code changes, or even to find that your sources won't build because by pure bad luck, you've picked a point to synchronize your sources, just when some unstable code was being checked in. Remember, the STABLE and CURRENT code branches are living, breathing creatures—they're not "release" quality, nor are they intended to be. Any interim code between releases should be regarded as beta-quality at best. Rebuilding the entire system between releases is really something you should do only if you're using your FreeBSD machine as a workstation or a small, non-critical server, or if there is absolutely no other way for you to get a critical bug fix or new feature.

If you do track either STABLE or CURRENT, it cannot be stressed enough that you should be subscribed to the `freebsd-stable@freebsd.org` or `freebsd-current@freebsd.org` mailing list (as appropriate). These lists serve as forums for anyone tracking the branch to discuss problems, new bug fixes or features, and possible pitfalls for anyone choosing to synchronize their sources at a particular time. A committer might post to `freebsd-stable@freebsd.org`, for instance, warning everyone not to `make world` for at least the next couple of weeks until they've had a chance to test the risky new feature they just put in. If you're not on the mailing list and the feature turns out to be less stable than they'd hoped for, you could end up with an unstable or insecure system, which is exactly what you're trying to avoid by tracking the sources.

> **Note**
>
> Both mailing lists are standard `majordomo` lists. You can subscribe to either one by sending an email to `majordomo@freebsd.org` (with the message body as follows):
>
> `subscribe freebsd-stable`
>
> *Do not send* the subscription request itself to `freebsd-stable` or `freebsd-current`! This is one of the Internet's most common mistakes! These addresses are for the actual list traffic, not for control commands.
>
> That's all there is to it. You will receive a confirmation message; return it to be added to the mailing list. To unsubscribe, do the same thing, except replace the word `subscribe` with `unsubscribe`.

It's important to note that even though you might choose not to run the `make world` process regularly, it's still an excellent idea, in almost all circumstances, to `track` the sources. All this does is synchronize your sources (everything within `/usr/src`) to the current state of either the STABLE or CURRENT code branch. It doesn't affect the operation of your system at all. You can then choose to `make world`—compiling all those sources into a completely new system—or, because the build process is as hierarchical as the filesystem in which it resides, you can simply go to any point within `/usr/src` and build that component individually. This is how you will generally patch your system in response to a security advisory. We will discuss security advisories in Chapter 29, "Network Security."

Above all, remember that upgrading a FreeBSD system is not a reversible process. You can't deinstall a newer version and have the older version still work as it used to. The best we can do is to take as many precautions as we can.

Bug Tracking and Problem Reports

The FreeBSD bug-tracking database is online. You can view the status of all open bugs and feature requests at http://www.FreeBSD.org/cgi/query-pr-summary.cgi, or go to http://www.freebsd.org and follow the links to "Bug Reports" and the GNATS bug database.

You can also submit bug reports of your own; indeed, that's how a lot of these bugs get filed. The tool to use is called send-pr. Simply run that command, and you will be placed into your preferred text editor with a template file that contains certain information about your system as well as a number of input fields that you need to fill out with the relevant data about the bug you're submitting. When you save and exit, the problem report will be sent directly into the GNATS database and reviewed by the committers.

Of course, you'll want to make sure that the bug you're reporting hasn't already been submitted. Search the preceding URL for any specific relevant text in any of the open reports. Also, you'll want to be subscribed to the appropriate mailing list: freebsd-stable or freebsd-current, as we discussed earlier. It's a good idea to post to the appropriate list before submitting a problem report, and ask whether anyone else has seen the problem before you send-pr it. It's fairly likely that someone will have already noticed it and may even have a temporary workaround to suggest to you.

Pre-make world Tasks

So, you've chosen to rebuild your system. Whether you're going to synchronize to interim sources along one of the development branches or whether you simply want to upgrade to the next RELEASE through this method, there are a number of things you'll need to do before embarking on the rather convoluted process. A lot of things can go wrong. It pays to follow the game plan.

The most crucial admonishment before you upgrade is to make a backup of your system. Many readers will undoubtedly ignore this warning and proceed anyway—I'm guilty of this myself—but if you can possibly manage the cost and hassle of setting up a backup solution, it's absolutely worth it. Nothing is more heartbreaking than performing a simple, routine upgrade, only to find that your filesystem is destroyed and all your users' data irretrievably lost. Backup solutions might include tape drives, optical disks (CD-R, DVD-RAM, DVD-R, and so on), a second hard drive that you mount only when you need to mirror your first drive's contents onto it, or a second machine that you keep synchronized via NFS or CVSup. (We'll cover some of these methods in Chapter 20, "FreeBSD Survival Guide.")

Pay attention to the mailing list for your chosen branch. Make sure this is an opportune time to upgrade. If it's not, and you desperately need just a certain patch or bug fix, see if there's a way to rebuild just that one component.

The next step, before you can really do anything further to prepare yourself for the build, is to synchronize your sources. The setup for this need only be done once. From then on, it's an automatable process.

Synchronizing Your Source Tree with the STABLE or CURRENT Tree or a RELEASE

There are a number of ways to synchronize your sources. The methods suggested by the FreeBSD developers include CTM, Anonymous CVS, and CVSup—and each one has its own particular advantages. You can read more about each of these at the FreeBSD Web site under the "Synchronizing Your Source" heading of the Handbook. Here, though, we'll only be covering CVSup because it's the most advanced and efficient (not to mention coolest) option available.

Using CVSup

We discussed how to set up CVSup in Chapter 15. The process described there is exactly the process you need to use here, so if you haven't set up CVSup using the cvsupit port, as described in that chapter, please refer to it now and follow the same procedure. There are a few differences to note, however.

1. When `cvsupit` prompts you for the source branch to use (the first screen), select the one appropriate to your system. If you're tracking the STABLE sources, select the topmost STABLE branch in the list that matches your system's version. For instance, if you're running 4.3-RELEASE, use `RELENG_4_3`. But if you're really cutting edge and want to use the latest and least tested code of all, select the very first entry: ".", the HEAD of the source tree.

2. In the next screen, simply hit Enter to select all available source components. It's not really advisable or necessary to pick and choose particular components; this capability is only there for experts who need that kind of flexibility.

3. Go ahead and accept the defaults to track the ports and doc collections as well. It's a good idea to synchronize those trees at the same time. However, you can disable these secondary updates by editing /etc/cvsupfile and commenting them out.

The cvsupit tool will offer to run the update now; go ahead and do this. After it finishes, you will probably want to add the update command to your daily periodic file, as described in Chapter 15. From now on, every day you'll have sources that are no less than a day old.

Pay attention to the contents of each update output mail you get! When you're tracking STABLE or CURRENT, these messages will tell you each day what has changed. This way, you'll know exactly when a crucial bug fix has been applied to a certain component you're watching.

Using CVSup to Synchronize to RELEASE Sources

CVSup is an excellent way to get the sources for a RELEASE snapshot, as well as to synchronize to interim sources. To do this, you simply need to use the branch tag that specifies the release you want (as discussed earlier in the chapter). However, cvsupit doesn't let you do this automatically.

Your best bet is to run cvsupit to create the /etc/cvsupfile and then elect not to run the update at this time. Exit from cvsupit and open /etc/cvsupfile in your editor. It will look something like Listing 18.1.

LISTING 18.1   Sample /etc/cvsupfile Created by cvsupit

```
*default   host=cvsup8.FreeBSD.org
*default   base=/usr
*default   prefix=/usr
*default   release=cvs
*default   tag=RELENG_4
*default   delete use-rel-suffix

src-all
*default tag=.
ports-all
doc-all
```

Simply change the tag line to the release tag you want. For example, 4.3-RELEASE sources can be had with the following line:

```
*default   tag=RELENG_4_3_0_RELEASE
```

Now, when you run the CVSup update from this file, you'll have the "frozen" sources for the release you've chosen, and (unlike with the constantly changing STABLE and

CURRENT branches) if you update again a week later, nothing will have changed. You can now `make world` from these sources, and change the release tag in `/etc/cvsupfile` back to what it was before; then, resume daily synchronizations so you can have all the latest source patches and updates at your disposal. This will probably be a more agreeable upgrade method for you if you have a critical server to keep updated.

Troubleshooting Questions

There are quite a number of things that can go wrong with CVSup, and because it's a type of task that has no analog on most other operating systems, it's hard to tell when the process has gone as planned, and when it has abjectly failed. Let's look at a few common problem areas and how to remedy them.

- **CVSup won't connect to the server I've selected (Connection refused).**

  Try picking a different CVSup server. The higher the number (for example, `cvsup8.freebsd.org`), the less traffic it is likely to be sustaining. Also, try to run CVSup at a time of day when traffic will be minimal (the middle of the night, for example).

- **CVSup connects, but nothing ever happens.**

  This might occur if you're behind a firewall or a NAT router that masks your IP address. CVSup is known to work with NAT-enabled network configurations, but a misconfigured one might cause problems. Also, make sure your firewall will allow CVSup traffic. The server port is 5999.

- **CVSup deleted my entire /usr/src directory!**

  This will occur if you've specified an invalid branch tag. If you give it a tag that the server doesn't recognize, it will respond by giving you the contents of the CVS tree at the branch you've specified—which is nothing. Make sure you've got the right branch tag, and you should be all right.

The UPDATING Text File

Now that your sources are updated, you'll have a current UPDATING file in `/usr/src`. This file is a "Late-Breaking News" bulletin that has important information on upgrading your system, almost guaranteed to be more current than anything you read in print or online (this book is no exception). UPDATING contains a reverse chronological listing (each with a date stamp) of notable changes to the build process that you should know about. Read all of them between the top of the file and the date of your last `make world`. If anything appears there that is not covered here, it's for an excellent reason.

Something to remember is that /etc is not altered automatically by the make world process. Any configuration files you have in there will not be overwritten. This ensures that your custom system setup won't be lost; it also means that whenever the default system configuration requires something new to be added to or deleted from /etc, you'll have to merge it in manually. The UPDATING file usually details cases like this. Fortunately, we have a neat tool called mergemaster, which allows for an easy merge of new files into /etc. We'll discuss mergemaster after we cover the make world process itself.

Merging /etc/group and /etc/passwd

Most of the /etc files will not affect your ability to build the system. However, occasionally new services are added that have to be installed with ownership matching a certain user and group. Remember that make world is not an installer application with built-in upgrade tasks; it's simply the process of recompiling and installing a new version of the operating system on top of the old. This means that it most likely won't create users and groups that it needs if they don't already exist. You can help avoid any collisions arising from this by merging any new entries into your /etc/group file.

The new version is in /usr/src/etc/group. It probably won't be any longer than 20 lines or so. Open /etc/group in another terminal window. Now, check to see if there are any entries in /usr/src/etc/group that are not in /etc/group. If there are, simply copy them over. Any new entries will likely have GIDs below 100.

One easy way to compare the two files is with diff, as shown in Listing 18.2.

LISTING 18.2   Comparing /etc/group and /usr/src/etc/group with diff

```
# diff -c /etc/group /usr/src/etc/group | less
*** /etc/group   Wed May  2 09:57:10 2001
--- /usr/src/etc/group   Fri Aug 27 16:23:41 1999
***************
*** 8,24 ****
  bin:*:7:
  news:*:8:
  man:*:9:
- wheel:*:10:root,frank,joe
  games:*:13:
  uucp:*:66:
  xten:*:67:xten
  dialer:*:68:
+ network:*:69:
- mysql:*:88:
- users:*:100:
  nogroup:*:65533:
  nobody:*:65534:
```

Groups in your existing /etc/group are shown with a -, and new groups in /usr/src/etc/group have a +. In our example, you will need to copy the network group into your /etc/group file.

It's important to preserve the GIDs suggested in the new group file. In the unlikely event that any of the GIDs don't match, you'll want to fix your existing /etc/group to match the new file. This might cause some existing files in your system (that were owned by that group) to lose their permissions. You can search the system for these files with the find command:

```
# find / -group <GID> -print
```

You can then fix the permissions on these files with chmod, as we saw in Chapter 10, "Users, Groups, and Permissions."

It's even less likely that any mismatches will occur in the user database; the sources don't include a passwd file, as a matter of fact—just a /usr/src/etc/master.passwd file. It's even shorter than the new group file. Quickly scan it and your /etc/master.passwd file for mismatches, and use adduser to insert any new users you find.

Merging /etc/make.conf

The make.conf files are the global configuration files that control all make operations, including make world. You don't have an /etc/make.conf file in a new installation of FreeBSD, but (in the same way that /etc/rc.conf and /etc/defaults/rc.conf work) there's an /etc/defaults/make.conf that specifies all the likely default settings. You'll most likely be okay leaving things as they are. However, you can speed things up a bit with the judicious use of a few options.

The FreeBSD handbook suggests enabling the following lines (by copying them out of /etc/defaults/make.conf into /etc/make.conf and uncommenting them):

```
CFLAGS= -O -pipe
NOPROFILE=     true    # Avoid compiling profiled libraries
```

There are other options you can set if you want to experiment, but that's beyond the scope both of this chapter and of this book.

Rebuilding Your System from Sources

We're now ready to go. This is a process consisting of a good number of steps, so we'll take our time with it.

The make world process itself consists of four main compilation steps, listed in Table 18.3. They can be reduced to two steps if you're feeling exceptionally confident. For this first time through the make world procedure, we'll take each step individually.

TABLE 18.3   Steps Involved in a Complete make world Process

Four-Step Command	Two-Step Command	Meaning
make buildworld	make world	Builds and installs everything but the kernel
make installworld	make buildkernel	Builds and installs the kernel
make kernel	make installkernel	

The make world and make kernel commands should be used only by seasoned veterans who really know what they're doing. For the rest of us, the four individual make commands are what we'll want to use. However, we won't be using those commands shown in the preceding order! We'll actually be building the world first; then building and installing the kernel; then installing the rest of the world. The steps for doing this are detailed as follows.

Cleaning Out `/usr/obj`

This step won't be necessary if this is the first time you've done a make world. If it isn't, you'll probably want to clean out everything in /usr/obj; it will speed things up and prevent collisions when the system runs into files it can't overwrite.

/usr/obj is where the object files (compiled components) are stored after being compiled and before being installed. Deleting them, however, isn't necessarily as easy as simply doing an rm -rf inside that directory. Making the world creates certain files with the schg flag (the "system immutable" flag), which means that the file can't be deleted even if you're root. This is a safety measure intended only to provide an extra means of protection against accidents (such as rm -rf \.*). To get around this and clean out the build directory properly, use the following commands:

```
# cd /usr/obj
# chflags -R noschg *
# rm -rf *
```

You won't be able to do this so easily if the securelevel is set to 1 or higher (this is a system-wide security setting that you select during installation or in /etc/rc.conf; see man securelevel and Chapter 29 for details); it will prevent you from unsetting the schg flags. You will have to reboot into single-user mode to complete this step properly.

Start an Output Log

You'll want to keep a log of the output from your make world; if anything goes wrong, you can review it for clues and (if necessary) post the relevant parts of it to the appropriate mailing list. Chances are that since an error will cause the compile to fail immediately, you'll have the relevant lines in your scrollback buffer, but it's still handy to have a transcript of the entire process to peruse if you need to.

Use the script command to accomplish this. This command effectively runs a shell-within-a-shell, capturing all output into the file you choose. You remain in the script shell until you type exit to return to your regular shell.

```
# script ~/buildworld.out
Script started, output file is ~/buildworld.out
# make buildworld

...

# exit
Script done, output file is ~/buildworld.txt
```

The argument to script specifies the target file that will contain all the build output. It's a good idea to name this file according to the build step you're about to capture. Since each time you run script with the same target filename it overwrites that file rather than appending to it, you'll probably want to run script separately—and have a separate target file—for each step in the make world process.

> **Caution**
>
> Don't specify a target file in /tmp! Files in /tmp are deleted on boot, so you won't have your output files when the system comes back up.

make buildworld

Here's where the fun really begins. Go to /usr/src, take a final look around to make sure everything looks okay, and enter the first make step.

```
# make buildworld
```

Now, sit back and watch. The buildworld process will probably take an hour or two, depending on your hardware. You can speed it up by using the `-j` option to run multiple simultaneous processes:

```
# make -j4 buildworld
```

This is useful even on a single-CPU system, but if you have multiple processors, you can get still more performance from higher values (try as many as 10).

The build process takes a vaguely alphabetical, recursive path through /usr/src. You can track its progress by looking through the directories in /usr/obj. Once you see it compiling things in /usr/src/usr.sbin, you'll know you're near the end.

Troubleshooting Questions

As with CVSup, the process of building a complete operating system is probably an unfamiliar one, and you will undoubtedly run into some problems. We will now look at a few of the more common ones.

- **The compiler fails with "signal 11" errors.**

  Signal 11 refers to a segmentation fault in the compiler, which most frequently occurs due to hardware issues. Check to see whether your CPU is overclocked; this can frequently cause problems with FreeBSD when you do processor-intensive things such as compiling software. If you're not overclocking, suspect your RAM or other hardware.

- **The compiler fails with a lot of "`*** Error code 1 ***`" lines.**

  This is the generic error when the build fails at any certain point. The buildworld won't proceed if any part of it fails, so the last few lines of output leading up to the failure are the most useful.

First, make sure you have completely removed the contents of /usr/obj before compiling. Leaving the objects from previous builds intact can save time, but it can also cause spurious failures if the compiler fails to realize it has to rebuild some component. Clean out /usr/obj, as shown earlier, and try again.

If this doesn't help, search the mailing list archives at http://www.freebsd.org (in the mailing list that pertains to your code branch—stable/freebsd-stable or current/freebsd-current) on the relevant keywords from your output. If you find nothing useful, post a question to the relevant mailing list, citing the output of uname -a, the time of your last CVSup, and the relevant final few lines from the compiler output.

Upgrading the Kernel

Okay, your "userland" (user-accessible files, or everything but the kernel) is now built and ready to be installed. First, though, we need to get the new kernel built and installed.

Upgrading a GENERIC kernel

If you're running a GENERIC kernel (see Chapter 17, "Kernel Configuration," for details), the process is simple:

```
# make buildkernel
# make installkernel
```

Or, even more simply:

```
# make kernel
```

Now your new kernel is installed as /kernel (/boot/kernel on FreeBSD 5.0) and the old one is at /kernel.old (/boot/kernel.old on FreeBSD 5.0).

Upgrading a Custom Kernel

This process is made a bit more complex if you're running a custom kernel. The adventurous might try building a new version of the custom kernel and running with that, but we're going to set up a safety net by building a GENERIC kernel first and keeping it on hand to boot with it if we have to. We'll also have our old kernel (the one currently running) as a fallback if all else fails.

Still within /usr/src, enter the following:

```
# make buildkernel KERNCONF=GENERIC
```

This is your first backup kernel, a GENERIC one built from the new sources. Now, if you haven't done this already, copy /boot/kernel to /boot/kernel.prev (or some other name to indicate that this is the kernel you were already running and that you know works). Next, install the newly built kernel:

```
# make installkernel KERNCONF=GENERIC
```

Next, copy this kernel to kernel.GENERIC:

```
# cp /boot/kernel /boot/kernel.GENERIC
```

Now, to build your first-choice kernel—the custom one built from the new sources:

```
# make buildkernel KERNCONF=CUSTOM
```

Naturally, replace CUSTOM with whatever the name of your custom kernel is. Now, install the new custom kernel as /boot/kernel:

```
# make installkernel KERNCONF=CUSTOM
```

So, to recap, here's our lineup of kernels, shown in Table 18.4.

TABLE 18.4   Newly Available Kernels (FreeBSD 4.4)

Kernel	Description
/kernel	New custom kernel
/kernel.GENERIC	New GENERIC kernel
/kernel.old	Old tried-and-true kernel

When you reboot, if the first kernel fails, try booting with the new GENERIC kernel (as described in Chapter 11). If that fails, boot with the previously working kernel, and you'll be back to where you started.

Troubleshooting Questions

Building and installing the kernel is the riskiest stage yet in the make world process, and the safeguards in the system that protect the kernel during this process add to the arcane nature of the procedure by being quite user-unfriendly. Here are a few common failure modes and their solutions.

- **The compiler fails.**

   The kernel sources can fail to build for the same reasons that building the rest of the system can fail. If you can't resolve the failure yourself, try the mailing lists.

- **The system won't let me install my new kernel!**

   If you've set the securelevel to 1 or higher, make installkernel won't be able to remove the schg flag on the kernel. You will have to reboot into single-user mode to complete each step of the process. Remember that when you boot into single-user mode (using boot -s from the loader prompt), none of the filesystems will mount automatically; you'll need to run mount -a before you can go into /usr/src and run the make installkernel process.

make installworld

After you've completed your kernels, it's time to reboot into single-user mode, which prevents multiuser processes (either run by other users or by daemons operating automatically) from altering files that we'll be upgrading. Collisions of this type can lead to serious instability. Single-user mode is also a good idea simply because of a slight speed advantage, and because it's nice to be able to bring the system back online completely upgraded and ready to go.

Reboot into single-user mode by using the reboot command. When you reach the loader (the countdown phase), press a key to get the loader prompt and then enter the boot -s command to bring the system up far enough for you to verify that the new kernel is working and to complete the installation.

> **Note**
>
> If the system fails to come up (it might crash, it may spew error messages, or there may be any number of different failure modes), reboot again, and try booting single-user with the backup kernel, as we saw a little earlier. Keep trying kernels until you reach the one you were previously using (which should boot without trouble—so far, the kernel is the only thing you've changed in the system). You may want to postpone your make world and try again from scratch after you've resolved the problem with your new kernel. Chances are that a kernel failure at this point is indicative of a more widespread and temporary problem that will be resolved in the source in the near future.

In single-user mode, you're root by default. Go back into /usr/src now and enter the final, most important part of the make world process. Installing the system binaries won't take as long as building them, but there is an equal chance of errors occurring—and this time, a failure will result in a partially altered system. Make sure to start your script output log before you begin this step.

```
# make installworld
```

After this step completes, your binaries and kernel should be compatible; try running utilities such as ps and top to make sure they work properly. You'll get errors if the kernel and the binaries aren't built from the same source base, so if the utilities work, you can be pretty confident that you successfully installed everything so far.

Troubleshooting Questions

Anything that goes wrong during the make installworld step is potentially dangerous—you will end up with a partially installed system, some of it compatible with the new kernel, some of it not. Fortunately, there are fewer things that can potentially go wrong than in the other stages.

- **The installer fails citing a problem with permissions or ownership.**

  This is the reason for synchronizing your /etc/group and /etc/master.passwd files before installing the world. Check again to make sure some user or group isn't missing and try again.

Using `mergemaster` to Check for Changed Configuration Files

There's only one step left to go: merging the /etc hierarchy (and other miscellaneous areas such as /var/log and /usr/share). As we discussed earlier, the `make world` steps don't touch /etc, in order to keep from stomping on heavily customized configurations. In earlier days, the only way to merge changes into /etc was to do it manually, a very painful and error-prone process. The `mergemaster` utility, a standard part of FreeBSD, makes this process a great deal simpler and safer.

There are a lot of safeguards built into `mergemaster`; it's a very safe tool to use. Nevertheless, there always exists the risk of damaging your configuration, so as a precaution, you should make a backup copy of /etc. Fortunately, this is easily done:

```
# cp -Rp /etc /etc.old
```

Typically, `mergemaster` doesn't really need any options; its defaults are set to sensible behaviors. This first time through, we'll probably want to add the -v option (verbose, to explain what it's doing at each step) and the -c option (to use contextual diffs instead of unified ones).

```
# mergemaster -cv
```

The first thing `mergemaster` does is create a temporary root directory and install everything from the relevant sources into it, including the various trees of files that need to be "installed" rather than simply copied over. This "staging area," by default, is in /var/tmp/temproot. It shows you a listing of files that only exist in /etc and not in the temporary root directory (generally, these are files you have added yourself, so it won't touch them.) Then, it proceeds to compare all the files in /etc and certain other locations with the new ones in /var/tmp/temproot; whenever it encounters files that don't match, it displays the `diff` output in whatever pager you have specified in the PAGER environment variable (or `more` by default). When you scroll to the bottom of the `diff` display, you are given a list of choices for what to do with the new file, similar to Listing 18.3.

LISTING 18.3   Options for Merging a File in `mergemaster`

```
***************
*** 321,326 ****
--- 327,333 ----
  kern_securelevel="-1" # range: -1..3 ; '-1' is the most insecure
  update_motd="YES"     # update version info in /etc/motd (or NO)
  start_vinum=""              # set to YES to start vinum
```

LISTING 18.3 continued

```
+ unaligned_print="YES" # print unaligned access warnings on the alpha (or NO).

  ################################################################
  ### Define source_rc_confs, the mechanism used by /etc/rc.* ##

  Use 'd' to delete the temporary ./etc/defaults/rc.conf
  Use 'i' to install the temporary ./etc/defaults/rc.conf
  Use 'm' to merge the old and new versions
  Use 'v' to view to differences between the old and new versions again

  Default is to leave the temporary file to deal with by hand

How should I deal with this? [Leave it for later]
```

As you can see, the default behavior is to do nothing, leaving the new file in /var/tmp/temproot for you to consider after you've finished running. This makes mergemaster a very safe utility to run.

If you select 'm' to merge the two files, you will be dropped into the sdiff environment. This shows you the old and new versions of the changed file, line by line, allowing you to choose between the left (old) and right (new) versions of each.

```
  *** Type h at the sdiff prompt (%) to get usage help

pccard_beep="1"        # pccard beep | pccard_beep="2"        # pccard beep
%
```

Since each changed line is shown on different halves of the same screen, sometimes the two sides will look the same because the only differences might be on the right side of the line. This isn't usually a problem (the only time it tends to crop up is on version-number lines in which a modification date appears toward the end of the line). You can get around it, though, by specifying a larger screen width with the -w option to merge-master:

```
# mergemaster -cv -w 120
```

The sdiff command options are available by typing 'h' at the prompt. Once you're done picking your way through the lines, you'll be brought back into mergemaster, where you are given yet another chance to review (or even re-merge) your changes before moving the new file into place.

Once you're all done, mergemaster asks you if you want to delete what's left of /var/tmp/temproot; if you've left unmerged files to deal with later, select "no". You'll exit from mergemaster and have the chance to go to /var/tmp/temproot to merge these remaining files by hand.

Troubleshooting Questions

The things that can go wrong with `mergemaster`, fortunately, aren't destructive to the system, especially if you have backed up your /etc directory. A few kinds of missteps are common, though, so let's look at them.

- **I accidentally overwrote a critical file in /etc with the generic new version!**

  Not to worry; if you kept a backup (for example, /etc.old), you can simply quit `mergemaster` with Ctrl+C, and copy the file out of the backup directory and back into /etc.

- **Mergemaster accidentally deleted the rest of the files in /var/tmp/temproot! I was going to get to those!**

  Just run `mergemaster` again, and ignore any files you already replaced or merged. Make sure to select "no" at the last prompt, where it asks if you want to delete the remainder of /var/tmp/temproot.

Rebooting After the Upgrade

Make a mental checklist:

- Have I synchronized to the latest sources?
- Have I done a `buildworld`?
- Did I compile a new kernel?
- Did the new kernel boot?
- Have I done an `installworld`?
- Do utilities such as `ps` and `top` work?
- Is /etc merged to my satisfaction?

If you can say "yes" to all of these, you're ready to reboot.

```
# reboot
```

When the system comes back up into multiuser mode, check `ps` and `top` again just to make sure everything's synchronized. Finally, run `uname -a` to see if you agree with the kernel version:

```
# uname -a
FreeBSD stripes.somewhere.com 4.3-STABLE FreeBSD 4.3-STABLE #0: Wed Jan 31
18:45:43 PST 2001 frank@somewhere.com:/usr/src/sys/compile/CUSTOM  i386
```

If it all checks out, congratulations! You've just completed a `make world`. You can rest easy—at least until the next time you decide to do it.

Understanding Hard Disks and Filesystems

This chapter will try to make sense of what is surely one of the ugliest parts of dealing with a UNIX system: disks. Compared to a Windows system (where a disk is automatically assigned a drive number by the BIOS) or a Macintosh (where a new disk simply appears on the desktop), UNIX systems require a deeper knowledge of geometry, partitions, access modes, and other such esoterica. FreeBSD is, unfortunately, no exception.

As we discussed in Chapter 9, "The FreeBSD Filesystem," the hierarchical filesystem structure of UNIX does allow us a more flexible way of dealing with files than is provided by traditional desktop operating systems (refer to Figure 9.2, illustrating the different "tree" metaphors of the two systems). This flexibility does come at a price. To add a new disk to the system, it must first be installed in the proper physical position; and then sliced, partitioned, labeled, and finally mounted at the selected mount point. This is a far cry from the two or three steps necessary in most desktop systems. Times are changing, though, and nowadays the progress of hardware standards has allowed us to dispense with some of the really nasty underlying pencil-and-paper work that used to accompany the installation of a new disk. With the right knowledge (and the help of our good friend `sysinstall`), we'll get the process the rest of the way under control.

IDE/ATA Access Modes

The most common type of hard disk for PC hardware is the IDE (Integrated Drive Electronics) interface, so named because the controller chips that control the disk are integrated into the drive itself rather than on a separate host adapter card (as with SCSI). The official name for this type of interface is ATA, or Advanced Technology Attachment, and ATA and IDE are often used interchangeably. We will discuss both IDE/ATA and SCSI disk systems in this chapter. You'll most likely be using IDE disks. They're inexpensive and ubiquitous, but they come with their share of annoyances and quirks. Paying the extra money for a SCSI disk system means you can avoid many of these troubles. Nonetheless, whether you use IDE or not, it's worthwhile to cover these issues so you can be prepared if the need arises.

When outfitting your system, you'll very likely choose IDE disks unless you're going to be running a high-profile server; IDE provides quite adequate speed, and it's the built-in standard on all x86-based motherboards currently on the market. You will have to make a couple of purchasing decisions based on the highest access modes supported by the disk, the motherboard, and FreeBSD. An informed decision on this subject requires a bit of access-mode history.

PIO Modes

Programmed I/O (PIO) modes were the original standard for data transfer on PC hardware using the ATA interface. To this day, they exist as a fallback method because PIO is a built-in part of the BIOS, and it requires no additional support by the operating system; just about every modern operating system has moved on to DMA and Ultra DMA since then, and unless you're using very old hardware it won't matter to you.

The five standard PIO transfer modes and their speeds are listed in Table 19.1.

TABLE 19.1   PIO Transfer Modes

PIO Mode	Maximum Transfer Rate	Defining Standard
Mode 0	3.3MB/s	ATA
Mode 1	5.2MB/s	ATA
Mode 2	8.3MB/s	ATA
Mode 3	11.1MB/s	ATA-2
Mode 4	16.7MB/s	ATA-2

> **Note**
>
> Most motherboards today use the PCI bus to talk to their hard drive chains. If, however, you've got a really old system with an ISA bus, the best it will be able to support is PIO Mode 2—anything faster is beyond the throughput limit of ISA.

DMA Modes

A fundamental problem with PIO is that it requires significant resources from the CPU to direct its data flow—something that originally was one of the biggest reasons to use SCSI rather than IDE disks because SCSI disks use an independent controller to take the load off the processor. DMA modes, introduced in the early 1990s and listed in Table 19.2, offer this same benefit to IDE disks by allowing the disk to communicate directly with the system RAM, bypassing the CPU. Naturally, this requires specialized electronics in the drive itself (particularly for first-party or "bus mastering" DMA disks), as well as operating system support, but this is almost universal nowadays.

19

UNDERSTANDING
HARD DISKS AND
FILESYSTEMS

TABLE 19.2   DMA Transfer Modes

DMA Mode	Maximum Transfer Rate	Defining Standard
Single Word Mode 0	2.1 MB/s	ATA
Single Word Mode 1	4.2 MB/s	ATA
Single Word Mode 2	8.3 MB/s	ATA
Multiword Mode 0	4.2 MB/s	ATA
Multiword Mode 1	13.3 MB/s	ATA-2
Multiword Mode 2	16.7 MB/s	ATA-2

You may not have heard much about plain DMA during its heyday. This is because, as you can see from the table, its transfer speeds were comparable to those of the PIO modes; whereas DMA disks did benefit from lower CPU overhead, this advantage was mitigated by poor support for the modes in the operating systems of the day, such as Windows 95. PIO was built-in, so there was little pressure on the industry to move away from it.

Ultra DMA (UDMA) Modes

That is, until the introduction of Ultra DMA. These enhanced DMA modes are now the ubiquitous industry standard, even giving SCSI a run for its money as far as performance goes, while remaining cheaper and better supported, even on low-end hardware.

Ultra DMA gave the data transfer speeds a significant and immediate boost over standard DMA by clocking its transfers on twice as many points in the interface strobe, on both the "rising" and "falling" edges of the signal waveform, a technique known as *double transition clocking*; this meant that without the controller having to reduce its cycle time, it could have a "free" doubling of data transfer speed to 33MB/s. Subsequent incremental improvements to Ultra DMA, shown in Table 19.3, have raised the bar ever higher, aided by a new IDE cable standard that uses 80 pins rather than the 40 of the previous standard.

TABLE 19.3   Ultra DMA Transfer Modes

Ultra DMA Mode	Maximum Transfer Rate	Defining Standard
Mode 0	16.7MB/s	ATA/ATAPI-4
Mode 1	25.0MB/s	ATA/ATAPI-4
Mode 2	33.3MB/s	ATA/ATAPI-4
Mode 3	44.4MB/s	ATA/ATAPI-5

TABLE 19.3 continued

Ultra DMA Mode	Maximum Transfer Rate	Defining Standard
Mode 4	66.7MB/s	ATA/ATAPI-5
Mode 5	100.0MB/s	ATA/ATAPI-6

Any hardware made after about 1998 is designed to work in UDMA mode, and you won't have to worry about a thing if you have these four components:

- A hard disk that supports Ultra DMA mode
- An 80-pin IDE cable
- A motherboard (or IDE controller) that supports Ultra DMA mode
- Support in the operating system (or BIOS) for Ultra DMA mode

If you're missing any one of these items, your system will still run—but in a reduced-speed mode, generally one of the PIO modes natively supported in the BIOS. Motherboards or controllers that don't support UDMA might prove troublesome. Issues with instability or lockups caused by controller issues can usually be solved either by upgrading the BIOS (to enable the controller to support UDMA) or by disabling UDMA in the disk itself through software utilities available from the manufacturer of the disk (which typically run only under DOS or Windows, and are either included with the disk or downloadable from the manufacturer's Web site).

FreeBSD fully supports Ultra DMA, making it perhaps the strongest link in this chain; you can see if all the necessary components are present by watching the device-probing messages during boot (or using dmesg afterwards):

```
ad0: 6194MB <HITACHI_DK239A-65> [13424/15/63] at ata0-master using UDMA33
```

If the UDMA capability isn't detected, and the hard disk is new but the rest of the machine's components aren't, you might want to find the disk manufacturer's drive management utility, boot the system from an MS-DOS floppy, and use the utility to disable the disk's UDMA capability. This will keep you running at a lower speed than the disk can go, but it's for the best—the alternative is to run the risk of crashes and lockups, and your system will thank you for not pushing it beyond its means.

SCSI Disks

If all this IDE nonsense is something you can afford to bypass, or if you will be attaching external disks to your system, your alternative is SCSI. At first glance, the litany of SCSI modes (shown in Table 19.4) looks hardly any less bizarre than that of IDE.

TABLE 19.4   SCSI Transfer Modes

Standard	Transfer Mode	Transfer Speed	Max Cable Length	Devices/ Ids	Connector
SCSI-1	SCSI	5MB/s	6m	8	50-pin
SCSI-2	Fast SCSI	10MB/s	3m	8	50-pin
	Wide SCSI	10MB/s	6m	16	68-pin
	Fast Wide SCSI	20MB/s	3m	16	68-pin
SCSI-3	Ultra SCSI	20MB/s	1.5m–3m	4–8	50-pin
	Wide Ultra SCSI	40MB/s	1.5m–3m	4–16	68-pin
	Ultra2 SCSI	40MB/s	12m	8	50-pin
	Wide Ultra2 SCSI	80MB/s	12m	16	68-pin
	Ultra3 SCSI	160MB/s	12m	16	68-pin
	Ultra160 SCSI	160MB/s	12m	16	68-pin
	Ultra320 SCSI	320MB/s	12m	16	68-pin

Nonetheless, for all its "can you top this?" naming conventions, SCSI is relatively well-behaved and predictable when it comes to its capabilities. Each successive standard is twice as fast as the previous, and while there are a truly astonishing number of different cable styles made for SCSI devices, the connector standard has remained mercifully steady over the years. This means that for the most part, any modern SCSI controller will recognize any SCSI device that was built to an earlier standard, and handle it properly.

A SCSI device chain can handle up to the number of devices specified by the standard, usually eight or 16—a far cry from the strictly regimented four (primary and secondary, master and slave) of the IDE/ATA structure. What's more, the order of these devices doesn't matter; there are no such things as "masters" or "slaves" in SCSI to dictate cabling order. There is only the controller, or host adapter (which takes up one of the device IDs), and the rest of the devices.

SCSI also has clear advantages if you're using external disks. IDE/ATA provides no good way to hook an external disk to the internal bus; sometimes you can get away with using the parallel (printer) port, as with Iomega ZIP drives, but this is an astoundingly slow interface, and unusable for any general purpose. SCSI is the only game in town for external disks until FireWire (IEEE 1394) becomes prevalent.

The biggest problem with SCSI is, simply, price. SCSI disks are generally pricier than similar-sized IDE disks by 50–100%. Beyond that, there's the sunk cost of the host adapter card, which you have to buy separately from the motherboard—very few motherboards today are made with built-in SCSI cards (though the number is, in fact, rising). These controllers aren't cheap.

If you're interested in going the SCSI route, there are more pitfalls to avoid that are beyond the scope of coverage here: terminators, the SCSI BIOS, setting device IDs (with jumpers), and what happens when you mix "narrow" and "wide" devices on the same chain. Further reference can be found in many books that are dedicated to the subject, or at the PC Guide Web site (`http://www.pcguide.com`).

Understanding Hard Disk Geometry

You'll see a lot of references to "hard disk geometry" in the online tutorials that explain how to prepare your disks, and you'll run into it every time you run `fdisk` (or the friendlier interfaces to `fdisk` that we'll be using). Fortunately, this is something that owners of newer hardware (that is, hardware manufactured after hard disks larger than 8GB were common) or owners of SCSI disks can skip or ignore. It's only there for informational purposes—its functional importance is now no longer the administrator's responsibility—it's the hardware's.

One of FreeBSD's strengths, though, is that it will run—efficiently—even on older hardware that is considered obsolete for desktop use or to run Windows. Your 166MHz Pentium motherboard will support FreeBSD just fine. But there's a trap: Try to plug in a new 70GB IDE hard disk, and the system might not realize that it's any larger than 8GB. This is where the unpleasantness of disk geometry comes into play. To use the disk, you will need to use some techniques that have otherwise been obsoleted by newer BIOS technology, and to know something about the history of hard disk development.

Back in the mists of time, when registers were made only as large as cost would allow, regardless of future scalability implications, IDE hard disks reported their size as a function of their physical geometry. Four dimensions—heads, cylinders, sectors, and bytes—described the layout of the disk and subsequently its size (see Figure 19.1), or the amount of data that could be stored on it. Hard disks still have the same internal geometry as they always did; it's just no longer as important to understand it thoroughly as it was back then.

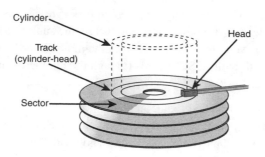

FIGURE 19.1

Hard disk geometry.

A disk is made up of a number of platters, stacked on a central spindle, with data stored on both sides of each platter and one or more magnetic *heads* reading each side. Thus, a disk with four platters and two heads per side would have 16 heads. Each platter is divided into concentric rings, or *cylinders* (not in a spiral configuration, as with optical disks such as CDs), and the combination of a cylinder and the head that reads it is called a *track* (or cylinder-head). Tracks are then divided into *sectors* (usually 64 of them, with 63 usable), and each sector stores a certain number of bytes (generally 512).

Each disk is shipped with information (usually on the label), showing how many of each of these subdivisions exist on the disk. You can calculate the total size of the disk by multiplying all of them together. The disk we used for the demonstration of `fdisk` back in Chapter 9 had the following information:

```
# fdisk /dev/ad1
******* Working on device /dev/ad1 *******
parameters extracted from in-core disklabel are:
cylinders=1247 heads=255 sectors/track=63 (16065 blks/cyl)
Media sector size is 512
```

Multiplying these figures together (ignoring the blocks-per-cylinder figure) and remembering that a cylinder-head is equivalent to a track (to keep our units straight), we get the following:

```
1247 cylinders x 255 heads x 63 sectors/track x 512 bytes/sector = 10.2GB
```

But wait a minute. 255 heads? Does that make sense at all? No, first of all we'd expect the number of heads to at least be an even number. Even if we allowed for that, we're talking about what appears to be at least 64 platters, which just isn't physically possible in a half-inch-high hard disk. What we've got here is a virtual disk geometry, made possible by two successive hacks by the hard disk industry, which get around register-size limitations imposed by the original design of the disk interface in the BIOS. We'll take a look at these two hacks (LBA and Extended INT13 modes) now.

LBA and the 528MB Limit

In the days of floppy disks, nobody ever thought that anyone would ever use a disk as gargantuan as 528MB; this is why that number was allowed to remain as the size limitation imposed by the number of bits the original PC BIOS allocated to each of the disk geometry dimensions, shown in Table 19.5.

TABLE 19.5 Dimensional Limits on Hard Disk Geometry

Dimension	Bit Size	Maximum Value
Cylinders	10 bits	$2^{10} = 1024$
Heads	8 bits	$2^8 = 256$
Sectors/Track	6 bits	$2^6-1 = 63$

So, a disk was allowed to have up to 255 heads, but no more than 1023 cylinders. Since the number of bytes per sector and the number of sectors per track are relatively fixed numbers (dependent on physical limitations such as rotation speed and read reliability), and because you can't really put more than a few platters and heads into a drive you want people to be able to lift, this meant that the cylinder number rapidly emerged as the limiting factor in a disk's ultimate size. Disk manufacturers eventually converged on the ATA standard of 16 physical heads in a disk, so this meant a size limit of 528MB. The manufacturers could produce disks larger than that size by adding more cylinders—which was easy because the stepper motor that moves the head's swingarm between cylinders is controllable very precisely—but the BIOS couldn't address any of the cylinders above 1024.

Around 1993, it became apparent that this wasn't going to fly as users' hunger for disk space continued to grow. A single video game could take up that much space! So, the BIOS manufacturers developed a scheme called *LBA*, or *Logical Block Addressing*, whose purpose was to augment the BIOS disk addressing method by remapping cylinders above 1024 to "virtual heads," thus taking advantage of all the available head numbers up to 255 that were going unused. For example, a disk with 1852 cylinders and only 16 physical heads could actually be thought of as having 463 cylinders and 64 heads. Now the disk's calculated size was unchanged, but both the cylinder and head values were within their BIOS-imposed limits. All was well once again...for a while.

Extended INT13 Modes and the 8.4GB Limit

The alert reader will have noticed that this scheme could only have been considered a temporary solution because eventually LBA would run out of room when both the cylinder and head numbers were completely filled—a disk size that works out to about 8.4GB. Indeed, it wasn't long—another four years or so—before disks were jostling at the 8.4GB barrier. (It should also be noted that 8.4GB was only a theoretical limit; many buggy BIOS implementations and supporting software tools used pseudo-LBA routines that introduced barriers at lower numbers.)

The solution was a newly redesigned BIOS interface, commonly called *Extended INT13*, which is now in general use in modern hardware and is used more and more commonly in the Windows world (where the software still must communicate with the disk through its BIOS, something FreeBSD doesn't need to do). This new interface abstracts the disk geometry addressing through a 16-byte Disk Addressing Packet, effectively removing any size limitation that we are ever likely to see. If your hardware is modern enough to understand the Extended INT13 modes, you're home free—disk geometry need only interest you for curiosity's sake. If you use a tool to try to extract the geometry information from a disk larger than 8.4GB, it will report 16383 cylinders, 16 heads, and 63 sectors per track—a "code" configuration that tells the operating system not to even try to compute the disk's size from its geometry. If you see this configuration being reported anywhere, rest assured that FreeBSD is taking care of all this "geometry" nonsense itself. At least, until IDE disks reach 137GB, where they will be blocked once again by the ATA standard-imposed limit of 65536 cylinders...

Practical Implications

If you're installing FreeBSD on older hardware, such as a motherboard from the days of LBA, you may well run into one of these limitations. You won't lose any data, but you may notice odd problems such as your 10GB disk only reporting 8.4GB total space. If it does, you'll know what the cause is.

Many motherboard and chipset manufacturers will provide BIOS upgrades, which can help get past these problems. Check with the maker of the motherboard or chipset (consult its Web site) to see whether a firmware update is available. If not, you may have no choice but to invest in a new motherboard and CPU, or else to use lots of small disks instead of one large one.

Of course, if you've chosen instead to use SCSI or FireWire (IEEE 1394) hard drives, none of this need apply to you. These interfaces were designed with much more scalability in mind than IDE/ATA was, and so their typically higher price is justified by their behavioral predictability.

Partitioning a Hard Disk

Okay, now that all the background is out of the way, it's time to get down to the action. Adding a new disk to the system involves four steps: installing it, partitioning it, labeling it, and mounting it. Depending on whether you've gone with a SCSI or IDE disk, the installation procedure will vary. The installation instructions that come with the disk will help.

For the following examples, we'll be assuming you've installed a new 40GB IDE disk as the primary slave. The device name, as you'll recall from Chapter 9, will be `/dev/ad1`. (A SCSI disk in a similar configuration would be `/dev/da1`; the rest of the instructions here apply just the same.) There's a lot more to a typical disk device name, though, as you'll also recall. The extensions beyond the initial `ad1` specify additional partitioning information. This is how you refer to specific parts of a disk that you've separated for different uses, either so you can run more than one operating system from the same disk, or so you can keep different parts of your system separate so they won't steal storage space from each other.

BIOS Partitions (Slices)

Every operating system allows you to partition your disk. The thing to remember about FreeBSD, though, is that it allows not one but *two* levels of partitioning. First come the BIOS partitions, addressed directly by the system BIOS in PC hardware; you can have up to four of these, which are what other operating systems think of as "partitions." If you partition your Windows or Macintosh disk, each partition is one of these BIOS partitions.

FreeBSD uses the term "slices" for these BIOS partitions. This is very important to remember. When FreeBSD refers to partitions, it's talking about the second level of partitioning, which occurs within the slices. This second level contains what are properly known as the "BSD partitions."

BSD Partitions

These subpartitions are the ones that separate different parts of a FreeBSD system from each other—`/var`, `/usr`, `/home`, and the like (as we saw in Chapter 9). Each partition has a single letter for a name, and there are eight BSD partitions available, shown in Table 19.6. When you divide a slice into BSD partitions (during the labeling process, which we will get to in a moment), the first few letters are reserved for special uses.

TABLE 19.6 BSD Partitions and Their Purposes

Partition	Purpose
a	Root partition (/)
b	Swap
c	Addresses the entire slice, or the entire disk in "dangerously dedicated" mode. ("Dangerously dedicated" was used in the past to get around geometry detection problems. It is deprecated in FreeBSD 4.4 and FreeBSD 5.0)

TABLE 19.6 continued

Partition	Purpose
d	General use (not used by the Disklabel Editor)
e	General use
f	General use
g	General use
h	General use

Figure 19.2 shows a fully specified device name. The first part (ad1) specifies the base device name. IDE/ATA disks can be ad0 through ad3 (primary master, primary slave, secondary master, secondary slave). Next comes the slice name, whose numbers start at 1 (s1). Finally, we have the BSD partition name (e).

FIGURE 19.2
Understanding a disk device name.

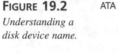 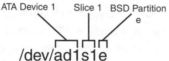

Foreign Extended Partitions

Some other operating systems have constructs analogous to FreeBSD's partitions; for instance, Extended DOS Partitions are a way to get subpartitions (logical partitions) into a DOS/Windows machine. Linux uses a functionally identical method. This is in many ways more awkward than the FreeBSD solution. Interoperability between different operating systems can be fairly tricky; partitions within Extended DOS Partitions are treated by FreeBSD as additional slices on the same level as regular DOS partitions, but starting at slice 5 (after the four regular DOS partitions). To mount the second logical partition within an Extended DOS Partition on a disk installed as ad3, you would address /dev/ad3s6 rather than trying to use BSD-style partition names within a slice.

Going the other direction is even trickier. You probably won't be able to mount a FreeBSD disk in a DOS/Windows system, but you may have to do something like that on a Linux machine. Linux treats its partitions (which we call slices) the same way that FreeBSD treats them, meaning that they're labeled numerically and sequentially, rather than hierarchically. To mount a FreeBSD slice under Linux, use Table 19.7 (which describes a primary slave disk with FreeBSD in its third BIOS partition/slice) for equivalency guidance.

TABLE 19.7 Linux-FreeBSD Disk Label Equivalence

Linux Label	FreeBSD Label
/dev/hdb4	/dev/ad1s3a
/dev/hdb5	/dev/ad1s3b
/dev/hdb6	/dev/ad1s3e
/dev/hdb7	/dev/ad1s3f

This is reliable only if you don't have any more Linux partitions after the FreeBSD slice! This is the peril of expanding a hierarchical structure into a sequential one.

The Slice Editor (`fdisk`) in `sysinstall`

As root, enter the `/stand/sysinstall` program, and select "Configure". Scroll down to the "Fdisk" option, labeled as the "Slice (PC-Style partition) Editor". Selecting this option gives you a list of all the disks the system has detected. Make sure that `ad1` (the primary slave, your new disk) is listed. If it isn't, the disk hasn't been installed properly. Check the `/var/run/dmesg.boot` file to see if the disk was detected at all when the machine booted; if it wasn't, you'll need to check your cabling and the jumpers on the disk. Remember that if you only had a single disk on the primary IDE chain before you installed the new one, its jumpers were probably set to the "Single" position; you'll have to make sure the primary disk's jumpers are set to "Master" and the new disk's jumpers to "Slave".

If your disk is listed, select it with the spacebar, and enter the visual `fdisk` ("fixed disk") editor. This is a utility that exists in some form on every operating system because every PC-hardware-based operating system needs a way to control its BIOS partitions (slices). You can use `fdisk` directly from the command line, but its many options and potential pitfalls make interfacing with it via `sysinstall` a good idea. It's not especially wise to "work without a net" around such things as disk reformatting and repartitioning tools!

Any pre-existing partitions will show up in the menu here; if it's a new unformatted disk, you'll have an essentially empty list of slices. You have a lot of flexibility here. If you really want to, you can do all your slicing here, setting up BIOS partitions for other operating systems or even for FreeBSD, in the Linux or DOS style; this is conventionally unnecessary, though. What you'll want to do, most likely, is to select the "A" option for "Use Entire Disk", whose results are shown in Figure 19.3. Don't worry about any of the other options—they're there for flexibility and compatibility.

19

UNDERSTANDING
HARD DISKS AND
FILESYSTEMS

Figure 19.3

The Slice Editor (after using the "Use Entire Disk" option).

You'll now have three entries: a small "reserved" space for the boot manager to be installed later, a single large FreeBSD slice (ad1s1), and a third "leftover" chunk of negligible space that could not be made part of the main slice.

Nothing has yet been done to the disk. Use the "W" option to write changes that modify the disk's layout; then select "Q" to quit the Slice Editor. You'll now be prompted for what kind of boot manager to install. If this is a secondary disk that you're adding to an already running system, select "None". Install the FreeBSD Boot Manager ("BootMgr") if you will be booting from this disk; for instance, if you're prepping this disk to be used in a new machine or to replace the existing disk in your current system. Otherwise, select "Standard" to do the equivalent of the DOS command fdisk /MBR, which removes operating-specific boot managers (such as Linux's LILO and FreeBSD's BootMgr) from the Master Boot Record and makes it available to other operating systems, for example if you're reusing the disk to make a new Windows machine.

Creating the Disk Labels

The disk is now sliced and made FreeBSD-friendly, but it still isn't formatted—you can't use it in your system yet. That's what we must do next, in the Disklabel Editor.

Still in sysinstall, select "Label", the Disklabel Editor. You'll again be asked to select from the list of installed disks; use the spacebar to select ad1. You'll now be presented with the Disklabel Editor screen, a visual interface to the command-line disklabel command. This is where you assign the BSD partitions and format the disk.

> **Note**
>
> FreeBSD's Disklabel Editor doesn't allow you to resize existing partitions. A partition can't be modified without reformatting it and losing its data, so consider carefully what your partitions will be used for before you commit your changes!

Creating a Complete FreeBSD Partition Layout

If you're just adding a new disk to the system, skip ahead to the "Adding a New Disk" section. This section demonstrates how to use the Disklabel Editor to assign BSD partitions and mount points for a complete FreeBSD system, including a root partition, /usr and /var partitions, and a swap partition. This is useful if you're going to be installing FreeBSD onto the new disk, for example if you're replacing your current disk with a larger one.

Press "A" to accept the "Auto Defaults for all!" settings. This automatically allocates a set of partitions that will be appropriate for most systems (see Figure 19.4), and you can probably go with the defaults if your FreeBSD system will be used as a workstation or a small server with only a few users.

FIGURE **19.4**

The Disklabel Editor (after using the "Auto Defaults for all!" option).

However, these defaults will almost certainly turn out to be woefully inadequate for a high-profile server. Mail and log files both live in the /var partition; if you have 100 users all storing their mail spools on the server, or if your Web server generates 100MB log files, the default /var size of 20MB will be exhausted almost before you can blink. We'll need to allocate some more space to /var; this gives us an excellent excuse to demonstrate some of the more flexible workings of the Disklabel Editor.

First, delete both the /var and /usr partitions. (Remember, nothing will be actually done to the disk itself until you press "W" to write changes; right now you're just setting up the configuration for it to write.) Delete these two partitions by selecting each of them and pressing "D". Now, scroll back up to the top of the screen, where the "Free:" field shows all the space you've recovered by deleting these two partitions. You can now reallocate that space as you see fit.

With the selector bar on the "Partition name: ad1s1" line, press "C" to create a new partition. You are given a dialog box asking how much space to dedicate to the new partition. Let's give /var 200 megabytes; that should be enough for a medium-sized server. (Give it an even higher number if you want to be really safe.) Assign this by deleting the

19

number displayed and entering "200m". Next, select "FS" to create a filesystem instead of a swap partition. You'll then be asked for the mount point; enter "/var". The partition is created and added to the list, and the "Free:" space listed at the top is updated accordingly.

Now you can repeat the process, this time accepting the default size for the remaining partition (to use all the rest of the space on the disk), and entering "/usr" for the mount point. The resulting list will be similar to Figure 19.5.

FIGURE 19.5

A customized partition layout.

Adding a New Disk

You can create up to eight BSD partitions on your new disk. Don't use the "A" option if you're simply creating more space to add to your current system; instead, with the "Partition name: ad1s1" line selected, press "C" to create a new partition. If you want to make one big BSD partition out of the disk (for example, if you want to add all 40GB to /home), accept the default value for the size of the partition—the entire available capacity of the slice you're in. Alternately, you might choose to specify a size (such as "20G") for one partition, and allocate the rest to another partition. It's up to you how to carve up the space.

Select "FS" to create a filesystem rather than swap space and then specify a mount point. This isn't really important in this case. This only specifies what will be written into /etc/fstab for the new filesystem, and this does not happen unless you're doing the initial system installation.

You can continue creating partitions this way until the available space is all consumed. Delete a partition by pressing "D" with that partition selected. Remember, this disk itself is not touched by any of these operations; no changes are written until you press "W".

Note

If you create more than four partitions, the "reserved" partition names will be used, beginning with a and b; c will be skipped because it has a specific

> reserved meaning. Beyond d, however, a "dummy" label of "x" will be used, and you won't be able to use the partition properly.

Writing Changes and Formatting the Disk

Formatting disks in FreeBSD is done with the `newfs` command, another command-line utility that is handled automatically by `sysinstall`. Each filesystem in the list that has a "Y" in the "Newfs" column will be formatted when you commit changes. You can toggle this on and off with the "T" key.

Take a good look at the partition labels that the editor is assigning. These are listed under the "Part" column; you'll notice that no matter how you set up your partitions, the a through d partitions are reserved for special uses, as shown in Table 19.6; the first partition you can create yourself is e. This means that our new mountable partitions, if you're adding space to the existing system, will be ad1s1e, ad1s1f, and so on. You'll need to remember these labels for when you mount the filesystems.

When you're happy with the partition layout, press "W" to write the changes. The disk will be partitioned, and `newfs` processes will be fired off to format each partition you've specified. Once this is done, press "Q" to exit, and then quit `sysinstall`.

Making the Filesystem Available for Use

We're almost done. All that remains now is to mount the new filesystems you've created. You may also want to set up /etc/fstab to mount the filesystems automatically on boot. A full discussion of the `mount` command and how to use /etc/fstab can be found in Chapter 9.

We're dealing with the simplest possible case, though: new, clean FreeBSD-formatted partitions. We can use the `mount` command in its most straightforward way.

Create a directory to act as the mount point, for example /mnt/newdisk. (This can be done anywhere in the filesystem.) Next, issue the `mount` command:

```
# mount /dev/ad1s1e /mnt/newdisk
```

Use the `df` command to verify that the disk is mounted. You can do the same for each new partition you created, placing each one at a different point in the filesystem. Unmount it with the `umount` command:

```
# umount /mnt/newdisk
```

Congratulations—you've tamed FreeBSD disk management!

CHAPTER 20

FreeBSD Survival Guide

The purpose of this chapter is to provide a rough guide to new users of FreeBSD: a trail map showing how to get the system up and stable as quickly as possible. It is especially targeted at administrators coming from other operating systems who will bring certain preconceptions about how FreeBSD might act; this chapter will serve as a guide to shifting those preconceptions to the point where common mistakes born out of inexperience or unfamiliarity can be avoided. If a reader is to choose only one chapter to read out of this book, this should be it.

The first few weeks with any new operating system are the riskiest—accidental misconfigurations can lead to security breaches, data loss, or general long-term disorganization. The key to surviving these first critical weeks is to get the platform-specific pitfalls out of the way and the necessary infrastructural safety nets in place so that you can take the more general administrative learning process more at your leisure.

Newbies and veterans alike should be able to find useful information in this chapter. It will summarize the philosophical differences between FreeBSD and Windows, and between FreeBSD and its much more similar cousin: Linux. It will also cover a set of general traps to avoid and useful tips to help keep the system running smoothly. Finally, we will look at the inevitable spectre of catastrophic system failure; the various weapons at our disposal for preparing for it; and, in the absence of the ability to turn back time, ways to recover from it.

Migrating to FreeBSD

At the time of this writing, and as accurately as these things can be measured (which is to say, not very), FreeBSD has approximately 15% of the open-source UNIX server market. The rest is almost all Linux, with the remainder comprised of NetBSD, OpenBSD, and a few other little-known variants. In the wider server market, Windows NT/2000 claims about a 20–30% share, with UNIX (both commercial and open-source) estimated at about 65%. By any measure, this means FreeBSD is not an especially large player. However, market share alone does not dictate the quality of a piece of software (as anyone reading this book likely knows).

FreeBSD usage is growing. There is a steady stream of Linux-based or commercial UNIX-based businesses moving to FreeBSD for its stability and its performance, desiring an open-source solution that is free of the distribution politics of Linux. Stories also abound of high-profile, Web-based services running on FreeBSD simply because it is the only solution that can handle the load, the services' parent companies' own operating systems notwithstanding. The end result is an increasing respect for FreeBSD in the server community; and a growing desire to move toward its tempting mixture of stability, standards compliance, openness, and power.

Migration away from Windows NT/2000 or Linux means a trade-off of two things: software availability and established practices. These two things are the largest stumbling blocks typically faced by seasoned server veterans eyeing FreeBSD for the first time—the former applying more significantly to Windows; the latter applying to both. We'll look at both of these migration paths in turn, and address these barriers as best we can.

Migrating from Windows NT/2000

Windows NT/2000 is almost exclusively GUI-based, without a mature or widely used remote administration method. This means that to use Windows NT/2000 effectively, you usually need to be physically sitting at the machine. Getting used to a command-line interface to do your work can be a daunting task, but it's crucial to UNIX systems' great advantage of remote accessibility.

> **Tip**
>
> Built-in and third-party components of Windows NT/2000 are gradually increasing the remote accessibility of the platform. These days, you can manage services remotely that are controlled through the Services control panel, and various methods exist to acquire a DOS command line on the server machine. However, these are both subsets of the complete functionality of a system—they're limited to the functionality explicitly built in to the control mechanism you're using. Complete configurability of installed server software often relies on administrative client programs, as we will discuss next.

Client-Server Applications

Most enterprise software for Windows servers is developed on a model in which you install the server portion physically (generally from CD), and then install an administrative portion—a client—on your desktop machine, and on anyone else's machine who will be administering the server. There are "terminal server" packages available, which allow you to control the server machine itself directly, but due to the extreme graphical intensiveness of the Windows GUI, these tools are not simple or elegant to use. There's a major philosophical shift to accept when moving to UNIX.

There are virtually no specialized client-server applications for FreeBSD. Some operate through a graphical Web-based interface accessed by a common Web browser (for example, streaming audio/video servers, calendaring servers, and the like), but for the most part all administration takes place through a remote terminal. Telnet (or SSH) is the dominant all-purpose tool for doing anything in the UNIX world. Technologically, it's one of the most efficient and streamlined methods imaginable of working with the server—all you're sending and receiving is text—but it's also the most versatile, giving you much wider access to the server's operations than any graphical tool could. Naturally, though, this also means you have more power to break things. It's a trade-off: the ease of use, safety, and directed functionality of Windows client-server software for the versatility, risk, and esoterica of terminal-based administration.

Security

Whole books have been written on Windows NT/2000's security model, and it's well beyond the scope of this one. However, if you're used to the Windows style of users, domains, and permissions and you're moving to FreeBSD, there are a few things you'll want to know that will help you keep your security model roughly intact.

The "root" account is the equivalent of "Administrator". That is hardly a secret. However, beyond that there are a few things you can do to keep your services running with their accustomed privileges, and to give your trusted administrators exactly as much power as they need—and no more. The first step is to know what some of the fundamental differences are between Windows NT/2000's and FreeBSD's security models.

- FreeBSD primarily uses the User, Group, and Other mode bits to specify ownership and permissions, whereas Windows NT/2000 uses Access Control Lists. In FreeBSD 5.0, usage of ACLs is also possible, as we discussed in Chapter 10, "Users, Groups, and Permissions," but in Windows NT/2000, it is much more prevalent than in FreeBSD.

- Windows NT/2000 has a concept of "trusted paths", allowing implicit authentication of users coming from specified hosts. For instance, you can tell Windows to "trust" any user connecting from a particular computer under some or all circumstances, eliminating the need for user authentication where it isn't necessary. FreeBSD doesn't have this capability unless you use Kerberos, as we will see in Chapter 29, "Network Security."

- Login names in FreeBSD must be 16 characters or fewer, and contain only lowercase characters or digits. No spaces or special characters are allowed.

- Windows NT/2000 has as many as 27 different assignable user rights for file modification and execution with various privileges. FreeBSD distinguishes between processes executed by root (the super-user); processes executed by individual users; and processes executed in "setuid" or "set-user-ID" mode, in which the process takes on the privileges of whoever owns the executed file.

- FreeBSD and UNIX don't have hierarchical groups. Windows NT/2000 allows you to place a group of users inside another group, to an arbitrary depth; this is not possible in FreeBSD. All groups exist at the same "level".

- Windows "domains" don't exist in the UNIX world. Instead, remote authentication services (as with the Domain Controller in Windows NT/2000) and security domains are handled by the NIS or "yellowpages" system. Details on NIS can be found in `man nis`.

- Peer-to-peer file sharing, done by NetBIOS under Windows, is typically done over NFS between UNIX systems. You can do Windows-style NetBIOS file and printer sharing in FreeBSD by using the Samba package. NFS is covered in Chapter 31, "The Network Filesystem (NFS)," and Samba is discussed in Chapter 32, "File and Print Sharing with Microsoft Windows."

- Windows uses the Authenticode scheme for verifying code authenticity in downloaded software packages. This is a signing scheme by which downloaded software must present a "certificate" to the user for acceptance or rejection, adding a layer of security against potentially malicious software. UNIX has no such standardized signing mechanism, but the FreeBSD ports/packages system provides centralized auditing and a measure of authenticity assurance suitable for nearly all applications. See Chapter 15, "Installing Additional Software," for more on the ports and packages.

Windows NT/2000 bills itself as being easier to use than UNIX and easier to make secure, but the number of necessary security certifications in the Windows world suggests that this is not universally true. Windows is potentially easier to make insecure through misconfigurations that are made with the best of intentions. Although this is also possible in FreeBSD, historical data shows that it is less common. This can be attributable both to the way UNIX is structured (a model that encourages tighter security as a result of actions a new user might take), and to the large amount of concise and useful information available online for securing UNIX systems. An excellent resource for such information is the SANS (System Administration, Networking, and Security) Institute, found at `http://www.sans.org`.

Software Equivalency

Let's take a look at some of the commonly used software on Windows servers, and what the equivalents would be under FreeBSD (see Table 20.1).

TABLE 20.1   Windows Server Software

Service	Windows NT/2000	FreeBSD	Availability
Mail (SMTP)	Microsoft Exchange	Sendmail	core system
Mail (POP)	Microsoft Exchange	qpopper	ports
MAIL (IMAP)	Microsoft Exchange	IMAP-UW	ports

20

FREEBSD SURVIVAL GUIDE

TABLE 20.1 continued

Service	Windows NT/2000	FreeBSD	Availability
News (NNTP)	Microsoft Exchange	`inn`	ports
System logging	Microsoft SMS	`syslogd`	core system
Web/HTTP	Microsoft IIS	Apache	ports
FTP	Microsoft IIS	`ftpd`	core system
Dynamic Web Content	Cold Fusion, ASP	PHP	ports
DNS	Microsoft Active Directory	BIND	core system
Remote Access	Microsoft Terminal Server	Telnet, SSH	core system
Directory Services	Microsoft Active Directory	OpenLDAP	ports

It's worth pointing out that in the Windows world, unwanted interactions between different pieces of server software are often such a risk that enterprises typically will not run more than one critical service on the same machine. There will be a dedicated mail server, a dedicated Web server, a dedicated name server—all different machines. The open-source UNIX community doesn't subscribe as commonly to that philosophy for two reasons:

- Open-source UNIX systems are often run for their low cost, so buying multiple servers often isn't within the budget of the operator or business.

- Software under UNIX typically is much better-behaved than under Windows, and detrimental interactions between services or daemons are much rarer and less potentially harmful.

You may or may not choose to follow the UNIX method. If you do, however, you can generally feel more at ease running multiple critical services on the same machine than you could if it were a Windows server.

Keeping Up to Date

Microsoft provides system updates through *service packs*: large collections of software revisions and binary patches that appear every six months or so. Quicker responses (for instance, in response to security bulletins) come in the form of binary *hotfixes*, which can be downloaded from Microsoft's Web site.

FreeBSD's method of keeping current can be a lot more complex, but once it's understood, it can be both easier and more effective. FreeBSD places a lot of emphasis on being available in source form for you to track if you like, keeping a local copy of the entire source tree synchronized at whatever frequency you choose. The CVSup tool makes this process both automatable and easy on bandwidth resources. If you prefer, you can also simply keep a source copy of the release version of FreeBSD that you have installed, as a substrate for source patches. This is probably what you'll want to do.

Any security bulletin that is sent out by the FreeBSD Security Officer contains a source patch or similar way to fix the problem. Line-by-line instructions are provided; all you really have to do is copy them verbatim to the command line, and you usually don't even need to reboot after you're done.

You can, if you choose, keep your system completely cutting-edge by rebuilding the entire thing from scratch, from your synchronized sources, however often you like. This process is known as make world, and is covered in detail in Chapter 18, "Keeping Up to Date with FreeBSD." This is probably not something you need to do as a newcomer to the FreeBSD world, but it might prove useful later as you build up experience with the system and want to work with the very latest state of the system. For now, though, use Chapter 18 as a reference for synchronizing your -RELEASE sources so you can apply security patches and keep your system fresh.

Migrating from Linux

Linux and FreeBSD are a lot more similar than Windows NT/2000 and FreeBSD are, naturally. They're both derived from the same UNIX tradition, they're both open-source, and their security models are almost identical. The same software (for the most part, especially if you take into account FreeBSD's Linux binary compatibility) is available for both platforms. The same kinds of system administration problems occur on both platforms, and the same kinds of solutions tend to work as well.

Migration difficulties from Linux to FreeBSD are much more technological than philosophical, and so this section will go into more administrative detail than the section on migrating from Windows has done.

Functional differences between Linux and FreeBSD can be boiled down to a few basic areas:

- Where everything in the system can be found
- Partitions and filesystem types
- Ports and packages
- Keeping in sync
- Technical esoterica

Where Everything in the System Can Be Found

The most important thing to remember about FreeBSD, which should be a mantra by now, is that everything that you install goes into /usr/local. FreeBSD maintains this model very carefully to prevent pollution of core system areas (/usr/bin, /var/lib, and so on). Let's take a look at a few common locations of resources that you'll need (see Table 20.2), bearing in mind that the Linux locations might vary from distribution to distribution.

TABLE 20.2 Comparison of Common Resource Locations Between Linux and FreeBSD

Resource	*Linux*	*FreeBSD*
Apache server root	/var/lib/apache	/usr/local/www
Apache configuration	/var/lib/apache/conf	/usr/local/etc/apache
Apache binaries	/var/lib/apache/sbin	/usr/local/sbin/
Sendmail executable	/usr/lib/sendmail	/usr/sbin/sendmail
MySQL database directory	/var/lib/mysql	/var/db/mysql
System Startup Scripts	/etc/rc.d	/etc/rc.*
User-installed Startup Scripts	/etc/rc.d	/usr/local/etc/rc.d
User-installed Executables	/usr/bin	/usr/local/bin
User-installed Libraries	/usr/lib	/usr/local/lib
User-installed Shared Files	/usr/share	/usr/local/share

Some of these differ because of the differences between the RPM method (the widely used Linux package manager) and the FreeBSD ports/packages method of software installation; others exist because of differences in the core system layout (Linux typically has more of a "System V" structure, whereas FreeBSD is…well, BSD-like). Refer to Chapter 15 for a fuller discussion of how ports and packages work under FreeBSD.

Partitions and Filesystem Types

The Ext2FS filesystem used by Linux takes a very DOS-like approach to disk partitioning: There are four primary BIOS partitions, one of which can be made into an "extended partition" with multiple "logical" partitions inside it. These partitions all appear on the same "level" to the user, even though it's in fact a hierarchical structure. The system can be booted only from a non-extended partition, leading to a lot of potential confusion.

FreeBSD's hierarchical partition structure is much more overt. BIOS partitions are called *slices*, subpartitions are called *partitions* or *BSD partitions*, and the boot process handles the different levels explicitly in order to remove the mystery associated with extended and primary partitions. Setting up a disk involves first slicing and then partitioning the disk. This process is described in detail in Chapter 19, "Understanding Hard Disks and Filesystems."

FreeBSD's native filesystem is UFS/FFS. You can use your Linux disks under FreeBSD without modification, but you will need to recompile the FreeBSD kernel to support Ext2FS. See Chapter 17, "Kernel Configuration," for instructions on how to enable this option and build yourself a new kernel.

Ports and Packages

Coming from a Linux background, you may be used to installing software through the RPM utility. This is not widely used or recommended in FreeBSD (and can in fact seriously damage your system by installing incompatible libraries into places like /usr/lib), though it is possible if you really need to. The preferred method of installing and maintaining software in FreeBSD is through the package tools (pkg_*) or the ports.

Packages and ports provide a centralized filtering mechanism to take software that may be written for Linux or other UNIX flavors, and tweak its build and installation options to ensure that it will compile properly under FreeBSD and install into the prescribed locations for user-installed materials. Ports and packages travel through the FreeBSD committers and the central download sites, rather than being available directly from the software developers themselves. This helps keep a FreeBSD system neat and tidy.

Chapter 15 covers the ports and packages in full detail.

Keeping in Sync

FreeBSD is more source-centric than Linux; since there is effectively only one "distribution" of the operating system, the entire installation is directly available in source form. The Linux world doesn't do this as effectively. Each distribution has its own structure and its own software selections; the only source subtree that you can be sure is the same as another Linux user's is that of the kernel itself. Different distributions have different philosophies toward making the rest of their source trees available for automatic download, synchronization, and building. FreeBSD provides these tools.

This means that to keep synchronized with the latest development code, all you have to do in FreeBSD is to CVSup your sources, as described in Chapter 18. Security patches and hotfixes (available in Linux variously as RPMs, source patches, or binary patches) are distributed in FreeBSD both in source patch form and by checking in fixes to the central source tree. You can update your system in response to a security bulletin either by following the line-by-line patch instructions in the bulletin, or by simply making sure that your source tree is synchronized to a point after the fix has been made, and rebuilding that part of the system.

> **Caution**
>
> Patching system components without rebuilding the entire operating system is a method that usually works (especially for small, non-critical elements of the system), but not always. The more fundamental to the system's operation a component is, the more likely it is that you will need to do a complete make world (as discussed in Chapter 18) in order to upgrade properly. Such fundamental areas of the system usually include the central libraries (items in /usr/lib) or headers (in /usr/include). Less-risky areas are the supporting binaries, in /usr/bin and /usr/sbin.

Password Files

Linux and FreeBSD both use *shadow passwords*, a security feature described in Chapter 10. However, while FreeBSD maintains an /etc/master.passwd file that contains all user data, with /etc/passwd being simply a subset (without the actual password strings), Linux does it a bit differently. Linux's /etc/shadow file doesn't contain any useful information other than the username and the hashed password.

With the combined /etc/passwd and /etc/shadow files from a Linux system, it's possible to put together a master.passwd that you can install into your FreeBSD machine and thus preserve all your users' login data. This can be done with a Perl script (available on the included CD-ROM as mkpasswd.pl), shown in Listing 20.1.

LISTING 20.1   Sample Perl Script to Convert a Linux User Database for Use in FreeBSD

```
#!/usr/bin/perl
# Set this to the location of bash on your FreeBSD machine (if installed),
# or to /bin/csh to switch /bin/bash users to csh
$newshell = "/bin/csh";

open (PASSWD,"/etc/passwd");
@passwd = <PASSWD>;                     # Read in the /etc/passwd file
close (PASSWD);
open (SHADOW,"/etc/shadow");
@shadow = <SHADOW>;                     # Read in the /etc/shadow file
```

LISTING 20.1   continued

```
close (SHADOW);

foreach $user (@shadow) {
  @sdata = split(/:/,$user);
  $passhash{@sdata[0]} = @sdata[1];  # Make a lookup table based on usernames
}
foreach $user (@passwd) {
  @pdata = split(/:/,$user);
  @pdata[6] = $newshell."\n" if (@pdata[6] eq "/bin/bash\n");
  @pdata[1] = $passhash{@pdata[0]};  # Replace the "x" with the password hash
  splice (@pdata,4,0,undef,"0","0"); # Splice in extra blank fields
  foreach (@pdata) {                 # Print the combined output line
    print "$_";
    print ":" unless ($_ =~ /\n/);
  }
}
```

Make sure this script is set executable, then run it as root on the Linux system, sending the output into a file:

```
% ./mkpasswd.pl > new.master.passwd
```

Transfer this `new.master.passwd` file to your FreeBSD machine, and put it into `/etc` (pwd_mkdb doesn't like working on input files and destinations that are on different filesystems). Open up the file in a text editor, and open FreeBSD's `/etc/master.passwd` in another window. You will need to modify the first block of about 15 usernames (such as daemon, bin, nowc, and other system pseudo-users whose UIDs are different in Linux and FreeBSD). Simply copy this block of users from FreeBSD's `/etc/master.passwd` into the `new.master.passwd` file, replacing the corresponding block in the new file.

Back up your existing `/etc/master.passwd` by making a copy of it. Finally, run pwd_mkdb to generate the new password files and hash databases:

```
# pwd_mkdb -p /etc/new.master.passwd
```

If this command completes without errors, don't log out yet—you need to test this while you're still root. You should be able to log in with a new terminal session. If you can't, run pwd_mkdb again on the backup file you created, and the databases will revert to their former state.

Technical Esoterica

There are a lot of extra little odds and ends that are different between Linux and FreeBSD. Here is a list of some of the most visible:

- FreeBSD doesn't have a `System.map` file. Linux uses this table to look up jump vectors for commonly used kernel symbols. FreeBSD builds these symbols into the kernel, so you don't need to worry about it.

- The default shell in FreeBSD is `tcsh`, not `bash`. `tcsh` and `csh` are hard-linked to each other, so `csh` is the same as `tcsh`. If you want `bash`, you'll need to install it out of the ports or packages.

- The Linux binary-compatibility package (which you really should install when given the chance) creates a `/compat/linux` tree that contains a basic Linux binary and library structure for Linux-packaged programs that really need them. It also creates a `linux.ko` kernel module (you can check its status with `kldstat`). These structures handle Linux executables mostly transparently; some anomalies may occur, but for the most part the handling is seamless. You will certainly want to install FreeBSD-native versions of anything you can, however, from the packages or ports if available.

- FreeBSD doesn't allow you to log in remotely as root unless you hack the `/etc/ttys` file (see Chapter 10 for details).

- As of version 5.0, FreeBSD uses the DEVFS device filesystem rather than a standard `/dev` directory populated with "special" files. See Chapter 17 for more information on how to work with DEVFS and device hints.

- Devices on the PCI bus in FreeBSD are numbered, starting with zero for on-board devices and then increasing as they move away from the motherboard down the PCI chain. In Linux, the on-board device is typically the highest-numbered one, and the numbers decrease with distance for the motherboard. This means that on a machine with two Ethernet cards, the devices that were `eth0` and `eth1` under Linux might become `fxp1` and `fxp0` (respectively) under FreeBSD.

- Trading in your Tux t-shirts and bean bags for Daemon ones can be a little discouraging due to incomplete market penetration as of this writing.

Aside from these, though, the transition from Linux to FreeBSD ought to be quite smooth.

"Do's" and "Don'ts" (Common Gotchas)

Every operating system has numerous pitfalls ready to snare the unwary, particularly successfully when the system is newly installed. We'll go over some of the most commonly made errors and some of the most valuable pointers for effective administration now.

DO:

- Do use the ports and packages to install software. It's possible to grab the source for a particular program directly from the developer and compile it using its built-in scripts, but all you'll do is pollute your core-system userland. If the program isn't available as a port, post to the `freebsd-ports@freebsd.org` mailing list and ask for it, or you can even learn the porting process and become a maintainer yourself.

- Do pay attention to the nightly, weekly, and monthly `periodic` output messages. Any setuid executable differences are flagged in the security report—as well as filesystem usage, rejected mail hosts, and many other forms of visibility that are an effective "closed-circuit TV" against intruders.

- Do become familiar with CVSup. CVSup is your friend. Not only can it keep your source and ports in sync at all times, it can also serve as an effective mirroring solution, as we will discuss a little later in this chapter.

- Do install `sudo` (`/usr/ports/security/sudo`), and encourage its use. If you have to share administrative privileges with others, giving them access to `sudo` is an excellent way to limit their potential to damage the system while enabling them to still effectively manage things.

- Do use `ntpd` and `ntpdate` to synchronize your system's clock. This is done by adding the following lines to `/etc/rc.conf`:

```
ntpdate_enable="YES"
ntpdate_flags="tick.usno.navy.mil"
xntpd_enable="YES"
```

  You can use any NTP server you like for `ntpdate`, which runs at boot time and corrects any gross time discrepancies before other services have a chance to run. You should also create an `/etc/ntp.conf` file to control `ntpd`, which runs as a daemon and keeps your clock synchronized with the NTP server (or servers) on an ongoing basis. See `man ntp.conf` for details on creating that file.

- Do be nice to the FreeBSD committers. There are only 15 or so of them, and the responsibilities of the entire operating system rest largely on their shoulders (as opposed to the collective shoulders of thousands of independent developers and distributors of Linux, or the corporate shoulders of Microsoft). That's a lot of responsibility. Be a cooperative and supportive user.

- Do decide what kind of security model you're going to have. Do you trust all your users? If so, you can get away with leaving a lot of system-level resources viewable, and when you have permissions collision problems such as Web applications that must store cleartext passwords or write to a world-writable directory, you won't have to worry about as much. If you don't trust all your users, though, you'll have to be much more careful. See Chapter 29 for a fuller discussion of security in a networked environment.

- Do subscribe to the appropriate mailing lists for your version of FreeBSD. Unquestionably, you should be on `freebsd-security@freebsd.org` if you're running a server; `freebsd-ports@freebsd.org` and `freebsd-questions@freebsd.org` are also useful; and if you're tracking the STABLE or CURRENT sources, subscribe to `freebsd-stable@freebsd.org` or `freebsd-current@freebsd.org` accordingly.

- Do monitor the size of your log files. Apache's `httpd-access.log` and `httpd-error.log` are notorious for eating up disk space if your Web server gets any kind of significant traffic. Use Apache's built-in `rotatelogs` utility, or run a `cron` job to flush the logs occasionally. If your `/var` partition fills up, your mail, databases, and runtime files will not work.

- Do fly the Daemon banner proudly!

DON'T:

- Don't use experimental features on a production server. This isn't the place to try out new ideas such as Soft Updates or unsupported filesystem kernel modules. Try these things out on a cheaply built "hobbyist" machine; then put them into practice only once you're comfortable with their use.

- Don't port-scan your server if you're running PortSentry, or another tool that blocks your route to the machine if it detects an intrusion coming from your IP address. You'll lose connectivity until you find an alternate direction from which to reach your server and delete the "black-hole" route.

- Don't use `shutdown` to drop to single-user mode (for high-privilege activities such as replacing the kernel) if you're running with the `securelevel` setting to 1 or higher; this won't decrement the kernel security level. Instead, reboot the machine, and enter `boot -s` at the loader prompt to boot into single-user mode. Simply exit the single-user shell to come back up the rest of the way. This must be done at the physical console!

- Don't get hung up on uptime. Remember, a system with 350-day uptime either means a system that has been sitting unused in a closet for a year, or a system that has not been conscientiously upgraded to keep up with security bulletins. It doesn't make for such great bragging rights as one might think.

- Don't forget to add yourself to the "wheel" group at installation time! Very little is more disheartening than to build a new server, drive fifty miles to the co-location facility, lock it in a cabinet, drive home, try to log in, and discover that you can't get root access.

- Don't make a habit of using filenames with spaces in them. It can be done (with backslashes in front of the spaces as with any special character, for example, `My\ Document.txt`), but there's no guarantee that software will handle the filenames properly. Most of the time, it will. There's still no guarantee.

- Don't write Perl or shell scripts on a local Windows machine, and then upload them in binary mode over FTP. Binary mode prevents proper translation of end-of-line characters, and although the body of the script might look perfectly fine, the return character at the end of the very first line (`#!/usr/bin/perl`) will be unrecognizable to the shell and cause the script to fail. If you're having trouble with CGI programming and scripts that mysteriously fail after uploading, check this first, and make sure you're uploading in ASCII mode. Better yet, do your programming directly on the server. There are excellent text-editing tools for just that purpose.

- Don't write Perl or shell scripts on a local Windows machine, and then upload them in binary mode over FTP. Binary mode prevents proper translation of end-of-line characters, and although the body of the script might look perfectly fine, the return character at the end of the very first line (`#!/usr/bin/perl`) will be unrecognizable to the shell and cause the script to fail. If you're having trouble with CGI programming and scripts that mysteriously fail after uploading, check this first, and make sure you're uploading in ASCII mode. Better yet, do your programming directly on the server. There are excellent text-editing tools for just that purpose.

Performance Tuning

In its default, "out of the box" configuration, FreeBSD is optimized for low-end hardware and to be extremely safe and reliable. This means that under heavy demand load, the system will perform much more poorly than similarly equipped Linux or Windows

20

FREEBSD
SURVIVAL
GUIDE

servers. This isn't because FreeBSD is an inferior platform; rather, it's because it needs to be tuned for high-performance operation. The other platforms to which it's compared tend to be optimized for high performance by default, to the exclusion of low-end hardware. Very few sites that run FreeBSD servers do so without tuning the system for higher performance.

Performance tuning involves several different areas of the system, some of which require kernel reconfiguration (as we saw in Chapter 17) and some of which do not.

Kernel Settings

You will need to tune your kernel to support high levels of traffic if your machine will be handling extreme load. The GENERIC kernel is tuned for workstation or low-load server use, so that its hardware requirements can be as low as possible; high demand for kernel resources can overload the system if it hasn't been optimized to support it. The kernel option to raise is MAXUSERS, which is set to 32 by default. This setting is analogous to the "licenses" concept in Windows; it doesn't actually set a limit on the number of users who can access the system at once. Rather, it sets a figure from which other tuning values (such as the number of network memory buffers, or NMBCLUSTERS) are derived. Set MAXUSERS to 128 or 256 (or higher) for extremely heavily-loaded systems.

Tip

The NMBCLUSTERS setting, derived as (MAXUSERS * 16) + 512, controls the number of available mbufs, which you can view with netstat -m; watch to see if they're being used up. If they are, and raising MAXUSERS doesn't help, you can tune NMBCLUSTERS independently from its derivation from MAXUSERS. Set it in the kernel to 16384 or 32768 (or higher) for heavily-loaded systems. Alternately, you can set it as a run-time kernel variable without rebuilding the kernel. Add the line kern.ipc.nmbclusters="16384" to /boot/loader.conf to set it at boot time.

Soft Updates and Asynchronous Writes

One of the features that allows FreeBSD to operate so safely on low-load systems is *synchronous writes*, meaning that the system has to wait while any write operations of filesystem meta-data take place. This ensures that a crash or power failure is much less likely to harm the filesystem than it otherwise would be. However, it also makes the system run noticeably more slowly than comparable platforms and introduces artificial performance ceilings that can be removed if you so desire.

In Chapter 9, we discussed Soft Updates, a technique by which disk write operations can be done in a software-controlled, orderly manner that will both speed up disk input/output (I/O) and ensure that the filesystem would remain safe should the system crash.

The Soft Updates mechanism is built into the GENERIC kernel and is available for use at any time. However, to enable it on a filesystem, you must use the tunefs utility, a support program for the FFS filesystem that FreeBSD uses natively. The tunefs program must be run in single-user mode for its changes to take effect, because filesystems on which it operates cannot be mounted at the time. Because tunefs is in /sbin, it is available in single-user mode without any additional filesystems needing to be mounted.

Reboot the system into single-user mode (enter boot -s at the loader prompt). At the shell prompt, enter the following commands:

```
tunefs -n enable /
tunefs -n enable /usr
tunefs -n enable /var
```

Repeat the command for any other regular filesystems on your disk. Note that you might have to substitute /sbin/tunefs for tunefs in these command lines.

An alternate way to get around the problem of synchronous writes, if Soft Updates is not an option, is to force the filesystems to be mounted *asynchronously*, or in such a way that write operations do not hold up system functions. This gives you the advantage of greatly enhanced speed; however, the safety of synchronous writes is lost this way. If the system should suddenly shut down while a write operation is pending, the filesystem could be damaged or even rendered irreparable.

To assume the inherent risk and mount a filesystem asynchronously, use the async option in the appropriate mount command or in /etc/fstab. A manual asynchronous mount would look like this:

```
# mount -o async /usr /dev/ad0s1f
```

To do asynchronous mounts automatically, add the async option to the fourth column in /etc/fstab:

```
/dev/ad0s1f            /usr           ufs     rw,async    2       2
```

Disk Geometry Concerns

If you're really interested in optimizing your system's disk access performance, you can squeeze a few extra horsepower from FreeBSD by arranging your partitions according to their placement on the disk. Because data can be transferred more quickly from the edge of a spinning disk than from the center (a disk spins at a constant speed, so more data can be packed into a single revolution near the edge than near the center), you can gain some speed benefits by placing your more active filesystems toward the edge.

The order in which you specify partitions in the partition table matters. The first entry in the table begins at the edge of the disk, and subsequent entries are placed further and further inward (the opposite of how data is arranged on a CD [md] which, incidentally, spins at different rates according to where the read head is). The root and swap partitions are accessed the most, so they should be placed as far outward as possible. Smaller filesystems also work better toward the edge than toward the center. With this in mind, the best layout is usually to start with a fairly small root partition, followed by a swap partition about twice the size of your physical RAM. Following this are your /var, /usr, and /home partitions, which generally tend to increase in size respectively.

> **Tip**
>
> In UNIX, the algorithms that control virtual memory are optimized to work best when the swap partition is about twice the size of your on-board memory. For instance, if you have 256MB of RAM, use a 512MB swap partition. A smaller swap volume can result in speed penalties as virtual memory paging operations start to overlap each other.

A Few `sysctl` Tune-Ups

The `sysctl` program controls numerous kernel state variables, such as the `kern.ipc.nmbclusters` variable which we saw earlier. The defaults for these variables, naturally, are such that a low-end system can operate smoothly and safely, but not with great top-end performance. You can tune a number of these to higher-performance values by adding them to /etc/sysctl.conf, which is evaluated at boot time. The /etc/sysctl.conf file doesn't exist in the default installation; you will need to create it and add the following lines:

```
vfs.vmiodirenable=1
kern.ipc.maxsockbuf=2097152
kern.ipc.somaxconn=8192
kern.ipc.maxsockets=16424
kern.maxfiles=65536
kern.maxfilesperproc=32768
net.inet.tcp.rfc1323=1
net.inet.tcp.delayed_ack=0
net.inet.tcp.sendspace=65535
net.inet.tcp.recvspace=65535
net.inet.udp.recvspace=65535
net.inet.udp.maxdgram=57344
net.local.stream.recvspace=65535
net.local.stream.sendspace=65535
```

Note that the meanings of these variables are largely opaque or undocumented. Before you reboot with the new /etc/sysctl.conf, you can use sysctl to view the default value of any of these variables:

```
# sysctl vfs.vmiodirenable
```

vfs.vmiodirenable: 0

You can then manually set any value with the –w flag:

```
# sysctl -w vfs.vmiodirenable=1
```

vfs.vmiodirenable: 0 > 1

Helpful Manual Pages

A wealth of information is available in the man tuning page. This document is an essay describing some of the ideas we've covered here, such as disk geometry issues and how to optimize a filesystem according to the read and write demand on it.

Similarly, read man tunefs for a fuller discussion of how the tunefs command can be used to take advantage not only of Soft Updates, but of many other performance enhancements that are a part of the FFS filesystem.

Finally, man sysctl offers a good description of the kernel state variable mechanism and how to use it to its full potential by tweaking the system's variables during run-time.

Preparing for the Worst: Backups and Mirrors

No matter how many precautions you take, no matter how much of a veteran you are, your system will one day be hacked, your hardware will fail, or something else will happen that will make your data unusable and recovery impossible. The only defense against this is to have the tools available for a complete rebuild from the ground up. Prepare for the worst, says one of the corollaries to Murphy's Law, and the worst will never happen. If precautions are the price we pay for safety, so be it.

Creating "Seed" Files

One way you can ensure that your custom configuration will survive a catastrophic failure is to gather together the "seed" files, which you can use to customize a new system that you build from scratch. These files can be preserved offline by burning them onto a CD, or in the absence of writable optical media, a floppy disk.

- `/etc/rc.conf`. The main system configuration file.
- `/etc/master.passwd`. The master user database. All other user databases can be generated from this one.
- `/etc/mail/myconfig.mc`. The sendmail "master config" file if you have a custom sendmail configuration.
- `/etc/fstab`. Important for re-creating your disk structure.
- `/usr/local/etc/*`. Individual config files for all the programs you've installed.

These are the most critical files—the ones that define your system and give it its identity. All told, they won't come to more than a few hundred kilobytes; those few hundred kilobytes can save weeks of painful tuning and trial-and-error when you rebuild the system.

You may even want to package these files together into a tarball and mail it to yourself (at an account *not* on your FreeBSD machine) on a daily basis. Here's a sample command to accomplish this:

```
# tar cvfz - /etc/rc.conf /etc/master.passwd /etc/fstab /usr/local/etc |
uuencode seedfiles.tar.gz | mail -s "Seed Files" me@myaccount.com
```

You can put this into a shell script in `/etc/periodic/daily` or into root's `crontab` file, as you prefer.

Backups

The importance of backups can hardly be overstated. Any system administrator will tell you this. Yet, it's also no secret that doing regular backups is tedious, annoying, and expensive. Many administrators will wax lyrical about how imperative it is to have a backup scheme in place, while not actually having one to wax lyrical about.

At the very least, we can go over the various options for doing backups, so that a missing backup solution won't be because of a lack of information on how to do it.

The built-in UNIX utility dump is the good old standby backup method. It operates based on dump levels specified in /etc/fstab (as we saw in Chapter 9, "The FreeBSD Filesystem"). They enable a fine-grained "delta dump" system, in which you can do one complete dump at the beginning and then subsequently dump only new or changed files, thus saving tape space and backup time.

You'll need a drive to use as the backup device. You can use a tape drive (/dev/rsa0, the default), an external hard drive, or basically any device that can be mounted and written to during normal operations. SCSI has always been the interface of choice for backup devices such as tape drives. You'll need a SCSI controller for this, which will hike up the price a bit, or alternatively you can wait until FireWire (IEEE 1394) devices have become fully mainstream and then use one of those. There are also IDE/ATAPI tape drives available. Make sure that FreeBSD supports the tape drive you like before you buy it! The device need not be mounted for the dump operation to work—it will write directly to the device specified.

The following command executes a baseline backup, a complete dump of the /home filesystem:

```
# dump -0u -f /dev/nrsa0 /home
```

The 0 option means to do a level 0 dump (back up everything, regardless of whether it needs to be backed up or not), and the u option tells dump to update the /etc/dumpdates file, a human-readable data file that dump reads to figure out whether incremental dumps need to back up certain files or not.

> **Note**
>
> The nrsa0 device is the same as rsa0, except it specifies a "non-rewinding" device—a confusing way to do it, certainly, but it has the effect of telling the tape drive not to rewind when it's done. Tape drives, particularly SCSI ones, use this convention to tell dump how to handle the tape, as shown in Table 20.3.

20

FREEBSD
SURVIVAL GUIDE

This is useful for when you're doing batch backups; specifying the nonrewinding tape device prevents it from rewinding after the first operation and overwriting the just-completed backup.

TABLE 20.3 Device Meta-Names as Control Options

Device Meta-Name	Effect
/dev/sa0	The actual device name
/dev/rsa0	Tells dump to rewind the tape when it's done
/dev/nrsa0	Tells dump not to rewind the tape when it's done
/dev/ersa0	Tells dump to eject the tape when it's done

After this is done, you can do incremental dumps with the same syntax, but a higher dump level number:

```
# dump -1u -f /dev/nrsa0 /home
```

The way the dump levels work is to dump only the files that have changed since the last dump of any lower level. So, if you do a level 3 dump and then a level 4 dump later, the level 4 dump will dump only files that have changed since the level 3 dump. If you then do a level 2 dump, everything backed up with the levels 3 or 4 dumps will be backed up again. The lower the dump level, the more backups will be "forced." A level 0 is the "ultimate" backup, dumping everything regardless of previous dump states.

The typical procedure is to do a level 0 dump at the outset; then a level 1 dump at the beginning of each week, using a different tape (or set of tapes) for each week. Each subsequent day, a higher-level dump is done, often in the staggered "Tower of Hanoi" sequence suggested in the man dump page.

Recovery

When it comes time to recover, you'll be using the restore utility. This can be used either in interactive or noninteractive mode; the former is helpful for specifying a particular set of files to restore, for instance if you've accidentally deleted a file and you need it back. First, cd to the directory where you want to extract the file and then enter the interactive restore program:

```
# restore -if /dev/nrsa0
```

Within this program, you have a number of commands available to you: cd, ls, pwd, add, and delete, among others. These commands allow you to navigate among the files in the tape's backed-up directory structure, view them, and add them to a list (with the add command). Remove files from the list (but not from the tape or disk) with the delete command. The extract command restores from the tape any files in the list at the time you issue it. Full syntax for each of the interactive restore commands can be found in the man restore page.

```
restore> add frank
restore> extract
```

Alternately, you can restore everything from a tape's backup session simply with the non-interactive options:

```
# restore -rf /dev/nrsa0
```

A tape often will have multiple sessions of backup data on it—multiple days' worth, for example. A single tape might have a week's worth of backups, beginning with a full backup followed by six incremental backups. If you want a file from a particular day's backup, you will need to position the tape to extract from that session. The tool that does this is mt, the "magnetic tape" manipulation utility.

When you first insert a tape into the drive, it is generally rewound automatically to the beginning. To wind it forward to the third session, use the fsf (fast forward) option with mt:

```
mt -f /dev/nrsa0 fsf 2
```

The fsf 2 tells mt to fast-forward two sessions, putting it at the beginning of the third session. To move back to the second session, rewind the tape to the beginning (also using mt) and then fast-forward it again:

```
mt -f /dev/nrsa0 rewind
mt -f /dev/nrsa0 fsf 1
```

There are a great many more details to the dump and restore procedures that need not be fully detailed here: Using the -s option with restore in non-interactive mode to specify a certain backup session on the tape, advanced usage of the mt utility, managing multiple tapes, remote backup devices, and so on. A good tutorial on dump and restore that covers these procedures can be found at http://www.nethamilton.net/dump.html. Also, read the man pages on dump, restore, and mt for documentation of all the capabilities of these tools.

Mirrors

Backups are certainly daunting, aren't they? It's small wonder that few people actually have the patience to do them. They do require a budgetary and time consideration appropriate to a small business at the least; a personal hobbyist system might find it difficult to justify the investment and aggravation. Fortunately, there's an alternative.

For just a little more money than it would take to set up a full-fledged tape backup system, you can instead create a mirror server, a second FreeBSD machine whose only purpose is to synchronize its files with the main server on a daily basis, to be swapped into place should anything happen to the main server. And the tool we'll use to do the mirroring? You guessed it: CVSup.

Ideally, your secondary server should be in a physically different location from the main server. CVSup's incremental backup system makes it possible to do this, even if the bandwidth available between the two systems is very limited. We'll now take a look at what needs to be done to set up a CVSup mirroring solution.

Let's say, for this example, that you want to mirror four directory structures: /home, /usr/local/www, /var/mail, and /etc. You may well want to do more than just these in your situation, but these will suffice for our example. The first step is to set up a base directory, a configuration staging area on the main server so that cvsupd (which is installed in /usr/local/sbin as part of the cvsup port or package, which hopefully you've already installed) will know what collections to serve to clients, such as your mirror machine.

Enter the following commands as root:

```
 cd /usr/local/etc
# mkdir -p cvsup/sup
# cd cvsup/sup
# mkdir home www mail etc
```

Now, in each of these four new subdirectories, we'll need to create two files: the .cvs file and the releases file. These files describe a "collection" to the cvsupd server and enable it to be served. In the home subdirectory, create a file called home.cvs with the following contents:

```
upgrade home
rsymlink *
```

Next, create a file called releases with the following contents:

```
home list=home.cvs prefix=/
```

Do this for each of the four subdirectories, changing the name of the .cvs file to match the name of the directory or collection, and altering the contents accordingly as well. When this is done, you can run the cvsupd server:

```
# cvsupd -b /usr/local/etc/cvsup -C 1 -l /dev/stdout
```

Now you're done with the main server; you can now move on to the secondary server.

Create a file in /etc called `mirror-supfile` or anything you like. The contents should be as shown in Listing 20.2, in which `server1.hostname.com` is the hostname of your main server.

LISTING 20.2   Example CVSup Configuration File (`mirror-supfile`)

```
*default host=server1.hostname.com
*default delete use-rel-suffix
*default compress
*default preserve

*default base=/usr
*default release=home
home

*default base=/usr/local
*default release=www
www

*default base=/var
*default release=mail
mail

*default base=/usr
*default release=etc
etc
```

Notice the final entry: it's not /etc that we're mirroring the main server's /etc into, but /usr/etc. The reasons for this should be obvious! In any case, this is a good excuse to demonstrate the flexibility of CVSup, showing how you can check out a collection into any location on the second server.

Once the mirror-supfile is created, you're ready to do your first mirroring operation. Start up the CVSup process:

```
# cvsup -L 2 /etc/mirror-supfile
```

You'll be flooded with output, telling you exactly what is being transferred and how. You can use Ctrl+C to break out at any time—CVSup will exit cleanly and pick up where it left off the next time through. This first transfer process will take a very long time—as long as it takes to transfer all the specified data from one server to the other via any other means. It's the subsequent processes that will be fast and efficient.

Once your /usr/etc has been transferred, you can copy the `master.passwd` file out of it and use `pwd_mkdb`, as we saw earlier in the "Migrating from Linux" section, to synchronize your users. You may choose to do this as a daily automated task if you have a lot of users or add them regularly; CVSup will skip any file that it can determine has the same checksum and the same ownership information, but the ownership information won't be the same if the users on one system don't match the other! If a file is owned by a user that doesn't exist on the secondary system, CVSup will "Rsync" it every time the mirror process is run, which doesn't take anywhere near as long as transferring the entire file, but takes much longer than simply skipping the file. Keeping the user database synchronized can speed up the CVSup process from 4 or 5 hours down to about 15 minutes.

Once the mirroring process is running smoothly each time you run it, you can add it to your /etc/periodic/daily or root's crontab, whichever you prefer. You'll get the verbose output mailed to you each night for your edification. Reduce the -L level if you want to see less output.

You can create more collections on the server side if you want; just make more directories in /usr/local/etc/cvsup/sup, and add them to the mirror-supfile. You don't need to restart the cvsupd process—it will pick up the new collections automatically.

Mirroring isn't a complete alternative to incremental backups. It's a solution for an administrator who doesn't need historical auditing, revision control, or offsite backup archives. Put simply, it isn't a perfect solution for a business using FreeBSD as its server platform. Mirroring provides a quick and easy solution to a sudden catastrophic failure. For business use, you really can't beat tape backups, tedious as they are.

CHAPTER 21

Introduction to Perl Programming

It's almost impossible to work in the UNIX world or the Internet in general today without at least some understanding of the Perl language. Despite many structural inconsistencies and quirks, Perl has managed to become the *de facto* default tool for writing quick but versatile programs for just about any purpose. The fact that it doesn't have to be compiled like C code, and that its lax syntax-checking and its built-in data typing and memory management eliminate many of the headaches of programming in more traditional compiled languages means that it can be used quite effectively with very little programming expertise. However, it also means that programs written in Perl are less efficient and capable than those written in C or C++, as are the majority of the components that make up FreeBSD.

This chapter will cover some of the basics of Perl so that you can take advantage of Perl's strengths without having to know enough about programming to be limited by its weaknesses.

What Is Perl?

Perl is an interpreted programming language, particularly suited for text processing, that is included by default in FreeBSD and is the basis for many crucial system tools. Its name stands for "Practical Extraction and Report Language" (although several less-flattering variants exist). Perl was written by Larry Wall as a replacement for the more limited awk. He is still its chief architect, and is currently (as of this writing) working on the newly redesigned Perl 6.

Many, many large books have been written on the subject of Perl. Its usefulness in today's world is so vast, its presence so ubiquitous, and its structure so complex that even those who can claim mastery of the language are frequently surprised by hidden quirks or tricks that the language can accomplish. This chapter will not attempt to get anywhere near such detailed coverage of Perl; rather, we will be looking at Perl in just enough detail to provide a useful base for writing simple scripts and understanding the concepts in more complex existing scripts. This way, you will be able to teach yourself further Perl techniques by example, using the Perl-based utilities in FreeBSD or any prewritten tools that you might download.

Perl in FreeBSD

About one-tenth of the programs that make up FreeBSD's core installation are actually Perl scripts. The rest are generally compiled binaries, built from source code written in C, C++, or a number of other popular languages. These binaries cannot be read by a human or easily decompiled back to source form. Perl code, on the other hand, does not

Introduction to Perl Programming
CHAPTER 21

543

21

INTRODUCTION TO
PERL
PROGRAMMING

need to be compiled. It exists as plain text, easily readable and editable, and is run with the help of the Perl *interpreter*, /usr/bin/perl.

We saw in Chapter 13, "Shell Programming," how to write scripts using the shell interpreter /bin/sh, by specifying the name of the interpreter on the first line of the script. Perl scripts work the same way. The difference is that while shell scripts are primarily useful as "batch programs" (in MS-DOS parlance) that execute sequences of system commands as they would be entered on the command line with simple variable substitution and flow control, Perl is a fully functional programming environment that allows you to write programs as complex as Web servers or database management systems. Because it's interpreted rather than compiled, Perl programs tend to be slower (especially to start) than their C counterparts. Perl's strengths are in string processing and text handling, however, so the ideal application for a Perl program is as a seldom-used script (such as adduser) that operates on string manipulation and files rather than on heavy-duty mathematics.

Perl is used in this capacity throughout FreeBSD. Some examples of system utilities written in Perl are adduser, pkg_version, and sockstat. It's still more widely found in third-party applications such as majordomo, the popular mailing list manager. Many programs that used to be Perl scripts have lately been rewritten in C for speed reasons. Still, you will run into Perl programs at least as frequently in FreeBSD as you will shell scripts, so it's important to know how to work with them.

Strengths of Perl

Perl strikes a balance between the ease-of-use of shell scripting (a high-level approach) and the versatility of C programming (a low-level approach). The result is a language that allows you to use variables of many different data types—including data structures, importable objects, associative arrays, multidimensional arrays, and I/O handles—without having to worry about casting variables from one type to another, allocating and freeing memory, predeclaring variables, dereferencing pointers, prototyping functions, or performing a number of the other onerous tasks associated with programming in C, including compiling binaries. Perl gives you extreme freedom to do what you like without getting bogged down in the convoluted and bug-prone details of low-level programming. The high-level tools that make Perl what it is are largely responsible for Perl's vast acceptance as the language of choice for CGI programming and server-side Web applications, a field that has grown explosively over the years of the growth of the Internet and e-commerce.

Perl's specific purpose is to provide superior string-manipulation tools: pattern matching, string replacement and translation, regular expressions, and a structure that makes it very straightforward to read and write text files using native arrays of strings. There is no need in Perl to declare a variable as being a string, an integer, a character, or any other type. Perl recognizes variable types in a cascading structure of appropriateness, assigning the necessary memory to each variable as it is modified, and applying operators appropriately according to the variable's type.

Perl gives you what is arguably the best mixture of ease-of-use and programming power of any widely used language. Its syntax is extremely lax and flexible, letting you get away with many minor mistakes that other languages would punish severely. It's extensible (with thousands of importable library modules available throughout the Internet), it's well-documented and well-supported, and it's available everywhere—on dozens of different platforms. You can be sure that a Perl script will operate the same no matter where you run it, whether it's on Linux, IRIX, Windows, or FreeBSD.

Weaknesses of Perl

Years of open-source development and incremental enhancement have turned Perl into something of a behemoth. Its syntax can hardly be called elegant. While Perl's strengths are very significant assets indeed, Perl is not widely regarded as a model of ideal language design.

Although Perl's laxness lets the programmer get away with many types of mistakes, this has the effect of encouraging sloppy code (much as a standards-lax Web browser will encourage invalid or incompatible HTML code). Perl accepts syntax that resembles C, BASIC, FORTRAN, or even common language in some cases. Although this gives the language great flexibility, it also means that the underlying structure is too complex to support certain crucial aspects of languages that are regarded with more esteem. Perl is in many ways the "black sheep" of the programming language community.

Python and Post-Perl Programming

Many new projects have attempted to fill in for Perl's shortcomings since its meteoric rise to prevalence. Many, such as REBOL, Java, and Ruby, have been under development since after Perl had already gained critical mass in the server programming world. The front-runner, however, is a language dating back to about the same time as Perl's beginnings: Python.

Python is an even more object-oriented language than Perl, and it has a much more regimented syntax. No C-style brackets are used; instead, tab indentations are significant, greatly simplifying the hierarchical nesting of flow-control blocks. Python also uses dotted-object hierarchies and tightly structured modules (or "dictionaries"), providing a much more direct and extensible interface to objects than Perl can.

While Perl programs are compiled with each runtime, Python generates compiled bytecode (a `.pyc` file) at the first run of a program, which speeds up execution on subsequent occasions. This is partially necessary because, as with all object-oriented programming environments, the trade-off is speed for structure. Python is potentially less susceptible to bugs than Perl is, as well as being easier to maintain because it is less prone to "spaghetti code." It is lacking in text-processing capabilities, though, which is the area where Perl shines the most.

While Python is not a part of the core FreeBSD system, it is available from the ports collection, in `/usr/ports/lang/python`. Perl itself once had to be installed from the ports; given Python's rapidly growing and enthusiastic user base, we might expect that it may show up in `/usr/bin` before too much longer.

Fundamentals of Perl Scripting

A Perl script is effectively similar to a shell script, such as those we saw in Chapter 13. The first line, the "interpreter line," tells the shell which interpreter to use to run the rest of the script's contents:

```
#/usr/bin/perl
```

The rest of the script, as in shell programming, is made up of variable assignments, flow-control blocks and loops, system calls, and operations on I/O handles—to name a few fundamental parts of a script's anatomy. Here's a simple example:

```
#!/usr/bin/perl

$string = "Hello world!";
$hostname = `hostname`;
if ($hostname eq "uncia") {
  print $string."\n";
  print `date`;
}
```

Notice the use of C-style curly brackets to delimit the `if` block, rather than the "if/fi" and "case/esac" syntax of shell scripting. Also as in C, each statement is terminated by a semicolon (`;`), allowing you to use multiline statements in most cases. The whitespace between the statements and operators is also optional: `"$a = 1"` is just as valid as `"$a=1"`. Perl's syntax much more closely resembles that of a simplified version of C than that of the shell language. Think of Perl as a cross between shell scripting and C, incorporating the best features of both.

A Perl script doesn't need to be compiled. This makes debugging very easy: Just edit the file, make a change, run it again, see what new errors there are, and edit it again. The Perl interpreter does the "compiling" at runtime, and doesn't write out any compiled bytecode. This makes Perl slower than full-fledged C—which is why almost all critical system functions are written in C—but it's fine for scripts that aren't especially time- or performance-sensitive, such as `adduser` or `majordomo`.

To run a Perl script, you have to set it executable. This is done with the `chmod` command:

```
# chmod +x myscript.pl
```

This should result in the following permissions, which we know as `0755` (see Chapter 10, "Users, Groups, and Permissions," for details on permissions):

```
-rwxr-xr-x  1 frank  frank  170 Jun 14  2000 myscript.pl*
```

Now, to run the script, you would use the `./` prefix to specify the script in the current directory because you most likely won't have "." (the current directory) in your path, especially as root:

```
# ./myscript.pl
Hello world!
Sat Apr 28 15:29:17 PDT 2001
```

Because Perl scripts are interpreted, you don't necessarily have to make them executable in order to run, or even to have the interpreter line at the top. If you prefer, though this method is less conveniently "encapsulated" than the previous method, you can run the script as an argument to `perl` itself:

```
# perl myscript.pl
```

There are some arguments to `perl` that can be used in either of these contexts. The `-w` switch turns on warnings, for example, and can be used in either of the following ways:

```
# perl -w myscript.pl
```

```
#!/usr/bin/perl -w
```

Variables and Operators

A variable in Perl is either a *scalar* or an *array*, which are two different ways of storing pieces of data. This data can take the form of a number (expressed in any of several different ways), a string of text, or other various types of what are known in Perl as *literals*. A scalar variable (the most common kind) has a name beginning with the dollar sign ($).

Introduction to Perl Programming

CHAPTER 21

547

21

INTRODUCTION TO
PERL
PROGRAMMING

The nice thing about Perl is that you never have to worry about whether a number is an integer, a float, a short, a long, or whatever. You also don't need to treat a string as an array of characters, a pointer to a string in memory, or anything like that. Perl handles all that stuff internally. You don't even have to convert strings to numbers or vice versa. Perl will recognize if a string has only numbers in it, and allow you to multiply it by a number or apply any mathematical operators to it. Everything from the first non-numerical character in a string onward is dropped, so "123blah" would be treated by numerical operators as "123", and "blah" would be treated as zero.

Operators are there to modify these variables. There are the mathematical operators you'd expect: +, -, =, and so on. C-style incrementation operators are available (++ and --), as are space-saving composite mathematical operators (+=, -=, *=, and so on). There are also extra operators such as exponentiation (**); modulus (%); and the comparison operators that are used in conditional clauses: >, <, =>, =<, ==, and !=. Strings can be concatenated with the . operator, or repeated any number of times using the string repetition operator (x). There are literally more operators in Perl than you are ever likely to need to know about, and a book dedicated to the subject of Perl will be able to provide full coverage of all of them.

A few simple lines of Perl that show the use of variables, literals, and operators are as follows:

```
$a = 5;
$a++;
$b = $a ** 2;
$c = "test" . $b;
print "$c";
```

This block of code would print out the string "test36". If that's clear to you, you understand the building blocks of Perl.

Scalars, Arrays, and Associative Arrays

Variables can be used individually or in arrays of arbitrary numbers of dimensions. We've already seen scalar variables, such as $a, $b, and $c in the previous example; a scalar variable contains a single number or string. But each of these variables travels separately, and there will be times when you will need to work with groups of associated pieces of data. This is where arrays come in:

```
@array1 = ("blah",5,12.7,$a);
@array2 = ($a, $b, $c);
```

An array has the same kind of naming conventions as a scalar variable, except that it has an "at" sign (@) at the beginning instead of a dollar sign. As these examples show, an array does not need to be declared with a certain size or to contain only a consistent type of data. Arrays can contain numbers, strings, other arrays, or whatever you like.

You can access an element of an array using square brackets. The third element of the previous @array1 array, a scalar value, would be $array1[2]. Remember that array element numbering begins at zero!

You will also see elements of arrays addressed with an @ prefix instead of $. This is because you can address a "slice" of an array by specifying more than one element; for example, @array1[1,2]. This is really an array in itself with two elements. If you say @array1[2], you're talking about a slice with one element, which is effectively the same thing as a scalar variable and works the same way; but for consistency's sake you may want to keep in mind that the "preferred" method is $array1[2].

There are various array operators, essentially built-in functions, which allow you to set up your arrays any way you like. Arrays are often also called "lists"; in that context, you can think of it in "stack" terminology, which gives you the push(), pop(), shift(), and unshift() operators. These operators are listed in Table 21.1, where @array1 undergoes each of them in turn.

TABLE 21.1   List Operators

Operator	Function	Syntax	Result
push()	Add a value to the end of a list	push(@array1,"test");	@array1 = ("blah", 5,12.7,6,"test")
pop()	Remove a value from the end of a list and return it	$d = pop(@array1);	@array1 = ("blah", 5,12.7,6), $d = "test"
unshift()	Add a value to the beginning of a list	unshift(@array1,"test");	@array1 = ("test","blah", 5,12.7,6)
shift()	Remove a value from the beginning of a list and return it	$d = shift(@array1);	@array1 = ("blah",5, 12.7,6), $d = "test"

> **Tip**
>
> Note that each of these operations can alternately be done by setting the output of the operator to a new array, or even to the same array. So, by saying @array3 = push(@array1, "test"), you can create a new array with the new lengthened contents, leaving the original array (@array1) untouched.

Introduction to Perl Programming

CHAPTER 21

549

21

INTRODUCTION TO
PERL
PROGRAMMING

A further useful array function is sort(); sort(@array1) would arrange all the elements in lexicographical order, treating them all as strings. You can specify an alternate sorting algorithm of your own construction to extend the functionality of the sort() routine to do whatever you like. For instance, if you create a subroutine called numerically(), which sorts two arguments in numerical order, you can sort numerically (@array1).

Arrays are especially useful when you're working with relational data, either through interfaces to real databases or simply delimited text files such as /etc/passwd. Arrays are also the way you would access the individual lines in a file that you've read in from standard input. We'll be looking at how that's done a bit later in the chapter.

> **Tip**
>
> You can get the size of an array by accessing it in "scalar context." The easiest way to do this is to assign the list to a scalar variable:
>
> ```
> $size = @array1;
> ```
>
> Now, $size is equal to 4.

An array can be created from a scalar string using the split() function. This will divide up the string based on whatever delimiter you specify, omitting the delimiter from each of the new array's elements.

```
$mystring = "Test|my name|Interesting data|123";
@mydata = split(/\|/,$mystring);
```

Note that slashes are used to delimit the delimiter expression, and you have to escape the pipe character (|) with a backslash to make sure that it's evaluated as a delimiter and not the "alternative" operator, which will make sense a little later, in the section on regular expressions. In any case, @mydata now contains the strings "Test", "my name", "Interesting data", and "123" as its elements.

A special kind of array is an *associative array*; this is equivalent to a hash table in which the different values in the array are stored as key/value pairs. The prefix for an associative array is the percent sign (%), but each value of the array is a scalar, so you use the scalar prefix ($) to refer to the individual elements. Here's how you set up an associative array:

```
$assoc1{key1} = "value1";
$assoc1{key2} = "value2";
```

You can then use any of several associative array operators on the array as a whole:

```
@myvalues = values(%assoc1);
while (($mykey,$myvalue) = each(%assoc1)) {
  print "$mykey -> $myvalue\n";
}
```

Associative arrays are very useful in applications such as server-side CGI programming, in which all the variables from HTML forms are sent to the server and read into an associative array based on the form field names.

Flow Control

What makes Perl a full-featured programming environment rather than a simple batch scripting language is its complete set of flow-control structures. These are what allow you to create complex data-flow paths and iterations in your programs.

if/elsif/else

The most common control structure is the `if` block:

```
if ($a == 5) {
  print "It's 5\n";
} elsif ($a > 5) {
  print "Greater than 5\n";
} else {
  print "Must be less than 5\n";
}
```

> **Note**
>
> Note that the conditional clause ($a == 5) must use the *equality operator*, ==, rather than a single = sign (the assignment operator). The == operator and other comparison operators, which we saw a little earlier, can always be used in conditionals. But if the items you're comparing are strings, you can use the string equivalents: eq for ==, lt for <, ne for !=, and others.

foreach

Another common flow-control player in Perl is `foreach`. This allows you to iterate over all the elements in an array.

```
foreach $line (@buffer) {
  print $line;
}
```

If you omit the optional variable name that refers to the element the loop is looking at ($line in this example), use the default $_ variable name to refer to the current element.

Introduction to Perl Programming
CHAPTER 21

551

21

INTRODUCTION TO
PERL
PROGRAMMING

It's a good idea to specify a variable name here in order to prevent confusion when you're doing multiple nested `foreach` loops.

for

There is also a standard `for` loop in Perl, which is almost identical to the `for` loop in C. The purpose of `for` is simply to iterate a specified number of times, rather than over the elements of an array. The `for` loop is controlled by an iteration variable—generally one that isn't used anywhere else in the script—which is iterated automatically by `for` until it reaches your specified limit. Its arguments, as in C, are separated by semicolons: the name of the iteration variable, the incrementation operation, and the end condition:

```perl
for ($i; $i++; $i<100) {
  print "$i\n";
}
```

This example `for` loop will print out 100 lines, numbered from 0 to 99. The first argument sets up `$i` as the iteration variable; the second says that `$i` should be incremented upward once; and the `for` loop will execute unless the condition specified in the third argument is false, which in this example occurs once `$i` has reached 100.

while/until/do

Finally, we have the `while` loop, which acts like a simplified version of `for` without the iteration variable. It has a conditional statement as its argument, evaluated every time the loop begins, and it keeps executing until the conditional is false.

```perl
while ($i < 100) {
  $1 += 5;
  $j++;
}
print "$j\n";
```

This loop will execute 20 times, and the output of the `print` statement will be `20`.

A variant of `while` is `until`, which has effectively the opposite meaning: It keeps executing until the conditional is true. The following example has the same effect as the previous `while` loop:

```perl
until($i == 100) {
  $i += 5;
  $j++;
}
print "$j\n";
```

Another way to do either `while` or `until`, which you may need to do on some occasions, is the `do...while` or `do...until` construct. This guarantees that the loop will execute at least once, and the `while` or `until` conditional is evaluated at the end, rather than the beginning:

```
do {
  $i += 5;
  $j++;
} while ($i < 100);
print "$j\n";
```

Backquotes (`` ` ``) enable Perl to execute any command as you would at the command line or within a shell script. Simply enclose your command in backquotes, and Perl will execute it using `/bin/sh`, waiting until the spawned process quits before proceeding. What's more, the output from the backquoted command is available as the return value, so you can put it into a variable for later use. Here's a commonly used example:

```
$date = `date`;
```

Note that this returned string generally has a `\n` at the end, so you can use `chomp()` to snip it off, either on a separate line or by enclosing the original assignment as an expression:

Caution

One thing to watch out for is that Perl won't necessarily know your command path; while it might work for you on your own machine, if you put the script on another system, it might fail through not being able to find the command you're trying to run. The best defense against this is to specify the full path to the command:

```
@who = `/usr/bin/who`;
```

```
chomp($date = `date`);
```

Command-Line Arguments

You can pass as many arguments as you want on the command line to a Perl program. These arguments, separated by whitespace (unless enclosed in quotes), are placed at runtime into the `@ARGV` array, and are available for any kind of use:

```
# ./myscript.pl test "My String" 123
```

@ARGV[0] is now "test", @ARGV[1] is "My String", and @ARGV[2] is "123". This also works on CGI programs, as we will see in Chapter 26, "Configuring a Web Server." If you specify a URL with arguments separated by + characters (the usual way of doing such things), @ARGV will be populated the same way:

```
http://www.some-host.com/myscript.cgi?test+My%20String+123
```

A Simple Perl Script

The following script (see Listing 21.1) doesn't really do anything useful except to use as many of the techniques as possible that we've covered so far, including some we haven't. This script is available on the included CD-ROM as simpledemo.pl.

LISTING 21.1   Simple Demo Perl Script (simpledemo.pl)

```perl
#!/usr/bin/perl

# <STDIN> is an I/O handle referring to the standard input. In this context,
# we're using it to read in text input from a prompt. The chomp operator removes
# any trailing newline/return characters from the end of the input.
print "Please enter your name: ";
chomp ($name = <STDIN>);

srand;   # Initialize the random number generator
@namelist = ("Bob","Jane","Frank");
@colorlist = ("green","red","blue","yellow");
foreach $testname (@namelist) {
  # You can select any random element of an array by using the rand() operator
  # on it.
  $colors{$testname} = $colorlist[rand(@colorlist)];
}
while (($name,$color) = each(%colors)) {
  print "$name: $color\n";
  undef ($n);    # The undef() function undefines a variable. Works like NULL.
  do {
    $color = @colorlist[$n+1];
    $n++;
  } until ($color eq "blue");
}
```

Advanced Perl Techniques

Now that we've covered the fundamentals of Perl, it's time to move on to some of the more interesting things we can do with it. So far we've seen nothing about file access, functions, modules, or even Perl's hallmark: its text-processing capabilities. Let's take a look at some of these now.

Text Processing

A regular ssion (also often called a *regexp*) is a very highly developed way of specifying a pattern to seek in a text stream. You can use regexps to do simple searches on strings, or you can modify one to include such constraints as the beginning or end of a line, groups of certain characters, included strings of arbitrary length, or any of a flexible number of occurrences of any pattern. Regexps are part of many different tools in UNIX, especially the pattern-matching tool grep and its variants. Perl gives you the same kind of flexibility as you have in grep, but embeds it in a full-featured programming environment. This is something that almost all other languages lack. For instance, in C you have to copy strings back and forth in memory, seek through them character-by-character—effectively, it's not possible without a lot of pain.

Regular Expressions

The simplest regexp pattern is a text string. To seek for a regexp in a string, use the =~ operator, and enclose the regexp in slashes:

```
if ($string =~ /abc123/) { ...
```

This can be simplified even more if you're receiving a text string already, such as from the "diamond operator" (<>), which allows you to loop through a text file specified on the command line (we'll look at this in the next subsection). If this is the case, and you already have a $_ variable (the "default" variable that we saw back in the section on foreach), you can search on it implicitly:

```
if (/abc123/) { ...
```

That's all well and good. But what about searching for a more complex pattern? For example, let's modify the pattern so that "abc123" will match only if it appears at the beginning of the line. This is done with the ^ anchor: /^abc123/.

There's an end-of-line anchor too, $, which is interpreted as such only if it's at the end of the regexp. Otherwise, it's treated as a variable name prefix. Using these two anchors together, we can change our pattern to only match if "abc123" is the whole line, with nothing else on it:

```
if (/^abc123$/) { ...
```

These are only the most basic of the regexp pattern controls. You can embed [abc] to specify a character "class", or any of the three letters a, b, or c. You can use quantifiers immediately after any character, class, or grouping to specify how many times it can appear in sequence. Table 21.2 shows a summary of these patterns (and not a complete one, at that).

TABLE 21.2 Regular Expression Syntax Operators

	Text	
.	Any single character	
[abc123]	Any of "abc123"	
[^abc123]	None of "abc123"	
[a-g]	All characters between a and g, inclusive	
abc1|abc2	Alternative: abc1 or abc2	
(abc123)	Grouping (for use with quantifiers or alternatives, or back references)	
	Quantifiers	
?	0 or 1 of the preceding text	
*	0 or *n* of the preceding text (*n* > 0)	
+	1 or *n* of the preceding text (*n* > 1)	
*?	Forces * to the minimal match (anti-greediness quantifier)	
{m}	Exactly m repetitions of the preceding text	
{m,n}	n through m repetitions of the preceding text	
{m,}	m or more repetitions of the preceding text	
	Anchors	
^	Start-of-line anchor	
$	End-of-line anchor	
\b	Word boundary	
\B	No word boundary	
	Escape Codes	
\X	Escapes (treats as a literal) any character X (for example, ".")	
\r	Carriage return	
\n	Line feed	
\f	Form feed	
\t	Tab	
\d	Digits (equivalent to [0-9])	
\w	Word characters (equivalent to [a-zA-Z0-9_])	
\s	Whitespace (equivalent to [\r\t\n\f])	
\D	NOT digits	
\W	NOT words	
\S	NOT whitespace	

TABLE 21.2   Continued

\###	ASCII character ### (in octal)
\cX	Control+x character (where X is any character)

> **Note**
>
> A word on precedence: When grouping within a regexp, parentheses have the highest precedence, followed by multipliers, then anchors, and then alternatives.

What's more, you can also add various switches to the end of the pattern, after the final slash, to change the sense of the match. An i makes it a case-insensitive search, for example: /abc/i

Regexps can be made as complex as the most obfuscated code you've ever seen in your life, and finishing a well-crafted regexp that does some incredibly obscure task can be one of the most satisfying parts of the UNIX lifestyle.

Translations

Of course, what's a search without the ability to replace? Perl has several built-in translation operators: the "substitution" operator (s///), "transliteration" operator (tr///), and explicit string-manipulation functions such as substr().

To do a substitution, you will still use the =~ operator, but this time as an assignment operator rather than a comparison. The argument to it is the s operator, then a regexp, then the replacement string, and finally any options. These are all separated by slashes:

```
$mystring =~ s/^test[0-9]/foo/g;
```

Here's a more useful example, which translates angle brackets into HTML escape sequences to display them literally in a Web page:

```
$myhtml =~ s/</&lt;/g;
$myhtml =~ s/>/&gt;/g;
```

The g at the end means "global", and tells the substitution operator to do a "replace all"—changing "test1", "test2", and so on, all to "foo"; if omitted, only the first match in the string would be substituted.

What if you wanted to preserve that number ([0-9]) in the previous example? That's where groupings and back references come in. Anything you put in parentheses in a regexp can be repeated or recalled by number. Within the regexp, you would use \#, where

is the number of the parenthesized grouping. For example, in the regexp `/abc(123)(.*)\1\2/`, `\1` is interpreted as `123` and `\2` is interpreted as `.*`. Note that this doesn't start at 0, confusingly enough, but 1. You can have as many of these patterns as you want.

Now, to apply this to a substitution, you can also refer to a regexp's parenthesized groupings from beyond the delimiting slash—not with `\1` and `\2`, but with `$1` and `$2`. These special read-only variables remain in memory after the match, too, so you can use them later on in your code. Here's how the previous example would look if we wanted to preserve the number:

```
$mystring =~ s/^test([0-9])/foo$1/g;
```

Okay...the substitution operator is all well and good, but for some functions—capitalizing all the letters, translating all 3s to 4s, and the like—it's cumbersome and sometimes prohibits what you want to do. That's a job for the transliteration operator (`tr///`).

The `tr` operator acts like a simplified and constricted version of the `s` operator, with a few of its functions held in check. Its operation takes a set of characters (not a regexp, just a group of characters or a range), a second set of characters, and maps the first set onto the second set. Be careful to note that we use the `=` operator with `tr`, rather than the `=~` (matching) operator. For example:

```
$mystring = "cat and dog";
$mystring = tr/abc/def/;
```

`$mystring` is now `fdt dnd dog`. The mappings can take on a number of interesting forms, especially if the new string is shorter than the old; if that happens, it simply wraps the shorter pattern around to make the matches fit. You can specify the `d` option (after the final slash) to make the matches "line up," deleting unmatched characters from the first set.

The most useful applications of `tr` are usually for things such as capitalization. This can be done by specifying a range on both sides:

```
$mystring = tr/A-Z/a-z/;
```

This example would force everything in `$mystring` to lowercase.

One of the more useful explicit text-processing functions is `substr()`. Its full usage is covered, along with all the other built-in functions in a good Perl reference; but the quick summary is that it takes a string, an offset, and a length—and returns just that substring. For example:

```
$mystring = "cat and dog";
$newstring = substr($mystring,0,3);
```

$newstring is now "cat". This is cool enough as it is, but substr() really comes into its own when used in conjunction with index(). This function will return the point in a string where a given substring appears:

```
$mystring = "cat and dog";
$newstring = substr($mystring,index($mystring,"cat"),index($mystring,"dog"));
```

This would assign "cat and " to $mystring, including the trailing space.

Working with Files

You can open a file, read it into an array, and write out a new one, or do many at once, through the use of *filehandles*. These are I/O methods that give you a way to direct your input and output to places other than the console (for example, in to and out of files).

The simplest filehandle is the "diamond operator," which doesn't really have a permanent filehandle at all—it's just a way to treat an incoming file (or set of files) from the command line as an input filehandle for as long as there are lines in the file to read. To use the diamond operator, use a loop like the following:

```
while (<>) {
  print $_;
}
```

Then, run your program with one or more filenames on the command line:

```
# ./myscript.pl file1.txt file2.txt ...
```

This will have the effect of printing out all the contents of the specified files, much in the way that cat would. This is a very convenient, quick way of operating on a file's contents. However, it's pretty limited; it's really a "degenerate case" of a true filehandle. Let's look at some properly specified ones and what they can really do.

A filehandle name by convention is in all caps. It is created with the open() command; and afterward you can read from it, print to it, and close it. Here's how to read a file's contents into an array:

```
open (FH,"/path/to/file1.txt");
@contents = <FH>;
close (FH);
```

It's possible for Perl to fail to open the file, either because it doesn't exist, its permissions don't allow you to read it, or any other of a number of reasons. You can trap for failures opening the file by using the die operator; if the evaluation of an expression falls through to die, it will print its argument (if any) to standard output, and the script will quit. Here's the most common way this is used with opening files:

```
open (FH,"/path/to/file1.txt") || die ("Can't open file1.txt!");
@contents = <FH>;
close (FH);
```

Writing to files is a bit more complex since there are so many different ways you can do it. The thing to remember is that you can write to any kind of handle you can use on the command line, which includes the > (overwrite) or >> (append) redirectors, or even the | (pipe) into a program. This is useful for, say, having your script write its output into an e-mail message.

```
open (FH,">/path/to/file2.txt");
print FH $_ foreach (@contents);
close (FH);

open (MAIL,"| /sbin/sendmail -oi -t");
print MAIL "From: me\@somewhere.com\n";
print MAIL "To: you\@somewhereelse.com\n";
print MAIL "Subject: Check it out!\n\n";
print MAIL $_ foreach (@contents);
close (MAIL);
```

Caution

Remember that when specifying @ characters in text strings (in email addresses, for instance), you need to precede them with backslashes to prevent Perl from treating them as array identifiers. If you don't, the script will fail with an error.

The filehandle goes as an argument to print; it's important here to realize that this argument is assumed to be the built-in filehandle <STDOUT> (standard output), unless a different one is specified. There is also a <STDIN> handle. To set the default input/output filehandle, use the select() function:

```
select (FH);
```

This way, you won't have to say print FH every time. However, you'll need to switch it back to STDOUT when you're done with FH.

Directories have corresponding opendir() and readdir() functions; you can open a directory and read its contents into an array like this:

```
opendir (DIR,"/path/to/dir");
@files = sort readdir (DIR);
closedir (DIR);
```

Using what we've seen so far, we can now do some pretty interesting stuff. Let's open up /etc/passwd, grab all the entries that have a UID greater than 1000, and print out their usernames and full names.

```
#!/usr/bin/perl

open (PASSWD,"/etc/passwd") || die ("Can't open passwd file!");
@passwd = <PASSWD>;
close (PASSWD);

foreach (@passwd) {
  @userdata = split(/:/,$_);
  if (@userdata[2] > 1000) {
    print "@userdata[0]: @userdata[4]\n";
  }
}
```

A useful tool already! This is what makes Perl so popular. There's very little effort involved in producing programs that make your life measurably easier.

Functions

Perl has hundreds of built-in functions, many of which we've already seen. These functions cover pretty much any general-purpose necessity of programming, especially once you know how to include Perl modules that expand your available functions as much as you want. However, there will come the time in your more complex Perl programs—especially programs that span multiple Perl scripts, such as server-side CGI suites—where you will want to define functions of your own (which Perl calls *subroutines*) to accomplish your common tasks.

You can define functions anywhere in your script that you want; they don't need to have already been "declared" in order to work. For neatness' sake you might choose to put your function definitions at the end, or you might want to put them all inline, or at the top—it doesn't matter.

Let's say we want to be able to pass an arbitrary number of values to a function, and have it add them together. The syntax for this would be as follows:

```
sub sum {
  $mysum += $_ foreach (@_);
  $mysum;  # This line evaluates $mysum and thus sets the function's return
value
}
```

The function would then be called with its name prefixed with the ampersand character:

```
$newsum = &sum(45,14,2134,89);
```

The @_ variable refers to the argument list, much in the same way that @ARGV represents the arguments passed to the program itself from the command line. To do a more "traditional" style of function, the kind that most other languages have (which accept a certain number of named variables), you can do something like this:

Introduction to Perl Programming

CHAPTER 21

561

21

INTRODUCTION TO
PERL
PROGRAMMING

```perl
sub printname {
  ($name, $number, $passwd) = @_;
  print "$name/$number" if ($passwd);
}
```

Functions bring up a common hornets' nest of issues surrounding "global" and "local" namespaces. The rule about Perl is that there are no local functions—they're all globally defined. Any variables that you define in a function are global, unless you say otherwise—for example, with the local() operator. The @_ array is already local; each time you call a function, its argument array is created as a brand-new local copy. Using local(), you can do the same with other variables, too, and have them be relevant only within the function and discarded when it's done:

```perl
sub sum {
  local($mysum);
  $mysum += $_ foreach (@_);
  $mysum;  # This line evaluates $mysum and thus sets the function's return
value
}
```

The my operator does the same thing, and it is more common nowadays. You can use my to specify a list of local variables:

```perl
my ($mysum, $name, $hash);
```

If you're running in "strict mode", Perl will complain unless you've properly specified your local variables within every function, and it won't let you use variables unless they're declared in a my statement. Keeping things tidy in memory isn't as big a deal in Perl because Perl programs tend to execute and quit without hanging around for a long time, but good code style does dictate practices such as these.

Perl Modules

Every good language has shared libraries of some sort, and Perl is no exception. In fact, Perl's libraries (called *modules*), which are chunks of non-executable Perl code with .pm extensions (for "Perl module"), have grown up as a very distributed Internet-wide grass-roots effort, much in the same way that FreeBSD's ports collection has grown. The ports and Perl modules do play an interrelated part, as a matter of fact—which we'll get to in a moment.

You can put Perl code into a .pm file in the same directory as your script (for instance, mylib.pm) and then call it using the use operator, minus the .pm extension:

```perl
use mylib;
```

Perl's support structure in FreeBSD is installed in /usr/lib/perl5. There aren't any Perl modules in there, though; it's up to you to install any modules that you need in the course of your system's life, and those go into (surprise!) /usr/local/lib/perl5. This directory forks in two directions, with man pages in one (named for the current version of Perl) and the actual modules in the other (site_perl). Inside this (one more level down) are various directories containing module groupings for any module set you've installed. There is also an i386-freebsd directory, which contains precompiled C code that some Perl modules use for performance reasons (mathematics-heavy algorithms, for example).

Modules come in groups, with a prefix and a module name separated by a double colon (::), as in C++ scoping. For example, Net::Telnet is the name of the Perl module that contains Telnet capabilities, and Net::DNS provides name-server lookup functions. These are kept in /usr/local/lib/perl5/site_perl/5.005, in the Net directory, as Telnet.pm and DNS.pm.

This directory is in Perl's search path. To bring a module into your script, use the use operator, like so:

```
use Net::Telnet;
```

Now, any function specified in that module can be used in your script as if you'd defined it within the script itself, simply by prepending an & to its name.

How do we find out which functions are in a module? By using perldoc, that's how. This utility works in a similar fashion to man, and assuming that you've installed your modules properly (for example, through the ports, as we'll see in a moment), you can look up any module's documentation the same way you'd specify it in a script. Here's part of the documentation for the Image::Size module (see Listing 21.2):

LISTING 21.2 Example Documentation for a Perl Module

```
# perldoc Image::Size

Image::Size(3) User Contributed Perl Documentation Image::Size(3)

NAME
        Image::Size - read the dimensions of an image in several
        popular formats

SYNOPSIS
        use Image::Size;
        # Get the size of globe.gif
        ($globe_x, $globe_y) = imgsize("globe.gif");
        # Assume X=60 and Y=40 for remaining examples

        use Image::Size 'html_imgsize';
```

LISTING 21.2   continued

```
# Get the size as "HEIGHT=X WIDTH=Y" for HTML generation
$size = html_imgsize("globe.gif");
# $size == "HEIGHT=40 WIDTH=60"

use Image::Size 'attr_imgsize';
# Get the size as a list passable to routines in CGI.pm
@attrs = attr_imgsize("globe.gif");
# @attrs == ('-HEIGHT', 40, '-WIDTH', 60)

use Image::Size;
# Get the size of an in-memory buffer
($buf_x, $buf_y) = imgsize($buf);
```

Documentation of this type will generally give you usable and accurate prototype code that you can insert into your scripts, as well as a complete listing of all available functions.

Perl Modules and the Ports Collection

What's the "correct" way to install Perl modules, you ask? Yes, it's our old friend the ports collection. Go into /usr/ports, and look through the various subdirectories. You'll see many ports beginning with p5-; these are Perl modules, which have been codified into proper FreeBSD ports. (Package versions of most of them exist, too.) Many modules have compiled C components, as well as multiple supporting modules and documentation, so it's definitely important to make sure that everything gets installed in the proper place. The ports make sure of that.

/usr/ports/net/p5-Net-Telnet is the port for Net::Telnet, and that's the naming scheme for all of them—a dash for the double colon. Some port categories have dozens of Perl modules, all of them added to the ports out of repeated usefulness. This distributed model allows Perl to be infinitely extensible while remaining fairly unencumbered in its default installation.

To install a module from the ports, simply build it as you would any port: cd into its directory, make, and make install. Perl modules have a built-in make test target, which tunes and evaluates how well the module will work on the system; this is run implicitly with the ports' make target.

You can use pkg_info and pkg_version to check which Perl modules you have installed; this is much easier than remembering to look in /usr/local/lib/perl5. The rest of the package tools work as well; you can pkg_add a Perl module from its tarball if you like, and pkg_update it when a new version comes out.

Useful Perl Resources

Because Perl is so widespread, it's little wonder that there are so many resources for it available in as many formats as you might want. Nearly everyone involved in content provider work on the Internet needs to have some familiarity with Perl, so computer bookstores do a brisk trade in books on the subject, and the most cursory or off-topic of searches on the Web will turn up discussions between Perl hackers on how to do this or that.

We'll now take a look at some of the more centralized and "official" sources of Perl information.

Web Sites

If you need a Perl reference, the first stop should be the Web. It's not as direct or definitive as a book, but if you don't have such a book, you're sure to find your answer on the Web in at least some form.

www.perl.org

www.perl.org is the "Perl Mongers" Web site, an independently run source of information and advocacy references. There are mailing lists you can join, as well as affiliated Web sites such as www.perldoc.com, the centralized Perl documentation database.

www.perl.com

The "official" Perl site, run by O'Reilly, is an aggregation of Perl news, tutorials, and discussions about all kinds of details of working with Perl. This is probably the most complete site for everyday Perl happenings, if not necessarily for definitive reference.

Books

Just about every Perl hacker has one of the popular O'Reilly Perl reference books on hand; for complete and easy-to-follow reference, these books are hard to beat.

The "Camel" Book

Programming Perl is the complete Perl reference book, written by Larry Wall (the father of Perl), Tom Christiansen, and Jon Orwant (O'Reilly, 2000). Nicknamed for the camel on the cover, which has become synonymous with Perl as a visual logo, this book is frequently revised to cover the most recent developments in the Perl world, and is widely accepted as the "definitive" work on the subject. One of its best features is an alphabetized function reference, an indispensable section.

The "Llama" Book

Learning Perl, by Randal L. Schwartz and Tom Phoenix (O'Reilly, 2001) is the "Camel" Book's little brother; the llama is its icon. It covers the basics of Perl (essentially the same topics covered in this chapter) in enough detail and with an engaging enough style to cover pretty much all you'll need to get you to where Perl is no longer a foreign language to you.

Perl Developer's Dictionary

Perl Developer's Dictionary by Clinton Pierce (Sams, 2001, ISBN: 0-672-32067-3) is a comprehensive reference of all Perl functions, and one of the most complete texts on the subject available today. It's ideal for the more advanced Perl hacker who needs reference on syntax and usage more than tutorials on how Perl works.

The CPAN

The *CPAN (Comprehensive Perl Archive Network)* is where all the modules across the Net are pulled together and made public. This also applies to binary distributions, scripts, and other tools; as well as source code for the brave of heart. Its primary usefulness, though, is for its comprehensive module list; if there's a module you want to install that isn't in the ports collection, you'll find it here, as well as all kinds of documentation that will help you use it.

The CPAN's central site is at `http://www.perl.com/CPAN-local/`. The CPAN's purpose is to provide numerous worldwide mirrors of its resources so that everyone will have quick access to it; you can use the sites list and map to find a mirror close to you and bookmark it for later reference.

FreeBSD Networking

PART
IV

IN THIS PART

Introduction to Networking

CHAPTER 22

There was once a time when there were two kinds of operating systems: those that were designed for networks, and those that weren't. The former category was dominated by mainframe-class UNIX flavors such as AIX, IRIX, Digital UNIX, BSDI, and more-specialized systems such as Novell NetWare and VMS. The latter category consisted of consumer-level desktop operating systems such as Windows and Mac OS. The two types of systems had very little in common, but the biggest architectural difference was that the network operating systems were robustly multiuser at the heart, with remote accessibility and networking capability built into the kernel. On the other hand, the desktop systems were single-user and much less robust, with no native networking support. Proprietary networking protocols existed (such as AppleTalk), but connecting a desktop system to the Internet required specialized, often third-party software of little maturity or integration into the operating system.

That has all changed. In the present day, the consumer-level, single-user, non-networked PC platform is giving way to operating systems whose robustness and networkability would have put to shame many of the mainframe-class systems of the old days. Mac OS X (with its FreeBSD architecture and Mach kernel) and Windows 2000/XP are both examples of platforms that were built around networking as a fundamental tenet, and are intended to replace older, formerly non-networkable systems. TCP/IP (the *de facto* transport protocol suite of the Internet) is woven tightly into the cores of these systems as it was in the mainframes, and as it is in FreeBSD.

The upshot is that FreeBSD is a system designed from the ground up to be a network-aware platform. Whether you're using it as a workstation or a server, chances are that you're using it for its networking strengths, and a FreeBSD machine without a network is frankly not a lot of use. It's certainly a great deal less fun.

In this chapter, we will cover the basic principles of networking as it applies to FreeBSD and its role in the Internet.

Introduction to Networking

Networking is the ability of two or more computers to be aware of each other's existence and exchange data. In the Internet age, this basic capability can mean anything from simple awareness sensing and topology mapping to e-mail traveling from server to server, Web browsers downloading HTML pages and large movie files from HTTP servers, and peer-to-peer MP3 sharing. A networked computer has the capability to expand its usefulness beyond what the user can buy off the shelf and install from CD, instantly and without any physical media being introduced. The advent of networking and what it means for business and recreation is what has fueled the computer revolution that is very likely behind your decision to use FreeBSD.

The *de facto* standard protocol suite that runs almost all active networks these days is TCP/IP (Transmission Control Protocol/Internet Protocol), and networking—especially FreeBSD networking—has become nearly synonymous with TCP/IP in recent years. TCP/IP, whose fundamental structure we will be examining in some detail later in this chapter, has enjoyed some thirty years of development and maturity, and its extensibility and modularity are part of what has contributed to its success. Although the first recognized computer network—the United States Department of Defense-funded ARPAnet—dates back to 1969, when its first four nodes were brought online at four universities in the western US, TCP/IP itself has its roots in a 1974 paper by Internet design pioneers Vint Cerf and Bob Kahn titled "A Protocol for Packet Network Interconnection." The Transmission Control Program, later to become split into TCP (Transmission Control Protocol) and IP (Internet Protocol), demonstrated a way that data could be sent reliably over the packet-switching networks that were then still newly discovering their usefulness. UNIX systems from Bell Labs, first released in 1977, helped to popularize the new protocol suite and some of the variants that fell into its layered structure, including UDP and ICMP. Thus, the foundations of FreeBSD's TCP/IP heritage were laid.

The TCP/IP suite forms the backbone for the Internet and all its trappings. It's just about the only game in town for network traffic over WAN (wide-area network) links, such as the telecommunications links between geographical regions; it's also quite prevalent in LANs (local-area networks), generally high-speed corporate enterprise or university networks connected directly through Ethernet or similar physical-link protocols. It's important to realize, though, that the IP layer—the component that corresponds to the "network" layer of the TCP/IP stack—is really the highest common element to the vast majority of Internet and LAN communications. Other protocols on the next level up, the "transport" layer (where TCP fits), cover the remainder: UDP, NetBIOS, ICMP, and other IP-based protocols don't use TCP, but are nonetheless still fairly common and have uses that aren't getting any less prevalent. Still more protocols, on the same level as IP (such as AppleTalk and IPX) are still widely used on LANs. We will be looking at how all of these protocols fit into the TCP/IP structure and how FreeBSD deals with them.

Network Topologies

Your FreeBSD machine might be installed on a university network, in a professional co-location facility, within a corporate enterprise network, or on a home dial-up network (or dialed-up directly)—and those are just the most common types of settings. Different network topologies, or logical layouts of devices and data link mechanisms, are as numerous as the individual networks in the world—no two are exactly the same. However, virtually all networks share a common basic topology and a few fundamental components.

In Figure 22.1, we can see the type of topology that would be found in a typical home network, but it's also serviceable as a simplified diagram of an enterprise or university network.

FIGURE 22.1

A basic network topology, showing a WAN and a LAN, separated by a router and comprising a number of different types of computers.

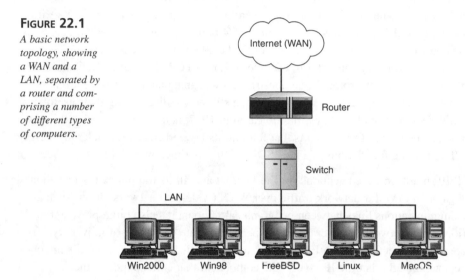

Each of these situations involves a WAN (wide-area network), generally a (relatively) low-speed serial link to the Internet such as a T1, T3, DSL, or cable modem connection—link types often referred to generically as "broadband," though the mechanisms for each are widely different. The bandwidth (or speed) of WAN links can range from the kilobits per second, in the case of 33–56Kbps modems, up through the massively infrastructural OC-3, OC-12, OC-48, and OC-192 links used between major telecommunications operators. Table 22.1 shows the equivalent speeds of most of the common WAN link types.

TABLE 22.1   Serial WAN Link Types and Corresponding Transfer Speeds

Link Type	Speed	Equivalency
Modem	Up to 56Kbps	
ISDN	56–128Kbps	
DSL	192kbps–1.5Mbps	
Cable Modem	1Mbps–5Mbps	

TABLE 22.1 continued

Link Type	Speed	Equivalency
T1	1.5Mbps	24 DS0 lines
T3	43.2Mbps	28 T1 lines
OC-3	155Mbps	100 T1 lines
OC-12	622Mbps	4 OC-3 lines
OC-48	2.5Gbps	4 OC-12 lines
OC-192	9.6Gbps	4 OC-48 lines

These WAN link types are designed to run over very long distances; because of their serial nature, they can carry traffic over telephone copper, fiber-optic lines, and any other infrastructure that carries standard telephone network "trunk" traffic. In fact, data traffic over these lines is indistinguishable from voice traffic; it's treated exactly the same way by phone switching equipment and travels from one geographical location to another, the same way a phone call would.

Another type of network topology is the Internet Service Provider (ISP) model, which involves a primary network like the one shown in Figure 22.1, as well as a secondary WAN connecting this network to a large number of home users dialing up via modems and phone lines. This is illustrated in Figure 22.2.

After the WAN traffic reaches a DSU/CSU and router, however, it makes the transition to LAN transport mechanisms such as Ethernet. This is a physical link mechanism that, unlike serial WAN traffic, can interface directly with any computer equipped with an Ethernet card.

In Figure 22.3, we can see a diagram of the bandwidth capacity of the entire path from one LAN to another, which is the path that Internet traffic usually takes from a server (such as a Web site) to a client (a user's Web browser). The WAN pipe, as a rule, is narrowest right before it hits the LAN router. Notice that although traffic in the middle of the WAN travels over lines with vastly more bandwidth than even the fastest LAN wiring, this bandwidth is divided among a great many more users than a typical LAN: thousands, even millions of users share the thickest trunk lines during peak usage periods. There are seldom more than a few hundred users competing for usage of a LAN.

22

INTRODUCTION TO NETWORKING

FIGURE 22.2

The ISP network topology; home users dial up through the telephone WAN over modems to the ISP's LAN, which then connects to the Internet WAN.

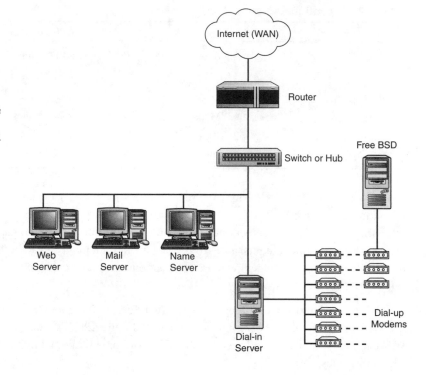

FIGURE 22.3

A schematic diagram of bandwidth availability throughout the path from one LAN (at the server end) to another LAN (at the client end), via a WAN of varying capacity.

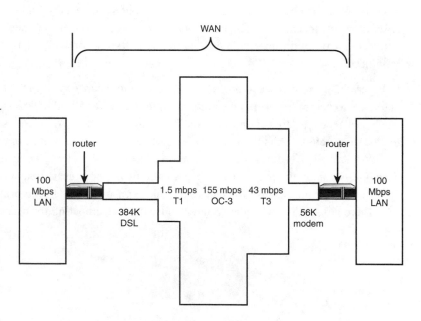

Network Components

We will be examining the various hardware components found in any network, so that you will have a working understanding of everything necessary to build a network of your own. The first topic to cover, because it's the component closest to the FreeBSD machine itself, is the cables.

Cables

The benefit of Ethernet and other LAN link types is that for very low cost, traffic can be carried between machines within a network at speeds that only the most expensive WAN links can reach: 10Mbps for "standard" Ethernet, 100Mbps for an enhanced and now nearly universally accepted variant (Fast Ethernet), and 1Gbps for the newest standard, Gigabit Ethernet. These speeds can be achieved with cheap cables and components, making networking between computers via Ethernet a joy compared to a low-speed WAN. The downside is that Ethernet can't be used over long distances. Because the signals aren't serialized or transmitted by equipment designed to support long-distance transmission, signals degrade with cable length, particularly in coaxial ("ThinNet" or "ThickNet") cables. Table 22.2 shows a summary of the different types of cables that can carry Ethernet traffic.

TABLE 22.2   Different Types of Ethernet Cables

Type	AKA	Speed	Cable	Connector	Maximum Length
10base-2	Thin Ethernet, ThinNet	10Mbps	Thin coaxial	DB-15 DIX/AUI (to transceiver)	185m
10base-5	Thick Ethernet, ThickNet	10Mbps	Thick coaxial	BNC	500m
10base-T	Ethernet	10Mbps	UTP (CAT3-CAT5)	RJ-45	100m
100base-TX	Fast Ethernet	100Mbps	UTP (CAT5)	RJ-45	100m
1000base-T	Gigabit Ethernet	1Gbps	UTP (CAT5)	RJ-45	100m

> **Note**
>
> A few acronym expansions:
>
> DIX: Digital, Intel, Xerox
>
> AUI: Attachment Unit Interface
>
> BNC: Bayonne Neil Councelman (or, alternately, British Naval Connector)
>
> UTP: Unshielded Twisted Pair

The most commonly used cabling these days is via twisted-pair cables, due to the relative simplicity and low cost of the cables and components. Whereas ThinNet and ThickNet must deal with terminators, segment-length limitations, repeaters, transceivers, BNC T-connectors (or "vampire tap" connectors for ThickNet), and unwieldy coaxial cables—instead, twisted-pair networks connect computers' network interface cards (NICs) directly to hubs and switches via cheap cables that can be coiled tightly and connected easily to RJ-45 phone-style jacks. Ethernet cards until recently came with multiple connectors to support all the different cable types described in Table 22.2 (see Figure 22.4), but today it's hard to find NICs with anything but the *de facto* standard RJ-45 connectors.

FIGURE 22.4

An Ethernet card showing the three common cable interfaces: RJ-45, DB-15, and BNC.

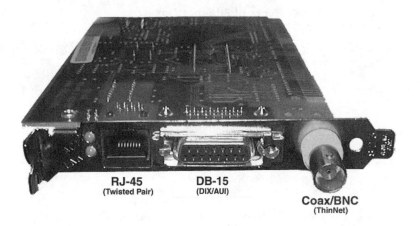

This standardization has resulted in an even lower cost in recent years for constructing Ethernet networks. Today, the only real use for BNC T-connectors and terminators is to make little metal sculptures, and ThickNet cable is useful only in hand-to-hand combat. The remainder of this chapter will concentrate on twisted-pair cable components because of their near ubiquity in today's networks.

Twisted-pair cables are cheap and flexible, and you can make your own if you want to save even more money. RJ-45 jack crimpers can be bought at any electronics supply store, as well as RJ-45 connectors and UTP cable. Refer to the section a little later in this chapter on "Straight-Through and Crossover Cables" for information on pinouts, so that you can attach the connectors correctly.

Refer to the next section for information on pinouts, so that you can attach the connectors correctly.

Straight-through and Crossover Cables

There are two types of twisted-pair cables: straight-through and crossover. The difference lies in whether the positions of two pairs of wires in the cable are reversed from one end to the other, and it's important to understand the different circumstances under which each are used.

Devices with RJ-45 connectors can be thought of as either "computer-type" or "hub-type" devices. Computers, routers, bandwidth managers, and other "endpoint" devices are considered "computer-type" devices, and hubs and switches are "hub-type" devices. The RJ-45 jacks on "computer-type" devices are all wired equivalently to each other, and "hub-type" devices are also all wired the same. Ethernet cables are wired to connect "computer-type" devices to "hub-type" devices.

To connect a computer to a hub, you need a straight-through cable. The same is true for connecting a computer to a switch or a router to a hub. These are all connections between "unlike" devices. However, to connect a hub to a hub or a hub to a switch, you need a crossover cable. You also need one to connect a computer to a computer; for instance, to play in two-player death-match mode. The rule to remember is this: Use straight-through cables between unlike devices, and crossover cables between like devices.

The tricky part is with the "uplink" port on hubs. This special port is wired as if it's a "computer-type" device, so you can connect a hub's "uplink" port to a standard port on another hub with a straight-through cable. This became necessary in large networks, in which a very long straight-through cable would be connected to a large enterprise-wide hub or switch (in the server room, for example), and wound through walls and conduits to emerge in another room. This cable couldn't be connected directly to a standard port on a smaller hub; it had to be fitted to an adapter and a short crossover cable before it could talk to the smaller hub. Replacing the Ethernet cable with a long crossover cable was impractical, to say the least. Hence the "uplink" port was born: a port that allowed a hub to be connected directly to another hub for which swapping out the cable for a crossover was not a viable option. Remember, though, that connecting two hubs' "uplink" ports together requires a crossover cable—that's a configuration that rather defeats the purpose, in any case.

How do you tell whether an Ethernet cable is a straight-through or a crossover cable? It's pretty easy: Hold up the two ends of the cable next to each other. If the color sequences of the wires match, it's a straight-through cable. If some of the wires appear out of place, it's a crossover cable.

The pinout for a straight-through cable is shown in Figure 22.5.

FIGURE 22.5

Straight-through cable wiring diagram.

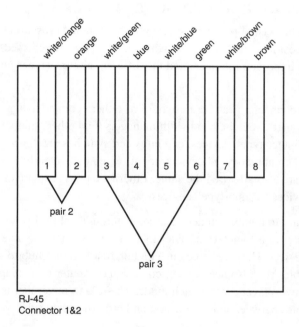

And to make a crossover cable, reverse the positions of pair 3 (wires 1/2) and pair 2 (wires 3/6), as shown when crimping the second end (see Figure 22.6).

Hubs

One end of the cable connects to your computer's Ethernet card; that much is clear. However, the other end needs to connect to something, too; far more often than not, what it connects to is a hub.

Figure 22.6

Crossover cable wiring diagram.

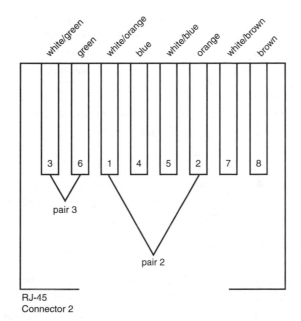

Hubs are devices with multiple RJ-45 ports, usually between four and 24, to which you can connect as many Ethernet cables as there are ports. These cables can connect to computers, other hubs, switches, or other network components as necessary. Hubs range in cost from about $40 to several hundred dollars depending on quality, number of ports, and the capability to operate simultaneously with 10base-T and 100base-TX devices. Many hubs can only do one or the other of the two popular speeds, and an auto-sensing hub (often referred to as "N-Way") can cost significantly more. Hubs range in size from small boxes no larger than your hand to full 19-inch rack-mountable units, and all require a power source. Some hubs are even "managed," meaning that you can telnet to them and configure each port's capabilities through a command-line interface. These hubs are naturally much more expensive than standalone hubs.

A hub is effectively a repeater, with all traffic appearing simultaneously on all ports, so a computer connected to one port on a hub will be able to see traffic to and from any other computer on the same hub. One port on a hub is usually reserved for "uplink"—a link to another hub, a switch, or a router higher up in the network hierarchy, as laid out in Figure 22.1; this "uplink" port is usually wired so that a crossover cable is not needed between the hub and its next upstream device. This port and one of the standard ports on the hub may also be wired so that they're mutually exclusive—a five-port hub might give you the option of hooking four computers together (ignoring the "uplink" port), or three computers to an upstream device (ignoring the fourth standard port). This might be hardwired, it might be controllable with a push-button or a DIP switch, or all the ports might be simultaneously usable. These are just some of the possible variations between different hubs.

Another matter that complicates the way hubs and other devices communicate with each other is that of half- and full-duplex. The difference is essentially that in half-duplex, a host can only be "listening" or "talking" at one time; whereas in full-duplex mode, twice as many wires are used, enabling the host to "listen" and "talk" at the same time. Thus, a 100Mbps Fast Ethernet link in full-duplex mode can transport up to 100Mbps on each direction simultaneously, whereas the same link in half-duplex can only do an aggregate total of 100Mbps in both directions.

Switches

Now that we know the nature and purpose of hubs, we can move on to switches. A *switch* looks like a hub that's a lot more expensive and usually has fewer ports. It has multiple RJ-45 ports, it ranges from hand-sized to rack-sized, and the same companies that make hubs make switches, so it's easy to mistake one for the other on store shelves. They even operate somewhat similarly—you can plug multiple devices into a switch, and a switch used in place of a hub in a network would usually give you what appears to be the same result. The difference between switches and hubs, however, is subtle yet crucial.

On a hub, all ports share the same internal wiring; all computers connected to the hub, as well as computers connected to other hubs connected to the first hub, exist on what's known as a "collision domain," in which a signal sent to one computer gets sent to all computers within the domain. It's up to each computer's Ethernet card to determine whether the signal is destined for it or not; and if it isn't, to throw it away.

A switch's internal wiring is much more complex. Each port comprises its own collision domain, and hosts connected to one port can't see any traffic destined for hosts on any of the other ports. Switches incorporate the software necessary to read each packet's Ethernet header and determine which port has the host that should get the packet, which means that a switch also stores an ARP cache, a lookup table of which hosts are on which ports. You can often confuse a switch by moving a computer from one port to another, so it may be necessary to power-cycle the switch in this circumstance. Managed switches, like managed hubs, have complete command-line interfaces and configurability, with the attendant high price and complexity.

Because each port on a switch has its own collision domain, this means that switched network traffic will be able to take fuller advantage of the available network bandwidth.

An eight-port, 100base-TX hub with all ports in use has to divide the available 100Mbps between the eight ports. If all eight ports are simultaneously trying to do bandwidth-intensive tasks and their aggregate bandwidth demand is greater than 100Mbps, "collisions"—cases in which two ports try to transmit or receive traffic at exactly the same time—will become much more common, resulting in retransmissions at the physical link level and performance degraded well below what each host would logically see as a share of the available 100Mbps. Switches alleviate this problem. Whereas a 100Mbps hub has 100Mbps of internal wiring in total, an eight-port switch has 800Mpbs worth of wiring—the full bandwidth duplicated for every port. This is why switches tend to have fewer ports than switches, and switches with many ports are quite expensive.

From a security standpoint, a fully switched network gives you the added benefit that machines in one collision domain can't see any traffic in any other collision domain. You can run a packet sniffer (such as `tcpdump` or EtherPeek) to put your Ethernet card into "promiscuous mode" (accepting all packets it sees whether or not they're destined for it) and spy on all other traffic within your collision domain; switches allow you to separate these domains so that this isn't possible. It also protects your network from being overwhelmed by a single host that floods the network with an aggressive traffic flow that uses all available bandwidth within the collision domain. The added cost of switches rather than hubs, along with careful network planning, can greatly increase the network's reliability, security, and performance.

Switches usually have no "uplink" ports, although occasionally (as with some two-port switches, which serve purely as a filter to keep out irrelevant traffic) one or both ports will have a push-button to select whether the port should need a straight-through or crossover cable. As a general rule, treat ports on a switch as "hub-type" devices, and use crossover cables to connect one switch to another, or a straight-through cable to connect a switch to a hub's "uplink" port.

Bridges

A *bridge* is a device that acts somewhat like a switch, but in a rather more complex way. To understand the function of a bridge, it's necessary to understand something of the four-layer structure of the TCP/IP stack. We will talk about TCP/IP in detail a little later in this chapter and cover the true function of a bridge; for now, think of a bridge as a type of switch that spans different networks, linking them together so that traffic from hosts on one network destined for another network can travel there directly without having to go to a router in the interim. This is useful for allowing traffic to pass from an Ethernet network to a Token Ring network, which is another style of LAN that is rapidly on the way out, so we won't bother discussing it.

Routers

A *router* is the most complex (and expensive) of all networking devices. Although we will be covering routing in detail later as well, it's necessary to know the function of a router as it applies to your network topology.

Routers have full operating systems and maintain tables that keep track of where entire networks can be found. Most networks have only one router, specifying which network numbers indicate your LAN and which ones should be forwarded on upstream into the WAN. You can have any number of routers in your network, though—each one managing a subnetwork and subservient to the topmost router.

What's more, routers use a variety of protocols to communicate with each other and plot out what's the best way for a packet to get from one place to another. When you send out a packet, it travels from router to router, further and further upstream by whatever route each router thinks is the best available, until it reaches a router that knows where *downstream* to find the destination network for your packet, and off it goes down through the downstream route until it reaches the destination LAN and, ultimately, the destination host. Routing is the backbone of the Internet and possibly the most complex part of the way TCP/IP networking operates, and we'll be spending more time both in this chapter and in Chapter 28, "Configuring an Internet Gateway," describing how it all works.

Most routers have either one or two LAN-side ports, either RJ-45 jacks or AUI ports that require transceivers to convert the interface to twisted-pair. On the other side of the router is a serial cable that connects to the DSU/CSU or other such high-speed serial converter, beyond which you have WAN traffic. Routers vary greatly in size, complexity, number and type of ports, manageability, and price; understanding how they work will be one of the most important things you can learn in the networking world.

Network Protocols

We've mentioned that most Internet traffic—HTTP, e-mail, FTP, and so on—use TCP/IP as their transport protocol, but also that it's more complicated than that alone. IP, the Internet Protocol, is the backbone of the vast majority of Internet traffic—the "network" layer of the TCP/IP stack—but TCP isn't the only commonly used "transport" layer protocol. There's also UDP, which differs from TCP in a few key ways. IP also isn't the only means of carrying traffic at the "network" level; it has a number of contemporaries, too, but they're mostly useful on LANs: AppleTalk, IPX, IGMP, and so on. Then there's ICMP, which exists partly on the "network" layer and partly on the "transport" layer; it's the mechanism by which the ping and traceroute utilities work. We'll talk about each of these protocols in some detail, but we'll leave the essentials of TCP/IP layering and header encapsulation until just a little later.

TCP: Transmission Control Protocol

TCP is *reliable*. That's the main distinguishing difference between TCP and UDP. TCP has lots of built-in features to make sure the traffic it carries arrives properly at its destination. It also has features to divide large packets into appropriately sized fragments so as to transmit more efficiently.

Also, TCP is a two-way mechanism. When a TCP packet is sent over the network, a timeout is set by the sender, which then waits for an acknowledgment (ACK) packet to come back from the other side. It then proceeds with the next packet. (Often, multiple packets can be sent at once, but this is a simplified example.) If the sender doesn't get the ACK from the other side within the specified timeout, it knows that either its own packet didn't make it, or the acknowledgment packet got lost on the way back, and so it sends the packet again and waits for the ACK again. This is what's known as a retransmission, and although it does provide reliability, it also decreases network efficiency— for each packet that must be retransmitted, that's twice as much traffic the infrastructure has to be able to support, which can lead to problematic congestion.

Because there is the concept of a "connection" fundamental to TCP, involving two endpoints and a fairly complex connection and disconnection procedure, you can tell quite accurately what TCP tasks your computer is doing. It's also a full-duplex connection, meaning that data can be sent and received at the same time, using the same packets. It's not uncommon for there to be a data payload on the ACK packets, for example. There are a number of other interesting features to TCP, such as a checksum that ensures the integrity of the data in the packet, automatic packet fragmenting and reconstruction, and out-of-order resequencing at the receiver level. These are all things that UDP doesn't do, or at least isn't required to do.

TCP is used in protocols in which data integrity is important and a connection can be ensured, such as Web surfing, e-mail, FTP, and the vast majority of other network applications.

UDP: User Datagram Protocol

The big thing to remember about UDP is that it's *unreliable*. There is no acknowledgment mechanism, no retransmission mechanism, and no true "connection" concept. UDP packets can be broadcast to anyone on the network, if so chosen; or a selected set of recipients, whether or not they're expecting to hear anything.

UDP packets can get lost along the way from the sender to the receiver, and neither can have any way of knowing that it missed anything. There are no sequence numbers in UDP as there are in TCP. A sender simply spews out the traffic, and the specified recipients can receive it or not—it's up to them and the network. Any reliability in a UDP flow must be added by application using it; an example of this is NFS, the Network File System protocol, which we'll talk about in Chapter 31, "The Network Filesystem." NFS is a UDP-based protocol. This seems strange; file management and transfer are very concerned with data integrity. Why would a protocol designed to handle files use UDP? The reason is that with NFS, many hosts on the network can be using an NFS resource, and any of them can drop off the network without warning. Rather than maintaining all the processing overhead necessary for keeping TCP connections with these ephemeral hosts, NFS chooses UDP as its transport and provides the data integrity necessary to file transfer at the application level. Information about the complete transfer is maintained in the packets' data, so NFS can know when it's missing any pieces, or if any are corrupt.

The biggest use for UDP these days, however, is in streaming media. Teleconferencing, streamed video, broadcast music—these protocols don't care if they miss a beat. They consist of long streams of datagrams (packets), usually very small ones, which are gathered in the order they're received by the application and then dumped to the screen or speakers. One lost packet probably won't even be missed. If network congestion occurs, the packets are simply lost at the router level (routers keep their own timeouts on their buffers), and the stream is resumed in real-time when the host becomes available again—not where it left off. There's no reason to queue up all the missed packets and dump them through at once. They're irrelevant. That's the utility of UDP.

ICMP: Internet Control Message Protocol

Some consider ICMP to exist on the "network" layer, equivalent to IP and IPX; others treat it as a "transport" protocol like TCP or UDP. The truth is that it has elements of both. The messages received by ICMP are handled at the "network" layer, but these messages contain IP header information, so it's difficult to say where it fits in the scheme of things.

ICMP is designed as a diagnostic protocol. The most common ways you'll use it are in the ping and traceroute tools, both of which return information fundamental to the ICMP datagram structure. Mostly, they're built on ICMP's capability to query remote hosts for timestamps or echoes, which come back with specialized codes. ICMP can also be used to provide error messages to "transport" layer protocols, such as the "Port Unreachable" error returned by ICMP to a UDP sender that tries to talk to an unavailable port on the recipient's machine. ICMP has 16 of these error conditions it can report, as well as about as many additional functions. You generally won't need to know about them because they're really of interest only to the applications that can read them.

TCP/IP

Now that we know something about different network components and protocols, let's take a look at how they all fit together. The *TCP/IP stack* is the collection of sequential layers of protocols and their handlers, which inherit tasks and data upward and downward from each other. As we can see in Figure 22.7, data travels down the stack from user-level applications through the various protocols we've discussed before reaching the wire.

FIGURE 22.7

TCP/IP stack layering diagram, showing common applications and their path to the Ethernet link.

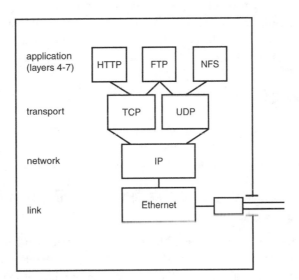

An application takes raw data and hands it to the transport layer (either TCP or UDP), which adds a TCP or UDP header containing information about how the remote TCP or UDP layer should decode it. The data packet now rolls down to the network layer, in which IP attaches another header containing information relevant to the remote network layer. Finally, it reaches the data link layer, in which the Ethernet driver encapsulates the whole packet in Ethernet headers and trailers, and sends it out through the Ethernet card onto the network.

A receiving computer passes an incoming packet up the stack, each layer stripping off a header and following its instructions before passing it to the next layer, until the application receives the raw data it needs. By this time, it's generally able to ignore any details about sessions, port numbers, hardware addresses, or anything else—the TCP/IP stack at the sender's end has handled all that automatically and packaged it neatly in the headers, and the recipient's TCP/IP stack has read it all out and presented it to the application free of complications.

Different network devices fit at different levels of the TCP/IP stack. A bridge links multiple networks at the data link level (for instance, Ethernet and Token Ring). A switch or a router links networks at the network level (where IP addresses are meaningful).

We will forgo a more detailed look into each of the headers the TCP/IP layers attach to a packet; that's a bit further into the mechanics of TCP/IP than we need to go to understand how it applies to FreeBSD because pretty much every operating system in the world handles TCP/IP the same way. A definitive reference for the structure of the protocol suite, regarded by many networking professionals as required reading, is *TCP/IP Illustrated* by W. Richard Stevens (Addison-Wesley, 1994). This multivolume text uncovers all the relevant details of how the protocols interrelate and interoperate, and presents them in an understandable manner.

IP Addresses

If you've ever done anything on the Internet at all, you're probably familiar with IP addresses—at least enough to know what they look like. An IP address is typically used as a way to refer to a specific computer on the Internet, though its meaning is actually a lot more flexible than "one IP address per machine." Most generally, it's a logical designation whose purpose is to locate a machine on the Internet so that IP routers can direct traffic between it and any other machine.

An IP address is a string of 32 bits in the IP header, which specifies either what machine a packet came from or where it is destined (both addresses are present in the header). The 32 bits can be thought of also as four 8-bit bytes, each of which is expressed as a number from 0 to 255—hence, our familiar four-part dotted-decimal notation (of the form 111.112.113.114). This allows it to be treated hierarchically when dealing with Class A, B, or C subnets, as we will discuss in a moment.

Typically, a single IP address is bound to a single Ethernet card; this is only by convention, though. The only constraint is that no two Ethernet cards on the same network can share the same IP address. You can bind multiple IP addresses to the same card, though, and every card needs to have at least one unique IP address to function. You might choose to install two Ethernet cards in your system in order to have access to two different networks at once, for example, or one address might be bound to an Ethernet card while another refers to your wireless 802.11 card. It all depends on how your network is set up.

You can find out the IP addresses of any Ethernet cards and other network interfaces in your system using the ifconfig utility, shown in Listing 22.1. The -a option shows all devices, or you can specify a specific interface (such as x10) to single out just that one. The inet line shows a configured IP address; the x10 interface in this example shows multiple IP addresses bound to a single card.

LISTING 22.1 Typical Output of ifconfig

```
# ifconfig -a
x10: flags=8843<UP,BROADCAST,RUNNING,SIMPLEX,MULTICAST> mtu 1500
        inet 64.41.131.102 netmask 0xffffff00 broadcast 64.41.131.255
        inet6 fe80::201:2ff:fe55:1256%x10 prefixlen 64 scopeid 0x1
        inet 209.154.215.246 netmask 0xffffffff broadcast 209.154.215.246
        ether 00:01:02:55:12:56
        media: autoselect (100baseTX) status: active
        supported media: autoselect 100baseTX <full-duplex> 100baseTX
10baseT/UTP <full-duplex> 10baseT/UTP 100baseTX <hw-loopback>
lp0: flags=8810<POINTOPOINT,SIMPLEX,MULTICAST> mtu 1500
gif0: flags=8010<POINTOPOINT,MULTICAST> mtu 1280
gif1: flags=8010<POINTOPOINT,MULTICAST> mtu 1280
gif2: flags=8010<POINTOPOINT,MULTICAST> mtu 1280
gif3: flags=8010<POINTOPOINT,MULTICAST> mtu 1280
lo0: flags=8049<UP,LOOPBACK,RUNNING,MULTICAST> mtu 16384
        inet6 fe80::1%lo0 prefixlen 64 scopeid 0x7
        inet6 ::1 prefixlen 128
        inet 127.0.0.1 netmask 0xff000000
ppp0: flags=8010<POINTOPOINT,MULTICAST> mtu 1500
sl0: flags=c010<POINTOPOINT,LINK2,MULTICAST> mtu 552
faith0: flags=8000<MULTICAST> mtu 1500
```

There are a few "special" IP addresses to keep in mind. First is the "network" address. This is an IP address in which one or more of its bytes are zero, such as 64.41.131.0. If the final byte is a zero, the address is a synonym for the entire 64.41.131 network, and generally used only when configuring routers. More important is if one or more of the trailing bytes are 255 (all bits set to 1). This is the "broadcast" address for the network; for example, 64.41.131.255 matches all hosts on the 64.41.131 network, and 64.41.255.255 matches all hosts on the 64.41 network. We will be discussing how these matching addresses work a little later when we discuss routing and subnets.

22

INTRODUCTION TO NETWORKING

IP Version 6 (IPv6)

32 bits' worth of IP addresses? That only works out to about 4.3 billion addresses in the entire Internet—and we already have about 30 million actively connected hosts, a number that's growing faster every year. It's looking like we'll be out of address space quite shortly, especially considering that the true address space is not actually 4.3 billion—it's actually considerably less because of the hierarchical nature of the dotted-decimal IP addressing scheme. There are only 256 Class A addresses spaces (for example, `114.xxx.xxx.xxx`), each with 16.7 million possible addresses within it. Many of the companies lucky enough to own Class A networks will never actually use anywhere near the full 16.7 million addresses they control, but because nobody else can use those addresses, effectively they're unavailable.

Many enterprises solve this problem by using NAT (Network Address Translation) and "IP masquerading" to make an entire network of hundreds or even thousands of internal IP addresses translate to only a single address as far as the outside world is concerned. This gives the enterprise as many addresses as it needs, but the downside is that outside hosts can't connect directly to any of the inside hosts because the translated IP addresses are meaningless outside the NAT translation point. The only way for true two-way accessible hosts to operate on the Internet is to have a legitimate IP address in the standard 32-bit address space.

This isn't going to scale for much longer. So various groups, such as the KAME project (`http://www.kame.net`), have been working recently on incorporating support for the next generation of IP—version 6, or IPv6—into FreeBSD. IPv6 provides a 128-bit address space, with addresses effectively four times the size in IPv4 (the current version). The result is address space for 3.4×10^{38} hosts—a number that we're unlikely to reach anytime soon, to say the least. Also included in IPv6 are a number of other enhancements, such as built-in encryption and authentication, connection differentiation (with "flow labels"), complete auto-configurability of hosts, and the abandonment of several outdated parts of IPv4 that are no longer used.

The trouble is that IPv6 is catching on only very, very slowly. Networks are expensive to build, and retrofitting them to be IPv6-compliant generally means replacing all existing equipment with newer, more expensive, less-mature hardware. Very few companies are willing to take that plunge just yet. But in the meantime, FreeBSD has full support for IPv6, and can take advantage of the various network resources currently available for IPv6, even if the infrastructure to support it isn't there yet. At least we can be sure that the relevant operating systems will be ready for IPv6 when it gets here!

ARP and the MAC Address

Although IP addresses are fairly visible to us as users because we can specify them directly in our networking applications such as Web and FTP programs, they are really just artificial constructs; they're bound to their hosts' Ethernet interfaces at the operating-system level, and can be changed at any time. At the bottom level of the TCP/IP stack, the data link layer, the IP address has no meaning—an Ethernet card knows nothing about what IP address the operating system has assigned to it or its hardware. Device drivers exist at a higher level than the one at which it communicates with the network.

What the network is really interested in is what's variously called the physical address, the hardware address, the Ethernet address, or the MAC (Media Access Controller) address. Every network interface device has a MAC address programmed into it at the factory—a unique one. The MAC address is theoretically supposed to be useful as a "fingerprint" identifier for an Ethernet card (and, thereby, a computer) because no two Ethernet cards in the world ideally share one. This doesn't work out in practice, though, because MAC addresses can be forged. There is no routing mechanism for a MAC address as there is for an IP address. It operates entirely at the physical link level on a LAN, and can't be forwarded by a router. The way it interoperates with IP addresses and routers is rather interesting; but first, let's take a closer look at what makes a MAC address tick.

The `ifconfig` output we saw a little earlier shows an `ether` line for the `xl0` interface card. This address shows us `00:01:02:55:12:56`, a typical MAC address for cards made by 3Com. The address itself is a string of six bytes (48 bits), expressed in hexadecimal and usually separated by colons. This makes for about 2,800,000,000,000,000 possible addresses—considerably more than the estimated 30 million networked computers online today. The first three bytes are used to identify the vendor (each vendor has one or more three-byte signatures assigned by the IEEE), and the other three are unique to the card. So, effectively, we really have the capacity for 16.7 million vendors, each with 16.7 million cards on the market. This does have the possibility of eventual scalability problems. It's probably for the best that the MAC address isn't used for routing!

Here's how it really works. When a newly created packet reaches the Ethernet layer of the sending TCP/IP stack, the Ethernet card must send it out onto the network and address it to the destination computer. It uses the MAC address instead of the IP address—because remember, the Ethernet cards on the network know nothing about IP addresses! But where does the TCP/IP stack get the MAC address of the remote computer? It has to ARP for it.

ARP stands for *Address Resolution Protocol*, and it's how IP addresses are mapped to MAC addresses. If your application wants to send a packet to the IP address `10.5.6.100`, it sends the packet down the stack to the link layer, where the stack consults the ARP cache, an OS-level table where known mappings between IP addresses and MAC addresses are stored. If it has never sent a packet to `10.5.6.100` before, that address won't be in the ARP table, and the TCP/IP stack must then perform an ARP. This is a broadcast packet, addressed to all Ethernet cards on the LAN (by setting the destination MAC address to `ff:ff:ff:ff:ff:ff`, or all bytes equal to 255, as with a broadcast IP address), with a payload of the IP address we're trying to look up: `10.5.6.100`. Every machine on the network receives this packet, but only the machine with the IP address we're looking for replies. After we get the reply packet, its IP address and MAC address go into our ARP cache for future use. The packet is then sent by our machine's TCP/IP stack onto the network destined for the intended recipient's MAC address only.

> **Note**
>
> Earlier in the chapter, we talked a little bit about how switches keep their own internal ARP caches. Now that we know how ARP is done, we can see how switches can keep track of which hosts are found on which ports through the use of ARP. A switch performs its own ARP queries to determine where to find a host to which it must send a packet that it receives. After it adds that ARP information to its own cache, it can direct future traffic to that destination address more quickly.

This is all well and good for machines on a LAN, but what if the machine you're sending the packet to isn't on the same network as the sender? Well, that's where routers come into play. A router receives an ARP packet like any other host, but when it looks up its IP address bindings to see whether it should reply to the ARP, it finds that it has internal routes set so that everything except traffic destined for the LAN it manages (the one you're on) should be sent out onto the WAN toward the next upstream router. The router's TCP/IP stack sees this as a claim that the router has all non-local IP addresses bound to its Ethernet card on the LAN. As far as the router is concerned, it *is* the computer you're looking for, and it replies to the ARP as though it were. When your packet goes out onto the network addressed for the router's MAC address, the router receives it and alters the MAC addresses in the packet's Ethernet headers. So the upstream routers think the packet came from it instead of from the sender, whose MAC address is meaningless after the packet leaves the LAN, and the destination address is changed to the MAC address of the next-hop router. This process continues until the packet reaches the destination LAN, in which the destination MAC address is looked up through ARP by the last router, the address fields are altered one last time so the source is the router's MAC address and the destination is the recipient host's MAC address, and the packet is delivered.

The arp Command

ARP is handled transparently by applications and the TCP/IP stack; you'll probably never have to actually ARP by yourself. However, there are some occasions when you'll need to tweak the ARP cache. You can check the contents of the cache by using the arp -a command:

```
# arp -a
w001.sjc-ca.dsl.cnc.net (64.41.131.1) at 0:0:c5:7c:7:f0 [ethernet]
w013.sjc-ca.dsl.cnc.net (64.41.131.13) at 0:30:65:a4:9a:5e [ethernet]
w063.sjc-ca.dsl.cnc.net (64.41.131.63) at ff:ff:ff:ff:ff:ff permanent [ethernet]
```

Entries in the ARP cache do time out after awhile, but there are times when you might need to clear the cache manually. Someone on the network might install a new Ethernet card in their machine and bind the old IP address to the new MAC address, which can make it unreachable if the old combination is still in your cache. You can delete cache entries by name, by IP address, or all at once (with -a).

```
# arp -d w001.sjc-ca.dsl.cnc.net
# arp -d 64.41.131.13
# arp -d -a
```

Subnets and the Network Mask

Netmasks, which travel hand-in-hand with IP addresses when configuring TCP/IP on a machine, are one of the most misunderstood parts of the whole structure, and yet potentially one of the most elegant when understood properly.

The purpose of the network mask (or *netmask*) is simply to tell a router or host whether a packet is supposed to go to the network it's on, or go upstream to the next router. This is the decision that is made in a situation such as the one we just discussed in the section on ARP. When a router receives a packet (not an ARP, a real TCP/IP packet), and it has to decide what to do with it, it checks the packet's destination IP address against its own netmask.

The netmask, a 32-bit string like an IP address, is usually of the form 255.255.255.0. Let's say we have a router managing the 64.41.131 network. The router receives a packet addressed for 64.41.131.45. This is matched against the netmask in an "and" fashion, and the result matches as far as 64.41.131, the address of the network our router manages. This packet is passed on to the network. Another packet now comes in, destined for 64.41.189.45; this match against the netmask fails, and the router passes the packet upstream to the next router.

A similar process takes place in individual hosts's TCP/IP stacks. If your host is sending a packet, it checks the destination IP address against its own netmask. If they don't match, the sender won't even ARP for the recipient's MAC address; it will simply send the packet to its own gateway router for it to route to the destination host. If it does match, however, the sender will ARP and send the packet directly.

This mechanism allows you to set up subnets within your network. Assume that you have a Class B address range to work with (64.41.xxx.xxx). Your network's main router, R1, manages this entire range, but you can put a router (R2) inside this network to manage two Class C address ranges: 64.41.131.xxx and 64.41.132.xxx. Hosts in the 64.41.131 network can be plugged into the same hub as hosts in the 64.41.132 network, as shown in Figure 22.8, but they won't speak directly to each other if their netmasks are set to 255.255.255.0, a Class C mask. Destination IP addresses in sent packets won't match the senders' netmasks. However, if a sender host (H1) in 64.41.131 sets its netmask to a Class B mask (255.255.0.0), the addresses *would* match, and the sender would be able to send the packet directly to H2—a host on 64.41.132. However, note that H2 wouldn't be able to send its replies directly back to H1 because its netmask prevents it! It has to send the reply back via R2, which has multiple network addresses and subnets bound to its internal interface. You'd need to set H2's netmask to 255.255.0.0 for it to talk directly to H1 without going through the router.

FIGURE 22.8

A network with subnets, demonstrating the packet path between two hosts whose netmasks don't permit them to communicate directly.

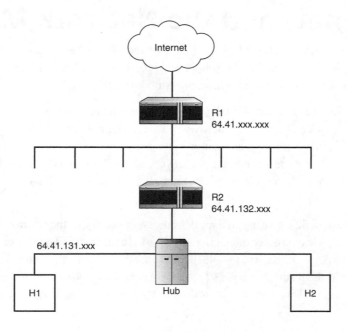

Netmasks don't need to be aligned on the byte boundary, either. For this reason, they're sometimes specified in pure hexadecimal format (for example, `0xffffff00` rather than `255.255.255.0`). You can specify a netmask of, for instance, `0xffffffc0`, or `255.255.255.192`. This mask will match a network of 64 hosts, the ones between 1 and 64.

Another notation used in specifying networks that incorporates the netmask is *CIDR*, or *Classless Inter-Domain Routing*, which takes the form of the network address, a slash, and the number of bits that make up the mask. For example, a mask of `255.255.255.0` on our `64.41.131` network would be written as `64.41.131/24` because the mask consists of three 8-bit bytes with all bits set to 1, or 24 bits. The `255.255.255.192` example, likewise, would correspond to a notation of `64.41.131/26`. This notation is seen in routing tables and other places where succinctness is useful.

Routing

We've already talked a little bit about how IP routing works, but we'll now cover it in a little bit more detail. Configuring routes properly is one of the great skills one can develop in networking, and it pays to be able to do it correctly—or at least to have a working understanding of it so that you can do administrative tasks that require interfacing with the routing table, such as `portsentry` (which we will discuss in Chapter 29, "Network Security").

Any router—by which we mean any device configured to act as a router, which includes actual routers or regular servers that will do their job in a pinch—works by maintaining a routing table, a set of rules that says where packets that match certain IP address criteria should be sent. Because FreeBSD can be configured as a router, let's look at its routing tables as an example, using the `netstat -rn` command:

```
# netstat -rn
Routing tables

Internet:
Destination          Gateway             Flags   Refs      Use    Netif Expire
default              hsrp-gw.netnation.  UGSc     126  1379327    xl0
64.41.53.101/32      localhost           UGScB      0        3    lo0
net-64-40-111.netn   link#1              UC         0        0    xl0 =>
ip3.somewhere.com    0:50:ba:b3:98:13    UHLW       2   357107    xl0    735
ip4.somewhere.com    0:50:ba:b3:95:bb    UHLW       0     2272    xl0    500
ip6.somewhere.com    0:1:2:55:12:56      UHLW       0   118941    lo0 =>
ip6.somewhere.com    localhost           UGScB      0        0    lo0
hsrp-gw.netnation.   0:0:c:7:ac:1e       UHLW     119     8814    xl0    405
64.77.63.139/32      localhost           UGScB      0        0    lo0
Toronto-ppp218408.   localhost           UGScB      0        0    lo0
```

```
localhost          localhost        UH       45 45210727     lo0
goo.cs.und.nodak.e localhost        UGScB     0        0      lo0
```

The information in the routing table includes the following fields for each entry:

- **Destination**. This can be an IP address, a hostname, a network address (which FreeBSD displays in CIDR format, as you can see in the preceding example), or one of several special destinations such as the "default route." This field matches the destination address of any packet the machine doing the routing sees.

- **Gateway address**. This is the "next-hop" router address where traffic to the specified destination should be sent. This can be a hostname or IP address, or for destinations on the LAN it can be a MAC address. FreeBSD also shows an entry for the link#1 gateway, which is a route matching the network of the primary network interface, from which new routes can be cloned on use (hence the C flag).

- **Flags**. These specify what kind of route it is. Each letter represents a different flag, so this example shows routes with between two and five simultaneous flags. See man netstat for the meaning of each of the flags.

- **Network interface**. When a packet matches a route in the table, it is passed out through this specified interface.

IP routing grew from the distributed, adaptive defense communications network envisioned by ARPA, and thus its nature is to dynamically update these routing tables according to network conditions. The large telecommunications hubs maintain immense routing tables with many backup links from any one place to any other place; when one route is found to be unavailable, the routing table shuffles the entries around until traffic is redirected to a working route. The result is a system in which no single router has to know anything about the route to a packet's destination other than where its own next-hop router is. Any address that isn't local (or, in other words, that isn't on the network managed by that router), is passed upstream to the next-hop router, and so on until the packet reaches a router that has an explicit entry in its routing table—with the appropriate netmask—for the network matching the packet's destination IP address. At that point, the packet is routed out that interface, and hopefully to its destination.

Notice that there's a susceptibility to misconfiguration here. On the way upstream, the packet will keep moving upward until it finds an explicit match for its destination address. This is pretty much guaranteed to work because someone has to explicitly add a bogus route to the table to hijack the packet on its way up the chain of routers. In its default state, the packet will reach the backbone routers without incident. However, after it starts downstream, every router along the way must be properly configured to route to the network that its upstream next-hop router thinks it's capable of routing! A packet might start on its way downstream, only to find that the router that was supposed to have a further route for it to the destination actually *doesn't* have one. Naturally, without an explicit route for the packet, the router will pass the packet back to its upstream router, which will then send it back downstream again, beginning what we frequently see as a "router loop":

```
traceroute to arclight.net (209.237.26.189), 30 hops max, 40 byte packets
 1  r2-72-core-van.netnation.com (10.10.4.253)  101.878 ms  135.377 ms  85.218
➡ms
 2  dis2-vancouver-atm1-0-0-33.in.bellnexxia.net (206.108.110.189)  132.023 ms
➡80.653 ms  81.686 ms
 3  core2-vancouver-pos11-1.in.bellnexxia.net (206.108.101.45)  102.365 ms
➡61.537 ms  68.561 ms
 4  core2-seattle-pos12-0.in.bellnexxia.net (206.108.102.209)  79.989 ms
➡109.389 ms  115.587 ms
 5  bx3-seattle-pos5-0.in.bellnexxia.net (206.108.102.202)  86.434 ms  109.678
➡ms  129.128 ms
 6  sea1-bellnexxia-oc12.sea1.above.net (208.184.233.73)  91.201 ms  67.287 ms
➡79.369 ms
 7  core2-core1-oc48.sea1.above.net (208.185.175.178)  74.219 ms  79.480 ms
➡93.121 ms
 8  sjc2-sea1-oc48.sjc2.above.net (216.200.127.117)  188.692 ms  212.627 ms
➡181.123 ms
 9  core1-sjc2-oc48.sjc1.above.net (208.184.102.25)  195.260 ms  194.973 ms
➡272.053 ms
10  main1-core1-oc12.sjc1.above.net (208.185.175.246)  344.104 ms  318.313 ms
11  core1-sjc2-oc48.sjc1.above.net (208.184.102.25)  195.260 ms  194.973 ms
➡272.053 ms
12  main1-core1-oc12.sjc1.above.net (208.185.175.246)  344.104 ms  318.313 ms
13  core1-sjc2-oc48.sjc1.above.net (208.184.102.25)  195.260 ms  194.973 ms
➡272.053 ms
14  main1-core1-oc12.sjc1.above.net (208.185.175.246)  344.104 ms  318.313 ms
15  core1-sjc2-oc48.sjc1.above.net (208.184.102.25)  195.260 ms  194.973 ms
➡272.053 ms
16  main1-core1-oc12.sjc1.above.net (208.185.175.246)  344.104 ms  318.313 ms
17  core1-sjc2-oc48.sjc1.above.net (208.184.102.25)  195.260 ms  194.973 ms
➡272.053 ms
18  main1-core1-oc12.sjc1.above.net (208.185.175.246)  344.104 ms  318.313 ms
```

This "bouncing" behavior will continue, preventing proper delivery of packets until the downstream router fixes its routing tables. Fortunately, usually when this occurs it's because work is being done on the router that's at fault, and the condition is temporary, resolving itself when the backed-up routing tables are restored.

Gateways and Network Address Translation

The term *gateway* is frequently used to mean *router*, and that isn't an inaccurate statement; we should clarify exactly what it means in today's parlance, though.

When you're configuring a machine's TCP/IP settings, you have to specify a gateway. This is simply the next-hop router for the machine you're configuring. Refer to Figure 22.7: H1 and H2 have to have a gateway configured so that they can operate with hosts whose addresses don't match their netmasks. Generally, in this type of topology, the gateway would be R2. Depending on the type of router, H1 and H2 might not be able to reach R1 directly. It's important to consider failure modes. If R2 should be shut down, it is unlikely that it would pass LAN traffic directly through; some network devices fail into a pass-through mode, but routers seldom fall into that category.

In another type of network topology, the subnets defined by R2 might be completely unlike the R1 subnet; for instance, R1 might specify the `64.41` network, but R2 would control subnets at `192.168.10` and `192.168.11`. In this case, it wouldn't do to set H1 or H2 to R1 as a gateway at all; traffic simply wouldn't reach it. The best practice is generally to set your machine's gateway to the nearest router, and make sure the router is properly configured to pass traffic to the upstream router and to its managed subnets.

The traditional meaning of "gateway", however, is the "edge device"—the point at which LAN traffic passes out onto the WAN. This device, generally a router, is also where network address translation (NAT) can be done. The NAT daemon on the router specifies aliases for internal routes and their translated addresses on the outside, and vice versa; NAT can be done in a one-to-one, many-to-one, or one-to-many fashion.

To use FreeBSD as a NAT router, you will want to configure and run the `natd` daemon; we'll discuss this in more detail in Chapter 28, "Configuring an Internet Gateway."

Host Names and Domain Names

Now that we have an understanding of the way MAC addresses and IP addresses work, we can apply yet another layer of indirection to the host-finding process: hostnames and DNS. Early in TCP/IP history, different networked machines were identifiable only by their IP addresses. This worked really well, except for the fact—increasingly important as more and more people came online—that keeping track of all the numbers involved was tedious and error-prone. Hence the introduction of the Domain Name System, a means of assigning common names to IP addresses, resulting in the much easier-to-use system we know today.

DNS records are kept in a centralized database on multiple *root servers* that are maintained by Network Solutions, Inc. These servers take their information from the DNS hosts they have designated as authoritative for any given domain name (for instance, `somewhere.com`). Each domain's authoritative DNS keeps the records in a database of its own, which varies from implementation to implementation. FreeBSD, like most UNIXes, uses BIND, which keeps its records in /etc/namedb. We will discuss how to set up DNS on FreeBSD in Chapter 30, "The Domain Name Server."

Within a domain, every machine listed in the domain's DNS records has a hostname, or a simple machine name such as tiger or pluto. Combined with the domain, you get a *fully-qualified domain name* (FQDN), such as tiger.somewhere.com.

What's important to understand for networking purposes is that the hierarchical structure of the domain name, hostname, and FQDN have no bearing on the hierarchical addressing conventions in IP addresses. The somewhere.com domain can have hosts with IP addresses all over the map—the DNS configuration just needs to point to them correctly. For instance, www.somewhere.com can be 64.41.131.45, and ftp.somewhere.com can be 213.11.31.221; it doesn't matter as far as TCP/IP is concerned. DNS is completely outside the TCP/IP stack.

Where DNS does come into play is at the application level, in which the hostname is used as an easier interface for the user than a bare IP address. A Web browser, for example, takes a DNS name and translates it into an IP address transparently before it even tries to connect to the requested host. To put it into the terms we've been using throughout this chapter, the abstraction that DNS provides over IP addresses is analogous to the abstraction that IP addresses provide over MAC addresses. Just as ARP associates IP and MAC addresses for use by the data link layer, a name lookup associates hostnames and IP addresses for use by the network layer.

DHCP

We've seen how an IP address can be bound to an Ethernet interface, and we'll go into the details of how it's done in the Chapter 23, "Configuring Basic Networking Services." One interesting twist, though, is DHCP: Dynamic Host Configuration Protocol, which assigns IP addresses to Ethernet interfaces on an as-needed basis.

When you configure an interface to be configured by DHCP, it sends out a request at boot time to the designated DHCP server. This request, which is really a RARP query (analogous to ARP, but operating in reverse) carries the MAC address of the interface in question to the DHCP server, which responds with an IP address (and other network settings, such as the netmask) that it knows is available. The booting host then assigns this address to the interface, and the DHCP server sets up a "lease" period, so that the host can boot with that same IP address on an ongoing basis.

We will be covering DHCP and how to configure FreeBSD for it in Chapter 33, "DHCP."

CHAPTER 23

Configuring Basic Networking Services

In the last chapter, we had a crash course in networking, the TCP/IP way. None of it, or very little, was FreeBSD-specific or really told you how to go about setting up your system to do networking properly. What it did do was to lay the groundwork so you could know what's going on in this chapter, in which we'll cover the various tools you can use to configure TCP/IP.

We won't be talking about specialized network services (such as Web/HTTP, mail/SMTP, FTP, and so on) in this chapter; those will be left until later, when we will tackle each of them in turn. Right now, we'll focus on the basics: getting the machine to be able to talk to its peers on your network.

Configuring the Network Card

As we discussed in the last chapter, a computer can have multiple Ethernet cards (interfaces), and each of those can have multiple IP addresses and related settings. Convention is for each machine to have one Ethernet card with one IP address, but there's no reason to limit ourselves in that regard; this chapter will show how to set up as many simultaneously installed cards as you like, as well as to bind as many IP addresses to each card as you see fit.

The first step is to make sure you have at least one Ethernet card that FreeBSD will work with. Table 23.1 lists all the cards that are supported in the GENERIC kernel. The system should recognize any of these, which comprise the vast majority of the hardware used these days, without any additional tweaking, particularly in the case of the PCI cards. A good many other cards are supported by FreeBSD but not included in the GENERIC kernel; refer to /sys/i386/conf/NOTES (as we discussed in Chapter 17, "Kernel Configuration"), and recompile the kernel to enable support for these cards.

> **Note**
>
> Be aware that the list of supported Ethernet cards changes fairly frequently. The devices listed in the GENERIC kernel config file on your system, /sys/i386/conf/GENERIC, will be the authoritative source for what's relevant to you.

TABLE 23.1 Ethernet Cards Supported in the Default (GENERIC) FreeBSD Kernel

	PCI Cards
de	Intel DC21x4x ("Tulip")
vx	3Com 3c590, 3c595 ("Vortex")
	PCI/MII Cards
fxp	Intel EtherExpress Pro/100B (82557, 82558)
tx	SMC 9432TX (83c170 "EPIC")
wx	Intel Gigabit Ethernet Card ("Wiseman")
dc	DEC/Intel 21143 and various workalikes
pcn	AMD Am79C79x PCI 10/100 NICs
rl	RealTek 8129/8139
sf	Adaptec AIC-6915 ("Starfire")
sis	Silicon Integrated Systems SiS 900/SiS 7016
ste	Sundance ST201 (D-Link DFE-550TX)
tl	Texas Instruments ThunderLAN
vr	VIA Rhine, Rhine II
wb	Winbond W89C840F
xl	3Com 3c90x ("Boomerang," "Cyclone")
	ISA Cards
ed	Novell NE1000/NE2000, 3Com 3c503, Western Digital/SMC 80xx
ex	Intel EtherExpress Pro/10 (82595)
ep	3Com 3c509
fe	Fujitsu MB86960A/MB86965A
ie	AT&T StarLAN 10 and EN100; 3Com 3c507; unknown NI5210; Intel EtherExpress
lnc	Lance/PCnet cards (Isolan, Novell NE2100, NE32-VL, AMD Am7990 and Am79C960)
cs	IBM Etherjet and other Crystal Semi CS89x0-based adapters
sn	SMC 9000
	PCMCIA Cards
wi	Lucent WaveLAN 802.11
an	Aironet 4500/4800 802.11
xe	Xircom/Intel EtherExpress Pro100/16

23

CONFIGURING BASIC
NETWORKING
SERVICES

Most Ethernet cards sold today for x86 hardware are PCI-based, which means that the PCI controller handles all the addressing automatically and you don't need to do any of the IRQ/DMA/memory address gyrations associated with ISA cards. If you're stuck with one of these older cards, though, there are a few things you need to do; for example, modifying the device hints for the card, which we'll cover shortly.

Configuring Network Settings with `sysinstall`

The simplest way to configure your Ethernet card, and probably the most familiar-looking to anyone who's gone through this process on a Windows machine or Macintosh, is our buddy `sysinstall`. The first time you ask `sysinstall` to do anything that requires a network connection (a net installation of the system, browsing packages, or various other tasks), it will bring up the network configuration window, in which you can set the TCP/IP options for your Ethernet card visually.

An easy way to get to this screen—if you're already up and running multiuser and not in the initial system installation process—is to run `/stand/sysinstall`, select "Configure" from the main menu, and scroll down to the "Media" option. In this submenu, select "FTP" and some FTP server (it doesn't matter which), and you'll see a dialog box that says "Running multi-user, assume that the network is already configured?" Choose "No" to enter the network configuration screens.

The first thing that appears is the Network Interface selection screen. You're presented with a list of the interfaces that FreeBSD has found in your system. You'll probably see a number of choices that don't make a lot of sense—aside from choices such as `lp0` (the parallel port) and various PPP or SLIP options on your serial ports, you'll see things like `gif0` and `faith0`. These are IPv6 devices; you can ignore them. The option you want is probably at the top. The one we're using in this example is `fxp1`, an Intel EtherExpress Pro/100B PCI card.

When you select your Ethernet card, you're given two dialog boxes: a choice to let the system try to configure the card automatically using IPv6 and then another choice to let it try using DHCP. Say "No" to both of these. You'll then be presented with the visual Network Configuration screen, as shown in Figure 23.1.

FIGURE 23.1

The visual Network Configuration screen in the sysinstall *program.*

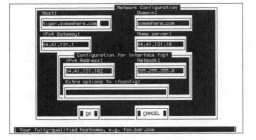

Each field in this screen has a short description at the bottom of the window, but we can explain it a little further here.

- *Host*: This is the hostname, which is just the first part of the machine's fully quali-fied domain name. For instance, if your machine is www.somewhere.com, the Host: field should be set to www.

- *Domain*: This is the rest of the domain name, or somewhere.com. This can be a composite domain for networks with named subnets, such as cslab.ivyleague.edu.

- *IPv4 Gateway*: This is the IP address of your gateway router. Use the next-hop router closest to your machine. This router will be responsible for transmitting any traffic between your machine and any other machines in the world.

- *Name server*: The IP address of the most reliable domain name server (DNS) in your network. You should use the DNS provided by your enterprise, ISP, or univer-sity network if at all possible; remote name servers are useful as backups, but they won't necessarily be set up to service non-local requests reliably.

- IPv4 Address: This is the IP address you're assigning to your Ethernet card. It needs to be on the same subnet as your IPv4 Gateway as matched against your net-mask, as we discussed in Chapter 22, "Introduction to Networking."

- *Netmask*: This is used to determine whether a packet's destination is on the local network or not. Set the field to 255.255.255.0 for a Class C network, 255.255.0.0 for Class B, and so on, as discussed in Chapter 22.

- *Extra options to* ifconfig: You most likely won't need to put anything in here unless you're a power user looking to tweak the performance of your interface card. Anything put in here will be added to the ifconfig command line that sysinstall issues in the background. We'll be covering ifconfig later in this chapter.

23

CONFIGURING BASIC
NETWORKING
SERVICES

After you've set all these options, select OK; the network settings will be applied to the card on the fly, and whatever you were doing in sysinstall will continue. If you're following the steps of this example, sysinstall will connect to your selected FTP server. If this isn't successful, there's likely a problem with the network settings you entered, and you'll have to go back in and troubleshoot your settings. If you're in an enterprise network and there's a network administrator handy, he or she will be able to give you the correct settings.

This process works in much the same way if you're doing a first-time installation of FreeBSD; you will be presented with this same configuration screen early in the install process, and if you're doing a network installation, it will use the settings to pull down the system distribution.

Coping with ISA Ethernet Cards

Most PCI Ethernet cards are very trouble-free. All you really need to do, especially if you have one of the commonly used cards supported in the GENERIC kernel, is plug it in, power up the machine, and watch the kernel identify it in the boot process:

```
fxp0: <Intel PLC 10/100 Ethernet> port 0xde80-0xdebf mem 0xff8fe000-
0xff8fefff irq 11 at device 8.0 on pci1
fxp0: Ethernet address 00:d0:b7:c7:74:f1
fxp1: <Intel Pro 10/100B/100+ Ethernet> port 0xdf00-0xdf3f mem 0xff700000-
0xff7fffff,0xff8ff000-0xff8fffff irq 11 at device 9.0 on pci1
fxp1: Ethernet address 00:d0:b7:bd:5d:13
```

However, if you're working with an old ISA card, the process can be trickier. ISA cards are set to a certain memory address and IRQ (interrupt request), and you have to pick them both so they aren't already used by some other device. Most Ethernet cards have memory addresses of 0x300 or 0x280, and an IRQ of 9 or 10; installing more than one of these cards means you have to configure the card itself to use an unused slot. Here's the really sticky part: This card configuration usually has to be done with a DOS utility that comes with the card.

It's fairly easy to see where the conflicts are between IRQs and memory addresses in the visual configuration menu during the initial installation of FreeBSD. Simply delete all the drivers you don't need, and if there's still a conflict between two installed devices, choose which one you want to change and what settings you want to switch to. Boot into MS-DOS with a DOS "rescue" floppy disk, and run the card's diagnostic program if you have its original disks. Ethernet cards' diagnostic programs typically have a selection of common memory addresses and IRQs to set the card to use; pick one that isn't used by any other device as reported in the visual configuration menu, set the card's firmware, and boot back into FreeBSD.

You might also need to alter the "device hints" (described in Chapter 17) for your card. These hints, kept in /boot/device.hints, control where FreeBSD expects to find the device; you can tweak them to match your card by editing that file. You should find lines like the following:

```
hint.ed.0.at="isa"
hint.ed.0.port="0x300"
hint.ed.0.irq="10"
```

Modify the port (memory address) and IRQ lines to match the settings of your card, and reboot to activate it.

Configuring Network Settings without `sysinstall`

Using `sysinstall` to configure your cards makes things easy in some ways (it's nice and visual, for instance, and it does everything in one place), but it's also less than versatile for many of the networking tasks you may need to do. We'll now cover how to access the network settings more directly from the command line. Naturally, you must be root in order to run these commands in a way that alters the system's configuration.

Caution

Some of the functions we will be discussing cannot be done in `sysinstall`, such as adding IP aliases or modifying the routing tables. In fact, if you have a customized IP setup (for example, a card with many IP aliases bound to it), and then you do an additional configuration of the card using `sysinstall`, you might lose your customized settings. Be aware that `sysinstall` is useful for the most basic and common of configuration tasks, but it should be avoided for more complex situations for which it is not intended.

Using `ifconfig` to Apply Network Settings

The InterFace Configurator, `ifconfig`, is the multipurpose tool for applying network settings on the fly. Its main purpose is to assign an IP address to an Ethernet card (interface), though naturally, as with most other UNIX tools, it can do a lot more, too. We'll be covering the most frequently used functions of `ifconfig` here. Further information can be found in the `man ifconfig` page.

First of all, let's use `ifconfig` to gather information on our network interfaces. In the previous chapter, we saw an example of `ifconfig -a`, which shows all interfaces and tells you which ones are available; it's an easy way to find out whether your Ethernet driver is `ed0`, `fxp0`, `xl0`, or what. After you know, you can specify that device name as a parameter to `ifconfig` to just get that interface's settings:

```
# ifconfig fxp1
fxp1: flags=8843<UP,BROADCAST,RUNNING,SIMPLEX,MULTICAST> mtu 1500
        inet6 fe80::2d0:b7ff:febd:5d13%fxp1 prefixlen 64 scopeid 0x2
        inet 64.41.131.102 netmask 0xffffff00 broadcast 64.41.131.255
        ether 00:d0:b7:bd:5d:13
        media: autoselect (100baseTX <full-duplex>) status: active
        supported media: autoselect 100baseTX <full-duplex> 100baseTX
10baseT/UTP <full-duplex> 10baseT/UTP
```

> **Caution**
>
> We're about to go through a few configuration examples that will almost certainly cause your Ethernet interface to lose connectivity to any connected sessions. If you want to try out the functionality of `ifconfig` on your own machine, you'll probably want to do it from the physical console rather than when connected via telnet or SSH!

If we want to only change our IP address, we use the following command:

```
# ifconfig fxp1 64.41.131.103
```

That's all there is to it. Note that if you don't specify a netmask, though, it's assumed that you're setting a Class A address—and the netmask and broadcast address are set accordingly, as we can see in the updated `ifconfig fxp1` output:

```
        inet 64.41.131.103 netmask 0xff000000 broadcast 64.255.255.255
```

Let's try this again, but this time we'll make it a Class C address, which means that we'll need to set our netmask, too. This is done with the `netmask` keyword in combination with the IP address. Note that `ifconfig` accepts netmasks in hex notation, dotted-decimal notation, or by a symbolic name defined in `/etc/networks`. So the following commands are equivalent:

```
# ifconfig fxp1 64.41.131.103 netmask 255.255.255.0
# ifconfig fxp1 64.41.131.103 netmask 0xffffff00
# ifconfig fxp1 64.41.131.103 netmask your-netmask
```

You can also specify the broadcast address, although this generally isn't useful except in really exceptional networks. Note that although the broadcast address is automatically extrapolated from the IP address and netmask if you omit it (as discussed earlier), the reverse is not true—omitting the netmask makes it assume a Class A mask. If you have to set the broadcast address, make sure to set both it and the netmask at the same time:

```
# ifconfig fxp1 64.41.131.103 netmask 255.255.0.0 broadcast 64.41.255.255
```

There are some conditions where you might need to set the MTU (Maximum Transmission Unit) of the interface. This value is usually 1500 for Ethernet cards, and it controls what the largest packet is that the card can send out (in bytes). Sometimes, you might want to set it to a smaller value to minimize latency on low-speed WAN links. This is usually taken care of by your router, though, so don't worry about this unless you have to and you know what you're doing:

```
# ifconfig fxp1 mtu 536
```

One final trick that `ifconfig` can use is the `media` keyword, which allows you to make the card switch between the various listed media types. This is very handy if you have a card with multiple interfaces (such as the card shown in Figure 22.3 in the last chapter), and you want to switch from the BNC connector to the RJ-45 (UTP) connector or the RJ-45 to the AUI connector. Similarly, if you have a 10/100 Ethernet card and an auto-sensing hub that has auto-negotiated a speed of 100Mbps full-duplex with your card, but you want to force it into 10Mbps mode, you can do that with the `media` and `mediaopt` keywords. First of all, let's take a look at what `ifconfig fxp1` reports to be the supported media types.

```
         media: autoselect (100baseTX <full-duplex>) status: active
         supported media: autoselect 100baseTX <full duplex> 100baseTX
10baseT/UTP <full-duplex> 10baseT/UTP
```

This tells us that we're in autoselect mode, in which the card will negotiate the highest possible speed with the hub to which it's connected. Let's set it instead to 10baseT mode. The `supported media:` line tells us that the keyword for this is `10baseT/UTP`, and that there's an option of `full-duplex` that we can set if we choose to (using the `mediaopt` keyword). Options are shown in angle brackets. Displayed more clearly, the media types and options for this example are as follows:

```
autoselect
100baseTX <full-duplex>
100baseTX
10baseT/UTP <full-duplex>
10baseT/UTP
```

23

CONFIGURING BASIC
NETWORKING
SERVICES

So, to set this interface to each of the two available 10baseT/UTP modes:

```
# ifconfig fxp1 media 10baseT/UTP
# ifconfig fxp1 media 10baseT/UTP mediaopt full-duplex
```

If you're doing this on a machine where you're sitting near the hub or switch where the Ethernet cable is plugged in, or you can see the back of the computer, check the lights. You should see that the "100" light has gone out, indicating that the connection has renegotiated to 10Mpbs mode. To switch back again to the previous mode:

```
# ifconfig fxp1 media autoselect
```

Recall that full-duplex mode is where the card can be both reading and writing at the same time, so 10baseT in full-duplex mode means 10Mbps total in each direction, whereas half-duplex mode means a maximum of 10Mbps as the aggregate total of both directions. A hub can't do full-duplex mode. You need a switch if you want to take full advantage of full-duplex mode.

> **Tip**
>
> You can also find out which media types and options your Ethernet card driver supports by reading its man page; for instance, man fxp for our example Intel driver.

Using `route` to Set the Gateway Router

We've now covered `ifconfig` in as much detail as you're likely to need. However, we haven't yet touched on how to set the gateway router or the DNS information from the command line, both of which are functions that the network configuration screen in `sysinstall` handles all at once. First, let's talk about gateway routers.

You don't set the gateway in `ifconfig` because a gateway address isn't bound to an individual Ethernet interface. Instead, FreeBSD's routing table—which allows the system to function as a full-fledged router in its own right (something you'll see how to do in Chapter 28, "Configuring an Internet Gateway")—has a single "default" route that receives all traffic not destined for any of the LANs accessible from your Ethernet cards, regardless of how many you have. This default route is what you set to specify your gateway router.

The `route` command is another large and complex beast, more so than `ifconfig`, in fact. However, because we're not actually setting up any routes right now, we need to concern ourselves only with the most fundamental functions: the `add` and `delete` keywords.

> **Note**
>
> Note that as long as you're on the same LAN as the FreeBSD machine, you can modify the routes—including the default route—without losing network connectivity. If you're going through these examples while connected via Telnet or SSH, you may have accidentally disconnected yourself with the `ifconfig` examples. This won't happen if you're just setting the router address, as long as there aren't any routers between you and the FreeBSD machine.

The first thing to do is to check the output of `netstat -rn`. This will show us what default route is currently set, if any:

```
# netstat -rn
Routing tables

Internet:
Destination        Gateway          Flags    Refs    Use    Netif Expire
default            64.41.131.1      UGSc      1       1      fxp0
...
```

It seems we already have a gateway router set. This will almost certainly be the case whether the network is running properly or not; there is little error-checking in `route`, and it's pretty easy to set up a default route that would be unreachable from any of your LANs. The system might also set up a dummy default route. In any case, setting a new router address is a two-step process: First, you must delete the existing default route; then, you must add the new one.

```
# route delete default
delete net default
# route add default 64.2.43.1
add net default: gateway 64.2.43.1
```

> **Note**
>
> It's worth pointing out that the `route` command is one of those parts of UNIX that gives people fits because it's implemented differently on almost every single UNIX variant on the planet. The differences are subtle and syntactical; although the functionality is pretty much the same whether you're on FreeBSD or Linux or Solaris or IRIX, the way you access that functionality is maddeningly varied. To get an idea of this lack of standardization, install `portsentry` (from `/usr/ports/security`), and look through `/usr/local/etc/portsentry.conf`. It lists no fewer than nine different ways (on nine different platforms) to use `route` to set up a "black-hole" route. It's a bit ridiculous, but that's part of the price we pay for the flexibility we demand from UNIX.

Using `hostname`

Setting your machine's hostname is dead simple. All it involves is the `hostname` command, with the desired hostname (as a fully-qualified domain name) as its argument:

```
# hostname tiger.somewhere.com
```

You can also print out the currently set hostname in either fully qualified or standalone format:

```
# hostname
tiger.somewhere.com
# hostname -s
tiger
```

Network Settings in `/etc/rc.conf`

Now that we have command-line tools at our disposal for setting the IP address, netmask, hostname, and gateway router, and now that we've seen how to set them manually on a one-time basis, it's time we made it so the system took care of all that for us. That's what `/etc/rc.conf` is for, as you no doubt recall from Chapter 11, "System Configuration and Startup Scripts."

Recall that the system's default settings are in `/etc/defaults/rc.conf` (which shouldn't be touched), and any overrides that supersede those defaults go into `/etc/rc.conf`. If you look in the defaults file, you'll find vague, generic, disabled settings for the various TCP/IP options. You'll be enabling your Ethernet cards permanently by putting everything relevant into `/etc/rc.conf`. If you've already configured the card using `sysinstall` (as we discussed earlier in the chapter), there will already be some settings in the file, such as the following:

```
# -- sysinstall generated deltas -- #
ifconfig_fxp1="inet 64.41.131.102  netmask 255.255.255.0"
network_interfaces="fxp1 fxp0 lo0"
defaultrouter="64.41.131.1"
hostname="tiger.somewhere.com"
```

Tip

Note that the order in which these options are specified doesn't matter; the startup scripts read them all into variables at once.

The values written into the file by `sysinstall` include `network_interfaces`, which sets an explicit list of the interfaces on your system; an `ifconfig_xxx#` line for each interface, which is precisely what is passed to `ifconfig` by the configuration scripts for each card specified in `network_interfaces`; `defaultrouter`, which sets just what you think it does; and `hostname`, which is the fully-qualified domain name. All these values are read into the resource configuration scripts when the system boots and passed to the appropriate utilities (`ifconfig`, `route`, and `hostname`) automatically.

If you're wondering "What about DNS?", we'll be getting to that shortly. DNS isn't really a part of the TCP/IP stack configuration; it's an application-level helper service, consulted independently by networking applications before any connections are really initiated, and we don't need it in place to get networking up and running.

Using `/etc/netstart`

A nice courtesy provided by FreeBSD is the `/etc/netstart` script. It's not a necessary part of the boot-time configuration process, and it can safely be removed from your system without hurting anything (though that would be silly, considering how useful it is). At one time, most network services were started explicitly within `/etc/netstart`, and back in the days when administrators had to edit scripts to add new services, it was a crucial part of the resource configuration process. Now, though, in keeping with FreeBSD's ideal of pushing all user-level and system-level script functions apart from each other, we now have `/etc/rc.network`—the system-level script that runs at boot time in a cascade with the rest of the resource configuration scripts—and `/etc/netstart`, a user-level script that can be run at any time.

The function of `/etc/netstart` is to read in any new configuration changes from `/etc/rc.conf` and start up the network—restarting it, effectively. If you take a quick look through the script, you'll see that there's not a lot to it: It reads in `/etc/defaults/rc.conf`, applies the overrides from `/etc/rc.conf`, and then runs `/etc/rc.pccard` and `/etc/rc.network` in sequence. Everything in `/etc/defaults/rc.conf` and `/etc/rc.conf` is available to `rc.network` when it's run at boot time, but not if you were to run it separately on your own; that's what `/etc/netstart` is for. It's a wrapper for `rc.network` that makes it behave as if the machine were just now booting.

The various command-line tools that we've just discussed—`ifconfig`, `route`, `hostname`, and the like—are all run from within `/etc/rc.network`, subject to various conditionals and consistency checks, and with syntax built up from the various settings to prevent input errors and potential illegal maneuvers. For everyday networking changes, `/etc/netstart` is the best and safest way to activate networking configuration changes, rather than running the various commands individually.

There's a caveat, however. The /etc/netstart script sets the default gateway using the route command, as we've seen; however, you can't add a new default route without deleting the old one first. The /etc/rc.network script doesn't issue a route delete default command—because it's designed to run at boot time, it shouldn't need to. So to use /etc/netstart, we have to delete the default route first. This makes using /etc/netstart a two-step process (shown in Listing 23.1).

LISTING 23.1   Restarting the Network Using /etc/netstart

```
# route delete default
delete net default
# /etc/netstart
Doing stage one network startup:
Doing initial network setup:.
fxp0: flags=8843<UP,BROADCAST,RUNNING,SIMPLEX,MULTICAST> mtu 1500
        inet6 fe80::2d0:b7ff:fec7:74f1%fxp0 prefixlen 64 scopeid 0x1
        inet 64.41.131.101 netmask 0xffffff00 broadcast 64.41.131.255
        ether 00:d0:b7:c7:74:f1
        media: autoselect (100baseTX <full-duplex>) status: active
        supported media: autoselect 100baseTX <full-duplex> 100baseTX
10baseT/UTP <full-duplex> 10baseT/UTP
lo0: flags=8049<UP,LOOPBACK,RUNNING,MULTICAST> mtu 16384
        inet6 fe80::1%lo0 prefixlen 64 scopeid 0x9
        inet6 ::1 prefixlen 128
        inet 127.0.0.1 netmask 0xff000000
add net default: gateway 64.41.131.1
Additional routing options: tcp extensions=NO TCP keepalive=YES.
Routing daemons:.
```

This will work fine if you're on the same LAN as the FreeBSD machine or logged in at the console; however, as you may have noticed, this will contain a nasty trap if you're controlling the machine from elsewhere in the Internet. When you delete the default route, you effectively make the machine unable to communicate with you further, so you can't issue the /etc/netstart command (which re-enables the default route). A trick to get around this is to put both commands on the same line, separated using a semicolon (;). This is risky—it still has the potential to result in a few dropped response packets— but if everything is configured properly in /etc/rc.conf, your terminal connection will pick back up where it left off after just a brief hiccup:

```
# route delete default; /etc/netstart
```

Creating IP Aliases

There's nothing to stop you from assigning as many IP addresses as you want to an Ethernet card. Recalling our discussion of ARP from the previous chapter, a new TCP/IP connection looks up a LAN host by its IP address, asking for the MAC address of whatever Ethernet interface has that IP address. It doesn't do the reverse. One MAC address can answer for many different IP addresses, but one IP address can't be assigned to multiple Ethernet cards without errors and collisions resulting.

The way to assign multiple IP addresses to a single card is through IP aliasing. As with the route command, every platform does aliasing slightly differently; syntax varies from system to system. On FreeBSD, alias is used as a keyword to ifconfig, appended after the address and all other parameters:

```
# ifconfig fxp1 64.41.131.103 netmask 255.255.255.255 alias
```

Note that the netmask is set to 255.255.255.255. This is required if the alias IP address is on the same subnet as the primary IP address for that interface. (If it's not, just use the regular netmask you would use for that subnet.) What does this mean from a TCP/IP standpoint? A netmask where all the bits are set to 1 ensures that the TCP/IP stack will only treat a packet where the destination address matches in all its bits as though it's on the local subnet; it's creating a "subnet" of just that one address. All packets to and from that address thus are sent to the router and not to the LAN. If multiple aliases had the same netmask, their broadcast addresses would be the same, which would confuse the TCP/IP stack. Using an all-1 netmask is how we trick ifconfig into allowing multiple IP addresses on a single interface.

To set up IP aliases in your /etc/rc.conf, you would use the ifconfig_xxx#_alias# keyword, which works syntactically just like ifconfig_xxx#. Here's how a set of aliases in /etc/rc.conf might look:

```
ifconfig_fxp1="inet 64.41.131.131 netmask 255.255.255.0"
ifconfig_fxp1_alias0="inet 64.41.131.132 netmask 255.255.255.255"
ifconfig_fxp1_alias1="inet 64.41.131.133 netmask 255.255.255.255"
ifconfig_fxp1_alias2="inet 64.41.131.134 netmask 255.255.255.255"
ifconfig_fxp1_alias3="inet 64.41.132.161 netmask 255.255.255.0"
ifconfig_fxp1_alias4="inet 64.41.132.165 netmask 255.255.255.255"
ifconfig_fxp1_alias5="inet 64.41.132.166 netmask 255.255.255.255"
```

Mapping Names to IP Addresses with the /etc/hosts File

We need a way for hostnames to map to IP addresses. Normally, this is done with DNS, but we don't have DNS set up yet. In the meantime, we can provide mappings for hosts we know about—such as hosts on our local network—with the /etc/hosts file.

/etc/hosts allows you to build a table in which each entry lists an IP address, its most common (or "official") hostname, and any aliases (additional names that map to the same IP address), separated by spaces or tabs. This table is consulted before any DNS queries are made, so /etc/hosts acts both as a backup to DNS (if it's not available) and an override (if it's not serving correct information). The aliases can even be used as a shorthand for favorite hosts whose names you don't want to have to remember, as with shell aliases (which we discussed in "Chapter 12, Customizing the Shell").

A sample few lines from /etc/hosts:

```
64.41.131.132        ns              ns.somewhere.com lion.somewhere.com
64.41.131.133        www2            www2.somewhere.com
64.41.132.165        www3            www3.somewhere.com
114.235.123.11       www.foobar.com  fred
```

With this table in place, you can connect to the listed hosts by name—either the "official" name in the second column or any of the aliases listed in the third column—even if no DNS servers can be reached.

Testing Network Connectivity with Ping

After you've finished your network configurations, setting them either with sysinstall or with /etc/netstart, you will want a quick way to make sure the settings are correct. The easiest solution is the ping program, a simple ICMP-based tool that checks for echoes from a specified host and reports the round-trip time it takes each packet to get to the host and back.

The use of ping is pretty simple. You can run it against either an IP address or a hostname (or /etc/hosts alias); it will run until you interrupt it with Ctrl+C:

```
# ping fred
PING fred (114.235.123.11): 56 data bytes
64 bytes from 114.235.123.11: icmp_seq=0 ttl=243 time=485.344 ms
64 bytes from 114.235.123.11: icmp_seq=1 ttl=243 time=351.589 ms
^C
-- fred ping statistics --
2 packets transmitted, 2 packets received, 0% packet loss
round-trip min/avg/max/stddev = 351.589/418.466/485.344/66.877 ms
```

This is a healthy TCP/IP configuration—the specified host replied to the ping. However, if the host isn't reachable, the ICMP packets will time out and report the failure to connect. If this happens, something's wrong with your configuration (or, of course, the remote host might actually be down—make sure to try multiple target hosts).

```
# ping 64.41.131.133
PING 64.41.131.133 (64.41.131.133): 56 data bytes
ping: sendto: Host is down
ping: sendto: Host is down
ping: sendto: Host is down
ping: sendto: Host is down
^C
-- 64.41.131.133 ping statistics --
10 packets transmitted, 0 packets received, 100% packet loss
```

Configuring DNS with the /etc/resolv.conf File

To use true DNS, we need access to at least one domain name server. It doesn't matter where this server is—most name servers are configured to allow queries from anywhere on the Internet, with no restrictions on who makes the queries. These servers are kept in the /etc/resolv.conf file.

```
search somewhere.com
nameserver 64.41.131.132
nameserver 207.78.98.20
nameserver 64.40.111.102
```

The nameserver keyword specifies a name server's IP address; you can have as many of these as you like, and the order in which they're listed is the order in which they're consulted. If one times out, the next server is queried. Many applications have their own internal timeouts on a DNS query that gets passed to the operating system to handle, though, so servers beyond the third or fourth probably won't provide much additional benefit.

The search keyword specifies the search domain—the string appended to hostnames that aren't fully qualified. For instance, if you were to do an nslookup www, the resolver would attach the search domain and perform the actual query on www.somewhere.com. You can list multiple search paths on the same line:

```
search somewhere.com foobar.com cslab.ivyleague.edu
```

Technically, /etc/resolv.conf is just a backup and override file such as /etc/hosts; ideally (or at least, according to design), a system should be running its own DNS daemon, which inherits its information from a master name server upstream, and DNS queries by default are always checked against the local system's DNS if it's running. However, in the real world, you don't want to be running DNS unless you have to. It's necessary these days to have an accurate resolv.conf file containing two or three remote name servers against which to do name lookups. If you want to run DNS on your own machine, we'll cover how to do it in Chapter 30, "The Domain Name Server."

> **Tip**
>
> Fortunately, /etc/resolv.conf can be edited and modified at any time, without any special tools to update any databases or anything. DNS lookups are only done on request by network applications, and the resolv.conf table is consulted only at those times and opened from the file on disk, not held in memory and queried constantly as with IP interface configuration. You can open /etc/resolv.conf in your favorite text editor, change or add nameserver entries, shuffle the order in which they're queried, and so on, and the next DNS query you make through any application will query against the newly modified /etc/resolv.conf.

A Look at Various Other Network Configuration Files

We've already seen just about all the files that contain network configuration information that you're ever likely to need to work with. There are, however, still a few more files worth listing and briefly describing. This doesn't count config files for major network services, though; we'll cover those in later chapters.

Most of these files have man pages; simply use man <filename>, without the path, to view it—for example, man inetd.conf.

- /etc/networks: As we've already seen, this file contains symbolic names for subnets that you might want to use in places such as the routing table.

- /etc/hosts.allow: This is a listing of fairly complex security rules for responding to connections of various types on a per-host basis. You can use hosts.allow to reject certain hosts, whether on a particular service or on all services, or to specify an action to take when such a connection attempt is made.

- /etc/inetd.conf: The inetd "super-server" is responsible for accepting connection requests for services specified in inetd.conf and spawning a process to handle each one. Services run from within inetd include Telnet, FTP, POP3, and various miscellaneous other services that you may want to disable if they're not needed. More on this will be in Chapter 29, "Network Security."

- /etc/services: A database of IP service types and the TCP and UDP ports each maps to. Some programs use this table to look up commonly used ports; it also provides a handy reference for what services are assigned what ports by the IANA (Internet Assigned Numbers Authority).

- `/etc/protocols`: Like `/etc/services`, this is a table providing keyword mappings for various IP subprotocol numbers. It is mostly of interest for its reference value.

- `/etc/rpc`: Another table of mappings, even less likely to be of interest to the administrator. RPC lookups provide port-mapping services to requests such as NFS, NIS, and various status-reporting programs.

- `/etc/pam.conf`: Pluggable Authentication Modules (PAM) are a way to assign cascading authenticators (S/Key, Kerberos, and the like) to various services. This will be of interest when we discuss network security in Chapter 29.

- `/etc/host.conf`: This file specifies the order in which name lookup sources are given priority and gives you the ability to set the search order of various sources for several kinds of information. For instance, the default configuration has the line hosts followed by the line bind, meaning that the local hosts database (`/etc/hosts`) should be consulted first for hostname data, followed by BIND (which is DNS). In FreeBSD 5.0, the `/etc/host.conf` file has been replaced with the more versatile `/etc/nsswitch.conf` file. It has a somewhat different format than /etc/host.conf. Consult man nsswitch.conf for more details if you are using FreeBSD 5.0.

23

CONFIGURING BASIC
NETWORKING
SERVICES

Connecting to the Internet with PPP

IN THIS CHAPTER

CHAPTER 24

PPP stands for *Point-to-Point Protocol*. It is the protocol that is used for most dial-up Internet connections. FreeBSD comes with two forms of PPP. The first is kernel PPP, which is the pppd daemon. As the name suggests, this form of PPP is implemented at a kernel level. User PPP on the other hand, runs in userland. Both forms have their advantages and disadvantages and will be discussed later in this chapter.

Choosing an ISP

Before you can connect to the Internet, of course, you will need an Internet service provider. Chances are that your city has a number of them to choose from, ranging from local independent providers to national providers such as AT&T and AOL. You will probably want to choose an ISP that allows you unlimited and unmetered access, so that you do not have to worry about monitoring the hours you spend online, and so on. Here are some other questions to ask when choosing an ISP:

- What is the subscriber-to-phone-line ratio? Expect a lot of busy signals if your ISP has a lot of customers and not so many lines.
- How much downstream bandwidth does the ISP have? ISPs with lots of subscribers and not enough bandwidth can result in slow connections.
- Will the ISP support FreeBSD? Many ISPs will not give you any support unless you are running Windows or a Macintosh. Avoid these types of ISPs, if possible.
- What value-added features does the ISP offer? Many ISPs offer value-added features such as free Web site space or multiple e-mail addresses for no extra charge. If these are features you want, ask the ISP whether they are included at no charge, or how much extra they cost if they do charge for these services.

In addition, you will want to avoid the so-called "on-line services" such as AOL and MSN. They can be difficult or impossible to get working properly with FreeBSD. For best results, stick with a plain old Internet service provider.

Gathering Needed Information

After you have signed up with an ISP, you will need to get several pieces of information:

- The communications port that your modem is on. If you know the DOS com port, the following FreeBSD devices correspond to the DOS com ports: COM1: cuaa0, COM2: cuaa1, COM3: cuaa2, COM4: cuaa3.
- The IP addresses of your ISP's DNS servers. These are used to resolve domain names to numerical IP addresses.

- Your ISP's dial-up phone number.
- Your user name and password.
- The type of authentication that your ISP uses. This should be either a standard shell login, PAP (password authentication protocol), or CHAP (challenge handshake protocol). More on the different authentication protocols will be covered later in the chapter.
- Whether you have a static IP address or a dynamic IP address. If you have a static IP address, you will need to know your IP number.

All of the information items except the first one can be obtained from your ISP.

User PPP versus Kernel PPP

The two types of PPP available with FreeBSD are user PPP and kernel PPP. Both have their advantages and disadvantages. User PPP is somewhat easier to debug than kernel PPP, but it uses a tunnel device, and is somewhat less efficient. Kernel PPP is a little more efficient, and runs as a daemon. It requires PPP support to be compiled into the kernel (it is there by default). We will cover kernel PPP first and then cover user PPP.

Configuring Kernel PPP

Kernel PPP is handled by the pppd daemon. The main configuration files for the pppd daemon are located in /etc/ppp. Other than the files located here, you will also need to edit the /etc/resolv.conf file.

/etc/resolv.conf

The /etc/resolv.conf file determines how FreeBSD resolves hostnames to numerical IP addresses. Each line in resolv.conf contains the keyword nameserver followed by the IP address of the DNS server. In addition, the keyword domain can be used in this file. If the domain keyword is present, FreeBSD will assume that any unqualified hostnames (hostnames that do not have a domain after them) are located in the domain specified after the domain keyword. Here is a sample of an /etc/resolv.conf file:

```
domain samplenet.org
nameserver 111.111.11.1
nameserver 222.222.22.2
```

You can edit the /etc/resolv.conf file with any text editor. You will need to be logged in as root to do so.

/etc/ppp/options

The /etc/ppp/options file is where most of the options for the PPP daemon go. It is read before any command line options.

The options that need to go in this file are different, depending on the type of authentication that your ISP uses. This is a sample file for using a simple shell login authentication and a dynamic IP address. PAP and CHAP will be covered in detail in the next sections.

```
/dev/cuaa0 115200
crtscts
modem
connect "/usr/sbin/chat -f /etc/ppp/opions/chat.script"
noipdefault
silent
domain samplenet.org
defaultroute
```

Here is what each of the options mean:

- **/dev/cuaa0**. This line sets the device that the modem is located on. In this case, this is equivalent to COM1. It also sets the port speed to 115200 bits per second.
- **crtscts**. This line sets the hardware flow control of the modem to on. Hardware flow control is required for high-speed communications.
- **modem**. This tells pppd to use the modem control lines, wait for carrier detect before opening the serial port, and so on.
- **connect**. This specifies the dialer program to run along with the script that should be used. The chat program can be used to automate the modem connection. This will be covered more in the next section.
- **noipdefault**. Use this option if you have a dynamic IP address (your ISP assigns you an IP address each time you log on). This option tells pppd to get an IP address from the dial-up server.
- **silent**. This tells pppd to wait for LCP packets.
- **domain**. The domain name of your ISP should go here. It may be used for authentication purposes. It appends the domain name onto the end of local hostnames.
- **defaultroute**. This will add a routing entry to the system routing tables while pppd is running. When pppd is terminated, the route will be removed.

If you have a static IP address, remove the line that says `noipdefault`, and replace it with a line that looks like the following:

```
111.111.111.11:222.222.222.22
```

The first number before the colon should be replaced with the IP address your ISP has assigned you. The number after the colon is the gateway address that your ISP has given you. If your ISP has not given you a gateway address, you can leave the second number off (you should include the trailing colon, however).

> **Tip**
>
> If you installed FreeBSD on an older system (486 or older) and you have an external modem, you may find that the preceding setup produces strange results. This is because older systems did not ship with a high-speed UART communication chip, and may not be able to handle a port speed of 115200. If you get strange results, try reducing the port speed to 57600.

The Chat Script

The `pppd` daemon has no built-in dialing capabilities. This is where the chat program comes in. The chat program allows an automated conversation with the modem. It uses a "send-response" syntax. In other words, the script contains what it should send, what the modem should respond with, what it should send next, and so on.

Here is a sample chat script. You may need to modify this script slightly to work with your particular modem, but this one should get you started. As root, open a new file in any text editor named `chat.script`, and enter the following, all on one line:

```
ABORT BUSY ABORT 'NO CARRIER' "" AT OK ATDT5551212 CONNECT "" TIMEOUT 10 ogin:-
\\r-ogin: foo TIMEOUT 5 sword: bar
```

The first part of this script tells it to abort if the modem should respond with either BUSY or NO CARRIER. Then, the script sends an AT command (which stands for "ATTENTION"), and waits for the modem to respond with "OK". When it does, the script uses ATDT (Attention Dial Tone), and dials the phone number given after ATDT. The script then waits for the modem to send CONNECT. When it has, it sets the timeout to 10 seconds. It then waits for the string `ogin:` (short for login) from the modem, which is the login prompt sent by the ISP. After the script has received the login prompt, it responds with `foo`, which should be replaced with your ISP login name. If the login prompt has not been received within 10 seconds, the script aborts. Assuming the script does receive the login prompt and sends the login name, the timer is then reset to five seconds, and the script waits to receive sword: (short for password). When it does, it ends bar, which should be replaced with the password you use to log in to your ISP. After the password has been sent, if your ISP's server automatically changes to PPP mode, the script is done. If instead, you are put into a login shell, you will need to find out from your ISP what shell command needs to be issued to start PPP. Then, you can simply add this command at the end of the script.

Tip

If you are unsure about which prompts your ISP sends, use a terminal emulator such as minicom (available in the ports tree) to dial your ISP's phone number and then do a manual login. This will enable you to observe what prompts the ISP's server sends when requesting various items of information.

Caution

If you want to allow non-root users to start the pppd daemon, the chat.script file will have to be world-readable. This can be a security hazard because any-one with a shell account on your system will be able to get your Internet pass-word from this file. Because of this, it is much better to use CHAP or PAP authentication if you want normal users to be able to start pppd. The chap-secrets and pap-secrets files (discussed as follows) need to be readable only by root, even if you are allowing normal users to start pppd. Also, if you do not want the rest of the world to be able to get your Internet password, don't forget to change the permissions on the chat.script file accordingly.

Starting the pppd Daemon

After you have completed the preceding tasks, the PPP connection should be ready to go. Simply type pppd at the command prompt to bring it up. If all goes well, your modem should dial and connect. If you have problems, please see the troubleshooting section at the end of this chapter.

To stop the pppd daemon, you can either find its PID number with PS and then issue a kill command, or you can use killall like this: killall pppd.

PAP and CHAP Authentication

Most ISPs these days support PAP or CHAP, and some support only PAP or CHAP. Both of these types of authentication do not use the shell, and both start off immediately in PPP mode. This makes them a little bit more efficient than a shell login. PAP and CHAP also have one other advantage over the shell login. The chat script has to be world-readable if you want any users other than root to be able to start pppd. With the shell login, it means that your password in the chat script is visible to everyone who has access to the system. With PAP and CHAP, the files that contain the passwords do not have to be world-readable, so they are more secure for a multiuser system. The configuration for PAP and CHAP is a bit more complicated, and requires some explanation.

Both CHAP and PAP start off right in PPP mode, and do not use a shell login. Also, both of them require authentication. The configuration is a little different. Let's start with the ppp options file.

At least one line will need to be added to the /etc/ppp/options file to determine what profile to use for logging in (more on the profile later).

The first line that needs to be added to the end of the options file is a user line. It corresponds to a profile name (the profiles will be added later in a different file). The user line looks like this:

```
user foo
```

Replace foo with the login name you use to log on to your ISP. The following is a list of other options you might need to include.

- **refuse-chap**. If this statement exists in /etc/options, pppd will refuse to authenticate using CHAP, even if the remote host requests it.
- **refuse-pap**. Like refuse-chap, except it applies to PAP instead.
- **require-chap**. If this option exists in /etc/options, pppd will require the remote host to authenticate itself using CHAP. Because your ISP's server likely does not authenticate itself to you, you will probably not use this line
- **require-pap**. Like require-chap, except that it applies to PAP instead.

If you do not include either the refuse-chap or refuse-pap statements in your options file, pppd will accept whichever authentication mechanism the ISP offers first. Note also that if you reject both PAP and CHAP, the connection will fail because your system will not have a way to authenticate itself to the ISP.

pap-secrets and chap-secrets

The /etc/ppp/chap-secrets and /etc/ppp/pap-secrets files contain the CHAP and PAP authentication information, respectively. The files follow the basic format of *username hostname password* where *username* is your ISP login name, *hostname* is the name of the host that this entry will also authenticate, and *password* is (of course) your Internet password. The hostname entry can be replaced with a wildcard (*) that tells pppd that this entry can authenticate to any host (this is probably what you will do for configuring your Internet account because if you dial in to your ISP, you are already assured that the host you are contacting is who it claims to be). A sample entry for either of these files might look like this

```
foo * bar
```

where *foo* is the username, * means that this entry is good for any host, and bar is the password.

There are other options that can be used in the chap-secrets and pap-secrets files, but they are generally used only if you are providing dial-in PPP service.

> **Caution**
>
> The /etc/ppp/chap-secrets and /etc/ppp/pap-secrets files should be readable only by root. Change the permissions accordingly. If you do not do this, anyone who has shell access to your system can get your Internet password from these files.

Dial-On-Demand and Persistent Connections

As the names suggest, *dial-on-demand* means that pppd will automatically dial out whenever it detects outgoing traffic that needs to be sent. A persistent connection, on the other hand, is always up and redials the connection immediately if pppd detects a disconnect. We will start with dial-on-demand.

Dial-On-Demand

Dial-on-demand will cause pppd to establish a dial-up connection any time it detects outgoing network traffic and the connection is not already up. The relevant statements in /etc/ppp/options are listed as follows:

demand	This statement turns on dial-on-demand.
idle *n*	Where *n* is a number representing seconds. This option causes pppd to automatically disconnect after this many seconds of being idle. *Idle* means that no traffic has been received or sent over the link for this many seconds.

After you have enabled dial-on-demand, you can create a startup script to automatically start the pppd daemon each time your system boots. There are a couple of ways to do this. The first is by simply adding the line pppd to the /etc/rc.local file. However, rc.local is deprecated. So a better option is to create a startup file in /usr/local/etc/rc.d with the single line pppd in it. This file can be called anything you want, but I suggest you call it ppp or something else that makes sense and tells you what it does.

> **Tip**
>
> If you have dial-on-demand enabled, and your Internet connection seems to be starting for no reason, a program is probably trying to do a DNS lookup. More often than not, the program that is causing problems will be Sendmail. Please see Chapter 25, "Configuring E-Mail Services," for information on how to stop Sendmail from doing this.

> **Tip**
>
> If you have dial-on-demand enabled, and you are running Fetchmail in daemon mode so it polls your mail server every so often, this might keep the connection open all the time in addition to causing pppd to dial on a regular basis. See the Fetchmail section in Chapter 25 for ways to stop this from happening.

Persistent Connections

You can also tell pppd to always keep the connection up. This is done by adding the persist statement to /etc/ppp/options. If this statement is present, pppd will automatically tell the modem to re-establish the connection if it is lost.

> **Caution**
>
> Even if your ISP tells you that you have unlimited access, make sure you read the fine print. There might be a "within reason" clause or something. If you are using the `persist` option to keep your Internet connection open 24 hours a day, 365 days a year, your ISP may terminate your account or ask you to purchase a dedicated line. The moral of this is that "unlimited access" does not always truly mean "unlimited access."

Running Commands on Connect and Disconnect

When `pppd` establishes a connection, it will check for the existence of a file called `ip-up` in `/etc/ppp`. Likewise, when the PPP connection goes down, `pppd` will check for the existence of a file called `ip-down` in `/etc/ppp`. If the file(s) exist, whatever commands are located in them will be executed. One example of when this could be useful is if you are traveling, and running FreeBSD on your laptop. You could read and respond to e-mail while on a plane. Then when you get to your destination and dial into your network, you could have `pppd` flush the mail queue (deliver all the mail you wrote on the plane), as well as run the Fetchmail program to download any new mail you had received. If you put the command to perform these options in `/etc/ppp/ip-ip`, they will automatically be performed when you type `pppd` to start your dial-up connection. You could than have the `ip-down` script automatically kill Fetchmail if it is running in daemon mode, so that it does not attempt to retrieve mail when the connection is not available.

User PPP

If, for whatever reason, you can't or don't want to use kernel PPP, FreeBSD also provides user PPP. User PPP does not run as a daemon, and does not require PPP support to be compiled into the kernel. It does, however, require a tunnel device to be compiled into the kernel because this is what it runs PPP through.

The first thing to do when setting up user PPP is to make sure that there is a tunnel device available (there should be unless you have built a custom kernel and removed it). If you have built a custom kernel, check your kernel configuration file in `/sys/i386/conf` for the line `pseudo-device tun 1`. If this line exists, your kernel is configured to use a tunnel device.

The `/etc/ppp/ppp.conf` File

The `/etc/ppp/ppp.conf` file is the configuration file for user PPP. There is a sample configuration file already present in `/etc/ppp` that you can use to get started. It is set up to use CHAP or PAP authentication. You will need to change several lines in it, however, to make it work with your ISP. Listing 24.1 is the sample configuration file included with FreeBSD, along with explanations of the items you may have to change. You will need to be root to edit this file.

LISTING 24.1 Sample User PPP Configuration

```
################################################################
# PPP  Sample Configuration File
# Originally written by Toshiharu OHNO
# Simplified 5/14/1999 by wself@cdrom.com
#
# See /usr/share/examples/ppp/ for some examples
#
# $FreeBSD: src/etc/ppp/ppp.conf,v 1.7 2001/02/22 23:28:12 brian Exp $
################################################################

default:
 ident user-ppp VERSION (built COMPILATIONDATE)

 # Ensure that "device" references the correct serial port
 # for your modem. (cuaa0 = COM1, cuaa1 = COM2)
 #
 set device /dev/cuaa1

 set log Phase Chat LCP IPCP CCP tun command
 set speed 115200
 set dial "ABORT BUSY ABORT NO\\sCARRIER TIMEOUT 5 \
         \"\" AT OK-AT-OK ATE1Q0 OK \\dATDT\\T TIMEOUT 40 CONNECT"
 set ifaddr 10.0.0.1/0 10.0.0.2/0 255.255.255.0 0.0.0.0
 set timeout 180                       # 3 minute idle timer (the default)
 add default HISADDR                   # Add a (sticky) default route
 enable dns                            # request DNS info (for resolv.conf)

papchap:

 #
 # edit the next three lines and replace the items in caps with
 # the values which have been assigned by your ISP.
 #

 set phone PHONE_NUM
 set authname USERNAME
 set authkey PASSWORD
```

Here is what the various options mean.

- **set device**. This option should point to the device name that your modem is on. Here is a list of the DOS equivalents: COM1: `/dev/cuaa0`, COM2: `/dev/cuaa1`, COM3: `/dev/cuaa2`, COM4: `/dev/cuaa3`.

- **set log**. This option controls what types of events get logged, and it can be useful for debugging connection problems. It will be covered more in the section on troubleshooting.

- **set speed**. This option sets the speed at which the serial port should run. The default of 115200 will work for most people. If you have problems with this on an older system, you may want to change this to `57600`.

- **set dial**. This option is the modem control string for the dialer. It is similar to the chat script used for kernel PPP. The default script will work for most people, so don't change this setting unless you have problems or you are familiar with your modem's command set.

- **set ifaddr**. The first number (`10.0.0.1/0`) should be replaced with the IP address assigned to you by your ISP. If you have a dynamic IP address, leave the number as is. The second number (`10.0.0.2/0`) should be replaced by the gateway address your ISP gave you. If your ISP has not given you a gateway address, leave this number as is. The third number (`255.255.255.0`) is the netmask. Unless your ISP has given you a netmask number that differs from this number, you should leave this number as is.

- **set timeout**. The number here is the number of seconds of inactivity (no outgoing or incoming traffic) that will pass before the connection is terminated. It is similar to the `idle` option in kernel PPP.

- **set default HISADDR**. This line adds a default route to the routing tables for your ISP's gateway. Note that this line must appear after the `set ifaddr` line; otherwise, PPP will not know what the gateway address is.

- **enable DNS**. This option causes PPP to check with your ISP to see whether the DNS servers you have listed in `/etc/resolv.conf` are correct or not. If they aren't, PPP will update them automatically.

- **set phone**. This option replaces PHONE_NUM with the phone number you use to connect to your ISP.

- **set authname**. This option replaces USERNAME with the login name that you use to connect to your ISP.

- **set authkey**. This option replaces PASSWORD with the password you use for your ISP.

If you can't use PAP or CHAP, and need to use a standard UNIX shell login instead, you will need to make some more changes to the default configuration file. First, remove the papchap section, including the `set phone`, `set authname`, and `set authkey` statements. Next, add the following lines after the `set dial` statement.

```
Provider:
        set phone "5551212"
        set login "TIMEOUT 10 \"\" \"\" gin:--gin: foo sword: bar"
```

Once again, replace `foo` and `bar` with your ISP login name and password, respectively. Also, as with kernel PPP, if you need to send any other commands to start PPP on the remote host, you will need to include these after the password. Like the chat script in kernel PPP, this script uses an "expect/send" syntax, in which you type what it should expect to receive from the server and then what it should respond with.

> **Tip**
>
> If you are unsure about which prompts your ISP sends, use a terminal emulator such as minicom (available in the ports tree) to dial your ISP's phone number and then do a manual login. This will enable you to observe what prompts the ISP's server sends when requesting various items of information.

Starting User PPP

If you are using PAP or CHAP authentication, you can start user PPP from the command line by typing `ppp -background papchap`. If you are using a shell login instead of CHAP or PAP, use the `ppp -background provider` instead. This will start user PPP in the background. If all goes well, you should hear your modem dial, and after a connection has been established, the system will respond with `PPP Enabled` and then return you to a command prompt.

To kill user PPP, you can either find its PID number with `ps` and then issue a `kill` command, or you can use `killall` like this: `killall ppp`.

Allowing Normal Users to Start User PPP

If you want to allow normal (non-root) users to start user PPP, add a line to `/etc/ppp/ppp.conf` that says `allow users`.

Dial-On-Demand and Persistent Connections

Like kernel PPP, user PPP also supports dial-on-demand and persistent connections.

Dial-On-Demand

To enable dial-on-demand for user PPP, you can type `ppp -auto papchap` or `ppp -auto provider` for CHAP/PAP or shell login, respectively. If you want to enable this by default at each system boot, you will need to add at least one line to `/etc/rc.conf`. The line to add is `ppp_enable="YES"`. This also sets a few other options that may or may not be correct for your system configuration:

- It sets the mode to auto so that PPP will dial automatically whenever it detects outgoing network traffic. The link will terminate when no incoming or outgoing traffic has been detected for the period of time specified in `set timeout` in `/etc/ppp/ppp.conf`.

- It sets the profile to `papchap`. If you are using a shell-based log into your ISP, you will also need to add a line that says `ppp_profile="provider"` to `/etc/rc.conf`.

- It enables *NAT (network address translation)*, which can allow other computers on the network that do not have a real IP address to access the Internet through this system. If this behavior is undesirable, you will need to add a line to `rc.conf` that says `ppp_nat="NO"`.

If you have made changes to `rc.conf` to enable dial-on-demand at system boot, you will need to reboot the system before these changes take effect.

Persistent Connections

To enable persistent connections for user PPP, you will first want to remove the `set timeout` line from `/etc/ppp/ppp.conf`, so that that the connection doesn't terminate after inactivity. From the command line, you can then start PPP in persistent mode with the command `ppp -ddial papchap` or `ppp -ddial provider` for CHAP/PAP or shell login, respectively. If you want to enable this by default at system boot, you will need to add the line `ppp-enable="YES"` to the `/etc/rc.conf` file. You will also need to add the line `ppp_mode="ddial"` to `/etc/rc.conf`. This also sets a few other options that you may need to change depending on your system configuration:

- It sets the profile to `papchap`. If you are using a shell-based login to your ISP, you will also need to add a line that says `ppp_profile="provider"` to `/etc/rc.conf`.

- It enables NAT (network address translation), which can allow other computers on the network that do not have a real IP address to access the Internet through this system. If this behavior is undesirable, you will need to add a line to `rc.conf` that says `ppp_nat="NO"`.

If you have made changes to rc.conf to enable persistent connections on system boot, you will need to reboot the system before these changes take effect.

Running Commands on Connect and Disconnect

Like kernel PPP, user PPP can also run commands on connect and disconnect. It reads the files /etc/ppp/ppp.linkup and /etc/ppp/ppp.linkdown files to run commands on connect and disconnect, respectively. The syntax looks like this:

```
papchap:
    commands to run here
```

The papchap tells PPP which profile the following commands apply to. If you are using a shell login, replace papchap with provider.

This could be used, for example, to automatically start Fetchmail and download new mail, as well as flush the mail queue and delivered queued mail automatically when PPP starts. This can be useful for a laptop user who travels (how to do this will be explained in Chapter 25).

Troubleshooting PPP

If you are having trouble getting PPP to work, here are a few suggestions for troubleshooting:

If the modem doesn't dial:

- Verify that you have selected the correct device for your modem.
- If you are using an older system, try reducing the speed to 57600. Some older systems without high-speed UARTs cannot handle 115200.
- Verify your chat script or set dial line. Check your modem documentation to see whether you need to be sending it some initialization string other than the default in the FreeBSD configuration files.

If the modem dials but fails to establish a connection:

- Verify that you are using the correct authentication type (CHAP, PAP, or shell login).
- Verify that you are using the correct login name and password for your ISP.
- Verify your chat script or set dial line. Check your modem documentation to see whether there is an initialization string you have to send.

24

CONNECTING TO
THE INTERNET
WITH PPP

- If you are using user PPP, you might want to try kernel PPP. This author had a modem/ISP combination once where kernel PPP worked fine; but user PPP, for whatever reason, simply refused to work with this particular ISP.

If a connection is made, but attempts to access remote hosts by host and/or domain name fail:

- Verify that you have the correct DNS servers listed in /etc/resolv.conf. Also, verify the correct setup of the /etc/host.conf file. It should have a line that says hosts followed by a line that says bind.

If the preceding suggestions do not correct the problem, try turning on logging and then attempt to connect again. This can be enabled by adding a line to /etc/ppp/options that says debug for kernel PPP, and by changing the set log line in /etc/ppp/ppp.conf to read All for user PPP. Messages from kernel PPP will be logged to /var/log/messages, and messages from user PPP will be logged to /var/log/ppp.log. You can monitor the messages as they are being sent by typing tail -f /var/log/messages or tail -f /var/log/ppp.log. This will show you the last 10 lines of the file and also update the display each time the file changes.

The information logged is fairly technical. You might be able to spot the problem yourself. If you can't, the contents of the log can still be useful in helping debug the problem. Your ISP might be able to use the log information to spot the problem. If they can't find it either, they might be able to call their RAS vendor and let them look at it to find the problem.

Final Thoughts

The information presented in this chapter should be enough to get most people up-and-running with their ISP. However, both kernel PPP and user PPP are extremely complex, and this chapter cannot cover all the options available. If you need to do more advanced configuration, both kernel PPP and user PPP have detailed man pages that describe all the options available. The kernel PPP man page can be accessed with man pppd, and the user PPP man page can be accessed with man ppp. In addition, there are sample configuration files located in /usr/share/examples/ppp.

Configuring E-mail Services

CHAPTER 25

What's the Internet without e-mail? Probably not even the Web, with its flashy graphics and its commercial opportunities, has quite the usefulness and cachet as the Internet's oldest application, electronic mail. It's omnipresent and indispensable. You can't get away from it. Part of the reason for this is that every UNIX server in the world has e-mail capabilities built in to it—not just the capability for users to send and receive it, but for the system itself to act as a full-fledged mail server. FreeBSD is no exception.

The catch is that configuring Sendmail, the venerable SMTP server application that forms the e-mail backbone of UNIX and the Internet, is perhaps the most daunting system administration task you'll face. After all, what can you say that isn't self-evident about a program that has a config file…for its config file? But don't worry; this chapter's aim is to outline the use of Sendmail to an extent where you can do what needs to be done for the sake of security and reliable performance, without covering enough ground for it to become overwhelmingly or needlessly complex.

We'll also cover the other side of e-mail, POP and IMAP—the protocols by which e-mail is received by remote clients. Fortunately, this is nowhere near as complicated as Sendmail. Let's get the big one out of the way first.

Introduction to SMTP

The *Simple Mail Transfer Protocol (SMTP)* is one of the oldest protocols on the Internet, nearly as old as e-mail itself, which began with Ray Tomlinson in 1971 (only two years after the first ARPA network was installed). SMTP's purpose is to transfer plain-text messages from one host to another—often in sequence, as when a dial-up client running Windows sends an e-mail message to the ISP's mail server, which then turns around and transfers it to the recipient's mail server. This sequential nature doesn't need to get much longer than this, though; it isn't like the Internet itself, with its router-to-router hopping of individual packets. The sender's SMTP server communicates directly with the recipient's SMTP server.

SMTP itself is, as suggested in its name, simple. A connection is initiated with a communication to TCP port 25 on the server, followed by an automated greeting code, some optional authentication commands, and a couple more commands to establish what the transaction is that the sender wants to do. Then, the recipient asks for the message, and the sender sends it. Finally, a termination command is sent, and the connection is closed. That's about all SMTP is ever really used for, and there really aren't many other capabilities designed into the protocol. No specialized software is necessary; in fact, you can execute a completely valid SMTP transaction right from the command line. Listing 25.1 is an example of such a transaction; bold type indicates your input during the session:

LISTING 25.1 Executing a Valid SMTP Transaction

```
# telnet destination.com 25
Trying 64.41.134.166...
Connected to destination.com.
Escape character is '^]'.
220 destination.com ESMTP Sendmail 8.11.1/8.11.1; Wed, 16 May 2001 22:55:37 -
0700 (PDT)
HELO stripes.sender.com
250 destination.com Hello w012.z064002043.sjc-ca.dsl.cnc.net [64.2.43.12],
pleased to meet you
MAIL From: frank@sender.com
250 2.1.0 frank@sender.com... Sender ok
RCPT To: bob@destination.com
250 2.1.5 bob@destination.com... Recipient ok
DATA
354 Enter mail, end with "." on a line by itself
From: frank@sender.com
To: bob@destination.com
Subject: Testing, 123...

This is a test message.
.
250 2.0.0 f4H5uCu53501 Message accepted for delivery
QUIT
221 2.0.0 destination.com closing connection
Connection closed by foreign host.
```

As you can see, communication between the two servers is done with four-letter command codes, by convention in caps, and with arguments that are incorporated into the message headers. The message that bob@destination.com receives will come up in his e-mail program with the following headers:

```
From: frank@sender.com
To: bob@destination.com
Subject: Testing, 123...
```

The headers are separated from the body of the message by a single blank line. A single dot on a line by itself marks the end of the message body; when the receiving SMTP program sees it, it delivers the message by appending it to the recipient's mailbox file (/var/mail/bob if it's a FreeBSD machine). And that's all there is to it. A full-featured SMTP program such as Sendmail transmits its messages using a few extra commands to enhance performance and efficiency, but functionally it uses exactly the same method as the example we've just seen during the actual connection. Sendmail's complexity lies mostly in areas outside the actual SMTP transaction.

The reason the client has to communicate first with its own ISP's SMTP server, rather than connecting directly to the recipient's, is to take advantage of queuing. This is a behavior of SMTP servers at the application level that enhances the functionality of SMTP, much in the way that DNS enhances the functionality of Internet applications while not actually being a part of the TCP/IP stack. With queuing, an SMTP server can keep each message it receives from a client—whether the client is on the local machine or sending the message from a different machine via its own SMTP connection—in a queue where it waits for a connection to the final recipient's SMTP server. This connection might be immediately available, in which case the message spends almost no time in the queue; if it isn't, however, the message sits in the queue until a connection becomes available, at which time the SMTP program sends it. The benefit this provides is that it removes from the dial-up client the burden of looking up the destination host's SMTP server, queuing the message, and retrying the connection at regular intervals; when the client dials up, it can make a single connection, upload all its pending e-mail messages into the outgoing SMTP queue, and then disconnect, freeing itself of the mail-sending task.

Mail Transfer Agents (MTAs) and Mail User Agents (MUAs)

The schematic diagram for an e-mail message's path from one person to another is shown in Figure 25.1. Whether the user is on a dial-up connection from a remote site or sitting at the console on the mail server itself, the path the message takes is the same: From the user's input into the Mail User Agent (commonly known as an e-mail client program), the message moves into the sending SMTP server's message queue, where the Mail Transfer Agent (MTA) (for example, Sendmail) pulls it out as soon as a connection to the receiving SMTP server becomes available and transmits it. (Since this process transmits a message that doesn't originate or terminate on the SMTP server machine itself, this step is known as *relaying*.) On the remote system, the MTA places the received message into the recipient's mailbox, where it can be read online with a server-side MUA or downloaded to a client-side MUA through POP3.

As a FreeBSD administrator, you'll be interested in the way Sendmail operates as an MTA, both in sender (relay) and receiver roles; we'll also be talking about how MUA programs, both the local kind that users run on the FreeBSD machine and the remote kind that operate by uploading and downloading messages, interact with the "holding areas" of the MTAs: the message queue and the user mailboxes.

FIGURE 25.1

Diagram of an e-mail message's path from one user to another, showing the roles of MUAs and MTAs.

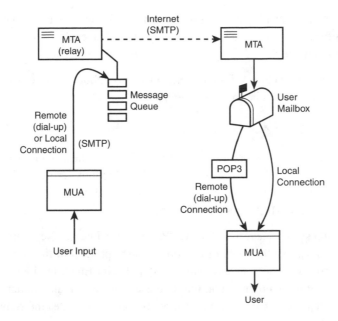

Common MTAs

Here are a few of the Mail Transfer Agent programs routinely used on the Internet:

- **Sendmail.** By far the most widely used MTA, it was developed by Eric Allman in 1983, and has developed into a cross-platform *de facto* standard with both a commercially supported and a freeware component. Sendmail, Inc. (http://www. sendmail.com) is a fully functional corporation that exists to support Sendmail for commercial UNIX and Linux resellers; the Sendmail Project (http://www. sendmail.org) is the free, volunteer-supported component, with grassroots resources positioned in the traditional open-source way for users of systems such as FreeBSD where Sendmail is bundled.

- **Microsoft Exchange.** The Windows equivalent of Sendmail, as well as of a multitude of other types of message transfer (such as POP3, NNTP, LDAP, and calendaring), Exchange is commercially developed and closed-source, in the Microsoft tradition.

- **Postfix.** Written by Wietse Venema as an alternative to Sendmail, it's designed to be faster, more secure, and easier to operate than Sendmail. We'll talk more about Postfix at the end of this chapter.

- **Qmail.** Another response to Sendmail, Qmail was written by Dan Bernstein and is gaining rapidly in popularity due to its reputation for security and speed (although Postfix is reputedly faster). Also, unlike Postfix (which attempts to mimic

25

CONFIGURING
E-MAIL SERVICES

Sendmail in its interactions with the system, for instance, where it keeps its spool and config files), Qmail uses its own structure and doesn't try to ease the transition for Sendmail users.

There are a great many more MTAs in general use throughout the Internet; the ones that are ported to FreeBSD can be found in `/usr/ports/mail`.

Common MUAs

Mail User Agents are even more numerous than MTAs. Because Windows and Macintosh e-mail clients (such as Microsoft Outlook/Outlook Express, Eudora, Apple Mail, Netscape Mail, and so on) are so widely understood, the following list contains only the more popular MUAs available for FreeBSD.

- **Pine.** Ostensibly an acronym for the "Program for Internet News and E-mail", rumors persist that the name of this open-source product of the University of Washington is actually an acronym for "Pine Is Not Elm". In either case, Pine is quite widely used, providing an intuitive user interface, many modern message-handling features, and a message composer that incorporates the stalwart `pico` editor, which comes packaged with Pine.

- **Elm.** The genesis of Pine (at least, if you believe the name), Elm evolved from the ancient `mail` and `mailx` programs that did e-mail duties for the university and government networks that predated the modern commercial Internet. Primitive by today's standards, Elm still claims many loyal users.

- **Mutt.** Conceived as a "mongrel" MUA and incorporating features from Elm, Pine, and a number of other programs, Mutt claims to be the most advanced of them all—and it may be right. It's got features the others don't, including many that require a graphical client-side MUA in other contexts, as well as a great deal of customizability.

Note that the e-mail agents listed here are all shell-oriented, meaning that they run in a Telnet or SSH session, monopolizing that session's window. This means they're (almost) exclusively text-oriented, and such things as inline images and HTML formatting won't work (although they can be configured to open attachments in helper applications, if you're running them on a graphical FreeBSD workstation). However, it also means that you can check your mail using these programs no matter where you're computing from—just open up a Telnet or SSH session from wherever you are. You'll also be virtually guaranteed to be safe from the Windows/Outlook-oriented viruses that plague the Internet.

For more information on mail user agents available for FreeBSD, see the e-mail section of Chapter 7, "Working with Applications."

Configuring Basic E-mail Services with Sendmail

FreeBSD comes with Sendmail installed and already configured to serve basic e-mail needs right out of the box. All you have to do to enable Sendmail (so that it starts at boot time) is add the following line to /etc/rc.conf:

```
Sendmail_enable="YES"
```

Once the system is up and running, you can send a message to anyone on the Internet, and they can send one to you—provided that you have a few things set up properly. For the most part, these aren't configuration items for Sendmail itself, but for the system in general—Sendmail relies on the system to have a few guarantees in place before it will operate without a hitch.

You can decide to replace Sendmail with another MTA, such as Postfix or Qmail; we'll talk about how to do that at the end of the chapter. Meanwhile, since Sendmail will do in its default configuration for the vast majority of servers, we'll talk about how to manage Sendmail effectively.

Sendmail File Layout

There are three places in the system that concern Sendmail:

- /etc/mail: Configuration files for Sendmail.
- /var/mail: User mailboxes.
- /var/spool/mqueue: Message queue files.

Sendmail itself is located at /usr/sbin/sendmail, and its log files are written to /var/log/maillog (which is rotated on a daily basis by the periodic job, which we discussed in Chapter 14, "Performance Monitoring, Process Control, and Job Automation."

> **Note**
>
> Some systems historically put the Sendmail binary in /usr/lib/sendmail. If you have to run programs that expect to find Sendmail there, such as certain old Web tools that were developed without FreeBSD or Linux in mind, you might want to violate the FreeBSD directory structure so far as to create a symbolic link from this historical location to the current one:
>
> ```
> # ln -s /usr/sbin/sendmail /usr/lib/sendmail
> ```

25

CONFIGURING E-MAIL SERVICES

The mailbox files (mail spools) in `/var/mail` are plain-text files, each named for the user who owns it and with permissions set to 600 (readable and writable only by the owner). New messages are appended to the end of the recipient's mail spool file. There are also temporary POP lock files, which have zero length and a name of the form `.username.pop`. They receive the contents of the corresponding mail spool file while a POP3 connection is open, and any untransferred remnants are then copied back into the mailbox. We'll be talking more about how the POP3 server works later in this chapter.

Configuration Files

Here are some of the files in `/etc/mail` that you'll find important when running Sendmail.

/etc/mail/sendmail.cf

This is the main Sendmail config file. However, unlike just about every other config file for every other program, you're not intended to edit this file to alter Sendmail's behavior. Rather, you should make changes at a higher "macro" level in the Master Config (`.mc`) file and then compile a `sendmail.cf` file from that.

The `sendmail.cf` file contains options, rulesets, and features; all in a format that can be very daunting and nearly not human-readable. It's best to leave `sendmail.cf` alone unless absolutely necessary.

/etc/mail/freebsd.mc

This is the "Master Config" file. It contains a list of features and options that override the defaults in the standard config file, much in the same fashion as `/etc/rc.conf` overrides `/etc/defaults/rc.conf`; here, though, the format of the settings is much more bizarre. Commands are given in the `m4` macro language (which is barely used outside of Sendmail configurations), and the `.mc` file is then compiled together with the default `cf.m4` file from the Sendmail source in `/usr/share/sendmail` or `/usr/src/contrib/sendmail` to create a `.cf` output file. You can then install this file as the new `sendmail.cf` file.

Sound confusing and backward? It is, yes. However, the process has come a long way in recent versions of FreeBSD. It used to be the case that to regenerate your `sendmail.cf` file, you had to go into the source directory on your own, figure out which `.mc` file was the one that most closely matched your system, make changes according to the online documentation as best you could, and then dig out the cryptic `m4` compilation command that produced the output file—which you then had to install by hand. The state of things today is greatly improved over that, although it's still not what anyone would call user-friendly.

Each line in the `m4` language contains the string `dnl` at some point; this stands for "delete through newline," and it marks the end of the readable line (each line must have one). To comment out a line, place the `dnl` at the beginning. Otherwise, put it at the end.

There's a `Makefile` in `/etc/mail`, which allows you to create a new `.cf` file from the `freebsd.mc` file simply by typing `make cf`. Then, install this output file (`freebsd.cf`) into `sendmail.cf` using `make install`.

```
# make cf
/usr/bin/m4 -D_CF_DIR_=/usr/share/sendmail/cf/ /usr/share/sendmail/cf/m4/cf.m4
freebsd.mc > freebsd.cf
# make install
install -c -m 444 freebsd.cf /etc/mail/sendmail.cf
```

The `/etc/mail/Makefile` has a number of other uses, as we'll see in a moment.

/etc/mail/aliases

There's a mailbox in `/var/mail` for every user on the system; however, for someone to have an e-mail address on your machine doesn't require that they have an account. You can always set up aliases to map incoming e-mail addresses to any other address, whether it's another account on your machine, an address somewhere else on the Internet, or even a pipe to a file or program. The default `/etc/mail/aliases` contains examples of all of these. An alias line contains the alias name, a colon, a space or tab, and the target address or pipe:

```
tiger: bob@stripes.com
fsmith: frank
pager: "|/usr/local/bin/pageme"
dump: ">>/home/frank/dump2me"
mylist:include:/home/frank/list.txt
```

This last example is an "include" alias, which reads in a list of addresses from a plain-text file at the specified location. This is an easy way to manage a mailing list: Just make changes to the included file, and the alias will always be up to date.

After you make any change to `/etc/mail/aliases`, you have to rebuild the `aliases.db` file, which is a hash table version of the `aliases` file that provides fast lookups (as with `/etc/master.passwd`, which we discussed in Chapter 10, "Users, Groups, and Permissions"). You can use the traditional `newaliases` command to do this, or for consistency's sake with the rest of the maintenance tasks, use `make aliases`:

```
# make aliases
/usr/sbin/sendmail -bi
/etc/mail/aliases: 22 aliases, longest 10 bytes, 213 bytes total
```

> **Note**
>
> Global aliases aren't the only way to redirect mail from one local address to another, or to an external address. For instance, if a user wants all his incoming mail to be forwarded automatically to some external address, you could use /etc/mail/aliases to do the trick, but this involves root access; there's a better way, if the user has a full account on the system.
>
> All a user has to do to forward mail to another address is to create a .forward file in his home directory, containing the forwarding e-mail address. This can be done with any text editor, or even simply with echo:
>
> ```
> # echo "frank@somewhereelse.com" > .forward
> ```
>
> Removing this file will cause mail forwarding to stop.

/etc/mail/access

The access database provides a way to apply certain rules to single hosts, subnets, or whole groups of addresses—an excellent anti-spam provision. Applicable rules include OK, REJECT, RELAY, DISCARD, or 550 <message>. The contents of the default /etc/mail/access file show examples of how the address/hostname field can be formatted:

```
cyberspammer.com          550 We don't acccpt mail from spammers
FREE.STEALTH.MAILER@      550 We don't accept mail from spammers
another.source.of.spam    REJECT
okay.cyberspammer.com     OK
128.32                    RELAY
64.2.43                   RELAY
RELAY
```

- OK accepts messages from the specified host, regardless of whether that host might fail other checks in the system (such as the anti-relaying provisions that we will discuss shortly).

- REJECT refuses connections initiated by the specified host.

- DISCARD silently drops messages after accepting them, making the sender think the message has been successfully delivered.

- RELAY enables relaying for the specified host, overriding other checks (as with OK).

- 550 <message> specifies a "rejection" message that is displayed to a sender matching the host specification. This message will appear during the SMTP session, and will be included in an error e-mail message that is sent back to the sender.

After you've made changes to /etc/mail/access, the access.db file must be regenerated. This is done with the make maps target, which regenerates any of the feature map files that have been changed since the last time make maps has been run. Follow this command with make restart to restart the Sendmail master process with the new access.db file:

```
# make maps
/usr/sbin/makemap hash access.db < access
# make restart
/bin/kill -HUP `head -1 /var/run/sendmail.pid`
```

/etc/mail/local-host-names

Formerly sendmail.cw, this file specifies all the hostnames that our server claims to be. This becomes especially important if you're hosting multiple domains and doing mail service for all of them (virtual hosting); if you don't add each relevant domain name to the local-host-names file, an incoming message destined for a domain you host will bounce back to the sender with the dreaded MX list for <domain> loops back to myself; local configuration error message.

The file doesn't exist in the default installation, but you'll need to create it if you add more domain or hostname aliases to your machine via DNS. After adding names to the list, run make restart to restart the server.

```
# make restart
/bin/kill -HUP `head -1 /var/run/sendmail.pid`
```

/etc/mail/virtusertable

Also on the subject of virtual hosting, /etc/mail/virtusertable provides a way to map addresses on one domain that you host to local accounts, other addresses, or error messages. This is somewhat like a hybrid of the access database and the aliases file.

Let's say you're hosting a secondary domain, mycave.org. You want webmaster@mycave.org to go to the local user bill, info@mycave.org to go to a remote address anne@elsewhere.com, and all other addresses @mycave.org to be rejected. This would be done with the following tab-separated rules:

```
webmaster@mycave.org    bill
info@mycave.org         anne@elsewhere.com
@mycave.org             error:nouser User unknown
```

Note that the order in which these rules are specified doesn't matter; when you build the virtusertable.db hash table, each rule has its own lookup value, and the ordering in the virtusertable file is irrelevant. As with the access database, you need to rebuild virtusertable.db and then restart the server:

```
# make maps
/usr/sbin/makemap hash virtusertable.db < virtusertable
# make restart
/bin/kill -HUP `head -1 /var/run/sendmail.pid`
```

An excellent and complete discussion of virtual hosting and the use of the
virtusertable file can be found at the Sendmail Consortium information site:
http://www.sendmail.org/virtual-hosting.html.

> **Note**
>
> By the way, /etc/mail/Makefile and all these convenient targets for rebuilding
> the various configuration databases are a FreeBSD addition, and not part of
> Sendmail as released by its developers. Other operating systems don't provide
> these conveniences. If you're going to be maintaining a Sendmail installation on
> a Linux system or some other platform, you'll want to know the underlying
> commands beneath each of the build targets in the Makefile, so you can accom-
> plish the same tasks. The documentation at http://www.sendmail.org is very
> helpful in this regard.

DNS Resolution Issues

Running a successful Sendmail server really requires that you have accurate DNS information set up for your machine. If you simply install FreeBSD, assign an available IP
address to it, and attempt to send mail, it might bounce back to you complaining that the
remote server "could not resolve your hostname". Many SMTP servers, including
Sendmail in its default configuration, do not accept mail from senders without fully
qualified domains in their addresses or resolvable DNS names.

Before you try to put Sendmail to full use on your machine, you'll need to make sure
that you have reverse DNS lookups correctly set up. You can check this with the
nslookup command, giving it your machine's IP address as an argument:

```
# nslookup stripes.somewhere.com
Server:  lion.somewhere.com
Address:  64.41.131.132

Name:    stripes.somewhere.com
Address:  64.41.131.102
```

This output shows a correctly resolving reverse DNS setup, one in which Sendmail will
work just fine. However, you may get something like the following:

```
# nslookup stripes.somewhere.com
Server:  lion.somewhere.com
Address:  64.41.131.132

*** lion.somewhere.com can't find stripes.somewhere.com: Non-existent
host/domain
```

This means you'll have problems sending and receiving mail until DNS is set up properly. Note that you'll want to check against a remote DNS to be absolutely sure of the DNS configuration; sometimes, a local name server will play tricks on you by reporting information that only it knows about and that hasn't propagated to the rest of the Internet.

We'll be discussing the proper operation of DNS in Chapter 30, "The Domain Name Server."

Controlling Sendmail

Sendmail operates by keeping a single "master" process running and listening on port 25 for incoming connections; and additional processes for handling queue runs, sending messages to remote recipients, and other tasks. The master process is started at boot time from /etc/rc. Starting and stopping the Sendmail master process is made easy by the Makefile and the integrated nature of the resource configuration files in /etc. To start the process, simply go into /etc/mail and enter make start:

```
# make start
(. /etc/defaults/rc.conf; source_rc_confs;  if [ "${sendmail_enable}" = "YES" -a
-r /etc/mail/sendmail.cf ]; then  /usr/sbin/sendmail ${sendmail_flags};  fi  )
```

Since this command echoes its actions, we can see that it pulls in relevant configuration details from the systemwide resource configuration files, in which flags such as -q30m (do a queue run every thirty minutes) and -bd (run as a background daemon) are centrally specified. It will even refuse to start the process if the sendmail_enable variable in the rc.conf files is set to NO.

Restarting or stopping the master process is equally simple:

```
# make restart
/bin/kill -HUP `head -1 /var/run/sendmail.pid`
# make stop
/bin/kill -TERM `head -1 /var/run/sendmail.pid`
```

You can see what state each Sendmail process is in by using ps in wide mode in conjunction with grep; each process reports its position in the queue as an argument against its name in the process table. The following example shows the master process (51248) and a process in the middle of a queue run (54150):

```
51248  ??  Ss     0:00.17 sendmail: accepting connections (sendmail)
54150  ??  I      0:00.02 sendmail: ./f4GKwVW16827 mail.backstreetboys.com.:
user open (sendmail)
```

The Message Queue

Messages waiting to be sent by Sendmail sit in `/var/spool/mqueue`. In Sendmail's default configuration, a new `sendmail -q` process is started every 30 minutes, stepping through each queued message and attempting to deliver it to its destination. This continues for five days, at the end of which an undeliverable message is returned to the sender with the relevant error headers attached.

If you have some messages in your queue, which you almost certainly will if you've been using the system for any length of time, you can browse through them at will. Unlike opaque systems like Microsoft Exchange, in which queue files are kept in a database without an easy way to tweak or even see the files waiting to be sent, Sendmail provides both. Queued messages are just plain-text files, able to be read and edited by regular text editors. This gives the administrator great control over how the mail system operates; however, it also provides an opportunity for the administrator to abuse his or her power by looking through pending messages' contents. If you run a system in which you trust your users, be sure they can trust you too!

The first tool that comes with Sendmail is called `mailq`, and it's a way to list the current state of all messages waiting in the queue.

```
# mailq
                /var/spool/mqueue (2 requests)
----Q-ID---- --Size-- -----Q-Time----- -----------Sender/Recipient-----------
f4H1Ahu36976    6246 Wed May 16 18:10 MAILER-DAEMON
                     (Deferred: Operation timed out with mlists.acmecity.com.)
                                    <fred@acmecity.com>
f4GKwVW16827     706 Wed May 16 13:58 www
                     (host map: lookup (hotamil.com): deferred)
                                    Bob bob@hotamil.com
```

Using `mailq`, you can keep an eye on what kind of mail transfer errors frequently occur on your system. If people often forget to specify complete e-mail addresses or misspell common mail server hostnames, you can address that problem through education and tutorials; if you're getting a lot of hostname lookup errors, it might point to a configuration problem on your end. It's an excellent diagnostic tool.

The queue also gives you the ability to fix mistakes in messages on the way out. Let's say, for instance, that you had an entry like the second one in the `mailq` output shown earlier. The erroneous recipient domain is the result of a simple typo; you can either wait five days for Sendmail to give up trying to find `hotamil.com` and send it back to you as an error—or you can fix this problem right in the queue.

To do this, go into /var/spool/mqueue, and look for the files matching the ID of the entry in the mailq output. These would be the files dff4GKwVW16827 and qff4GKwVW16827; the first contains the message body, and the second contains the message headers in an interim format. Simply open up the file with the headers (qff4GKwVW16827) in a text editor, replace all occurrences of hotamil.com with hotmail.com, save the file, and wait for the next queue run. The message will go through cleanly this time.

If you can't wait that long, force a queue run by running sendmail -q -v. This gives you the added bonus of a look into exactly how Sendmail does its SMTP transactions with all the remote systems; with each message it processes, it will echo to the session all the output from the transaction, just as in our example at the beginning of the chapter. You'll get to see all the interesting greeting messages that various administrators program into their MTAs, visible only to other MTAs, and therefore often quite creative. You can use Ctrl+C to exit at any time—messages are removed from the queue only after they've been successfully transferred.

Notes on Relaying

One of the most recent additions to Sendmail is protection against spam (unsolicited e-mail) through anti-relaying rules. These rules have been available for a long time, but only recently—as of Sendmail version 8.9—has the default configuration been to disallow relaying of messages from one server to another.

For a legitimate dial-up or remote user to use your SMTP server to send a message to another remote recipient, your server has to act as a relay, forwarding the message on to the recipient even if the message didn't originate from and wasn't addressed to anyone on its machine. Functionally, as illustrated in Figure 25.2, this is exactly how a spammer would send an unsolicited message to the same recipient through the same SMTP server: It must relay.

Relaying is usually allowed by what's known as the "MX record", a line in the SMTP server's network DNS database (either served from the same machine as the SMTP server or another server in the same network), which tells all the machines within that network that your SMTP server (S1) is a legitimate Mail eXchanger for them. Sendmail, in its default configuration on FreeBSD, will accept mail from senders whose MX record points to S1, defining it as the MTA for the network. This prevents people from outside the network from using S1 as a relay; if they try, they'll get their messages bounced back with a Relaying denied error.

FIGURE 25.2

Relaying. Spammers and legitimate users, if they're not local to S1, must use S1 as a relay to forward their messages to S2.

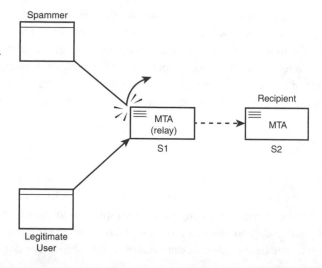

Note

You can find out what the registered MX host is for a domain by using the `host` command:

```
# host somecompany.com
somecompany.com has address 164.199.3.78
somecompany.com mail is handled (pri=30) by mail-1.somecompany.com
```

You can then connect directly to this host to perform raw SMTP transactions (for testing purposes, for example).

The problem commonly faced, though, is that this is great for ISPs or enterprise networks that have a fully defined network, DNS entries for all its hosts, and a proper MX record pointing to the relaying SMTP server. But what about standalone Internet hosts, which might have users all over the world trying to use it to transmit mail? Each of these users, when trying to send a message through S1 from wherever they happen to be, will get a `Relaying denied` error back unless S1 has been specifically configured to allow them to relay. There are a number of ways to do this, many of which are extremely inadvisable.

- Add "trusted" sender domains to the file `/etc/mail/relay-domains`, which doesn't exist in the default installation. Any host within a listed domain will be permitted to relay through your server. You have to restart Sendmail after modifying this file. This is easy and effective, but as soon as you add a large, popular domain to this file that might contain spammers as well as legitimate senders, its benefit is lost.

- Use the access database (/etc/mail/access). This feature allows you to set up an OK or RELAY rule for each known host or domain from which your users will be connecting. This works well for small impromptu networks or for a few remote hosts at easily identifiable addresses, but it doesn't scale well for lots of users on dynamic addresses.

- Enable any of the five or six relaying exception features available in Sendmail by adding them to /etc/mail/freebsd.mc and regenerating the sendmail.cf file (as we showed earlier). There's a feature that lets you allow relaying based on whether the From: header is set to an address at your domain (relay_local_from), though this is easily forged by spammers and therefore the feature isn't usually advisable. There's also an optional feature to perform a check against the *Realtime Blackhole List (RBL)*, a centrally maintained database of known spammers. This feature is in the default freebsd.mc, but commented out; to enable it, move the dnl to the end of the line, and rebuild the config file.

- As an absolute last resort, turn off relay checking altogether by enabling the promiscuous_relay feature. This will allow any valid user to send mail through your Sendmail server; however, it will also allow any spammer to do the same. There are independently run databases on the Internet which keep records of all "open" mail servers, and some service providers use these databases as "blackhole" lists of their own. You don't want your server to end up in these databases! If it does, some legitimate mail from your users or their correspondents may be blocked due to their ISPs blocking mail to or from your server. It's an incredibly bad idea to run an open mail server.

As a general rule, the best solution to the relaying problem is simply to instruct all your users to use the SMTP servers provided by their own dial-up Internet Service Providers. These services will always have their own SMTP servers that are open to their own customers. Since the headers in a mail message (such as the From: address) are all derived from the message body and therefore completely under the control of the e-mail client program, there's no reason for a remote user to want to use your SMTP server if he already has one of his own.

The Sendmail Consortium has an excellent page on relaying rules and your various available configuration options at http://www.sendmail.org/tips/relaying.html.

Introduction to POP3

We've now taken care of SMTP and Sendmail, and we have the tools we need to configure it according to the needs of almost any typical Internet server. But SMTP is only half of the equation. For e-mail to get completely from one user to another, there's another process that needs to take place: downloading the mail through POP.

The Post Office Protocol became necessary once it was clear that there would ultimately be a great many more Internet users who used graphical client-side e-mail programs on their own dial-up computers, rather than server-side shell clients such as Pine and Mutt, which read mail directly out of the user's mailbox file. To use an MUA such as Microsoft Outlook or Qualcomm's Eudora, the client has to connect to the mail server in which the user's mailbox file is stored (refer to Figure 25.1); determine whether there are any new messages since the last time it checked; and if so, download them. The client program then displays these new messages, and optionally deletes them from the mailbox file on the server.

Unlike SMTP, POP3 (the current and standard version of POP) requires authentication. This is sensible because although security really isn't an issue for sending mail, it's absolutely essential to receiving mail. After all, anybody can drop a letter in the outgoing post office mailbox, but only the legitimate receiver can open his or her mailbox and retrieve it. This makes it a little less easy to simulate a POP transaction than an SMTP one, though it's also a lot less necessary—largely because POP3 requires very little in the way of configuration. There's not a lot that can go wrong. However, the POP3 server, qpopper, is not included in the core FreeBSD installation. To enable POP3 service you must install qpopper out of the ports (/usr/ports/mail/qpopper). This program is derived from the original Berkeley POP server program, but is currently developed semi-commercially (but in a free and open-source fashion) by Qualcomm, the makers of Eudora.

The POP3 server runs from out of inetd, the "super-server." inetd listens for TCP and UDP connections, and upon receiving one on TCP port 110, it looks up the service name in /etc/services, determines how to handle requests for that service type, and fires off a qpopper process from /usr/local/libexec/qpopper. (This location—in the libexec directory—tells you that qpopper is not a program intended to be run from the command line. Rather, it's only supposed to be invoked by other programs.) This process handles the transaction, authenticates the user, locks the user's mailbox, figures out which messages need to be downloaded, and serves them. This works just fine for most systems. Although qpopper does in fact provide a rather large number of configuration options, most of them are useful only for tweaking extra performance out of the server—a valuable thing to know how to do if your server is a high-profile one. For most purposes, all you have to do is install the port and enable the service.

> **Note**
>
> You may have your system configured so that `inetd` is not running (for example, for security reasons—which we will outline in Chapter 29, "Network Security"). If this is the case, qpopper can be run in standalone mode, like Sendmail. We will discuss how this is done in a moment.

One fairly important thing to note about POP3, though, is that by default its transactions are done in cleartext, which means that it's a source of potential password leaks and a security risk. In version 4.0, qpopper enables encrypted connections through the Secure Sockets Layer (SSL) libraries, which are part of FreeBSD and also used in such protocols as SSH (Secure Shell) and secure HTTP. We'll talk about how to configure qpopper to take advantage of this security measure.

Configuring a POP3 Server with qpopper

There are several levels to which you can take your POP3 server configuration. You can simply install the server and let everyone use it; you can run it in standalone mode, which avoids having to run `inetd` if you don't want to; you can enable "server mode," which enhances performance depending on your circumstances; and you can enable encrypted sessions through TLS/SSL. These latter options are not mutually exclusive. We'll be looking at each of them in turn.

Basic qpopper Installation and Configuration

To get POP3 service up and running without concerning yourself too much about performance or security, it's a simple matter. Go to the qpopper directory in the ports collection (`/usr/ports/qpopper`), and build and install it from there, as described in Chapter 15 "Installing Additional Software;" or install the qpopper package using `sysinstall` or the package tools. After this is done, you'll need to enable the POP3 service in the `inetd` super-server. This is done by adding a line to `/etc/inetd.conf`.

Open up the `inetd.conf` file, and find the lines regarding POP3 as shown. Add or uncomment the pop3 service using the following syntax:

```
# example entry for the optional pop3 server
#
#pop3   stream  tcp     nowait  root    /usr/local/libexec/popper        popper
pop3    stream  tcp     nowait  root    /usr/local/libexec/qpopper       qpopper -s
```

> **Note**
>
> For legacy purposes, there's a port that's simply called popper. It is actually
> qpopper in an earlier form, and it's generally deprecated by this point. The one
> you want to use is qpopper.

Now, restart inetd by using killall:

```
# killall -HUP inetd
```

You can check to see if the POP3 service is available now by connecting to port 110 on
your machine via Telnet. Type **QUIT** to exit the session.

```
# telnet localhost 110
Trying 127.0.0.1...
Connected to localhost.
Escape character is '^]'.
+OK Qpopper (version 4.0.2) at stripes.somewhere.com starting.
<4763.990313780@stripes.somewhere.com>
QUIT
+OK Pop server at stripes.somewhere.com signing off.
Connection closed by foreign host.
```

If you get this response from the server, congratulations—you have a working POP3
server.

Enabling Standalone Mode

Certain security settings turn off the inetd super-server; for instance, if you chose a
Medium or High security setting during your system installation, it would have added the
following line to your /etc/rc.conf, preventing inetd from being run at all:

```
inetd_enable="NO"
```

On a security-conscious system, you don't want to have to re-enable inetd just so you
can run POP3 services. This is what standalone mode is for. It isn't an option available
by default, but a quick tweak to the Makefile makes it pretty easy.

In /usr/ports/mail/qpopper, edit the Makefile and alter the CONFIGURE_ARGS to add
the --enable-standalone option:

```
CONFIGURE_ARGS= --enable-apop=${PREFIX}/etc/qpopper/pop.auth \
                --enable-nonauth-file=/etc/ftpusers \
                --with-apopuid=pop --without-gdbm \
                --enable-keep-temp-drop \
                --enable-standalone
```

Now, run `make` and `make install` to build a version of qpopper that runs in standalone mode. It will still be installed in `/usr/local/libexec`, though; don't move it from this location, or deinstallation will be made more difficult later.

You'll need to start up the standalone qpopper process from a script during system boot; this can be done by creating a startup script in `/usr/local/etc/rc.d` called (for example) `qpopper.sh`, as we saw in Chapter 11, "System Configuration and Startup Scripts." Make sure that qpopper isn't enabled in `inetd` if you do this!

Enabling Server Mode

If your system has *only* users who access their mailboxes through POP3—where none of the users have shell access or run shell-based, server-side mail programs—you might choose to enable server mode for qpopper. This mode allows it to run in a streamlined fashion: Instead of copying the mail spool file to a temporary copy, locking it, making changes, keeping track of mail that arrives during the session, and merging the locked session spool back to its original location, the server can instead work directly from the mailbox file itself. This is more dangerous, particularly if you have users who access their mail spool files through other methods, which is why you ought to consider server mode only if your system serves mail exclusively through POP3, and if it's under enough load for you to consider this performance-boosting measure to be necessary.

There are a number of ways you can enable server mode. The easiest is to use the `-S` switch on the command invocation line, whether in `inetd.conf` or on the command line if you're using standalone mode:

```
pop3    stream  tcp    nowait  root   /usr/local/libexec/qpopper      qpopper
-s -S
```

This will put qpopper into server mode for all users at all times. You can do it per-user, though, or per-group, if you prefer. Group control is best done through a configuration file. To make qpopper use a config file, create one in `/usr/local/etc/qpopper` (for example, `qpopper.conf`) and then indicate it on the command line in `inetd.conf` with the `-f` option:

```
pop3    stream  tcp    nowait  root   /usr/local/libexec/qpopper      qpopper
-s -S -f /usr/local/etc/qpopper/qpopper.conf
```

Now, in the `qpopper.conf` file, specify the name of a group to include or exclude from server mode using the `group-server-mode` or `group-no-server-mode` keywords. The following example turns server mode on for members of group1 and group2, and off for members of group3:

25

CONFIGURING
E-MAIL SERVICES

```
set group-server-mode=group1
set group-server-mode=group2
set group-no-server-mode=group3
```

You can also do it on a per-user basis. To do this, you need to add the `-u` switch to the command invocation line (to enable per-user configuration files). Then, each user to which the mode should apply needs to have a file in his or her directory called `.qpopper.options`, which contains the line `set server-mode`. Alternately, if you don't want each user to be able to modify his or her `.qpopper.options` file, use the `-U` switch instead of `-u`, and place a corresponding per-user file in `/var/mail` called `.<user>.qpopper.options` (where `<user>` is the username in question). This allows you to turn on server mode on an individual basis. Don't use the `-S` global server mode switch if you do it this way!

Enabling SSL Encryption

By default, qpopper will build with implicit TLS/SSL support. However, to take advantage of it, you need to create and install security certificates. First, create a directory for your certificates:

```
# mkdir -p -m665 /etc/mail/certs
# chown root:mail /etc/mail/certs
# chmod 660 /etc/mail/certs
```

Next, use openssl to generate a certificate request. This will require you to enter several accurate pieces of information about your organization. Afterward, make sure that the permissions on the private key file (`cert.pem`) only allow root to view it.

```
# openssl req -new -nodes -out req.pem -keyout /etc/mail/certs/cert.pem
...
# chmod 600 /etc/mail/certs/cert.pem
# chown root:0 /etc/mail/certs/cert.pem
```

Once this is done, you'll need to register the certificate with a Certifying Authority (CA) such as VeriSign; submit the certificate request in `req.pem` to the CA, and you'll get back a signed certificate. Concatenate this onto the end of `cert.pem`:

```
# cat signed_req.pem >> /etc/mail/certs/cert.pem
```

Now, add TLS/SSL support to the config file at `/usr/local/etc/qpopper/qpopper.conf`, restart the server (if running in standalone mode), and SSL encryption is yours. Any client that supports SSL will now be able to negotiate a secure connection if configured to do so.

```
set tls-support = stls
set tls-server-cert-file = /etc/mail/certs/cert.pem
```

If you want, you can emulate a Certifying Authority yourself to create a self-signed certificate that you can use to make sure the system works. However, SSL-enabled clients won't trust this certificate, and will require the user to manually approve it before continuing.

First, create the test CA's private key (making sure to remember the passphrase you enter) and then create the CA certificate:

```
# openssl genrsa -des3 -out ca.key 1024
...
# openssl req -new -x509 -days 365 -key ca.key -out ca.crt
```

Now, you can self-sign the certificate request you created earlier (req.pem):

```
# openssl x509 -req -CA ca.crt -CAkey ca.key -days 365 -in req.pem -out signed-
req.pem -Cacreateserial
```

This should allow you to run an SSL-enabled qpopper server so as to test its functionality. Make sure to get the real CA-signed certificate at some point!

For More Information

The official Web site for qpopper is http://www.eudora.com/qpopper. It has a lot of useful information, including a PDF document (in the Documentation section) that definitively describes all the possible configuration options of qpopper. It is from a Linux viewpoint, so many of the pathnames quoted in the documentation are slightly different from your installation.

Even more information, particularly on the use of configuration files, can be found in the man qpopper page.

Configuring an IMAP Server with IMAP-UW

IMAP (Internet Message Access Protocol) is an alternative to POP that some users prefer, and you will probably want to support it on your mail server, along with POP and SMTP services, to make the package complete. The fundamental difference between IMAP and POP is that whereas POP downloads each message from the server and stores it in the mail program, IMAP mail is accessed and manipulated wholly on the server. An IMAP client, like a server-side shell-based mail client, can have multiple mail folders and transfer messages between them as if they were local. Messages are transferred to the client only when requested, and are not deleted unless the user explicitly deletes them. This provides the mobile flexibility of shell-based MUAs such as Mutt and Pine with the user convenience of graphical client-side mail programs such as Outlook and Eudora. Most, if not all, mail clients that support POP also support IMAP.

The most popular UNIX IMAP server is IMAP-UW, by the University of Washington (the same group that produces Pine, a popular MUA that we will discuss shortly). It's available in the ports, at /usr/ports/mail/imap-uw, or in the packages collection. Refer to Chapter 15 for details on installing software from the ports or packages. Add USE_SSL=YES to both the make and make install command lines to build with SSL support.

> **Note**
>
> The IMAP-UW port warns of a security issue where known buffer overflows in the server daemon allow IMAP users to gain shell access with their own user privileges. This may or may not be an issue for you. If you allow shell access to your users anyway, it won't be a problem. If you don't allow shell access, though, this represents a security hole. Your choices are to wait for an update that fixes the problem, to look for alternative IMAP servers, or to disable IMAP altogether and rely on POP for your clients' mail services.

The IMAP-UW package consists of a mailbox test program (mboxtest) and four daemon executables that go into /usr/local/libexec. Two of these, ipop2d and ipop3d, are POP servers (for POP2 and POP3, respectively), which you don't need to install if you're already running qpopper. However, these POP daemons do have the capability to pipe POP commands to the IMAP server, so they can provide an upgrade path for existing POP clients to move to IMAP if you want to migrate to an exclusively IMAP environment.

Installation of IMAP-UW is fairly simple. There are no configuration files to edit for the program itself; all that is necessary is a modification to /etc/inetd.conf (because the IMAP server operates out of inetd, like qpopper) and optionally to /etc/pam.conf.

The commented-out line in /etc/inetd.conf will work just fine for IMAP-UW. Just uncomment it:

```
# example entry for the optional imap4 server
#
imap4   stream  tcp     nowait  root    /usr/local/libexec/imapd        imapd
```

Then, restart inetd:

```
# killall -HUP inetd
```

The IMAP daemon listens on TCP port 143. You can test whether it's set up properly by connecting to port 143 via Telnet. End the session by pressing Ctrl+] and typing `quit`.

```
# telnet localhost 143
Trying 127.0.0.1...
Connected to localhost.somewhere.com.
Escape character is '^]'.
* OK [CAPABILITY IMAP4 IMAP4REV1 LOGIN-REFERRALS AUTH=LOGIN]
localhost.somewhere.com IMAP4rev1 2001.303 at Sun, 10 Jun 2001 11:21:26 -0700
(PDT)
^]
telnet> quit
Connection closed.
```

The installation script suggests changing the `imap` entries in `/etc/pam.conf` (which controls cascading authentication layers) to be a little more strict. Do this by replacing the following line:

```
imap    auth    required        pam_unix.so                     try_first_pass
```

with these lines:

```
imap    auth    required        pam_unix.so
imap    account required        pam_unix.so                     try_first_pass
imap    session required        pam_deny.so
```

You can do the same for the pop3 rules:

```
pop3    auth    required        pam_unix.so
pop3    account required        pam_unix.so                     try_first_pass
pop3    session required        pam_deny.so
```

> **Note**
>
> You may notice warnings in your `/var/log/messages` file or your IMAP client software that the mailbox is "vulnerable," urging that `/var/mail` should have "1777 protection." This is a security check done by the IMAP-UW server (Pine does it, too).
>
> FreeBSD's mail directory permissions are 775, meaning that all programs that access or create files in `/var/mail` must be `setgid` to the mail group. However, IMAP-UW does not run `setgid`, and so to create lock files (preventing mailboxes from delivering mail while receiving new messages), it can't do so in `/var/mail`. The suggested workaround is to change the permissions on `/var/mail` to 1777, allowing non-privileged users to add and delete files, but only the proper users can modify their own files. This isn't an ideal solution, but it will suffice in most cases.

You can use SSL/TLS encryption with IMAP just as with POP3. When building it from the ports, use `make USE_SSL=YES` and `make install USE_SSL=YES` instead of simply using `make` and `make install`. You can then generate a certificate using `make cert`, or simply copy the certificate file you may have created for qpopper into `/usr/local/certs` (where IMAP-UW expects to find it). For consistency's sake, you might want to alter your qpopper configuration to point to the same certificate in `/usr/local/certs` if you will be using it for both secured services.

An alternate way to provide security for both POP3 and IMAP is with `stunnel`, which we will cover in Chapter 29.

E-mail for Standalone Workstations

Knowing how to run a full-fledged e-mail server is an excellent system administration skill; however, it doesn't help you much if your FreeBSD machine isn't intended to be an Internet server providing mail services for dozens of users. What if you're just running a workstation, in the same way that someone might run a Windows desktop machine, with a Gnome or KDE desktop and graphical productivity applications instead of server tools?

Fortunately, as you might guess, a standalone workstation's e-mail setup is much less complex than that of a full-scale server. Still, it's no less important an environment to know how to control, and there are some interesting tricks that will make standalone computing with FreeBSD quite convenient.

Using Fetchmail to Retrieve E-mail from POP3 and IMAP Servers

Most consumer operating systems have e-mail client programs (such as Outlook, Eudora, Netscape Messenger, and so on) that have their own internal, built-in mechanisms for checking POP3 or IMAP (Internet Message Access Protocol) servers. Each one gets your mail in its own way and then stores it in its own fashion internally. Some MUA programs of this type exist for FreeBSD, and they work just fine.

However, you might choose instead to run an MUA such as Mutt, Elm, or Pine on your workstation, just as you would on a server. These programs operate directly on the system's central `/var/mail` directory and your mail spool file inside it, rather than keeping their own internal cache of downloaded messages. This allows you to share the mailbox between programs, search through it using command-line tools, and participate in any number of other testaments to the versatility of UNIX.

But to get the messages from the POP3 or IMAP server where your e-mail address stores them (for instance, all mail to a `frank@earthlink.net` address would collect on the `earthlink.net` servers) to your local FreeBSD workstation, something needs to make the POP3 or IMAP connection and deliver the new messages from the remote mailbox to your local one. That something is Fetchmail, a small but versatile utility written by Eric Raymond.

Fetchmail can be installed out of the ports (`/usr/ports/mail/fetchmail`) or packages. It operates on the basis of a `.fetchmailrc` file in your home directory; this file specifies remote POP3 or IMAP servers to poll for new mail, the intervals at which to check, and numerous other options. Fetchmail then retrieves new mail as specified and relays it to port 25 on your workstation, where Sendmail is listening (in the default configuration); it then will deliver it to your local mailbox according to all the rules that would normally apply, such as `.forward` files and mail aliases.

Once Fetchmail has been installed (it is available in the FreeBSD ports collection in the `mail` directory), you will need to configure the `.fetchmailrc` file in your home directory before you can use it. This can be done in one of two ways.

The first method involves using the "fetchmailconf" program. This is a graphical configuration program for Fetchmail that is written in Python and uses the TK toolkit (a toolkit for building graphical user interfaces in X Windows. Although `fetchmailconf` comes with the Fetchmail program, it requires Python and TCL/TK to be installed in order to work. (Python and TCL/TK are both popular languages available for many different platforms.)

The second method of configuring Fetchmail involves creating the `.fetchmailrc` file manually. The format of the configuration file is straightforward, and the Fetchmail man page is extremely good, covering in detail every option that can go in the `.fetchmailrc` file. This is the method we will cover in this chapter.

Configuring the `.fetchmailrc` File

In your home directory, open a new file in your favorite text editor called `.fetchmailrc`. The `.fetchmailrc` file you create here will contain three sections. Note that it is very important that these sections appear in exactly the order shown as follows. Also note that no options that belong to a previous section can be used after a new section has been started. One of the most common causes of errors in `.fetchmailrc` files is having options in the wrong order or in the wrong place.

We will not cover all of the options available here because there are far too many for the available space. However, we will create a sample setup for retrieving mail from a POP3

server. As mentioned before, the man page for Fetchmail is extremely detailed and informative. Use the information presented in this section as a starting point for getting
Fetchmail up and running. Then, refer to the man page for Fetchmail for any advanced
configuration you wish to do.

The first section of the `.fetchmailrc` file contains the global options. These options will
apply to all of the mail servers and user accounts that will be listed later on in the configuration file. It is possible to override some of the global options with server- or user-spe-
cific options, but as a general rule, these will apply to all of the servers and accounts that
Fetchmail checks. Here is a sample of a simple global configuration section and the
options it might contain:

```
set daemon 600
set postmaster foobar
set logfile ./.fetchmail.log
```

The first line causes Fetchmail to run in daemon mode and check for new mail every 600
seconds (10 minutes). When Fetchmail is started, it will check for new mail and move
itself into the background as a daemon. After that, it will check for new mail every 600
seconds. If this line is not present, when you invoke Fetchmail, it will check for new
mail and then terminate immediately and not check again.

The second line is the fallback address. Basically, any mail that Fetchmail receives that is
not addressed to a local user will be sent to this account on the local system. You should
probably set this to the same user that you will be running Fetchmail as.

Finally, the third option sets a log file in which Fetchmail will log its activity.
Alternatively, you can use the line `set syslog` instead, which will cause Fetchmail to use
`syslogd` for logging. `syslogd` is the system-logging daemon that handles the logging of
other system events.

These are the most common options that will be used in the global section.

The next section of the `.fetchmailrc` file is the server section, which contains information on each mail server that should be checked for mail. Here is a sample server section
that is configured to check one e-mail server:

```
poll mail.samplenet.org
proto pop3
no dns
```

The first line causes the server `mail.samplenet.org` to be checked for new mail at the
interval configured by the `set daemon` option in the global section, as well as each time
Fetchmail is invoked manually. The alternative would be `skip mail.samplenet.org`.
In this case, this server would be skipped and not checked for new mail at the regular

intervals or when Fetchmail is invoked manually. If the skip option is used, the server will only be checked for new mail when it is specified on the command line when invoking Fetchmail.

The second line tells Fetchmail the protocol to use with this server. In this case, it is POP3. Other legal options are POP3, IMAP, APOP, and KPOP.

The third option tells Fetchmail not to perform DNS lookups on multidrop. If you are running over a dial-up Internet connection, you will probably want to include this line.

There are several other server options available. See the Fetchmail man page for full details.

The third and final section of the `.fetchmailrc` file is the user section, which contains information about the account itself. Here is a sample user section of `.fetchmailrc`:

```
user foobar
pass secretword
fetchall
flush
```

The first and second lines contain the user name and password, respectively, that you use to access the mail on your ISP's mail server.

The third line tells Fetchmail that it should retrieve all messages from the server, including those that have already been read.

Finally, the fourth line tells Fetchmail that it should flush the server (delete the messages it downloads off the server). This line would not have been strictly necessary since this is the default.

There are several more user options available, including options that cause Fetchmail not to delete mail off the server that it downloads, and so on. See the Fetchmail man page for full details.

The complete Fetchmail configuration file looks like this:

```
set daemon 600
set postmaster foobar
set logfile ./.fetchmail.log

poll mail.samplenet.org
proto pop3
no dns

user foobar
pass secretword
fetchall
flush
```

From top to bottom, this file basically says "Check for new mail every 600 seconds. Send any unaddressed mail to the user 'foobar'. Log the actions to `.fetchmail.log`. Check the server `mail.samplenet.org` for new mail every 10 minutes using the POP3 protocol, and do not attempt to do DNS lookups. Use the user name `foobar` and the password `secretword` to log in to the server, fetch all of the messages, and delete the messages off the server after they are downloaded."

> **Caution**
>
> Because the `.fetchmailrc` file contains your user name and password for the mail server, its permissions should be set so that only you can read it. The permissions should be no higher than 600. You can set the permissions to the correct value by typing `chmod 600 .fetchmailrc`. This will allow only the owner of the file to read or write to it. Fetchmail will complain and refuse to run if you attempt to start it with a `.fetchmailrc` file that has permissions greater than this.

Once again, this has been a fairly brief introduction to Fetchmail that should get you up-and-running with a basic configuration. For more advanced options, see the man page for Fetchmail. It is very detailed and fully explains all of the options available for the `.fetchmailrc` file.

Sendmail Configuration for Standalone Workstations

For Fetchmail to work, Sendmail (or some equivalent) has to be running on port 25 to accept incoming messages. However, Sendmail is also useful for outgoing mail, so it's not generally a good idea to run your workstation with no MTA at all. For example, Mutt and other shell-based mail clients send messages by passing them directly to Sendmail, rather than by connecting remotely to some external SMTP host. This prevents relaying-related issues, as we discussed earlier.

Still, there are a few things you can do to tweak Sendmail's performance and configuration so that it's optimized for use in a system that isn't connected to the Internet at all times. The first major one is the "smart" mail host, and the second is an automated mail spool run.

In `/etc/mail/freebsd.mc` you'll find the following lines:

```
dnl Dialup users should uncomment and define this appropriately
dnl define(`SMART_HOST', `your.isp.mail.server')
```

Uncomment the `define` line by moving the `dnl` to the end, and change `your.isp.mail.server` to the appropriate mail server name. Rebuild the config file by running `make cf` and `make install` from inside `/etc/mail`.

This allows your workstation to operate like any desktop operating system in which the mail clients each make its own SMTP connections to the SMTP server provided by the dial-up ISP, which then relays the mail on to its final destination. Since you might be using shell-based MUAs such as Mutt or Pine, which send mail by passing it directly to Sendmail rather than trying to make their own in-program SMTP connections to a defined SMTP relay, you need a centralized way to make these mail clients behave like their commercial Windows counterparts. Defining `SMART_HOST` forces Sendmail to direct all outgoing mail to your dial-up SMTP server.

The purpose of all this, as you will recall from our discussion of relaying and DNS issues, is that most SMTP servers will reject mail that comes from an unresolvable IP address, and many ISP networks don't provide DNS lookup information for their dial-up clients. This would prevent your FreeBSD workstation from being able to send mail reliably to a good percentage of the mail hosts on the Internet. However, since you have an available SMTP server at your ISP, and because this server will relay mail from all its dial-up customers (because that's how Windows MUAs work), you can rest assured that defining `SMART_HOST` will get all your messages to their destinations.

Another configuration item you may want to tweak is the outgoing message queue. By default, Sendmail does a queue run every 30 minutes (using the `-q30m` command-line option, set in `/etc/defaults/rc.conf`). If you're a dial-up user who connects for only brief periods, this interval might be too long. You can add a line to `/etc/rc.conf` overriding the default interval:

```
sendmail_flags="-bd -q10m"
```

However, an even more efficient way to handle this is to leave the default `-q30m` untouched and to simply do a queue run as soon as you connect to the Internet. As you recall, you can initiate a queue run with the `sendmail -q` command, optionally adding `-v` for entertainment or debugging purposes.

Doing this by hand is sure to become tedious, though, so you can add `sendmail -q` to your `ppp-up` script, which we discussed in Chapter 24, "Connecting to the Internet with PPP."

A Look at Some Sendmail Replacements

While Sendmail is still widely recognized as the industry-leading MTA by a wide margin, it's not without its faults. It is widely criticized, and one might say rightly so, for its barely comprehensible configuration files, the "Master Config" file in its otherwise almost-unknown m4 format, the proliferation of different runtime files (such as the access database and virtusertable file), and its comparative bulk and sluggishness. If you're comfortable with the way Sendmail works in its default configuration (which usually doesn't take much extra effort), you may have no need to complain. However, if you find you need more speed, less resource consumption, better configurability, or just an alternative, you're not alone. Would-be replacements for Sendmail abound, each with its advantages, disadvantages, and die-hard supporters.

Postfix

Perhaps the largest and most compelling Sendmail alternative right now is Postfix, developed by Wietse Venema with primary goals of speed and security. Also, its structure tends to be very "Sendmail-like," which makes it a good choice for an administrator of a large and entrenched Sendmail system that needs to be given a performance boost.

The speed of Postfix is reported to be extremely good, easily faster than Qmail, for example, although these are difficult things to measure empirically. The downside to Postfix is that it's still quite new, and therefore doesn't have the maturity or the advanced features that Sendmail or Qmail has.

The Postfix home page is at http://www.postfix.org.

Qmail

Dan Bernstein wrote Qmail specifically to provide an alternative to Sendmail that was fast and secure. On those fronts it succeeds quite well, and is gaining popularity in a lot of high-profile Internet services such as Hotmail, Network Solutions, and Yahoo! mail. The internal structure of Qmail is built up from scratch, not adapted from the Sendmail structure; this means that the configuration and the file structure for a Qmail installation don't much resemble their counterparts in Sendmail. Qmail is a good choice for an administrator who wants speed and security, but doesn't know enough about Sendmail to be attached to it.

The Qmail home page is at http://www.qmail.org.

Exim

Developed at Cambridge University, Exim offers a Sendmail alternative whose chief advantages are a helpful complement of documentation, developer support, and mailing lists. It's also reputed to be very easy to configure, largely due to these sources of help, and more mature than some of the other alternatives.

However, Exim has had historical problems with security, and is one of the poorer choices of Sendmail alternatives when it comes to modularity or advanced features. It's still a very high-performance server, though, and can speed up SMTP services by a significant amount over Sendmail.

The Exim home page is at `http://www.exim.org`.

Smail

An older MTA, Smail claims easy configurability and tight security as its hallmarks; its configuration structure is nowhere near as complex as Sendmail's (its nearest relative is Exim), but its command-line syntax has some similarities with that of Sendmail. However, Smail appears to be on its way out as a viable Sendmail alternative; development efforts seem to be petering out.

Configuring a Web Server

CHAPTER 26

Whether e-mail or the Web is the true "killer app" of the modern Internet is really a toss-up these days. While e-mail, the venerable workhorse of online applications, has quietly changed the way we communicate forever, there isn't anything quite like the flash of the Web and its potential as a full-fledged entertainment and commerce medium. It's the age-old contrast between the stodgy and reliable, and the glamorous and risky. A lot of Web companies have gone out of business since first conceiving their lofty ambitions, but e-mail services have seldom lacked for a profit.

It's probably pretty safe to assume that if you're setting up a FreeBSD server, you want it to be a Web server as well as providing e-mail and shell access. This isn't universally the case, though, so while FreeBSD ships with Sendmail installed to do e-mail services with almost no additional configuration, there is no equivalent Web server application installed by default. You have to get your own from the ports or packages. However, for 90 percent of the reasons to need a Web server, Apache is the server of choice. There are a number of other servers you can use instead, such as Roxen and AOLserver, but Apache has slowly built up so much of the market share in polled Internet servers over the years since it was first released as an enhanced alternative to NCSA httpd that it's the leading choice by a wide margin.

Apache does get a fair amount more respect than Sendmail does these days, and there isn't as much pressure to use newer and better-written alternatives. The Apache Project is one of the best examples of the open-source philosophy at work, producing software that gets the job done better and in more compliance with published standards than just about all the alternatives. It's also suitable for all kinds of environments—from small, low-traffic informational Web sites to full-scale e-commerce sites with hundreds of concurrent connections—with the addition of plug-in modules allowing you to take advantage of such server-side technologies as database connectivity and built-in Perl scripting.

This chapter will discuss how to configure Apache for each of these types of installations.

Introduction to the HTTP Protocol

The HyperText Transfer Protocol (HTTP) is the backbone of the World Wide Web. Developed in 1993 to support information exchange at CERN in Switzerland, it's a very simple protocol, involving no authentication and only a few possible client commands. It's optimized for the lightweight serving of small (several kilobytes at most) text files, in keeping with the original intent of HTTP as a means of disseminating interlinked informational pages in the newly developed markup language understood by HTTP browsers, known as the HyperText Markup Language, or HTML.

As you no doubt well know, the use of HTTP has expanded well beyond its original design specifications. It's now used for the transfer of large binary files, often including many inline images requested at once from an HTML page as it renders, which was seldom done in the early days of the Web (GIF and JPEG image support in 1994 was sporadic across various platforms). In response to this, certain augmentations have been made to the HTTP specification since it was first implemented, most importantly the HTTP/1.1 standard, which provides features such as *pipelining* (combining the responses to many simultaneous requests into a single response stream), though the standard is still only partially supported in most browsers.

Unlike SMTP, FTP, and many other such popular protocols, HTTP is stateless, meaning that there isn't a concept of a "session" where a client connects to a server, performs several transactions, and then ends the connection. HTTP permits only a single request per connection, and therefore it's really not possible to determine how many users are connected to a Web server at any given time, except for downloads that are currently in progress. This also means there aren't any of the topological issues that are associated with protocols such as SMTP: relaying, MX records, queues, and so on, aren't relevant to HTTP. Instead, the problems that an HTTP server administrator faces have mostly to do with bandwidth, CPU, and memory resources, and with their most efficient use as concurrent activity grows with the popularity of the Web site.

The structure of an HTTP/1.0 request is about as simple as it can get. You can simulate an HTTP transaction by connecting to port 80 of an HTTP server, issuing a GET request that can contain multiple lines in the following form:

```
# telnet www.somewhere.com 80
Connected to www.somewhere.com.
Escape character is '^]'.
GET / HTTP/1.0

HTTP/1.1 200 OK

Date: Sun, 20 May 2001 22:45:55 GMT
Server: Apache/1.3.20 (Unix)
Content-Location: index.html
Vary: negotiate,accept-language,accept-charset
TCN: choice
Last-Modified: Fri, 31 Mar 2000 01:45:46 GMT
ETag: "6531f-54e-38e4034a;3a977613"
Accept-Ranges: bytes
Content-Length: 1358
Connection: close
Content-Type: text/html
Content-Language: en
Expires: Sun, 20 May 2001 22:45:55 GMT

<HTML>
```

```
<TITLE>test page</TITLE>
<BODY>
test
</BODY>
</HTML>
```

You could instead issue a HEAD request of the same form, to retrieve the headers only, not the message body. You enter a blank line to indicate the end of the multiline request (press Enter twice).

The first block of response lines are the headers. This way, you can easily tell what kind of HTTP server is at the other end; each HTTP server has its own unique signature on the Server: line. The rest of the lines, especially the Content-*: lines, contain information that help the Web browser lay out the page. For instance, Content-Length:, when present, allows the browser to report how much data there is left in the download; and Content-Type: tells the browser how to render the requested file (as HTML, plain text, GIF or JPEG image data, and so on).

An HTTP/1.0 request allows a number of extra lines to be included in the request, including lines specifying cookies, accepted encodings, preferred languages, and so on. Aside from the request line, which must appear first, the order of the rest of the lines doesn't matter. However, these are optional; only one line (the request line itself) is required. An HTTP/1.1 request is almost the same as HTTP/1.0, except that a second line is also required—the Host: line. This is an addition to the protocol intended to support virtual hosting, where a single Web server can answer for many different hostnames. This means that the client has to specify the hostname whose Web content it wants to see. Because a Web browser looks up the server's IP address from the hostname the user specifies and then makes the HTTP connection based on the IP address (which is how TCP/IP applications operate, as we saw in Chapter 22, "Introduction to Networking"), the server knows nothing about what hostname the user is trying to reach unless the client supplies the Host: header.

```
# telnet www.somewhere.com 80
Connected to www.somewhere.com.
Escape character is '^]'.
GET / HTTP/1.1
Host: www.somewhere.com
```

All major browsers today, including text-only browsers such as Lynx, support HTTP/1.1-style Host: headers. (However, whether they formulate their requests to claim HTTP/1.1 support is inconsistent. Netscape Navigator, for instance, supports many HTTP/1.1 features, but it issues its requests as HTTP/1.0 anyway.) This means that virtual hosting based on the Host: header (rather than by IP address and network-level IP aliases) is now almost exclusively the method of choice, greatly simplifying matters. We'll talk more about virtual hosting later in this chapter.

Response Codes and Redirects

While there are only a few request methods (GET, HEAD, and POST, plus several more for HTTP/1.1), there are a wide variety of responses the server can return. These are three-digit numeric codes, and they're grouped on meaning by the first digit. Table 26.1 shows the complete set of HTTP response codes and what they mean, particularly in the context of Apache and its features.

TABLE 26.1 HTTP Response Codes

Numeric Code	Name	Meaning
2xx—Success		
200	OK	Standard success code
201	Created	
202	Accepted	
203	Partial Information	
204	No Content	
3xx—Redirection		
300	Multiple Choices	MultiViews or CheckSpelling found multiple matches
301	Moved Permanently	Trailing slash was omitted
302	Moved Temporarily	Redirect found
304	Not Modified	Cached copy is OK to use
4xx—Client Error		
400	Bad Request	
401	Unauthorized	Must authenticate to continue
403	Forbidden	Server permissions or configuration do not permit access
404	Not Found	File does not exist
5xx—Server Error		
500	Internal Server Error	Server-side (CGI) program failed
501	Not Implemented	
502	Bad Gateway	
503	Service Unavailable	Resources to process the request are not available

You're probably quite familiar with 404 and 403 errors, and 500 errors will be familiar to you if you're ever done any CGI programming. However, one little-understood code is 304. This is never seen by a user because it's intended purely for a browser's use; nonetheless, it's one of the most commonly used codes by a production server, as you would see if you were to look through the access log (/var/log/httpd-access.log).

When a client has to make a request for a file that it already has in its cache (such as an inline GIF image in an HTML page), it performs a GET request with the If-Modified-Since field set to the date and time the image was last downloaded. This causes the server to evaluate whether the file has been changed on the server since that time. If it has, it sends the file (with a 200 success code); if it hasn't, it returns a 304 (Not Modified) code—telling the browser that it's okay to display the copy that it has in its cache, thereby saving the trouble of serving the file all over again.

Another code frequently seen by browsers but not people is 301 (Moved Permanently). This most often occurs when someone requests a URL of the type http://some.host.com/Subdirectory, where Subdirectory is the name of a directory on the server. The correct form of the URL that accesses the index of that directory is http://some.host.com/Subdirectory/ with a trailing slash. Notice, however, that if you enter the URL without the trailing slash, you'll still get the page—but the browser attaches the slash for you. This is because it received a 301 code for the first request, redirecting it to the same URL with the slash appended. The URL in your browser was updated, the browser made a second request, and the correct page was served. For this to work seamlessly, the server needs to know exactly what its hostname is; this is the purpose of the ServerName directive in Apache, which we will discuss a little later in this chapter.

More information—exhaustive and authoritative—can be found at the W3 Consortium Web site, www.w3.org/Protocols. The original HTTP/1.0 specification is laid out in RFC 1945, and HTTP/1.1 is RFC 2068.

Obtaining and Installing Apache

Apache, its name derived from its original nickname "A Patchy Server" (since it grew out of a series of patches applied against the industry-standard but limited NCSA httpd server in early 1995), is one of the most widely ported pieces of software in the world today. It runs on dozens of different operating system platforms, from AIX to Windows to BeOS to Mac OS X, as well as, of course, FreeBSD. Probably the most complete HTTP implementation available anywhere, it's also seen by many as the epitome of the open-source ideal, showing how a free, grass-roots development effort can earn its way to being the *de facto* standard solution for a problem where competing offerings include large, commercially developed packages by market-leading software companies. Apache claims at least a 60% market share at the time of this writing—a figure that continues to grow.

Obtaining Apache is a matter of installing it from the ports (/usr/ports/www/apache13) or packages. At the time of this writing, Apache 1.3 is the mature code branch, with most of its bugs and security issues solved long ago; it's the codebase that has built Apache's popularity and reputation, and it will probably do everything you need it to do. However, it has a few structural quirks (such as a forking model, where it spawns a new Apache process to handle every single request), and Apache 2.0 is a complete rewrite that incorporates kernel threading and greater modular architecture for major performance benefits. It's in alpha development right now, though, and so this chapter will cover working with the established Apache 1.3 codebase rather than the newer version, which is available at /usr/ports/www/apache2 if you should wish to try it out.

One interesting advantage that Apache has for FreeBSD users is that many parts of it were developed explicitly in a FreeBSD environment, such as the URL Rewrite module (mod_rewrite) by Ralf Engelschall, and a number of performance-tuning options. It also means that Apache fits well into the FreeBSD directory structure, as we'll discuss in a moment.

The Apache source distribution is available from a number of worldwide mirror sites, if your ports collection is unable to get it from the main, central one. These mirrors, as well as the definitive collection of Apache documentation, can be found at http://httpd.apache.org.

Apache File Layout

After installing Apache, you'll notice that a new directory has been created in /usr/local for the server's root directory. This new directory, /usr/local/www, contains several subdirectories for various purposes, some of which are symbolic links. The map of Apache's file layout is shown in Figure 26.1. As is surely not a surprise by now, everything installed as part of Apache is underneath /usr/local, except for log files (which go into /var/log with all the rest of the system's log files).

Actually, a few of these directories are in a temporary, installation-only file structure that prevents the install script from "clobbering" existing files on a live server. For instance, /usr/local/www/data.default is a symlink to /usr/local/share/doc/apache, but /usr/local/www/data (which is where the configuration expects to find the document root, the directory that has the main server HTML pages) is a separate symlink to the same place, which you can alter if you want to. Similarly, /usr/local/www/cgi-bin is a symlink to /usr/local/www/cgi-bin.default, itself a regular directory. If you put files into cgi-bin, they will actually go into the cgi-bin.default directory, unless you change cgi-bin to be its own regular directory.

FIGURE 26.1

Map of the Apache file layout, showing the relationship of config files, the server document root, and support binaries.

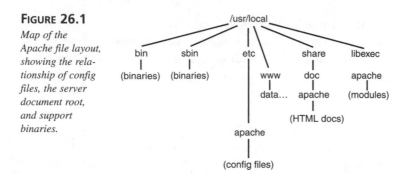

Files in /usr/local/etc/apache, which we will discuss in a moment, also have .default variants—there are no symbolic links here, but the .default files are the only ones that are touched when you reinstall or upgrade. This gives you a "safety net" and reference file in case you change something in your live configuration files that you can't fix without hints.

As with Sendmail, this file layout is considerably different from the layout in an Apache installation on other platforms. Each one differs slightly, so knowing the FreeBSD layout well won't necessarily help you if you have to maintain Apache on Linux or Solaris or Windows.

One tip that may help: There's usually a "server root" directory, such as /usr/local/www on FreeBSD, in which everything Apache-related lives. On Linux, this is often in /var/lib/apache; however, in this style of installation, very nearly everything associated with Apache—including config files, binaries, logs, sources, and build configuration scripts—lives in or under that one directory. While this doesn't have the benefit of FreeBSD's rigid and consistent structure, at least you'll be able to find just about everything in one place in such an installation.

Configuring Apache

Just as in /etc/mail (which we saw in Chapter 25, "Configuring E-mail Services"), /usr/local/etc/apache (the Apache configuration directory) contains a number of files, some of which are of interest to us and some of which are not. Let's take a look at each of them in turn:

- **httpd.conf**—This is the main Apache configuration file. These days, everything is consolidated into this one file, rather than being grouped into as many as three more specific files.

- **mime.types**—This file provides a lookup table between filename extensions and MIME types (Content-Type headers) in files that Apache sends. This is how browsers know how to handle files they download.

- **magic**—An alternative method to MIME types is "magic", which tries to determine a file type by looking for certain patterns within the file, making filename extensions unnecessary. This is the same method that's used by the file command.

- **access.conf and srm.conf**—These files used to contain certain parts of what is now incorporated into httpd.conf. They will still be read if you put configuration items into them, which is why they're still here (to maintain compatibility with legacy installations), but these days they're unnecessary and can be ignored.

Again, note that .default versions of all of these files exist. Immediately after a clean installation, these are copies of the regular versions of each file. After you've made changes to the regular versions over the course of regular usage, though, if you install a newer version of Apache, only the .default files will be touched by the installation scripts. This allows you to upgrade your system and merge in new configuration options at your leisure, using diff or some other method.

Using httpd.conf

The httpd.conf file is long and detailed, but (unlike /etc/mail/sendmail.cf) it's entirely human-readable and very well commented. Every one of the configuration directives is set to a sensible default value; you can modify any of them that you want, and the inline documentation explains quite clearly what each one does. If you misconfigure something, Apache will tell you exactly what's wrong when you try to start it up.

Immediately after installation, Apache can be started up and will serve requests properly. However, just to be safe, there are a couple of configuration directives you should set. Find each of these in the httpd.conf file, and alter it accordingly:

```
#
# ServerAdmin: Your address, where problems with the server should be
# e-mailed.  This address appears on some server-generated pages, such
# as error documents.
#
ServerAdmin you@your.address

#
# ServerName allows you to set a host name which is sent back to clients for
# your server if it's different than the one the program would get (i.e., use
```

```
# "www" instead of the host's real name).
#
#ServerName new.host.name
```

This second one, ServerName, is what's used in 301 redirections (which we discussed earlier in the chapter). If the trailing slash is left off of a request for a directory index or listing, Apache responds with a 301 code (Moved Permanently) and the URL to which the browser should go. Apache has to construct this redirection URL from the information it has from the client's request, which (as we've seen) contains only the portion of the URL beginning with the slash after the hostname—if the requested URL was http://some.host.com/images/foo, the request is /images/foo. If it's an HTTP/1.1 request, it contains a Host: header, which Apache can use to rebuild the full URL, but otherwise it's on its own unless you've specified the server's hostname with the ServerName directive.

HTTP/1.1 does cause a few other repercussions regarding the ServerName directive. If you're doing name-based virtual hosting, which we'll get to shortly, Apache uses ServerName to match a virtual host with a request based on its Host: header. Each virtual host must have a ServerName specified; but even if you're not doing virtual hosting, it's a good idea to define the ServerName to help Apache construct its redirection URLs and match requests with the single main host configuration—effectively treating the default configuration as a virtual host that must match a Host: header.

We could go through all the available configuration directives here, but there are too many of them that are equally important relative to each other and unimportant relative to the default configuration to justify going into them in too much detail. Authoritative documentation can be found at the Apache Group's Web site at http://httpd.apache.org/docs/.

Using .htaccess Files and Overrides

While httpd.conf provides global configuration options, many of them can be overridden on a per-directory basis without the server having to be restarted. You do this by placing a file called .htaccess, containing any directives you want to override, into the directory to which you want it to apply. On every request that comes in, the global configuration that was loaded into memory from httpd.conf is consulted, followed by every per-directory configuration file (.htaccess) sequentially down the path to where the requested file is. Each successive .htaccess file can override previously seen directives, but otherwise an .htaccess applies to its own directory and all subdirectories.

Whether .htaccess files can be used depends on the AllowOverride directive. As you can see by reading through httpd.conf, AllowOverride is set to None at the operating system root level and again on the /usr/local/www/data directory; thus, .htaccess files are ignored by default. However, you can turn them on by replacing AllowOverride None (in the /usr/local/www/data block) with any of the directives in Table 26.2, or any combination thereof (for example, AllowOverride AuthConfig Limit).

TABLE 26.2   AllowOverride Configuration Options

Directive	*Allows* .htaccess *Files to Override*
AllowOverride Options	The Options directive
AllowOverride FileInfo	File-typing directives, such as AddType and ErrorDocument
AllowOverride AuthConfig	Authorization directives, such as Require and Auth*
AllowOverride Limit	Host access directives, such as Allow, Deny, and Order
AllowOverride All	All of the above

> **Note**
>
> The Options directive is one of the largest and most versatile configuration items in Apache; it controls the availability of many of Apache's most significant features, such as ExecCGI (the ability to execute CGI scripts), Includes (server-side includes), and MultiViews (versatile content negotiation). These features can be added to or subtracted from the current configuration at any level in the hierarchical directory structure. Refer to http://httpd.apache.org/docs/mod/core.html#options for full coverage of the Options directive and how to use it.

After changing httpd.conf accordingly, restart the server (as we will discuss in a moment); you can now put a .htaccess file into any Web-accessible directory and place into it any configuration directives that Apache allows in .htaccess files (for details on these, see http://httpd.apache.org/docs/).

The httpd.conf file contains a commented-out block for controlling user directories (in /home); if you plan to run a server where your users can have sites of their own, but you want to make sure browsers that support various data-changing HTTP/1.1 methods (such as DELETE, COPY, and MOVE) can't exercise them, you might want to uncomment this block:

```
#
# Control access to UserDir directories.  The following is an example
# for a site where these directories are restricted to read-only.
#
#<Directory /home/*/public_html>
#    AllowOverride FileInfo AuthConfig Limit
#    Options MultiViews Indexes SymLinksIfOwnerMatch IncludesNoExec
#    <Limit GET POST OPTIONS PROPFIND>
#        Order allow,deny
#        Allow from all
#    </Limit>
#    <LimitExcept GET POST OPTIONS PROPFIND>
#        Order deny,allow
#        Deny from all
#    </LimitExcept>
#</Directory>
```

Note that the `AllowOverride` here allows `.htaccess` files to override `FileInfo`, `AuthConfig`, and `Limit` directives, but the `Options` directives are set at the global level.

> **Note**
>
> In accordance with historical convention, per-user document directories are called `public_html`; a request for `http://some.host.com/~user/` would show the documents in `/home/user/public_html`. Also traditionally, if there's an `index.html` file present, Apache will serve that file instead of the directory listing. (Microsoft servers generally use `Default.htm` for this function.) You can specify as many of these index filenames as you like using the `DirectoryIndex` directive. Apache will try each filename you specify, in the order in which you enter them.

Starting and Stopping the HTTP Daemon

The Apache installation process in the ports collection will start the server automatically. You can verify this by looking for `httpd` processes using `ps` and `grep`:

```
# ps -waux | grep httpd
root     220  0.0  2.0  4436 2456  ??  Ss   Sat02PM  0:02.79
/usr/local/sbin/httpd
nobody   303  0.0  2.0  4496 2548  ??  I    Sat02PM  0:00.01
/usr/local/sbin/httpd
nobody   304  0.0  2.0  4460 2452  ??  I    Sat02PM  0:00.00
/usr/local/sbin/httpd
```

```
nobody   305  0.0  2.0  4460 2452  ??  I   Sat02PM  0:00.00
/usr/local/sbin/httpd
nobody   306  0.0  2.0  4460 2452  ??  I   Sat02PM  0:00.00
/usr/local/sbin/httpd
nobody   307  0.0  2.0  4460 2452  ??  I   Sat02PM  0:00.00
/usr/local/sbin/httpd
nobody 13963  0.0  2.0  4468 2468  ??  I   Sat10PM  0:00.00
/usr/local/sbin/httpd
```

Note that Apache uses a forking model, where one "master" process (the one owned by root in the previous output) listens on port 80 for incoming requests, and forks off a copy of itself (owned by the unprivileged pseudo-user nobody) as a child process to handle each request. The master process never actually serves any requests on its own—it's very dangerous to have a Web server that can serve requests as root, since that means it can execute programs as root—a situation that's one small CGI script away from an exploit that can wipe your entire hard disk clean.

Under the forking model, where dozens of httpd processes might be running simultaneously, killing and restarting every one of these processes is impractical, to say the least. There's a better way, though. All you have to do if you want to stop the server is to kill the master process; to restart the server, send the master process a HUP signal, upon which it will kill all its child processes, restart itself, and respawn its children.

This is still fairly messy, though, and it involves using tools such as ps and grep and kill in a fairly arcane manner. Fortunately, Apache provides us with a handy tool for this purpose: apachectl, which is installed into /usr/local/sbin and is therefore part of your default program path. Starting and stopping Apache using apachectl is quite easy:

```
# apachectl start
/usr/local/sbin/apachectl start: httpd started
# apachectl stop
/usr/local/sbin/apachectl stop: httpd stopped
```

After you've made any changes to any of the files in /usr/local/etc/apache, you must restart Apache. This is also made easy by apachectl:

```
# apachectl restart
/usr/local/sbin/apachectl restart: httpd restarted
```

The apachectl restart command does the equivalent of sending a kill -HUP to the master httpd process: All child processes will be killed, even if they're in the middle of serving files to clients—those clients will have the connection abruptly dropped. If you want to restart Apache in a less-intrusive way—for example, if you have a high-load server whose data integrity is critical—you might choose instead to do a "graceful restart," which uses a SIGUSR1 instead of a SIGHUP. This less-urgent signal allows the master process to restart itself without killing its child processes, meaning that in-progress transfers will not be dropped.

```
# apachectl graceful
/usr/local/sbin/apachectl graceful: httpd gracefully restarted
```

One other common use for apachectl is the configtest command. This will cause Apache (whether it's running or not) to read in the config files from /usr/local/etc/apache and report any configuration errors, just as the start command would—except that it does not actually start the server if it finds no errors. This is an excellent diagnostic tool, besides which it is an implicit part of both the restart and graceful commands: apachectl uses configtest to determine whether the configuration is valid before trying to restart the server; and if it isn't, it leaves the running processes alone. This prevents a restart or graceful command from inadvertently killing your server:

```
# apachectl graceful
/usr/local/sbin/apachectl graceful: configuration broken, ignoring restart
/usr/local/sbin/apachectl graceful: (run 'apachectl configtest' for details)
```

> **Tip**
>
> If Apache isn't running, apachectl restart or apachectl graceful will start it.

Basic Access Control with Apache

Certain parts of your Web site will almost certainly need to be protected from being viewed by the general public; access control allows you to restrict these sections to authorized users either by hostname/IP address, or by password authentication. We'll take a look at both of these methods.

Access Control by Address

Let's say you want to restrict a certain file, directory, or set of files and directories to a short list of fixed IP addresses or hostnames. You can do this at the global (httpd.conf) level; or more efficiently, you can use a .htaccess file in any directory at or above the level of the items you want to protect.

First of all, you need to make sure that .htaccess overrides are enabled in the part of the site that you want to protect. As we saw earlier, you can use AllowOverride Limit, at the /usr/local/www/data level or further down in the directory structure with another <Directory> container, to enable the use of the access-control directives we're about to use: `Allow`, `Deny`, and `Order`. Since Apache directives are all read in at the same time, we need to specify the order in which to read our `Allow` and `Deny` directives, or else they'll override each other in ways we didn't intend.

To close off a directory to everyone but certain specified addresses or hostnames, put a `.htaccess` file in that directory with the following contents:

```
Order deny,allow
Deny from all
Allow from 64.41.131.102
Allow from stripes.somewhere.com
Allow from nowhere.com
Allow from 10.5.100
Allow from 10.67.22.211/255.255.255.0
```

As you can see, a number of different address formats are allowed; these are just matching rules, where if the connecting host matches any of these hostname or network patterns, it will be allowed access. Similarly, you can have the directory open to everybody *except* certain hosts:

```
Order allow,deny
Allow from all
Deny from l33t.hacker.com
Deny from 192.168
```

You must place these commands inside a `<Directory>` or `<Location>` block if you're doing this in `httpd.conf`; you can also use `<Files>` or `<FilesMatch>` to list certain files, wherever in the system they might be, which should be subject to the access control

```
<Files "*.jpg">
  Order deny,allow
  Deny from all
  Allow from 64.41.131.102
</Files>
```

`FilesMatch` can be used to specify filenames matching regular expressions, as in this example, which would match all `.gif`, `.jpg`, `.jpeg`, and `.png` files:

```
<FilesMatch "\.(gif|jpe?g|png)$">
  Order deny,allow
  Deny from all
  Allow from 64.41.131.102
</FilesMatch>
```

Note, however, that `<Directory>` and `<Location>` are not available in `.htaccess` files.

The `<Limit>` block, despite its name, is not required for the previous access controls to work. Rather, its purpose is to list certain access methods to which the access controls should apply. For instance, you might choose to limit only `GET` and `POST`, but leave all other methods unrestricted. Likewise, you could use `<LimitExcept>` to specify the only methods to which the access controls should *not* apply. We saw an example of this earlier, in the commented-out block controlling user directories within /home.

Access Control by Password

Sometimes, it's not practical or desirable to limit access by address. A privileged portion of your site might be made available to registered users who have paid a fee, for example, and these users might not come from a predictable IP address. This is where it's much more sensible to use password authentication for access control.

Apache stores its own username and password databases, distinct from the systemwide one in /etc/master.passwd and its relatives. This is for security purposes, and it's an extremely bad idea to try to merge the two authentication schemes together, so don't even think about it. The FreeBSD password database is for authenticating shell users who actually have an account on the system, while the Apache authentication databases control access to certain parts of your Web site from Web surfers. You might have a situation in which these two areas of functionality overlap (such as an intranet server for a company), but don't be tempted to try to serve both from the same database. If you succeed, it will be a study in insecurity and irresponsible system administration technique, explicitly discouraged by the Apache Group, and will earn you a great deal more scorn than respect from your peers. It's not worth it.

To password-protect a portion of your Web site, you'll need to use an .htaccess file (or equivalent configuration in httpd.conf)—including the appropriate use of `<Directory>`, `<Location>`, and `<Files>` blocks—just as with per-address access control. The contents of this file or configuration block are considerably different, though, involving an entirely different module in Apache to do the access control. A simple example block follows:

```
AuthType Basic
AuthName "Restricted Area"
AuthUserFile /usr/local/www/.htpasswd
Require valid-user
```

This is the minimum number of directives needed to make it work. Each of these, or their alternatives, is required. These directives are a little confusing, so let's look at them individually:

- **AuthType**—This can be either Basic or Digest; Basic is the only one that really concerns us.

- **AuthName**—This is just a name for the "realm" or the area you're protecting. This name pops up in the authentication window in the user's browser (for example,

"Enter username for 'Restricted Area' at `www.somewhere.com`"), helping to tell the user which area he or she is entering and which username and password it needs. It can be anything you want, except that it must be enclosed in quotes if there are spaces in the name.

- `AuthUserFile`, `AuthDBUserFile`, and `AuthDBMUserFile`—One of these directives must be used to specify the location of the file that contains the user/password database for the realm. (Each realm can have a different user database file if you like.) If it's a pure text file, use `AuthUserFile`; if it's in db or dbm format for lookup speed purposes (a good idea if there are a lot of users in it), use `AuthDBUserFile` or `AuthDBMUserFile` accordingly. We'll cover how to create plain text or db/dbm user databases in a moment.

- `AuthGroupFile`, `AuthDBGroupFile`, and `AuthDBMGroupFile`—These directives work in the same way as the `AuthUserFile` ones, except that they specify groups of users from the `AuthUserFile`, allowing you to restrict access to a group rather than just to certain users. This directive isn't required, but if you do use it, an `AuthUserFile` needs to be present for its users to be recognized as part of the listed groups.

- `Require`—This tells Apache how to authenticate the user. The argument can be `valid-user` (any user present in the `AuthUserFile` who enters the correct password), `user <username> <username>`... (a list of users), or `group <groupname> <groupname>`... (a list of groups).

Adding Users

Once you have the access control block set up and `apachectl configtest` reports that the configuration is OK, it's time to add users. First, let's see how to make a plain-text user database, the kind for which you'd use an `AuthUserFile` directive. The command to use is `htpasswd`, which in FreeBSD is in `/usr/local/bin` and therefore part of your path:

```
# htpasswd -c /usr/local/www/.htpasswd frank
```

The `-c` flag is only necessary the first time; this tells `htpasswd` to create the file, since it doesn't exist yet. You will then be prompted for the user's password, which you must enter twice (as usual). To do this in a script, you can use the `-b` option and specify the password as another argument:

```
# htpasswd -b /usr/local/www/.htpasswd joe Pr1d3L4ndz
```

Another useful option is `-m`, which causes `htpasswd` to use an MD5-based encryption algorithm rather than the system's `crypt()` routine; this may provide you with better security. Other options can be found in the `man apachectl` page.

> **Caution**
>
> The user database file can be anywhere in the system that the Web server user (nobody) can read, and it can be named anything you want, though having the name begin with .htpasswd is traditional and protected from view by the default server configuration. However, it's a very bad idea to put the file anywhere where it can be accessed by a user with a Web browser! To wit, don't put it anywhere inside /usr/local/www/data or in any user's public_html directory; instead, use Web-inaccessible locations such as /usr/local/www or directly inside a user's home directory. You don't want people downloading your user database and cracking it!

Plain-text user databases work great for small lists of users; however, once you start working with dozens or hundreds of users, the time it takes to look up a user's password makes the authentication process cumbersome or even non-functional. The solution to this is to use a true database file, either in db or dbm form, and to use the appropriate AuthDBUserFile or AuthDBMUserFile directives. The support program that allows you to work with the database files is /usr/local/bin/dbmmanage:

```
# dbmmanage /usr/local/www/.htpwddb adduser frank
New password:
Re-type new password:
User frank added with password encrypted to NtMDxy6jwyW7A using crypt
```

This example will create a db-style database file called /usr/local/www/.htpwddb, which you can then access with the AuthDBUserFile directive. The dbm equivalent can also be used if necessary, but you shouldn't have to. See man dbmmanage for further details on the user management commands you can use.

Adding Groups

Listing groups in a plain-text file (AuthGroupFile) is quite easy. Each line contains the group name, a colon, and then the list of users in the group:

```
mygroup: frank joe alice
```

The group file should probably be kept in the same place as the user file, and with a similar name; however, since the group file doesn't contain any passwords, security considerations aren't quite as critical.

Group files can be managed with dbmmanage as well, but this practice is usually unnecessary because (as with /etc/group) there are seldom anywhere near as many groups as there are users. You can use AuthGroupFile in conjunction with AuthDBUserFile if you wish to mix formats; this is probably the simplest way to maintain a large user list along with a small group list.

Access Control by Address and Password

It's possible to require that a user satisfy both address restrictions *and* password authentication before access control allows access to a restricted area. This is done with the `Satisfy` directive:

```
Allow from 64.41.131.102
Require valid-user
Satisfy all
```

`Satisfy all` is the default setting if both `Allow` and `Require` directives are present; this behavior means that the incoming user must meet the `Allow` requirements *and* supply a valid username and password before access will be granted. You can also use `Satisfy` any to tell the server that the user must supply a valid password *or* be coming from an `Allowed` address; this is useful if you want users at certain locations to have unconditional access to an area, but require authentication from all other users (for instance, if you're providing a service that you must administer as a regular user, but you don't want to be forever entering passwords for access).

Virtual Hosting

Virtual hosting is the practice of keeping the Web site contents for multiple different domains or hostnames on the same server; a single installation of Apache serves requests for all of them. For instance, www.mystore.com and www.frankspage.com might both be configured in DNS to point to the same IP address on your FreeBSD machine, and Apache is responsible for serving both of them, as well as its own hostname (as specified in the `ServerName` directive).

As we've seen, HTTP/1.0 provided no indication of what hostname the HTTP client was trying to reach (as specified by the user), so in earlier days, virtual hosting had to be done by pointing each hostname to a separate IP address and then binding each IP address as an IP alias to the same Ethernet card. Each virtual host was then specified by IP address, so a request coming in from a Web browser would always be sure to get the correct Web site in response. The downside was that binding these large blocks of IP addresses to the same card became unwieldy, and it caused unnecessary consumption of IP address space (which, as we saw in Chapter 22, is not infinite).

Now that we have HTTP/1.1, though, this cumbersome process is much alleviated. The mandatory `Host:` header specifies what hostname the client is trying to reach, and so "name-based" virtual hosts are the norm on the modern Web. Clients that don't support the Host: header are almost unheard-of these days, so we will be discussing only name-based virtual hosts; if you're interested in address-based virtual hosts, you can find information on them at the Apache Web site.

The bulk of the httpd.conf file specifies the "default" server—a global set of definitions that apply to all requests that Apache receives. In the default server, the ServerName directive is used primarily for constructing 301 redirection URLs, as we discussed earlier. However, you can then set up small sets of overrides to these global settings, which are used if the Host: header matches a certain specified hostname. These groupings of overrides make up what we know as virtual hosts.

Let's say your server is called stripes.somewhere.com, and that's what your main ServerName directive specifies. To configure name-based virtual hosts, you need a NameVirtualHost directive with an argument of * (the wildcard specifies "all hostnames"), followed by as many different <VirtualHost *> blocks as you like:

```
NameVirtualHost *

<VirtualHost *>
  ServerName www.somewhere.com
  DocumentRoot /usr/local/www/data
  ServerAdmin webmaster@somewhere.com
  ErrorLog logs/www.somewhere.com-error_log
  CustomLog logs/www.somewhere.com-access_log common
</VirtualHost>

<VirtualHost *>
  ServerName www.frankspage.com
  ServerAlias frankspage.com
  DocumentRoot /home/frank/public_html
  ServerAdmin frank@frankspage.com
  ErrorLog logs/www.frankspage.com-error_log
  CustomLog logs/www.frankspage.com-access_log common
</VirtualHost>
```

Inside a <VirtualHost> container, the ServerName directive determines the hostname to match against the client's Host: header, and a match will result in the corresponding set of overrides (the appropriate <VirtualHost> being applied to the configuration). DocumentRoot specifies where in the filesystem the incoming request should be mapped, and the ErrorLog and CustomLog directives specify alternate log files for each virtual host. ServerAlias provides a way of listing multiple alternate matching hostnames for a virtual host. You can also include any other directives you like, as long as they're allowed inside a <VirtualHost> block—apachectl configtest will tell you if they're not allowed.

It's important to note, though, that in the setup shown earlier, a request for the default server (`stripes.somewhere.com`), or for any other hostname that maps to the server's IP address but doesn't match any of the `<VirtualHost>` blocks, will not be answered by the default server; the default server never answers requests for any address that is specified for name-based virtual hosts (in the `NameVirtualHost` directive)—it exists only to specify the default configuration set. Since we've used the `*` wildcard to specify name-based virtual hosts on all IP addresses, the default server will never itself service a request. In the absence of a `<VirtualHost>` matching the requested hostname, the server that responds will be the first `<VirtualHost>` that appears in the config file (`www.somewhere.com` in this case).

A more correct configuration than the previous one, then, would be this:

```
NameVirtualHost *

<VirtualHost *>
  ServerName stripes.somewhere.com
</VirtualHost>

<VirtualHost *>
  ServerName www.somewhere.com
  ServerAlias *.somewhere.com
  DocumentRoot /usr/local/www/data
  ServerAdmin webmaster@somewhere.com
  ErrorLog logs/www.somewhere.com-error_log
  CustomLog logs/www.somewhere.com-access_log common
</VirtualHost>

<VirtualHost *>
  ServerName www.frankspage.com
  ServerAlias frankspage.com
  DocumentRoot /home/frank/public_html
  ServerAdmin frank@frankspage.com
  ErrorLog logs/www.frankspage.com-error_log
  CustomLog logs/www.frankspage.com-access_log common
</VirtualHost>
```

Virtual hosts can be done in a myriad of other ways, allowing you to specify different IP addresses and ports to match certain groups of `<VirtualHost>` blocks. Examples of the syntax for these methods can be found at `http://httpd.apache.org/docs/vhosts/`.

Introduction to Apache Modules

One of Apache's greatest strengths is its modular structure. All configuration directives are part of one module or another, and while in earlier versions of Apache these modules were all painstakingly turned on or off at compile time, nowadays almost all modules are available as dynamic shared objects (DSOs) and can simply be loaded at runtime.

Built-in Modules

To see which modules are compiled statically into Apache, use `httpd -l`:

```
# httpd -l
Compiled-in modules:
  http_core.c
  mod_so.c
suexec: disabled; invalid wrapper /usr/local/sbin/suexec
```

This means that the directives in the `Core` module and the `mod_so` module are the only ones guaranteed to be available. The `Core` module provides access to the most fundamental directives without which Apache could not run at all; `mod_so` enables DSO support, which makes it possible to load all the approximately thirty-two further modules that ship with Apache, as well as any additional modules that you might choose to install.

> **Note**
>
> Ignore the note about `suexec`; this is a utility that allows Apache to run in a setuid wrapper, executing requests as a specified user (usually different for every virtual host). The `suexec` wrapper isn't installed by default; you can read more about it at `http://httpd.apache.org/docs/suexec.html`. Also, in Chapter 29, "Network Security," we cover CGIwrap, a more versatile alternative to `suexec`.

Dynamically Loaded Modules

Dynamic modules allow you to trim down the size of your running `httpd` processes by eliminating modules you don't need. This can easily be done at runtime by commenting out the unnecessary modules from `httpd.conf`. If you decide later that you need the functionality in a certain module, just re-enable it and restart Apache. A complete listing of all the Apache modules and which directives are part of each module can be found at `http://httpd.apache.org/docs/mod/`.

To enable a module, you need both the `LoadModule` directive (which dynamically links the module into the `httpd` process) and the `AddModule` directive (which enables the module's directives in the correct order for further use in the configuration file). If you look in `httpd.conf`, you'll find `LoadModule` and `AddModule` directives for all the bundled Apache modules, which are installed into `/usr/local/libexec/apache`. Something to note about `LoadModule` is that each `LoadModule` directive is processed inline before proceeding, so the order in which the modules are specified matters. If a module depends on another module already being linked in, the dependency must be invoked first. The default configuration has all this correctly handled for you.

Third-Party Modules

The real strength of Apache's modular structure comes with third-party modules. These modules are linked in at runtime with the rest of the available Apache modules, providing additional functionality and configuration directives—usually to give Apache the ability to process certain kinds of server-side content more efficiently. One popular module is mod_perl, which embeds a Perl interpreter into Apache, greatly speeding up Perl CGI scripts by obviating the need for Apache to start up a subshell process and execute the CGI program within it. Another is mod_php4, a module that gives Apache the ability to parse and serve dynamic PHP pages (the UNIX analog of Microsoft's ASP technology). There are some 34 third-party Apache modules available in the ports collection in /usr/ports/www; they're the ones beginning with mod_.

Building Modules with apxs

Early in the development of the first third-party modules, when DSO support was experimental at best, compiling a third-party module meant having the Apache source available, tweaking the build configuration files in both the Apache source and the module's source, and cross-compiling them into a single, hybrid binary. While this was technically a "modular" approach (which is to say that it was better than having to patch in the code manually into the Apache source itself), it still wasn't what anyone would call easy to handle. It still involved building a new executable each time a new version of either Apache or the module became available, and it still involved a fair amount of code hackery to get it to work.

Enter apxs, the APache eXtenSion tool. This support program, residing in /usr/local/sbin, is built along with Apache to take advantage of the already compiled binary's DSO support (the statically compiled mod_so module) to provide a self-contained build framework that's fully aware of all the capabilities of your httpd binary. You no longer have to have the Apache source code around in order to build third-party modules; apxs compiles and converts modules in raw source form or already compiled objects into .so objects that can be loaded into Apache with the LoadModule directive, along with the rest.

You will most likely never need to use apxs directly; it's a compile-time tool used transparently by the build tools in the ports collection. All you have to do to build a third-party module, just as with any other port, is to go into the module's directory in /usr/ports/www and type make; apxs does the rest. If a new version of Apache is released, it can be built and installed on its own, and third-party modules will continue to work; likewise, if a module is updated, you can simply rebuild and reinstall it. This is true modularity at its best.

mod_perl

One of the most popular third-party modules is `mod_perl`. While Perl is still the most popular choice for CGI programming (which we'll discuss shortly), executing Perl scripts means a fair amount of overhead for Apache. When an HTTP request is made for a Perl CGI program, Apache must start a shell process and run the script within it, feeding the results back to the client.

With `mod_perl`, a Perl interpreter is built directly into Apache. Specialized directives define certain file types as executable Perl scripts that Apache can execute itself; further, each Perl script that Apache executes is held in compiled form in memory for later use. This eliminates the startup overhead usually associated with CGI execution, making the response of server-side programs a great deal faster.

More information on `mod_perl` is available at `http://perl.apache.org`.

mod_python

In keeping with the rise of Python as the likeliest inheritor of Perl's crown as the server-side programming language of choice in the future, `mod_python` provides the same kind of benefit to Apache for Python that `mod_perl` does for Perl. The Python interpreter is made directly available to the Apache executable, allowing Apache to run Python programs without any of the execution overhead of doing it through CGI.

The `mod_python` home page is at `www.modpython.org`.

mod_php

PHP, the wildly popular dynamic page-generation tool for UNIX, is made a part of Apache through the `mod_php3` and `mod_php4` modules. The directives enabled by this module family let Apache serve `.php` files completely natively, executing their embedded scripting functionality to generate the final form of a page before sending it to the client. When you build and install `mod_php4`, your `httpd.conf` file is automatically updated to provide support for the `.php` and `.phps` file types.

More information on PHP and `mod_php4` can be found at `www.php.net`.

A great many more modules are available, providing Apache with enough expanded functionality to keep you busy for a long time. Apache's modularity has only fairly recently become completely entrenched, and the widespread availability of standardized third-party modules, coupled with the FreeBSD ports collection, makes for an unprecedented new era in extensible HTTP server administration.

Server-Side Includes

One popular feature of Apache is the ability to process server-side includes, or calls to internal Apache functions that are embedded into plain HTML files and processed by Apache before being sent to the browser. *Server-side includes* let you perform feats from simply echoing environment variables into a page to importing modular HTML fragments or executing server-side programs each time the page is requested.

Server-side includes are embedded into what's known as *parsed HTML*, which is effectively just regular HTML that Apache parses when the page is requested, searching through it for server-side includes and processing each one in turn before sending it on to the client. Each include is of the following form:

```
<!--#command attribute=value attribute=value ... -->
```

In this generic example, `command` can be any of `include`, `exec`, `config`, `echo`, or a few other possibilities. The `attribute=value` pairs are ways of setting or reading variables, which you can set yourself using includes or read in from the available environment variables.

First, to turn on server-side includes in Apache, uncomment the following two lines in `httpd.conf` (or add them to the appropriate `.htaccess` file):

```
AddType text/html .shtml
AddHandler server-parsed .shtml
```

Next, add the `Includes` option to the `<Directory>` or `<Location>` block (or `.htaccess` file) that controls the area of the Web site that concerns you:

```
Options +Includes
```

The `AddType` directive maps a class of files (by their filename extensions) to a MIME type, extending the basic set which is stored in `/usr/local/etc/apache/mime.types`; the `AddHandler` assigns a handler (an internal way for Apache to process a file that is requested by the user) to a certain extension—in this case, `.shtml` (the traditional extension for HTML files that you want Apache to parse before serving). With these two directives in place, any `.shtml` file will be parsed for server-side includes on its way to the client.

Caution

Aside from containing server-side includes, the only difference between `.html` and `.shtml` files is the filename extension. They're both regular HTML files. If you put a server-side include into an `.html` file, simply rename it to have a `.shtml` extension if you want it to be parsed before being sent to the browser. A server-side include in an `.html` or `.htm` file will show up unparsed in the client's HTML source for the page.

A few examples of useful server-side includes follow:

- `<!--#echo var="HTTP_USER_AGENT"-->`—Prints the user's browser identifier string into the page. A fuller discussion of the available environment variables will appear later in this chapter where we cover CGI programming.

- `<!--#set var="e-mail" value="me@somewhere.com"-->`—Sets the variable called e-mail to the string me@somewhere.com for the remainder of the page (unless overridden later with a similar directive).

- `<!--#include virtual="/toolbar.html"-->`—Embeds the contents of /toolbar.html into the page. SSIs are parsed recursively, so a file included this way can have its own includes.

- `<!--#config timefmt="%A %B %d, %Y"-->`— Sets the time format for any server-side includes that output a date and time. The format string is the same as for the date command; see man date for more details.

- `<!--#flastmod file="index.shtml"-->`—Displays the date and time that index.shtml was last modified, in the time format specified in the config timefmt example.

- `<!--#exec cgi="/cgi-bin/counter"-->`—Executes a CGI script called counter and displays its output.

If you put directives like these into a .shtml file and they don't seem to be working, view the page's source. The directives should not appear in their server-side include form in the HTML code. If you see any, it means they haven't been parsed out, which means the Apache configuration hasn't been set up properly to support server-side includes. Make sure that your AddType and AddHandler directives are correctly specified and that they apply to the part of the site that you're using.

> **Tip**
>
> The default page displayed in a directory when no filename is specified is index.html, but using the DirectoryIndex directive, you can change this or even specify a list of filenames to try:
>
> `DirectoryIndex index.php index.php3 index.html index.shtml`
>
> Apache looks for each of these files in turn in a bare directory request, and only if none are found (and Options Indexes is enabled) will it display a file listing for that directory.
>
> If you prefer, you can simply use the following instead:
>
> `Options +MultiViews`
> `DirectoryIndex index INDEX`

`MultiViews` tells Apache to look for any file matching the requested base file-name (without the extension), and `DirectoryIndex index` says that any file in the directory called `index.*` (with any extension) should be served, generally in alphabetical preference. This way you can account for `index.htm`, `index.HTM`, and `INDEX.HTML` files, however your users happen to name their files.

A full tutorial on server-side includes, showing everything from conditional flow-control to external CGI execution, can be found at `http://httpd.apache.org/docs/howto/ssi.html`.

Introduction to CGI

Conventional Web sites made up of static HTML pages are fine in their way. Server-side includes let you embed a lot of useful functionality into regular HTML pages. However, for true Web applications (such as e-commerce sites, message boards, databases, and anything where the system tailors its content to the actions of the user), you need a server-side programming environment to handle the user's input and control the requested output. The standard way to do this is *CGI*, the *Common Gateway Interface*.

CGI exists as a "mediator" protocol, a layer of the Web server that allows you to use HTML forms to take in users' data, which the server (through CGI) feeds in a common format to any program on the server, regardless of what language it's written in. A CGI program can be a Perl script, a compiled C binary, a shell script, or anything else that can be executed by the Apache user (nobody). The output of the program is routed back through Apache directly to the Web browser. This means that (for example) you can write a CGI program that reads in variables from an HTML form, processes them, opens a pipe to Sendmail to mail the contents of the variables to you, and prints out an HTML response to the user. We'll see how to do this in a simple Perl script in just a moment.

Enabling CGI in Apache

There are two ways to use CGI programs in Apache. The first, cleanest way is with the `ScriptAlias` directive, which defines a certain directory as containing only CGI pro-grams, and maps it to a virtual path (as seen by the Web browser):

```
ScriptAlias /cgi-bin/ "/usr/local/www/cgi-bin/"
```

This line, which is enabled in `httpd.conf` by default, tells Apache that the `/cgi-bin/` URL (`http://stripes.somewhere.com/cgi-bin/`) is a designated CGI directory, and that everything in it should be treated as a CGI program. If you put anything in this directory that isn't a CGI program, it will return a 500 Server Error code, a failure to execute it as a CGI. You can add as many additional ScriptAlias lines as you like. The filesystem path to the CGI directory (for example, /usr/local/www/cgi-bin/) need not even be in the normally Web-accessible path; you can point the alias to anywhere in the system that's readable by the nobody user. This prevents people from being able to look at the contents of the directory or navigate to it from other directory listings. You generally don't want people to be able to access your CGI programs directly, anyway—they're typically called from links or as form actions, which we will discuss shortly.

> **Note**
>
> Note that the trailing slash on /cgi-bin/ is specified. This is another security measure, designed to prevent unauthorized access to the directory listing. A CGI program as Apache sees it through ScriptAlias is the name of the program (for example, script.cgi) that is appended to the ScriptAlias virtual path (for example, /cgi-bin/), so the slash is required in order for the server to construct the proper path (for example, /cgi-bin/script.cgi). 301 redirects don't apply here.

The other way to enable CGI programs is to use the Options directive to add the ExecCGI option to an area of the server specified by a <Directory> or <Location> block. This is useful for enabling CGI programs in your users' public_html directories, allowing the server to execute programs as CGI based on their filename extensions (for example, .cgi) and whether they're set executable. The following example will turn on CGI execution of all users' executable .cgi files, no matter where they are:

```
<Directory /home/*/public_html>
  Options +ExecCGI
  AddHandler cgi-script .cgi
</Directory>
```

If a CGI file (whether in a ScriptAlias directory or mapped to a handler by extension) can't be executed for any reason, the user will get a 500 Server Error message; you can look at Apache's error log to get a more detailed diagnostic message. Here's an example of an error log from an unsuccessful request for a Perl script called blah in /usr/local/www/cgi-bin:

```
# tail /var/log/httpd-error.log
syntax error at /usr/local/www/cgi-bin/blah line 3, at EOF
Execution of /usr/local/www/cgi-bin/blah aborted due to compilation errors.
[Tue May 22 22:06:26 2001] [error] [client 64.2.43.44] Premature end of script
headers: /usr/local/www/cgi-bin/blah
```

The first two lines of output are directly from Perl, exactly the same as if the script had been run on the command line. The third line is Apache telling us that it tried to execute the script, but it quit before printing out any HTTP headers, such as Content-type: (which is required for a valid CGI script). Our task, then, is to make sure the program is written correctly for CGI execution.

Writing CGI Programs

The format in which CGI variables are passed to a server-side program is as a URL-encoded text string, with each variable separated from its value by an equals sign (=) and from other variables by ampersands (&). The script sees it as being fed in via standard input (STDIN).

Perl is the most common language for CGI programming, and therefore the two terms are (incorrectly) often used synonymously. Don't confuse the two: Perl is useful for a great many things besides Web programming, and CGI encompasses all conceivable languages, even ones that don't exist yet. Still, the prevalence of Perl in the CGI programming world makes it the object of our attention right now.

Perl's strengths, as we saw in Chapter 21, "Introduction to Perl Programming," are in text processing and ease of development; this makes it an ideal candidate for situations when you need to read in variables from an HTML form (such as a user's name, e-mail address, mailing address, and comments), and process them into a form you or the system can use. A typical Perl CGI program is invoked as the action of the HTML form:

```
<FORM NAME="myform" METHOD="POST" ACTION="/cgi-bin/post2me">
```

When the user submits this form, all of its variables are submitted through the CGI interface to post2me, the Perl program whose job it is to handle them. The first thing this script must do is read in the variables from standard input and format them into an associative array for easy access:

```
read(STDIN, $buffer, $ENV{'CONTENT_LENGTH'});
@pairs = split(/&/, $buffer);
foreach $pair (@pairs)
{
    ($name, $value) = split(/=/, $pair);
    $value =~ tr/+/ /;
    $value =~ s/%([a-fA-F0-9][a-fA-F0-9])/pack("C", hex($1))/eg;
    $value =~ s/~!/ ~!/g;
    $FORM{$name} = $value;
}
```

This code does some security parsing to prevent malicious form input from being sent to the program. Specifically, if you write a CGI program that prints a user's form input out into an HTML file, a user can embed some malicious HTML code into his input, which calls a server-side include that runs some program on the server. Because any program executed through HTTP requests is run by the unprivileged `nobody` user, this usually amounts only to an annoyance. Still, it's a security hole that must be addressed, and this code block disables any potentially malicious HTML tags by inserting spaces and dashes where appropriate.

After your script has read in the form input, each form variable is available as a key in the `%FORM` array; the contents of the HTML input field called `e-mail`, for instance, are in `$FORM{'e-mail'}` and can be used however you like.

Next, your script must print out a valid HTML header. You have two choices here: You can print HTML code to standard output, effectively writing a new HTML page from within the script; or you can redirect the user to a different URL while the script does its work. The former is done with a `Content-type:` header, which can be any valid MIME type (it's up to the browser to know how to handle it), followed by a double newline, the standard signal for the end of the header block:

```
print "Content-type: text/html\n\n";
```

Anything printed out by your script after this header is part of the response body, rendered as HTML by the browser. You can use a type of `text/plain` to force the browser to display it as plain text, or any other type according to your needs.

The latter method, a redirect, is done with a `Location:` header and a redirection URL:

```
print "Location: http://www.somewhereelse.com/path/to/file.html\n\n";
```

Anything printed after this header vanishes because the browser will have already moved on to this new URL.

Environment variables are also available to CGI programs, and an HTTP connection comes with a great many pieces of interesting information. Some of these include `HTTP_REFERER` (the referring URL), `HTTP_USER_AGENT` (the browser the user has), `REMOTE_HOST` (the user's hostname), and many more. You can see them all by accessing the `printenv` script, which is included as part of the default Apache installation in the `/usr/local/www/cgi-bin` directory; you can access it at the URL `http://www.somewhere.com/cgi-bin/printenv`, substituting your FreeBSD machine's hostname or IP address as appropriate. Within Perl, your environment variables are accessible as keys in the `%ENV` array, so you can access the `REMOTE_HOST` variable as `$ENV{'REMOTE_HOST'}`.

Let's look at a simple Perl CGI program, which reads in three variables—called "name", "e-mail", and "comments"—from an HTML form, mails them to you, and prints a formatted thank-you note to the user. This script, which is shown in Listing 26.1, is available on the included CD-ROM as sendcomments.cgi.

LISTING 26.1   A Sample Perl CGI Program

```perl
#!/usr/bin/perl

read(STDIN, $buffer, $ENV{'CONTENT_LENGTH'});
@pairs = split(/&/, $buffer);
foreach $pair (@pairs)
{
    ($name, $value) = split(/=/, $pair);
    $value =~ tr/+/ /;
    $value =~ s/%([a-fA-F0-9][a-fA-F0-9])/pack("C", hex($1))/eg;
    $value =~ s/~!/ ~!/g;
    $FORM{$name} = $value;
}

print "Content-type: text/html\n\n";

open (MAIL,"| /usr/sbin/sendmail -oi -t");
print MAIL "From: $FORM{'name'} <$FORM{'e-mail'}>\n";
print MAIL "To: you\@your.hostname.com\n";
print MAIL "Subject: Form output\n\n";
print MAIL "$FORM{'name'}, from $ENV{'REMOTE_HOST'} ($ENV{'REMOTE_ADDR'}), has
sent you the following comment:\n\n";
print MAIL "$FORM{'comment'}\n";
close (MAIL);

print qq^<HTML>\n<HEAD>\n<TITLE>Thank you!</TITLE></HEAD>\n^;
print qq^<BODY><H3>Thank you!</H3>\nThanks for your
comments!</H3>\n</BODY>\n</HTML>^;
```

You'll want to tune this script to your own needs—replace the dummy To: header with one that mails to your real e-mail address, making sure to keep the backslash in front of the @ symbol. This example script doesn't do very much in and of itself, but after some experimentation you'll find that the basic principles we've covered here form the heart of server-side programs, from the smallest feedback forms to the largest online databases and e-commerce systems.

A CGI program does not have to be called from an HTML form or with the POST method. You can use a direct URL to call a CGI script that doesn't need to have any variables posted directly into an associative array such as %FORM. Such a URL would look like this:

```
http://www.somewhere.com/cgi-bin/sysinfo?frank+3
```

This URL calls the sysinfo program in the /cgi-bin/ directory. Everything after the question mark is known as the *query string*, and its contents are available to the script as elements of the @ARGV array. Arguments are separated by plus signs (+). The sysinfo program would have the string frank available as $ARGV[0] and the number 3 as $ARGV[1].

> **Tip**
>
> You can also access the entire query string as the environment variable QUERY_STRING, or $ENV{'QUERY_STRING'} in Perl.

CHAPTER 27

Configuring an FTP Server

Once the foremost method of transferring files from one point in the Internet to another, the File Transfer Protocol (FTP) is now becoming eclipsed by the more glamorous and versatile HTTP. However, although FTP is a very rudimentary protocol, it is designed more specifically for large file transfer than HTTP is, and therefore is able to do a number of things that HTTP cannot. FTP's prevalence is fading, but it will always have a place in the Internet, as long as such services as authenticated downloads and two-way transfers are needed.

FreeBSD comes with an FTP server built in, and you can replace it with a different server if you desire. The built-in one is quite complete and secure and it allows you to transfer files to and from your FreeBSD machine without any additional setup. The default configuration of the FTP server is quite basic though, and in order to take advantage of the more advanced features available to us, we will have to examine some details about how the FTP protocol works.

Introduction to the FTP Protocol

To the uninitiated, FTP and HTTP seem to be quite similar. Both allow file transfers, both support a form of user authentication, and the two protocols often appear to be used interchangeably on the Web—a binary package or large multimedia file might be linked from a Web site via either the `http://` or the `ftp://` protocols, which seem to do the same thing with regard to downloading the file to your computer. However, a little further investigation shows us that the two protocols are designed for considerably different purposes, and therefore support widely different feature sets. Table 27.1 shows a contrast of these crucial areas of difference.

TABLE 27.1 Comparison of FTP and HTTP Functionality

Feature	FTP	HTTP
Session-based	Yes	No
User authentication built in	Yes	No
Primarily intended for transferring	Large binary files	Small text files
Connection model	Dual connection	Single connection
Primarily geared toward download/upload	Both	Download
Supports ASCII and binary transfer modes	Yes	No
Supports content typing (MIME headers)	No	Yes
Supports file system operations (`mkdir`, `rm`, `rename`, and so on)	Yes	No

The biggest difference between FTP and HTTP is that FTP is session-based, meaning that a complete connection is initiated between the client and server, multiple commands are sent back and forth, and finally, the client terminates the connection by choice. (HTTP, as you will recall, is a stateless protocol—a single request, followed by a single or pipelined response, comprises the whole HTTP "session.") FTP goes even beyond a single connection, as a matter of fact. A complete FTP session contains two connections: one for passing commands and status messages back and forth ("control connection"), and another to handle the actual file transfers ("data connection"). Figure 27.1 shows a diagram of a complete FTP connection.

FIGURE 27.1

An FTP session, with both the control and data connections established.

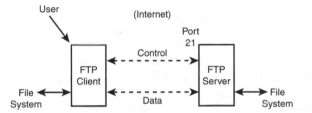

An FTP client, such as the `ftp` command built in to FreeBSD, opens the control connection to TCP port 21 on the FTP server. This connection remains open throughout the session. When the user enters a command, such as `ls` or `get picture1.gif`, the client and server negotiate a pair of TCP ports between which they will open the data connection, which exists for as long as the response listing or file is being transferred, after which it is closed. A separate data connection is opened for each such transfer. A complete typical FTP session is shown in Listing 27.1.

LISTING 27.1   A Command-Line FTP Session

```
# ftp spots.somewhere.com
Connected to spots.somewhere.com.
220 spots.somewhere.com FTP server (Version 6.00LS) ready.
Name (spots.somewhere.com:frank):
331 Password required for frank.
Password:
230 User frank logged in.
Remote system type is UNIX.
Using binary mode to transfer files.
ftp> cd mydir
250 CWD command successful.
```

LISTING 27.1   continued

```
ftp> ls
150 Opening ASCII mode data connection for '/bin/ls'.
total 484
-rw-r--r--  1 frank   frank     43175 Apr  8 01:14 addresses.txt
-rw-r--r--  1 frank   frank    100523 Apr  8 01:14 contents.html
-rw-r--r--  1 frank   frank     37864 Apr  8 01:14 directions
-rw-r--r--  1 frank   frank     37308 Apr  8 01:14 lk_logo.gif
-rw-r--r--  1 frank   frank     52427 Apr  8 01:12 picture1.gif
-rw-r--r--  1 frank   frank     18648 Apr 24 13:04 picture2.jpg
-rw-r--r--  1 frank   frank    175325 Apr  8 01:14 resume.html
226 Transfer complete.
ftp> get picture1.gif
local: picture1.gif remote: picture1.gif
150 Opening BINARY mode data connection for 'picture1.gif' (52427 bytes).
100% |**************************************************| 52427        00:00 ETA
226 Transfer complete.
52427 bytes received in 4.99 seconds (10.25 KB/s)
ftp> quit
221 Goodbye.
```

The first part of the connection is a username and password authentication stage, just as you would get in a Telnet connection. Unlike HTTP user authentication, which is actually a function of Apache and not of HTTP itself and requires Apache's own user databases to be separately maintained, FTP user authentication operates directly on a user's account information on the machine running the FTP server. FTP operates very much like Telnet in this regard. In order to log in via FTP, the user must either have a valid user account on the server machine, or must log in via "anonymous FTP" if the server allows it—a common practice that we will cover later in this chapter.

A number of user commands are available in FTP, behaving in much the same way as their familiar shell counterparts: ls, cd, mkdir, pwd, and so on. These commands help you navigate through the directory structure and modify remote files as if they were on the local (client) machine. There is also an lcd command that allows you to change directories on the client machine, in case you want to download a file to a different location from the one where you started the FTP program. Additionally, there are the put (upload), get (download), mput (multiple upload), and mget (multiple download) commands, which control the file transfers themselves. These user commands are translated into client commands (such as RETR, STOR, CWD, and LIST) that the FTP server understands, responding with three-digit response codes much as in HTTP. The meanings of the response codes aren't especially important to know, so we won't cover them here. See man ftpd if you're interested in seeing the complete list of FTP client commands.

> **Note**
>
> FTP file transfers can be done in one of two modes: ASCII (plain text, in which all data is transferred as alphanumeric characters and end-of-line symbols are translated to whatever the client's platform uses, such as CR/LF for DOS/Windows, CR for Macintosh, and LF for UNIX) or Binary (a stream of untranslated data). Some FTP clients, such as the built-in FreeBSD one, automatically detect which type is appropriate and then switch to that mode when the transfer begins. Other clients require that you select either ASCII or Binary mode before transferring files. Use the bin and asc commands to switch modes.
>
> It's very important, especially when transferring files from one platform to another, to use ASCII mode to transfer plain-text files such as HTML pages and Perl scripts. This ensures that end-of-line characters are translated properly. Binary mode can cause Perl scripts to fail to run if uploaded from a non-UNIX client. Binary mode, however, is necessary for images, executables, and any other kind of binary data; binary files transferred in ASCII mode will be corrupted on the destination machine.

The default FTP server that ships with FreeBSD, which we will be covering in this chapter, is the standard BSD ftpd daemon. It runs from within the inetd super-server, like telnetd and Qpopper, not as a standalone daemon. It lacks a few features supported by some of its alternatives (such as WU-FTPD and ProFTPD), but it also lacks a number of security holes that are inevitable with more complex software. We will be taking a closer look at these alternative daemons at the end of this chapter; meanwhile, let's see how to make the most of the FreeBSD FTP server.

Overview of the FTP Directory Structure

Unless you've enabled anonymous FTP logins, which we will discuss how to set up a little later, the file layout of the FTP server is very simple and integrated with the system in the same way that most other core services are. There are several configuration files in /etc, some of which do double duty as system-wide resource files used by other services. Individual users' home directories are considered part of the FTP server layout, since each authenticated user connects directly into his or her home directory.

If you've enabled anonymous FTP, there's a server root area just as in Apache; this is created at the time when you elect to enable anonymous FTP, as we will see. The default location for the FTP server root is /var/ftp, and there are several subdirectories that exist to help the server manage FTP users who don't actually have user accounts on the system.

Authenticated and Anonymous FTP

When a user who has an account on the server logs in via FTP with his or her username and password, the server provides access to the user's home directory and all its files. The user can enter an ls command to verify this. Each regular user thus connects into a different point on the FTP server when logging in as a user: his or her home directory. However, anonymous FTP provides a way for a user without an account to connect. An anonymous user opens the connection, enters anonymous or ftp as his or her username, and any text string (conventionally the user's e-mail address, though this isn't enforced or authenticated in any way) for the password. The user is then given access to a "public" FTP area: /var/ftp, the home directory of the ftp user (which is also created when anonymous FTP is enabled).

There's a fundamental difference between regular account users and anonymous FTP users, though. Anonymous FTP is in a chroot "jail" by default, meaning that to the user, /var/ftp appears to be the server root /. Nothing outside /var/ftp is accessible or even visible. A regular account user can enter a command such as cd /usr/local to move to any part of the system and access files with the same readability permissions as in a terminal session, but an anonymous FTP user can't get out of /var/ftp at all. An anonymous user who enters cd /pub will be taken to /var/ftp/pub.

You can specify additional users who must be "chrooted" in the same way as anonymous FTP logins by adding them to the /etc/ftpchroot file. That's just one example of the configuration files that control the FTP server.

Configuring the FTP Server

The FTP service involves a fairly large number of configuration files; some of them exist in /etc, and some are in /var/ftp/etc. The reason for this is that some of the files have to be accessible by anonymous FTP users, and, as we've seen, such users can't see any files outside of /var/ftp. Let's look at a few of the files in /etc, which apply globally to the FTP server as a whole.

- /etc/ftpusers. A "blacklist" of users who are disallowed FTP access. Add usernames to this file to prevent them from logging in via FTP.

- /etc/ftpchroot. Any users listed in this file will be placed in a chroot "jail" similar to that of anonymous FTP, limiting the user's access solely to his home directory.

- /etc/ftphosts. Allows you to configure virtual hosts, much like with Apache (as we saw in Chapter 26, "Configuring a Web Server"). We will discuss virtual hosting in more detail later.

- /etc/ftpwelcome. A welcome notice. The contents of this file are displayed to everyone who connects, immediately after the connection is opened, before the login prompt.

- /etc/ftpmotd. A second welcome notice ("Message Of The Day"); this one appears after a regular account user has logged in.

- /etc/shells. We encountered this file in Chapter 12, "Customizing the Shell." Its purpose is to ensure that anybody logging in to the system has a valid shell, thus preventing people from logging in to accounts such as bin, tty, and nobody, which don't have shells listed in this file.

Beyond the config files in /etc, there are a number of additional files that control anonymous FTP. These aren't just config files, either. If /var/ftp is mapped to / for anonymous users, that means the tools in the system binary directories (such as /bin) are as inaccessible as the files in /etc. The FTP server relics on a few system tools—notably /bin/ls and /bin/date—to generate file listings to send to the client. These tools have to available to anonymous users, too; that's what the /var/ftp/bin directory is for.

The /var/ftp tree contains the following files and directories. Any anonymous user can see these files, but none of them are inherently "dangerous" for users to see (the /var/ftp/etc files don't contain any passwords, for example).

- /var/ftp/bin. This directory contains ls and date executables. These are provided because they're necessary for the FTP server to be able to generate directory listings, and the system /bin/ls and /bin/date programs are not available if you've configured the server to chroot, or limited the anonymous FTP user's access, to within /var/ftp. (This is the default behavior.)

- /var/ftp/etc/passwd, /var/ftp/etc/group. As with the tools in /var/ftp/bin, these are copies of the default /etc/passwd and /etc/group, whose purpose is to provide file ownership mappings during directory listings. Since anonymous FTP access is limited to what's in /var/ftp, these files must exist in order to show who owns the various files in /var/ftp. Typically, any files in the public FTP area will be owned by root or another system account because they will be put there by you as the administrator. Other usernames, because they don't exist in /var/ftp/etc/passwd, will not be mapped and will appear to FTP users as raw UIDs for files owned by them.

- /var/ftp/etc/ftpmotd. Operates the same way as /etc/ftpmotd, except that this one is displayed to anonymous FTP users instead of regular login users. From their perspective (with the chroot making /var/ftp appear to be / to them), this *is* /etc/ftpmotd.

- /var/ftp/pub. Visible to anonymous FTP users as /pub, this is where all down-loadable files should go. The hierarchy under /pub is up to you to determine, but convention says at least that /pub should contain everything that's meant to be of interest to the public.

- /var/ftp/incoming. This optional directory has world-writable permissions with the "sticky bit" set (1777). This means that any anonymous user can upload files into this directory. This can be dangerous; having an open upload directory is an invitation for people to use it as a trading point for MP3 files and pirated software. Use this option only if you really need to!

One final configuration file that concerns the FTP server is /etc/inetd.conf. As we have mentioned, ftpd runs as a subsidiary to the inetd super-server, and as such it won't work if inetd isn't running. First, use ps to check to see if the daemon is serving requests:

```
# ps -waux | grep inetd
root    1640  0.0  0.6  1048   780  ??  Ss   Thu08PM    0:00.15 inetd -Ww
```

If you don't see the inetd process running, you may have turned it off in /etc/rc.conf; check there for the inetd_enable="NO" line, and remove or disable it if it's present. Second, open up /etc/inetd.conf, and make sure the ftpd service is enabled:

```
ftp     stream  tcp     nowait  root    /usr/libexec/ftpd       ftpd -l
```

If this line is commented out, uncomment it, and restart inetd (using the killall -HUP inetd command). Check your configuration by trying to connect to the server (ftp localhost). If you are presented with a login prompt, you're in business. If not, look over the preceding steps again; kill inetd completely, and restart it if necessary.

Controlling FTP Access

FTP access is not something you should enable lightly; although it's crucial for your users to have access to it for uploading files (such as Web pages) to your server, it's also a potential source of security issues—it's a cleartext mechanism, meaning that all data (including passwords) is transmitted unencrypted and available to anybody eavesdropping with packet-sniffing software. As we will see in Chapter 29, "Network Security," most major cleartext services can be superseded by a secure equivalent: Telnet with SSH, HTTP with Secure HTTP, and POP3 and IMAP with their own built-in encryption layers.

FTP, however, is inherently insecure, and although several secure solutions have been put forth (such as Brian Wellington's `sftp` and corresponding `sftpd`), unencrypted FTP holds out as the last widely used insecure data transfer protocol, difficult to replace and a virtual requirement for a fully functional server. We will talk more about how to secure it in Chapter 29; meanwhile, be aware that special care must be taken when enabling FTP access to your users to ensure your system's security.

With this in mind, we need a way to lock out certain users from being able to connect to the system via FTP. This can be done in a number of ways. The two most convenient involve the `/etc/ftpusers` and `/etc/shells` files. A third, `/var/run/nologin`, controls whether the server accepts connections at all.

The `/etc/ftpusers` File

The simplest way to forbid a certain individual user or a group of users from connecting to the FTP server is to add that user's login name to the `/etc/ftpusers` file, which exists in the default FreeBSD installation and contains the names of the various system pseudo-users (such as `operator`, `bin`, `tty`, and so on). These users have null passwords, and `ftpd` will not allow anyone with a null password to connect; keeping the usernames in `/etc/ftpusers` provides an extra layer of security.

You can add any username to the file, and because `ftpd` reads all relevant configuration files with each new connection, there's no need to restart any processes. Try connecting to the FTP server as a disallowed user, and you should get a response like the following:

```
# ftp localhost
Connected to localhost.somewhere.com.
220 stripes.somewhere.com FTP server (Version 6.00LS) ready.
Name (localhost:frank):
530 User frank access denied.
ftp: Login failed.
ftp>
```

27

CONFIGURING AN
FTP SERVER

> **Note**
>
> Note that the `access denied` message appears immediately after the server receives the username—it doesn't prompt for a password. This prevents passwords from being sent over the wire, providing an extra security precaution in the case that you've disabled a user out of concern regarding an eavesdropper sniffing for passwords.

You can also add any group name to /etc/ftpusers; simply precede the name with an "at" symbol (@); for example, @users. Any user who is part of any group listed in the file will be disallowed access.

The /etc/shells File

After seeing whether the user is listed in /etc/ftpusers, ftpd checks the shell associated with the user, and sees whether it's listed in /etc/shells. If it isn't, the user will get the same kind of access denied message as with /etc/ftpusers. You can leverage this functionality to prevent a user from logging in with a terminal program or with FTP, by changing the user's shell to /sbin/nologin (which we saw in Chapter 12—it simply prints out an account not available message and exits, and is not listed in /etc/shells) or something similarly constructed.

The /var/run/nologin File

To turn off FTP logins completely, without modifying /etc/inetd.conf or any other such config files, you can simply place a file called nologin in /var/run; if ftpd sees this file, it will respond to all connections as follows:

```
# ftp localhost
Connected to localhost.somewhere.com.
530 System not available.
ftp>
```

You can use touch /var/run/nologin to create the file (with zero length) and disable FTP logins. Remove the file (rm /var/run/nologin) to re-enable the FTP server.

Allowing Anonymous FTP Access

By default, anonymous FTP is not enabled; the easiest way to enable it, if you choose to do so, is through sysinstall. Run /stand/sysinstall; then enter the Configure and Networking sections. Scroll to the Anon FTP option, and press the spacebar to enter the Anonymous FTP Configuration screen, shown in Figure 27.2.

The default options are generally appropriate for a typical FreeBSD system. The UID, Group, and Comment fields control how the new ftp user will be created. This user's home directory is set to /var/ftp, which is how anonymous FTP works—the ftp login is treated as a regular user that behaves as if it's listed in /etc/ftpchroot, so anybody logging in as ftp (or its alias, anonymous) will be put into a chroot jail at /var/ftp.

FIGURE 27.2

Anonymous FTP configuration options.

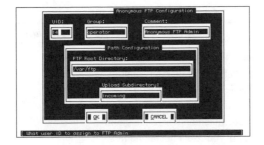

You can change any of the fields to suit your system (for instance, if you already have a user with a UID of 14, or if you want a name for the upload directory that's different from incoming). When you select OK at the bottom of the screen, the ftp user will be created, as will the /var/ftp tree with its necessary subdirectories.

/stand/sysinstall doesn't provide the capability to disable anonymous FTP after it's been enabled, but you can do this a number of ways:

- Remove the /var/ftp tree.
- Remove the ftp user.
- Add the ftp user to /etc/ftpusers (probably the easiest and cleanest method).

Similarly, you can disable the upload (incoming) directory by simply removing it, or else by changing its permissions to 755 (the default directory permissions, in which only the owner—root—can write into it). Re-enable it (or any other directory to which you want anonymous users to be able to upload files) by changing its permissions to 1777—for instance, chmod 1777 /var/ftp/incoming.

Virtual Hosting

If you have multiple IP addresses bound to your machine, you can map different FTP server behaviors to each one. This virtual hosting mechanism is controlled with the /etc/ftphosts file, which does not exist in the default FreeBSD system (you need to create it).

Each virtual host is defined on its own line, with fields specifying alternate config files for each host separated by whitespace. Table 27.2 describes the various fields, their meanings, and the default values (the ones that the server uses without an /etc/ftphosts file present).

TABLE 27.2   Virtual Hosting Table Fields in /etc/ftphosts

Field	Description	Default
Hostname	The hostname or IP address of the virtual host. Note that FTP has no equivalent of the Host: header of HTTP/1.1, so FTP virtual hosts are defined purely on the IP address of your machine where the client is connected. If you use a hostname in this field, ftpd uses the IP address to which it resolves. Bear this in mind when adding virtual hosts.	N/A
User	The user whose home directory is used for anonymous FTP access in this virtual host. Anonymous users are jailed (via chroot) into this directory, so equivalents of /var/ftp/etc and /var/ftp/bin should be present.	ftp
Statfile	The log file that tracks all FTP transfers for the virtual host.	/var/log/ftpd
Welcome	The welcome message displayed upon the initial connection to the FTP server.	/etc/ftpwelcome
MOTD	The second welcome message, presented after a successful user login.	/etc/ftpmotd

A few example virtual hosts in /etc/ftphosts follow. If a field is left blank or has a hyphen (-), the default value is used.

```
64.41.131.106      frank   /var/log/ftpd-frank   /home/frank/welcome
/home/frank/welcome2
ftp2.somewhere.com ftp2    -                     /etc/ftpd2welcome   -
64.41.131.107      ftp3    /var/log/ftpd-3       -                   -
```

Using Alternate FTP Servers

Many alternate FTP server packages exist; the two most popular are Washington University's WU-FTP and the highly configurable ProFTPD.

WU-FTPD

Originally developed at Washington University to host what was once one of the most popular file-sharing and distribution locations on the Internet, the WUarchive,

WU-FTPD, has gained in popularity to become the most frequently used FTP server in the world. It's the default FTP daemon in Linux and many commercial UNIX brands; its configuration differs from FreeBSD's default `ftpd` in a few subtle ways, but it has a few features that our `ftpd` does not, such as a configuration checking tool, on-the-fly compression and archiving, and limitations on access and transfers by time and date. You might choose to install WU-FTPD to maintain compatibility with an existing non-FreeBSD system.

WU-FTPD is available as a package or in the ports (`/usr/ports/ftp/wu-ftpd`). After installing it, you can switch to it from the FreeBSD `ftpd` by commenting out the `ftp` line in `/etc/inetd.conf` and replacing it with one that points to the new `ftpd`:

```
ftp     stream  tcp     nowait  root    /usr/local/libexec/ftpd ftpd -l
#ftp    stream  tcp     nowait  root    /usr/libexec/ftpd       ftpd -l
```

27

CONFIGURING AN
FTP SERVER

> ### Tip
>
> WU-FTPD is installed as `/usr/local/libexec/ftpd`, and its man page can't be accessed directly with `man ftpd`—you'll get the page for the default system `ftpd`. To see the correct page, use the `-M` option to use an alternate man path:
> `man -M /usr/local/man ftpd`

More information on WU-FTPD is available at `http://www.wu-ftpd.org`.

ProFTPD

ProFTPD was developed with the intention of creating an FTP server that could be managed with configuration files that resembled those of Apache. The server's config file has hierarchical configuration blocks like those in `httpd.conf` (as we saw in Chapter 26) and directives that are similar in style to those of Apache. The result is a server that has very Apache-like, access-limiting features; and has a high level of configurability, especially for administrators familiar at all with Apache. It's available as a package or from the ports (`/usr/ports/ftp/proftpd`).

One difference between ProFTPD and its relatives is that it can be run in standalone mode, like Apache, rather than from `inetd`. If you do run it from `inetd`, replace the default `ftp` line with one pointing to `/usr/local/libexec/proftpd`:

```
ftp     stream  tcp     nowait  root    /usr/local/libexec/proftpd      proftpd
#ftp    stream  tcp     nowait  root    /usr/libexec/ftpd       ftpd -l
```

The ProFTPD home page, `http://www.proftpd.org`, has much more information on its capabilities and configuration directives.

CHAPTER 28

Configuring an Internet Gateway

Routing and gateways were covered briefly in Chapter 22, "Introduction to Networking," as was the concept of NAT (network address translation). Chapter 23, "Configuring Basic Networking Services," also covered routing a little bit, but mostly in the context of configuring a host to use a router. This chapter will cover how to configure FreeBSD to serve as a router or a gateway. It will also cover how to set up network address translation. We will start with a few short definitions of each of the items we will be discussing.

What Is a Router?

Like its name suggests, a *router* is a network device that determines how datagrams sent over the network get to their final destination. This is a very simple definition. A more accurate definition is that a router connects two networks together, and determines how datagrams get from one network to another.

> **Note**
>
> A *datagram* is a packet of digital information. A datagram contains addressing information, as well as the data to be transmitted. Not all datagrams necessarily take the same route to get to their destinations, even if they all have the same origin.

To better understand what a router does, look at the following two figures. Figure 28.1 shows two sample networks for a fictional global company that has offices in New York and Denmark.

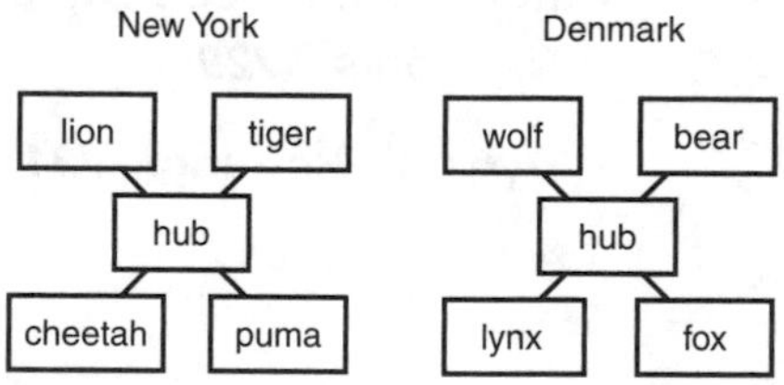

FIGURE 28.1

A sample global network for a fictional company. There are several hosts in its New York office, and several hosts in its Denmark office.

In the network in Figure 28.1, the hosts named lion, cheetah, tiger, and puma all know about the existence of each other, and can communicate with each other at the New York Office. And the hosts named wolf, bear, fox, and lynx all know about each other, and can communicate with each other at the Denmark office. The problem here is that the networks are isolated. None of the hosts in the New York office know anything at all about any of the hosts in the Denmark office, and vice versa. There is no way for network information to travel between the two offices. In order for data to be able to flow between these two offices, we need to install a couple of routers. Figure 28.2 shows the same network, but this time we have installed a router at each office.

FIGURE 28.2

The same network as shown in Figure 28.1, except that in this one, there is a router installed on each end of the network.

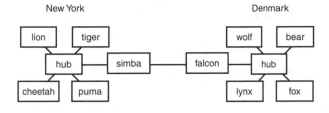

After the router is installed, one change needs to be made to the hosts on the network: They simply need to be told about the existence of the router in the office. (See Chapter 23 for information on how to tell the hosts about the existence of the router.)

So what has changed about this setup? Well, the hosts in the New York office still know nothing at all about the hosts in the Denmark office, and the reverse is also true. But there is one very important difference. The hosts in the network now know about the existence of the router in their office. If each host is configured to use this router as the default router, any outgoing traffic it has for a host that it knows nothing about, will simply be sent to the router. The router then worries about routing the network traffic to the correct destination.

For example, suppose that cheetah wants to establish a network connection with lynx. As mentioned before, cheetah knows nothing about the existence of lynx. So, when cheetah generates traffic to lynx, it will simply pass it off to simba, which is the router in the New York office. simba does know about the existence of lynx, and it also knows that it can get network traffic to lynx by passing it to the router in Denmark (falcon). The router in Denmark than sends the traffic to lynx.

This is a very simple example. In a real scenario (especially when sending transoceanic network traffic), there will usually be several routers involved, each passing the traffic to another until it gets to the proper destination. If you want an analogy, you can think of routers as being like air traffic controllers, and network traffic as being like aircraft. An aircraft in route from New York to Denmark will be handed off between several different air traffic controllers until it finally reaches its destination.

28

CONFIGURING AN
INTERNET
GATEWAY

Okay. So why do we need a router? Why not just tell the hosts in New York about the hosts in Denmark, and vice versa, so that they can communicate with each other directly? There are two primary reasons why it is not done this way:

- **Ease of maintenance**. This might not seem like a big deal when dealing with only eight systems. But now think of a network the size of the Internet. Without routers, every single system connected to the network would have to know how to contact every other system on the network. Obviously, when you are dealing with millions of systems, that would quickly become a maintenance nightmare.

- **Reducing traffic congestion**. If the two offices were just connected by one big network, then all network traffic would have to be sent to all computers. If, for example, lion sends network traffic to cheetah (both in the New York Office), this traffic would also get sent through the pipe, across the Atlantic Ocean, and into the Denmark office. This would occur even though the hosts in Denmark couldn't care less about this traffic since it is not for them. Imagine the network congestion if any time any host on the Internet sent network traffic to another host, it had to also go to every single other host on the Internet. And besides that, transoceanic leased lines are expensive—you are usually charged by the amount of bandwidth you use. That means you don't want to use the line when you don't have to. The router acts as a "door" that keeps traffic intended for one of the local hosts inside the local network. Only traffic not intended for one of the local hosts will be sent outside of the local network. (This also increases security since you don't have internal network traffic being broadcast over the Internet and such.

What Is a Gateway?

In general network terminology, a *gateway* is a router that allows the rest of the clients on the internal LAN to access the outside world, hence the name "gateway." Because of this, the terms "default router" and "gateway" are virtually interchangeable in most networking circles these days. In our example in the previous section, the routers simba and falcon could be called gateways.

If you want to get really technical, the definition of a gateway just given is not correct. According to the technical definition, a gateway is a router that can route between two different types of networks. However, virtually no one goes by this definition anymore, so we are not going to, either. Instead, we will use the commonly accepted definition throughout this chapter, and the terms "default router" and "gateway" will be used interchangeably.

One of the most common uses of a gateway is to allow multiple hosts to share a single Internet connection.

What Is NAT?

NAT, which stands for *Network Address Translation*, is a way for multiple hosts to connect to the Internet using a single IP address. The magic involved in how this works is beyond the scope of this book, but basically NAT works by having a NAT gateway attached to the network in question. When the internal hosts want to send or receive Internet content, their request goes through the NAT gateway. The NAT gateway "hides" the internal IP address, and sends all requests from the hosts connected to it out on the Internet with a single IP address (which is the IP address owned by the NAT gateway). Responses that are sent back are sent to that single IP address (which is owned by the NAT gateway). The NAT gateway then routes the data to the proper internal host, which does not need to have a registered IP address. There are two primary advantages of this method:

- It conserves IP addresses. The IP address pool is a limited resource. And there is no reason to waste IP addresses where they are not needed. NAT prevents you from having to register an IP address for each one of your systems.

- If you are a home or small office user, it allows you to share a single Internet connection with multiple computers, and you won't have to purchase additional accounts from your ISP. You can also share a single modem and a single phone line, preventing you from having to install additional phone lines if more than one computer will use the Internet at the same time.

We will look at a few scenarios in this chapter of ways to configure various types of routing services on FreeBSD. We will start by looking at sharing a single modem and Internet connection at home or in a small office.

Configuring a NAT Gateway in FreeBSD

In this scenario, you will generally have a single Internet connection, which may or may not be over a modem. You have several systems that need to access the Internet. Figure 28.3 shows an example.

A variation of this system might be that you have a classroom, and you want to provide laptops with wireless Internet access. This will also be discussed later on in this section because it is just a variation of a NAT Gateway.

FIGURE 28.3

A simple gateway setup. simba has a connection to the Internet via a modem. The idea is to allow lion, tiger, cheetah, *and* puma *to share this modem and access the Internet through* simba.

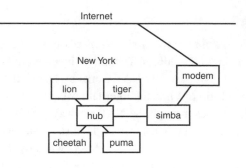

In this type of setup, your system will have two network interfaces in it. For example, ppp0 will be the modem interface. It is the interface to the Internet. The other interface will usually be an Ethernet interface (for example, ed0). This interface will be the interface to the internal network. The job of the gateway is to act as a "door" between these two interfaces by passing packets back and forth between them. It connects the Internet with your internal network. When traffic comes in from the Internet over interface ppp0, it will be passed to interface ed0 to be sent to the proper host on the network. When outgoing traffic for a host on the Internet arrives from a host on the local network through ed0, it will be passed to the ppp0 interface so that it can be sent out over the Internet to the remote destination. Before this can occur, however, you need to enable packet forwarding so that network traffic can flow between the two interfaces.

Enabling Packet Forwarding

In order for your system to act as a gateway, it must be able to forward packets between network interfaces. Your system will be handling incoming and outgoing Internet traffic for other computers on your network so when the system receives a packet that is not addressed to it, it needs to forward it to the correct destination. By default (and to conform with Internet standards), packet forwarding is turned off, so FreeBSD will drop any packet it receives that is not addressed to the system it is running on.

You can enable packet forwarding in one of two ways. The first goes through the Sysinstall program. However, it is easier to do it manually since only one line needs to be added to a single file to enable packet forwarding. The manual method is the one we will cover here.

Open the file /etc/rc.conf in your favorite text editor, and add the following line:

```
gateway_enable="YES"
```

Once you have restarted the system, packet forwarding will be enabled, and the system can now forward packets between interfaces.

If all of the systems on your network have real static IP addresses, this is all you need to do. You can now configure the other systems on the network to use the host `simba` as their gateway. These hosts in turn will send any traffic that they do not know how to deliver to the system that is configured as the default gateway. The default gateway system will then worry about handling this traffic.

> **Note**
>
> This section and the ones that follow assume that you already have a working Internet connection on the system that you wish to configure as the gateway to the Internet. If this is not the case, please see Chapter 23 for setting up network access on a LAN (this chapter also applies to you if you are accessing the Internet through ADSL or a cable modem). If you need to configure an Internet connection over a modem, please see Chapter 24, "Connecting to the Internet with PPP" for more information on setting up a modem Internet connection.

Most of the time, however, if you are configuring an Internet gateway, the other systems on the network will not have a real IP address that is registered. Instead, they will just be using internal IP addresses. In this case, you still have a little more work to do. You will have to enable NAT for these other systems to be able to access the Internet.

Enabling NAT

If you are using PPP over a dial-up Internet connection, the method used to enable NAT will depend on whether you are using User PPP or Kernel PPP. If you have not set up an Internet connection yet, I recommend you use User PPP if you want to use NAT because it is the easier of the two to configure to work with NAT.

If you are using Kernel PPP, or you need to set up NAT for an Internet connection that is not PPP, the procedure is a bit more complex.

The NAT setup procedure has been divided into two sections below. You only need to read the section appropriate to your situation.

Using User PPP

The User PPP program in FreeBSD has NAT capability built in to it, so it is very easy to enable. You can simply use the -nat option to ppp to enable NAT. Simply add it to whatever other options you are currently using to start PPP (see Chapter 24 for more details).

The only other thing you should need to do is configure your Windows, Macintosh, or other client to use the new gateway server. This will be covered later on in this chapter in the "Client Configuration" section.

Using Kernel PPP or a Dedicated Ethernet Connection to the Internet

If you are using kernel PPP, or you have a dedicated Internet connection (ADSL, cable, T1, OC3, etc.), the configuration is a little more complicated. In this case, you will need to use the NAT daemon (natd), which requires a firewall in order to work. To enable the firewall, you will need to build a new kernel. This is not difficult to do, however. You can simply add the following two lines to your kernel configuration file:

```
options IPFIREWALL
options IPDIVERT
```

There are various other options that can also be added to the kernel configuration file that have to do with the firewall—such as logging. A detailed discussion of firewalls is beyond the scope of this chapter, but you may want to read the "Configuring a Firewall" section of Chapter 29, "Network Security," before you build a new kernel with firewall support. This way, you won't have to build yet another kernel if you later decide you want another option for the firewall that you didn't include in the kernel the first time around.

Also, if you are unclear about how to build a new kernel, see Chapter 17, "Kernel Configuration," for more details.

Once you have finished building a new kernel, you will need to enable natd.

Configuring and Enabling natd

natd can be enabled either by configuring network settings in Sysinstall, or by manually editing the /etc/rc.conf file. Once again, if you already have basic networking set up, it is easier to simply make the necessary changes manually rather than go through Sysinstall, so this is the method we are going to cover here.

Open the file `/etc/rc.conf` in your favorite text editor, and add the following lines:

```
natd_enable="YES"
natd_interface="ppp0"
```

The `natd_interface` in the previous example assumes that you have a modem connection to the Internet and that it is on the interface `ppp0`. If you have a dedicated connection over an Ethernet device (such as ADSL, cable, T1, or OC3), you should replace `ppp0` with whatever network interface your connection to the outside world runs on.

There are a few other options to `natd` that control things such as logging. If you are interested in the other options, see the man page for `natd`.

Don't exit and save the modified `rc.conf` file yet because there is at least one more option you have to add. This has to do with the firewall.

Enabling and Configuring the Firewall

At a minimum, you will need to add the following line to `/etc/rc.conf` to enable the firewall:

```
firewall_enable="YES"
```

There are various ways to configure the firewall rules, and you should see Chapter 29 for full details. But here is a quick description of my preferred method.

In addition to the previous line, add the following line to `/etc/rc.conf`:

```
firewall_type="/usr/local/etc/firewall.conf"
```

Save the changes you made to `/etc/rc.conf`, and exit your editor. You can then create the file `/usr/local/etc/firewall.conf`, in which you simply put the firewall rules (except for the default rule, which by default will deny anything that is not specifically allowed—see Chapter 29 for more details).

If you do not want to deny any types of network traffic, and simply want to pass everything through, the following rules will work in `/usr/local/etc/firewall.conf`:

```
add divert natd all from any to any via ed0
add allow all from any to any
```

This will basically have the same effect as not having a firewall at all since it simply passes all traffic and doesn't deny anything.

It can be a security hazard to allow people to see the firewall rules that your system is using, so you should set the permissions on the file so that only root can read it. The command `chmod 600 /usr/local/etc/firewall.conf` will do the trick.

> **Caution**
>
> The firewall rules described previously are very insecure since they allow all types of network traffic from any source, and will happily pass that content to any one of the systems that is using this gateway. This compromises the security of your network. Because of this, allowing all traffic is not recommended. You should see the section "Configuring a Firewall" in Chapter 29 for information on how to configure the firewall to block potentially dangerous types of traffic.

Once you have completed all the previous steps, reboot the system for the kernel changes to take effect and for the firewall and `natd` to load. Your gateway should now be configured. The only thing left to do is inform the clients of the existence of the gateway. The configuration of various clients will be covered below. For client types that are not covered, please see your system documentation.

Configuring Clients to Use the New Gateway

The procedures for configuring a client to use the gateway vary, depending on the type of operating system you are running. We will cover configuring Windows, Macintosh, FreeBSD, and Linux clients below.

Note that all of the following configuration instructions assume that you already have basic networking configured, and will just show you how to set up the system to use the gateway. If you do not have basic networking configured on the system yet, see the documentation for your system for instructions on how to do this.

Configuring Windows 95/98 Clients

To configure a Windows 95 or 98 client to use the gateway, double-click the My Computer icon, double-click Control Panel, and double-click Network. This will bring up the dialog box shown in Figure 28.4.

From this dialog box, click TCP/IP and then click the Properties button. This will take you to the TCP/IP configuration dialog box. Click on the Gateway tab, and you will be given the dialog box shown in Figure 28.5.

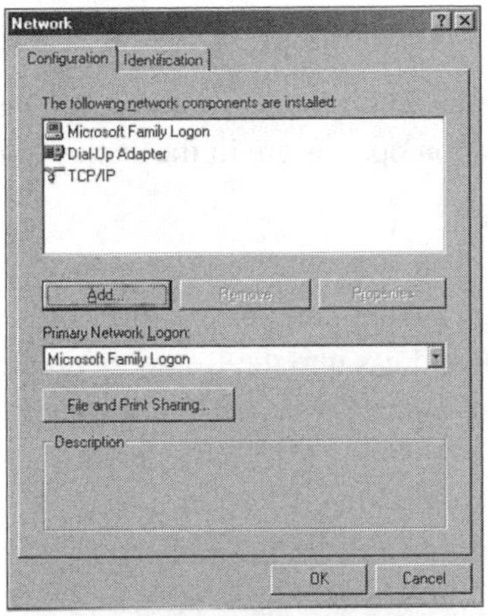

FIGURE 28.4

The Network Configuration dialog box in Windows 98. Windows 95 and Windows ME may look slightly different.

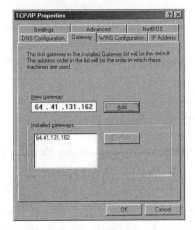

FIGURE 28.5

The Gateway configuration tab and its dialog box in Windows 98.

Simply enter the IP address of the gateway in the New gateway box, as shown. (Assuming, in this case, that the IP address of the gateway system is 64.41.131.162. Then, click the Add button, and it will show up in the list of Installed gateways. Click OK to save the changes and then click OK again to leave the network configuration dialog box. In Windows 95 or 98, you will have to restart your computer for the changes to take effect, and you will be informed of this fact. Windows ME will probably not require a reboot.

After the reboot is complete, you should now be able to access the Internet from the Windows system.

Configuring Mac OS and Mac OS X Clients

Macintosh clients are potentially easier to set up to use your FreeBSD gateway than Windows because all TCP/IP configuration options are in the same window, and no reboot is necessary.

In the classic Mac OS (version 9 or earlier), open the TCP/IP control panel, as shown in Figure 28.6, and select Manually from the Configure: drop-down menu if it is not already selected. Put your gateway's IP address into the Router address: field. When you close the window, it will prompt you to save the changes. When you do so, the new settings will be immediately applied.

FIGURE 28.6

Configuring the TCP/IP settings under Mac OS 9.

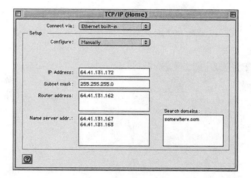

In Mac OS X, open the System Preferences and then select the Network panel, shown in Figure 28.7. As in Mac OS 9, select Manually from the Configure: menu, and fill in the gateway IP address in the Router: field. Click Save to commit the changes. The new network settings are immediately in effect.

In both these situations, you have the option to configure the built-in Ethernet card, the AirPort wireless card, or other network devices. Make sure you repeat this process for all relevant devices.

FreeBSD

To configure FreeBSD for a default gateway, add the following line to the /etc/rc.conf file:

```
defaultrouter="64.41.131.162"
```

Of course, you will need to replace the IP address in the previous sample with the IP address of the gateway interface on the FreeBSD system that is serving as a gateway.

FIGURE 28.7
Configuring the TCP/IP settings under Mac OS X.

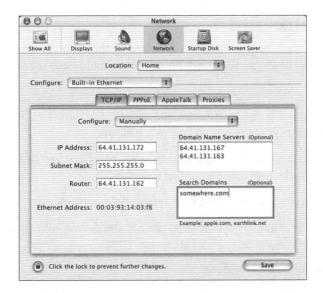

The change will not take effect until you have rebooted the system.

If you don't want to restart the system, you can add the default route manually with the following command issued from a root shell:

```
route add default 64.41.131.162
```

Configuring Linux Clients

Because of the lack of standardization in Linux, how you configure your Linux system to use the FreeBSD gateway will depend on the distribution you are using. We will not cover all of the distributions here, but we will cover some of the more popular ones. If your distribution is not covered, see the documentation for your distribution for more instructions.

> **Caution**
>
> Because there is a lack of standardization between Linux distributions, the examples in this section may not work for your distribution. See the documentation for your particular Linux distribution if you need help configuring your system to use a gateway.

28

CONFIGURING AN
INTERNET
GATEWAY

Red Hat Linux

Red Hat Linux network configuration is controlled by the file `/etc/sysconfig/network`. To use the new FreeBSD gateway, the following line should exist in the file:

```
GATEWAY=64.41.131.162
```

Replace the IP address in the previous sample with the IP address of the gateway interface on the FreeBSD system that is serving as a gateway.

Make sure you check to see if the line already exists before adding this line because having two GATEWAY lines could cause a conflict.

You will need to restart the Red Hat Linux system before the changes take effect.

If you don't want to restart the system, you can add the default route manually with the following command issued from a root shell:

```
route add default gw 64.41.131.162
```

Slackware Linux

In Slackware Linux, the initial part of the network setup is controlled by the file `/etc/rc.inet1`. This file handles basic network setup, including routing. To use the new FreeBSD gateway, the following line should exist in the file:

```
GATEWAY="64.41.131.162"
```

Replace the IP address in the previous sample with the IP address of the gateway interface on the FreeBSD system that is serving as a gateway.

Make sure you check to see if the line already exists before adding this line because having two GATEWAY lines could cause a conflict.

You will need to restart the Slackware Linux system before the changes take effect.

If you don't want to restart the system, you can add the default route manually with the following command issued from a root shell:

```
route add default gw 64.41.131.162
```

Configuring Wireless Internet Access

Wireless network access has recently become very popular since it does not require wires to be strung around, and it also does not require network connection jacks. It also eliminates the problem of not having enough network connection jacks. Any PC that has a wireless networking card can communicate with the network. Indeed, many notebook computers are shipping with wireless networking capabilities built in to them.

One of the most common applications of this technology is Internet sharing for school classrooms. Each student can have a notebook computer on their desk and have access to the Internet through a central server.

Configuring FreeBSD to work as a wireless gateway for this type of setup is almost identical to configuring a normal gateway as already discussed. The only real difference is that you will need to have a wireless networking card installed in the FreeBSD system.

Table 28.1 shows a list of the wireless network interfaces that FreeBSD currently supports, along with the corresponding devices that need to be present in the kernel configuration file.

TABLE 28.1 Wireless Network Interfaces that FreeBSD Currently Supports

Wireless Interface	*Kernel Device*
Aironet 4500/4800 802.11	device an
AMD Am79C930-based cards	device awi
Xircom CNU/Netware Airsurfer	device cnw
Lucent WaveLan 802.11	device wi
Lucent WaveLan (ISA only)	device wl

With the exception of the cnw and wl devices, support for these adapters is included in the default GENERIC kernel. So, unless you have a device wireless network card that requires the cnw device or the wl device, you should be okay unless you built a custom kernel and removed support for these devices.

If you do need to build a new kernel to support your wireless network card, see Chapter 17 for details on how to do this.

Once you have your wireless network card working, simply follow the same procedures mentioned earlier in this chapter to configure the gateway and the clients.

Routing Between Three or More Networks

In all of the situations up to this point, the router configuration has only needed one route. For example, our simba gateway only has one connection to the Internet, and only serves one network. Figure 28.8 shows how this works.

28

CONFIGURING AN
INTERNET
GATEWAY

FIGURE 28.8

The gateway simba *here only needs to route packets between two networks, which are the local LAN, and the Internet.*

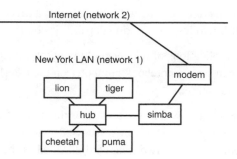

In this simple example, the hosts lion, tiger, cheetah, and puma use simba as their default gateway to communicate with systems on the Internet. Likewise, simba also has a default router, and it is set to the router at your ISP. For a dial-up PPP connection, this is transparent to you since the default route will be added automatically when the PPP connection is established, and will be deleted automatically when the PPP connection terminates. You do not need to worry about this, but you should be aware that your gateway has a default router it uses, just as your clients that use the gateway use it as a default router.

However, sometimes you might have a more complex configuration such as that shown in Figure 28.9. In this situation, simba acts as the default router for its own network as well as serving as the default router for falcon, which is itself a default router for another network.

FIGURE 28.9

A more complex gateway setup. In this case, simba *acts as a default router for its own network, as well as serving as the default router for* falcon, *which is itself a default router for another network.*

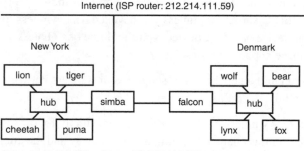

In this example, in addition to serving the clients on its own network, simba is actually serving as an Internet service provider to the network served by the router falcon. This means that simba now needs to route between three networks. For this to work, we need to add another route to simba so that it knows what packets should be routed to the network served by falcon, as well as how to get them there.

The network served by falcon owns a class C address block. Notice that all the addresses on the network begin with the base address of 205.211.117.xx. Also, notice that falcon has an IP address of 169.151.116.121. To get simba to route packets to the network served by falcon, we can add the following lines to /etc/rc.conf:

```
defaultroute="212.214.111.59"
static_routes="falcon"
falcon="-net 205.211.117.0 169.151.116.121"
```

In this case, the IP address 212.214.111.59 is the default router for simba. In other words, any packets that simba receives that are for hosts it doesn't know about will be sent to this router. 212.214.111.59 is the router at the Internet backbone provider that serves simba.

We have also added what is called a *static route*. This is an entry in the routing table that is static, or does not change. In this case, we have told simba that any packets it receives that have a destination with a base address of 205.211.117.0 should be routed to the address of 169.151.116.121. This is the IP address of falcon, which itself serves as a router for another network. As you can see, all the hosts on the network served by falcon begin with the IP address of 205.211.117.xx. So any packets that simba receives that are intended for any of these hosts will be routed to falcon, rather than to the default route of 212.214.111.59. In addition, any packets received by simba that are intended for clients on its own network will be routed directly to those clients rather than sent to the default route.

In order for the static routes to take effect, you will need to reboot the system. It is recommended that you reboot the system, but if you do not want to, you can add the static routes manually so they will take effect immediately. In the previous example, this can be done with the following command from a root shell:

```
route add -net 205.211.117.0 169.151.116.121
```

Dynamic Routing

All of our examples so far have used static routes, which are routes that never change. This is because in our examples up to this point, the routers have only had one connection to the Internet. For example, in the previous section, simba accessed the Internet through the router at its ISP. And falcon accessed the Internet through simba. In both cases, these were the only access points that the router had to the Internet.

Sometimes however, you may have multiple Internet connections, or multiple routes to the same network. In this case, static routing does not work well. This is where dynamic routing comes in.

28

CONFIGURING AN
INTERNET
GATEWAY

Dynamic routing uses a routing daemon along with a routing protocol to discover new routes, and dynamically adds them to the routing table. In addition, dynamic routing automatically deletes routing entries from the routing table when they are no longer valid.

There are several router daemons available for FreeBSD. The one that is included with the FreeBSD base system is called routed. It is a fairly old program and it uses a fairly old routing protocol known as RIP (Routing Information Protocol). RIP has some security problems, so there are better choices available for routing than routed. Other routing daemons available in the FreeBSD ports collection include gated and zebra, both in the "net" directory of the ports tree. For more information on installing software using the FreeBSD ports collection, see Chapter 15, "Installing Additional Software."

A discussion of how to configure the routing daemons is beyond the scope of this book. See the man pages and documentation for the routing daemon that you decide to use for more information.

The good news is that you probably won't need to run a routing daemon, anyway. As mentioned before, the only time you will need a routing daemon is if you have multiple routes to get to the same network (for example, multiple Internet connections). If you don't have multiple routes to the same network, static routing entries as discussed previously will work fine.

Enterprise Routing and DMZ

A variation of the previous concept of routing between multiple networks is the DMZ concept, which is fairly common in enterprise environments.

The problem here is that you may need some systems behind the gateway to have real IP addresses (such as Web servers), but you want the rest of the systems to use NAT. This is usually done by having a gateway that has three network interfaces in it. One interface is the outside link to the Internet, the second is for the systems that should use NAT, and the third is for the systems that should not use NAT. The interface that serves the systems with the real IP addresses is known as the *DMZ*, or *Demilitarized Zone*. More information on DMZ setups can be found in Chapter 29.

Network Security

CHAPTER 29

Of all the topics near to a system administrator's heart, none is so hot as system security. It's arguably the most important part of any administrator's job, whether it's a Windows server, a commercial UNIX system, or FreeBSD. More books have probably been written about security theory, security practice, security neutralization, security philosophy, and so on, than about any other topic—and with good reason. It's an immensely complex subject. We can't hope to cover it all in this chapter alone, but it's so crucially important to the success of a networked system that a reference on FreeBSD would be critically deficient without as complete a discussion of security as possible.

The Internet today is not an especially friendly place for servers. The proliferation of "rootkit" tools and published attack scripts, combined with countless individuals with nothing better to do than pursue destructive hobbies, make for an atmosphere where you as an administrator must always fear and prepare for the worst. You must assume that your system is being probed for security weaknesses at all times around the clock, the situation growing more dangerous with each new exploit published. The only defense is to keep your system as up to date as possible, act on new security advisories as soon as they're released, and be educated about the real dangers and where your greatest risks lie.

Security risks for a network server can be grouped into three major categories:

- **Root compromise.** An attacker takes advantage of unencrypted transmissions or known programming weaknesses in server software (most commonly "buffer overflows") to gain super-user access to the system. He then installs tools of his own to conceal his presence from your system-monitoring tools (such as `last` and `ps`), and can steal any of your critical data or use your system as a base point for further hacking activities.

- **Privacy compromise.** If network traffic to and from your system is not encrypted (scrambled), an attacker can view any of it, including passwords (potentially leading to root compromise) or any user's critical or private communications.

- **Denial of service.** An attacker uses brute-force methods such as flooding your server with large amounts of legitimately constructed traffic, swamping its ability to serve traffic to normal clients and potentially crashing the system.

This chapter will help you develop a security policy for your FreeBSD system based upon the risk factors it faces in its role as a server or workstation. Reality does dictate that no security model can be perfect, and only superhuman effort can keep a system so completely buttoned-up that no attack will ever get through. "Perfect security" is a myth. The next best thing, however, is to mitigate the greatest risk areas through knowing their nature and how they can be combated.

Security Models

There are several models of security that you can adopt for your system; depending on your circumstances, any of these models might apply to you. The model you choose will dictate how careful you will need to be about certain administrative duties, such as password policies, open services, encrypted traffic, and so on.

- **"I trust everybody on the Internet."** Most certainly an inadvisable model, this is nonetheless how a lot of amateur servers are run, and they pay the price for it. Often found on university systems, especially those that have been around for many years (since before the Internet became so rich in hacker activity), these types of systems have many open services, don't require encrypted logins, have a loose account and password policy, and are easy targets for hack attacks.

- **"I trust anybody on my system's network."** Common in enterprise networks, this model tends to exist where the server is protected from the general Internet by a firewall, and the internal network is made up of employees of a company or a department at a university. Malicious users on the internal network are rare, and so the system can afford to provide unencrypted services and even have disabled login security. A server in this environment, where the firewall is reliable, can have the loosest security model of all and get away with it.

- **"I trust my local users."** Somewhat more paranoid than the first two models, this scheme dictates a tight network security policy: screening of users before new accounts are granted, encrypted network services (either required or encouraged), unnecessary services turned off, and crack resistant passwords. However, local users are allowed to access internal services and see sensitive information (such as encrypted password strings). The idea is that once users are approved and given accounts, they can have the run of the system, and betrayal of that trust is grounds for removal from the system. This model is appropriate for hobbyist systems that serve a "low-risk" audience (for example, a fan Web site or community e-mail service), or for high-profile commercial Internet servers where only a few people actually have user accounts.

- **"I trust only myself and other administrators."** The most paranoid of all, this model not only has tight network security as the preceding model, but tight local security as well. Regular users are denied access to system configuration files and server-side program code through carefully crafted permissions. The administrator must watch each user carefully to make sure that nothing unauthorized is being done, and special measures (such as custom shells, `chroot` jails, and the disabling of certain commands) are often taken to restrict each user's access to the system's

29

NETWORK
SECURITY

resources. This model is useful for high-profile servers that provide e-mail or Web hosting services to hundreds or thousands of users from indeterminate or anonymous backgrounds.

Once you've decided what model is appropriate for you and your system for network and user-level security, you need to decide where the risk areas are for that model and what you can do to combat the exploitability of those areas. The most common risk areas to address are as follows:

- Insecure (weak) passwords
- Cleartext services
- Unnecessary and exploit-prone services
- Open SMTP relaying
- Unfiltered network access
- Outdated and vulnerable software

Each of these areas is a potential problem on FreeBSD in its default configuration. This chapter will address each of them and more, giving you the necessary tools to maintain a system that will stand up to the inevitable hacker (or, more properly, "cracker") attacks that will be leveled against it.

Note

Open SMTP relaying is more a matter of being a good Internet citizen rather than a security issue; it's discussed in detail in Chapter 25, "Configuring E-mail Services," rather than here.

Password Policies

If your users have insecure passwords, all the other security measures you might take may well be moot. Probably the most responsible thing you can do as the administrator of a FreeBSD system is to institute a password policy, requiring (or at least encouraging) your users to use passwords that cannot be easily guessed or decoded.

Users frequently find passwords inconvenient, and strict password policies doubly so. If allowed, a user will try to use his or her username, telephone number, hostname, a word such as "password," or strings of convenient-to-type characters such as repeated letters or numbers. If you choose to expire users' passwords after some period, the first thing a user will try, when prompted to choose a new password, is to reuse the password from the previous period. However, an axiom of security is that "convenience and security are mutually exclusive"—meaning that to increase one, you must sacrifice the other. Increased convenience brings about decreased security. There's no easy way around that truth.

When a user chooses a password using the system's `passwd` program or a script that calls the same routines that `passwd` uses, a few loose checks are performed. By default, passwords must be at least six characters in length, but that's about the only built-in measure that prevents people from choosing weak passwords. Let's take a look at a couple of methods you can use to take your password policy to the next level.

Enforcing Secure Passwords with `Crack`

An ideal password is at least eight characters long (the longer the better, actually); and contains a mixture of capital and lowercase letters, numbers, and punctuation marks or "meta-characters." We need a way to ensure that users have to follow these guidelines when picking a password with the `passwd` program.

Again, the only limit enforced by the default `passwd` is that passwords must be at least six characters long. Efforts are underway in the FreeBSD development community to incorporate further weak-password checks into the `passwd` program, preventing users from choosing insecure passwords in the first place. As of this writing, though, the best way to make sure your users aren't using easily guessable passwords is to periodically try to guess them yourself. This is done with a tool called `Crack`, available in the ports collection at `/usr/ports/security/crack`. While it may appear to be a "hacker" tool, `Crack` is primarily intended as a security auditing tool for system administrators, allowing you to perform "dictionary" attacks (trying a plethora of English words as potential passwords) as well as a number of other commonly used "convenience" passwords: repeated strings, the user's login name, groups of numbers, and so on). The goal is to show you which users are using insecure passwords, allowing you to contact them directly and ask them to adhere to the password rules you set.

After you've built and installed the `Crack` port (see Chapter 15, "Installing Additional Software," for details), a new `/usr/local/crack` directory is present; this directory's permissions are such that only root can list its contents or run any of its programs. To check your system's user database for weak passwords, go into `/usr/local/crack` and run the `Crack` program like so (noting the capitalization):

```
# ./Crack -fmt bsd /etc/master.passwd
```

The Crack program will build some utilities and compile some dictionaries; then, it will launch its arsenal against /etc/master.passwd, sending its output into runtime files that can be analyzed with the Reporter program as shown:

```
./Reporter -quiet
---- passwords cracked as of Sun Jan 14 12:17:41 EST 2001 ----

979693112:Guessed frank [frank] Frank Jones [/etc/master.passwd /bin/tcsh]
979693187:Guessed joe [password] Joe User [/etc/master.passwd
/usr/local/bin/bash]

---- done ----
```

Only the users whose passwords were successfully guessed are reported. In the example output, the cracked passwords are shown in the first set of brackets; Frank's password is frank, and Joe's password is password—both very weak passwords that can be guessed by an attacker with little effort. You can then contact these users and remind them of the password policy, requiring them to change to stronger passwords.

Once you're done running Crack, clean up the runtime tools and output files with the following two commands:

```
# make tidy
# rm run/F-merged
```

> **Note**
>
> As FreeBSD continues to develop, it's highly likely that there will be support in the passwd program for automatic password-strength checking such as that done manually by Crack; in fact, the libraries that Crack uses are available at /usr/ports/security/cracklib. On systems such as Linux, cracklib has been developed into a pluggable authentication module (PAM), a mechanism that FreeBSD supports as well (see man pam), but FreeBSD doesn't have cracklib support fully integrated into PAM as of this writing. For now, though, if you're an adventurous sort willing to work with source code and experimental software, and you're interested in incorporating the cracklib routines into the passwd program, a discussion of how to do it can be found at http://www.kearneys.ca/~brent/FreeBSD/passwd42.html.

Expiring Passwords

By default, passwords in FreeBSD do not expire. However, one common part of a secure password policy is to require users to change their passwords every so often, with the expiration interval chosen by you.

To do this in FreeBSD, you need to modify the /etc/login.conf file. This file is a centralized way to control capabilities and behaviors (such as the number of allowed processes, the maximum allowed process size, the allowed number of simultaneous open files, certain shell behaviors, and many more that are listed in man login.conf). Each of these properties can be assigned to a "class" of users, which you can assign with the chfn command (as we have seen earlier); normally, users aren't associated with any particular class, and so the values in the default class apply to everybody:

```
default:\
        :passwd_format=md5:\
        :copyright=/etc/COPYRIGHT:\
        :welcome=/etc/motd:\
        :setenv=MAIL=/var/mail/$,BLOCKSIZE=K,FTP_PASSIVE_MODE=YES:\
        :path=/sbin /bin /usr/sbin /usr/bin /usr/games /usr/local/sbin
/usr/local/bin /usr/X11R6/bin ~/bin:\
        :nologin=/var/run/nologin:\
        :cputime=unlimited:\
        :datasize=unlimited:\
        :stacksize=unlimited:\
        :memorylocked=unlimited:\
        :memoryuse=unlimited:\
        :filesize=unlimited:\
        :coredumpsize=unlimited:\
        :openfiles=unlimited:\
        :maxproc=unlimited:\
        :sbsize=unlimited:\
        :priority=0:\
        :ignoretime@:\
        :umask=022:
```

The backslash (\) characters "escape" the line-breaks, allowing you to specify all these properties on different lines, keeping the file readable.

Setting a password expiration date involves putting an extra line into the default class, specifying the passwordtime property; it can go into the block at any point, but the easiest place to add it is right at the top, between the class name and the first existing property line:

```
default:\
        :passwordime=90d:\
        :passwd_format=md5:\
        :copyright=/etc/COPYRIGHT:\
        :welcome=/etc/motd:\
```

This example will set passwords to expire after 90 days. You can also use time values like 2y (2 years), 6w (6 weeks), or 24h (24 hours). Now, because /etc/login.conf is a database that must be compiled into a hash table (as with the tables in /etc/mail, which you will remember from Chapter 25), you must run the `cap_mkdb` program to generate the hash table and enable your changes:

```
# cap_mkdb /etc/login.conf
```

From now on, if it's been over 90 days since a user last changed his or her password, the login procedure will require the user to choose a new password. Note that when the `passwordtime` property is set, `passwd` writes the time of the last password change into the sixth field of `/etc/master.passwd`:

```
frank:$1$LXZkCuzD$70a8LyRf5jYOb.XrXiB3d.:1060:100::999066364:0::/home/frank:/bin
/tcsh
```

> **Tip**
>
> You can also use `login.conf` to alter the default minimum password length. This is done with the `minpasswordlen` value:
>
> ```
>         :minpasswordlen=8:\
> ```
>
> This sets the minimum acceptable password length to eight characters.

Assigning Initial Passwords

It can be tempting to set a simple initial password for every new user, such as `Temp123` or `ChangeThis`. However, this is quite insecure in itself, especially if you use the same password for every new user you add.

You can mitigate this risk by coming up with a random password for each user; you can use any scheme you want to generate passwords (such as the first initials of song titles), but doing it yourself can become tiresome quickly. One good way to generate a unique and unguessable password is with the `md5` tool and a few randomly pressed keys:

```
# md5 -s "asdsad"
MD5 ("asdsad") = b5b037a78522671b89a2c1b21d9b80c6
```

You can then assign the first seven or eight characters of this string (for example, `b5b037a7`) as the new user's password, with instructions telling the user how to use `passwd` to change the password to something more memorable. You might choose to incorporate this scheme into a small Perl script that does an MD5 hash on the output of `rand()` to generate a new password.

Onetime Passwords with S/Key

If you're really serious about password security, you can do what they do at government offices and super-secure businesses: You can assign onetime passwords to your users, shifting part of the security burden from your own shoulders onto those of your users. Onetime passwords are generated by the key program, which has variants on all major platforms, and even a platform-agnostic Java key calculator at http://www.cs.umd.edu/~harry/jotp/src.html. (FreeBSD uses MD4 for its calculations.)

Onetime passwords are good candidates for use on systems in which you don't obligate your users to use SSH instead of Telnet (as we will discuss shortly). Because a new password has to be generated by the user with the key program on a local system, with the user feeding into it the server's "challenge" phrase and the user's own secret password, which is never transmitted over the wire (except during initial key setup), an eavesdropper can never get any useful data by sniffing the connection. Once the password is used once, it can't be used again. The user can transmit his onetime password in cleartext without fear.

> **Note**
>
> S/Key is as much a tool for a security-conscious user as it is a way for the administrator to enforce good security practices. Many parts of S/Key setup, for example, the keyinit program, are the user's responsibility to maintain. If a user feels strongly about keeping his passwords private, he might choose to use onetime passwords, even if he has the option to do otherwise.

Let's say you want to make it so that the user Frank cannot log in with his usual UNIX password from a remote host, but instead must use S/Key onetime passwords. While logged in to the server (preferably securely, as with SSH), he must use the keyinit program to set up S/Key authentication:

```
# keyinit
Adding frank:
Reminder - Only use this method if you are directly connected.
If you are using telnet or rlogin exit with no password and use keyinit -s.
Enter secret password:
Again secret password:

ID frank s/key is 99 st28077
COL APT HELM TAB DRY TRIM
```

> **Note**
>
> If Frank is not securely connected to the server (as with a cleartext Telnet con-
> nection), he ought to use `keyinit -s`. Without the `-s`, `keyinit` incorporates the
> `key` program into its own operation. Frank enters his secret key-generating
> password (which is used only for calculating S/Key onetime passwords, and
> shouldn't be the same as his UNIX password), and transmits it over the network
> to the server. If the connection isn't secure, the secret password is susceptible to
> interception, making any further attempts at security moot. The `-s` option
> requires Frank to use the `key` program locally—on his own Windows, Macintosh,
> or UNIX machine—to generate a password that he must then enter into
> `keyinit` at the `s/key access password:` prompt (which only appears if the `-s`
> option is used).

After Frank has used `keyinit` to set up his S/Key mechanism, adding an entry for his
login to `/etc/skeykeys`, you must create the file `/etc/skey.access` (if it doesn't already
exist), and add the following line:

```
deny user frank
```

The `/etc/skey.access` file tells FreeBSD under what conditions a remote user is permitted to use his regular UNIX password, and under what conditions he must use an
S/Key onetime password. A line in `skey.access` specifies a rule beginning with `permit`
(allowing either an S/Key or UNIX password) or `deny` (requiring an S/Key password),
followed by as many conditions as you like. These conditions, described fully in `man`
`skey.access`, can specify certain users, groups, remote hostnames or networks, or login
terminals. The example line we just saw requires that when Frank tries to log in, only an
S/Key password will be permitted—not his UNIX password.

The next time Frank uses Telnet to connect to your system, his login prompt will look
like this:

```
# telnet stripes.somewhere.com
Trying 64.41.131.102...
Connected to stripes.somewhere.com.
Escape character is '^]'.

FreeBSD/i386 (stripes.somewhere.com) (ttyp2)

login: frank
s/key 99 st28077
Password:
```

Frank must now use the key program (or its equivalent) on his own machine to figure out what password to enter. He has to feed into it the challenge information presented by the server: the iteration count (99 in this case, meaning that there are 99 logins left before Frank must run keyinit again), followed by the "seed" string (st28077 here, the same as we saw in the keyinit example). These numbers, combined with Frank's secret password, generate an S/Key password made up of six short, uppercase English words:

```
# key 99 st28077
Reminder - Do not use this program while logged in via telnet or rlogin.
Enter secret password:
COL APT HELM TAB DRY TRIM
```

Frank now enters this string of words as his password, and is granted access. An attacker, if he intercepted the words, would be out of luck—they only went across the wire once (on the way to the login prompt). The next time the system asks for Frank's S/Key password, the iteration number will be 98, and the password will be different. The iteration keeps counting down until it hits zero, at which time Frank must run keyinit again to set the counter back to 99, or else he will be denied access and you'll have to get involved (by changing his rule in /etc/skey.access from deny to permit until he's reinitialized S/Key).

> **Tip**
>
> If he wants, Frank can generate multiple keys at once by using key with the -n option. He can then print out these keys and take them with him if that's more convenient or secure for him:
>
> ```
> # key -n 5 50 st28077
> Reminder - Do not use this program while logged in via telnet or rlogin.
> Enter secret password:
> 41: SHOT YOU BIEN GIN JUDD AS
> 42: CHOW AVIS DOES EMIT FLAM WORK
> 43: DOCK ATE ANN WAS JOCK OAT
> 44: WALE AWL ELK LETS AWK WALE
> 45: GIFT BERT ROD GRIN YANG EAST
> ```

The S/Key password challenge is also issued as part of the su command, helping to prevent the actual root password from being transmitted over the network at any time.

To turn off S/Key for a user, remove that user's entry from /etc/skeykeys and any mention of him from /etc/skey.access.

Kerberos

One last authentication method that deserves mention is Kerberos. Developed as a centralized login management system at the Athena cluster at MIT, Kerberos provides a way for users to authenticate with a central server on a network and be issued "tickets" for performing tasks such as Telnet, FTP, POP3, and NFS without having to log in each time. As long as the hosts on your network between which you're running traffic support Kerberos and subscribe to the master server, the Kerberos subsystem takes care of all the authentication chores for you. FreeBSD allows you to set up a Kerberos master server to which other hosts in the network subscribe, or to simply support Kerberos in a network where it's already running.

Until fairly recently, Kerberos has been a scheme that was really useful only in legacy situations or at MIT. Its usefulness is in streamlining often-used tasks in large LANs such as those found at universities or hierarchical enterprise networks, and there aren't many situations left where Kerberos is especially important in today's networking atmosphere. It's less a security measure than a way of eliminating unnecessary work in pure UNIX environments. However, because many enterprise networks use Kerberos to provide centralized, encrypted login services, and because Windows 2000's security model is largely tied together with Kerberos (albeit a somewhat modified version), it's once again becoming increasingly important and ubiquitous. You may need to set up your FreeBSD machine to integrate with it.

If you want to enable Kerberos in FreeBSD, you can do so.
`kerberos_server_enable="YES"` in `/etc/rc.conf` will start up the services that manage a master Kerberos server; if you're working with an existing master server, you can uncomment the appropriate lines in `/etc/pam.conf` to enable centralized authentication for the services that support it, for example:

```
login   auth    sufficient      pam_kerberosIV.so              try_first_pass
```

Further documentation on Kerberos can be found in the man `kerberos` page and in the online FreeBSD handbook (`http://www.freebsd.org/handbook`).

Problems with Cleartext Services

It may seem that your transmissions between your client machine and the server (in applications such as Telnet, e-mail, and HTTP) are secure; after all, your passwords are hidden (or at least, they seem to be), and everything travels in tiny packets of data that flow out onto the network along with so many millions of other tiny packets that it might

seem silly to think that someone could have the patience to apply the networking equivalent of a wiretap and piece together the fragments of an interesting transaction. They'd
have to be on the same network segment as your LAN or the LAN at the opposite end, or
at some trunk service provider along the way—and they'd have to possess stealth and
equipment befitting James Bond. And even if they did, they'd have to eavesdrop on many
different such sessions in order to unearth anything they could use. Who could have that
kind of spare time?

Anybody, that's who. Security in cleartext services (applications that don't encrypt, or
scramble, their transactions) is a myth. Even more importantly, *security through obscu-
rity*—the notion that your communications or services are secure because you think
nobody pays attention to them—doesn't work. That's another axiom that has been proven
wrong repeatedly over the years, and you would be well-advised not to fall prey to the
temptation to ignore security in cleartext services out of the belief that hackers wouldn't
be interested in cracking your system. You should always assume the worst—that your
traffic is constantly being maliciously watched.

Using `tcpdump` to Monitor Traffic

You can illustrate the risks inherent in your network's cleartext services by using a
packet sniffer, a software tool that watches all packets on your network segment and displays the ones that interest you. A sniffer operates by putting your Ethernet card into
"promiscuous mode," where it accepts all packets that it sees on the network, rather than
discarding packets not addressed to it (as you will recall from Chapter 22, "Introduction
to Networking"); it then applies all kinds of highly configurable filters to the traffic it
sees. This is how an eavesdropper can extract the relevant packets from the storm of traffic to capture a transaction with ominous ease.

FreeBSD's built-in packet sniffer is `tcpdump`, available in /usr/sbin. Its use is barred to
regular users, who will get a `Permission denied` error on the /dev/bpf0 (Berkeley
Packet Filter) device; only the administrator (root) can use the program. The purpose of
`tcpdump` is not to log the actual data of the TCP/IP packets it sees (you might want to
look into WildPackets' EtherPeek for that functionality); rather, `tcpdump` is much like
`Crack` in that it's intended as an administrative security-auditing tool that allows you to
see how much unencrypted traffic is being sent to and from your system, and to watch
for suspicious network activity that might indicate illicit pursuits on the part of your
users.

29

NETWORK
SECURITY

> **Note**
>
> It's possible to use `tcpdump` to spy on the activities of your users, whether they're doing anything wrong or not. A warning in the GENERIC kernel configuration file reminds you to consider the ethical issues involved with using a packet sniffer—it all depends on what kind of system you're running, naturally, but packet sniffers are the equivalent of telephone wiretaps or hidden security cameras, and you should use `tcpdump` only under circumstances in which you would be comfortable using wiretaps and hidden cameras to gather information.

The configuration of `tcpdump` is quite complex, and it allows you to do a lot of very useful and versatile things. All we're interested in right now, though, is demonstrating the dangers of cleartext TCP/IP traffic. Let's set up a simple monitoring filter on the Telnet port (TCP port 23):

```
# tcpdump -x port 23
tcpdump: listening on fxp0
20:14:19.076941 w044.z064002043.sjc-ca.dsl.cnc.net.54109 > w012.z064002043.sjc-
ca.dsl.cnc.net.telnet: S 1972342903:1972342903(0) win 32768 <mss 1460,nop,wscale
0,nop,nop,timestamp 465710 0> (DF) [tos 0x10]
                      4510 003c e44b 4000 4006 8024 4002 2b2c
                      4002 2b0c d35d 0017 758f 9077 0000 0000
                      a002 8000 001b 0000 0204 05b4 0103 0300
                      0101 080a 0007 1b2e 0000 0000
20:14:19.077050 w012.z064002043.sjc-ca.dsl.cnc.net.telnet > w044.z064002043.sjc-
ca.dsl.cnc.net.54109: S 1734674412:1734674412(0) ack 1972342904 win 17520 <mss
1460> (DF)
                      4500 002c c9c2 4000 4006 9acd 4002 2b0c
                      4002 2b2c 0017 d35d 6765 07ec 758f 9078
                      6012 4470 349c 0000 0204 05b4
...
20:14:19.677472 w044.z064002043.sjc-ca.dsl.cnc.net.54109 > w012.z064002043.sjc-
ca.dsl.cnc.net.telnet: . ack 195 win 33580 (DF) [tos 0x10]
                      4510 0028 e458 4000 4006 802b 4002 2b2c
                      4002 2b0c d35d 0017 758f 910a 6765 08af
                      5010 832c 0c49 0000 5555 5555 5555
^C
134 packets received by filter
0 packets dropped by kernel
```

Since `tcpdump` is not designed as "spyware," the output (specified with the `-x` option) is shown in hexadecimal format, which you can convert to plain, human-readable text with a hex editor. This data isn't encrypted at all. It only takes a little bit of effort to be able to see the complete contents of every packet sent via Telnet. It's even easier with tools that do the packet decoding for you, such as EtherPeek. If these packets contained a user's login session, an attacker using `tcpdump` or EtherPeek would now know it and be able to log in to your system. This is true of POP3, IMAP, FTP, and HTTP traffic, too, as well as just about every small and non-essential service such as Finger and Syslog; it's especially important where passwords or any other sensitive data is transferred. It's as much a privacy issue as it is a security concern.

Fortunately, there's a way to combat these problems. Encrypted alternatives to each of the major data transfer protocols exist, many of which are part of the default FreeBSD installation. It's only a matter of knowing they exist, implementing them, and convincing your users to adopt them.

Securing Terminal Traffic (OpenSSH)

Terminal traffic, which is typically done with the Telnet or `rlogin` applications, is probably the riskiest type of cleartext traffic, and is the easiest to fix. FreeBSD comes with a complete SSH (Secure Shell) package designed to supplant Telnet and `rlogin`, allowing your users to establish a completely encrypted tunnel to your server, protecting their login passwords and any command-line activity from snooping intruders. This is OpenSSH, developed originally for OpenBSD and now incorporated into FreeBSD.

SSH runs on port 22, and it runs as a standalone daemon that spawns off new sshd processes (like Apache does) when new connections come in. To enable the SSH server, add the following line to /etc/rc.conf (if it's not already there), and then reboot (or simply type sshd):

```
sshd_enable="YES"
```

The SSH client is a replacement for Telnet. All you have to do to use it instead of the command-line `telnet` program is to use the `ssh` command instead:

```
# ssh stripes.somewhere.com
```

SSH itself prompts for your password, assuming the remote username is the same as the local one. You can specify an alternate username with either of a couple of different methods:

```
# ssh stripes.somewhere.com -l frank
# ssh frank@stripes.somewhere.com
```

The `ssh` program establishes the encrypted connection, and passes the login data to the server in a secure fashion. From that point on, it acts just like a regular Telnet

29

NETWORK
SECURITY

connection—there's no difference as far as the user is concerned. This is how a user on a FreeBSD, Linux, UNIX, or Mac OS X system would connect to your machine.

Users on desktop client systems such as Windows or classic Mac OS have a little bit more work to do. These platforms have no command-line SSH client programs, but there are some excellent graphical terminal programs that incorporate both Telnet and SSH functionality: Windows users have SecureCRT (from Van Dyke, http://www.vandyke.com) or SSH (from SSH Communications Security, http://www.ssh.com), and Mac users can use NiftyTelnet/SSH or MacSSH. The Windows programs tend to be commercial products, whereas the Mac ones more frequently are shareware.

Your task lies in convincing your users to switch to SSH rather than using Telnet. You can let them all know via your published server policy that they are advised to use SSH to protect themselves at their option; however, this doesn't guarantee that they will use it, and you as the administrator are still faced with the threat of an attacker who sniffs the connection of someone who has chosen not to use SSH. A more heavy-handed, but more complete approach is to disable Telnet entirely and require your users to use SSH instead. To disable Telnet, comment out the telnetd line from /etc/inetd.conf:

```
#telnet  stream  tcp    nowait  root    /usr/libexec/telnetd    telnetd
```

Then, restart the inetd process:

```
# killall -HUP inetd
```

> **Note**
>
> SSH has two popular protocol flavors: SSH1 and SSH2. FreeBSD supports both, but SSH1 is less well-designed and potentially more likely to display security vulnerabilities than SSH2. You can disable SSH1 by adding the following line to /etc/ssh/ssh_config:
>
> ```
> Protocol 2
> ```
>
> However, note that not all consumer SSH clients have full support for SSH2. Don't worry about disabling SSH1 unless you have to.

Securing E-mail Services (POP3 and IMAP)

Perhaps even more of a risk than Telnet for password sniffing (but a little harder to defend against) is the cleartext nature of POP3 and IMAP. If your users have set their e-mail clients to connect to the server every five minutes or so to check for new messages, a plainly visible login and password transaction occurs with each one of these connections, resulting in an even higher likelihood of password compromises—especially because these services send their sensitive data at predictable, regular intervals. If you're enforcing SSH rather than Telnet on your server, it's in your interest to do the same for your e-mail services.

We talked in Chapter 25 about how to secure the qpopper program to use the built-in SSL (Secure Sockets Layer) tools in FreeBSD to encrypt POP3 connections, and the same method can be used for IMAP using the IMAP-UW software package. You can enable SSL support in IMAP-UW by generating a certificate with a certifying authority, as we saw in Chapter 25; if you already have a certificate for your site, generated for a different service (qpopper, for example), you can use the same certificate for IMAP-UW. Refer to the IMAP-UW documentation at http://www.washington.edu/imap/ for more details.

An alternative way to encrypt both POP3 and IMAP, managing your SSL certificates centrally and without using each service's built-in SSL support, is to use the stunnel program. Also available in the ports (/usr/ports/security/stunnel), it allows you to set up a universal SSL tunnel for any service on the system that you choose. Most commonly, it's used to encrypt POP3 and IMAP traffic; if you install it from the ports, its default startup script (/usr/local/etc/rc.d/stunnel.sh.sample) starts a listener process on port 993 (for IMAP) and 995 (for POP3), which are the generally accepted ports for the secure versions of these protocols, as you can see in /etc/services.

Note

Remember to rename stunnel.sh.sample to stunnel.sh, as we discussed in Chapter 11, "System Configuration and Startup Scripts." The .sample is there to make sure you look at the script's contents to ensure that the paths to the .pem certificate files are correct.

If you choose to use stunnel, you'll still have to generate a certificate, just as with qpopper and IMAP-UW. The stunnel certificate should be placed at /usr/local/etc/stunnel.pem. Once it's in place, your POP3 and IMAP clients should be able to connect to the appropriate ports to establish a secure connection: 993 instead of 143 for IMAP, and 995 instead of 110 for POP3.

The problem is that not all e-mail client programs support SSL encryption for POP3 and IMAP. Many of the popular ones do—Microsoft Outlook, for example—but others have support for only one of the two, or none, or the support is incomplete or optional. Requiring users to use SSL might mean requiring them to switch e-mail programs, something not many people like to do. Also, note that `stunnel` is not a replacement for POP3 or IMAP—it's an augmentation, the generalized addition of SSL capability to any specified service. This means that the regular POP3 and IMAP services must still be enabled; you can't remove these services from `/etc/inetd.conf`. You'll need to use IPFW (as we will see later in this chapter) to disallow connections to these ports from any host other than `localhost` if you want to enforce a "secure connections only" policy.

Securing FTP

FTP, as we saw in Chapter 27, "Configuring an FTP Server", is another cleartext service that has inherent password authentication, and therefore has the potential to be compromised by an attacker watching the wires. It's about as much of a risk to the system as Telnet is because it's used frequently by users to do things such as uploading Web pages, but it isn't used at predictable, regular intervals like POP3 or IMAP. This makes it a bit less risky than Telnet, but still worth securing.

Fortunately, secure FTP is just as easy to implement as SSH. If you've enabled SSH on your system (as we saw earlier), secure FTP is available; encrypted FTP sessions actually operate over the SSH channel, with the SSH client establishing a terminal connection, starting the `/usr/libexec/sftp-server` program on the server end, and opening the necessary connections back to the client over encrypted channels. The secure FTP client then operates just like a regular FTP program, transparently to the user.

On FreeBSD, the built-in `sftp` program that's a part of OpenSSH serves the purpose of handling the client end of a secure FTP session. On Windows, the SSH Communications Security package provides a secure FTP client that works with FreeBSD. The previously mentioned Mac OS clients also have secure FTP capabilities.

An alternate way to do file transfer over a secure channel is to use `scp`. This enables you to copy files to and from a remote server using login authentication, much in the same way that `rcp` works (see `man rcp` and `man scp` for details), except that `scp` operates via the encrypted SSH tunnel. Some SSH clients, such as NiftyTelnet/SSH for the Mac, support file transfer via this method.

To `scp` a file from your local machine to a remote SSH server, use a command like the following:

```
# scp file.txt stripes:
frank@stripes's password:
file.txt              100% |*****************************|   511      00:00
```

The remote hostname is specified with a trailing colon (:), and can be either the source or destination argument; either of these arguments can also contain full pathnames to the file's location. This is a quick way to transfer files securely if you don't need all the features of full-fledged FTP.

Securing Apache

Finally, we come to HTTP. Secure HTTP is vitally important to e-commerce, protecting clients' credit card numbers and billing information rather than their login names and passwords—arguably just as critical, especially if your business depends on your clients' confidence in the privacy with which you handle their information.

Securing HTTP was one of the earliest widespread uses for SSL, and although that security package has today become adopted for nearly all popular services, Apache's integration with it still shows signs of the disorganization with which the early years of SSL were plagued. There are two different, unrelated, SSL-enabled versions of Apache that are being simultaneously developed: Apache-SSL and mod_ssl. Both integrate FreeBSD's OpenSSL libraries and tools, but they're maintained by different groups and attempt to solve somewhat different problems.

> **Note**
>
> Secure and cleartext HTTP are intended to operate side-by-side; it's not a good idea, and very seldom done, to serve all HTTP requests through SSL. This is partly for performance reasons (high-traffic Web sites would suffer a speed impact from the processing overhead of encrypting every page and image, whether it contains sensitive information or not), and partly out of convenience and convention. Most public Web data has no need for encryption—after all, it's public. But switching to secure mode when a customer enters an online purchasing page or information-gathering form helps to provide your Web users with assurance that they're now in a more heavily protected area. Remember, you're serving the user's expectations and confidence as much as the user's data.

Apache-SSL

The "official" secure implementation of Apache, Apache-SSL is maintained by the Apache Group itself, and has a more limited feature set than mod_ssl, being primarily concerned with stability and performance rather than with advanced features. Development on Apache-SSL is not very active these days, largely because of the tightly controlled feature set and the lack of known bugs.

The Apache-SSL binary is called httpsd rather than httpd; the idea is that you would run a regular httpd to serve regular HTTP requests on port 80, and httpsd to handle encrypted requests on port 443. Of course, this means you would have to have a version of Apache without SSL installed as well to accomplish this.

You can install Apache-SSL from the ports at /usr/ports/www/apache13-ssl, and the official Web site is at http://www.apache-ssl.org.

Apache with `mod_ssl`

A more complete and active implementation of SSL on HTTP than Apache-SSL, mod_ssl is a standard Apache module that links OpenSSL into Apache, taking advantage of the modern modular architecture of the software. It's more streamlined than Apache-SSL, incorporating many more features and a more versatile configuration model. For instance, the apache13-modssl port installs a single httpd executable, just like the regular apache13 port, except that the configuration files have special tuning to enable SSL connections when requested:

```
<IfDefine SSL>
Listen 80
Listen 443
</IfDefine>
```

You can add further modules to Apache with mod_ssl, such as mod_perl, mod_php, and all the rest in /usr/ports/www. The focus of mod_ssl is a rich and complete feature set and easy configurability, so it's not necessarily as fast or robust as Apache-SSL. Statistics on this are scarce, however.

Apache with mod_ssl can be installed from /usr/ports/www/apache13-modssl; the official Web site is http://www.modssl.org.

Running a Secure Web Server

Whether you decide to go with Apache-SSL or Apache with mod_ssl, maintaining your Web server will necessarily become a little more complex than without it. As mentioned earlier, Apache-SSL operates under the assumption that you will want to run a regular httpd to handle regular cleartext HTTP connections, and httpsd for encrypted requests on port 443. This means that there's a separate httpsdctl program that controls Apache-SSL, operating the same way as apachectl with the regular Apache, and an httpsd.conf in /usr/local/etc/apache in parallel with httpd.conf. These will not be present if you install Apache with mod_ssl instead—the functionality is rolled into a single set of files, the ones we saw in Chapter 26, "Configuring a Web Server."

The ports (both apache13-ssl and apache13-modssl) install complete Apache directory trees—including icons, sample HTML pages, dynamic modules, and configuration files. For this reason, you will want to take care when updating the parallel installations of Apache-SSL and regular Apache. The mod_ssl version only has a single installation, replacing the standard Apache installation, so the maintenance is potentially much simpler.

Your OpenSSL certificates are read much more interactively by a Web browser than by other secure services, so you'll have to make especially sure that the certificates match reality. If the hostname in the certificate doesn't match the server's hostname or if the certificate isn't signed by a recognized certifying authority (in other words, if it's self-signed), the user will get a dialog box showing all the information about your certificate and asking for confirmation on whether the browser should accept it, potentially bewildering the user and dissolving his confidence in your site's security. Even if your certificate matches your site's information properly, the user can view the certificate's contents through the Security Information feature of his browser, so all the fields you specify when generating the certificate request will be visible to any interested party. Bear this in mind—it's fairly difficult to change the information on a certificate once it's been signed.

Poorly Written CGI Scripts

Cleartext traffic isn't the only potential security hole in an Apache installation. Something you should be equally worried about, especially if your security model is one where you don't necessarily trust your local users, is the possibility of users' CGI scripts running amok on the system (whether intentionally or accidentally) and destroying files. Because many files in Apache's document root are owned by the nobody user (especially files created dynamically by your own server-side programs), and because the same nobody user executes every user's CGI programs as well, it's a simple matter for a user CGI program to be able to delete or modify anything else on the server owned by nobody.

It's easier than you might think for this to happen. All it takes is for a CGI program to be designed to remove a user's own unneeded files, but to be mistakenly coded to prepend the wrong path to the filenames. The same might happen in a program that prints data

out into a file, potentially corrupting other users' data. Even the most seasoned CGI veterans have fallen prey to this trap before. The danger is naturally much higher if you have a malicious user on your system who decides intentionally to write a destructive script to be executed by Apache as `nobody`.

The solution to this problem is to run Apache within a "wrapper" program that intercepts user CGI programs, performs security checks on them (making sure their permissions are appropriate), and executes them as the users who own them rather than as `nobody`. This has traditionally been done with the `suexec` wrapper that comes with Apache, but an easier-to-use and more flexible solution is another wrapper, CGIWrap by Nathan Neulinger.

Making CGI Scripts Safer with CGIwrap

CGIWrap, available in the ports at `/usr/ports/www/cgiwrap`, provides the double advantage of protecting users and the server root from attack by poorly written CGI scripts while also enabling users' CGI programs to write files that the users themselves can modify or delete in the shell. When you think about it, it makes a lot more sense for a user CGI program to be executed by the user who owns it rather than by the unprivileged `nobody` user. In an ideal world, where programs are always written perfectly and nobody tries to sabotage others' files, this would be the default way all Web servers would work.

However, it's not an ideal world—people write buggy CGI scripts, and hackers abound. It's a fairly simple matter for a user to create a CGI program owned by root and put it in his directory, and wait for it to be executed as the owner, the super-user, unleashing its destructive payload against any files in your system.

CGIWrap protects your system against such problems. It's not a complete or ideal solution, of course, but it reduces the vast majority of the security risks associated with user CGI scripts to the point where you can put your administrative efforts elsewhere. By running security checks against all user CGI programs before executing them, and by running each program as its owner, the risks inherent in a badly written CGI are shifted from you onto the script's owner.

When you install CGIWrap from its port directory, the `cgiwrap` program (a precompiled binary) goes into your top-level `cgi-bin` directory, `/usr/local/www/cgi-bin`. Rather than operating as a wrapper around Apache itself as `suexec` does, CGIWrap has to be called explicitly by your users, with a URL of the following form:

```
http://www.somewhere.com/cgi-bin/cgiwrap/frank/myscript.cgi
```

Or as a server-side include:

```
<!--#include virtual="/cgi-bin/cgiwrap/frank/myscript.cgi"-->
```

This executes the myscript.cgi program in /home/frank/public_html/cgi-bin. All of a user's CGI programs must go inside his public_html/cgi-bin directory, which the user needs to create if it doesn't exist already. CGI programs outside that location will not be run through CGIWrap, so it's important that you disable CGI execution outside the server DocumentRoot by making sure that you don't have an Options +ExecCGI directive in a block that defines your users' directories.

The official CGIWrap home page is at http://cgiwrap.unixtools.org/ for further reference.

System Security Profiles and Kernel Security (securelevel)

The FreeBSD kernel runs with five different levels of security, controlled by the kern_securelevel option in /etc/rc.conf—levels -1 through 3. Each of these settings corresponds to a profile that controls such things as whether the kernel can be replaced on the disk, whether kernel modules can be loaded or unloaded, whether certain file permissions and flags can be set or altered, whether filesystems can be mounted on demand, and whether utilities such as IPFW (the built-in firewall, which we will discuss shortly) can be disabled or modified. As we saw in Chapter 17, "Kernel Configuration," the securelevel can be raised only during runtime—it can never be lowered except by rebooting. More information on kernel security can be found in man securelevel.

There's a second multilevel network security profile set in FreeBSD as well. You saw it during installation, and you can see it again in /stand/sysinstall, under "Configure" followed by "Security". This menu allows you to choose between four different system-wide security profiles: Low, Medium, High, and Extreme. These profiles control whether services such as Sendmail, sshd, and inetd should be run, and they also have a very rough correspondence to the kernel security levels. Table 29.1 shows a breakdown of each of these security profiles and what options each sets in /etc/rc.conf:

TABLE 29.1 System-wide Security Profiles

Profile Name	/etc/rc.conf *Settings*
Low	sendmail_enable="YES"
	sshd_enable="YES"
	portmap_enable="YES"
	inetd_enable="YES"

TABLE 29.1 continued

Profile Name	/etc/rc.conf *Settings*
Medium	sendmail_enable="YES"
	sshd_enable="YES"
	inetd_enable="YES"
High	kern_securelevel="1"
	kern_securelevel_enable="YES"
	sendmail_enable="YES"
	sshd_enable="YES"
	portmap_enable="NO"
	nfs_server_enable="NO"
	inetd_enable="NO"
Extreme	kern_securelevel="2"
	kern_securelevel_enable="YES"
	sendmail_enable="NO"
	sshd_enable="NO"
	portmap_enable="NO"
	nfs_server_enable="NO"
	inetd_enable="NO"

As you might expect, the "Extreme" profile is restrictive, almost to the point where the system isn't useful. The kernel securelevel is set to 2, meaning that the kernel can't be modified (with kernel modules) or replaced without rebooting into single-user mode, and the only way to mount or unmount filesystems is explicitly with the mount and umount commands (implicit, on-demand mounting, as with amd, is not allowed). Additionally, inetd, Sendmail, sshd, the NFS server, and other services are not enabled.

The "High" profile is a little less restrictive, with a securelevel of 1, meaning that filesystems are more easily mountable but the kernel still cannot be modified. Sendmail and sshd are enabled, but the rest of the services from the "Extreme" profile are not.

Of course, because the security profiles work purely by setting options in /etc/rc.conf, you can mix the settings from Table 29.1 to your taste, creating a security profile that fits the model by which you're running your system. Generally, you should never enable a service that you don't think you'll need. If it doesn't serve a useful purpose for you, the only possibilities are that it will continue to be useless but harmless, or that a security vulnerability will be found in it that opens your system up to security breaches. Play it safe wherever possible.

Using a Firewall

It's undeniable that *firewalls*, or machines that operate as routers with filters, are an increasingly important—even indispensable—part of maintaining an Internet server. Easily accessible hacking tools, run incessantly by "script kiddies" with nothing better to do, make it imperative that you have some kind of protection layer beyond simply electing not to run certain services and keeping on top of security bulletins. You need a generalized shield at the kernel level that prevents your system from being accessed at all on certain ports, from certain hosts, or over certain protocols. Firewalls, particularly the IPFW firewall that comes with FreeBSD, are an answer to this need.

A firewall can prevent the vast majority of casual attacks by only allowing through the traffic that you designate as valid. However, yet another axiom of network security is that even the most expensive and robust firewall can be made useless through a simple misconfiguration. Most cases of ineffective firewalls are the result of misconfigurations rather than the quality of the firewalls. There is no substitute for a well-maintained, properly designed security policy in conjunction with a competent firewall, so don't be fooled into thinking that if you just buy a more expensive firewall, your problems will be solved. That's the thinking that leads to a great many security breaches on the Internet today.

You can do two basic things with a firewall. Foremost is the capability to filter packets based on the criteria you specify, discarding unwanted traffic at the kernel level (before it reaches any critical system services). Secondly, you can do accounting, keeping statistics on the usage of your system and seeing how much traffic comes from where. IPFW does both of these things; you can run it directly on your FreeBSD machine, or you can use it on a system acting as a gateway router protecting multiple hosts on the inside LAN. Figure 29.1 shows this latter case, with a FreeBSD machine with three Ethernet cards acting as a gateway router (as we saw in Chapter 28, "Configuring an Internet Gateway"), passing packets between the inside (LAN), "demilitarized zone" (DMZ), and outside (WAN) networks.

FIGURE 29.1

A diagram of a gateway router providing firewall services—showing the LAN, DMZ, and WAN interfaces.

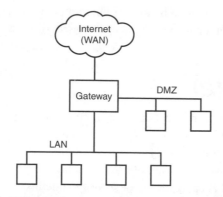

> **Note**
>
> The "demilitarized zone" is a network that is exposed to the WAN traffic directly, rather than on the LAN. Particularly useful in cases where the IP addresses on the LAN are translated (as we saw in Chapter 22), a DMZ provides an enterprise or ISP with a network on which to place untranslated "edge" machines such as Web servers, mail gateways, and other hosts that need to be accessible from the general Internet.
>
> A DMZ may or may not be configured to be protected by the firewall rules in the gateway router. Usually this is desirable, but some specialized cases require that the DMZ be exempt from the LAN's firewall rules. Your network situation will dictate your needs.

Enabling the Firewall

IPFW is not supported in the GENERIC kernel. There are some options you can compile into a custom kernel to enable it, as we saw in Chapter 17: IPFIREWALL, IPFIREWALL_VERBOSE, and IPFIREWALL_VERBOSE_LIMIT=10. However, it's really not necessary to go to all the trouble of building a new kernel in order to use IPFW; it's available as a kernel module, which is loaded automatically by the /etc/rc.network script. To enable the firewall without rebuilding the kernel, add the following lines to /etc/rc.conf:

```
firewall_enable="YES"
firewall_type="open"
```

If you don't specify that the firewall type should be open, the only rule that IPFW will start with is the default one, with an index of 65535 (the maximum), specifying deny ip from any to any. In other words, if you reboot with IPFW in its default configuration, your machine will be completely blocked off from the network, and you'll have to have physical console access to it in order to get it back.

> **Caution**
>
> It's very dangerous to experiment with IPFW if you don't have console access because it's very easy to put your machine into an unreachable state. Until you are comfortable enough with IPFW to know exactly what you're doing, always make sure you can access the machine via the console in case something goes wrong.

The open setting will change the default rules so that IP traffic is passed (allowed) by default, rather than blocked. Bear in mind that a truly secure system should deny access to all hosts unless specifically told otherwise, rather than allowing access except for a few blocked exceptions. The latter scheme can never be made completely secure. However, such a restrictive scheme as the former is probably overkill for systems that are in already secure environments.

Once your /etc/rc.conf is set up properly, reboot—or alternately, run the /etc/netstart script from the physical console (not from a remote terminal—this is very dangerous!). You will know the firewall has been enabled properly if you see the following lines:

```
Kernel firewall module loaded
Flushed all rules.
00100 allow ip from any to any via lo0
00200 deny ip from any to 127.0.0.0/8
00300 deny ip from 127.0.0.0/8 to any
05000 allow ip from any to any
Firewall rules loaded, starting divert daemons:.
```

You can also use kldstat to check whether the IPFW module has been loaded automatically:

```
# kldstat
Id Refs Address    Size    Name
 1    3 0xc0100000 355be4  kernel
 2    1 0xc0eee000 6000    ipfw.ko
 3    1 0xc0f19000 12000   linux.ko
```

You now have full access to the ipfw command, which lets you set rules on what kinds of traffic to allow and view the accounting information accumulated by IPFW.

> **Caution**
>
> If you will be using NATD to share an internet connection as described in chapter 28, "Configuring an Internet Gateway", you will still need to build a custom kernel since NATD requires the IPDIVERT option to be enabled in the kernel. See chapter 28 for more details.

29

NETWORK SECURITY

Configuring IPFW

The `ipfw` command is used to either `add` or `delete` rules from the kernel filter and accounting system. The rules are constructed in a syntax that flows somewhat like natural English; it's made up of an action (such as `deny`), a protocol to which the action applies (such as `tcp`), and an address specification involving a `from` clause and a `to` clause. For example, a rule that would block TCP traffic from a host called `badhost.com` would look like `deny tcp from badhost.com to any`, and you would add this rule to the kernel firewall like this:

```
# ipfw add deny tcp from badhost.com to any
```

A number of variations on this theme are possible. You can specify an address based on a network mask either with a mask pattern (for example, `255.255.255.0`) or with a CIDR bit-mask (for example, `/24`). You can also block individual ports rather than an entire system, which is useful for preventing hosts within a large ISP with unpredictable IP addresses from targeting a single service on your machine. Such a rule might look like this:

```
# ipfw add deny all from evil.isp.com/16 to www.somewhere.com 80
```

Similarly, you can exempt hosts from earlier rules by following them with `allow` rules, like so:

```
# ipfw add allow all from goodhost.evil.isp.com to www.somewhere.com 80
```

Note that IPFW rules are entered in a "chain," in which each rule is evaluated in the order it was specified. Each rule has an index number, normally spaced by 100 from its neighbors, which you can control by specifying the index number after the `add` or `deny` keyword in an `ipfw` command; this is how you can indicate the execution order of your rules. View the existing rule set with `ipfw -a list`:

```
# ipfw -a list
00100    0     0 allow ip from any to any via lo0
00200    0     0 deny ip from any to 127.0.0.0/8
00300    0     0 deny ip from 127.0.0.0/8 to any
00400    0     0 deny tcp from badhost.com to any
00500    0     0 ipfw add deny all from evil.isp.com/16 to www.somewhere.com 80
00600    0     0 ipfw add allow all from goodhost.evil.isp.com to
www.somewhere.com 80
65000 1214 79688 allow ip from any to any
65535    1    40 deny ip from any to any
```

The index number is shown in the first column; the number 65535 rule, as we saw earlier, is the default `deny` rule that rejects anything that falls through from above. Our open setting puts an `allow` bucket above it, but still with a high index number so that it should come after any other rules that you might add through regular usage.

The second and third columns show usage statistics, displaying the number of packets and bytes that have matched each rule, respectively. This is how you can tell whether your rules are being effective.

You can specify a number of different firewall types in /etc/rc.conf. Each keyword has a different meaning, as shown in Table 29.2. The exact definitions of these profiles can be deciphered from the shell script code in /etc/rc.firewall.

TABLE 29.2 Available Firewall Types

Keyword	*Meaning*
open	Allows access to all, from all
closed	Disables all IP except on the loopback (lo0) interface
client	Sets up rules designed to protect just this machine
simple	Sets up rules designed to protect the whole network
unknown	Loads no rules except for the default deny rule at index 65535
<filename>	Loads rules from <filename>

For your purpose, a "canned" IPFW profile such as client or simple might be appropriate. However, you're likely to need a specialized configuration as your system continues to evolve. Your specialized rule set will need to be put into a configuration file of your choice; let's call it /etc/firewall.conf. List your desired rules in that file, omitting the ipfw command itself:

```
add deny tcp from badhost.com to any
add deny all from evil.isp.com/16 to www.somewhere.com 80
add allow all from goodhost.evil.isp.com to www.somewhere.com 80
add 65000 allow all from any to any
```

Now, change the firewall_type in your /etc/rc.conf file:

```
firewall_type="/etc/firewall.conf"
```

The next time you reboot or run /etc/netstart, the rules from /etc/firewall.conf will be loaded with indexes of 100, 200, 300, and so on. An allow all rule at index 65000 provides a default behavior of passing traffic rather than denying it, if you want it.

For further reading on IPFW, see the man ipfw page and the online *FreeBSD Handbook* at http://www.freebsd.org/handbook.

29

NETWORK SECURITY

Preventing Intrusions and Compromises

Firewalls, password policies, and encryption go a long way toward protecting your system from malicious access. They still aren't enough, though, to defend against a really determined hacker who has a "rootkit" or other tool designed to take advantage of some known weakness in one of your system's services. There is a variety of tools you can use that go beyond the functionality of a simple firewall, dynamically blocking suspicious hosts, monitoring for intrusions, and controlling access to individual services on a host-by-host basis. Let's go over a few of these tools.

Using PortSentry

PortSentry, from Psionic Software, is a daemon that monitors all incoming network traffic, listening on all of a list of specified ports, and attempts to detect traffic that might indicate a port scan—a preliminary attack where a hacker probes your system for open services to try to exploit. When such traffic is detected, PortSentry blocks that host from accessing your system by wrapping it in a black-hole route or IPFW rule, where all future connection attempts from the offending host are discarded. PortSentry monitors both TCP and UDP traffic, dynamically building a "killfile" table of sorts that acts like an antibody against a virus, reacting to suspicious activity by blocking it before it has a chance to cause any damage.

Being open-source, PortSentry can be installed out of the ports (/usr/ports/security/portsentry). The portsentry binary is installed into /usr/local/bin, and the configuration file is /usr/local/etc/portsentry.conf. Open this file in your favorite text editor; it needs to be edited in order for PortSentry to work properly.

The first decision to make is which set of ports you want PortSentry to monitor. There are three available sets, in pairs beginning with TCP_PORTS and UDP_PORTS. The first set is quite large; it is intended for a very strict security policy in which any remotely suspicious port will trigger a blocking rule. The second set is more moderate, and the third is minimal—watching only the ports that a remote user can't possibly be contacting unless he's doing a port scan or trying to run an exploit. The middle set, the "if you want to be aware" grouping, is enabled by default. To switch to one of the other two, comment out the middle set and uncomment the one you want. If you like, you can create your own set. Make sure that none of the ports used by your core services are included in this list! For example, port 143 is listed in all three example sets, but 143 is the IMAP port. If you're running IMAP services, make sure to remove port 143 from the list. If you're not, however, leave it in—it will trap attackers who try to exploit IMAP-related security flaws.

Next, you have to choose a method by which to block suspicious hosts. You can do this in one of two ways: through IPFW (if you're running it, as we discussed earlier in the chapter), or through black-hole routes (if you're not running IPFW). Choosing a method involves uncommenting a single line beginning with KILL_ROUTE, which specifies the system command that PortSentry should use to block an offending host.

For a system running IPFW, uncomment the line containing /sbin/ipfw like so:

```
# For those of you running FreeBSD (and compatible) you can
# use their built in firewalling as well.
#
KILL_ROUTE="/sbin/ipfw add 1 deny all from $TARGET$:255.255.255.255 to any"
```

If you're not using IPFW, use the black-hole route method—which, despite the comments, works just as well as IPFW:

```
# FreeBSD (Not well tested.)
KILL_ROUTE="route add -net $TARGET$ -netmask 255.255.255.255 127.0.0.1 -
blackhole"
```

Once you've enabled a blocking method, PortSentry is ready to run. However, as of this writing, the PortSentry port doesn't come with an automated startup script. You can use the script shown in Listing 29.1 (available on the companion CD as portsentry.sh); make sure it's set executable, and copy it into your /usr/local/etc/rc.d directory to start up PortSentry each time your system boots.

LISTING 29.1 Sample PortSentry Startup Script

```
#!/bin/sh

PORTSENTRY="/usr/local/bin/portsentry"

case "$1" in
    start)
        ${PORTSENTRY} -tcp && echo " Starting PortSentry TCP mode..."
        ${PORTSENTRY} -udp && echo " Starting PortSentry UDP mode..."
        ;;

    stop)
        killall `basename ${PORTSENTRY}`
        ;;
    *)
        echo ""
        echo "Usage: `basename $0` { start | stop }"
        echo ""
        ;;
esac
```

> **Tip**
>
> While PortSentry is running, you can see which ports it's listening on by using
> the `sockstat` command:
>
> ```
> # sockstat
> USER      COMMAND    PID    FD PROTO  LOCAL ADDRESS          FOREIGN ADDRESS
> root      portsent   2432   0 udp4   *:1                    *:*
> root      portsent   2432   1 udp4   *:7                    *:*
> root      portsent   2432   2 udp4   *:9                    *:*
> root      portsent   2432   3 udp4   *:69                   *:*
> root      portsent   2432   4 udp4   *:161                  *:*
> root      portsent   2432   5 udp4   *:162                  *:*
> ...
> ```

Each time an attack attempt is detected, the offending host and the ports it scanned that
triggered the detection are listed in `/usr/local/etc/portsentry.blocked.tcp` for TCP
attacks, and `/usr/local/etc/portsentry.blocked.udp` for UDP attacks; this is how
PortSentry keeps track of which hosts it has already blocked so that it doesn't try to
block them again later. You can also use these files to see what hosts have been caught by
your attack detection system. These files are cleared out automatically each time
PortSentry starts up. Note that when you reboot, both IPFW and the routing table are
cleared of any entries that were added during runtime, so a host that was blocked once
will have access to you again if you reboot—at least until it tries to probe your ports
again.

> **Tip**
>
> If you're using the IPFW `KILL_ROUTE` method, view the current blocking rules
> with `ipfw -a list`:
>
> ```
> # ipfw -a list
> 00001    1       44 deny ip from 209.237.26.165 to any
> ```
>
> If you're using black-hole routes, use `netstat -rn`:
>
> ```
> # netstat -rn
> Routing tables
>
> Internet:
> Destination        Gateway          Flags   Refs    Use    Netif Expire
> ...
> 209.237.26.165/32  127.0.0.1        UGScB     0      0      lo0
> ```
>
> The B flag indicates a "black-hole" route, in which packets are simply discarded.

> **Tip**
>
> Additionally, each time an attack is detected, /var/log/messages receives lines indicating what PortSentry is doing about it:
>
> ```
> Jun  2 23:50:56 stripes portsentry[2430]: attackalert: Connect from host:
> 209.237.26.165/209.237.26.165 to TCP port: 1
> Jun  2 23:50:56 stripes portsentry[2430]: attackalert: Host 209.237.26.165
> has been blocked via wrappers with string: "ALL: 209.237.26.165"
> Jun  2 23:50:56 stripes portsentry[2430]: attackalert: Host 209.237.26.165
> has been blocked via dropped route using command: "/sbin/ipfw add 1 deny all
> from 209.237.26.165:255.255.255.255 to any"
> ```
>
> Another tool from the makers of PortSentry is Logcheck (available in /usr/ports/security/logcheck); it analyzes this and other log files and sends you a daily report on any unusual activity or detected attacks.

> **Caution**
>
> As with IPFW, be careful when testing PortSentry. It's very easy to trigger it so that the system from which you're administering your FreeBSD machine becomes blocked, for instance if you Telnet to port 1 to see what happens. What will happen is that your host will be blocked, and further connection attempts will simply time out. You will have to connect from a different host or the physical console to remove the mistakenly applied rule, either through an ipfw delete 1 or route delete <IP address>/32 command.
>
> If you want to protect certain hosts (such as your own machines) from ever being blocked by PortSentry, add their IP addresses to the /usr/local/etc/portsentry.ignore file.

29

NETWORK
SECURITY

Using /etc/hosts.allow

The /etc/hosts.allow file lets you block certain hosts from accessing certain services on your system. It's like a manual version of PortSentry; you can specify a block of rules for a given service, each rule applying to a certain IP address or set of addresses, and with each rule either allowing or denying matching hosts access to the service. Here's an example block of rules from the default /etc/hosts.allow file, with a few extra lines added to show example syntaxes:

```
sendmail : localhost : allow
sendmail : .nice.guy.example.com : allow
sendmail : .evil.cracker.example.com : deny
sendmail : 231.21.15.0/255.255.255.0 : deny
```

```
sendmail : 12.124.231. : deny
sendmail : ALL : allow
```

Since we've seen how IPFW works, the format of these rules is pretty easy to figure out. A rule has at least three fields: the service (specified by process name), the matching hostnames or IP addresses, and the action to take (or multiple actions, if there are four or more fields). The first two columns can be lists (multiple entries separated by spaces), and the host column can match a variety of different ways: a leading dot to specify an entire DNS subnet or a trailing dot to do the same for an IP address. Separate an IP address and a netmask with a slash to specify a network. The block should end with a "default" rule, specifying whether to allow or deny access to the service by default. Generally, if you're running the service, there's a good reason for it; you'll probably want your default rule to be "allow".

Something interesting you can do with /etc/hosts.allow is to specify actions other than simply "allow" and "deny". You can also make it so unauthorized access to a service triggers an e-mail to you, or executes a program that does some kind of reverse probing against the remote host (though this is probably not a good idea). Any shell command can be executed whenever a given rule is matched. The default rule for the fingerd service shows an example of this type of configuration:

```
fingerd : ALL \
        : spawn (echo Finger. | \
        /usr/bin/mail -s "tcpd\: %u@%h[%a] fingered me!" root) & \
        : deny
```

The %u, %h, and %a codes and additional configuration options are described in man 5 hosts_access and man hosts_options.

Using Tripwire

Beyond outright blocking of suspicious hosts lies intrusion detection. A sufficiently wily hacker will be able to get past your security checks, no matter how carefully you set them up. If that happens, you need to be able to see whether he got into the system and caused any damage. If your system has been "owned," you want to know about it as soon as it happens, and the exact extent of the damage.

A widely used tool for this task is Tripwire, available at /usr/ports/security/tripwire. This tool keeps an authenticity record of every program on the system, comparing each one on a daily basis to an "authoritative" record that it compiles the first time it is run, which occurs upon installation. If any differences are detected, for example if the sshd executable has suddenly changed size or had its contents or meta-data altered in any way, Tripwire notifies you via e-mail. This way, you can tell at a glance whether your system has been compromised.

When you first install Tripwire, it builds its initial database of program "fingerprints" during the `make install` phase, and writes it out into a file in the `/var/adm/tcheck` directory. However, this is a potential security risk; an attacker who gains access to your system, if he sees that the Tripwire database exists, will simply alter the database so it doesn't notice his presence. This is a reason to keep the database somewhere off the machine, either on a different system or—most conveniently—on a floppy disk.

FreeBSD provides a streamlined way to create this archive floppy. All you have to do is put a floppy into the drive before running the `make install` phase and then add the `TRIPWIRE_FLOPPY=YES` variable assignment to your `make install` command line:

```
# make install TRIPWIRE_FLOPPY=YES
...
### Phase 3:    Creating file information database
###
### Warning:    Database file placed in ./databases/tw.db_stripes.somewhere.com.
###
###             Make sure to move this file file and the configuration
###             to secure media!
###
###             (Tripwire expects to find it in '/var/adm/tcheck/databases'.)
# preparing the floppy
/dev/rfd0c:     2880 sectors in 80 cylinders of 2 tracks, 18 sectors
        1.4MB in 5 cyl groups (16 c/g, 0.28MB/g, 32 i/g)
super-block backups (for fsck -b #) at:
 32, 632, 1184, 1784, 2336
mount /dev/fd0c /mnt
# transferring things to the floppy
# Do not forget to remove and write-protect the floppy.
```

Your floppy now has a copy of the initial Tripwire database, along with the `tripwire`, `twcheck`, and `gunzip` tools; and a copy of the `tw.config` file—all that you need to recover the known good database from the disk.

From now on, you can have the system run `tripwire` every night in the `periodic` tasks, which we saw how to do in Chapter 14, "Performance Monitoring, Process Control, and Job Automation." When `tripwire` is run with no arguments, it operates in consistency check mode, scanning all the files specified in `/var/adm/tw.config` for mismatches against the database of file fingerprints. If any inconsistencies are found, it reports them, as with this example in which the file modification time of `/usr/sbin/sshd` has been changed:

```
# tripwire
...
### Phase 3:    Creating file information database
### Phase 4:    Searching for inconsistencies
###
```

29

```
###                     Total files scanned:        16803
###                            Files added:         0
###                          Files deleted:         0
###                          Files changed:         14321
###
###                     After applying rules:
###                        Changes discarded:        14320
###                        Changes remaining:        1
###
changed: -r-xr-xr-x root       197940 (null) /usr/sbin/sshd
### Phase 5:   Generating observed/expected pairs for changed files
###
### Attr         Observed (what it is)         Expected (what it should be)
### ===========  =============================  =============================
/usr/sbin/sshd
      st_mtime: Sun Jun  3 00:55:51 2001       Sat Apr 28 21:17:19 2001
      st_ctime: Sun Jun  3 00:55:51 2001       Sat Apr 28 21:17:19 2001
```

It may well be that you expect this file to be different from what Tripwire expects; you may have installed an updated version of sshd, for example. Whenever you update files that Tripwire is monitoring, you should update the Tripwire database to reflect the new information. This is done with the -update option:

```
# tripwire -update /usr/sbin/sshd
```

This creates a databases directory within your current directory, containing the new database file (which you should move to /var/adm/tcheck/databases) and a backup copy of the old one. It's uncompressed; you may want to gzip it and copy it to your Tripwire floppy disk as well:

```
# gzip databases/tw.db_stripes.somewhere.com
# mount /dev/fd0 /floppy
# cp databases/tw.db_stripes.somewhere.com /floppy
# umount /floppy
```

Air Gaps

The concept behind keeping your Tripwire database on a floppy disk is that of an *air gap*, a security concept that describes a condition where no automated process can possibly get data from one side of the "gap" to the other. Any system in which data can move via software from point A to point B is potentially susceptible to penetration by a sufficiently ingenious hacker. Given enough time and effort, someone intent on infiltrating your data will be able to access your archives—even if you go to such lengths as having a second "hidden" hard drive that mounts itself automatically during the night to perform a backup operation. That's still an automated procedure, and therefore vulnerable to anyone willing to try to break its security.

An air gap is a "last resort" security measure, the ultimate in decreased convenience for the sake of guaranteed security. If you keep your data in a physically separate location from any machine connected to the network, no hacker can break into it. This is how properly designed hospital and government networks are managed: Critical databases are maintained on machines that have no connection to any machines that are on the network; they're separated by an air gap, and therefore secure… at least, as long as the administrators physically in charge of the systems can be trusted.

When you keep your crucial data on a floppy disk, CD-R, or other removable media, you are employing an air gap; you're keeping the "keys to the city" where they can't be compromised, even if the entire networked system has been infiltrated. That is, of course, unless you leave that removable disk in the drive…

If You Think You've Been Hacked…

No matter how careful you are or how many precautions you take, it's simply not possible to be 100% sure that your system is secure. Total security is as inaccessible an ideal as absolute zero or a perfect vacuum. And as long as there's even the slightest chance of a security breach occurring in your system, there remains the necessity for you to assume the worst if there's any doubt.

While Tripwire and PortSentry can take a great deal of the drudgery of intrusion prevention and detection off your shoulders, you should still be on the alert for subtle and subjective changes in how the system behaves. Keep an eye on top, monitor what your system's load is over long periods, and see if it gradually gets higher; if it does, investigate to see what might be causing it. Don't ignore mysterious behavior changes such as login prompts that seem to be formatted wrong or command-line output that doesn't look right. Look through /tmp and /var/tmp periodically, watching for anything executable or setuid or very large, and clear out those directories regularly. Watch your system's log files in /var/log; be on the lookout for messages that seem suspicious, such as anything with long strings of garbage characters—these are almost certainly hack attempts probing for buffer overflows. In short, be constantly on the lookout for anything out of the ordinary. Such ad-hoc watchfulness is sometimes the only way to notice that your system isn't behaving the way it should.

> **Note**
>
> A favorite place to find evidence of hacker activity is in /dev. That's where packet-sniffing tools are often placed by intruders running pre-packaged "rootkits" or scripts. However, because FreeBSD now uses a dynamically generated DEVFS device filesystem, this is less of a worry—but it still doesn't hurt to keep an eye out.

If you do suspect that you've been hacked, though, and especially if you find any evidence of it, you must assume that the damage is greater than it appears. The most common mistake for an administrator to make who has discovered evidence of a security breach is to simply disable a few services and assume that the attacker has gone away. Often, this may be the case; however, treating all such incidents in this manner is an invitation to disaster. All it takes is for the attacker to have installed a "back-door" of some kind that lets him return and cause much more destructive damage than before.

If you suspect that you have been hacked or "owned," there are a few steps you must take:

1. Disconnect the system from the Net immediately. No matter what back-doors the attacker has installed in your system, he can't do anything if the system isn't on the network (behind an air gap). This prevents a hacker who realizes that he's been discovered from covering his tracks by wiping your hard disk clean.

2. Check /var/cron/tabs and /etc/crontab for new entries; also check atq for jobs the attacker has left to be run in his absence. The system may be off the network, but cron jobs will still run, and the hacker can still trash your system in this way unless you clear out any suspicious pending jobs.

3. Don't try to contact the attacker or let him know that you're onto him. Even after you've removed your system from harm's way, the attacker will vanish if he realizes you're trying to track him down, and law enforcement will have a much harder job finding him. Let him think you've simply taken the machine offline to recover from the damage.

4. Gather together your log files from /var/log and wherever else your programs might have them, and comb them for entries that might indicate where the attacker came from and how he gained access. If you are running any services for which security bulletins have been recently posted, and you haven't updated those services to remedy their vulnerabilities, it's almost a certainty that that's how the attacker gained access.

5. Take as much useful information as you can find to the National Infrastructure Protection Center (NIPC) Web site: `http://www.nipc.gov` (or the equivalent for your country's cybercrime investigation agency, if you're not in the United States), and fill out an incident report. This arm of the FBI is in charge of investigating cybercrime and hacker activity, and provided they have enough concrete information from your affected data, they can swiftly track down the perpetrator. Most hacker activity is committed by "script kiddies"—casual vandals who use tools prepackaged by others to exploit certain known vulnerabilities. These types of hackers usually can be found and prosecuted quite successfully.

6. Back up your important data—Web documents, configuration files, home directories, and everything in `/usr/local`—and reinstall the operating system. To be really thorough, wipe the hard disk clean, reinstall FreeBSD from scratch, and restore the local data. Use the daily output of Tripwire to tell you to what extent you need to "nuke and pave" the machine; beware of back-doors that may have been installed among your own installed programs in `/usr/local`.

7. Update all your services to the most recent versions, referring to all relevant security bulletins, before putting the system back online. Be especially vigilant for the first few days after bringing the system back up; the hacker may continue to try to break in. Pay especially close attention to your log files during this period; the more evidence you can gather, the easier it will be for the NIPC and FBI to do their job.

Denial of Service (DOS) Attacks

While it isn't technically a security issue, another type of malicious network activity has nonetheless become quite important to system administrators recently. This is the Denial of Service, or DOS, attack.

DOS attacks don't involve any compromise of a system's security or privacy. Rather, they are simply brute-force floods, sending so much traffic over a network that legitimate traffic is lost in the shuffle. The goal is often to crash the server through sheer overwhelming volume of data and number of requests. These kinds of attacks are much harder to defend against than directed hack attacks, which can be foiled through the use of IPFW, PortSentry, and the other tools we have already discussed. The impact of a DOS attack cannot be eliminated; it can only be mitigated because DOS attacks are made up completely of legitimate traffic, indistinguishable from your actual mission-critical data flow. The problem is just that there's too much of it.

Sometimes, a DOS attack can be identified as coming from a certain source, and you can block it by adding a firewall rule to deny traffic from or to that source. However, many recent attacks hide the actual source—ping (ICMP) broadcast attacks look as if they're coming from a certain source address, which is actually the victim address that receives the brunt of the attack. Distributed DOS, or DDOS, attacks work even more insidiously, with hundreds or even thousands of compromised desktop machines unwittingly taking part in the attack, so that tracking down the actual culprit is pretty much impossible.

Certain configuration options in various servers and in the kernel can help to prevent your system from completely submerging during a DOS attack. We will look at a few of these measures now; however, bear in mind that they can only serve to increase your system's chances of surviving a DOS attack—they can't neutralize the attack itself, nor can they guarantee that the attacker won't simply try harder until your system does succumb.

Limiting Server Forks

Many DOS attacks are targeted against services such as Apache, Sendmail, or others that operate by "forking" a new process to handle each incoming request. If an attacker sends an overwhelming number of requests to the service, it will fork off so many processes that the CPU and memory will eventually become exhausted, possibly destabilizing your system. You can mitigate the risk of a server fork attack by making sure that all your forking services have built-in limits to the number of simultaneous child processes they can have. These limitations can impact the services' ability to fulfill legitimate requests during normal operation, but that trade-off may be what saves you during a DOS attack.

Apache has a `MaxClients` directive, by default set to 150, which keeps more than that number of requests from being serviced at once. However, a complicating factor is that a wily attacker can repeatedly request a processor-intensive CGI script until Apache is creating executable processes faster than they can complete, leading to a runaway server much more easily than requests for static HTML pages. Often, the only way to recover from this situation, if you can even get the system to accept a Telnet or SSH login, is to shut down Apache (`apachectl stop`) until the attack is over. Fortunately, most HTTP DOS attacks are traceable to a single client IP address, which you can block with IPFW rules or with a `deny from` directive in Apache itself. If this doesn't work, though, you can always decrease `MaxClients` to the point where even if maxed-out, the clients can't swamp the server.

There's a similar feature in Sendmail: `MaxDaemonChildren`, disabled by default, which you can enable by uncommenting it in `/etc/mail/sendmail.cf` directly and restarting the server (`make restart`). Apart from this, Sendmail has a built-in brake that prevents it from starting new processes if the system load is over 12; however, this mechanism has too much lag during a fast-moving attack for the server to respond well, so it may be necessary to explicitly limit the number of children Sendmail can have at a time.

A potential general solution to fork attacks, even defending against those that might originate from your own system (a renegade or clumsy user, for example), is to modify /etc/login.conf to put limits on the CPU, RAM, and open file usage that a user can have. Create a class for the user that runs the service in question—nobody in the case of Apache, or an individual local user whose resources you want to limit—and use chfn to put the user into the class. An example login.conf class might look like this:

```
baduser:\
        :cputime=30m:\
        :openfiles=24:\
        :maxproc=32:\
        :memoryuse=16m:\
        :tc=default:
```

Then, use cap_mkdb /etc/login.conf to enable this new class and enforce these limits on any user in it.

Defending Against Springboard Attacks

A "springboard" attack leverages the resources of your own network to achieve its ends. While brute-force or forking attacks must involve a high-powered attacker doing a lot of work, in a springboard attack an attacker only needs to inject a carefully constructed set of requests so that the network's own infrastructure becomes its own worst enemy. For example, a broadcast ping (or "smurf") attack involves an attacker sending normal ping requests to your network's broadcast address (which multiplexes the requests out to all hosts on the network), with the requests' source address spoofed to appear to be a different host—a hapless victim, who suffers a lot more than you do in this type of attack because every host in your network turns around and floods the victim with ping responses. The multiplication effect of this kind of attack can be disastrous for the victim, and the source is very difficult (if not impossible) to trace. Another kind of springboard attack injects a UDP packet between two servers' echo service ports, causing them to enter into an "echo war" that can be stopped only by shutting off the echo port (which is already done by default in FreeBSD).

29

NETWORK
SECURITY

Springboard attacks are best prevented at the network's edge router. Smurf attacks can be prevented by configuring your router not to respond to broadcast ping requests; if your router is a FreeBSD machine, the icmp_bmcastecho="NO" setting in /etc/defaults/rc.conf prevents it from responding to these kinds of requests, which are almost never used for any good purpose.

An option that's compiled into the GENERIC kernel by default is ICMP_BANDLIM, which limits the rate at which responses to ICMP error messages (another common springboard attack) are sent, limiting such an attack's effectiveness.

Physical Security

Even after every possible measure has been taken to ensure network security, there is still the overriding issue of physical or "presence" security. The most secure system in the world can always be compromised if there's a possibility that an unauthorized person can gain physical access to the server machine itself because no amount of software security can defend against someone with a screwdriver.

Secure co-location facilities are vital for a commercial or otherwise high-profile Internet server. Such a facility provides locked server cabinets in locked machine rooms, and only employees of the facility are generally allowed to open the cabinets to touch the machines. Your system might itself be in a rack-mounted case with a locked front panel and BIOS security measures that warn you if the panel has been removed.

Anybody with physical access to the machine can reboot it into single-user mode, which doesn't prompt for the root password in the default configuration. You can change it so it does prompt for a password by telling /etc/ttys that the console is "insecure," meaning that you can't guarantee that anybody accessing it is authorized:

```
console none                         unknown off insecure
```

However, this doesn't stop an intruder from being able to boot from a floppy disk or CD-ROM to compromise your system. Other devices attached to the machine can also be used to gain unauthorized access: modems, for example, or wireless networks, which should not be a part of any machine from which you're trying to restrict physical access. The bottom line is that without a guarantee of physical security, complete security is not attainable.

Other Security Resources

This chapter has covered a few general security topics as they apply specifically to FreeBSD. However, the subject of network security is vast, and it grows each day as more and more malicious users try to find ways to bring down the Internet's core services.

There are a number of excellent resources on security, both FreeBSD-specific and general, that you would do well to check out.

The man security Page

Compiled by Matthew Dillon, the man security page contains a long discussion of general security topics and good administrative habits, as well as miscellaneous tips for preventing break-ins and DOS attacks. This page is the basis for a number of online resources, including part of the FreeBSD Handbook.

Mailing Lists

Join the freebsd-security@freebsd.org mailing list. Do this by sending a message to majordomo@freebsd.org, with subscribe freebsd-security in the message body. This list is where the most up-to-date discussion of security issues takes place; as an administrator, you will need to keep abreast of the most recent developments so you can defend against each new vulnerability as it becomes known.

Another useful security list, geared toward UNIX security issues in general, is Bugtraq. This list receives advisories of all major issues that arise in Internet security, sometimes before their full impact on FreeBSD is known. Bugtraq is hosted at http://www.securityfocus.com, where you can subscribe to the list or search its archives.

FreeBSD Security Advisories

Security advisories are sent out by the FreeBSD Security Officer onto the freebsd-announce@freebsd.org and freebsd-security@freebsd.org lists to warn of newly discovered vulnerabilities. Each advisory is also archived at http://www.froobsd.org/security/.

An advisory contains a complete discussion of the nature and impact of a vulnerability, whether it exists in part of the core FreeBSD system or in a program in the ports collection, whether it's FreeBSD-specific or not, and how to work around or solve the problem. Because it would be inviting hackers to a free lunch to disclose the exact nature of a vulnerability before a fix is available, advisories are released only after a solution has been found. This is one good reason to be subscribed to freebsd-security@freebsd.org because there will be discussion of a vulnerability there even before the advisory is released.

Fixes to vulnerabilities in ports or packages usually mean simply synchronizing your ports tree and rebuilding the port in question (see Chapter 15). A fix to the core FreeBSD system, though, is usually checked into the appropriate -STABLE or -CURRENT source tree; to take advantage of it, you will need to rebuild that part of your system after synchronizing your sources. If the fix is in a sufficiently fundamental part of the system code, you may need to do a complete make world to make your system secure. Instructions on how to do this are in Chapter 18, "Keeping Up to Date with FreeBSD."

Web Resources

The FreeBSD Security Information page, `http://www.freebsd.org/security/`, contains resources and links geared toward the FreeBSD administrator or developer. Security advisories are archived here, as are various tips and tricks for reducing your risk factors.

The FreeBSD Security How-To (`http://people.freebsd.org/~jkb/howto.html`) is a lengthy discussion of various methods by which you can secure your FreeBSD system. It covers many topics discussed in this chapter, and many more that are not.

CERT (`http://www.cert.org`), the Internet's foremost security advisory site, maintains resources on security vulnerabilities in all different operating systems, and is widely regarded as the authoritative source of alerts and recovery information. CERT also handles incident reports; you can report a break-in there, and they will work with the proper authorities to catch the perpetrator.

SecurityFocus, the site that hosts Bugtraq, is a security news site covering topics from intrusion detection systems to virus protection. It also has numerous articles on good security practices and how to run a system responsibly. It doesn't have much in the way of FreeBSD-specific material, but much of its information can be applied to any platform. The URL is `http://www.securityfocus.com`.

Books

Two books suggested in `/etc/rc.firewall` include *Firewalls & Internet Security* by William R. Cheswick and Steven M. Bellowin for general network security topics, and *Building Internet Firewalls, 2nd Edition* by Brent Chapman and Elizabeth Zwicky for fuller coverage of firewall theory and practice.

Further books and papers on security are listed and scored for usefulness at the SecurityFocus site, under the "Library" link.

CHAPTER 30

The Domain Name Server

We have seen in earlier chapters—particularly Chapter 22, "Introduction to Networking," and Chapter 23, "Configuring Basic Networking Services"—how DNS (the Domain Name System) provides a common naming scheme for finding hosts on the Internet, rather than everyone having to memorize IP addresses. We have covered the process of setting up a FreeBSD machine to gather domain name information from a designated server. However, we must now come to the topic of configuring the FreeBSD machine to act itself as a domain name server, providing lookup information to itself and to any client machines that wish to use it.

Domain name service is one of the most complex single subjects in network administration. While it's fairly easy to set up a Web server on each of as many different servers as you might install in a network, the installation of a name server is something that typically is only done once, often by a "guru" whose efforts quickly become folklore to the rest of the network staff, resulting quite often in a DNS setup that is hard to maintain or even understand. Administrators who know DNS inside and out are far less numerous than those who don't. This chapter cannot attempt to describe DNS exhaustively. For that purpose, there are whole books that are quite thick in themselves. This chapter's purpose is to enable you to set up FreeBSD as a name server in any of several common configurations.

DNS software is ubiquitous. For UNIX systems, which account for the vast majority of name servers on the Internet, the software of choice is BIND by the Internet Software Consortium (ISC).

Introduction to BIND

BIND, short for *Berkeley Internet Name Domain*, consists of one major daemon program (named), a set of resolver libraries that provide the ability to perform name lookups, and various administrative tools. BIND is built into FreeBSD, though it is not enabled by default.

Structure of DNS

DNS is a hierarchical protocol, operating across the Internet in a fashion similar to how routing works. There are a number of "root servers" maintained by Network Solutions, Inc., and other bodies, distributed geographically around the Internet for redundancy reasons. Each domain name (for example, somewhere.com) is defined in backward order from the root zone, with the domain suffix—com, org, net, and so on—being the topmost layer of the hierarchy directly under the . (a single dot) that refers to the root zone. Below each of the suffixes (commonly known as top-level domains, or TLDs) are the regular domain names, each typically defined not by the root servers but by individual DNS hosts on the Internet. For instance, the `somewhere.com` domain would have its DNS administered by a server on its own network (for instance, `ns1.somewhere.com`). This server is the "authoritative" DNS host for that domain. A central registry—also maintained by Network Solutions—keeps records of these individual domains so that the root servers can provide authoritative lookup information on them. You define these "host records" when setting up a new name server by submitting a form to Network Solutions or any or its peer registrars.

When a client makes a DNS request, it queries the name server configured in its TCP/IP settings—usually a server on its own network, as shown in Figure 30.1. If that server cannot answer the request, it passes the request on to its upstream DNS forwarder if one is available. If not, the request goes directly to the root servers.

The root servers don't maintain any authoritative DNS data of their own. All they have are host records, which we will come to know as NS records, which point to the authoritative name servers for each domain. The root servers send back a DNS response that refers the requester to the authoritative name server for the domain the client wants to find out about. This server sends back the requested DNS data to the local DNS machine, which passes it back through to the client.

FIGURE 30.1

Diagram of a DNS lookup, showing the path from a client to the local DNS, the root servers, and the authoritative name server.

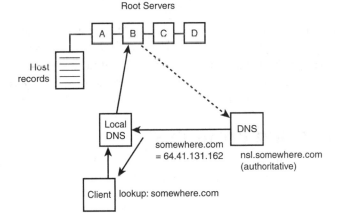

The local DNS might keep lookup information around in its cache for a period of time specified by the authoritative name server. This speeds up the query process, allowing local clients to get immediate responses to their DNS queries from the local server without the queries having to travel out over the Internet. However, this means that changes to DNS records at the authoritative DNS will not be available to the client until the expiration period has passed. Until that time, the DNS information the client sees is "stale" and potentially inaccurate. We will cover name server caching and data expiration later in this chapter.

Zones

BIND allows you to define *zones*, which are logical groupings of IP addresses and hostnames that exist at a certain level in the DNS naming hierarchy. For example, `com.` is a zone under the root (`.`) zone, and `somewhere.com.` is a zone that exists underneath the `com.` zone. Note that zone names always end in a dot, referring to the root zone—this will be important when you create your zone files! *Subdomains* are zones managed by the individual domain name servers; `cluster.somewhere.com.` is a zone that can have multiple machines inside it—indeed, it can have as many further subdivisions within it as you are willing to configure. These zones provide *forward DNS lookups*, or mappings from names to IP addresses.

Similarly, *reverse DNS lookups*—or mappings from IP addresses to hostnames—are managed in zones. Because DNS and IP addresses have their roots in the ARPAnet (see Chapter 22 for details), and have not changed fundamentally in structure since that time, a reverse DNS zone name is of the form `CCC.BBB.AAA.in-addr.arpa`. This is a name constructed of the IP address space in reverse order with `.in-addr.arpa` appended to it. For example, the `64.41.131.*` network would be defined by the zone `131.41.64.in-addr.arpa`.

Each zone that your name server will manage must be defined in a *zone file*—a formatted set of definitions that maps hostnames to IP addresses (or vice versa) within the zone. A zone file also contains parameters for the behavior of the zone, such as the caching expiration period. The zone files are the most critical part of proper DNS configuration; we will be discussing them in detail later in this chapter.

BIND Files and Programs

Because BIND is a built-in part of FreeBSD, you don't need to worry about installing it or making sure the proper files are in the proper places. It is worthwhile, though, to know what programs are involved in name server operations and where you will be making your configuration changes.

- `/usr/sbin/named`—The name server daemon itself. It listens on port 53 for DNS lookup requests.

- `/usr/sbin/ndc`—The name daemon controller program. This is the tool that you will use to start, stop, reload, and monitor the `named` server.

- `/etc/namedb`—All your BIND configuration and runtime status files, including zone definition files, are in this directory (or any subdirectories of it that you create).

- `/etc/namedb/named.conf`—The master BIND configuration file. This tells BIND which domains we are to manage, and how to handle each one.

Enabling the Name Server Daemon

Enabling BIND in FreeBSD is the simplest part of configuring it. All you have to do, just as with other built-in FreeBSD services that we have discussed, is add the following line to `/etc/rc.conf`:

```
named_enable="YES"
```

With this option set, `named` will run automatically at boot time. To start it without rebooting, use the `ndc` tool:

```
# ndc start
new pid is 12717
```

The server should now be running. However, this is only scratching the surface of a complete BIND configuration.

> **Note**
>
> For maximum efficiency, put a `nameserver` line into your `/etc/resolv.conf`, referring to the loopback address (127.0.0.1) as your primary name server. This way, you will be able to do DNS lookups the quickest way of all: from your own machine. Make sure this line appears before any additional servers:
>
> ```
> search somewhere.com
> nameserver 127.0.0.1
> nameserver 64.41.131.167
> ```

Running BIND in a Sandbox

As we saw in Chapter 27, "Configuring an FTP Server," it's sometimes advisable (for security purposes) to run certain services within what's known as a "sandbox", or a directory structure that's been pruned off so as to appear that it's all that exists in the filesystem. In FTP, we know this as a "`chroot` jail"; the effective "root" of the filesystem

30

THE DOMAIN NAME SERVER

is changed so the server and processes that it creates cannot see outside its own directory structure above a certain point. BIND provides the same kind of capability, though most of the documentation refers to it as a "sandbox" rather than as a "chroot jail". The concept is the same, however.

A common sandbox configuration is to have a directory called sandbox within /etc/namedb, with named pruning itself off into that directory as soon as it is started. This ensures that if named is compromised (which is possible because vulnerabilities continue to be found in versions of BIND to this day), the damage is restricted to that directory. Create the /etc/named/sandbox directory, and change its ownership and permissions to the unprivileged bind user and group:

```
# chown -R bind:bind /etc/namedb/sandbox
# chmod -R 750 /etc/namedb/sandbox
```

Next, create /etc and /var/run subdirectories inside the sandbox. Copy /etc/localtime into /etc/namedb/sandbox/etc. The server will write runtime files into /var/run, and it needs the localtime file to process the serial numbers found in zone files and to log dates properly.

```
# mkdir /etc/namedb/sandbox/etc
# cp /etc/localtime /etc/namedb/sandbox/etc
# mkdir -p /etc/namedb/sandbox/var/run
```

Finally, add the following line to /etc/rc.conf:

```
named_flags="-u bind -g bind -t /etc/namedb/sandbox"
```

Note that when using the ndc program to control named (as we will see in this chapter), you must use the -c option if you're running named in a sandbox. The syntax would take the following form:

```
# ndc -c /etc/namedb/sandbox/var/run/ndc start
```

Also note that if you configure named to log to a file, the file must be inside the sandbox for named to be able to write to it.

BIND Configuration File (named.conf)

In order to make your name server do anything useful, you need to make sure that it is topologically in the right place with respect to its clients and the rest of the network, and that it is configured to interoperate properly with other name servers. A misconfigured name server can result in deluges of DNS traffic between your server and the root servers as it tries futilely to synchronize its data. Your `/etc/namedb/named.conf` file must be constructed properly, and so it needs to be understood properly.

Fortunately, BIND 8 (the version included in FreeBSD at the time of this writing, probably soon to be replaced with BIND 9) greatly simplifies many of the esoteric details of name server configuration that were the norm in BIND version 4 and earlier. BIND 8, which immediately replaced BIND 4, introduced a lot more configurability, and at the same time eliminated many elements that were obsolete or poorly designed. Listing 30.1 shows a sample `named.conf` file, giving an idea of its syntax and structure.

LISTING 30.1 Sample `/etc/namedb/named.conf` File

```
/*
 * A simple BIND 8 configuration
 */

logging {
    category lame-servers { null; };
    category cname { null; };
};

options {
    directory "/etc/namedb";
};

zone "somewhere.com" {
    type master;
    file "somewhere.com";
};

zone "131.41.64.in-addr.arpa" {
    type master;
    file "131.41.64.in-addr.arpa";
};

zone "elsewhere.com" {
    type slave;
    file "slave/elsewhere.com";
    masters { 113.125.2.145; };
};

zone "." {
    type hint;
    file "named.boot";
};

zone "0.0.127.in-addr.arpa" {
    type master;
```

LISTING 30.1 continued

```
    file "localhost.rev";
};

zone "0.0.0.0.0.0.0.0.0.0.0.0.0.0.0.0.0.0.0.0.0.0.0.0.0.0.0.0.0.0.0.0.IP6.INT" {
        type master;
        file "localhost.rev";
};
```

As shown in the listing, a configuration file consists of a number of blocks (or "statements") in C-style syntax, with substatements allowed within curly brackets ({}). All possible statements are listed and described in the man `named.conf` page. Some of the most useful ones are `options`, `controls`, `logging`, and `zone`.

Comments in `named.conf` are also C-style; single-line comments are done with double slashes (`//`), and block comments are done with the `/* comment */` syntax. Shell-style comments (`#`) are also supported.

The `named.conf` file that exists in the default installation of FreeBSD has a few of the statements shown in Listing 30.1 and a few that are not. It also has a lot of inline documentation that describes how to use each of them.

Whenever you make a change to `named.conf` or to any of the zone files (which we will discuss later in this chapter), restart `named` using the `ndc` program:

```
# ndc reload
Reload initiated.
```

Using a Forwarder

Recalling the topology shown in Figure 30.1, a *forwarder* is a name server at an "upstream" network—a larger network "closer" to the root servers—that allows you to request DNS information from it. (Note that access to a name server can be restricted, as we will see.) A good candidate for a forwarder is your uplink ISP's name server, if your FreeBSD machine is acting as a name server for a home network. Normally, if your machine can't answer a DNS request on its own, it must query the root servers (found in `/etc/namedb/named.root`) for the authoritative reply. These extra steps take time and add to the packet traffic on the network.

It really isn't necessary for everyone to get authoritative answers all the time. It's perfectly acceptable in most cases to work from non-authoritative DNS information, such as that from a caching name server:

```
# nslookup www.freebsd.org ns.somewhere.com
Server:  ns.somewhere.com
Address:  64.41.131.172

Non-authoritative answer:
Name:    freefall.freebsd.org
Address:  216.136.204.21
Aliases:  www.freebsd.org
```

Configuring your FreeBSD system to query one or more forwarders allows it to benefit from the cache of the upstream name server, rather than to fetch authoritative data on every query. The downside (as we discussed earlier) is that the cached data can become "stale" by as much time as the authoritative server's zone file specifies it should (a period frequently measured in days). Figure 30.2 shows a DNS query path in which a forwarder is involved. The forwarder does most of the work, building up its cache through queries of its own and in service to its own clients. The downstream DNS that points to it needs only query the forwarder, preventing unnecessary lag and query traffic.

> **Tip**
>
> The deluges of DNS traffic that we mentioned earlier are often caused by name servers that are improperly configured, never to take advantage of caching name servers. These forwarders are what prevent too much unnecessary traffic from swamping low-bandwidth links—for instance, in cases where a DNS host serving as the authoritative name server for a domain is on a small DSL or dial-up link. Without caching name servers, every host on the Internet would have to send DNS queries to it directly. With forwarders, the load on the target host's link is greatly reduced. Using a forwarder is a way to act as a good network citizen and make your own queries faster and more efficient.

FIGURE 30.2

Diagram of a DNS lookup involving a forwarder providing cached DNS information in a nonauthoritative capacity to the local DNS and the client.

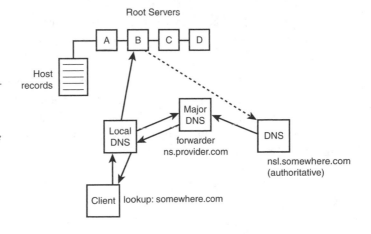

To enable a forwarder, replace 127.0.0.1 in the forwarders block of the options statement with the upstream name server's IP address (127.0.0.1, the localhost address,
will not work here), and uncomment the block by removing the /* and */ comment tags.

```
/*
        forwarders {
                127.0.0.1;
        };
*/
```

You can specify as many forwarders as you like, and named will consult each one before
giving up and querying the root servers. You can additionally uncomment the forward
only; statement in the options block to force named to consult only the forwarders on
all queries. Normally, your machine will consult the forwarders for DNS data unless it
appears that the forwarders are unreachable or broken, in which case it makes full
queries to the root servers. Setting the forward only; option prevents it from making
root server queries on any occasion.

Master and Slave Configurations

Each zone block defines a domain or subdomain that your FreeBSD machine will administer. Most commonly, a zone block defines a domain of the form somewhere.com:

```
zone "somewhere.com" {
    type master;
    file "somewhere.com";
};
```

All that's absolutely necessary in this block is the name of the domain or subdomain
(without the trailing dot that will usually be associated with a zone name), the type statement that defines whether it's a master or slave configuration for that domain, and the
filename that contains the zone information. Let's examine what it means for a name
server to act as a master or a slave for a particular zone.

The type substatement can be master, slave, stub, forward, or hint. The most commonly used of these are master and slave; the rest are used in special circumstances
only, which we will look at shortly.

A master zone indicates that the server is authoritative for the zone; it means the server
has a master copy of the zone file, defining name-to-address mappings that are to propagate throughout the Internet, and any changes to it must be made manually—but those
changes override the information in every other name server's DNS cache when the
existing information expires.

A `slave` zone is a replica of the master, with a zone file derived from the one that the master has. Slave servers can provide authoritative answers to DNS queries. A `slave` zone block looks like this:

```
zone "elsewhere.com" {
    type slave;
    file "slave/elsewhere.com";
    masters { 113.125.2.145; };
};
```

The `masters` substatement contains a semicolon-delimited list of master servers from which to transfer zone information. These masters can be actual authoritative master zone servers or they can be other slaves. The `file` statement in a `slave` zone refers to the name of the autogenerated zone file that `named` will create when it transfers it from the master. In this example, the `elsewhere.com` file is created within the `/etc/namedb/slave` subdirectory; you can use a directory structure like this to separate out your authoritative (master) zone files from the autogenerated (slave) files.

> **Tip**
>
> When you set up a slave zone on your server, run `ndc reload` to cause BIND to do a zone transfer and create the new zone file at the location you specify in the `file` statement. Sometimes, the file will not be updated immediately if you make a change to the master zone file, even if you do an `ndc reload`. If this is the case, simply delete the slave zone file and reissue the `ndc reload` command to transfer the zone data again and re-create the file.

Other Zone Types

As described in `man named.conf`, you can have three other types of zone blocks.

- **stub**—A `stub` zone works in the same way as a `slave` zone, except that it transfers only the NS records—the records specifying where clients can find valid DNS information for the specified domain.

- **forward**—You can use a `forward` zone type to forward all requests for the zone to another server or set of servers. A `forwarders` block can be specified in this type of zone statement, operating like the global one in the `options` block; this enables you to override the global `forwarders` list.

- **hint**—A `hint` zone is only really used in one case: the initial list of potential root servers, found in `/etc/namedb/named.root`. This is not actually the authoritative list of root servers; it's a list of "hints" for BIND, specifying servers that will have the current true list of root servers, which has a habit of changing as network conditions vary.

Restricting DNS Access

BIND has the capability to restrict access based on Access Control Lists, or ACLs. An ACL is specified in an `acl` statement, which defines a name for the list and contains the criteria for which hosts are included in the list. These criteria can take a number of forms, and they can be recursive; in other words, an ACL can contain other ACLs. The following ACLs are built-in:

- **any**—Allows all hosts.
- **none**—Denies all hosts.
- **localhost**—Allows the IP addresses of all interfaces on the system.
- **localnets**—Allows any host on a network for which the system has an interface.

Other types of list elements that are allowed can be IP addresses (for instance, 111.112.113.114), networks in CIDR format (for instance, 111.112.113/24), a "negated" version of either of these (!111.112.113.114, which means "any host but 111.112.113.114"), or a key statement (used in secure DNS transactions, which are beyond the scope of this chapter). When compiling a list of ACL elements, it's best to put the more specific elements before the broader ones because the list is evaluated in the order in which it's specified. If a host matches any element, it will be allowed, regardless of whether a later "negation" element would have matched it. Put all such exceptions toward the beginning of the list.

Because `named.conf` is read sequentially, an ACL must be specified in the file before it can be referred to later in other statements. For best results, put all `acl` statements toward the top of your `named.conf` file, above the `options` block. A sample ACL would be the following:

```
acl "my_list" {
  localhost;
  localnets;
  another_list;
  !132.112.14.124;
  132.112.14/24;
};
```

Once you have a list specified, you can use it along with other address list elements later in a `zone` statement (to control access to requests for just that zone) or in the global `options` statement. Available access-control statements are the following:

- allow-query { *address_list_elements*; ... };—Specifies which hosts are allowed to perform ordinary DNS queries. `allow-query` may also be specified in a `zone` statement, in which case it overrides the `options allow-query` statement. If not specified, the default is to allow queries from all hosts.

- allow-transfer { *address_list_elements*; ... };—Specifies which slave servers are allowed to receive zone transfers from this server. allow-transfer may also be specified in the zone statement, in which case it overrides the options allow-transfer statement. If not specified, the default is to allow transfers from all hosts.

- allow-recursion { *address_list_elements*; ... };—Specifies which hosts are allowed to make recursive queries through this server. If not specified, the default is to allow recursive queries from all hosts.

- blackhole { *address_list_elements*; ... };—Specifies a list of addresses that the server will not accept queries from or use to resolve a query. Queries from these addresses will not be answered.

For example, you could restrict queries globally to members of the my_list ACL that we specified earlier; furthermore, you could restrict queries for the somewhere.com domain to the members of my_list as well as to an additional network, and restrict zone transfers only to two specified slave servers with the following partial configuration:

```
options {
    directory "/etc/namedb";
        allow-query { my_list; };
};

zone "somewhere.com" {
    type master;
    file "somewhere.com";
        allow-query { my_list; 64.2.43/24; };
        allow-transfer { 64.2.40.107; 120.15.221.0; };
};
```

Creating a Zone File

The zone file is where the mappings for hostnames to IP addresses within a domain or zone are defined; it's also where the most mistakes are commonly made in a BIND configuration, so we will cover it in detail.

The format of a zone file (often referred to as a *Master Zone File* or simply *Master File*) is quite complex and regimented, although there are certain things you can get away with. A "living" zone file in an existing BIND setup can be all but incomprehensible. It helps to understand what kinds of primitives (directives) are allowed and how each one is specified, as well as the shortcuts that are allowed and commonly used.

First, we will look at an example zone file, shown in Listing 30.2, and dissect its components. Note that semicolons (;) are the comment characters in zone files.

LISTING 30.2   Example Zone File for the somewhere.com Domain

```
$TTL 3600

        somewhere.com. IN SOA stripes.somewhere.com. root.somewhere.com. (
                                20010610        ; Serial
                                10800           ; Refresh
                                3600            ; Retry
                                604800          ; Expire
                                86400 )         ; Minimum TTL

        ; DNS Servers
        @       IN NS           stripes.somewhere.com.
        @       IN NS           spots.somewhere.com.

        ; Machine Names
        localhost       IN A    127.0.0.1
        ns1             IN A    64.41.131.162
        ns2             IN A    64.41.131.163
        mail            IN A    64.41.131.167
        @               IN A    64.41.131.162

        ; Aliases
        www             IN CNAME        @
        ftp             IN CNAME        www.somewhere.com.

        ; MX Record
        @               IN MX   10      mail.somewhere.com.
```

While it may look as though this is an unformatted mess, there is in fact a distinct structure to it. Listing 30.2 consists of six basic elements:

- A $TTL directive
- The SOA (Start-of-Authority) record
- A block of NS (Name Server) records
- A block of A (Address) records
- A block of CNAME (Canonical Name) records, which define aliases
- An MX (Mail Exchanger) record

Aside from the directives, each element of the file is a Resource Record (RR), defining
the properties of a name within the zone relative to a certain "origin." We will now look
at each of these elements in turn.

Directives

The zone file format allows for a number of different basic directives. These are global settings for the entire file, and each one is specified in capital letters beginning with a dollar sign ($). Directives can appear anywhere in the zone file, and each subsequent directive of the same type overrides any previous ones.

Of all the available directives, only $ORIGIN is generally very useful in practice.

- $ORIGIN—Syntax: $ORIGIN <domain-name> [<comment>]

  $ORIGIN is what will be appended to any unqualified name in a record. An unqualified name is, for instance, www; if www is listed in a record in a zone file with the $ORIGIN set to somewhere.com., the record will be defined as www.somewhere.com. (with the trailing dot).

  If $ORIGIN is not set within the zone file, it is assumed to be the same as the name of the zone specified in the zone statement that refers to it. If an $ORIGIN directive doesn't have a trailing dot, it is not "absolute", meaning that it will be appended to any previous $ORIGIN strings. For example, the following

  ```
  $ORIGIN com.
  $ORIGIN somewhere
  www                    IN  CNAME stripes
  ```

  is equivalent to

  ```
  www.somewhere.com. IN  CNAME stripes.somewhere.com.
  ```

- $INCLUDE—Syntax: $INCLUDE <filename> [<origin>] [<comment>]

  The $INCLUDE directive imports the file specified by <filename> and processes it as if it were a part of the zone file at the point where the $INCLUDE appears. For the duration of the included file, the $ORIGIN is set to <origin> if specified.

- $TTL—Syntax: $TTL <default-ttl> [<comment>]

  $TTL sets the default Time-to-Live for any records where the TTL value is not set. Generally, this is useful only for such things as *negative caching*, where BIND caches the fact that a record does not exist for a certain period (in other words, the TTL). In a Resource Record (RR), the TTL is the field that appears before the class column—blank in the records shown in Listing 30.2 (the IN field is the class). These records inherit the value of $TTL shown at the top of the listing, which is 3600 seconds in our example.

- $GENERATE—Syntax: $GENERATE <range> <lhs> <type> <rhs> [<comment>]

  $GENERATE is used to create a range of records that differ by an *iterator*, or a step value. In other words, you can automatically specify a large list of name records whose names and mapped IP addresses fit a certain formula.

30

THE DOMAIN NAME SERVER

- `<range>`—This can be one of two forms: `start-stop` or `start-stop/step`. If the first form is used, `step` is set to 1.
- `<lhs>`—This describes what will vary between the newly created records on the left-hand side of the record. Any single $ symbol within the left-hand side is replaced by the iterator value. If `<lhs>` is not an absolute name, the current `$ORIGIN` is appended to it. Use a 0 as a placeholder if nothing on the left-hand side should be iterated.
- `<type>`—Can be any of `PTR`, `CNAME`, or `NS`.
- `<rhs>`—Does the same as `<lhs>`, except for the right-hand side of the record.

The following `$GENERATE` directives

```
$ORIGIN 0.0.192.in-addr.arpa.
$GENERATE 1-2    0 NS     ns$.somewhere.com.
$GENERATE 1-127 $ CNAME $.0
```

...are expanded by BIND into the following:

```
0.0.0.192.in-addr.arpa. NS     ns1.somewhere.com.
0.0.0.192.in-addr.arpa. NS     ns2.somewhere.com.
1.0.0.192.in-addr.arpa. CNAME 1.0.0.0.192.in-addr.arpa.
2.0.0.192.in-addr.arpa. CNAME 2.0.0.0.192.in-addr.arpa.
...
127.0.0.192.in-addr.arpa. CNAME 127.0.0.0.192.in-addr.arpa.
```

SOA Records

Next we come to the first Resource Record in a zone file: the Start-of-Authority (SOA) record. This is the most important part of a zone file, and the most commonly botched. This is because so much of it is counterintuitive in style. We will need to look at it piece by piece.

The example SOA record in Listing 30.2 was as follows:

```
somewhere.com. IN SOA stripes.somewhere.com. root.somewhere.com. (
                   2001061000       ; Serial
                   10800            ; Refresh
                   3600             ; Retry
                   604800           ; Expire
                   86400 )          ; Minimum TTL
```

The SOA, like all records, has the following basic form:

```
<name> [<ttl>] [<class>] <type> <value>
```

If `<name>` is not absolute, the current `$ORIGIN` is appended. In this case, the name is absolute (it ends with a dot).

The <ttl> field is omitted because our example file has a global $TTL directive specifying it. IN (for "Internet") is the class; BIND supports other kinds of classes, but we're not interested in them here. If in was specified in the zone statement in named.conf, this field is redundant and can be omitted.

The <value> field for most records is quite simple: an IP address, a hostname, or some symbolic name. For the SOA record, though, it's much more complex. It begins, first of all, with the name of the authoritative name server for the zone (stripes.somewhere.com). The next piece of information is the e-mail address of the administrator of the domain, with the @ sign replaced by a dot. It also has a trailing dot at the end. In our example, the administrator (root@somewhere.com) is specified as root.somewhere.com., and will be used by BIND to mail status notifications to the responsible party.

> **Note**
>
> The reason for the @ sign in the administrator e-mail address being replaced with a dot is that the @ symbol, in a zone file, has a special meaning. It's a shorthand for the current value of $ORIGIN, and will be expanded by BIND into a fully qualified domain name.
>
> Note that the @ symbol must be the complete key if you use it; it can't be expanded implicitly, as in www.@ or similar constructs.

Following the administrator address is a parenthesized block of settings; the parentheses specify a block in which line breaks are ignored, so you can format the values for better clarity. These are the numbers that define how the zone data will behave on the Internet.

- Serial Number—The serial number is the way BIND keeps track of how recent a zone file is. Each time you update the zone file, you must increment the number so that BIND knows to refresh its information from the file. Standard practice is to use the format YYYYMMDDNN for this number; the final two digits are for revisions within a day. Update the number to reflect the current day when you make a change.

> **Note**
>
> When you use ndc reload to refresh a master zone file's information, BIND will automatically determine that the data needs to be refreshed, regardless of the serial number. However, keeping the serial number accurate is a good habit to be in; it will ensure proper operation in cases such as manually refreshing slave zone data.

- Refresh—This number, in seconds, specifies how frequently slave servers should check the master for updated zone data. If the master's serial number has changed since the last zone transfer, a new zone transfer will be performed.

- Retry—If the master server cannot be contacted, the slaves will retry at intervals specified by this number (in seconds).

- Expire—If the master server cannot be contacted within this time (in seconds), the slave servers discard all their data for the zone.

- Minimum TTL—This number (in seconds) specifies how long "negative cache" responses (which indicate the absence of a piece of data) should be kept.

NS Records

Listing 30.2 listed the following example Name Server (NS) records:

```
; DNS Servers
@          IN NS          stripes.somewhere.com.
@          IN NS          spots.somewhere.com.
```

These records specify the DNS servers that are allowed to give authoritative answers to queries about the zone. Note that the @ symbol refers to the current $ORIGIN (somewhere.com.), and that both server names have trailing dots (indicating that they are absolute).

You can create NS records for subdomains, or zones within the current zone. For instance, suppose you have a cluster of machines within a zone called cluster.somewhere.com., with their DNS information handled by their own name server (ns.cluster. somewhere.com). A valid NS record for that server, allowing external hosts to query it for the cluster's IP addresses, would be

```
cluster IN NS          ns.cluster.somewhere.com.
```

Recall that by leaving the trailing dot off of cluster, the current $ORIGIN (somewhere.com.) is appended to it by BIND.

A Records

The Address (A) record is what you use to associate a hostname with an IP address. Our example had the following records:

```
; Machine Names
localhost      IN A    127.0.0.1
stripes        IN A    64.41.131.162
spots          IN A    64.41.131.163
mail           IN A    64.41.131.167
@              IN A    64.41.131.162
```

The meaning of these records is fairly straightforward. The unqualified names on the left-hand side are expanded with the current $ORIGIN, so mail.somewhere.com would resolve to 64.41.131.167. Similarly, the @ symbol expands so that a query for somewhere.com would return 64.41.131.162.

Names that are defined in A records are known as *canonical names*, as opposed to *aliases* (which are defined by CNAME records).

CNAME Records

Canonical Name (CNAME) records are used to create aliases. The terminology is such that in our example from Listing 30.2:

```
; Aliases
www             IN CNAME        @
ftp             IN CNAME        www.somewhere.com.
```

The alias name www (which expands with $ORIGIN to www.somewhere.com.) points to the canonical name @, or somewhere.com. (whose IP address is defined in the A block).

CNAME records are often useful in that they are not immediately bound to an IP address. You can use CNAME records to point to names in another zone, for example, which can then be controlled by the owner of that zone. Also, CNAME records are helpful in reducing the number of changes that must be made in a zone file if an IP address changes.

MX Records

Mail Exchanger (MX) records define which hosts are to be used for mail delivery to addresses in the zone. Sendmail (and other MTAs) look up the highest-priority MX record within a zone and open a connection to it; you can find out the MX hosts for a domain with the host command:

```
# host somecompany.com
somecompany.com has address 207.114.98.18
somecompany.com mail is handled (pri=100) by mail.uu.net
somecompany.com mail is handled (pri=5) by mx-1.somecompany.com
```

Lower-priority numbers are tried first and then increasingly higher numbers are tried until a successful SMTP connection can be made. The priority is specified as part of the value field in the record, as in our example:

```
; MX Record
@                   IN MX   10 mail.somewhere.com.
```

> **Caution**
>
> An MX record cannot point to an IP address. Also, many MTAs and mail clients will complain if they detect an MX record that points to a CNAME. Make sure your MX records point to defined names specified elsewhere with A records!

PTR Records

Pointer (PTR) records are the reverse of A or CNAME records, and are used in reverse DNS zone files (for example, 131.41.64.in-addr.arpa) to map IP addresses to domain names. An example reverse DNS zone file is shown in Listing 30.3.

Because a reverse DNS lookup only returns a single name, multiple PTR records for the same IP address are useless and only confuse matters. For this reason, reverse files are often shorter than their forward counterparts.

Reverse DNS Zone Files

A reverse DNS zone file, defining a zone of the form 131.41.64.in-addr.arpa, is used to map IP addresses to names. Files of this sort are referenced in named.conf and propagated to slave servers just like forward DNS zone files. Listing 30.3 shows an example reverse DNS zone file.

Listing 30.3   Example Reverse DNS Zone File for the 131.41.64.in-addr.arpa Zone

```
$TTL 3600

131.41.64.in-addr.arpa.  IN SOA stripes.somewhere.com. root.somewhere.com. (
                          2001061000      ; Serial
                          10800           ; Refresh
                          3600            ; Retry
                          604800          ; Expire
                          86400 )         ; Minimum TTL

@       IN NS   stripes.somewhere.com.
@       IN NS   spots.somewhere.com.

162     IN PTR  stripes.somewhere.com.
163     IN PTR  spots.somewhere.com.
167     IN PTR  mail.somewhere.com.
```

Note the use of PTR records instead of A or CNAME records. The name that each PTR points to is the true canonical name for that IP address. There is also no need for an MX record in a reverse file because MX records cannot be associated with IP addresses in the first place.

Making a `localhost` Zone File

A special zone file must exist for the localhost zone (0.0.127.in-addr.arpa) to work properly. There's a shell script in /etc/namedb to help you create one. The script is called make-localhost, and it reads in a template (PROTO.localhost.rev) and fills in information that it derives from your input. Because it isn't set executable, you must run it with the sh command:

```
# sh make-localhost
Enter your domain name: somewhere.com
```

The resulting file, localhost.rev, should look something like Listing 30.4.

LISTING 30.4 Autogenerated localhost.rev Zone File

```
;       From: @(#)localhost.rev 5.1 (Berkeley) 6/30/90
; $FreeBSD: src/etc/namedb/PROTO.localhost.rev,v 1.6 2000/01/10 15:31:40 peter
Exp $
;
; This file is automatically edited by the `make-localhost' script in
; the /etc/namedb directory.
;

$TTL    3600

@       IN      SOA     stripes.somewhere.com. root.stripes.somewhere.com. (
                                20010612        ; Serial
                                3600    ; Refresh
                                900     ; Retry
                                3600000 ; Expire
                                3600 )  ; Minimum
        IN      NS      stripes.somewhere.com.
1       IN      PTR     localhost.somewhere.com.
```

Make sure to create this file before fully deploying your DNS service!

Configuring a Caching Name Server

It's entirely possible to run a name server that is not authoritative for any zones. This is what's known as a caching name server, and its job consists solely of making DNS queries when prompted by clients and storing the results for later use. This is the opposite effect of the `forward only;` option that we discussed earlier in this chapter: Whereas a `forward only;` name server would pass off all requests to its forwarder to handle, a caching name server performs all requests that are asked of it by itself and caches the results. Other name servers can use this server as a forwarder, leveraging the work that it has already done.

To configure a caching name server, simply omit any `zone` statements from your `named.conf` file other than the ones necessary for its own operation. Listing 30.5 shows such a configuration.

LISTING 30.5   Sample `/etc/namedb/named.conf` File

```
/*
 * A simple BIND 8 configuration
 */

logging {
    category lame-servers { null; };
    category cname { null; };
};

options {
    directory "/etc/namedb";
};

zone "." {
    type hint;
    file "named.boot";
};

zone "0.0.127.in-addr.arpa" in {
    type master;
    file "localhost.rev";
};

zone "0.0.0.0.0.0.0.0.0.0.0.0.0.0.0.0.0.0.0.0.0.0.0.0.0.0.0.0.0.0.0.0.IP6.INT" {
        type master;
        file "localhost.rev";
};
```

Because a caching name server is simply a "degenerate case" of a fully configured name server, you can easily expand your server's functionality by adding additional zones as time goes on. There is no real fundamental difference between the two "modes."

Your DNS configuration will change with time as your network evolves. Each time a new host is added to your network or changes its name, and each time you take on or remove the name service authority for a zone, you will need to make changes to the configuration. It's a good idea to keep in practice with DNS administration so that these tasks become more natural with time.

CHAPTER 31

The Network Filesystem (NFS)

NFS, the *Network Filesystem*, is the UNIX way of performing file sharing. Windows and Mac OS both have their own file-sharing mechanisms, enabling networked computers to access files on remote machines on a LAN as if they were local. NFS provides the same benefits, with a few extra features that other sharing protocols don't have.

This chapter will describe how to configure your FreeBSD machine to operate as an NFS client and/or server, sharing files with other UNIX machines on your LAN or across the Internet.

Introduction to NFS

Windows uses NetBIOS for its file sharing, and Macintoshes use AppleTalk. These are both peer-to-peer protocols, with each system broadcasting its presence onto the LAN, and all machines being able to mount each other's shared folders dynamically. NFS is a bit different in that it's a client-server protocol, with designated servers sharing items that can be mounted remotely by specified NFS clients. This model is designed for centralization in an enterprise or university network, rather than for peer-to-peer file transfers, as other protocols tend to operate. However, with proper configuration, NFS can do almost everything that the other protocols can do and more, with the exception of server discovery.

Under both Windows and Mac OS, the built-in file-sharing protocol on a computer broadcasts information about its own shared folders (or "shares"), and asks for responses about other available shares on the network. These "discovery" queries and responses, sent out by each machine on the network and triggering frequent responses from all other machines, make for a very "chatty" network environment. NFS doesn't have a corresponding discovery mechanism. As we will see, each NFS client has to know where to find each server, and mount it manually. However, this does mean that the network is much quieter due to a lack of discovery traffic.

There are benefits to the less-convenient structure of NFS. A server can control exactly which clients are able to connect to it, for example, by hostname or IP address; or by centralized login, as with NIS or Kerberos. Another feature of NFS is that because it does not depend on LAN broadcasts for server discovery, it can be used across the Internet just as easily as across the LAN. A client in Boston can mount a share from a server in San Francisco, if necessary. By contrast, NetBIOS and AppleTalk only can operate within "domains" or "zones" on the local network.

As far as FreeBSD is concerned, NFS is a filesystem just like any other. You can mount an NFS share over the network just as if you were mounting a floppy disk or a new hard drive partition, as we saw in Chapter 9, "The FreeBSD Filesystem." Shares will even be mounted automatically if their resources are requested and the client machine is properly set up to do it. We will go over the procedure of mounting an NFS share later in this chapter.

The client-server structure of NFS is designed so that you can centralize the resources in your network. For example, an enterprise might give all its employees home directories on a central UNIX machine, and every other system in the network that supports NFS will be able to mount those home directories and access them remotely, rather than requiring each machine to have its own copy of every home directory. Figure 31.1 shows this kind of network topology in action. The same can be done for build directories (in a software development environment) or shared applications that are centrally installed (as in a university workstation cluster). NFS mounts can be used in conjunction with NIS (centralized login management) to provide the entire network with user authentication; then, file ownership and permissions on every file in a mounted share will work just as on the NFS server machine itself. You can even install FreeBSD over NFS if you mount the installation CD-ROM on the NFS server and point Sysinstall toward it.

FIGURE 31.1

An enterprise net-work with central NFS-mounted home directories.

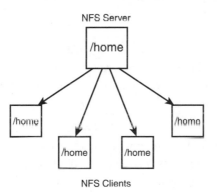

An interesting aspect of NFS is that it's primarily based on UDP, rather than TCP. As we discussed in Chapter 22, "Introduction to Networking," UDP has none of the reliability or connection-centric structure of TCP, and is inherently unreliable. Although it seems odd that a data-conscious network protocol would use UDP as its transport mechanism, spewing datagrams from server to client without any guarantee of their integrity, NFS is actually one of the best examples of UDP used properly. Full TCP connections aren't really needed, especially on a LAN. NFS clients come and go as machines on a network come up and shut down, and TCP connections would just get in the way of data streams sending files and directory information back and forth between the endpoints on request. An NFS mount can stay dormant for days and then suddenly be called into use again.

UDP allows the shared resources to be immediately available without connection startup overhead or lag time, and if a host drops off the network, it's no big deal to the server.

Data integrity is maintained by the NFS software itself, keeping checksum and sequencing information in the packets' payload and doing all the work that TCP would otherwise have done. However, NFS clients that operate over TCP do exist, and the NFS server supports them too. NFS over TCP is primarily intended for mounts that take place over a WAN, in which dropped packets are much more likely, and the benefits of full TCP connections mitigate the benefits that UDP offers on LAN connections.

> **Note**
>
> One downside to using UDP, though, is that if a client tries to contact an NFS server that isn't there, it can take forever to time out. The lack of a full TCP connection means that more primitive methods are necessary to determine whether a server is not responding. We will talk about some of the ways to avoid running into the lengthy NFS timeout later in this chapter.

NFS doesn't have any built-in security or encryption, so it should be used over the Internet only if you're working with files that can safely be exposed to the public. Mission-critical or sensitive data should never be sent over wide-area NFS, except inside a LAN protected by a firewall or through an encrypted VPN tunnel.

A FreeBSD machine can be configured to be an NFS server, an NFS client, or both. Depending on how you configure it, the system will run a few different processes that manage its end of the NFS connections it will handle. We'll talk first about setting it up as an NFS server and then about configuring it as a client.

Configuring an NFS Server

Setting up your FreeBSD machine to be an NFS server involves a one-line addition to /etc/rc.conf:

```
nfs_server_enable="YES"
```

Also, make sure that portmap_enable is set to "YES" (as it is by default unless you override it). The portmap daemon needs to be running in order for NFS to work because the NFS server needs a mechanism by which to tell its clients which port to connect to. UDP services operate with only one "connection" per port, so while initial connections to the NFS server take place on the server port 2049, these connections are mapped by RPC (remote procedure call) services, provided by portmap, to a new and unused server port.

Note that portmap services are fairly insecure and subject to a number of recurring security issues; for this reason, it's not a good idea to have an NFS server exposed to the Internet without a firewall protecting it. See Chapter 29, "Network Security," for more on firewalls.

When you set the nfs_server_enable option and reboot, FreeBSD starts two kinds of daemon processes—three if you count portmap—after reading the contents of the /etc/exports file to determine what to share via NFS. Let's look at each of these components to see what they do and how to control them.

NFS Daemon (nfsd)

The NFS server daemon, the equivalent of sshd or httpd, is nfsd. A certain number of nfsd processes are started when the network is initialized (the default is four); these processes are assigned to service NFS clients when they connect, one process per client. In the default configuration, a maximum of four clients can connect to your NFS server at the same time. You can tune this with the nfs_server_flags setting in /etc/rc.d:

```
nfs_server_flags="-u -t -n 4"
```

The -n flag can be set to any number you like; set it to the highest number of concurrent NFS clients you expect to be connected to your server at any one time. The -t and -u flags tell the nfsd processes to serve both TCP and UDP clients. Other flags are available for you to tweak, if you like. For instance, specify -h 64.41.131.102 among the other flags to bind the NFS servers to the interface with the address 64.41.131.102. (You can also use a hostname instead of an IP address.) This can be necessary if your server has multiple network interfaces; the UDP mechanism is such that if you don't tell nfsd for which specific IP addresses it should serve requests, its responses are not guaranteed to come from the address that the client contacted. You can list as many addresses as you need with multiple -h flags. For example, let's say you have a server acting as a gateway with two network cards, one on the "inside" and one on the "outside" of the network. Your "inside" card has two IP addresses bound to it, and you want to serve NFS shares only to clients on the inside. You can set up NFS like this:

```
nfs_server_flags="-u -t -n 4 -h 64.41.131.102 -h 64.41.131.116"
```

Then, you can block access to the NFS service on the outside interface with an IPFW rule, like so:

```
ipfw add deny udp from any to 64.41.131.10 nfsd
```

Refer to Chapter 29 for more information on how to configure firewall rules using IPFW.

NFS Mount Daemon (mountd)

While nfsd is the program that provides the connection end of each individual NFS mount, a second program is in charge of listening for new NFS client requests (on TCP port 2049). This program is mountd, the mount daemon. It is executed automatically along with the nfsd processes during the network setup procedure at boot time if nfs_server_enable is set to "YES".

mountd takes incoming NFS connections, and passes them to nfsd processes. It's also in charge of keeping track of the NFS shares that you have specified in /etc/exports; to restart NFS services after making changes to /etc/exports, you need to send a HUP signal to mountd, as we will see shortly.

There aren't too many useful options for mountd. The default settings in /etc/defaults/rc.conf, which you can override in /etc/rc.conf, are as follows:

```
mountd_flags="-r"
```

The -r flag allows mountd to serve regular files rather than only directories, to maintain compatibility with certain diskless workstations that boot via NFS. The -l flag allows you to log all NFS mount requests, and the -n flag allows NFS shares to be mounted to remote systems such as Windows PCs that don't share the same ownership and permissions model as UNIX.

Determining What to Share with the /etc/exports File

The /etc/exports file lists what directory trees should be shared via NFS, and who should be allowed to share them. If /etc/exports does not exist or is not readable at the time the network is started, the nfsd and mountd processes are not started.

The full format of /etc/exports is defined in man exports. A basic export line specifies one or more directories that should be exported (shared), any of several options, and then an optional list of hosts (by IP address, network, netgroup, or hostname) that are allowed to share the specified directories. For example, the following line shares the /home directory and all its subdirectories to anybody who connects:

```
/home -alldirs
```

Note that the -alldirs option can only be specified if the share is the mount point of a filesystem (for example, /usr or /home). If it isn't, the share will not be made available.

A share that can be accessed only by three specified hosts and is read-only would look like this:

```
/usr2 -ro -alldirs stripes.somewhere.com spots.somewhere.com 64.41.131.165
```

> **Tip**
>
> You can create groups of hosts by specifying them in the file /etc/netgroup. A group can be specified in the following form:
>
> ```
> groupname (host, user, domain) (host, user, domain) ...
> ```
>
> For instance, to create a group called desktops that contained three particular hosts (named sol, luna, and terra), the line would look like this:
>
> ```
> desktops (sol,,) (luna,,) (terra,,)
> ```
>
> A netgroup defined on usernames would look like this:
>
> ```
> developers (,frank,) (,bob,) (,alice,)
> ```
>
> You can then use any of these netgroup names instead of hostnames in /etc/exports to confine an NFS share to members of that group.

File ownership in an NFS share is mapped based on the UIDs of each file and directory. If the usernames and UIDs on the server and client machines are the same (for instance, if the machines' logins are synchronized via NIS or Kerberos), the permissions will match. However, if the UID 1045 maps on the server to the username bill, but UID 1045 on the client is john, John will own the files in the share that the server thinks Bill owns. When exporting a share containing files owned by many different users, make sure the infrastructure is in place to provide consistent mappings between UIDs and usernames on all the machines on your network.

You can use the -maproot=<username> or -maproot=<UID> options to map ownership so that the username matching <username> or with the user ID <UID> on the client machine will have full root permissions in the share. For example, to share the entire filesystem of the NFS server with anybody in the 64.41.131 network, with the client user frank having full read/write access to all the files:

```
/ -maproot=frank -network 64.41.131 -mask 255.255.255.0
```

After making any changes to /etc/exports, you need to restart the mountd process. Do this by accessing the runtime PID file:

```
# kill -HUP `cat /var/run/mountd.pid`
```

> **Note**
>
> You can't have multiple export lines for mount points within the same partition or filesystem. This is to prevent problems in cases where the export permissions for different shares in the same filesystem would conflict. NFS clients cannot access one filesystem from within another that it has mounted, and the same access permissions must apply for all shares within a filesystem. The following setup is illegal:
>
> ```
> /home/frank 64.41.131.102
> /home/joe 64.41.131.102
> ```
>
> But the following is correct:
>
> ```
> /home/frank /home/joe 64.41.131.102
> ```

You can use the `showmount` program to display the valid shares and their permissions. This is how you can tell whether your `/etc/exports` setup is valid:

```
# showmount -e
Exports list on localhost:
/usr                        Everyone
/home/frank                 64.41.131.102
/home/joe                   64.41.131.102
/                           64.41.131.0
```

Starting NFS Services Without Rebooting

The cleanest way to start NFS services is to reboot the system. However, if you need to start the services and you don't want to reboot, simply issue the following commands as root (omitting the `portmap` command if it's already running):

```
# portmap
# nfsd -u -t -n 4
# mountd -r
```

Then, use `showmount -e` to make sure that the NFS shares are being exported properly.

Configuring an NFS Client

If your FreeBSD machine will be mounting NFS shares from other servers, you will need to configure it as a client. Technically this isn't really necessary—you can mount an NFS share in a rudimentary fashion right out of the box. However, configuring the system as an NFS client gives you a few features that ensure speedy and reliable performance.

To set up an NFS client machine, simply enable the following line in `/etc/rc.conf`:

```
nfs_client_enable="YES"
```

This setting enables the NFS Input/Output Daemon, `nfsiod`, which helps to streamline NFS client requests and tunes a few kernel settings to improve access time. This is all handled automatically in the `/etc/rc.network` script at boot time, along with the NFS server settings (which we saw earlier).

NFS Input/Output Daemon (`nfsiod`)

The `nfsiod` daemon isn't required for proper NFS client operation, but it helps to speed things up. It operates by allowing NFS read and write operations to be done in an asynchronous manner, with "read-ahead" and "write-behind" operations occurring in the background, rather than having to wait for each sequential step in the process to complete. Just as with `nfsd`, there should be as many `nfsiod` processes running as there are mounted NFS shares on the client machine. You can tune this with the `nfs_client_flags` setting in `/etc/rc.conf`, set to 4 by default:

```
nfs_client_flags="-n 4"
```

There aren't any other settable options for `nfsiod`. To start it without rebooting the machine, simply run it from the command line:

```
# nfsiod -n 4
```

Mounting Remote Filesystems

Mounting an NFS share is done with the `mount_nfs` command, which is a shorthand command for `mount -t nfs` (as we saw in Chapter 9). In its most common form, you would pass to it two arguments: the host and share names in a combined string, and the local mount point:

```
# mount_nfs spots:/home /home2
```

A successful mount will result in no output. Check that the mount was successful with the `df` command:

```
# df
Filesystem        1K-blocks      Used     Avail Capacity  Mounted on
/dev/ad0s1a          992239     54353    858507     6%    /
/dev/ad0s1f        26704179   4872963  19694882    20%    /home
/dev/ad0s1e         9924475   1642343   7488174    18%    /usr
procfs                    4         4         0   100%    /proc
spots:/home         9924475   1642343   7488174    18%    /home2
```

If you go into the /home2 directory, you'll see all the directories within /home on the NFS server, with each file's ownership mapped based on UID, as we discussed earlier. The filesystem will remain mounted until you explicitly unmount it with the umount command:

```
# umount /home2
```

Caution

Remember to leave any NFS-mounted directory before you try to unmount it with umount! You will get a "device busy" error if you try to unmount a filesystem while you're still inside it.

NFS shares can be mounted in a great variety of different ways, and the options are laid out in the man mount_nfs page. Some of the more useful are the -T option, which forces TCP transport rather than UDP (useful for mounts done over WAN links); and the -s and -x <seconds> flags, which allow the mount to time-out and disappear after a specified period and fail (a "soft" mount).

```
# mount_nfs -s -x 60 spots:/home /home2
```

Tip

Another useful option is -i, which enables interruptibility. Normally, if you have mounted an NFS share and the server becomes unresponsive or unreachable, any filesystem calls you make (commands that deal with the shared files, such as ls) can hang in such a way that even pressing Ctrl+C won't stop them. The -i option makes it so Ctrl+C (the termination signal) will force the command to fail, returning control to you.

As with other filesystem types, you can add NFS mounts to /etc/fstab to set up predefined mount points, simplifying the mount process. Place any options that you would otherwise pass to mount_nfs in the Options column, separated by commas:

```
# Device            Mountpoint      FStype  Options         Dump    Pass#
spots:/home         /home2          nfs     rw,-T,-i,noauto 0       0
```

With a table entry like this, you can mount an NFS filesystem with the mount command:

```
# mount /home2
```

Mounting Remote Filesystems Automatically at System Boot

All filesystems in `/etc/fstab` are automatically mounted at boot time, as we saw in Chapter 9, unless the `noauto` option is present. You can specify that remote NFS shares should be mounted at startup by simply adding them to `/etc/fstab`, as we just saw. However, there are a few things to watch out for.

Most notably, NFS has an extremely long default timeout period, and the phase during startup when filesystems are mounted is a synchronous, blocking process. If your NFS server or servers cannot be found—for instance, if the server machine isn't running, or if your own machine's network connection is not configured properly—the boot process can hang for an intolerably long period before giving up and finishing the boot procedure.

You can solve this problem by placing the `noauto` option in `/etc/fstab`, as we saw in our earlier example. However, this means that you have to mount each NFS share manually after the system is fully booted. There's a better way to handle this: the `-b` option.

```
# Device              Mountpoint    FStype  Options    Dump    Pass#
spots:/home           /home2        nfs     rw,-b      0       0
```

The `-b` option tells `mount` to make a quick attempt to contact the server, and if it can't, to fork off a child process to continue trying to connect while the boot process continues on. Similarly, if you mount a share from the command line using `-b`, the process forks into the background and returns you to the command prompt. The following is the output you would get when trying to mount the share specified in the preceding example `/etc/fstab` line, after trying for 60 seconds:

```
# mount /home2
NFS Portmap: RPC: Port mapper failure - RPC: Unable to send

mount_nfs: Cannot immediately mount spots:/home, backgrounding
```

The background `mount_nfs` process will keep trying to mount the share until it's successful. This method is particularly useful in computing clusters or labs in which NFS-mounted resources are nice to have but not required for correct operation—for example, a cluster in which an NFS mount contains popular user programs or games, but all critical system functions are available on disks on the local system.

Auto-Mount Daemon (amd)

Something that makes NFS mounts even more convenient is the auto-mount daemon, `amd`. This daemon allows you to mount NFS shares (and other filesystem types, as a matter of fact) dynamically, simply by working in the directory in which the share would be mounted, without ever having to bother with `mount` commands.

FreeBSD provides a basic way to set up `amd`. Simply add the following line to `/etc/rc.conf`:

```
amd_enable="YES"
```

When the system is booted with this option, `amd` runs with the options specified in the `amd_flags` setting, which are such that anything in the `/host` or `/net` directories—both of which are created automatically by `amd`—will auto-mount by name. You can also start it in the same way as it would be at boot time by issuing the following command:

```
# amd -a /.amd_mnt -l syslog /host /etc/amd.map /net /etc/amd.map
```

With `amd` running, `cd` into the `/host` directory and look around. It's empty.

```
# cd /host
# ls
#
```

However, try listing by name as if there were a directory there with the same name as a known NFS server on the network:

```
# ls stripes
home
```

So, it seems that there's indeed a directory called `stripes` in the `/host` directory, and inside it is a `home` directory—which contains everything that the `stripes:/home` share has. You've just auto-mounted that share into the `/host` directory, simply by listing it as a directory name. `/host/stripes/home` is functionally the same thing as the `/home2` mount point we manually created in our earlier example. The `df` command will verify it:

```
# df
Filesystem          1K-blocks     Used    Avail Capacity  Mounted on
stripes:/home        9924475  1642345  7488172    18%
/.amd_mnt/stripes/host/home
```

> **Note**
>
> Notice that NFS shares mounted in this manner actually appear to be mounted inside a directory called `.amd_mnt` in the root directory. This directory doesn't actually exist; it's just a shorthand used by the `amd` daemon for bookkeeping purposes.

To specify a permanent location for a mountable NFS resource, simply make a symbolic link to the appropriate path within /host or /net:

```
# ln -s /home2 /host/stripes/home
```

From now on, whenever you go into the /home2 directory, the stripes:/home share will automatically mount and give you access to its files. When the share is no longer in use, it will automatically unmount.

> **Tip**
>
> You can specify much more complex amd mount maps, which are more direct methods of mounting filesystems at particular points, with the /etc/amd.conf file. This file doesn't exist in the default FreeBSD installation; see man amd.conf for details on its format and capabilities.

CHAPTER 32

File and Print Sharing with Microsoft Windows

NFS is an excellent solution for file sharing between UNIX machines, where UNIX permissions and file meta-data (such as modification times) must be preserved from machine to machine. However, NFS isn't widely supported on many consumer operating systems. Windows and classic Mac OS support it only through third-party applications, and—more importantly in an enterprise environment—there isn't any "discovery" mechanism built in to NFS to allow clients to browse lists of available servers.

When you put a FreeBSD machine into an existing network, chances are that most of the computers already there will be running Windows. True interoperation with these clients and with existing Windows file servers require that FreeBSD share files the same way Windows does. This method is *SMB*, the *Server Message Block* protocol, and the *Common Internet File System (CIFS)*, which is gradually replacing it.

File sharing over SMB/CIFS is not a built-in part of FreeBSD. However, an add-on package called *Samba* gives a FreeBSD machine the ability to act as a Windows file server and participate in all the same file-sharing activities as true Windows clients can.

Introduction to Samba

Samba is an open-source, volunteer project originally begun by Andrew Tridgell and now developed collaboratively by the general UNIX community. It provides a UNIX machine (such as FreeBSD) with the capability to do everything that Windows file sharing can do, including appearing in network browsing lists, securing connections based on NT domain and username logons, and providing network print services. There are also tools that provide many of the administrative functions that a Windows NT/2000 server has. With the addition of the smbfs port, which we will examine later in this chapter (allowing FreeBSD to operate as a Windows file-sharing client), we have a complete suite of software that allows us to use a FreeBSD machine in a Windows network environment with just as much functionality as a native Windows machine would have.

The official Web site for Samba is at `http://www.samba.org`, from which you can select any of a number of different geographical mirror sites.

SMB/CIFS Explained

SMB, dating back to documents published in 1985 by IBM and later further expanded by Microsoft and Intel, is a generalized system for sharing all kinds of system resources over a local network. Such resources include files, printers, serial ports, and software abstractions such as named pipes. It's a protocol that operates in a client-server fashion, even if Windows file sharing on the surface appears to be a peer-to-peer structure. SMB is a fundamental part of many operating systems, including MS-DOS, Windows, OS/2, and Linux—although the primary uses for SMB today are in Windows and promulgated by Microsoft.

SMB and CIFS commands are sent over network protocols such as IPX, NetBEUI, Banyan VINES, and DECnet. These protocols operate at the "network" level of the stack, the same level as IP (as we saw in Chapter 22, "Introduction to Networking"), and are therefore not limited to TCP/IP transport. However, the most commonly used transport for SMB is NetBIOS (Network Basic Input/Output System, described in RFCs 1001 and 1002) traveling over IP, operating with both TCP and UDP components. This is the protocol used in Windows file sharing.

Browsing

An advantage that SMB has over protocols such as NFS is that it supports automatic server discovery, or browsing. In Windows, if you open the Network Neighborhood or My Network Places window, it will display the names of all the available SMB servers on the local network. This list is built up dynamically, with each machine sending out periodic broadcast packets looking for the "master browser" of the network (a computer with a definitive list of local and remote SMB hosts) and announcing its own presence. Every other machine on the network builds its "browse list" from those broadcasts.

The name of each machine, as it appears in the network browser window (as shown in Figure 32.1), is its "NetBIOS name," a designation that Windows allows to be up to 15 characters long. Although Windows makes you input a NetBIOS name in uppercase, it shows up in the network browser window in initially capitalized, lowercase form. Under other operating systems (such as FreeBSD), the NetBIOS name is the same as the machine's hostname, truncated to 15 characters if necessary.

FIGURE 32.1

The Windows network browser window, showing a FreeBSD machine running Samba.

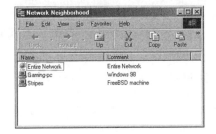

NetBIOS names are handled by a form of name service, somewhat like DNS names, but mapping the displayed NetBIOS machine names to particular machines based on other criteria as well as the IP address (because NetBIOS isn't restricted to IP). Samba's name server component is separate from the actual SMB data server, as we will see.

One drawback to NetBIOS is that it operates only on a LAN; NetBIOS packets are broadcast-based, and therefore aren't forwarded by routers. The WINS (Windows Internet Name Service) protocol exists to link Windows sharing zones on different networks, mitigating this issue somewhat.

Security, Workgroups, and Domains

Access to SMB shares is controlled at various levels. The topmost level restricts access based on host IP address or by password authentication from viewing any of the file server's contents. Beneath that, each individual share (a directory, printer, or other resource) has its own access permissions and optional host/password restrictions as well. Finally, within a share, individual files are subject to access permissions based on the authenticated user or host that has gained access to the share.

User authentication with passwords can be handled in a distributed way (by each individual sharing host) or in a centralized way (by a central network logon server). This is the difference between "workgroups" and "domains" in Windows. A *workgroup* is a collection of machines that agree to appear in one another's network browser windows, and each individually handles its own authentication and security. A *domain* is a group of machines whose security duties are handled by a central server to which all member machines must be subscribed.

Samba provides the ability to restrict access on all of these levels, as well as to act itself as a "master browser" (in workgroup context) or as a domain controller (the central logon authority in a domain environment). We will see how this is done shortly.

File and Print Sharing with Macintosh Clients Using AppleTalk

While Samba provides SMB/CIFS sharing capabilities for interoperability with Windows clients, you'll need to consider AppleTalk—another LAN-level protocol suite operating over its own transport layer or over IP—to talk to Macintosh clients. Because many enterprise and university networks do have significant AppleTalk file-sharing and printer management zones, it may be a good idea to consider supporting it with your FreeBSD system as well.

The software package that provides AppleTalk functionality to UNIX platforms, called *netatalk*, is available in the ports collection. It's another open-source community effort developed at SourceForge, and it is undergoing continual development.

To install AppleTalk support, build netatalk from the ports at /usr/ports/net/netatalk. You can safely ignore the netatalk-asun port because the enhancements in that port by Adrian Sun have been rolled into the basic netatalk port, which tracks a more advanced version anyway. Don't install both ports at once, or AppleTalk won't work at all.

For netatalk to operate correctly, you will need to enable the NETATALK option in your kernel configuration. See Chapter 17, "Kernel Configuration," for information on building a custom kernel. The netatalk port installs a number of configuration files—one for each necessary daemon—along with .dist (or distribution) reference copies. The daemons will all run in the default installed configuration, though you will probably want to change some of the config files to tweak their behavior. Every Macintosh on the network will see the machine in its AppleShare zone in the Chooser (or in the Connect to Server window in Mac OS X), as shown in Figure 32.2.

32

FILE AND PRINT
SHARING WITH
MICROSOFT WINDOWS

FIGURE 32.2

The Mac OS Chooser, showing a file server running netatalk available in the AppleShare zone.

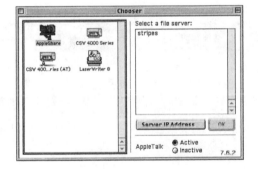

See the official netatalk Web site at http://netatalk.sourceforge.net/ for fuller descriptions of the various tools in the netatalk package and links to other documentation (largely Linux-oriented, but still useful).

Installing and Configuring Samba

Samba is available in the ports at /usr/ports/net/samba or in the packages. Refer to Chapter 15, "Installing Additional Software," for details on how to install a package or port.

Once you have installed the Samba package, there will be a variety of new items installed: daemon executables (in /usr/local/sbin), administrative tools (in

/usr/local/bin), documentation and examples (in /usr/local/share), and configuration files that go into /usr/local/etc. Some of the possible config files don't exist in the default installation; you have to create them from scratch if you want to take advantage of their functionality. There are also code pages (in /usr/local/etc/codepages) that map Windows character sets to UNIX ones.

The only configuration file that exists in the package is smb.conf.default, which you must rename to smb.conf for it to work. Similarly, the /usr/local/etc/rc.d/samba.sh.sample startup script must be renamed to samba.sh. In the very easiest way to get Samba running, you only need to edit smb.conf and modify the workgroup line to reflect the workgroup or domain of which your machine is a part:

```
# workgroup = NT-Domain-Name or Workgroup-Name, eg: REDHAT4
    workgroup = MYGROUP
```

Samba will now be started automatically when the system boots. To start it manually, run the samba.sh script with the start parameter:

```
# /usr/local/etc/rc.d/samba.sh start
  Samba#
```

> **Note**
>
> Note that there is no line break in the script output after the service name
> Samba. This cosmetic flaw exists because during startup, each service in
> /usr/local/etc/rc.d is started sequentially, and the echoed output of each
> startup script all goes onto the same line. Being able to start services from
> the rc.d startup scripts is a convenience feature, not the primary intended
> functionality.

The smbd and nmbd Daemons

If the samba.sh script runs successfully, you will notice two new processes running: smbd and nmbd:

```
# ps -waux | grep mbd
root    3855  0.0  1.5  2368 1816  ??  Is   2:43PM  0:00.00
/usr/local/sbin/smbd -D
root    3857  0.0  1.2  1940 1496  ??  Ss   2:43PM  0:00.02
/usr/local/sbin/nmbd -D
```

The smbd daemon is the actual data server, the process that handles SMB/CIFS requests from connected Windows clients—file transfers, print jobs, listings, and so on. Unlike NFS, SMB doesn't require a separate process to be running for each simultaneous connection; the master `smbd` process forks off a new copy of itself for each new client session, and handles all of that client's requests for the duration of the session. The `-D` option specifies that `smbd` should operate as a standalone daemon, listening for requests on TCP port 139.

Operating in parallel with `smbd` is `nmbd`, the NetBIOS name server. It's the process that allows Windows clients to see the FreeBSD machine in the network browser view, as we saw in Figure 32.1. It also has the job of responding to client requests for a particular NetBIOS host if it's specified by name; if a Windows client uses the `\\<name>` syntax to connect to a particular server by name, the client sends out a broadcast name request asking for the IP address of the server with that NetBIOS name. It's the job of `nmbd` to send back a response with the requested host's IP address so the client can open an SMB request directly to the server. It's somewhat like DNS (in that it maps a common name to a direct address), and also has a lot in common with ARP (in that it operates on a LAN through broadcast name requests, rather than to a designated central name server).

smb.conf and SWAT

The main configuration file for Samba is `/usr/local/etc/smb.conf`, in which you can set any of dozens of different options, and create shares with customized settings. In this file, lines beginning with # or ; characters are comments; the usage in `smb.conf.default` (the example config file) is to use the # characters as comments and the ; characters to enable and disable configuration lines.

Each option is pretty well documented in comments in `smb.conf.default`. However, it can become very daunting to try to keep track of everything in that file because there are so many possible options (listed in `man smb.conf`) that you can set, with so many subtle differences between them. There's an alternative method to administering `smb.conf`, however, if your network circumstances permit it. This method is *SWAT*, the *Samba Web Administration Tool*, which is shown in Figure 32.3.

SWAT comes with the Samba port, and allows you to configure Samba graphically through a Web browser interface. The advantage of this is greatly increased simplicity in managing the `smb.conf` file, and a reduced risk of errors. The disadvantage is that by its nature as a Web application, the security risks are significant. SWAT authenticates users against the system user database in `/etc/master.passwd`; authentication passwords are sent in cleartext over the network from your client machine to the Samba server you want to configure; and unless you're configuring it from the local machine (`localhost`, using X-Windows), this presents a security risk. The risk can be managed a number of ways, but it's still not foolproof. You must take one of the following routes when deciding to run SWAT.

FIGURE 32.3
SWAT, the
Samba Web
Administration
Tool.

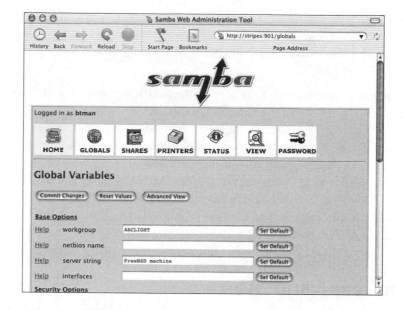

- Access SWAT only from `localhost`. This prevents any traffic from being sent over the wire at all.

- Operate entirely behind a firewall that allows no traffic from the outside. The `smb.conf` file is owned by root by default, so your browser must log in to SWAT using the root password, sent over the network in cleartext, with each HTTP request you make to the SWAT program. This should never be done on a network in which the password could be exposed to a malicious eavesdropper.

- Create a "dummy" user (for example, `smbowner`), and change `smb.conf` to be owned by that user (using `chown`). When running SWAT, log in as that user, not as root. Don't use the dummy username for any other tasks on the server; and don't give the user any privileges, a shell, or a home directory. Be aware that if the password for this user is sniffed, an intruder can easily alter your Samba configuration. However, he won't be able to do anything else.

If the security risks are acceptable to you, and you can adhere to one of these methods of accessing SWAT, you can enable it by adding the following line to `/etc/services` in the appropriate spot (901 is a suggested port—any unused TCP port will do):

```
swat        901/tcp
```

Next, add the following line to `/etc/inetd.conf`:

```
swat    stream  tcp     nowait  root    /usr/local/sbin/swat    swat
```

Finally, restart `inetd`:

```
# killall -HUP inetd
```

You can now access SWAT by the URL `http://stripes.somewhere.com:901`, substituting your Samba server's hostname or `localhost` as appropriate. You will be prompted for a username and password. Use the system username you have decided to use for SWAT access: root, if your security situation allows it, or the dummy user otherwise.

SWAT allows you to access and modify your shares and printers as well as global settings; you can also view the current status of the server and do Samba user management. If SWAT recognizes that the username under which you are logged in has full access to the `smb.conf` file, you will see all seven action buttons shown in Figure 32.3. Otherwise, you will see only four, allowing you to view Samba information and status, but not make any configuration changes.

Because SWAT operates as a front-end to `smb.conf`, and because SWAT is not necessarily a viable administrative option, the rest of this chapter will concentrate on configuring Samba through `smb.conf` directly—not on SWAT's equivalent actions.

Sharing Directories

Many examples for how to configure a shared directory can be found in `smb.conf.default`. To enable any of them, make the appropriate change in `smb.conf`; then stop and restart Samba:

```
# /usr/local/etc/rc.d/samba.sh stop
# /usr/local/etc/rc.d/samba.sh start
```

Example shares are displayed below the `===== Share Definitions =====` line in `smb.conf`. Each share's name is listed in brackets, and the configuration lines following it apply until the next bracketed block. The `smb.conf` file begins with a `[global]` block, allowing you to set global parameters; the rest of the blocks each define a share whose settings override the previously defined global settings, much in the same way as `httpd.conf` works for Apache (as we saw in Chapter 26, "Configuring a Web Server").

> **Tip**
>
> The `man smb.conf` page lists all available configuration parameters and describes in detail what each does. However, you may find it easier to view the page in HTML format, in which headings and examples are set apart with text formatting and made easier to read, as well as being contextually hyperlinked. Refer to the online documentation at `http://samba.org/samba/docs/man/smb.conf.5.html` for the formatted version.

To share a regular public directory, define a share block like this:

```
[my-public]
   comment = Public Stuff
   path = /usr/local/share/samba-stuff
   public = yes
   writeable = yes
   printable = no
   write list = @staff
```

With this share enabled, a client will see a share called my-public at the top level of the server's share listing. However, unless the user is authenticated and is a member of the UNIX group staff, the files in the share will be read-only. Remove the write list line to make the share writeable by all users. Note that writeable = yes is equivalent to saying read only = no.

By default, a [homes] share is defined and enabled; this special share is built-in, allowing access to each user's home directory on the Samba server if the Windows client connects to it with the proper credentials. (We will be discussing user-level and share-level security a little later.)

```
[homes]
   comment = Home Directories
   browseable = no
   writeable = yes
```

Because this share is set as not browsable, home directories that are not owned by the client user are not displayed; if a client connects as a valid user with a home directory on the Samba server, his or her home directory (labeled with his or her username because that's the name of the directory in UNIX) appears as one of the available shares. No other users' home directories appear.

Sharing Printers

Like [homes], [printers] is a special share that behaves a little differently from regular shares. Under FreeBSD, all attached printers that are defined in /etc/printcap are available to Samba users. Chapter 16, "Printing," explains how to set up your FreeBSD machine to support local printers in /etc/printcap.

By default, the [printers] share is set up like this:

```
[printers]
   comment = All Printers
   path = /var/spool/samba
   browseable = no
# Set public = yes to allow user 'guest account' to print
   guest ok = no
   writeable = no
   printable = yes
```

As stated in the embedded comment, you can make your printers public so that anyone on the network can use them. This involves the use of a *guest user*, which we will discuss next. Note that public is a synonym for guest ok, so you would change the guest ok line to yes instead of adding a public = yes line to allow the guest user to print.

In Samba 2.2.0 and later, Windows 2000/NT printing RPCs are supported, meaning that you can push the appropriate printer drivers to a client that lacks them. For documentation on this feature, see the Samba Web site.

Access Control

Samba access control involves a number of abstract concepts that can be very difficult to reconcile. Windows user authentication schemes include LAN Manager (LANMAN), Windows NT/2000, Windows 95/98/Me, and Windows for Workgroups—all subtly different in how they handle encryption, login names, and challenge-response handling.

In Samba, there are two widely used ways to do access control: user-level and share-level. The default setting is user-level, defined by the security option:

```
# Security mode. Most people will want user level security. See
# security_level.txt for details.
   security = user
```

User-Level Access Control

In *user-level* security, the client presents a username/password pair to the server upon the initial setup of the connection. The server determines whether to accept the client based on the username/password pair and the identity of the client machine itself. If it accepts the client, all shares are accessible.

It can be tricky to set up user-level security properly. The Windows username, which is defined either when logging in to a local profile or to a domain controller in a Windows session, must exist on the Samba server as a regular UNIX user (or mapped to a UNIX user). For instance, if the Windows user Harris logs on to his Windows machine, opens up the Network Neighborhood window, and tries to connect to our Samba server, he will be denied access (and given a password prompt for a share called \\STRIPES\IPC$) unless the user harris exists on the UNIX machine.

> **Note**
>
> In Windows NT/2000, the password prompt allows you to enter a username as well as a password. However, in Windows 95/98/Me, all you get is a password prompt, and the username is derived from the login name.

Samba users must exist in a password database at /usr/local/private/smbpasswd, sim-
ilar to /etc/master.passwd in that encrypted passwords are stored in it for each local
UNIX user. When Samba is installed, users from /etc/master.passwd are converted into
Samba format and placed into /usr/local/private/smbpasswd, with both the LAN-
MAN password and the Windows NT password (both are present for compatibility) set
to strings of 16 X characters—indicating that the user cannot log in.

To enable a user, you must set the password to something valid. This is done with the
smbpasswd program. It works similarly to passwd, prompting you for your old Samba
password and then requiring you to enter a new one twice, unless you're root—in which
case, you need not supply the old password, and you can change any user's password as
well as your own.

```
# smbpasswd harris
New SMB password:
Retype new SMB password:
Password changed for user harris.
```

By default, early versions of Windows 95 and NT did not use encrypted passwords. They
sent passwords in cleartext over the wire, as with UNIX. With an update to Windows 95
and with Windows NT service pack 3, encrypted passwords became the default behavior,
alterable only by changing Registry keys. To integrate properly with recent versions of
Windows NT/2000, and with Windows 98 and later, you will need to enable password
encryption in Samba. This is done by enabling the encrypt passwords parameter after
reading the document at /usr/local/share/doc/samba/textdocs/ENCRYPTION.txt,
which describes the mechanism of encrypted passwords in detail. Refer also to
Win95.txt and WinNT.txt in the same directory.

```
# You may wish to use password encryption. Please read
# ENCRYPTION.txt, Win95.txt and WinNT.txt in the Samba documentation.
# Do not enable this option unless you have read those documents
  encrypt passwords = yes
```

As the documents explain, encrypted passwords—although they seem like a sensible
security measure—actually decrease security on the server end because the encrypted
Samba passwords that are stored in the /usr/local/private/smbpasswd file are the
same as the passwords that are sent over the wire, and therefore are equivalent in security
to passwords stored in cleartext. An intruder who gains access to the smbpasswd file
could immediately log in as any user (including root) through Samba, whereas the
encrypted passwords in /etc/master.passwd must be cracked through some brute-force
method. Guard the smbpasswd file just as carefully as you would master.passwd, if not
more so!

Tip

You can map Windows users on a many-to-one basis to UNIX users, allowing you to give groups of Windows users the same privileges as a single UNIX user. To do this, create a file containing mappings, for example, `/usr/local/etc/smbusers.map`. The format of this file is with one mapping per line, as follows:

`<unix-user> = <win-user-1> [<win-user-2> ...]`

Next, enable it by adding the following anywhere in the `[global]` section of `smb.conf`:

`username map = /usr/local/etc/smbusers.map`

Each aliased Windows user must log in with the correct password for the UNIX user to which he maps.

Share-Level Access Control

In *share-level* access control, a client can connect to the Samba server without any username/password authentication and receive the list of shares; the client will be refused access only if denied by IP address in the `smb.conf` file (the `hosts allow` line). However, each share has its own user authentication, using the same password scheme as we already saw in the discussion on user-level access control. A public share, in which access is open to all, can be entered without any barriers; however, a share that is restricted to a particular user (such as a home directory from the `[homes]` block) presents the same username/password challenge as user-level security presented at the initial connection.

More details on the workings of user-level and share-level security can be found in the documentation file at `/usr/local/share/doc/samba/textdocs/security_level.txt`.

Guest User

For some Samba services, notably printing, you will want any user on the network to be able to have access regardless of authentication. This is done with a *guest account*, an unprivileged user account that has access as a UNIX user to the service you want to provide, but to nothing unnecessary. Note that guest users are primarily intended for Samba servers running in share-level security mode, because guest user access is allowed or disallowed on a share-by-share basis.

To enable a guest user, uncomment the `guest account` line in `smb.conf`:

```
# Uncomment this if you want a guest account, you must add this to /etc/passwd
# otherwise the user "nobody" is used
  guest account = pcguest
```

You must then add the `pcguest` account (or any other name you choose) to the system using `adduser`. Use `chfn` to tune the user's capabilities; the `ftp` user (created by `sysinstall` if your system allows anonymous FTP—see Chapter 27, "Configuring an FTP Server," for details on FTP server setup) is a good model for the Samba guest account.

With this account enabled, any Windows user connecting to the Samba server will have full access to any share where the `guest ok` or `public` parameter is set to `yes`. No authentication challenge will be presented for that share.

The `guest only = yes` parameter can be specified to indicate that only guest connections are permitted for a service.

Samba Log Files

In `/var/log`, there are various log files for Samba, one for each type of service and for each client that has connected. These files' names are of the form `log.<service>`:

```
# ls -l /var/log/log.*
-rw-r--r--  1 root  wheel   468 Jun  9 12:42 /var/log/log.gaming-pc
-rw-r--r--  1 root  wheel  2343 Jun  9 14:49 /var/log/log.nmb
-rw-r--r--  1 root  wheel  1606 Jun  9 14:44 /var/log/log.smb
```

The `log.nmb` and `log.smb` files report status and error conditions for the `nmbd` and `smbd` servers, respectively. Additionally, whenever any errors are reported for any connecting client host (such as authentication failures), these messages are printed into a `log.<name>` file for that client. Note that this can result in a lot of files cluttering up your `/var/log` directory. You can switch to a combined log format by commenting out the `log file` line in `smb.conf`:

```
# this tells Samba to use a separate log file for each machine
# that connects
;   log file = /var/log/log.%m
```

SMB errors for individual hosts will go into `log.smb` with this line commented out.

Another useful line to modify is the `max log size` line; set to 50Kb by default, this control allows you to set the "rollover" size for any of the log files. When any Samba log file reaches this size, it's renamed by appending `.old` to the filename, and new log entries are added to a new file. The `.old` file is overwritten at the next rollover.

```
# Put a capping on the size of the log files (in Kb).
  max log size = 50
```

Samba Variables

Configuration parameters in `smb.conf` don't have to be hard-wired; you have a number of variable substitutions at your disposal, so you can set certain options to be dynamically determined, depending on the conditions of the connection. For example, you can set an option to reflect the client's username with the `%u` variable, allowing you to set a parameter such as `path = /usr/local/share/user-files/%u`. The user `harris` would thus receive the path `/usr/local/share/user-files/harris`.

A few of the most useful variables are as follows:

- `%u`—The client's username.
- `%g`—The primary group name of `%u`.
- `%S`—The name of the current service, if any.
- `%H`—The home directory of the user given by `%u`.
- `%h`—The Internet hostname of the Samba server.
- `%M`—The Internet hostname of the client machine.
- `%L`—The NetBIOS name of the Samba server. This allows you to change your config based on what the client calls you; your server can have a "dual personality."
- `%m`—The NetBIOS name of the client machine.
- `%I`—The IP address of the client machine.
- `%T`—The current date and time.
- `%$(envvar)`—The value of the environment variable envvar.

The complete list of variable substitutions is available in `man smb.conf`.

Other Samba Components

The Samba package includes a number of additional tools. These are each described in `man samba`; we will also cover each one briefly here. Each one has its own man page for further details.

- `smbclient`—A simple FTP-like client that allows you to connect to remote SMB shares and print to remote Windows printers.
- `testparm`—A configuration file syntax checker that tests your `smb.conf` for correctness; similar to `apachectl configtest` for Apache.
- `testprns`—Tests whether the printers specified in `/etc/printcap` will work properly with Samba.

- smbstatus—Displays current connections to the Samba server. SWAT, as we saw earlier, has a page that shows the formatted output of this command in a Web browser.
- nmblookup—Allows you to make NetBIOS name queries like those made by Windows hosts connecting directly to SMB shares by name.
- make_smbcodepage—A tool that allows you to create new SMB code page definitions for Samba.

These are in addition to the smbd, nmbd, and smbpasswd utilities that we have already discussed. Each of these has its own man page as well.

Future Samba Development

At the time of this writing, the most recent version of Samba in the ports is 2.0.9; Samba 2.2.0, the next major revision, has only just been released, and it or a later version will probably be the official version in /usr/ports/net/samba by the time you read this.

Version 2.2.0 incorporates many enhancements to Windows networking, enabling features that are new in Windows 2000 and increasing the level of interoperability between Windows and UNIX file servers. Some of the new features are as follows:

- Automatic downloading of Windows NT/2000 printer drivers from the Samba server, if they are not present on the client machine
- Unification of Windows NT/2000 and UNIX Access Control Lists (ACLs), and remote manageability of such lists from Windows machines
- Built-in Windows NT/2000 login authentication
- Microsoft Distributed File System (DFS) support and capability to act as a DFS server for Windows clients

See the documentation at http://www.samba.org for further details on these and other new features.

smbfs Filesystem

SMB file sharing can work both ways. Samba allows you to set up your FreeBSD machine as an SMB server only, but there is a way to set it up as a client and mount a remote SMB share like any other filesystem. This is smbfs, available in the ports at /usr/ports/net/smbfs.

An smbfs implementation has existed for Linux for some time; the FreeBSD implementation is new and native to the platform because as a filesystem, it has to be integrated into the kernel—and the kernels are the least compatible parts of any two operating systems. The smbfs port for FreeBSD creates an smbfs.ko kernel module in /modules and a mount_smbfs tool in /sbin that works like all the other mount_* tools that we saw in Chapter 9, "The FreeBSD Filesystem." The best documentation for smbfs is found in the man mount_smbfs page.

After installation, you will need to rename /usr/local/etc/nsmb.conf.sample to nsmb.conf and /usr/local/etc/rc.d/smbfs.sh.sample to smbfs.sh. The former sets defaults for certain SMB hosts and globally for all smbfs mounts, and the latter is a script that mounts smbfs shares at boot time that are listed in /etc/fstab.

To mount an SMB filesystem using smbfs, use mount_smbfs with a few basic options. The -I flag specifies the hostname or IP address, and the two remaining arguments are the remote share name (of the form //<user>@<NetBIOS name>/<share name>) and the local mount point. To mount the share called public from a Windows machine called gaming-pc onto the local /smb/public directory, use the following syntax:

```
# mount_smbfs -I 64.41.131.139 //guest@gaming-pc/public /smb/public
```

You will be prompted for a password. Use a blank password if the share is set to allow full access; use the appropriate password if the share is set to read-only or password-protected mode.

> **Note**
>
> The smbfs.ko kernel module is loaded automatically when needed by mount_smbfs. If you want to, you can load it at boot time by adding the following line to /boot/loader.conf:
>
> ```
> smbfs_load="YES"
> ```
>
> However, this is probably not necessary.

To add an SMB share to /etc/fstab, use the following syntax:

```
//guest@gaming-pc/public    /smb/public      smbfs  rw,noauto 0    0
```

The /usr/local/etc/rc.d/smbfs.sh script will mount this share when the FreeBSD system boots.

DHCP

CHAPTER 33

DHCP, which stands for *Dynamic Host Configuration Protocol*, is a network protocol that allows a client to obtain its IP address, name server information, gateway server information, and several other network configuration options from a server that is running a DHCP server.

How DHCP Works

A detailed discussion of how DHCP works is beyond the scope of this book, but here is a basic rundown of what happens.

In FreeBSD, there is a client program called dhclient that allows FreeBSD to act as a DHCP client. When a system configured to use DHCP boots and dhclient starts, it will send out broadcast requests on port 68. These requests are sent in UDP format.

If there is a DHCP server on the network, it will be listening to port 68 for these requests. When it receives a request for configuration information, it will check its database for a free IP address that can be assigned to the client. It will then send back all of the configuration information that the client requests on port 67, once again using UDP. The IP address that is assigned to the client will be removed from the pool of available addresses so that it is not assigned to another client that requests DHCP configuration information.

The client that is running DHCP will be listening on port 67 for this configuration information from the server. When it receives it, it will configure itself to use the information that the server sent.

IP Address Leases

When the DHCP server assigns an IP address to a client, the client does not own the address. Instead, the address is leased. The lease term is configured on the DHCP server. The information about how long the lease is good for is sent to the client along with the configuration information.

The leasing of IP addresses serves two purposes:

- If the DHCP server cannot be contacted, the client will check its database to look for a lease that is still valid. Assuming it has a valid lease, the client can continue to function normally, even if the DHCP server is currently down.

- It automatically places IP addresses that are not in use back in the pool after the lease expires. This helps conserve IP addresses. For example, if a guest from a branch office visits, he can plug his laptop into your network and be assigned an IP address so he can use your network. When he leaves, that IP address will eventually expire and be placed back into the pool for others to use. This way, IP addresses are not being wasted on systems that do not exist anymore.

Advantages of DHCP Over Static IP Addresses

Depending on your situation, DHCP may have several advantages over simply assigning each system its own static IP addresses. These advantages include the following:

- **Ease of maintenance.** DHCP automatically keeps track of which IP addresses are in use and which ones are free. This prevents the system administrator from having to keep track of which IP addresses can be assigned to new clients, as well as having to remember to reclaim old IP addresses when clients are permanently removed from the network. All of this is handled automatically with DHCP.

- **Ease of installing new clients.** When new clients are installed, you (or the user) do not have to worry about setting up the network information. You can simply ask the new client to obtain its information via DHCP, and all of the networking information will be configured automatically.

- **Ease of use for travelers.** If your users travel to branch offices, DHCP makes their life a lot easier. With DHCP, they can simply plug their laptop into the network at the branch office and have all the network information configured for them automatically. At the next branch office they go to, they can do the same thing. This way, your users do not have to reconfigure their network settings at each office they go to. It also makes life easier for the network administrators because they do not have to worry about making IP addresses available for these traveling users.

- **It conserves IP addresses.** This is true, especially if you have traveling users who go to branch offices occasionally and plug their laptops into the network. DHCP allows these IP addresses to be automatically reclaimed after the traveling user leaves. This way, you don't have IP addresses wasted on systems that are rarely plugged in to the network anyway.

- **It eliminates problems caused by IP address conflicts.** It only takes one user to make one typing mistake when setting up a system to cause all kinds of problems on a network if the IP address the user enters conflicts with another system on the network, especially if that address conflicts with the IP address assigned to a server. DHCP eliminates these problems by assigning IP addresses automatically and keeping track of ones that are in use so they do not get assigned to multiple systems.

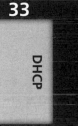

Of course, if you are running a small network of only 10 or 15 systems, and you rarely or never have visitors that need to plug into your network, these issues are not all that important, and DHCP is probably not worth installing. However, DHCP is definitely worth considering if you have several hundred or thousand clients on a network, or if you expect your small network to grow to a large number like this over time. If you anticipate this kind of growth, you may want to go with DHCP now, even if you currently have only 10 or 15 clients. It is much easier to configure DHCP when you still have only a small number of clients than it is to try to convert an existing network of several hundred systems over to DHCP.

Kernel Configuration for DHCP

In order to configure FreeBSD as a client on a DHCP network, you will need to have the Berkeley Packet Filter device installed in the kernel. This is installed by default in the GENERIC kernel, so unless you built a custom kernel and removed it, you shouldn't have to do anything.

To verify that the Berkeley Packet Filter device is installed in the kernel, look for the following line in your kernel configuration file:

```
device bpf
```

If this line exists in your kernel configuration file, there is nothing you need to do here. If the line does not exist, you will need to add it and then rebuild your kernel. Complete instructions on kernel building can be found in Chapter 17, "Kernel Configuration."

Caution

There is a slight security risk involved with the Berkeley Packet Filter. The bpf device allows packet sniffers to be run. Packet sniffers can be malicious because they can display passwords and such being sent across the network. Although only the root user can run the packet sniffers, this is something you still should be aware of if you are in an environment in which security is absolutely critical. That being said, on a very large network, the benefits of DHCP probably outweigh the very slight risk involved with running bpf.

Enabling DHCP

Once you have made sure the kernel is configured for DHCP, you can enable it in one of two ways. The first is by going through the sysinstall program. The second is by manually editing the configuration files. The sysinstall method will be covered first.

DHCP through `sysinstall`

If you are installing FreeBSD for the first time, simply answer yes to the post-installation question when you are asked if you want to try DHCP configuration of the network. If you have already installed FreeBSD, perform the following steps to enable DHCP from sysinstall:

1. As the root user, type **sysinstall** at the command prompt to start the sysinstall program.

2. At the main menu, select the Configure option. Note that you cannot use the mouse in sysinstall. You must use the arrow keys and the Enter key to make selections.

3. At the Configuration menu, select the Networking option. This will bring up the Network Services Menu (see Figure 33.1).

FIGURE 33.1

The Network Services Menu portion of sysinstall.

4. Select the Interfaces option by using the arrow keys to make sure it is highlighted and then pressing the spacebar.

5. Select the network interface that you want to configure from the next menu (see Figure 33.2).

FIGURE 33.2

Selecting the network interface to configure. Many of the devices listed here are pseudo-devices, not real network devices.

6. Answer No to the question that asks if you want to try IPv6 configuration of the interface.

7. Answer Yes to the question that asks if you want to try DHCP configuration of the interface.

When you have answered Yes to the question about trying DHCP configuration of the interface, the `dhclient` will start and begin broadcasting a request for configuration information over the network. If it successfully receives configuration information back from a DHCP server, it will automatically fill in the values on the next screen that asks you to supply the network values. You can then select OK to accept the values that were supplied by DHCP.

If this is not a new installation (you are making changes to an existing installation), you will need to exit the `sysinstall` program and reboot the system before the new DHCP settings will take effect.

Manual Configuration of DHCP

You can also configure DHCP manually by editing the `/etc/rc.conf` file. To do so, you will need to add an `ifconfig` line to the file for the device that you want to configure with DHCP. For example, if your Ethernet device is `ed0`, the following line would be added to `/etc/rc.conf`:

```
ifconfig_ed0="DHCP"
```

If the network interface you want to configure with DHCP is not `ed0`, you will, of course, want to replace it with whatever the name of the device is that you want to configure.

If there is already an existing line in `/etc/rc.conf` for the device you want to configure, and it contains something else, it is probably currently set up to use static IP. In this case, either delete the existing line and replace it with the earlier line, or comment out the existing line by placing a hash mark in front of it (#) and then add the line above.

After you have made this change to the `/etc/rc.conf` file, reboot the system for the new DHCP changes to take effect.

dhclient Program

The dhclient program is the client portion of DHCP. It is run automatically at each system boot if you have any network interfaces that are configured to use DHCP.

If you need to modify the default behavior of dhclient, you can do so by supplying flags to it with an option in /etc/rc.conf.

If you do need to modify the default behavior of dhclient, the following line should be added to /etc/rc.conf below the ifconfig line where the DHCP interface is configured:

dhcp_flags="*flags*"

where *flags* is a list of options for dhclient. Table 33.1 shows the valid options that can be used.

TABLE 33.1 Valid Options for dhclient

Option	Action
-d	This will force dhclient to stay in the foreground rather than move to the background after it gets its configuration information. This should be used only for debugging purposes, and should probably never be used from /etc/rc.conf.
-cf *filename*	By default, dhclient reads its operating system-specific configuration information from the file /sbin/dhclient-script. The -cf option can be used to tell dhclient to read from a different configuration file where *filename* is the name and path of that file.
-lf *filename*	By default, dhclient stores information on its leases in the file /var/db/dhclient.leases. The -lf option can be used to tell dhclient to use a different file for this, where *filename* is the name of the file and path where this information should be stored.
-pf *filename*	By default, dhclient stores its process ID (PID) information in /var/run/dhclient.pid. The pf option can be used to change this. *filename* is the name of the file that should be used to store this information.
-q	This tells dhclient to be quiet when it runs. In other words, dhclient will not be so verbose about the messages it prints.
-1	This causes dhclient to try only once to get a lease on an IP address. If this fails, dhclient will exist with a status of 2.

33

DHCP

/sbin/dhclient-script

This is the operating system-specific configuration file for dhclient. You shouldn't need to make any changes to this file, and it is best left alone unless you are sure you know what you are doing.

/etc/dhclient.conf

This is the configuration file for dhclient, in which you can control various options about its behavior. The file must exist for dhclient to run, although by default, the file contains nothing but comments. dhclient has reasonable default values that will work fine for most users, so most users will not have to worry about this file.

However, you should be aware of some of the options that can be controlled in this file. Table 33.2 lists some of them.

TABLE 33.2 Some dhclient.conf Options

Option	Action
timeout *n*	Where *n* is the number of seconds dhclient should wait for a response when trying to contact a DHCP server before giving up and deciding the server is unavailable. By default, this is 60 seconds.
retry *n*	Where *n* is the number of seconds dhclient should wait before trying to contact the DHCP server again if the first request timed out. By default, it will wait five minutes.
select-timeout *n*	Some networks may have more than one DHCP server on them. In this case, the client may receive multiple offers for configuration information. The first offer received is not always the best offer (for example, if the second offer received contains the same IP address the client has, it is preferable to an offer where the IP address is different). *n* here is the number of seconds dhclient should wait after receiving a first offer to see if any other servers respond with offers.
reboot *n*	When dhclient starts, it will try to obtain the same IP address it had last time. If it cannot, it will then accept a different IP address. *n* here is the number of seconds that dhclient will wait before giving up and deciding it can't get the same IP address it had last time. The default is 10 seconds.

TABLE 33.2 Some `dhclient.conf` Options

Option	Action
request *option*	The client will request information for the specified options from the DHCP server. See the `dhcp-options` man page for information on the available options.
require *option*	The client will require information for the specified options from the DHCP server. If the required information is not provided, the client will reject the offer. See the `dhcp-options` man page for information on the available options.
default *option value*	If the DHCP server does not provide information for the specified option, then *value* will be used for that option. See the `dhcp-options` man page for information on the available options.
supersede *option value*	The specified options will always use *value*, even if the DHCP server sends a different value for that option. See the `dhcp-options` man page for information on the available options.
reject *address*	Any offers sent from the DHCP server with the IP address of *address* will be rejected.

There are many more options that can be used in the `/etc/dhclient.conf` configuration file. See the `dhclient.conf` man page for more information on options available in this file. Also, see the `dhcp-options` man page for more information about the DHCP options that can be requested or required from the DHCP server.

As mentioned previously, most users will not need to make any changes to `/etc/dhclient.conf` because the default `dhclient` values will usually work fine.

DHCP Server Daemon

FreeBSD does not come with the software required to run a DHCP server. However, there is free software available in the FreeBSD ports collection for running a DHCP server. The port, called `isc-dhcp3`, is available in the `net` directory of the ports tree. See Chapter 15, "Installing Additional Software," for information on how to install ports.

In addition, there is a program called `dhcpconf`, which is also available in the FreeBSD ports collection under the `net` directory, which helps you create the configuration files necessary to run a DHCP server on FreeBSD.

33

DHCP

When `isc-dhcp3` is installed, it will create a startup file in `/usr/local/etc/rc.d` called `isc-dhcpd.sh.sample`. The next time you restart your system, this file will cause the DHCP server to start automatically on system boot. The default startup file will work fine for a basic DHCP server configuration. See the `dhcpd` man page for the various options available to `dhcpd`.

You may want to rename the startup file in `/usr/local/etc/rc.d` to something that is easier to remember and type. For example, you might want to call it `dhcpd`. Assuming you rename it, you can now control the operation of the DHCP server by using the following commands as root.

This command will start the DHCP server:

`/usr/local/etc/rc.d/dhcpd start`

This command will stop a DHCP server that is currently running:

`/usr/local/etc/rc.d/dhcpd stop`

This command will stop and then restart a DHCP server that is currently running:

`/usr/local/etc/rc.d/dhcp restart`

Before you start the DHCP server for the first time, you will need to create a configuration file for it.

dhcpd Configuration File

The configuration file for the DHCP server, named `dhcp.conf`, is located in `/usr/local/etc`. When you installed `dhcpd`, it placed a sample configuration file in the directory called `dhcpd.conf.sample`.

There are two ways to configure the `dhcpd.conf` file. The first way is manually. The second is with the `dhcpconf` program. If you have never configured `dhcpd` before, I recommend that you install and use the `dhcpconf` program. You can then look through the `dhcp.conf` file that `dhcpconf` creates to see how the file looks.

dhcpconf Program

`dhcpconf` is a menu- and dialog-driven program that helps you set up a basic DHCP server configuration. Once you have it installed, you can start it by typing `dhcpconf` at the command prompt as root. You will get an About dialog box that tells you a little about the program. Press Enter to continue on to the main screen. Figure 33.3 shows the main screen of `dhcpconf`.

FIGURE 33.3

The main
dhcpconf *menu.*

Note that the mouse cannot be used in this program. You will need to use the arrow keys, Enter key, and Tab key to navigate in the program.

The first menu option (Common) sets options that apply to all IP addresses assigned. This is the default configuration information that will be sent to clients. Press Enter to select it. Figure 33.4 shows the Common dialog box.

FIGURE 33.4

*Options common
to all IP
addresses, as well
as default options.*

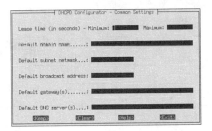

Most of the options listed here are self-explanatory, with the exception of the first one that defines the minimum and maximum lease periods.

The *minimum* lease is also the default lease period. This is the default time in seconds that a lease will be good for. The *maximum* time is the maximum amount of time that the server will lease an IP. The client can request a longer lease than the default defined in minimum, but the server will never lease an IP for longer than the value defined here in maximum.

The default minimum lease period is 600 seconds (10 minutes), and the default maximum lease period is 7200 seconds (120 minutes). The client must renew its lease before the maximum lease period is up, or it will lose the lease, and the IP address it has will be placed back into the pool of available addresses.

Once you have filled in all the values here, tab to the <Keep> button and press Enter. This will take you back to the main screen.

Fixed-host Entries

Sometimes, you might need to reserve static IP addresses (IP addresses that never change) for some systems. This is usually done for systems that are acting as servers. The second option, DHCP Configurator, allows you to do this. Figure 33.5 shows the Fixed-host Entries configuration dialog box.

FIGURE 33.5

Configuring information for systems that require static IP addresses.

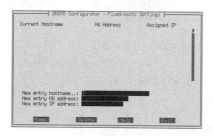

Table 33.3 shows the options in this dialog box and what they do.

TABLE 33.3   Fixed-host Configuration Options

Option	Description
New entry hostname	This is the hostname of the system that is being configured for static IP. You should provide only the hostname here, not the domain name, because the domain information was provided in the Common options.
New entry HW address	Enter the hardware address of the network card on the host that is being configured for static IP here.
New entry IP address	This is the static IP address that the host being configured for static IP will use.

Once you have finished entering the information, in the last field, press Enter to add the host to the list. You can then enter more hosts if you want, or tab down to <Keep> to return to the main menu. Note that you must press Enter after filling in the last entry. If you do not, and you simply tab to <Keep>, the entry will be lost.

Subnet Ranges

Finally, you need to configure the IP addresses ranges that are available on various subnets. Select the Subnet option from the main menu to do this. Figure 33.6 shows the Subnet configuration dialog box.

FIGURE 33.6

The Subnet dialog box, which looks and behaves very much like the Fixed-host entries dialog box discussed in the previous section.

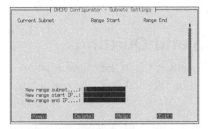

Table 33.4 shows what these options do.

TABLE 33.4   Subnet Range Options

Option	Description
New range subnet	This is the subnet that this range of IP addresses will affect.
New range start IP	This is the first IP address that will be available to DHCP clients on this subnet that are receiving dynamic IP addresses.
New range end IP	This is the last IP address that will be available to DHCP clients on this subnet that are receiving dynamic IP addresses.

As with the Fixed-host configuration, you must press Enter here after entering the range end IP address for the entry to be added to the list and for changes to take effect. After you have done so, you can add more entries if you want.

If you want to have multiple IP address blocks available to a single subnet, simply create a new entry for the same subnet as an existing entry, and include a different IP address range. Both of the entries will be valid, and both of the ranges of IP addresses will be available to the subnet.

Once you have finished creating all the entries you want, tab to <Keep>, and press Enter to return to the main menu.

> **Tip**
>
> If you are unclear about some of the networking terminology in this chapter such as subnets, and so on, please see Chapter 22, "Introduction to Networking," for information on these various networking concepts.

Saving the Information and Quitting

From the main menu of DHCP Configurator, tab to the <Save> button, and press Enter. The program will create the configuration file, and exit. The configuration file will be located in /etc/dhcpd.conf.

The instructions presented in this section should get you up and running with a basic DHCP server setup. For more advanced configuration, see the man pages for dhcpd, and also for dhcpd.conf, which contains all the options that can be configured in the dhcpd.conf configuration file.

X-Windows

PART
V

Advanced X-Windows Configuration

CHAPTER 34

By default, FreeBSD installs XFree86 3.3.6. This version is rather old, and is rapidly becoming obsolete. Although we did cover basic configuration of this version in chapter 2, "Installing FreeBSD,", we are not going to give it any detailed coverage here. Instead, we will cover upgrading XFree86 to version 4.1, and then configuring this version.

Upgrading from 3.3.6 to 4.x

As of this writing, the most current version of XFree86 is version 4.1. If you've decided that you want to use XFree86 4.1 instead of XFree86 3.3.6, you will need to install the 4.1 package from the CD included with the book. The package is located in the `pack-ages/x11` directory of both the 4.4 and 5.0 CD's included with the book. The name of the package is `XFree86-4.1.0_4.tgz`. A full discussion of installing packages is beyond the scope of this chapter, (this is covered in chapter 15, "Installing Additional Software Packages"), but in a nutshell, here is how to install XFree86 4.1. As root, issue the following commands:

```
# mount /cdrom
# cd /cdrom/packages/x11
# pkg_add -v XFree86-4.1.0_4.tgz
```

The package is quite large and will take some time to install. So be patient.

Once the package has finished installing, there are a couple more things you must do to configure it for use.

The first thing you need to do, is update `/etc/make.conf` so to reflect that you have XFree86 4 installed rather than XFree86 3. To do this, as root, open the file `/etc/make.conf` in your favorite text editor (if the file does not exist, create it), and add the following line:

```
XFREE86_VERSION= 4
```

The next thing you need to do is install the `Xwrapper` program. Although you could avoid doing this by setting the `XFree86` binary to run as the root user, this is a major security hazard and should not be done. The `Xwrapper` program provides a way around having to do this.

Unfortunately, the `Xwrapper` program is not included on the CD, so you will need to install it from the FreeBSD ports tree. To do so, you will need to have a working Internet connection (see the relevant networking chapters for how to configure this). The `Xwrapper` program is located in `/usr/ports/x11/wrapper`. A full discussion of installing software is beyond the scope of this chapter. (It is covered in chapter 15, "Installing Additional Software.". But here is the basic procedure you will need to follow to install `Xwrapper`. As root, issue the following commands:

```
# cd /usr/ports/x11/wrapper
# make
(several lines of status messages will appear here...)
# make install
(more lines of informational messages)
#
```

Finally, remove your old /etc/XF86Config file to avoid the possibility that it could cause problems with the new configuration. (rm /etc/XF86Config issued as wroot will do the trick.)

Once you have completed these steps, you may continue on with the next section of this chapter to begin configuring XFree86 4.1.

Using SuperProbe

The SuperProbe program will probe your video hardware and attempt to determine what type of video card is installed in the system, the amount of video RAM it contains, and so on. SuperProbe cannot detect all hardware, nor can it detect all the information on some of the hardware it does know about. Still, it can be very useful if you do not know what kind of video hardware is installed on your system, and you need to find out in order to install X-Windows.

> **Caution**
>
> There is a chance that SuperProbe could cause your system to hang when it is run. Because of this, make sure that you have saved any documents that you are currently working on in case your system hangs and you need to reset it.

34

ADVANCED
X-WINDOWS
CONFIGURATION

You need to be root in order to run SuperProbe.

Once you are logged in as root, type SuperProbe at the command prompt to start it in its most basic form (options to modify the behavior of SuperProbe will be covered later in this section). You will be given a warning message about the possibility that SuperProbe could hang your system, as well as five seconds to interrupt SuperProbe before it actually tests your video hardware. If you do want to interrupt the program, you can do so by pressing Ctrl+C to exit the program and return to the prompt.

Once the five seconds are up, SuperProbe will probe your video hardware and print the results of what it finds. On my system, the output of SuperProbe looks like this:

```
First video: Super-VGA
        Chipset: Matrox (chipset unknown) (PCI Probed)
                Signature data: 50 (please report)
        RAMDAC:  Generic 8-bit pseudo-color DAC
                (with 6-bit wide lookup tables (or in 6-bit mode))
```

You should write down the information discovered by SuperProbe so that you can use it later on in the X-Windows configuration.

There are several options to SuperProbe that modify its default behavior. One of the most common is the -verbose option, which causes SuperProbe to display more information about what it is doing. See the man page for SuperProbe for a complete description of all the options available.

Configuring X-Windows with the xf86config Script

If for whatever reason, you cannot use or do not want to use the graphical configuration tool described in Chapter 2, "Installing FreeBSD," there is an older shell script-based configuration tool available in X-Windows. This tool will ask you a series of questions and configure X-Windows based on the answers you provide.

Caution

Improper use of this tool when configuring video settings could actually cause physical damage to your hardware. Although most monitors have built-in protection circuits these days, and will shut themselves down if you try to drive them with a refresh rate higher than they support, some monitors will try to display the screen at the given refresh rate, even if the monitor's hardware is not capable of handling it. The result could destroy your monitor.

Caution

The xf86config program will overwrite your existing Xf86Config file. If you have a working XF86Config file, and you want to experiment with a new configuration, you should back up your existing file first. The file is located in /etc/X11/XF86Config. Make a copy of this file to /etc/X11/XF86Config.bak or some other name before continuing. This way, you can restore your previous configuration easily if your new configuration does not work by simply copying the backup file back to /etc/X11/XF86Config.

You will need to be root to use this program. As the root user, type `xf86config` at the command prompt, and press Enter. You will see a screen like the following:

```
This program will create a basic XF86Config file, based on menu selections you
make.

The XF86Config file usually resides in /usr/X11R6/etc/X11 or /etc/X11. A sample
XF86Config file is supplied with XFree86; it is configured for a standard
VGA card and monitor with 640x480 resolution. This program will ask for a
pathname when it is ready to write the file.

You can either take the sample XF86Config as a base and edit it for your
configuration, or let this program produce a base XF86Config file for your
configuration and fine-tune it.

Before continuing with this program, make sure you know what video card
you have, and preferably also the chipset it uses and the amount of video
memory on your video card. SuperProbe may be able to help with this.

Press enter to continue, or ctrl-c to abort.
```

Once you have read the information, simply press Enter to continue. The first thing you will be asked to configure is your mouse.

Caution

Double-check your typing when entering values in `xf86config`. The program is not very forgiving of mistakes and typos. If you accidentally make a wrong entry, and don't catch it before you have pressed Enter, there is no way to back up and fix it. You will have to press Ctrl+C to exit the program and then start completely over again.

Configuring the Mouse

The mouse configuration screen of `xf86config` looks like the following:

```
First specify a mouse protocol type. Choose one from the following list:

 1.  Microsoft compatible (2-button protocol)
 2.  Mouse Systems (3-button protocol)
 3.  Bus Mouse
 4.  PS/2 Mouse
 5.  Logitech Mouse (serial, old type, Logitech protocol)
 6.  Logitech MouseMan (Microsoft compatible)
 7.  MM Series
 8.  MM HitTablet
 9.  Microsoft IntelliMouse
```

If you have a two-button mouse, it is most likely of type 1, and if you have a three-button mouse, it can probably support both protocol 1 and 2. There are two main varieties of the latter type: mice with a switch to select the protocol, and mice that default to 1 and require a button to be held at boot-time to select protocol 2. Some mice can be convinced to do 2 by sending a special sequence to the serial port (see the ClearDTR/ClearRTS options).

```
Enter a protocol number:
```

Simply enter the number representing the type of mouse you have, and press Enter. Here are some guidelines for determining what type of mouse you have:

- If your mouse has a 9-pin, D-shaped connector where it plugs into your computer, it is a serial mouse. Use either 1, 2, 5, or 6. Note that most serial mice will work with either 1 or 2, and that all newer Logitech mice will use either 1 or 6. 5 is only for older Logitech mice.

- If your mouse has a small round connector where it plugs into your computer, it is a PS/2 mouse. Any PS/2 mouse should use 4. Even if you have a Microsoft mouse, you should use 4 if it has a PS/2 connector. The Microsoft mice listed are only for serial mice.

- If you are installing FreeBSD on a laptop or notebook computer, the built-in pointing device will probably work with 4 because it is most likely running on a PS/2 port. This includes touch-pads and touch-points.

Once you have entered the type of mouse you have and pressed Enter, you will be asked the following:

```
If your mouse has only two buttons, it is recommended that you enable
Emulate3Buttons.

Please answer the following question with either 'y' or 'n'.
Do you want to enable Emulate3Buttons?
```

This really should say it is required that you enable Emulate3Buttons if you have a two-button mouse instead of being only recommended. X-Windows makes use of all three buttons on the mouse. If you have only a two-button mouse, you need to answer y here. Doing so will cause clicking both mouse buttons at the same time to emulate clicking the middle button on a three button mouse.

You will then be asked for the device that the mouse is on:

```
Now give the full device name that the mouse is connected to, for example
/dev/tty00. Just pressing enter will use the default, /dev/mouse.

Mouse device:
```

Unless you have symlinked the actual device that your mouse is on to /dev/mouse, you will need to enter the device that your mouse is on here. Table 34.1 shows guidelines on what should be entered here, depending on what type of mouse you have.

TABLE 34.1   Device Names for Various Mouse Types

Mouse Type	Mouse Device
PS/2 mouse (or laptop)	/dev/psm0
Serial mouse on COM 1	/dev/cuaa0
Serial mouse on COM 2	/dev/cuaa1
Serial mouse on COM 3	/dev/cuaa2
Serial mouse on COM 4	/dev/cuaa3
Bus mouse	/dev/mse0

Enter the corresponding mouse device at the prompt for the type of mouse you have and then press Enter.

Selecting the Keyboard

The next screen will ask you to select the type of keyboard you have:

```
Please select one of the following keyboard types that is the better
description of your keyboard. If nothing really matches,
choose 1 (Generic 101-key PC)

  1  Generic 101-key PC
  2  Generic 102-key (Intl) PC
  3  Generic 104-key PC
  4  Generic 105-key (Intl) PC
  5  Dell 101-key PC
  6  Everex STEPnote
  7  Keytronic FlexPro
  8  Microsoft Natural
  9  Northgate OmniKey 101
 10  Winbook Model XP5
 11  Japanese 106-key
 12  PC-98xx Series
 13  Brazilian ABNT2
 14  HP Internet
 15  Logitech iTouch
 16  Logitech Cordless Desktop Pro
 17  Compaq Internet
 18  Microsoft Natural Pro

Enter a number to choose the keyboard.
```

Notice that there are more keyboard layouts available than can fit on one screen. Pressing Enter will show you the next screen full of layouts. When the list gets to the end, it will start over at the beginning if you press Enter again.

If you have a U.S. keyboard, you will want to select 1 here and press Enter. You will then be asked the following:

```
Please enter a variant name for 'us' layout. Or just press enter
for default variant
```

There is probably no reason for you to change the default here, so you can simply press Enter to continue on to the next question.

```
Please answer the following question with either 'y' or 'n'.
Do you want to select additional XKB options (group switcher,
group indicator, etc.)?
```

Select n here unless you want to remap some keys. If you do want to remap some keys (or you just want to see what is available), press y. Pressing y will take you to a couple of menus in which you can do various things such as make the Caps Lock key into a Ctrl key (useful for Emacs gurus) or swap the Caps Lock key with the Ctrl key. Enter the number of an option you want to perform and then press Enter. If you want to exit the menu without doing anything, simply press Enter without selecting a number first.

Configuring the Monitor

In this section you will configure various aspects of your monitor, including the horizontal and vertical refresh rates. You will see this screen first:

```
The next section you will be taken to will help you configure the refresh rates
for your monitor:
Now we want to set the specifications of the monitor. The two critical
parameters are the vertical refresh rate, which is the rate at which the
the whole screen is refreshed, and most importantly the horizontal sync rate,
which is the rate at which scanlines are displayed.

The valid range for horizontal sync and vertical sync should be documented
in the manual of your monitor. If in doubt, check the monitor database
/usr/X11R6/lib/X11/doc/Monitors to see if your monitor is there.

Press enter to continue, or ctrl-c to abort
```

Press Enter at this message to continue. You will then be asked to set the horizontal sync range of your monitor:

```
You must indicate the horizontal sync range of your monitor. You can either
select one of the predefined ranges below that correspond to industry-
standard monitor types, or give a specific range.
```

It is VERY IMPORTANT that you do not specify a monitor type with a horizontal sync range that is beyond the capabilities of your monitor. If in doubt, choose a conservative setting.

```
    hsync in kHz; monitor type with characteristic modes
1   31.5; Standard VGA, 640x480 @ 60 Hz
2   31.5 - 35.1; Super VGA, 800x600 @ 56 Hz
3   31.5, 35.5; 8514 Compatible, 1024x768 @ 87 Hz interlaced (no 800x600)
4   31.5, 35.15, 35.5; Super VGA, 1024x768 @ 87 Hz interlaced, 800x600 @ 56 Hz
5   31.5 - 37.9; Extended Super VGA, 800x600 @ 60 Hz, 640x480 @ 72 Hz
6   31.5 - 48.5; Non-Interlaced SVGA, 1024x768 @ 60 Hz, 800x600 @ 72 Hz
7   31.5 - 57.0; High Frequency SVGA, 1024x768 @ 70 Hz
8   31.5 - 64.3; Monitor that can do 1280x1024 @ 60 Hz
9   31.5 - 79.0; Monitor that can do 1280x1024 @ 74 Hz
10  31.5 - 82.0; Monitor that can do 1280x1024 @ 76 Hz
11  Enter your own horizontal sync range
```

Enter your choice (1-11):

> **Caution**
>
> The next few questions in the configuration are the parts that could potentially damage your monitor if not configured correctly. Make sure you do not select frequency ranges higher than your monitor can support.

If you know the exact horizontal frequency range that your monitor can support, select 11 to enter the range manually. If you do not know the exact range, you might be able to find it in the file /usr/X11R6/lib/X11/doc/Monitors.

Unfortunately, this file is not in a readable format, but you can still find information in it if you look. Basically, the file contains the configuration for several types of monitors. The following shows a sample entry from the file:

```
Section "Monitor"
    Identifier "ELSA GDM-17E40"
    VendorName "ELSA GmbH"
    ModelName "GDM-17E40"
    BandWidth 135
    HorizSync 29-82
    VertRefresh 50-150
    ModeLine "640x480" 25 640 664 760 800 480 491 493 525
    ModeLine "640x480" 31 640 664 704 832 480 489 492 520
    ModeLine "800x600x32" 45 800 820 904 964 600 601 604 621
    ModeLine "1024x768x16" 78.7 1024 1044 1140 1264 768 770 773 796
    ModeLine "1152x875" 135 1152 1416 1456 1664 875 875 877 906
    ModeLine "1152x900" 135 1152 1400 1440 1648  900 901 905 935
```

```
    ModeLine "1280x1024i" 80 1280 1296 1512 1568 1024 1025 1037 1165 interlace
    ModeLine "1280x1024" 110 1280 1328 1512 1712 1024 1025 1028 1054
    ModeLine "1280x1024" 135 1280 1312 1456 1712 1024 1027 1030 1064
EndSection
```

The lines that begin with `Section` and `EndSection` mark the beginning and end of a single monitor definition.

For now, you do not need to worry about what most of the lines in the section mean—you are concerned only with five lines.

The first three lines you are concerned about are the ones that begin with `Identifier`, `VendorName`, and `ModelName`. These lines identify the type of monitor that this section is for. Look for the vendor name and model of your monitor in these lines.

The final two lines you are concerned with are the ones that begin with `HorizSync` and `VertRefresh`. If you find a section for your monitor, write down these two values for use in the configuration; then select 11, and enter the horizontal sync rate that you wrote down.

If you can't find this information in your monitor's manual, and you can't find an entry in the Monitors file, select one of the predefined entries where the listed resolution and refresh rate does not exceed a refresh rate that you know your monitor can handle.

Tip

Many hardware vendors are now making documentation and technical specifications for their products that are available online at their Web sites. If you can't find the printed documentation for your monitor, it might be worth a trip to the vendor's Web site to see if it has documentation and technical specifications available online.

Once you have selected one of the predefined entries or entered your monitor's horizontal sync range, press Enter to move to the next screen, where you will be asked to set the vertical refresh rate:

```
You must indicate the vertical sync range of your monitor. You can either
select one of the predefined ranges below that correspond to industry-
standard monitor types, or give a specific range. For interlaced modes,
the number that counts is the high one (e.g. 87 Hz rather than 43 Hz).

  1   50-70
  2   50-90
```

```
3  50-100
4  40-150
5  Enter your own vertical sync range

Enter your choice:
```

Once again, it is very important that you do not select a refresh rate higher than your monitor can handle, or else you may cause damage to your monitor. If you know the vertical refresh rate for your monitor, select 5 and then enter the refresh range for your monitor. Otherwise, you can select 1–4 for one of the predefined types. Press Enter after you have made your selection.

```
You must now enter a few identification/description strings, namely an
identifier, a vendor name, and a model name. Just pressing enter will fill
in default names.

The strings are free-form, spaces are allowed.
Enter an identifier for your monitor definition:
```

This is the information that will show up in the XF86Config file that the program will generate after you have finished entering all the values. You can just press Enter here to accept the defaults.

Configuring the Video Card

Next, you will be given some information about configuring the video card. Press Enter after you have read the information to get to the card database. It will look like the following:

```
0   2 the Max MAXColor S3 Trio64V+       S3 Trio64V+
1   2-the-Max MAXColor 6000              ET6000
2   3DLabs Oxygen GMX                    PERMEDIA 2
3   928Movie                             S3 928
4   AGX (generic)                        AGX-014/15/16
5   ALG-5434                         CL-GD5434
6   AOpen PA2010                         Voodo Banshee
7   ASUS 3Dexplorer                      RIVA128
8   ASUS PCI-AV264CT                     ati
9   ASUS PCI-V264CT                      ati
10  ASUS Video Magic PCI V864            S3 864
11  ASUS Video Magic PCI VT64            S3 Trio64
12  AT25                                 Alliance AT3D
13  AT3D                                 Alliance AT3D
14  ATI 3D Pro Turbo                     ati
15  ATI 3D Pro Turbo PC2TV               ati
16  ATI 3D Xpression                     ati
17  ATI 3D Xpression+                    ati
```

```
Enter a number to choose the corresponding card definition.
Press enter for the next page, q to continue configuration.
```

Once again, there are many more cards listed in the database than can fit on one screen. Press Enter to get to the next page. When you reach the end of the list, pressing Enter will start the list over at the first page.

If you can't find your exact video card in this list, simply press q to quit. Don't select a model just because it looks similar because this could cause problems. Models that have similar names do not necessarily have similar hardware.

If you do find the make and model of your video card in the list, enter its number and then press Enter. You will then receive information about the video card you selected. For example:

```
Your selected card definition:

Identifier: Matrox Millennium G400
Chipset:    mgag400
Driver:     mga
Do NOT probe clocks or use any Clocks line.

Press enter to continue, or ctrl-c to abort.
```

Pressing Enter here will continue on to the next question. Pressing Ctrl+C to abort will abort the entire program and cancel the configuration. If you do this, you will have to rerun xf86config and start over.

After this, you will need to give some more information about your video card, starting with the amount of RAM it contains:

```
Now you must give information about your video card. This will be used for
the "Device" section of your video card in XF86Config.

You must indicate how much video memory you have. It is probably a good
idea to use the same approximate amount as that detected by the server you
intend to use. If you encounter problems that are due to the used server
not supporting the amount of memory you have (e.g. ATI Mach64 is limited to
1024K with the SVGA server), specify the maximum amount supported by the
server.

How much video memory do you have on your video card:

 1  256K
 2  512K
 3  1024K
 4  2048K
 5  4096K
 6  Other

Enter your choice:
```

Unless you have a very old video card, you probably have more RAM than any of the default options here, so you will want to select 6 and then enter the amount of RAM manually.

If you do this, you will be asked to enter the amount of video RAM installed in the system in kilobytes. Remember that in binary math, a kilobyte is equal to 1024 bytes and not 1,000 bytes. Table 34.2 shows the value to enter for various amounts of video RAM.

TABLE 34.2 Video RAM in Megabytes and the Corresponding Kilobyte Values

Video RAM in Megabytes	Amount of Memory in Kilobytes
8	8192
16	16384
32	32768
64	65536
128	131072

Enter the number under Amount of memory in Kbytes and then press Enter to continue.

```
You must now enter a few identification/description strings, namely an
identifier, a vendor name, and a model name. Just pressing enter will fill
in default names (possibly from a card definition).

Your card definition is Matrox Millennium G400.

The strings are free-form, spaces are allowed.
Enter an identifier for your video card definition:
```

If you selected a video card type from the card list, there will already be a suggested identification/description string listed here. I suggest that you accept the default that is given. If you can't find your card in the list, enter a description of your video card here and then press Enter.

Depending on whether or not you selected a card definition from the database, you will be presented with a different set of questions. Please read the appropriate section below depending on whether you did or did not select a card definition from the database.

Selecting One of the Cards from the Database

If you selected a card definition from the database list, you will be presented with a menu of currently configured video modes. The following shows an example of what this might look like:

For each depth, a list of modes (resolutions) is defined. The default
resolution that the server will start-up with will be the first listed
mode that can be supported by the monitor and card.
Currently it is set to:

```
"640x480" "800x600" "1024x768" "1280x1024" for 8-bit
"640x480" "800x600" "1024x768" "1280x1024" for 16-bit
"640x480" "800x600" "1024x768" "1280x1024" for 24-bit
```

Modes that cannot be supported due to monitor or clock constraints will
be automatically skipped by the server.

```
1  Change the modes for 8-bit (256 colors)
2  Change the modes for 16-bit (32K/64K colors)
3  Change the modes for 24-bit (24-bit color)
4  The modes are OK, continue.
```

Enter your choice:

You will probably want to make some changes here because by default, X-Windows will
start up in a resolution of 640×480, which is virtually unusable. If you have a 17-inch
monitor, you will probably want to go with at least 1024×768, and you may want to go
even higher. If you have a 19- or 21-inch monitor, you can definitely go higher than
1024×768. If you have a 15-inch monitor, you might want to try 1024×768, but this
might be too small and you will have to go down to 800×600. If you have a 14-inch
monitor, 1024×768 will likely be too small, and you will want to go down to 800×600 or
possibly even stay with 640×480.

Also, you will want to decide what color depth to use. As a general rule, the higher the
color depth, the better. If you have a small amount of video RAM, though, color depth
and resolution may be a trade-off. In general, you will not notice a difference in most
applications between 16-bit and 24-bit color. However, there will be a big difference
between 8-bit color and 16-bit color. Although personal preference has to be the govern-
ing factor here, here are my recommendations:

- If the resolution you want to run does not allow more than 8-bit color (256 colors),
  it is probably better to reduce the resolution to a level that allows 16-bit color.
  However, if getting more than 256 colors requires you to reduce the resolution to a
  value lower than 1024×768, you may want to reconsider this.

- If the resolution you want to run does allow 16-bit color, but does not allow 24-bit
  color, it is probably not worth reducing the resolution to allow 24-bit color. In most
  cases, unless you are doing something in which the number of colors is extremely
  important, you are not likely to notice a huge difference between 16-bit and 24-bit
  color.

Once you have decided on the default color depth that you want to run, you will want to make changes to the mode line for that color depth (unless you plan on running 640×480 resolution by default, in which case you do not have to make any changes.

Select the number of the mode line you want to make changes to and then press Enter. For example, if you plan to run 24-bit color by default, you would select 3 in the sample given previously. This will take you to a screen similar to the following.

Select modes from the following list:

```
1   "640x400"
2   "640x480"
3   "800x600"
4   "1024x768"
5   "1280x1024"
6   "320x200"
7   "320x240"
8   "400x300"
9   "1152x864"
a   "1600x1200"
b   "1800x1400"
c   "512x384"

Please type the digits corresponding to the modes that you want to select.
For example, 432 selects "1024x768" "800x600" "640x480", with a
default mode of 1024x768.

Which modes?
```

Select the number corresponding to the default resolution that you want to use when X-Windows first starts up. For example, if you want X-Windows to start in 1024×768 resolution by default, select 4.

If you want to be able to switch between different resolutions, you can enter multiple numbers here. The first number will be the default resolution, and the numbers listed after that will be cycled through in the order they are listed when you issue the command to change the screen resolution. For example, if you want the default resolution to be 1024×768, the next resolution displayed when you cycle to be 800×600, and the final resolution displayed when cycling to be 640×480, you would enter the number 432 here.

Most people are not in the habit of changing the resolution on their screens at all once they have it initially set up. If you never changed the screen resolution on your Windows or Macintosh system, chances are you won't in FreeBSD, either. Unless you anticipate having to flip back and forth between various resolutions for some reason, you can probably just set one resolution here.

34

ADVANCED
X-WINDOWS
CONFIGURATION

When you have selected the resolution(s) that you want for this color depth, press Enter to continue. You will than be asked about virtual screens:

```
You can have a virtual screen (desktop), which is screen area that is larger
than the physical screen and which is panned by moving the mouse to the edge
of the screen. If you don't want virtual desktop at a certain resolution,
you cannot have modes listed that are larger. Each color depth can have a
differently-sized virtual screen

Please answer the following question with either 'y' or 'n'.
Do you want a virtual screen that is larger than the physical screen?
```

A virtual screen that is larger than the physical screen will cause parts of the desktop to be off the edge of the screen. To see the different parts of the desktop, you will need to scroll up, down, left, and right by dragging the mouse pointer off the end of the screen.

In my opinion, virtual screens are extremely annoying and difficult to work with. The only time they might make sense is if you are forced to use a very low resolution (640×480 or less). Even then, you will probably find the virtual screen intolerable and extremely difficult to work with. Because of this, I highly suggest that you select n here.

If you do decide that you want a virtual screen, you will be asked for the resolution that you want the screen to be. Select the desired resolution, and press Enter.

If you decide that you do not want a virtual screen, you will be taken back to the mode line configuration screen shown earlier. Another sample is shown as follows:

```
For each depth, a list of modes (resolutions) is defined. The default
resolution that the server will start-up with will be the first listed
mode that can be supported by the monitor and card.
Currently it is set to:

"640x480" "800x600" "1024x768" "1280x1024" for 8-bit
"640x480" "800x600" "1024x768" "1280x1024" for 16-bit
"1024x768" for 24-bit

Modes that cannot be supported due to monitor or clock constraints will
be automatically skipped by the server.

   1  Change the modes for 8-bit (256 colors)
   2  Change the modes for 16-bit (32K/64K colors)
   3  Change the modes for 24-bit (24-bit color)
   4  The modes are OK, continue.

Enter your choice:
```

Notice that the mode lines for 24-bit color have changed. It now has only 1024×768 resolution.

Unless you plan to run multiple color depths, you can leave the other color depths alone. If you do plan to switch between color depths, simply select the number for the next color depth you want to configure and repeat the previous steps to configure the resolutions for that color.

When you have finished configuring all the modes you want to configure, select 4 (The modes are OK, continue) to move on to the next section.

You will then be asked to specify the default color depth that you want to use:

```
Please specify which color depth you want to use by default:

   1   1 bit (monochrome)
   2   4 bits (16 colors)
   3   8 bits (256 colors)
   4   16 bits (65536 colors)
   5   24 bits (16 million colors)

Enter a number to choose the default depth.
```

Simply select the number for the color depth that you decided on earlier and then press Enter.

Saving the Configuration File

After you have selected the desired color depth, you will be asked whether you want to save the changes:

```
I am going to write the XF86Config file now. Make sure you don't accidentally
overwrite a previously configured one.

Shall I write it to /etc/X11/XF86Config?
```

Select y to write a new XF86Config file. If you already have an XF86Config file, it will be overwritten with the new file.

Once you have selected y here, xf86config will respond with the following:

```
File has been written. Take a look at it before running 'startx'. Note that
the XF86Config file must be in one of the directories searched by the server
(e.g. /etc/X11) in order to be used. Within the server press
ctrl, alt and '+' simultaneously to cycle video resolutions. Pressing ctrl,
alt and backspace simultaneously immediately exits the server (use if
the monitor doesn't sync for a particular mode).

For further configuration, refer to /usr/X11R6/lib/X11/doc/README.Config.
```

At this point, you will be returned to the command prompt. You can skip the next section and continue on with the section "Testing the X-Windows Setup" that follows.

34

ADVANCED
X-WINDOWS
CONFIGURATION

If You Did Not Select One of the Cards from the Database

If you did not select one of the cards from the card list database, the first question you will be asked is what default color depth you want to use:

```
Please specify which color depth you want to use by default:

    1   1 bit (monochrome)
    2   4 bits (16 colors)
    3   8 bits (256 colors)
    4   16 bits (65536 colors)
    5   24 bits (16 million colors)

Enter a number to choose the default depth.

Please specify which color depth you want to use by default:

    1   1 bit (monochrome)
    2   4 bits (16 colors)
    3   8 bits (256 colors)
    4   16 bits (65536 colors)
    5   24 bits (16 million colors)

Enter a number to choose the default depth.
```

Select the number corresponding to the default color depth that you want, and press Enter.

You will then be asked if you want to save the changes:

```
I am going to write the XF86Config file now. Make sure you don't accidentally
overwrite a previously configured one.

Shall I write it to /etc/X11/XF86Config?
```

Select y here to write the configuration file. This will overwrite any existing configuration file that you may have. Once you have written the changes, xf86config will respond with the following message and then exit:

```
File has been written. Take a look at it before running 'startx'. Note that
the XF86Config file must be in one of the directories searched by the server
(e.g. /etc/X11) in order to be used. Within the server press
ctrl, alt and '+' simultaneously to cycle video resolutions. Pressing ctrl,
alt and backspace simultaneously immediately exits the server (use if
the monitor doesn't sync for a particular mode).

For further configuration, refer to /usr/X11R6/lib/X11/doc/README.Config.
```

By default, X-Windows will start in 640×480 resolution. You will probably want to change this to a higher resolution. You will need to edit the XF86Config configuration file manually in order to do so. The XF86Config file is covered in the next section.

Understanding the XF86Config File

Like most other aspects of configuring FreeBSD, the X-Windows configuration is controlled by a configuration file that is plain text. The primary X-Windows configuration file is located in /etc/X11 and is called XF86Config. This is the file that is created and/or modified by xf86cfg (the GUI interface for X-Windows configuration) and also by xf86config (the text-based interface for X-Windows configuration that was covered in the previous chapter. These configuration tools have made X-Windows configuration much easier than it used to be when these files had to be edited by hand.

However, there are still some situations in which you might need to make changes to the configuration file by hand. For example, if your video card was not listed in the card database, you may need to make changes to this file by hand. Another situation in which you may need to make changes by hand is if you configured X-Windows by using xf86config, and you want to make changes to the mouse (such as the speed of the mouse). If you simply want to make one or two minor changes to X-Windows, it may be desirable to edit the file by hand rather than go through a complete configuration with xf86config.

To make changes to the XF86Config file, first make a backup copy of the file so that it will be easy to undo your changes if they cause problems. For example, you might want to copy /etc/X11/XF86Config to /etc/X11/XF86Config.bak. Once you have a backup copy, open the file /etc/X11/XF86Config in your favorite text editor (see Chapter 7, "Working with Applications," if you need information on how to use one of the text editors included with FreeBSD.

Tip

Remember that FreeBSD (and other UNIX-like operating systems) are case-sensitive. Do not confuse the text-based configuration program (xf86config) with the actual configuration file (XF86Config). Because of the case-sensitivity, they are two completely different files.

XF86Config Syntax

The XF86Config file is divided into several sections. Each section relates to a specific device or configuration issue. Each section begins with the keyword Section followed by the section name in quotes. Each section ends with the keyword EndSection. The body of the section is indented for readability purposes. Comments begin with a pound sign (#) and go to the end of the line. The following is an example of a section in the XF86Config file:

```
Section "Module"

# This loads the DBE extension module.

    Load        "dbe"    # Double buffer extension

# This loads the miscellaneous extensions module, and disables
# initialization of the XFree86-DGA extension within that module.
    SubSection  "extmod"
      Option    "omit xfree86-dga"   # don't initialize the DGA extension
    EndSubSection

# This loads the Type1 and FreeType font modules
    Load        "type1"
    Load        "freetype"

# This loads the GLX module
#    Load        "glx"

EndSection
```

The comments before this section are not shown, but in the XF86Config file, they explain what the section is for. In this case the Module section loads dynamic modules when the server starts to support various things. For example, the part of this sample that begins with # This loads the Type1 and FreeType font modules loads dynamic modules to support various types of fonts. In this case, the first Load line loads a module that supports Adobe Type 1 fonts. The second Load module loads the freetype module, which is a freely available module that allows X-Windows to use TrueType fonts.

In addition to main sections, there are also subsections that can be embedded within the sections. These begin with the keyword SubSection followed by the name of the subsection in quotes. They end with the keyword EndSubSection. Like the main sections, they are also indented for readability purposes.

The following sections take a look at the various sections and subsections in the XF86Config file.

Section "Modules"

The module section is where modules can be dynamically loaded to support things such as various font types. Dynamically loaded modules are not a part of the X binary, but are loaded dynamically when X-Windows starts. The advantage of dynamically loaded modules is that they are loaded only if they are needed. Modules that are not needed are not loaded, and therefore do not waste memory and system resources. For example, if you don't have any TrueType fonts on your system, there is little point in having TrueType font support in X. You can comment out the Load "freetype" line.

Modules that are to be loaded begin with the keyword Load followed by the name of the module in quotes. For example, the following line loads the module that supports TrueType fonts:

```
Load "freetype"
```

Section "Files"

This is sort of like the X-Windows PATH environment variable. It tells X-Windows where it can expect to find various files.

About the only portion of this section you may ever want to modify is the section that tells X-Windows where to look for fonts. Each one of the font directories begins with the keyword FontPath, followed by a directory enclosed in quotation marks. For example, the following line is where the Adobe Type 1 fonts are located:

```
FontPath    "/usr/X11R6/lib/X11/fonts/Type1/"
```

This is also the directory in which you would install new Adobe Type 1 fonts that you may download or purchase. Details on X-Windows fonts will be covered later on in this chapter.

If you do add new font directories, the name of the directory is not really important. For example, there is nothing that says that Adobe Type 1 fonts have to be stored in a directory called Type1. This convention is just followed to make it easier for you to guess what types of fonts are in a directory.

Section "ServerFlags"

The server flags section of the file contains some global options that control the behavior of X-Windows. Some of the available options are present in the configuration file generated by xf86config, and include comments about what they do. All of the options are commented out by default.

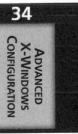

34

ADVANCED
X-WINDOWS
CONFIGURATION

All of the options in this section begin with the keyword `Option`, followed by the option in quotes. For example, the following line will disable the Ctrl+Alt+Backspace sequence that kills the X-Server immediately:

```
Option "DontZap"
```

(You definitely will not want to uncomment this option until you have tested your X-Windows system and are sure that you have a working setup.)

In the following sections we do not cover all the options, but we cover some of the ones you will be most likely to use.

Option "NoTrapSignals"

If this option is uncommented, X-Windows will not exit cleanly when there is a problem. Instead, it will write a core dump file. This can cause problems with the console not working correctly after X-Windows has terminated incorrectly.

You should probably leave this line commented out unless you are experiencing consistent X-Server crashes. In this case, the core dump file that uncommenting this option will create is invaluable for troubleshooting purposes. Even if you are not a programmer and cannot make heads or tails of the dump file, it will be invaluable if you want to file a bug report with the Xfree86 project.

Option "DontZap"

If this option is uncommented, you will not be able to kill the X-Server by Using the Ctrl+Alt+Backspace key combination. You should definitely not uncomment this line until you have tested your X-Windows configuration and are sure that it is working correctly. Even then, there is little reason to uncomment this line. About the only reason you would need to do so is if you have programs that run under X-Windows that use this key combination for some other function. Then, you might need to uncomment this line to prevent the X-Server from catching the combination and exiting.

Option "DontZoom"

If this option is uncommented, it will disable video mode switching using the Ctrl+Alt+keypad+ and Ctrl+Alt+keypad-. By default, these key combinations will allow you to cycle between different video modes if you have configured multiple video resolutions.

About the only reason for uncommenting this would be if you have programs that require these key combinations for some other use. In this case, uncommenting this line will prevent the X-Server from intercepting the combination and causing the video modes to switch.

Option "DisableVidModeExtension"

If this option is uncommented, it will prevent the xvidtune program from making any changes to the video system. If this is a multiuser system, it may be a good idea to uncomment this line to prevent users from being able to use xvidtune because the improper use of xvidtune can damage your monitor. Note that if the line is uncommented, xvidtune can still be loaded. But you will not be able to make any changes to the video system with it.

Most of the other options in this section that are present in the configuration file generated by xf86config should probably be left alone.

There are several other options that may be of interest that are not present in the default configuration file generated by xf86config. We are not going to discuss all of them here, but many of the more useful ones are discussed. If you want to add any of these options, simply add the line in bold text to this section in XF86Config.

Option "AllowMouseOpenFail"

By default, if the X-Server cannot open the mouse or other pointing device, the server will not start and will exit with an error. Adding this line will allow the server to start, even if the mouse or other pointing device cannot be accessed.

Unless you are trying to use X-Windows without a mouse or other pointing device, there is probably no reason to change this option.

Option "BlankTime" "n"

This option will cause the screen to go blank after the number of minutes represented by *n*. If this option is not present, the default is 10 minutes.

Option "StandbyTime "n"

This option will cause the monitor to go into standby mode after the number of minutes represented by *n*. If this option is not present, the default is 20 minutes.

This option is not supported by all video drivers, and it only works with monitors that support DPMS. The monitor section of XF86Config (discussed later in this chapter) must specifically specify that the monitor can support DPMS for this feature to apply.

Option "SuspendTime" "n"

This option will cause the monitor to go into suspend mode after the number of minutes represented by *n*. If this option is not present, the default is 30 minutes.

34

ADVANCED
X-WINDOWS
CONFIGURATION

This option is not supported by all video drivers, and it only works with monitors that support DPMS. The monitor section of XF86Config (discussed later in this chapter) must specifically specify that the monitor can support DPMS for this feature to apply.

Option "OffTime" "n"

This option will turn the monitor off after the number of minutes represented by *n*. If this option is not present, the default is 40 minutes.

This option is not supported by all video drivers, and it only works with monitors that support DPMS. The monitor section of XF86Config (discussed later in this chapter) must specifically specify that the monitor can support DPMS for this feature to apply.

Option "NoPM"

This option will disable some events that relate to power management. By default, power management is enabled on systems that can support it. You should need to add this option only if you are experiencing strange problems that seem to be related to power management events.

There are a few other options that can be included in this section, but they are less commonly used. If you are interested in some of the other options available, see the man page for XF86Config.

Section "InputDevice"

This section is where the input devices are configured. There can be multiple InputDevice sections in the configuration file. Usually there will be at least two: one for the keyboard, and one for the mouse or other pointing device.

InputDevice sections have several keywords associated with them.

The first is the Identifier keyword. It is followed by a name that identifies this device. X-Windows doesn't really care what you call the device, but it is best to use a descriptive name that defines the device.

The second is the Driver keyword. It is followed by the name of the driver for this device in quotes. The most common drivers are "keyboard" and "mouse", but there are a few others such as "microtouch" for a touch screen.

The final part of the InputDevice section consists of options for the device.

In the following sections we will look at the two most common InputDevice sections: the keyboard and the mouse. We will also look at some of the option lines that are available.

Keyboard

Here is a sample of the first part of the InputDevice section for the keyboard:

```
Section "InputDevice"

    Identifier  "Keyboard1"
    Driver      "Keyboard"
```

Option "Protocol"

If this option is omitted or commented out, the default value of "standard" will be used. There is probably no reason to change this.

Option "AutoRepeat" "x y"

This option controls the repeat rate of the keys on the keyboard. The number represented by *x* is the delay in milliseconds before the key starts repeating. The number represented by *y* is the number of times the key will repeat each second.

The default is 500 milliseconds before the key starts to repeat, and 30 times per second that it will repeat.

Option "XkbRules" "xfree86"

This option determines the way various aspects of the keyboard are interpreted. In most cases, you will want to leave this set to "xfree86" unless you have the Japanese PC-98 platform, in which case it should be "xfree98".

Option "XkbModel" "pc104"

If you have a 104-key Windows keyboard, this will be "pc104". If you have a 101-key keyboard that does not have the windows keys, it will be "pc101". These values will also work for laptops. Even though laptops usually have fewer keys, they generally have ways of emulating the additional keys.

Option "XkbLayout" "us"

This will usually be set to "us". But if you are using the Japanese PC-98 platform, you will want to change it to "nec/jp".

Option "XkbOptions" "ctrl:swapcaps"

If this line is uncommented, it will cause the Caps Lock key to become a Ctrl key and the left Ctrl key to become a Caps Lock key. You may want to uncomment this line if you are an Emacs guru (Emacs relies heavily on the Ctrl key) or if you are used to a UNIX keyboard layout in which the Ctrl key is placed in the position that the Caps Lock key is placed in on PC keyboards.

There are a few more options available for controlling keyboard behavior, but these are the ones that you will use most commonly.

Mouse

Here is a sample of the first part of the `InputDevice` section for the mouse:

```
Section "InputDevice"

# Identifier and driver

    Identifier   "Mouse1"
    Driver       "mouse"
```

The following sections describe some of the most commonly used options.

Option "Protocol" "*protocol*"

In this option, *protocol* represents the type of mouse that your system has. This option is required, and the X-Server will not work if it is not present.

Many users will be able to get away with specifying `Auto` here to have the X-Server automatically attempt to determine the protocol that the mouse uses. There are several other options available. Here are the valid protocol types: `Auto`, `Microsoft`, `MouseSystems`, `MMSeries`, `Logitech`, `MouseMan`, `MMHitTab`, `GlidePoint`, `IntelliMouse`, `ThinkingMouse`, `AceCad`, `PS/2`, `ImPS/2`, `ExplorerPS/2`, `ThinkingMousePS/2`, `MouseManPlusPS/2`, `GlidePointPS/2`, `NetMousePS/2`, `NetScrollPS/2`, `BusMouse`, `SysMouse`, `WSMouse`, `USB`, `Xqueue`.

And here are some guidelines for choosing the correct protocol:

- The Logitech protocol is used only by older Logitech serial mice. If you have a newer Logitech serial mouse, use the Microsoft or MouseMan protocols.
- Use the PS/2 protocol for any PS/2 mouse, no matter who the manufacturer is. You have a PS/2 mouse if the mouse connector is a small round one.
- If this is a laptop or notebook system, the built-in pointing device such as a track pad or track point will probably work with the PS/2 protocol.

I suggest that you try using `Auto` first and then change it only if your mouse is not detected or is not working properly.

Option "Device" "*devicename*"

This option specifies what device the mouse is on. The option is required, and the X-Server will not work if this option is missing.

Table 34.2 lists some of the common device names where your mouse may be located.

TABLE 34.2   Device Names for Various Mouse Types

Mouse Type	*Mouse Device*
PS/2 mouse (or laptop)	/dev/psm0
Serial mouse on COM 1	/dev/cuaa0
Serial mouse on COM 2	/dev/cuaa1
Serial mouse on COM 3	/dev/cuaa2
Serial mouse on COM 4	/dev/cuaa3
Bus mouse	/dev/mse0

devicename in this option should be replaced with the mouse device.

Option "Buttons" "*n*"

In most cases, the number of buttons on the mouse will be automatically detected. But if they are not, this option can be used to tell the X-Server how many buttons are on the mouse.

n here represents the number of buttons on the mouse. The most common values are 2 and 3, although numbers up to 5 are supported. If you happen to have a mouse with five buttons on it, go for it.

Option "Emulate3Buttons"

This line allows a two-button mouse to emulate a three-button mouse. If you have a two-button mouse, you will want to uncomment this line because X-Windows make extensive use of all three mouse buttons.

If you do uncomment this line, the middle mouse button is emulated by pressing the left and right mouse buttons at the same time.

Option "Emulate3Timeout" "*n*"

If the Emulate3Buttons option is set, this option will control the number of milliseconds that can elapse between clicking the left and right mouse buttons before X-Windows will no longer interpret the action to be a middle click. In other words, both the left and right mouse buttons must be pushed within this time frame in order for the action to be interpreted as a middle click. *n* is the number of milliseconds that can elapse.

If this line is not present, and the Emulate3Buttons option is enabled, the default Emulate3Timeout will be 50 milliseconds.

These are the most common options for configuring the mouse.

Section "Monitor"

This is where you configure the horizontal and vertical refresh rates for your monitor. It consists of the `Identifier` keyword followed by a name in quotes to identify this monitor. The name you choose is not very important.

Two other keywords are required to be present in this section. They are listed as follows.

HorizSync

This is the horizontal sync rate in kilohertz that the monitor supports. It can be specified in several ways:

- **As a range**—This is normally the method used to configure multisync monitors (and virtually all monitors are multisync these days). For example, `HorizSync 44-76` would be used for a monitor that can support horizontal refresh rates ranging from 44 to 76 kilohertz.

- **As a single value**—If you have a fixed frequency monitor that supports only one frequency, it is simply listed after `HorizSync`.

- **As a list of frequencies**—If your monitor supports several fixed frequencies, you can supply a list of the fixed frequencies that it supports, separated by commas. For example `"HorizSync 31.5, 35.2"`.

- **As multiple ranges of frequencies**—If your monitor supports more then one range of frequencies, but has a gap in the middle that it does not support, you can list multiple ranges here. For example `"HorizSync 15-25, 30-50"`.

VertRefresh

This is the other keyword that must be present in this section. It simply lists the vertical refresh rate that your monitor can support. It can take its value in any one of the formats that the `HorizSync` keyword can use.

> **Caution**
>
> Supplying values for `HorizSync` and `VertRefresh` that are outside the range of what your monitor can support can damage or destroy your monitor. Be extremely careful that you do not supply values outside the supported range. See your monitor's documentation or check the manufacturers Web site for technical specifications to find the values that your monitor can support.

There are a few more options that can be used with the Monitor section, but they are not as common. For full details on all the available options, see the man page for XF86Config.

Section "Device"

This section is where you configure your graphics adapter. Like most other sections, it begins with the keyword Identifier, followed by a name in quotes to identify the device.

The Driver keyword is also required, followed by the name of the driver for your card in quotes. For example, if you have an NVIDIA TNT2, the line would look like this:

```
Driver "nv"
```

If you have a supported video card, it is much easier to go through xf86config (explained earlier in this chapter) to set up the graphics device than to do it manually in the XF86Config file. However, if for whatever reason you need to or want to do it manually, a full list of the supported cards, along with the driver that should be used to support that card, is available at www.xfree86.org/current/Status.html.

The other keyword that is most commonly used here is the VideoRam keyword to specify how much video RAM the video card has. For example, if your video card has 16MB of RAM, the line would look like this:

```
VideoRam 16384
```

The amount of Video RAM is specified in kilobytes. Remember that in binary math, a kilobyte is actually 1024 bytes. Table 34.2 lists the number that should be entered for various amounts of video RAM.

There are some more options available for graphics devices, but most of them will not be needed for most video cards. See the man page for XF86Config for full details on all of the available options.

Also, you will probably want to have a look at the Web page located at http://www.xfree86.org/4.0.2/index.html to see if there are any notes regarding your particular type of video card and any specific options you need to supply for it.

34

ADVANCED X-WINDOWS CONFIGURATION

> **Note**
>
> If you cannot find a driver for your video card, all may not be lost. You might be able to get the card working with the Vesa driver. The Vesa driver is a generic super VGA specification that a lot of cards support to some extent. If you have to use this driver, the accelerated features of your card will not be fully supported. Also, it may not support all the resolutions and color depths that your video card can support. But it is better than nothing, and may allow you to use a card for which there is no driver currently available for X-Windows. If you do end up doing this, check the supported card database often because support for new cards is being added on a regular basis.

Section "Screen"

The `Screen` section is where a monitor is combined with a graphics card to make a display that will work with the X-Server. It starts with the `Identifier` keyword that contains a name enclosed in quotes, after which it gives this screen a name. There can be multiple screen sections present in the `XF86Config` file. The first one encountered will be the one that is used unless specified otherwise in the `ServerLayout` section.

After you have specified an identifier for the screen section, the following keywords are required to be specified.

Device "*devicename*"

This is the name of the graphics device that should be used for this screen configuration. *devicename* here is whatever string appears in the `Identifier` section of the graphics device that should be used for this screen setting.

Monitor "*monitorname*"

This is the name of the monitor that should be used for this screen configuration. *Monitorname* here is whatever string appears in the `Identifier` section of the monitor that should be used for this screen setting.

DefaultDepth "*n*"

This is the default color depth that should be used for this screen configuration. Valid values for *n* are 8, 16, and 24, assuming that your video card supports all three color depths.

There are some other options that are available but will not be used by most people. See the man page for XF86Config for details on these options.

Once you have configured the screen section, you will need to configure the display subsection(s) for the screen.

SubSection "Display"

The display subsection is where the resolutions and the order that they are cycled in are given for each color depth. There must be at least one display subsection for the default color depth, or the X-Server will not start. However, there can be more then one display subsection. There is one display subsection for each color depth.

The first line in the subsection will be the keyword Depth followed by the color depth that this subsection is for. Here is a sample of what the first two lines of this subsection might look like:

```
Subsection "Display"
    Depth        24
```

The third line that is required here is a mode line. It is simply the keyword Modes followed by a list of the resolutions that you want to have supported. The first resolution listed will be the default. The resolutions listed after that will be cycled through when the Ctrl+Alt+keypad+ or Ctrl+Alt+keypad- key combinations are used.

Here is a sample mode line:

```
Modes "1024x768" "800x600" "640x480"
```

In this example, the default resolution will be 1024×768 for this color depth. Pressing Ctrl+Alt+keypad+ or Ctrl+Alt+keypad- will also allow the resolutions of 800×600 and 640×480 to be used.

X-Windows allows you to have a virtual screen that is larger than the resolution that you have configured. For example, you can have your screen resolution set to 800×600 and have a virtual screen size of 1024×768. This was discussed in a previous section of this chapter when we talked about configuring X-Windows with the xf86config program.

If you decide that you want to use a virtual screen, the following options can be used to configure how the virtual screen behaves.

Virtual *resolution*

This is the resolution that the virtual screen should be. For example, "Virtual 1024X768" will set the virtual screen size to 1024×768. If the actual screen resolution is lower than this, only part of the screen will be visible. To see the portions of the screen

34

ADVANCED
X-WINDOWS
CONFIGURATION

that are not visible, you will need to drag the mouse pointer off the edge of the screen. This will scroll the screen left, right, up, or down—depending on which edge of the screen you are.

There are some other options available here, but they are not commonly used. For a list of all the options that are available in the display subsection, see the man page for XF86Config.

Section "ServerLayOut"

The ServerLayout section is optional. If it does not exist, the first screen listed and the first keyboard and mouse input devices listed will be used. If the ServerLayout section does exist, it is used to select the screen entry and keyboard and mouse entries to be used for the X-Server.

The Identifier keyword is required, and it is followed by a string in quotes that gives this ServerLayout a name. Here are some of the other things that will commonly be used in the ServerLayout section:

Screen "screenname"

This is the screen configuration that should be used for this device. The screenname here is the name listed in the Identifier keyword for the screen section that is to be used for this ServerLayout.

InputDevice "keyboardname" "CoreKeyboard"

This determines which keyboard entry should be used for this ServerLayout. keyboard-name is the name listed in the Identifier keyword for the keyboard section that you want to use.

The CoreKeyboard option that follows sets this keyboard to the default keyboard.

InputDevice "mousename" "CorePointer"

This is like the keyboard entry, except that it determines the mouse that should be used for this ServerLayout. Once again, the CorePointer option that follows sets this mouse to the default mouse.

Option lines can also be included in the ServerLayout section. If they are included, and if they conflict with options listed in other sections, the options listed here will override the other options.

There are various other options available for all aspects of the XF86Config file, but most of them are rarely used. Once again, see the man page for XF86Config for full details of all the available configuration options.

Testing the X-Windows Setup

Once you have finished with xf86config, and/or hand-edited the XF86Config file and saved your changes, you are ready to test the X-Server.

Type startx at the command line to start the X-Windows system. If all goes well, your screen will go blank for a moment, and you should soon see a checkered background with a small x in the middle. The x is the mouse pointer. After a few more seconds, the window manager should come up, and you should be able to move the mouse around on the screen.

If you can't move the mouse, or if X-Windows seems to start, but then quits with an error message, double-check your XF86Config file to make sure that you have everything configured properly.

> **Caution**
>
> If you start X-Windows and your screen appears to be garbled, and/or you hear a high-pitched whine coming from your monitor, IMMEDIATELY turn your monitor off and/or press Ctrl+Alt+Backspace to kill the X-Server. Either one of these symptoms indicates that you are probably driving the refresh rate of your monitor higher than it can tolerate, and the flyback transformer in your monitor is getting ready to fry. After you have killed the X-Server, reconfigure the sync rates and/or resolutions for your monitor in XF86Config or with the xf86config script, and try again.

If you type startx and your monitor goes blank and then seems to turn off or go into a suspend mode (the power light changes color, starts blinking, or you can hear the static on the monitor discharging), it probably means you have driven your monitor past the specs that it can tolerate. Press Ctrl+Alt+Backspace to kill the X-Server. This should restore your screen and give you the command prompt back. Then, reconfigure your refresh rates and/or resolutions in XF86Config or with the xf86config script, and try again.

Once you have a working X-Windows setup, you may want to make some customizations to the way it works. The next section covers your personal .xinitrc file in your home directory.

34

ADVANCED
X-WINDOWS
CONFIGURATION

Your Personal .xinitrc File

Changing the .xinitrc file in your home directory is the primary way of making changes to the basic X-Windows setup. One of the things controlled by this file is which window manager is used by X-Windows. Other attributes that you can control from this file include causing certain applications to start automatically every time you run X-Windows, setting the background color of the screen, and setting an image to display in the background. Each of these operations will be covered separately in the sections to follow. All of them will involve making changes to your personal .xinitrc file.

Changing the Window Managers

Chapters 4, 5, and 6 dealt primarily with the Gnome Desktop Environment. However, as has been mentioned in multiple places in the book, you can always choose to run a different window manager if you do not like Gnome.

Two popular window managers for X-Windows are Blackbox and WindowMaker. Both of these window managers are available in the FreeBSD ports collection in the x11-wm directory. See Chapter 15, "Installing Additional Software," for information on how to work with the FreeBSD ports collection.

Figures 34.1 and 34.2 show the Blackbox window manager and the WindowMaker window manager, respectively.

FIGURE 34.1

Blackbox is a very small and fast window manager. It contains few frills and takes up very few system resources.

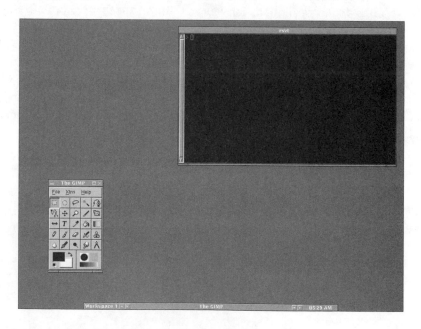

FIGURE 34.2
WindowMaker is based on the windowing system that came with the NextStep operating system.

Blackbox is an ideal window manager for those who do not want the window manager to get in the way. It is also ideal for systems that are low on memory. Blackbox is a common window manager on servers.

One of WindowMaker's more interesting and powerful features is the dock on the right side of the screen. There are many dockable applications that can be loaded here that do things such as monitor network bandwidth, display a clock, check e-mail, or even play CDs.

Once you have installed one or both of these window managers, you will need to make changes to your personal .xinitrc file to cause one of these window managers to be used instead of Gnome.

Open the .xinitrc file located in your home directory in your favorite text editor. If the file does not already exist, it will be created.

In this case, all we want to do is tell X-Windows what window manager we want to use, so we only need to add one line to the file.

For WindowMaker, the line to add is

```
wmaker
```

For Blackbox, the line to add is

```
blackbox
```

34

ADVANCED
X-WINDOWS
CONFIGURATION

Once you have added one of these lines to the .xinitrc file, save the file, and exit the editor. The next time you start X-Windows, you will be placed in the new window manager instead of in Gnome.

Configuration of these two window managers is beyond the scope of this book. If you are interested in learning more about either Blackbox or WindowMaker, see their Web pages, located at http://blackbox.alug.org and www.windowmaker.org, respectively.

There are many more window managers available than the two that have been listed in this chapter. Many of them are available in the FreeBSD ports collection under the x11-wm directory.

For information, including screen shots of many of the more popular window managers, see www.xwinman.org.

Starting Applications Automatically

If you want to have applications start automatically each time you start the X-Windows system, you can add them to your .xinitrc file. Any applications that you want to start automatically should be added before the window manager, and should end with a & so they start in the background. If you don't end them with a &, they will start in the foreground, and the window manager will never get started.

Here is an example of an .xinitrc file that starts an X terminal window and an X clock along with the Blackbox window manager.

```
xterm &
xclock &
blackbox
```

Setting a Background Color or Background Image

Many window managers and desktop environments such as WindowMaker and Gnome have the capability built in to them to set their own background colors or background images. However, some of the simpler window managers such as FVWM and wm2 do not. There are a couple of ways that the background color or background image can be set by calling external programs from the .xinitrc file.

Setting the Background Color

By default, X-Windows has a rather ugly checkered background that is hard on the eyes.

The program xsetroot allows you to set the background color to a solid color or to a tiled bitmap from an image. There is a text file that lists all of the available colors located in `/usr/X11R6/lib/X11/rgb.txt`. Here is an example of how the background color can be set to a solid color:

```
xsetroot -solid ForestGreen
```

You can type this from an X terminal window to set the background to forest green.

If you want this change to be permanent, you can add this command to your `.xinitrc` file before the window manager starts. For example, the following line will set the background color to forest green and then start the `twm` window manager:

```
xsetroot -solid ForestGreen &
twm
```

The color you use must be a valid color that is listed in the `rgb.txt` file, and if the color has a space in it, the name of the color must be enclosed in quotation marks.

In addition to setting the background color or pattern of the desktop, `xsetroot` can also change the appearance of the mouse pointer.

See the `man` page for `xsetroot` for details on how to configure bitmapped backgrounds and also change the mouse pointer to a different bitmap.

You can create your own bitmaps to use as the background and as the mouse pointers with the bitmap program. Figure 34.3 shows the bitmap program.

FIGURE 34.3
The bitmap program, which can be used to create bitmaps for use as background patterns and mouse pointers with `xsetroot`.

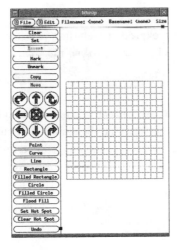

34

ADVANCED
X-WINDOWS
CONFIGURATION

Configuring a Background Image

X-Windows does not come with any program that allows you to set a background image. However, there is a program available in the FreeBSD ports collection called `xv` that can handle this for you. xv is available in the ports collection under the graphics directory. Figure 34.4 shows xv running in interactive mode.

FIGURE 34.4

xv can do far more than just set the background image in X-Windows. It is also a full-featured image viewer that can be used interactively.

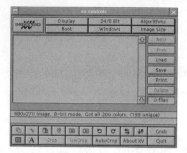

xv supports most common image formats including GIF, JPEG, and BMP; and can set any one of these formats as a background image.

The following command is an example of how xv can be used to load an image as a background image for X-Windows:

```
xv -root -quit /hone/foobar/images/myimage.jpg
```

This tells xv to load the image myimage.jpg onto the root window (which is the background of the window manager). It also tells xv that it should quit as soon as it has loaded the image.

In order to have this image loaded as the background each time you start X-Windows, you could do something like the following in your .xinitrc file:

```
xv -root -quit /home/foobar/images/myimage.jpg
twm
```

Some of the other options you may want to use with xv when using it to load background images are -max, which will cause the image to be resized and take up the entire available screen size; or -maxspect, which will cause the image to be resized to take up the entire available screen size within the limits of maintaining the proper aspect ratio of the image.

Working with Fonts

Sooner or later, you will probably want to install additional fonts in X-Windows for your applications (such as GIMP).

Although X-Windows supports several types of fonts, the most common ones you will likely install are Adobe Type 1, and TrueType. Both are extremely popular because they are supported by Windows and Macintosh, as well as newer versions of Xfree86. There are thousands of Type 1 and TrueType fonts available free for download from various places on the Internet, as well as commercial fonts available for purchase in both formats.

Because these are the most common types of fonts you are likely to want to install, they are the types that this section will focus on.

Checking the XF86Config File

The first thing you will need to do is make sure that the XF86Config file contains the proper modules to support the fonts that you want to use. The XF86Config file was covered in detail under the section "Understanding the XF86Config File" earlier in this chapter.

Basically, you need to check the file /etc/X11/XF86Config for the appropriate Load line under the Modules section. These lines are as follows.

This line is necessary to support Adobe Type 1 fonts:

```
Load "type1"
```

This line is necessary to support TrueType fonts:

```
Load "freetype"
```

These lines need to be located under the heading in XF86Config that looks like this:

```
Section "Modules"
```

You will also need to make sure that an appropriate font directory exists in the files section to hold the new fonts.

Look for the lines in XF86Config that begin with FontPath. If you are installing a TrueType font, I suggest that you add the following line after the last FontPath statement in the file to hold all your TrueType fonts:

```
FontPath   "/usr/X11R6/lib/X11/fonts/TrueType/"
```

After you add this line, save the file and then exit the editor.

Creating the Directories and Installing the Fonts

Now, you will need to create the directory. As root, issue the following command:

```
mkdir /usr/X11R6/lib/X11/fonts/TrueType
```

34

ADVANCED
X-WINDOWS
CONFIGURATION

This will create the directory for the TrueType fonts.

Once you have a directory for the fonts, copy the font files for the fonts you want to add into the appropriate directory. Type 1 fonts should be copied into /usr/X11R6/lib/X11/fonts/Type1, and TrueType fonts should be copied into /usr/X11R6/lib/X11/fonts/TrueType. The fonts only need read access, so you may want to change the permissions on the font so that they only have read access for everyone. You can do this with the following command

```
chmod 444 fontname
```

where `fontname` is, of course, the name of the font you just installed. (Make sure you are currently in the right font directory. If you need help with basic shell commands and navigation through the directories, please see Chapter 8, "Working with the Shell").

After this has been done, you will need to run a couple of programs to set up the fonts correctly.

For TrueType fonts, you will need the program `ttmkfdir`. It is available in the FreeBSD ports collection under the directory `x11-fonts`. For Adobe Type 1 fonts, you will need the program `type1inst`. It is also available in the FreeBSD ports collection under the `x11-fonts` directory. See Chapter 15 for information on how to install software from the ports collection.

After you have copied the fonts to the appropriate directory, make sure you are in that directory, and type one of the following commands at the command prompt.

For TrueType fonts:

```
ttmkfdir > fonts.scale
```

For Adobe Type 1 fonts:

```
type1inst > fonts.scale
```

Once this has been done, there is one more command left to run. You need to run the `mkfontdir` command to recognize the new fonts and add them to the font configuration file. For scalable fonts such as Type 1 and TrueType, you need to run it with the `-e` option. Once again, making sure you are in the proper directory where you copied the fonts to, issue the following command from the prompt:

```
mkfontdir -e /usr/X11R6/lib/font/encodings
```

Once you have done this, restart X-Windows if you are currently in it, and your new fonts should be available for use.

You need to repeat `ttmkfdir` or `type1inst`, followed by `mkfontdir` procedure, whenever you add any new fonts to the system.

Using Remote X-Windows Clients

Because of the design of X-Windows, applications can be run on a host and have their output and input redirected to a remote host. This can be useful, for example, if you have graphical applications on a server and you need to be able to control them from a workstation. In a way, it is similar to simply using Telnet or SSH to log in to a remote system and then run a text-based application. The application is actually running on the server. The output and input is just being sent to your system. X-Windows extends this concept to graphical applications as well as text-based applications. However, this capability is disabled by default and needs to be enabled before it can be used.

The confusing aspect of this is that the terms *client* and *server* are reversed when dealing with X-Windows. In networking terminology, you think of a client as being a host that runs applications located on another system known as a server. In X-Windows, however, the server is running on the local system, and the client is located on a remote system. Basically, a client in X-Windows is any program that runs under the X-Windows system. To make things even more confusing, your X-Server may be running a client located on a remote system, which is actually a server. For example, you might load a graphical database administration client located on a remote system onto your X-Server. In this case, your client is located on a remote system, but the remote system is a database server.

In order for any of this to work, the system on which you want to display the output of and control the input of the remote X-Windows application must be running an X-Server. However, the X-Server does not have to be on the same type of system. The X-Server can be running on another FreeBSD system, a Linux system, a Solaris system, or a Mac OS X system. The system doesn't even have to be a UNIX-based system. There are X-Servers available for Windows that can display remote X applications running on FreeBSD. Right now, the large majority of them are commercial. But Xfree86 is being ported to Windows, so soon a freely available X-Server will be available for Windows systems.

By default, your X-Server will not allow remote applications to be displayed on your screen. There are a few common ways to allow this. The most common, but also the least secure, is by using xhost.

Using xhost to Allow Remote Applications to Be Displayed

xhost will allow remote applications running on a different system to be displayed locally on your system and take their input from your system. To see the current xhost configuration settings, type xhost with no arguments. Here is what the default xhost configuration will return:

```
bash$ xhost
access control enabled, only authorized clients can connect
bash$
```

In this case, only applications being run on remote systems that appear in this system's authorization list will be allowed to be displayed on this system. Also, the list is currently empty, meaning that no clients are currently authorized to send their display to this system.

If you want to be able to run remote applications on the host named lion, you need to add it to the authorization list. To do this, you use the following command:

```
bash$ xhost +lion
lion being added to access control list
bash$
```

If you type xhost now without any arguments, the system responds with this:

```
access control enabled, only authorized clients can connect
INET:lion.samplenet.org
```

The remote host lion can now display its X-Windows applications on the local system.

The problem with this setup is that anyone who has an account on lion can send the display to your system. This can be a major security problem in an environment with untrusted users. Therefore, it is not a good idea to use xhost in these environments. There are some other methods available that are more secure, which are discussed briefly later in this chapter.

Also, if you do use xhost, it is probably a good idea to authorize a host only just before you need it, and then remove the authorization as soon as you are done working with the remote application. To revoke authorization from a host, you can use a command like the following:

```
bash$ xhost -lion
lion being removed from access control list
bash$
```

The remote host lion can no longer display applications on this system.

There is also a way to completely disable access control in xhost so that any clients can connect to the system. This is probably never a good idea because it is a serious security hazard. But if for some reason you want to do it, you can use the following command:

```
bash$ xhost +
access control disabled, clients can connect from any host
bash$
```

To enable access control again, type xhost -. The system responds with this:

```
access control enabled, only authorized clients can connect
```

Caution

Because of the security hazards involved with xhost, at a minimum you will want to have a firewall configured that blocks unauthorized users from outside the internal network from accessing the ports that xhost uses. xhost uses ports 6000 through 6063. See the "Configuring a Firewall" section of Chapter 29, "Network Security," for more information on configuring a firewall.

After you have configured the system to allow a remote application to display on it, you need to connect to the remote system and start the application. You can do this through Telnet, SSH, or rlogin if the remote system supports rlogin from your system.

Tip

If you are connecting to the remote system by using an X-Server running on Windows, make sure that you use the Telnet or SSH application included with your X-Server software. Because the Windows Telnet application knows nothing about the X-Server, it does not work correctly for the procedures described in the following chapters.

Starting a Remote Application

To start an application on the remote host and have it display its output on the local system, you need to set the DISPLAY environment variable on the remote host to your local system. You can do this from the Telnet, SSH, or rlogin session. In your connection window to the remote host, you can usually use something like the following to start a remote application and display it on your system (this example assumes that your local host is named simba):

```
bash$ DISPLAY=simba:0; export DISPLAY
bash$ xcalc &
```

This code is for a bourne-style shell (that is, bourne, korn, or bash). If you are using a C shell (or tcsh), then replace the first line with the following:

```
% setenv DISPLAY simba:0
```

This code should start an `xcalc` on the remote host and display the output on your screen.

The `DISPLAY` environment variable has the following syntax:

```
DISPLAY=hostname:display#:screen#
```

display# is almost always be set to 0, and you can usually eliminate *screen#* unless you are on a system that has multiple screens attached to it.

> **Tip**
>
> Make sure that you enter the information in the Telnet or SSH window that is connected to the remote host. Entering the information on a local `xterm` window will not have the desired effect.

Other Client Access Controls

There are other ways to control which hosts can display applications on the local host. Some of these ways are more secure than using the `xhost` method described previously. The other methods and their configuration are beyond the scope of this book. However, you might want to read the man page for `Xsecurity` to get you started. (Note that it is case-sensitive when you try to access the man page.)

xdm

`xdm` is a graphical login manager for the X-Windows system. When it is run, at system startup, it displays a graphical login prompt rather than the text-based login prompt at the console. The graphical login prompt is similar to a Windows NT/2000 login screen.

If you want to use `xdm`, you should create a file called `.xsession` in your home directory. This file is the `xdm` equivalent of the `.xinitrc` file that the console login uses. It should contain the command to start your desired window manager, as well as the commands to start any applications you want to run automatically at boot time. All the commands in the `.xsession` file should end with an `&` so they start in the background. The following is what a sample `.xession` file could look like:

```
wmaker &
xterm &
```

This would start the WindowMaker window manager and also start an `xterm` automatically after login.

Note that unlike the `.xinitrc` file, the `.xsession` file needs to be executable, or it will not work.

There are a couple of ways you can have `xdm` start automatically at each system boot. But the method we will look at here is the safest because it allows you to access a text-based login prompt on another virtual terminal if you accidentally mess up your X-Windows configuration and end up with `xdm` not working correctly. The safest way is to create a file that looks similar to the following in `/usr/local/etc/rc.d`:

```
#!/bin/sh
case "$1" in
    start)
        echo "**************************************************"
        echo "* Starting the XDM login manager. Please wait... *"
        echo "**************************************************"
        xdm
        ;;
    *)
        : #do nothing
        ;;
esac
```

Make the file executable and reboot the system. `xdm` should start automatically on the next system boot.

`xdm` is very configurable, and details of its configuration are beyond the scope of this book. See the man page for `xdm` for information on the various configuration files available to configure `xdm`.

Appendixes

PART
VI

Command Reference and Configuration File Reference

This appendix contains a reference of common FreeBSD commands It is divided into
sections for commands related to files and directories, system administration, and so on.
Each entry gives a short description of the command along with the chapter in which
more information can be found. It also contains a list of some of the common FreeBSD
configuration files.

Command	*Action*
File- and Directory-Manipulation Commands	
cd *dirname*	Change to the directory *dirname*; if path is notspecified, *dirname* is assumed to be relative to the current path. (Chapter 8, "Working with the Shell") .
ls	Lists the contents of the current directory. Popular options include -l to list the attributes of each entry, -a to list hidden files, and -F to help differentiate different types of files (Chapter 8)
cp *oldfile newfile*	Copies *oldfile* to *newfile*. If no directory path is specified for either file, they are both assumed to be in the current directory. Common options include -r to recursively copy a directory and -i to do an interactive copy that prevents clobbering existing files. (Chapter 8)
mv *oldfile newfile*	Moves *oldfile* to *newfile*. If no directory is specified for either file, they are both assumed to be in the current directory. Common options include -r to recursively move a directory and -i to do an interactive copy that prevents clobbering existing files. This command is also used to rename files and directories. (Chapter 8)
rmdir *dirname*	Removes the directory *dirname*, assuming that it is empty. (Chapter 8)
touch *filename*	Updates the access time on *filename*. If the file does not already exist, it is created. (Chapter 8)
mkdir *dirname*	Creates the directory *dirname*. (Chapter 8)
ln *file1 file2*	Creates a link named *file2* that points to *file1* (like a shortcut in Windows). (Chapter 8)
mount *filesystem mountpoint*	Mounts the filesystem represented by *filesystem* on the directory represented by *mountpoint* to make it available for use. (Chapter 9, "The FreeBSD Filesystem")

Command	Action
File- and Directory-Manipulation Commands	
umount *mountpoint*	Unmounts the filesystem mounted on the directory *mountpoint*, making it unavailable for use. (Chapter 9)
Security-Related Commands	
chmod [permissions] *filename*	Changes the access permissions on *filename*. (Chapter 10, "Users, Groups, and Permissions)
chown *username* *filename*	Changes the ownership of *filename* to the user *username*. (Chapter 10)
chgrp *groupname* *filename*	Changes the group ownership of *filename* to the group *groupname*. (Chapter 10)
passwd	Changes your login password. The root user can specify a name after passwd to change the password of that user. (Chapter 10)
adduser	Runs a script that adds a new user to the system. (Chapter 10)
rmuser	Runs a script that removes a user from the system. That user will no longer be able to log in to the system. (Chapter 10)
vipw	Allows you to edit the /etc/master.passwd file directly, and updates the database when exiting. (Chapter 10)
Common Shell Commands	
grep [pattern] *filename*	Searches the file *filename* for the specified pattern. (Chapter 8)
more *filename*	Views the contents of *filename* one screen at a time. (Chapter 8)
less *filename*	Views the contents of *filename* one screen at a time. Like more, but less actually has more features than more. (Chapter 8)
cat *filename*	Displays the contents of *filename*. Catcat is normally used with redirection or pipes. (Chapter 8)
wc *filename*	Displays the number of words, lines, and characters in *filename*. (Chapter 8)
diff *file1* *file2*	Compares the contents of *file1* with the contents of *file2*, and displays the differences between the files. (Chapter 8)

Command	Action
Common Shell Commands	
`fmt` *filename*	Formats *filename* into a format suitable for e-mailing. Output is sent to STDOUT by default. (Chapter 8)
`cut` [option] *filename*	Displays only a particular column or field from *filename*. Output is sent to STDOUT by default. (Chapter 8)
`head` *filename*	Displays the first 10 lines of *filename*. (Chapter 8)
`tail` *filename*	Displays the last 10 lines of *filename*. (Chapter 8)
`sort` *filename*	Sorts the contents of *filename* into alphabetical order. Output is sent to STDOUT by default. (Chapter 8)
`cal`	Displays a calendar for the current month. (Chapter 8)
`date`	Displays the current date and time. The root user can also use this command to change the date and time. (Chapter 8)
`man` *command*	Displays the manual page for *command*. (Chapter 8)
`vi`	Invokes the `vi` text editor. If a filename is specified, that file will be opened. (Chapter 7, "Working with Applications")
`ee`	Invokes the FreeBSD Easy Editor. If a filename is specified, that file will be opened. (Chapter 7)
System Utilities and Maintenance-Related Commands	
`ps`	Displays the list of processes running on the system. Common options include `-l` for a detailed list, `-a` for all processes, and `-x` to display daemon processes as well. (Chapter 14, "Performance Monitoring, Process Control, and Job Automation")
`top`	Displays a list of processes and their resource usage statistics that is updated on a regular basis. (Chapter 14)
`kill` *n*	Where *n* is a process ID number that you wish to kill. Options are available to send different signals to the process. (Chapter 14)
`killall` *pnameI*	Where *pname* is the name of a process to kill. All processes that match and belong to you will be killed. Options are available to send different signals to the process. (Chapter 14)
`at`	Schedules a job or command to run at a specified time. (Chapter 14)

Command	Action
System Utilities and Maintenance-Related Commands	
crontab *filename*	Schedules jobs or commands to run on a regular basis. *filename* is the name of the crontab file you want to edit. (Chapter 14)
shutdown	Shuts down or reboots the system. (Chapter 4, "Your First Session with FreeBSD")
halt	Halts the system. (Chapter 4)
reboot	Reboots the system. (Chapter 4)
Printer-Related Commands	
lpr	Sends a job to the printer. (Chapter 16, "Printing")
lprm *n*	Where *n* is a job number. This removes the job from the printer. Other options allow removing jobs for a particular user, and so on. (Chapter 16)
lpq	Displays the list of jobs currently in the printer queue. (Chapter 16)
lpc	Controls the printer queues and the print daemons. (Chapter 16)
Software Installation and Removal Commands	
pkg_info	Displays a list of packages installed on the system along with a short description of each package. (Chapter 15, "Installing Additional Software")
pkg_add *packagename*	Installs the software package *packagename* onto the system. (Chapter 15)
pkg_delete *packagename*	Removes the software package *packagename* from the system. (Chapter 15)
make	When issued from a port directory, obtains the port files and builds the port. (Chapter 15)
make install	When issued from a port directory, installs the port if it has already been built. If not, obtains the necessary files and builds the port first. (Chapter 15)
make deinstall	When issued from a port directory, removes the installed port from the system. It will also remove any dependencies that are not required by some other installed port or package. (Chapter 15)

A

COMMAND
REFERENCE

Command	Action
Software Installation and Removal Commands	
`make clean`	When issued from a port directory, removes the work files and object files created when building the port, reclaiming the hard disk space used by them. (Chapter 15)
`make distclean`	When issued from a port directory, removes the work files and object files created when building the port as well as the source distribution files that were obtained, reclaiming the hard disk space used by them. (Chapter 15)
Common Configuration Files	
`.profile`	The configuration file for Bourne-style shells (`sh`, `ksh`, and `bash`). (Chapter 12, "Customizing the Shell")
`.login`	The configuration file for C- style shells (`csh`, `tcsh`). (Chapter 12)
`.cshrc`	Configuration options for C- style shells (`csh`, `tcsh`) that affect subshells as well as login shells. (Chapter 12)
`.bashrc`	Configuration options for the `bash` shell that affect subshells as well as login shells. (Chapter 12)
`/etc/csh.login`	Default global configuration options for C-style shells (`csh`, `tcsh`) that affect all users. (Chapter 12)
`/etc/profile`	Default global configuration options for Bourne-style shells (`sh`, `ksh`, `bash`) that affect all users. (Chapter 12)
`.forward`	Controls e-mail forwarding. (Chapter 25, "Configuring E-mail Services")
`.xinitrc`	Controls X-Windows options. (Chapter 34, "Advanced X-Windows Configuration")
`/etc/rc.conf`	Main system configuration file that controls startup options for FreeBSD. (Chapter 11, "System Configuration and Startup Scripts")
`/etc/X11/XF86Config`	The main configuration file for the X-Windows system. (Chapter 34)

Hardware
Compatibility Lists

This appendix lists the hardware that FreeBSD is known to work with, as well as the video cards that are supported by the X-Windows system.

System Requirements

Minimum:

- Intel 386sx or compatible CPU
- 4MB of RAM

My recommended minimum configuration:

- Intel 486DX2/66 or compatible CPU
- 32MB of RAM
- At least 1GB of free disk space for a full install (with X-Windows), in which third-party applications will be added on a workstation. Servers may require much more space, depending on number of users and the services the server is providing.

In addition, if you plan to run the X-Windows system, I recommend the following additional minimum system configuration:

- Monitor that can do 1024×768 resolution (comfortably)
- Supported SVGA video card (see video card list) with at least 1MB of video RAM
- Three-button mouse

Supported Hardware

The following hardware is known to work with FreeBSD.

Disk Controllers (Non-SCSI)

Any generic MFM or RLL (WD1003)

Any generic IDE (WD1007)

ATA controllers

FreeBSD supports UDMA mode on EIDE controllers that can use it.

Disk Controllers (SCSI)

Note that some SCSI controllers (such as the SoundBlaster SCSI controllers) use a chipset from another manufacturer such as Adaptec. If you don't find your actual card listed here, check to see what chipset it uses. In some cases, the chipset will be in the following list.

Adaptec:

174X series EISA SCSI controllers in standard and enhanced mode

274X/284X/2920C/294X/2950/3940/3950 (Narrow/Wide/Twin) series EISA/VLB/PCI SCSI controllers

AIC-7850, AIC-7860, AIC-7880, AIC-789X on-board SCSI controllers

1510 series ISA SCSI controllers (not for bootable devices)

152X series ISA SCSI controllers

AIC-6260 and AIC-6360-based boards, which include the AHA-152X and SoundBlaster SCSI cards

AdvanSys:

All AdvanSys SCSI controllers are supported.

AMI:

Amy AMI FastDisk disk controller that is a true BusLogic MultiMaster clone

BusLogic:

MultiMaster "W" Series Host Adapters including BT-948, BT-958, BT-9580

MultiMaster "C" Series Host Adapters including BT-946C, BT-956C, BT-956CD, BT-445C, BT-747C, BT-757C, BT-757CD, BT-545C, BT-540CF

MultiMaster "S" Series Host Adapters including BT-445S, BT-747S, BT-747D, BT-757S, BT-757D, BT-545S, BT-542D, BT-742A, BT-542B

MultiMaster "A" Series Host Adapters including BT-742A, BT-542B

Compaq:

Intelligent Disk Array Controllers: IDA, IDA-2, IAES, SMART, SMART-2/E, Smart-2/P, SMART-2SL; Integrated Array; and Smart Arrays 3200, 3100ES, 221, 4200, 4200, 4250ES

DPT:

SmartCACHE Plus, SmartCACHE III, SmartRAID III, SmartCACHE IV, and SmartRAID IV SCSI/RAID are supported. The DPT SmartRAID/CACHE V is not yet supported. The DPT PM3754U2-16M SCSI RAID Controller is also supported.

DTC:

EISA SCSI controller in 1542 evaluation mode

SymBios (also NCR):

53C810, 53C810a, 53C815, 53C820, 53C825a, 53C860, 53C875, 53C875j, 53C885, and 53C896 PCI SCSI controllers including ASUS SC-200; Data Technology DTC3130 (all variants); Diamond FirePort (all); NCR cards (all); SymBios cards (all); Tekram DC390W, 390U, and 390F; and Tyan S1365

QLogic:

1020, 1040, 1040B, and 2100 SCSI and Fiber

> **Note**
>
> FreeBSD supports SCSI-I and SCSI-II devices. However, CD-RW and WORM devices are supported only in read-only mode by the driver included with FreeBSD. To get write access to these devices, install `cdrecord` from the FreeBSD ports tree.

CD-ROM Drives

Any ATAPI-compliant drive

SCSI-based drives

Matsushita/Panasonic (Creative Labs SoundBlaster) proprietary drives (562/563 models)

All Sony proprietary drives

Network Cards

Adaptec:

Duralink PCI Fast Ethernet adapters based on the Adaptec AIC-6195 Fast Ethernet controller chip, including the following:

>   ANA-62011 64-bit single port 10/100baseTX adapter
>
>   ANA-62022 64-bit dual port 10/100baseTX adapter

ANA-62044 64-bit quad port 10/100baseTX adapter

ANA-69011 32-bit single port 10/100baseTX adapter

ANA-62020 64-bit single port 100baseFX adapter

Allied-Telesyn:

AT1700 and RE2000

Alteon Networks:

Alteon Networks PCI Gigabit Ethernet NICs based on the Tigon 1 and Tigon 2 chipsets, including the Alteon AceNIC (Tigon 1 and 2), 3Com 3c985-SX (Tigon 1 and 2), Netgear GA620 (Tigon 2), Silicon Graphics Gigabit Ethernet, DEC/Compaq EtherWORKS 1000, NEC Gigabit Ethernet

AMD:

PCnet/PCI (79c970 and 53c974 or 79c974)

RealTek:

8129/8139 Fast Ethernet NICs, including the following:

Allied-Telesyn AT2550

Allied-Telesyn AT2500TX

Genius GF100TXR (RTL8139)

NDC Communications NE100TX-E

OvisLink LEF-8129TX

OvisLink LEF-8139TX

Netronix Inc. EA-1210 NetEther 10/100

KTX-9130TX 10/100 Fast Ethernet

Accton "Cheetah" EN1207D (MPX 5030/5038; RealTek 8139 clone)

SMC EZ Card 10/100 PCI 1211-TX

Lite-On:

98713, 98713A, 98715, and 98725 Fast Ethernet NICs, including the following:

LinkSys EtherFast LNE100TX

NetGear FA310-TX Rev. D1

Matrox FastNIC 10/100

Kingston KNE110TX

Macronix:

98713, 98713A, 98715, 98715A, and 98725 Fast Ethernet NICs, including the following:

NDC Communications SFA100A (98713A)
CNet Pro120A (98713 or 98713A)
CNet Pro120B (98715)
SVEC PN102TX (98713)

Macronix/Lite-On:

PNIC II LC82C115 Fast Ethernet NICs, including the LinkSys EtherFast LNE100TX version 2

Winbond:

W89C840F Fast Ethernet NICs, including the Trendware TE100-PCIE

Via Technologies:

VT3043 "Rhine I" and VT86C100A "Rhine II" Fast Ethernet NICs including the Hawking Technologies PN102TX and D-Link DFE-530TX

Silicon Integrated Systems:

SiS 900 and SiS 7016 PCI Fast Ethernet NICs

Sundance Technologies:

ST201 PCI Fast Ethernet NICs, including the D-Link DFE-550TX

SysKonnect:

SK-984x PCI Gigabit Ethernet cards, including the following:

SK-9841 1000baseLX (single-mode fiber, single port)
SK-9842 1000baseSX (multimode fiber, single port)
SK-9843 1000baseLX (single-mode fiber, dual port)
SK-9844 1000baseSX (multimode fiber, dual port).

Texas Instruments:

ThunderLAN PCI NICs, including the following:

Compaq Netelligent 10, 10/100, 10/100 Proliant, 10/100 Dual-Port, 10/100 TX Embedded UTP, 10 T PCI UTP/Coax, and 10/100 TX UTP

Compaq NetFlex 3P, 3P Integrated, and 3P w/BNC

Olicom OC-2135/2138, OC-2325, OC-2326 10/100 TX UTP

Racore 8165 10/100baseTX and 8148 10baseT/100baseTX/100baseFX multipersonality cards

ADMTek:

AL981-based and AN985-based PCI Fast Ethernet NICs

ASIX Electronics:

AX88140A PCI NICs including the Alfa Inc. GFC2204 and CNet Pro110B

DEC:

EtherWORKS III NICs (DE203, DE204, and DE205)

EtherWORKS II NICs (DE200, DE201, DE202, and DE422)

DC21040-, DC21041-, or DC21140-based NICs (SMC Etherpower 8432T, DE245, etc.)

FDDI (DEFPA/DEFEA) NICs

Efficient:

ENI-155p ATM PCI

FORE:

PCA-200E ATM PCI

Fujitsu:

MB86960A/MB86965A

HP:

PC Lan+ cards (model numbers: 27247B and 27252A)

Intel:

EtherExpress ISA (not recommended due to driver instability)

EtherExpress Pro/10

EtherExpress Pro/100B PCI Fast Ethernet

Isolan:

AT 4141-0 (16-bit)

Isolink:

4110 (8-bit)

Novell:

NE1000, NE2000, and NE2100

PCI network cards emulating the NE2000, including the following:

> RealTek 8029
>
> NetVin 5000
>
> Winbond W89C940
>
> Surecom NE-34
>
> VIA VT86C926

3Com:

3C501

3C503 Etherlink II

3C505 Etherlink/+

3C507 Etherlink 16/TP

3C509

3C579

3C589 (PCMCIA)

3C590/592/595/900/905/905B/905C PCI and EISA (Fast) Etherlink III / (Fast) Etherlink XL

3C980/3C980B Fast Etherlink XL server adapter

3CSOHO100-TX OfficeConnect adapter

Toshiba:

All Toshiba Ethernet cards

PCMCIA cards:

PCMCIA Ethernet cards from IBM and National Semiconductor

USB Devices

USB keyboards

USB mice

USB printers and USB to parallel printer conversion cables

USB hubs

Sound Devices

16550 UART (Midi) (experimental, needs a trick in the hints file)

Advance Asound 100, 110, and Logic ALS120

Aureal Vortex1/Vortex2 and Vortex Advantage-based sound cards by a third-party driver

Creative Labs SB16, SB32, SB AWE64 (including Gold), Vibra16, SB PCI (experimental), SB Live! (experimental), and most SoundBlaster-compatible cards

Creative Labs SB Midi Port (experimental), SB OPL3 Synthesizer (experimental)

Crystal Semiconductor CS461x/462x Audio Accelerator; the support for the CS461x Midi port is experimental

Crystal Semiconductor CS428x Audio Controller

CS4237, CS4236, CS4232, CS4231 (ISA)

ENSONIQ AudioPCI ES1370/1371

ESS ES1868, ES1869, ES1879, ES1888

Gravis UltraSound PnP, MAX

NeoMagic 256AV/ZX (PCI)

OPTi931 (ISA)

OSS-compatible sequencer (Midi) (experimental)

Trident 4DWave DX/NX (PCI)

Yahama OPL-SAx (ISA)

B

HARDWARE COMPATIBILITY LISTS

Miscellaneous Devices

AST 4-Port serial card using shared IRQ

ARNET 8-Port serial card using shared IRQ

ARNET (now Digiboard) Sync 570/i high-speed serial

Boca BB1004 4-Port serial card (Modems *not* supported)

Boca IOAT66 6-Port serial card (Modems supported)

Boca BB1008 8-Port serial card (Modems *not* supported)

Boca BB2016 16-Port serial card (Modems supported)

Cyclades Cyclom-y serial board

Moxa SmartIO CI-104J 4-Port serial card

STB 4-Port card using shared IRQ

SDL Communications RISCom/8 serial board

SDL Communications RISCom/N2 and N2pci high-speed sync serial boards

Specialix SI/XIO/SX multiport serial cards, with both the older SIHOST2.x and the new "enhanced" (transputer-based, aka JET) host cards; ISA, EISA, and PCI are supported

Stallion multiport serial boards: EasyIO, EasyConnection 8/32 & 8/64, ONboard 4/16 and Brumby

Connectix QuickCam

Matrox Meteor Video frame grabber

Creative Labs Video Spigot frame grabber

Cortex1 frame grabber

Various frame grabbers based on the Brooktree Bt848 and Bt878 chip

HP4020, HP6020, Philips CDD2000/CDD2660 and Plasmon CD-R drives

Bus mice

PS/2 mice

Standard PC Joystick

X-10 power controllers

GPIB and Transputer drives

Genius and Mustek hand scanners

Floppy tape drives (some rather old models only; driver is rather stale)

Lucent Technologies WaveLAN/IEEE 802.11 PCMCIA and ISA standard speed (2Mbps) and turbo speed (6Mbps) wireless network adapters and workalikes (NCR WaveLAN/IEEE 802.11, Cabletron RoamAbout 802.11 DS)

Video Cards Supported by X-Windows

The following is a list of the video cards that XFree86 currently supports. The list was taken from the XFree86 Project's Web site. If you cannot find an exact match for your card, see if you can find out what chipset your card uses and find a match there.

2 the Max MAXColor S3 Trio64V+

3DLabs Oxygen GMX

928Movie

AGX (generic)

ALG-5434

ASUS 3Dexplorer

ASUS PCI-AV264CT

ASUS PCI-V264CT

ASUS Video Magic PCI V864

ASUS Video Magic PCI VT64

AT25

AT3D

ATI 3D Pro Turbo

ATI 3D Pro Turbo PC2TV

ATI 3D Xpression

ATI 3D Xpression+

ATI 3D Xpression+ PC2TV

ATI 8514 Ultra (no VGA)

ATI All-in-Wonder

ATI All-in-Wonder Pro

ATI Graphics Pro Turbo

ATI Graphics Pro Turbo 1600

ATI Graphics Pro Turbo with AT&T 20C408 RAMDAC

ATI Graphics Pro Turbo with ATI68860 RAMDAC

ATI Graphics Pro Turbo with ATI68860B RAMDAC

ATI Graphics Pro Turbo with ATI68860C RAMDAC

ATI Graphics Pro Turbo with ATI68875 RAMDAC

ATI Graphics Pro Turbo with CH8398 RAMDAC

ATI Graphics Pro Turbo with STG1702 RAMDAC

ATI Graphics Pro Turbo with STG1703 RAMDAC

ATI Graphics Pro Turbo with TLC34075 RAMDAC

ATI Graphics Ultra

ATI Graphics Ultra Pro

ATI Graphics Xpression

ATI Graphics Xpression w/ ATI68860 RAMDAC

ATI Graphics Xpression w/ ATI68860B RAMDAC

ATI Graphics Xpression w/ ATI68860C RAMDAC

ATI Graphics Xpression w/ ATI68875 RAMDAC

ATI Graphics Xpression w/ AT&T 20C408 RAMDAC

ATI Graphics Xpression w/ CH8398 RAMDAC

ATI Graphics Xpression w/ Mach64 CT (264CT)

ATI Graphics Xpression w/ STG1702 RAMDAC

ATI Graphics Xpression with STG1703 RAMDAC

ATI Graphics Xpression with TLC34075 RAMDAC

ATI Mach32

ATI Mach64

ATI Mach64 3D RAGE II

ATI Mach64 3D RAGE II+DVD

ATI Mach64 3D Rage IIC

ATI Mach64 3D Rage Pro

ATI Mach64 CT (264CT), Internal RAMDAC

ATI Mach64 GT (264GT), aka 3D RAGE, Int

ATI Mach64 VT (264VT), Internal RAMDAC

ATI Mach64 with AT&T 20C408 RAMDAC

ATI Mach64 with ATI68860 RAMDAC

ATI Mach64 with ATI68860B RAMDAC

ATI Mach64 with ATI68860C RAMDAC

ATI Mach64 with ATI68875 RAMDAC

ATI Mach64 with CH8398 RAMDAC

ATI Mach64 with IBM RGB514 RAMDAC

ATI Mach64 with Internal RAMDAC

ATI Mach64 with STG1702 RAMDAC

ATI Mach64 with STG1703 RAMDAC

ATI Mach64 with TLC34075 RAMDAC

ATI Pro Turbo+PC2TV, 3D Rage II+DVD

ATI Ultra Plus

ATI Video Xpression

ATI Video Xpression+

ATI WinBoost

ATI Win Boost with AT&T 20C408 RAMDAC

B

HARDWARE
COMPATIBILITY
LISTS

ATI WinBoost with ATI68860 RAMDAC

ATI WinBoost with ATI68860B RAMDAC

ATI WinBoost with ATI68860C RAMDAC

ATI WinBoost with ATI68875 RAMDAC

ATI WinBoost with CH8398 RAMDAC

ATI WinBoost with Mach64 CT (264CT)

ATI WinBoost with STG1702 RAMDAC

ATI WinBoost with STG1703 RAMDAC

ATI WinBoost with TLC34075 RAMDAC

ATI WinCharger

ATI WinCharger with AT&T 20C408 RAMDAC

ATI WinCharger with ATI68860 RAMDAC

ATI WinCharger with ATI68860B RAMDAC

ATI WinCharger with ATI68860C RAMDAC

ATI WinCharger with ATI68875 RAMDAC

ATI WinCharger with CH8398 RAMDAC

ATI WinCharger with Mach64 CT (264CT)

ATI WinCharger with STG1702 RAMDAC

ATI WinCharger with STG1703 RAMDAC

ATI WinCharger with TLC34075 RAMDAC

ATI Win Turbo

ATI WinTurbo with AT&T 20C408 RAMDAC

ATI WinTurbo with ATI68860 RAMDAC

ATI WinTurbo with ATI68860B RAMDAC

ATI WinTurbo with ATI68860C RAMDAC

ATI WinTurbo with ATI68875 RAMDAC

ATI WinTurbo with CH8398 RAMDAC

ATI WinTurbo with Mach64 CT (264CT)

ATI WinTurbo with STG1702 RAMDAC

ATI WinTurbo with STG1703 RAMDAC

ATI WinTurbo with TLC34075 RAMDAC

ATI Wonder SVGA

ATI Xpert 98

ATI Xpert XL

ATI Xpert@Play PCI and AGP, 3D Rage Pro

ATI Xpert@Play 98

ATI Xpert@Work, 3D Rage Pro

ATI integrated on Intel Maui MU440EX motherboard

ATrend ATC-2165A

AccelStar Permedia II AGP

Actix GE32+ 2MB

Actix GE32i

Actix GE64

Actix ProStar

Actix ProStar 64

Actix Ultra

Acumos AVGA3

Alliance ProMotion 6422

Ark Logic ARK1000PV (generic)

Ark Logic ARK1000VL (generic)

Ark Logic ARK2000MT (generic)

Ark Logic ARK2000PV (generic)

Avance Logic 2101

Avance Logic 2228

Avance Logic 2301

Avance Logic 2302

Avance Logic 2308

Avance Logic 2401

Binar Graphics AnyView

Boca Vortex (Sierra RAMDAC)

COMPAQ Armada 7380DMT

COMPAQ Armada 7730MT

California Graphics SunTracer 6000

Canopus Co

Canopus Total-3D

Cardex Challenger (Pro)

Cardex Cobra

Cardex Trio64

Cardex Trio64Pro

Chips & Technologies CT64200

Chips & Technologies CT64300

Chips & Technologies CT65520

Chips & Technologies CT65525

Chips & Technologies CT65530

Chips & Technologies CT65535

Chips & Technologies CT65540

Chips & Technologies CT65545

Chips & Technologies CT65546

Chips & Technologies CT65548

Chips & Technologies CT65550

Chips & Technologies CT65554

Chips & Technologies CT65555

Chips & Technologies CT68554

Chips & Technologies CT69000

Cirrus Logic GD542x

Cirrus Logic GD543x

Cirrus Logic GD5446 (noname card) 1MB upg

Cirrus Logic GD544x

Cirrus Logic GD5462

Cirrus Logic GD5464

Cirrus Logic GD5465

Cirrus Logic GD5480

Cirrus Logic GD62xx (laptop)

Cirrus Logic GD64xx (laptop)

Cirrus Logic GD754x (laptop)

Colorgraphic Dual Lightning

Creative Blaster Exxtreme

Creative Labs 3D Blaster PCI (Verite 1000)

Creative Labs Graphics Blaster 3D

Creative Labs Graphics Blaster Eclipse (OEM Model CT6510) XF86_SVGA

Creative Labs Graphics Blaster MA201

Creative Labs Graphics Blaster MA202

Creative Labs Graphics Blaster MA302

Creative Labs Graphics Blaster MA334

DFI-WG1000

DFI-WG5000

DFI-WG6000

DSV3325

B

HARDWARE COMPATIBILITY LISTS

DSV3326

DataExpert DSV3325

DataExpert DSV3365

Dell S3 805

Dell onboard ET4000

Diamond Edge 3D

Diamond Fire GL 1000

Diamond Fire GL 1000 PRO

Diamond Fire GL 3000

Diamond Multimedia Stealth 3D 2000

Diamond Multimedia Stealth 3D 2000 PRO

Diamond SpeedStar (Plus)

Diamond SpeedStar 24

Diamond SpeedStar 24X (not fully supported)

Diamond SpeedStar 64

Diamond SpeedStar A50

Diamond SpeedStar HiColor

Diamond SpeedStar Pro (not SE)

Diamond SpeedStar Pro 1100

Diamond SpeedStar Pro SE (CL-GD5430/5434)

Diamond SpeedStar64 Graphics 2000/2200

Diamond Stealth 24

Diamond Stealth 32

Diamond Stealth 3D 2000

Diamond Stealth 3D 2000 PRO

Diamond Stealth 3D 3000

Diamond Stealth 3D 4000

Diamond Stealth 64 DRAM SE

Diamond Stealth 64 DRAM with S3 SDAC

Diamond Stealth 64 DRAM with S3 Trio64

Diamond Stealth 64 VRAM

Diamond Stealth 64 Video VRAM (TI RAMDAC)

Diamond Stealth II S220

Diamond Stealth Pro

Diamond Stealth VRAM

Diamond Stealth Video 2500

Diamond Stealth Video DRAM

Diamond Stealth64 Graphics 2001 series

Diamond Stealth64 Graphics 2xx0 series (864 + SDAC)

Diamond Stealth64 Graphics 2xx0 series (Trio64)

Diamond Stealth64 Video 2001 series (2121/2201)

Diamond Stealth64 Video 2120/2200

Diamond Stealth64 Video 3200

Diamond Stealth64 Video 3240/3400 (IBM RAMDAC)

Diamond Stealth64 Video 3240/3400 (TI RAMDAC)

Diamond Viper 330

Diamond Viper 550

Diamond Viper PCI 2MB

Diamond Viper Pro Video

Diamond Viper VLB 2MB

Digital 24-plane TGA (ZLXp-E2)

Digital 24-plane+3D TGA (ZLXp-E3)

Digital 8-plane TGA (UDB/Multia)

Digital 8-plane TGA (ZLXp-E1)

B

HARDWARE
COMPATIBILITY
LISTS

EIZO (VRAM)

ELSA ERAZOR II

ELSA GLoria Synergy

ELSA GLoria-L

ELSA GLoria-L/MX

ELSA GLoria-S

ELSA GLoria-XL

ELSA Gloria-4

ELSA Gloria-8

ELSA VICTORY ERAZOR

ELSA Victory 3D

ELSA Victory 3DX

ELSA WINNER 1000/T2D

ELSA Winner 1000 R3D

ELSA Winner 1000AVI (AT&T 20C409 version)

ELSA Winner 1000AVI (SDAC version)

ELSA Winner 1000ISA

ELSA Winner 1000PRO with S3 SDAC

ELSA Winner 1000PRO with STG1700 or AT&T RAMDAC

ELSA Winner 1000PRO/X

ELSA Winner 1000TRIO

ELSA Winner 1000TRIO/V

ELSA Winner 1000TwinBus

ELSA Winner 1000VL

ELSA Winner 2000

ELSA Winner 2000/Office

ELSA Winner 2000AVI

ELSA Winner 2000AVI/3D

ELSA Winner 2000PRO-2

ELSA Winner 2000PRO-4

ELSA Winner 2000PRO/X-2

ELSA Winner 2000PRO/X-4

ELSA Winner 2000PRO/X-8

ELSA Winner 3000

ELSA Winner 3000-L-42

ELSA Winner 3000-M-22

ELSA Winner 3000-S

EPSON CardPC (onboard)

ET3000 (generic)

ET4000 (generic)

ET4000 W32i, W32p (generic)

ET4000/W32 (generic)

ET6000 (generic)

ET6100 (generic)

ExpertColor DSV3325

ExpertColor DSV3365

Generic VGA compatible

Genoa 5400

Genoa 8500VL(-28)

Genoa 8900 Phantom 32i

Genoa Phantom 64i with S3 SDAC

Genoa VideoBlitz III AV

Hercules Dynamite

Hercules Dynamite 128/Video

Hercules Dynamite Power

Hercules Dynamite Pro

Hercules Graphite HG210

Hercules Graphite Power

Hercules Graphite Pro

Hercules Graphite Terminator 64

Hercules Graphite Terminator 64/DRAM

Hercules Graphite Terminator Pro 64

Hercules Stingray

Hercules Stingray 128 3D

Hercules Stingray 64/V with ICS5342

Hercules Stingray 64/V with ZoomDAC

Hercules Stingray Pro

Hercules Stingray Pro/V

Hercules Terminator 3D/DX

Hercules Terminator 64/3D

Hercules Terminator 64/Video

Hercules Thriller3D

Integral FlashPoint

Intel 5430

Interay PMC Viper

JAX 8241

Jaton Video-58P

Jaton Video-70P

Jazz Multimedia G-Force 128

LeadTek WinFast 3D S600

LeadTek WinFast 3D S680

LeadTek WinFast S200

LeadTek WinFast S430

LeadTek WinFast S510

Leadtek WinFast 2300

MELCO WGP-VG4S

MELCO WGP-VX8

MSI MS-4417

Matrox Comet

Matrox Marvel II

Matrox Millennium 2/4/8MB

Matrox Millennium (MGA)

Matrox Millennium G200 4/8/16MB

Matrox Millennium G200 SD 4/8/16MB

Matrox Millennium II 4/8/16MB

Matrox Millennium II AGP

Matrox Mystique

Matrox Mystique G200 4/8/16MB

Matrox Productiva G100 4/8MB

MediaGX

MediaVision Proaxcel 128

Mirage Z-128

Miro Crystal 10SD with GenDAC

Miro Crystal 12SD

Miro Crystal 16S

Miro Crystal 20SD PCI with S3 SDAC

Miro Crystal 20SD VLB with S3 SDAC (BIOS 3)

Miro Crystal 20SD with ICD2061A (BIOS 2)

Miro Crystal 20SD with ICS2494 (BIOS 1)

Miro Crystal 20SV

Miro Crystal 22SD

Miro Crystal 40SV

Miro Crystal 80SV

Miro Crystal 8S

Miro Crystal DVD

Miro miroCRYSTAL VRX

Miro miroMedia 3D

Miro MiroVideo 20TD

Miro Video 20SV

Neomagic

Number Nine FX Motion 331

Number Nine FX Motion 332

Number Nine FX Motion 531

Number Nine FX Motion 771

Number Nine FX Vision 330

Number Nine GXE Level 10/11/12

Number Nine GXE Level 14/16

Number Nine GXE64

Number Nine GXE64 Pro

Number Nine GXE64 with S3 Trio64

Number Nine Imagine I-128 (2-8MB)

Number Nine Imagine I-128 Series 2 (2-4MB)

Number Nine Imagine-128-T2R

Number Nine Revolution 3D AGP (4-8MB SGRAM)

Number Nine Visual 9FX Reality 332

Oak 87 ISA (generic)

Oak 87 VLB (generic)

Oak ISA Card (generic)

Ocean (octek) VL-VGA-1000

Octek AVGA-20

Octek Combo-26

Octek Combo-28

Octek VL-VGA-26

Octek VL-VGA-28

Orchid Celsius (AT&T RAMDAC)

Orchid Celsius (Sierra RAMDAC)

Orchid Fahrenheit 1280

Orchid Fahrenheit VA

Orchid Fahrenheit-1280+

Orchid Kelvin 64

Orchid Kelvin 64 VLB Rev A

Orchid Kelvin 64 VLB Rev B

Orchid P9000 VLB

Orchid Technology Fahrenheit Video 3D

PC-Chips M567 Mainboard

Paradise Accelerator Value

Paradise/WD 90CXX

PixelView Combo TV 3D AGP (Prolink)

PixelView Combo TV Pro (Prolink)

RIVA TNT

RIVA128

Rendition Verite 1000

Rendition Verite 2x00

Revolution 3D (T2R)

S3 801/805 (generic)

S3 801/805 with ATT20c490 RAMDAC

S3 801/805 with ATT20c490 RAMDAC and ICD2061A

S3 801/805 with Chrontel 8391

S3 801/805 with S3 GenDAC

S3 801/805 with SC1148{2,3,4} RAMDAC

S3 801/805 with SC1148{5,7,9} RAMDAC

S3 864 (generic)

S3 864 with ATT 20C498 or 21C498

S3 864 with SDAC (86C716)

S3 864 with STG1703

S3 868 (generic)

S3 868 with ATT 20C409

S3 868 with ATT 20C498 or 21C498

S3 868 with SDAC (86C716)

S3 86C260 (generic)

S3 86C280 (generic)

S3 86C325 (generic)

S3 86C357 (generic)

S3 86C365 (Trio3D)

S3 86C375 (generic)

S3 86C385 (generic)

S3 86C391 (Savage3D)

S3 86C764 (generic)

S3 86C765 (generic)

S3 86C775 (generic)

S3 86C785 (generic)

S3 86C801 (generic)

S3 86C805 (generic)

S3 86C864 (generic)

S3 86C868 (generic)

S3 86C911 (generic)

S3 86C924 (generic)

S3 86C928 (generic)

S3 86C964 (generic)

S3 86C968 (generic)

S3 86C988 (generic)

S3 86CM65

S3 911/924 (generic)

S3 924 with SC1148 DAC

S3 928 (generic)

S3 964 (generic)

S3 968 (generic)

S3 Aurora64V+ (generic)

S3 Savage3D

S3 Trio32 (generic)

S3 Trio3D

S3 Trio64 (generic)

S3 Trio64V+ (generic)

S3 Trio64V2 (generic)

S3 Trio64V2/DX (generic)

S3 Trio64V2/GX (generic)

B

HARDWARE
COMPATIBILITY
LISTS

S3 ViRGE (generic)

S3 ViRGE (old S3V server)

S3 ViRGE/DX (generic)

S3 ViRGE/GX (generic)

S3 ViRGE/GX2 (generic)

S3 ViRGE/MX (generic)

S3 ViRGE/MX+ (generic)

S3 ViRGE/VX (generic)

S3 Vision864 (generic)

S3 Vision868 (generic)

S3 Vision964 (generic)

S3 Vision968 (generic)

SHARP 9080

SHARP 9090

SNI PC5H W32

SNI Scenic W32

SPEA Mercury 64

SPEA Mirage

SPEA/V7 Mercury

SPEA/V7 Mirage P64

SPEA/V7 Mirage P64 with S3 Trio64

SPEA/V7 Mirage VEGA Plus

SPEA/V7 ShowTime Plus

STB Horizon

STB Horizon Video

STB LightSpeed

STB LightSpeed 128

STB MVP-2

STB MVP-2 PCI

STB MVP-2X

STB MVP-4 PCI

STB MVP-4X

STB Nitro (64)

STB Nitro 3D

STB Nitro 64 Video

STB Pegasus

STB Powergraph 64

STB Powergraph 64 Video

STB Powergraph X-24

STB Systems Powergraph 3D

STB Systems Velocity 3D

STB Velocity 128

STB Velocity 64 Video

STD nvidia 128

SiS 3D PRO AGP

SiS 5597

SiS 5598

SiS 6326

SiS SG86C201

SiS SG86C205

SiS SG86C215

SiS SG86C225

Sierra Screaming 3D

Sigma Concorde

B

HARDWARE
COMPATIBILITY
LISTS

Sigma Legend

Spider Black Widow

Spider Black Widow Plus

Spider Tarantula 64

Spider VLB Plus

TechWorks Thunderbolt

Techworks Ultimate 3D

Toshiba Tecra 540CDT

Toshiba Tecra 550CDT

Toshiba Tecra 750CDT

Toshiba Tecra 750DVD

Trident 3DImage975 (generic)

Trident 3DImage975 AGP (generic)

Trident 3DImage985 (generic)

Trident 8900/9000 (generic)

Trident 8900D (generic)

Trident Cyber 9382 (generic)

Trident Cyber 9385 (generic)

Trident Cyber 9388 (generic)

Trident Cyber 9397 (generic)

Trident TGUI9400CXi (generic)

Trident TGUI9420DGi (generic)

Trident TGUI9430DGi (generic)

Trident TGUI9440 (generic)

Trident TGUI9660 (generic)

Trident TGUI9680 (generic)

Trident TGUI9682 (generic)

Trident TGUI9685 (generic)

Trident TVGA 8800BR

Trident TVGA 8800CS

Trident TVGA9200CXr (generic)

Unsupported VGA compatible

VI720

VL-41

VidTech FastMax P20

VideoLogic GrafixStar 300

VideoLogic GrafixStar 400

VideoLogic GrafixStar 500

VideoLogic GrafixStar 550

VideoLogic GrafixStar 560 (PCI/AGP)

VideoLogic GrafixStar 600

VideoLogic GrafixStar 700

ViewTop PCI

WD 90C24 (laptop)

WD 90C24A or 90C24A2 (laptop)

Weitek P9100 (generic)

WinFast 3D S600

WinFast 3D S600

WinFast S200

WinFast S430

WinFast S510

XGA-1 (ISA bus)

XGA-2 (ISA bus)

B

HARDWARE
COMPATIBILITY
LISTS

APPENDIX C

Troubleshooting Installation and Boot Problems

This appendix is designed to help you solve various installation and booting problems. Installation problems are covered first, followed by booting problems.

Installation Problems

This section of the appendix covers various installation problems you may encounter and possible solutions to these problems.

Booting from Floppy Causes System to Hang or Reboot

There are a few things that can cause this to happen. The first is simply a bad floppy. Remember that the boot image is written to the floppy without checking the format, and that the entire floppy is used. Even a single bad block on the floppy can cause problems. Try writing the boot disk to a new floppy, and see if it fixes the problem.

If using a new floppy does not fix the problem, make sure that you used binary mode and not ASCII mode to transfer the floppy in your FTP client.

Another thing that can sometimes cause this problem is virus protection on the motherboard. This can be disabled in the system's BIOS setup utility.

Finally, make sure that you created the floppy from DOS mode, not from a DOS prompt in Windows. This has been known to cause problems on occasion.

Boot Floppy Hangs at "Probing Devices"

The boot floppy sometimes gets confused by IDE Zip and Jaz drives. If you have one of these drives, try removing it and see if the system will boot. If it does, you can install FreeBSD and than reconnect the drive after the installation is complete.

System Boots from CD, but Installer Shows That CD-ROM Was Not Found

This is probably caused by an improperly configured CD-ROM drive. Some systems ship with the CD-ROM drive as a slave drive on the secondary controller and have no master drive on the secondary controller. To fix this, you will need to change your CD-ROM drive to the master if it is on the secondary controller. This can usually be done via a jumper on the back of the CD-ROM drive (you will need to go inside your case).

Hard Disk Geometry Is Not Detected Properly

If FreeBSD cannot detect your hard disk geometry correctly, there are two ways this can usually be fixed.

The first is by creating a small DOS partition at the beginning of the disk. This will usually cause FreeBSD to see the right geometry.

The second way is with the `pfdisk` program included on the CD-ROM. `pfdisk` runs under DOS, and will usually detect the proper geometry of the hard disk. You can then give the FreeBSD partition the proper geometry manually.

Micron System Hangs When Booting

Some Micron systems have buggy PCI BIOS routines. This can cause PCI devices to be configured incorrectly when they are probed. You can work around this problem by disabling the plug-and-play operating support in the BIOS setup utility.

3Com PCI Network Card Doesn't Work with Micron System

This is related to the previous problem of the buggy PCI BIOS routines in Micron systems. Once again, disable plug-and-play operating system support in the BIOS to work around this problem.

HP Netserver SCSI Controller Is Not Detected

This has to do with an address conflict between the EISA SCSI controller and the PCI bus. The EISA SCSI controller with this system uses slot 11, which conflicts with PCI address space. To fix this problem, enter the plain command-line interface of `UserConfig` when prompted to do so during the install. Note that the visual mode will not work. You will have to use the command-line interface. At the command prompt for `UserConfig`, enter the following commands:

```
eisa 12
quit
```

This should allow FreeBSD to detect the controller and install. After the installation is complete, you will also want to build a custom kernel with the line:

```
options     EISA_SLOTS=12
```

This should take care of the problem.

C

TROUBLESHOOTING
INSTALLATION AND
BOOT PROBLEMS

Screen Goes Blank with ATI Mach64 Video Card

This is a problem with the ATI Mach64 video card having an address conflict with the fourth serial port. To fix this problem, enter the UserConfig program when prompted during the installation. From here, disable sio0, sio1, sio2, and sio3. Then, exit and continue booting.

In order to use your serial ports, you will need to make a modification to the kernel source file /usr/src/sys/i386/isa/sio.c. Find the string 0x2e8 and remove it and the preceding comma. Then rebuild the kernel. (See Chapter 17, "Kernel Configuration," for details on how to rebuild the kernel).

Devices Needed to Install FreeBSD Are Not Being Detected

First of all, check the hardware compatibility list in Appendix B, "Hardware Compatibility Lists," to make sure that your hardware is supported. If it is, and it is not using the default resources, you will have to configure it manually with UserConfig, as well as eliminate any resource conflicts that may cause with other hardware.

The UserConfig program can be entered from the screen in the install process that looks like this:

```
                    Kernel Configuration Menu

Skip kernel configuration and continue with installation.

    Start kernel configuration in full screen Visual mode.
    Start kernel configuration in CLI mode.

Here you have the chance to go into kernel configuration mode, making
any changes which may be necessary to properly adjust the kernel to
match your hardware configuration.

If you are installing FreeBSD for the first time, select Visual Mode
(press Down-Arrow then ENTER).

If you need to do more specialized kernel configuration and are an
experienced FreeBSD user, select CLI mode.

If you are certain that you do not need to configure your kernel then
simply press ENTER or Q now.
```

Use the full-screen visual mode.

The idea in this program is to reduce the number of conflicts to zero.

Boot Problems and Other Non-Installation Problems

This section covers problems related to booting as well as other non-installation related problems.

FreeBSD Says `Missing Operating System` When Trying to Boot

This usually means that FreeBSD did not correctly detect your hard disk's geometry when it installed. There are two solutions to this problem:

- Create a small DOS partition at the beginning of the drive, and install a bare minimum copy of DOS on it. This should cause FreeBSD to detect the right information for partitioning.

- Use the `pfdisk.exe` program found on the CD to detect the hard disk geometry and then set it manually in the FreeBSD partition editor.

Either way, you will have to reinstall FreeBSD to get things working.

FreeBSD's Boot Manager Hangs at "F?"

This is usually caused by FreeBSD not detecting your hard disk geometry properly. See the previous section for solutions to this problem.

FreeBSD's Boot Loader Says `Read Error` and Hangs

Once again, this is usually caused by FreeBSD not detecting the hard disk geometry correctly. See the previous two sections for solutions to this problem.

There Is No Boot Manager; System Boots Right into Windows

Either the boot manager didn't get installed when you installed FreeBSD, or if you did something in Windows (`fdisk /mbr` or something), it clobbered the FreeBSD boot manager. Fortunately, it is relatively easy to restore.

Boot from the included CD or from the install disks you created. After you have gotten into the `Sysinstall` program, select `Configure` and then `Fdisk` (see Chapter 2, "Installing FreeBSD," if you need a refresher on `Sysinstall`). If you have multiple hard disks in your system, you will be prompted for which system you want to run Fdisk on. Select the primary disk that your system boots from. Once you are in Fdisk, simply select W to write changes. You will be given a warning, telling you that it should be done only when making changes to an existing installation. Select Yes and press Enter. When the system asks about the boot loader, select Master Boot Record. Once you have completed this process, the boot manager should be back in operation.

FreeBSD Detects Less RAM Than Is Really in System

FreeBSD can't always get the proper amount of memory in your system from the BIOS. Usually, this results in FreeBSD detecting only 64MB of RAM, even if you really have more.

To fix this problem, you will need to add the following option to the kernel configuration file:

```
options      "MAXMEM=n"
```

where *n* is the amount of memory you have in kilobytes. Remember that in binary math, a kilobyte is actually 1024 bytes instead of 1000 bytes. A megabyte is actually 1,048,576 bytes instead of 1,000,000 bytes. In binary math, there are 1024 kilobytes in a megabyte rather than 1000 kilobytes. So, you basically end up with $k = m * 1024$ where k is the number of kilobytes and m is the number of megabytes. For example, if you have 128MB of RAM, the number you would enter here is 131072 (131072 = 128 * 1024).

After you have made this change, you will need to rebuild the kernel (see Chapter 17, "Kernel Configuration," for detailed information on rebuilding the kernel).

FreeBSD Complains Device Not Configured While Trying to Mount CD-ROM

This can be caused by a few things. The first and easiest to fix is if there is no CD in the drive. Simply insert a CD and try again.

The second possibility is that an ATAPI CD-ROM drive is configured as the slave drive on the secondary controller and there is no master drive on the controller. You will need to reconfigure your CD-ROM drive as the master if this is the case (this can usually be done from jumpers on the back of the CD-ROM).

The third possibility if you have a SCSI CD-ROM drive is that it is not getting enough time to answer the bus reset request when the kernel is started. If this is the case, find the options SCSI_DELAY line in the kernel configuration file, and change it to read and increase the time. (The time is given in milliseconds. By default, it is set to 15000, or 15 seconds.) You will then need to rebuild the kernel (see Chapter 17).

Programs Crash with Signal 11 Errors

This is somewhat like an illegal operation error in Windows. It basically means that a program tried to access memory that was not allocated to it. This could be the result of a bug in the program, or, if it is occurring with utilities included with FreeBSD, a bug in FreeBSD itself.

A third potential cause of this problem is flaky hardware. If the problems occur at random points while compiling software, you can be almost sure that flaky hardware is the culprit. Common hardware that causes such problems is defective RAM, a CPU that is overheating (Is your CPU fan running? Are you overclocking?), defective cache memory, or a flaky power supply.

Strange Error Messages When Running top, ps, and Other System Utilities

This is almost always caused by your world and your kernel being out of sync. Often, the culprit is that you used make world to build the system from source and then you didn't build a new kernel. The reverse could also be true. You built a new kernel with sources that you downloaded, but did not do a make world first.

Since it is much quicker to rebuild the kernel than to rebuild the world, you should probably simply try making a new kernel and rebooting first (see Chapter 17 for detailed information on rebuilding the kernel).

If rebuilding the kernel doesn't fix the problem, try rebuilding the world. (See Chapter 18, "Keeping Up to Date with FreeBSD," for details on doing a make world.)

Finally, if neither of these options solves the problem, getting the latest source (see Chapter 18), making the world, and then rebuilding the kernel should fix this problem.

Forgotten Root Password

If you have forgotten your root password, you can boot into single-user mode to recover it.

To get into single-user mode, press any key when you boot the system to see the countdown. Once you have pressed any key, the boot will be interrupted. You will get a prompt that simply says

Ok

At this prompt, type `boot -s`, which will boot the system into single-user mode. When you are asked which shell to use, simply press Enter for the default. You should then get a root user prompt that looks like this:

```
#
```

At the prompt, type `mount -u/` and then press Enter to remount the root filesystem read/write. Then, type `mount -a` to mount all the other filesystems. You can now type `passwd root` to change the password for the root account. You will not be asked for the old password. Simply enter the new password you would like to use, press Enter, confirm it, and press Enter again. After this, reboot your system with `shutdown -r now`. When your system finished rebooting, the system should be back to normal.

APPENDIX D

Sources for More Information

FreeBSD is a large and growing community of users and developers, with many sources of information available on FreeBSD and related products. This appendix lists some of those sources.

FreeBSD-Specific Resources

Web Sites

www.freebsd.org

This is the official Web site of the FreeBSD project. It is the place to go for news, updates, and information on ports and packages. It is also where the online handbook and various tutorials are located.

www.freebsddiary.org

This site is a gold mine of FAQS and how-to articles on a large number of subjects. It is also the home of some FreeBSD discussion forums, including the one and only "FreeBSD Pets" forum. Yes, it really is what the name says. Are you a FreeBSD user? Do you have a pet? Post a message here about your pet along with a link to a picture of your pet for all other FreeBSD users to see.

www.freebsdzine.org

An online magazine covering FreeBSD-related topics. It is written by people in the FreeBSD community for people in the FreeBSD community.

www.freshports.org

The place to get the latest news regarding new and updated FreeBSD ports.

www.freebsdmall.com

The source to purchase all things FreeBSD. Here, you can get CDs, T-shirts, jackets, mouse pads, coffee mugs, hats, books, and so on. You can also purchase professional support services for FreeBSD here.

Mailing Lists

All of these mailing lists are official project mailing lists. To subscribe to any one of these lists, send an e-mail to `majordomo@freebsd.org` with the following in the body of the message:

```
subscribe list-name
```

where `list-name` is, of course, the name of the list you want to subscribe to. You can unsubscribe to any of these lists by sending an e-mail to `majordomo@freebsd.org` with the following in the body of the message:

```
unsubscribe list-name
```

Many of the lists are high volume, and will generate a lot of e-mail. If you wish to avoid this, you can subscribe to many of the lists in digest form. If you do this, you will only be sent an e-mail from each list you subscribe to when the number of messages posted has exceeded 100KB. All the messages will be sent in the single e-mail.

General Lists

Anyone can subscribe and participate in the general lists. However, you should read the list's guidelines (which will be sent to you when you subscribe) before posting to the list. Here are the general lists and a short description of what each one is used for.

freebsd-advocacy

A list for discussing the benefits of FreeBSD and different ways of promoting FreeBSD.

freebsd-announce

Important announcements regarding FreeBSD. This is a read-only list that is pretty low volume.

freebsd-arch

Discussions regarding architecture and design.

freebsd-bugs

Bug reports for FreeBSD. Note that you should not actually send bug reports to this list. Rather, you should submit a problem report into the GNATS database using the form located at `http://www.freebsd.org/send-pr.html`. Your submitted problem report will then be posted on the list for those subscribed to it to see.

freebsd-chat

General, nontechnical discussion for the FreeBSD community.

freebsd-commit

Changes made to the FreeBSD source tree are posted to this list. This is a read-only list.

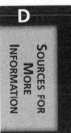

D

SOURCES FOR
MORE
INFORMATION

freebsd-config

A list for discussions regarding FreeBSD installation and configuration tools (such as new GUI installation tools that will probably eventually replace Sysinstall). Mostly of interest only to developers and programmers.

freebsd-current

If you are tracking the CURRENT branch of FreeBSD, you NEED to be subscribed to this list. Among other things, reading this list can prevent you from making world when the source tree is broken, and possibly rendering your system unusable. You should not be tracking CURRENT unless you are tech savvy and are willing to deal with problems like this. This means that you should not post general "how-to" questions to this list. Only technical questions regarding behavior in CURRENT should be posted to this list. Other questions will either not get a response at all, or likely you will simply be told to repost your question in freebsd-questions.

freebsd-isp

A discussion list for Internet service providers using FreeBSD. Note that this list is for providers, not users. In other words, if you are having problems getting FreeBSD to connect to your Internet service provider, this is NOT the place to post that question.

freebsd-jobs

If you are a FreeBSD guru looking for a job, you will find job announcements on this list. If you are an employer and you need a FreeBSD guru, you can post your "help wanted" ad to this list.

freebsd-newbies

A discussion list for users new to FreeBSD. Note that this is not a help list. Rather, it is a list for newbies to swap stories about their experiences with FreeBSD and such. Questions should be posted to freebsd-questions, not to freebsd-newbies.

freebsd-policy

Policy decisions made by the FreeBSD core team. It is low volume and read-only.

freebsd-questions

The place to post technical questions about FreeBSD. If you post a question here, please be specific. In other words, don't post a question that says "I can't get pppd to work. What am I doing wrong?" That is not useful at all for troubleshooting. To get a useful answer, you will need to provide details such as the contents of any error messages that are written to the logs, what kind of configuration you are trying to use, etc. Also, please be polite, and don't flame the list if you don't get an answer right away. Remember—the people staffing this list are here on their own time and are entirely volunteers. Most of them have real jobs, and are devoting part of their free time to reading and responding to this list. No one on this list gets paid to help you. Note that you do not need to be subscribed to this list in order to post to it. But make sure you provide a valid e-mail address so that people have a place to send answers to your questions.

freebsd-stable

This list is for discussion regarding the FreeBSD STABLE tree. Like CURRENT, if you are tracking STABLE, you NEED to be subscribed to this list. Although serious problems that break the distribution and can render a system unbootable are much more rare in STABLE than in CURRENT, they can and do happen sometimes. The FreeBSD developers and committers are only human, and like everyone else, they occasionally make mistakes. This list will tell you when there are problems with the tree and also let you know when it is safe to use the tree again.

freebsd-security-notifications

Although the FreeBSD project considers this a technical list, I am putting it in here because everyone using FreeBSD in a production environment should subscribe to it. This is where notifications regarding FreeBSD security holes will be posted, as well as instructions for fixing the holes. Unless you don't mind having an insecure system, you should be subscribed to this list.

Technical Lists

There are many different technical lists for FreeBSD related to such issues as porting to different platforms, porting various software to FreeBSD, using FreeBSD in embedded systems, and so on. Because these lists are not of interest to most people, I am not going to list them here. But a full list of the technical lists can be obtained from `http://www.freebsd.org/doc/en_US.ISO_8859-1/books/handbook/eresources.html#ERESOURCES-MAIL`.

As the category suggests, these lists are quite technical in nature. Do not post questions of a general nature to the lists that are considered "technical lists." Virtually all of these lists have guidelines for the way they are to be used. So, you should read the charter that is e-mailed to you when subscribing to any of these lists before posting to them.

USENET Newsgroups for FreeBSD

The following FreeBSD-related newsgroups are available on USENET (contact your ISP to find out what news server you should be using to access USENET):

- `comp.unix.bsd.freebsd.announce`
- `comp.unix.bsd.freebsd.misc`

IRC Channels

There are several IRC channels available for FreeBSD. I'm not going to list all of them here because some of them are general discussion channels in which the topic is rarely about FreeBSD. But here are the two in which you are likely to be able to get help for FreeBSD:

- On EFNet: `#freebsdhelp`
- On Undernet: `#freebsd`

Note that depending on the time of day you show up, these channels may have a lot of people in them and still be very quiet. It may look like people are ignoring you. Chances are, they are not. Many people are working and are simply logged in to the channel as well. Also, during periods of high net congestion, IRC can have very high lag times between the time you post your message and the time some people actually get it. Keep this in mind as well when you don't seem to be getting any responses (and possibly switch to a different server if it seems your lag time is very high).

Expect to be treated the way you treat others on IRC. If you are rude because you are not getting answers or not getting the answers you want, expect that people will either be rude back to you, that you will be ignored, or that a channel operator will ban you from the channel. Remember, like the `freebsd-questions` mailing list, no one here is paid to help you. They are helping you on their own free time. So, keep that in mind before you get mad at someone on IRC.

Other BSD-Related Resources

These are resources that are related to BSD in general, but are not FreeBSD-specific. Since FreeBSD is the most popular of the BSD-based operating systems, most of these resources cover FreeBSD extensively. You will find coverage of other BSD-related things here as well, though.

Web Sites

www.daemonnews.org

The premier site for news on all things BSD-related. This site also has forums and runs how to articles. It is also home of the "Source Wars" comics.

www.bsdtoday.com

This is another Web site that contains daily updated news on items of BSD interest.

www.maximumbsd.com

Another site that contains news of BSD interest. This site also has some good archives and links to tutorials.

USENET Newsgroups

The following BSD-related newsgroups are available on USENET (contact your ISP to find out what news server you should be using to access USENET):

- comp.bugs.4bsd
- comp.bugs.4bsd.ucb-fixes
- comp.unix.bsd

Other Internet Resources

This section covers other resources on the Internet that are somehow related to FreeBSD in a general sense. Included in this section are the home pages for some of the software that was used and described in this book.

D

SOURCES FOR MORE INFORMATION

Web Sites

www.slashdot.org

"News for nerds. Stuff that matters." This is the premier nerd news site. Here, you will find articles on everything ranging from open-source software, to nerdy movie reviews, to the latest findings in nuclear fusion technology. The subjects that slashdot covers are wide and varied, and often technical or scientific. There is never a boring moment at slashdot.

www.xfree86.org

This is the home page for the XFree86 project, which is the free implementation of X-Windows included with FreeBSD. This is where you will find documentation and such related to the X-Windows system.

www.gnu.org

The home page for the GNU (a recursive acronym that stands for GNU's Not UNIX) project. Many of the utilities included with FreeBSD—such as the GCC compiler, the GAWK pattern matching language, the EMACS editor, and the f77 FORTRAN compiler—are from the GNU project. This site contains information on almost all of the GNU project's software.

www.gnome.org

The home page for the Gnome Desktop Environment project. News, tutorials, etc., on Gnome can be found here.

www.kde.org

The major competitor to Gnome. If you prefer KDE, this is your site.

www.apache.org

This is the home page for the Apache Web server project—the most popular Web server in the world. It is free and is the Web server of choice for FreeBSD.

www.mysql.com

The open-source SQL database of choice for FreeBSD. This site contains documentation, tutorials, and so on, for the MySQL database software.

www.postgresql.org

Another open-source SQL database available for FreeBSD. This one has more features than MySQL, but is somewhat slower.

www.php.net

The home page of the embedded scripting language of choice for building Web-based applications. PHP is an open source competitor to Active Server Pages (ASPs).

www.perl.com

Information and tutorials on the Perl programming language, which is included as a standard part of FreeBSD.

www.python.org

The home page for the Python programming language, which is a popular alternative to Perl.

www.sendmail.org

The home page of the Sendmail mail transfer agent, which is the default mail transfer agent included with FreeBSD.

www.postfix.org

A popular alternative mail transfer agent for Sendmail. Postfix is a drop-in replacement for Sendmail. It is my favorite mail transfer agent. New users will find it much easier to configure than Sendmail.

USENET Newsgroups

The following non-FreeBSD-specific newsgroups are available on USENET (contact your ISP to find out what news server you should be using to access USENET).

General UNIX Newsgroups

- comp.unix
- comp.unix.questions
- comp.unix.admin
- comp.unix.programmer
- comp.unix.shell
- comp.unix.user-friendly
- comp.security.unix
- comp.sources.unix
- comp.unix.advocacy
- comp.unix.misc

X-Windows Newsgroups

- comp.windows.x.i386unix
- comp.windows.x
- comp.windows.x.apps
- comp.windows.x.announce
- comp.windows.x.intrinsics

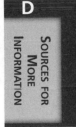

D

SOURCES FOR MORE INFORMATION

- `comp.windows.x.motif`
- `comp.windows.x.pex`
- `comp.emulators.ms-windows.wine`

INDEX

What's on the CD-ROMs

The companion CD-ROMs contain Disc 1 of FreeBSD 4.5 and a Disc 1 pre-release snapshot of FreeBSD 5.0.

FreeBSD Installation Instructions

The FreeBSD 4.5 operating system installation routine is on Disc 1 and the FreeBSD 5.0 pre-release snapshot installation routine is on Disc 2. Depending on the age of your computer and the security settings in the BIOS, you can choose to install FreeBSD by booting directly from the CD-ROM, or you can create a boot diskette to start the installation program. FreeBSD may also be installed from diskettes, FTP, or NFS, but we will only describe how to install using the enclosed CD-ROM. Other types of installations are covered in the INSTALL.TXT file on the top-level directory of the CD-ROM.

Start Installation with a Bootable CD-ROM

You may need to change your BIOS settings to boot directly from a CD-ROM drive. If you are not sure if you can boot from a CD-ROM, then you should start or reboot your computer and go into the computer's BIOS setup utility. Hitting the Delete or the F2 key usually accesses this utility while the computer is starting up. Once in the BIOS setup utility, look for a boot priority option. If your computer is capable of booting from a CD-ROM, your CD-ROM drive will be listed. Make sure the CD-ROM drive has a higher boot priority than your hard drive(s) to enable booting from a CD-ROM.

Once you have determined that you can boot from the CD-ROM, start or reboot your machine with Disc 1 (for FreeBSD 4.5) or Disc 2 (for FreeBSD 5.0) in your CD-ROM drive. After a few moments, you should see the FreeBSD installation routine. For more details on the installation routine, please see the section Installation Quick Start Guide.

Create a Boot Diskette

To start the FreeBSD install process from a diskette, you will need two formatted 1.44 MB 3.5" diskettes or one formatted 2.88 MB 3.5" diskette. Label the two disks appropriately, such as BOOT and MFS ROOT, or label the one disk as BOOT.

1. Insert Disc 1 (for FreeBSD 4.5) or Disc 2 (for FreeBSD 5.0) into your computer's CD-ROM drive. If you are using UNIX without a volume manager, you will need to mount the disc.

2. Go to the command line.

3. Navigate to the TOOLS directory on the CD-ROM.

4. Insert one of the two formatted diskettes (BOOT) and, if using DOS or Windows, type:

   ```
   fdimage ../FLOPPIES/KERN.FLP a: [ENTER]
   ```

   Or, if using UNIX, type:

   ```
   dd if=../floppies/kern.flp of=/dev/floppy [ENTER]
   ```

5. When the first image has been written, remove the first diskette and insert the second diskette (MFS ROOT). Use the same command as in Step 4, but this time use MFSROOT.FLP.

> **Note**
>
> If you formatted one 2.88 MB 3.5" diskette, use the same command as in Step 4, but use the BOOT.FLP image instead.
>
> When you are through creating the boot diskette(s), leave the FreeBSD CD-ROM in your CD-ROM drive and see the section Start Installation with a Boot Diskette.

Start Installation with a Boot Diskette

You may need to change your BIOS settings to boot from a diskette drive. If you are not sure your computer is set to boot from a diskette, then you should start or reboot your computer and go into the computer's BIOS setup utility. Hitting the Delete or the F2 key usually accesses this utility while the computer is starting up. Once in the BIOS setup utility, look for a boot priority option. Make sure the diskette drive has a higher boot priority than your hard drive(s) to enable booting from the diskette drive.

Insert the BOOT diskette and start or reboot your computer. If you are using the two diskette option, you will be prompted to insert the MFS Root diskette after a few moments to a few minutes. After a few moments, you should see the FreeBSD installation routine. For more details on the installation routine, please see the section Installation Quick Start Guide.

Installation Quick Start Guide

Once the root file system has been loaded, you will be presented with the Kernel Configuration Menu. While a detailed walkthrough is not presented here, we can offer a few installation tips. If your system is pretty standard, you can probably just press Q and continue with the installation. If your system hung and you are at this step again or you have a non-standard system, you should choose the full-screen visual mode kernel configuration. Go through the menus and determine if the hardware listed matches your system. Pay special attention to anything flagged with CONF in reverse video as this signifies that one or more drivers in the default configuration conflict with the resources you have in your system. Once you are done, press Q to continue installing.

If everything went well, you will be presented with the FreeBSD Installation Main Menu (called /stand/sysinstall Main Menu). The Usage menu option will describe the installation options in detail, so you should read this guide before you do anything else.

Once you choose an installation option, follow the on-screen prompts to finish the installation.

The Healthy Heart Cookbook for Dummies®

By
James M. Rippe, M.D.
Amy G. Myrdal, M.S., R.D.
Angela Harley Kirkpatrick, R.D.
Mary Abbott Waite, Ph.D.

EasyRead Large

Copyright Page from the Original Book